QM Library

D1766424

RUSSIA'S POST-COMMU

HC

Russia's Post-Communist Economy

Edited by

BRIGITTE GRANVILLE
PETER OPPENHEIMER

OXFORD
UNIVERSITY PRESS

QM LIBRARY
(MILE END)

This book has been printed digitally and produced in a standard specification
in order to ensure its continuing availability

OXFORD
UNIVERSITY PRESS

Great Clarendon Street, Oxford OX2 6DP

Oxford University Press is a department of the University of Oxford.
It furthers the University's objective of excellence in research, scholarship,
and education by publishing worldwide in

Oxford New York

Auckland   Cape Town Dar es Salaam   Hong Kong   Karachi
Kuala Lumpur Madrid Melbourne Mexico City   Nairobi
New Delhi Shanghai Taipei Toronto
With offices in
Argentina Austria Brazil Chile Czech Republic France Greece
Guatemala Hungary Italy Japan South Korea Poland Portugal
Singapore Switzerland Thailand Turkey Ukraine Vietnam

Oxford is a registered trade mark of Oxford University Press
in the UK and in certain other countries

Published in the United States
by Inc., New York

© Oxford University Press 2001

Not to be reprinted without permission
The moral rights of the author have been asserted
Database right Oxford University Press (maker)

Reprinted 2005

All rights reserved. No part of this publication may be reproduced,
stored in a retrieval system, or transmitted, in any form or by any means,
without the prior permission in writing of Oxford University Press,
or as expressly permitted by law, or under terms agreed with the appropriate
reprographics rights organization. Enquiries concerning reproduction
outside the scope of the above should be sent to the Rights Department,
Oxford University Press, at the address above

You must not circulate this book in any other binding or cover
And you must impose this same condition on any acquirer

ISBN 0-19-829525-1

Antony Rowe Ltd., Eastbourne

Contents

List of Figures

List of Tables

List of Abbreviations

ADRs	American Depository Receipts
AKKOR	Association of Independent Peasant Farms and Co-operatives
ARKO	Agency for the Restructuring of Credit Organizations
BOP	Balance of Payments
BRU	Banking Review Unit
CBR	Central Bank of Russia
CHP	Combined heat and power plants
CIS	Commonwealth of Independent States
CMEA	Council for Mutual Economic Assistance (in Russian, SEV: *Sovet Ekonomicheskoi Vzyaimopomoshchi*)
CPRF	Communist Party of the Russian Federation
CPSU	Communist Party of the Soviet Union
DNs	*de novo* firms
EBRD	European Bank for Reconstruction and Development
ECE	East and Central Europe
EFF	Extended Fund Facility (category of IMF credit)
FBA	Federal Bankruptcy Agency
FBS	Family Budget Survey
FFST	Federal Fund for Financial Support of the Territories
FIDP	Financial Institutions Development Project
FIG (in Russian, FPG)	Financial Industrial Group
FRP	Foundation for Enterprise Restructuring
FSC (in Russian FKTs B)	Federal Securities Commission
FSRs	Former Soviet Republics
FSU	Former Soviet Union
FTDM	Foreign Trade Domestic Market
GAO	Gross Agricultural Output
Gazprom	The Russian monopoly gas enterprise
GIL	Gross International Liabilities
GKI	State Property Committee (*Goskomimushchestvo*)
GKO	*Gosudarstvennye kratkosrochnye obyazatel'stva* (State short-term obligations or treasury bills)
Goskomstat	Committee for State Statistics
IBRD	International Bank for Reconstruction and Development
IET	Institute for (the Study of) Economies in Transition (in Russian, IEPPP: *Institut Ekonomicheckikh Problem Perekhodnogo Perioda*)

IMF	International Monetary Fund
IO	firms with majority private ownership, but insider-dominated. IOs are divided into worker-dominated ('WO') and manager-dominated ('MO').
KOs	*Kaznacheiskiye obyazatel'stva* (treasury promissory notes)
KNOs	tax offset certificates
MBMW	machine-building and metal-working
MICEX	Moscow Currency Exchange
MT index	Moscow Times Index
MZRF	*Ministerstvo Zdravookhraneniya Rossiiskoi Federatsii* (Federal Ministry of Health)
MB	monetary base
MOL	Ministry of Labour
MFER (in Russian, MVES)	Ministry for Foreign Economic Relations
MFT	Ministry of Foreign Trade
MIWM	medical industry wholesale market
MSI	minimum subsistence income
MSM	Medical Services Market
NDA	Net Domestic Assets
NEP	New Economic Policy
NIR	Net International Reserves
OECD	Organization for Economic Co-operation and Development
OO	firms with majority private ownership, but outsider-dominated
OPEC	Organization of Petroleum Exporting Countries
PO	Private owners
PSO	firms which have been partially but not majority privatized
RECEP	Russian European Centre for Economic Policy
RPI	Retail Price Index
RLMS	Russian Longitudinal Monitoring Survey
RSFSR	Russian Soviet Federal Socialist Republic
SCC	State Customs Committee
SGM	Soviet Growth Model
SIC	strategically important commodities
SKSNG	*Statisticheskii Komitet Sodruzhestva Nezavisimykh Gosudarstv* (Statistical Committee of the CIS)
SO	State Owners
SSO	firms which remain 100 per cent state-owned
STE	Soviet-type Economy
STF	Systemic Transformation Facility (of the IMF)
STS	State Tax Service

UNDY	United Nations Demographic Yearbook
USDC	US Department of Commerce
USSR	Union of Soviet Socialist Republics
VIOCs	vertically integrated oil companies
VPK	*Voyenno-promyshlenniy kompleks* (military-industrial complex)
VTsIOM	All-Russia Centre for Research on Public Opinion
WHO HFA	World Health Organization Health for All Database
WHO WHSA	World Health Organization World Health Statistics Annual
WIDER	World Institute for Development Economics Research

List of Contributors

Anders Åslund, Senior Associate, Carnegie Endowment for International Peace, Washington, DC, USA

Simon Commander, Adviser to the Chief Economist at the European Bank for Reconstruction and Development (EBRD); Visiting Fellow, Centre for New and Emerging Markets and the Economics Department, London Business School, UK

Christopher Davis, Lecturer in Russian and East European Political Economy, University of Oxford and Fellow, Wolfson College, University of Oxford, UK

Mikhail Dmitriev, Scholar-in-residence of Moscow Carnegie Center of Carnegie Endowment for International Peace

John S. Earle, Associate Professor of Economics at the Stockholm Institute for Transition Economics (SITE), Sweden

Saul Estrin, Professor of Economics and Deputy Dean (Faculty and Academic Planning) at the London Business School, UK

Clemens Grafe, Economist, EBRD and London School of Economics (LSE), London, UK

Brigitte Granville, Head of International Economics Program, The Royal Institute of International Affairs, London, UK; Director of CAIS, Moscow, Russia

Christopher Granville, Chief Strategist at United Financial Group, Moscow, Russia; formerly Fellow of All Souls College, University of Oxford

Philip Hanson, Professor of the Political Economy of Russia and Eastern Europe, University of Birmingham, UK

Barry W. Ickes, Professor of Economics, Pennsylvania State University, USA

Jeni Klugman, Lead Economist, Poverty Reduction and Economic Management Network, The World Bank, Washington, DC, USA

Andrei Lushin, Alternate Executive Director for Russia, IMF, Washington, DC, USA

Sheila Marnie, Consultant on the socio-economic aspects of transition in the Former Soviet Union

Mikhail Matovnikov, Chief Expert, Center for Economic Analysis, Interfax Information Agency

Leonid Mikhailov, Director, Center for Bank Analysis, Central Economics and Mathematics Institute, Russian Academy of Science (CEMI RAS)

Nat Moser, Consultant on oil and industrial restructuring issues, Moscow, Russia

Peter Oppenheimer, Student (i.e. fellow) of Christ Church, University of Oxford; formerly (until March 2000) tutor in Economics. Since April 2000, President, Oxford Centre for Hebrew and Jewish Studies

Kaspar Richter, Economist at the World Bank, Washington, DC, USA

Carol Scott Leonard, University Lecturer and Fellow of St Antony's College, University of Oxford, UK

Eugenia Serova, Deputy Head for the Real Economy, Institute for the Economy in Transition, and Head of Department, Higher School of Economics, Moscow, Russia

Irina Starodubrovskaya, Deputy Director, Foundation for Enterprise Restructuring and Financial Institutions Development, Moscow, Russia

Ludmila Sycheva, Leading Researcher, Problems of Financial Sector Laboratory, Institute for the Economy in Transition

Eugene Timofeyev, Senior Researcher, Problems of Financial Sector Laboratory, Institute for the Economy in Transition

Andrei Tolstopiatenko Economist at the World Bank, Washington, DC, USA

Dirk Willer, Researcher, Emerging Markets Group, Centre for Economic Performance, London School of Economics, UK

1

Introduction

BRIGITTE GRANVILLE AND PETER OPPENHEIMER

The present volume offers a multi-author survey and analysis of economic developments in the Russian Federation since the collapse of Communism and the break-up of the Soviet Union, in 1989–91. This introduction sets out the international and historical context and focuses on key aspects, including some involving insights from a number of chapters without being specifically emphasized in any of them.

1.1. THE OUTPUT STORY

All the former Communist/Socialist countries of central and eastern Europe experienced a substantial (20–40 per cent) fall in national output at the onset of transition, with patchy recovery following in the later 1990s. At the end of the decade only one country—Poland—had a real GDP significantly above that of 1989. A few others (the Czech and Slovak Republics, Hungary, Slovenia) had more or less regained the 1989 level.[1] The Russian Federation's recovery was slower than most, and was additionally interrupted by the financial upheaval of August 1998 (government debt default, sharp devaluation of the currency, and bank failures). Two points about the initial decline in output are significant. First, it did not reflect the impact of western-style fiscal and monetary stabilization programmes. Except in Poland no such programmes had been put in place. Rather, it reflected two interconnected elements associated with the more or less abrupt termination of central output planning ('the command-administrative system'). To begin with, the change in the composition of output demanded by the population with the advent of market freedom was on a scale that no economic system could have realized without severe disruption. The point was most vividly reflected in

---

[1] EBRD, Transition Report (1999), p. 73.

the behaviour of international trade. During the Cold War era the countries of the Communist bloc had been required to conduct the bulk
of their external trade with each other through the COMECON or
CMEA apparatus. With the crumbling of the Communist system there
was a rush to switch trade to western partners. Western goods were better
quality and more varied. Western prices for exports of basic commodities
and semi-manufactures were often higher. The main immediate effect,
however, was a drastic and at first uncompensated contraction of intra-
COMECON trade, as erstwhile member countries rejected each other's
products and sought to sell their own outputs for hard currency only.[2]

Simultaneously with the upheaval in demand patterns came the disappearance of supply links and marketing channels. Enterprise managers
had previously been subject to—and had relied upon—ministry instructions as the basis of both input sourcing and product disposal. When these
vertical lines of communication were removed, horizontal networks
among firms, as well as direct linkages (such as market-research mechanisms) between firms and final purchasers, were almost wholly lacking and
had to be created from scratch.

Admittedly the command system had been rough and ready and
had depended a good deal on improvization for its practical functioning. However, while the spirit of improvization is often valuable, the
specific arrangements developed under Communist planning were
seldom helpful to the subsequent transition process. One example was
the tendency on the part of large enterprises to spread their own productive capacity down the supply chain, as a safeguard against interruptions to
component deliveries from elsewhere. In the context of the command-
administrative regime such 'insurance' may well have been warranted
and efficient. From the standpoint of eventual transition to a market
economy it was deplorable, fostering piecemeal agglomeration of production units in ever more sprawling and ramshackle organizations,
rather than flexible independent businesses. Another example, similarly
associated with the *ad hoc* management of over-large factories rather than
the systematic development of small businesses, were the so-called fixers
(*tolkachi*) who ran informal networks between suppliers and clients.

The second point about the drop in output at the onset of transition was
that it was entirely unforeseen by western observers, whether or not they

[2] EBRD, *Transition Report* (1994), table 8.2. See also Rodrik, D. (1994). 'Foreign Trade in
Eastern Europe's Transition: Early Results', in O. Blanchard, K. Froot, and J. Sachs (eds.),
The Transition in Eastern Europe, vol. 2, Chicago: NBER and University of Chicago Press.

had previously claimed expertise on Communist economics. The history of western judgements on the economic performance of the planned and latterly the transitional economics does indeed merit a book to itself. In the 1950s and 1960s, when the Cold War was at its height, the threat of the Soviet Union overhauling the West in economic as well as military terms was taken seriously. It gradually ceased to be so in the 1970s and 1980s, not least because the West's economic pre-eminence came under more evident challenge from quite different sources—first the OPEC oil exporters and then the newly industrializing countries of East Asia. None the less, Communist economic performance continued to be overrated, partly under the influence of propaganda both from Communist governments (the German Democratic Republic a conspicuous source alongside the USSR) and from the CIA, the latter aptly dubbed by Rodric Braithwaite 'the Nostradamus of the modern world'.[3]

As soon, however, as the failure of Communist economics was admitted by its former adherents, the consensus expectation in western circles swung to the opposite extreme: if the command-administrative system was such a disaster, then surely its abandonment must bring an instant improvement. Not so, alas.

1.2. SEQUENCING

The western misassessment pointed also to the superficiality of discussions then customary about the so-called sequencing problem, i.e. the preferred order in which key features of the market economy should be introduced. Three main features were distinguished: liberalization (of prices, of inter-enterprise transactions, and of foreign trade); privatization (of enterprises, housing, and land); and competition.[4] Events showed before long that governments had much less freedom of manœuvre than was presupposed by such grand conceptual debate.

A substantial measure of *price liberalization* was the unavoidable corollary of the abandonment of state controls over the production and

---

[3] Braithwaite, R. (1999). *Russia in Europe*. London: Centre for European Reform, p. 24. This is not the only lapidary comment in Braithwaite's booklet. Connoisseurs will appreciate, for instance, his remarks on western economic advisers in Russia (p. 34), who 'after a brief visit leave the country like Hilaire Belloc's doctors, "saying as they took their fees, there is no cure for this disease".'

[4] See, for example, *Journal of Economic Perspectives*, 5/4 (1991), Symposium on Economic Transition in the Soviet Union and Eastern Europe. Also Kaser, M. C. (1990). 'The Technology of Decontrol: Some Macro-economic Issues', *Economic Journal* 100: 596–615 and Rybezynski, T. M. (1991). 'The Sequencing of Reform', *Oxford Review of Economic Policy*, 7: 26–34.

distribution of goods. In the dying years of the USSR (to 1991) the Soviet authorities resisted the former while largely accepting the latter. To the extent that official prices were remote—and increasingly so—from market equilibrium levels, the result was a growing deflection of production and distribution activity away from inherited authorized structures into unofficial, irregular ones. The irregular structures involved a good deal of inter-firm barter and direct supply of wage goods by firms to their employees. Given the Soviet system's neglect of distribution and the tendency to wasteful inventory accumulation at all levels (another part of the effort to forestall shortages and supply interruptions), some of the barter mechanisms which emerged in the system's twilight were arguably more efficient than previous official channels. This applied, for instance, to the network of commodity exchanges which flourished briefly across the country in 1990–2 and represented a kind of generalization of the *tolkachi*.[5] Similarly with inter-firm investment agreements, which amounted to a primitive capital-market mechanism. Profitable export enterprises in climatically severe regions (for example, the diamond producers in Yakutia) provided investment funds to farming co-operatives in southern Russia or central Asia in return for guaranteed food supplies over the succeeding year or two.

The snag was, however, that such individual elements of rational enterprise did not lend themselves to aggregation. The systemic effect of allowing producers freedom to determine outputs but not to negotiate market prices was a progressive fragmentation of the economy. During 1991 attempts were made to limit the damage by freeing many wholesale prices. But with retail prices still controlled this only added to confusion, besides greatly aggravating the state budget deficit because of the need for larger subsidies. Particularly affected by the turmoil was the delivery of wage goods to households. Traditional shopping channels, long erratic in their functioning, seemed for a brief period in 1991–2 to be heading for total collapse (empty shelves in the shops, etc). The threat was lifted and a semblance of normality restored by the wide-ranging price liberalization introduced by the Gaidar government in the first quarter of 1992. The decisive nature of this move must be emphasized. The resurgence of barter later in the 1990s had quite different causes (to be sketched below) and did not stem from any attempts to reimpose price controls.

[5] See Oppenheimer, P. M. (1992). 'Economic Reform in Russia', *National Institute Economic Review*, London.

In relation to *international trade*, liberalization was mostly a corollary of the geographical upheaval noted earlier. The reorientation meant that prices of exports and imports in international trade ceased automatically to be determined by national government decision or negotiation as in the Communist era. To be sure, *internal* prices of traded goods, as well as trade volumes, remained subject to government influence through taxation and subsidization and in special cases quotas. But this was no different in principle from the situation in any established market economy.

One way of facilitating enforcement of trade taxation and/or quotas was to retain centralized organization of external trade, through either government agencies or government-approved private ones. In Russia the government for a few years designated trading companies as special export agencies to handle exports of oil and other commodities on behalf of producers. The designation was lucrative and a focus of rent-seeking and corruption. Other elements of monopoly also played a part, either because of intrinsic market or technological factors (as in the cases of diamonds, aluminium, and pipeline transmission of oil and gas) or for political reasons (e.g. Gazprom). The preservation of Gazprom as a single organization reflected—apart from personal power politics and greed—both protectionist attitudes and great-power chauvinism.

Analogous motives operated in relation to other sectors. Banking was a notorious example. In the event, Russia's first decade of post-Communist transition saw no serious progress towards the creation of a professional and trustworthy banking system outside the state Savings Bank—which itself relied on a government guarantee of deposits. The monetary lifeline for the household sector was currency liberalization or 'internal convertibility of the rouble', i.e. the fact that the population was free from early on in the transition process—in effect, from the establishment of a unified rouble exchange rate in summer 1992—to maintain unlimited holdings of hard currency. For a time the dollar made inroads as a transactions currency also. This was halted by new rules in 1995 requiring internal transactions to be settled in roubles only. Exceptions remained in street markets and the like. The main effect of the rules was to increase vastly the volume of exchange transactions between roubles and dollars. An estimated two-thirds or more of household liquid assets were still held in dollars, a phenomenon that could be labelled the poor man's capital flight. Predictions of systematic 'de-dollarization' in the wake of the introduction of the rouble exchange-rate corridor in mid-1995 proved to be premature. As a result, in August 1998, when government debt default, seventy-per cent devaluation of the rouble, and insolvency of the private banking system led western commentators to speak of financial 'meltdown' in the Russian economy, the vast majority of Russian citizens (and enterprises, too, for that matter) had protected their savings by holding the greater part of them in cash dollars. Of course, real wages were affected by the devaluation: rouble prices of importables rose sharply, and money wages did not fully catch up for two years. But this in itself was not a crisis or breakdown phenomenon. It was a matter of normal market adjustment to a normal, if painful, market shock.

With respect to *privatization*, policymakers had in some respects more freedom of action. Certainly its accomplishment took much longer than liberalization. In most of eastern Europe it was far from complete after a decade. The situation in Russia was that land privatization remained stalled, for historical and ideological reasons. Housing privatization was extensive, though marred by failure to privatize responsibility for maintenance of common areas and facilities in urban apartment blocks. A market, or series of markets, in dwellings had none the less developed. As regards privatization of enterprises, Russia was from 1994 onwards in the group of leading countries—ahead of Poland and only slightly behind Hungary and the Czech Republic (and later Albania and Estonia). EBRD guesstimates for 1999 showed about 70 per cent of Russia's GDP being produced by the private sector.[6]

As in other countries, a distinction was drawn between small-firm and larger-firm privatization. The latter, unlike the former, required the preliminary step of formation of corporate share capital. Thereafter, the main wave of privatization of larger firms was conducted in 1993–4 under the direction of Privatization Minister Anatoliy Chubais. There were two component procedures. The main one was the sale to employees and management at peppercorn prices of a significant proportion of their enterprise, the precise terms depending on a workforce vote among three alternative blueprints. The other component, far less important but internationally more publicized, was a universal distribution—following Czechoslovak precedent—of privatization vouchers entitling each holder or bearer (the vouchers being transferable and tradable) to acquire by June 1994 10,000 roubles' work of shares at privatization auctions.[7]

At the time the government, or rather the state, retained significant, often controlling, shareholdings in major enterprises of sectors viewed as critical to the national interest, such as energy and defence. Partial sales of

[6]   EBRD (1999), *Transition Report*, p. 93.
[7]   The best single account of Russia's industrial privatization is Blasi Joseph R., Kroumova Maya, and Kruse, Douglas (1997). *Kremlin Capitalism*. Ithaca, NY: Cornell University Press.

these holdings for cash began in 1994. Such sales were severely discredited by the notorious 'loans-for-shares' scheme of 1995–7, whereby proprietary control of some of the most profitable segments of the nation's capital stock passed to a handful of unscrupulous banker 'oligarchs' at a negligible price.

The relationship between this calamity and the earlier Chubais privatization strategy needs careful pondering. The difference between the two was that 'loans-for-shares' for the first time in Russian experience gave control to private outsiders rather than to the insiders who were managing the enterprise. Furthermore, the outsiders were generally bent not on strengthening the enterprise's business, but on plundering its revenue stream at the expense of minority shareholders and employees alike. This highlighted the insecurity of business property rights in Russia and the irrelevance for the time being of western, especially Anglo-Saxon, notions of corporate governance.

These shortcomings were, however, equally present when insiders had unfettered control—the situation which arose in practice as soon as planning controls were abolished in the late 1980s. Managers became autonomous in their decision-taking on output and capital investment. And many of the new private ('co-operative') firms created in the final Gorbachev years were in fact parts of long-existing enterprises appropriated by their management. In short, managers were stealing state assets. There were two ways to stop them. One was to reassert the old Communist-style state controls. Chubais's overriding priority was to prevent this. The other was to strip the state of its property rights and put management's control onto a legalized basis. Accordingly, under Chubais's privatization programme, managers went through the motions of purchasing their controlling interests, in part direct from the state but mainly from consenting or semi-consenting employees and voucher holders. The key point is that the government was acting from a position of weakness.[8]

Although there was no democratic alternative, the outcome was unsatisfactory. Mere withdrawal of the state from ownership of productive assets could not create the legal and juridical framework necessary to

---

[8] The point is emphasized by Vladimir Mau (2000), in *Russian Economic Reforms as Seen by an Insider*. London: Royal Institute of International Affairs, refuting the suggestion of Joseph Stiglitz that Russia could have stopped short at a kind of semi-privatization stage, with the state granting orderly leases to managers of enterprises over which it still exercised serious supervision. The same point had been made earlier, in 1992, by Vitaly Naishul, 'Economic Reforms: a Liberal Perspective', in Anders Aslund (ed). (1994). *Economic Transformation in Russia*. London: Pinter Publishers.

secure the new private ownership rights against theft or misappropriation by other private agents. Hence the atmosphere of banditry in corporate governance. Chubais's associates—especially Dmitri Vasiliev, head of the Federal Securities Commission in the late 1990s—soon found themselves embroiled in the issue.[9]

While privatization was merely blemished by insecurity of property rights, *competition (or anti-monopoly) policy*—the third item in the original sequencing trio—was totally sidelined. In theory it might be possible to develop anti-monopoly policies while simultaneously establishing basic ownership rights. In practice the two are scarcely compatible. Effective anti-monopoly measures in Russia would appear as simply one more source of vulnerability of industrial property rights. Struggles over legitimacy and entitlement would be further complicated. In obedience to western notions of economic correctness, the Russian authorities did indeed set up a committee, elevated in due course to a ministry, of anti-monopoly policy. Its activities have been entirely vacuous, focused on such matters as registering the names of individuals who sit on more than one corporate board of directors. Worthwhile forces of competition in post-Communist Russia have come mainly from imports, especially the 50 per cent or more import penetration in consumer expenditures (of which more below). In some service industries structural change has brought competitive benefits, the clearest example being internal air passenger transport, with the break-up of the old Aeroflot monopoly into numerous separate, mostly regional companies.

1.3. INSTITUTION-BUILDING

Property rights are a vital constituent of the institutional infrastructure of a market economy. The task of institution-building, barely mentioned at the onset of transition, moved steadily to the centre of western attention in the course of the 1990s, as may be seen by its increasing prominence in the annual Transition Reports of the EBRD. Many of the institutions in question involve the law, its enforcement, and the judicial process, together with the competence and impartiality of judges.

Apart from shareholders' rights and other business property law, key areas are the law of contract and commercial law, including bankruptcy

---

[9] For a detailed account (by lawyers) of the banditry, see Black, Bernard, Kraakman, Reinier, and Tarassova, Anna (1999). 'Russian Privatization and Corporate Governance: What Went Wrong?', Stanford Law School, processed. See also Moser and Oppenheimer in this volume.

regulations. Adjacent domains are accountancy standards and corporate financial relations. Beyond them lie the business networks referred to earlier as relevant to input supplies, technical services, product design, marketing, and so forth.

All these institutions—both physical and psychological—have in common the fact that they take time, in many instances a considerable time, to establish. Complex learning processes are involved. Some are connected with 'restructuring' (see below) and the creation of unfamiliar types of business organization. Beyond that, the key general difference between planning and market mechanisms is that the latter are non-hierarchical and involve bargaining and co-operation rather than obedience to orders. Co-operation in turn rests ultimately on awareness of mutual interests.

The classic study by Robert Axelrod models the process of learning to co-operate in terms of strategy selection in repeated games (prisoner's dilemmas).[10] This is illuminating for cases of direct confrontation between two equally favoured parties, and by extension for small numbers. With growing numbers, growing distance, and growing inequality of starting-points, progressively greater reliance has to be placed upon habitual compliance with the law, honesty, and trust. These characteristics are, in technical parlance, intermediate public goods. That is, they are non-exhaustible inputs into economic transactions. But not all the benefits they generate accrue exclusively to those who supply the inputs; so the amounts supplied tend to fall short of the ideal. In plain terms, cheating may pay. Social enforcement procedures can help to minimize cheating; but their power is intrinsically limited, not least by the personal attitudes of those entrusted with their operation. In countries with small populations—such as the Baltic states—informal enforcement pressures may be effective, based on the fact that 'everybody knows everybody else' and behaviour of persons in positions of responsibility is directly observed. With bigger populations, such neighbourhood pressures are weaker, and the formalities of the law become increasingly dominant as the only convincing enforcement mechanism. However, laws and law courts are useful only if most people are law-abiding anyhow and judges are not corrupt.

In any event, the statute book cannot be relied upon to indicate the state of institutional development. The EBRD in its Transition Reports presents and employs various numerical indicators of progress in transition on a scale from 1 to 5. Some of these relate to physical networks (telephone, electricity grid, transport systems) whose extent and condition are in principle quantifiable. Other indicators are heavily dependent on

---

[10] Axelrod, Robert (1990). *The Evolution of Co-operation*. London: Penguin Books.

opinion surveys and individual judgement, for example measures of legal 'extensiveness' and 'effectiveness'. The 1999 report cites among others an 'Index of shareholder rights' for the main groups of transition economies, compared with the same index for some advanced western countries.[11] These show that in 1998 shareholder rights in the CIS (including Russia), though less extensive than in Britain, were substantially greater than in France and Germany, and significantly greater than in Scandinavia. This is a striking indicator of the hollowness of such law in Russia (the CIS). As the EBRD remarks, USAID consultants succeeded in persuading the Russian authorities to legislate for protection of minority shareholders, but without practical effect. 'Major improvements in the state's capacity for rule enforcement will be required before the changes that have been made in the formal set of rules will affect economic outcomes.'[12]

The alignment of Russia's juridical realities with its legal dreams is, or would be, a praiseworthy aspiration—after all, even Britain and the United States accorded much less legal protection to shareholders in the nineteenth century than they do nowadays. But progress is unlikely to be swift. The inherited culture which needs displacing is that not merely of Communism but of Russia's entire history. Law in Russia has throughout been the creature of autocratic or authoritarian governments, a means for these wielding power to impose their will upon the population. It has never hitherto acquired the status of constitutionality, of being itself the acknowledged ultimate source of authority.

Moreover, the concept of economic (mainly landed) property was bound up with that of serfdom and oppression. Even after releasing the serfs, in 1861, Alexander II continued to limit their freedom of movement and occupation as well as their rights of ownership. All in all, law in the economic domain is viewed in Russia as an obstacle to be manipulated or side-stepped, and respected only if it happens to serve one's immediate interest.

1.4. ARREARS, OFFSETS, AND BARTER

Perhaps the most basic institution of the well-functioning market economy is the cash or 'hard' budget constraint. It is this which allows decision-taking on the use of resources to be decentralized to individual economic agents. One of the dysfunctional symptoms of the Russian

[11] EBRD (1999), *Transition Report*, pp. 36–9.

[12] Ibid., p. 37. The legal survey was carried out by Katherina Pistor of the Max Planck Institute for Foreign and International Law in Hamburg, following methodology developed by La Porta, Lopez de Silanes, Shleifer, and Vishny (1996) in 'Law and Finance' (National Bureau of Economic Research Working Paper No. 5661, Cambridge, Mass.).

economy is the difficulty which it has manifested in coming to terms with hard budget constraints. In the face of a 'shortage of money', Russian enterprises and other organizations resort to payment delays (arrears), offsets (paying, or seeking to pay, a creditor by transferring the entitlement to collect sums due from a debtor), and barter (including barter offsets, settling tax bills, for example, through the delivery of goods and services to third parties). The extent of recourse to such devices has fluctuated. In 1997–8, according to various reported estimates, barter accounted on average—albeit with a wide dispersion—for about half of enterprise turnover, compared with no more than 5 per cent in 1992.[13] The proportion fell back sharply in the aftermath of the 1998 devaluation.

The phenomenon has led to puzzlement regarding its consistency with normal economic behaviour (inclination to use barter 'ought' to be held in check by escalating transaction costs), and to a certain amount of rather inconclusive research seeking to discover why some enterprises choose barter when they could use cash, and whether proneness to engage in barter varies with economic sector, size of firm, market structure or region.[14] One difficulty for such research is that when barter accounts for half of corporate sector turnover, it will be difficult for any enterprise to stand aside from this method of doing business, whatever its own initial preferences; and there will be a natural tendency to husband cash where possible, against the risk that a sudden jump in barter receipts and/or in emergency cash disbursements will drain the firm's liquidity. In short, barter will have become institutionalized and the original chain of causation obscured.

As was pointed out earlier, familiarity with barter was part of the legacy of the Soviet era, and especially of its very last years when little remained of the command–administrative system except price controls. After 1992, however, markets were generally free to operate. Price controls were invoked only as a rare emergency and in a few regions. So the systemic resurgence of non-payments and barter in this period requires fresh explanation.

Initially, in 1992–3, inter-firm arrears predominated. Their order of magnitude in relation to turnover was not grossly out of line with the volume of receivables and payables typical in western firms, especially considering the inadequacy of Russian banking facilities. The difference was that criteria of normality of payment terms were not clearly established in the former Soviet Union, and the culture of the soft budget

---

[13] See 'Russia's Barter Economy' in E. Berglöf and R. Vatilingam (eds.) (1999), *Stuck in Transit: Rethinking Russian Economic Reform* (Stockholm: SITE, London: CEPR, and Moscow: RECEP), pp. 43–7.

[14] Ibid., pp. 44–6, reporting work by Guriev and Ickes, and by Guriev and Kvasov.

constraint was still a powerful collective memory. So firms' comparative unconcern about accumulating payables went together with anxiety about the ultimate riskiness of their receivables.

Increasingly, however, tax and wage arrears became more prominent, and these are phenomena unknown on any scale in the West. The challenge is to identify their fundamental causes. This is more straightforward for wages than for taxes. Wage arrears are, together with barter, an employers' substitute for downsizing and restructuring. They constitute a line of least resistance in the face of conflict among management responsibilities on the one hand and worker passivity on the other. Enterprises not paying their way are reluctant to dismiss workers, or to cut wages overtly. The government, unable to finance all of its desired commitments by a combination of taxes and prudent borrowing, is reluctant to reduce numbers in the armed forces (already heavily cut), or the civil service, or to authorize charges for health care and education.

The employees' reaction for the most part involves a measure of fragmented, third-best restructuring after all. Additional employments, or other productive activities such as home horticulture, are widely engaged in. Whereas a complete walk-out from one's principal employment is risky, not least because it threatens pension rights, part-time absence is seldom an issue. The exceptions are the armed forces (where desertion is still a rarity) and to a lesser extent the civil service. Health services have been subject to partial informal privatization through doctors levying charges. Teachers, too, at any rate in the larger cities, earn private fees on the side (sometimes corruptly, for instance in connection with admission procedures to universities). Where some wages are paid by barter—typically in a factory's own product, be it refrigerators, car parts or furniture—workers must allocate time to marketing or exchanging such goods for items that they actually want.

Tax arrears do not have such a clear-cut explanation. Given half a chance, most people in most countries would rank punctuality of tax payments low on their list of priorities. In Russia the problem is compounded by nostalgia for soft budget constraints, as well as by the government's own arrears in its payments to suppliers. This causes genuine difficulty to affected enterprises, besides encouraging a tit-for-tat attitude—an obvious vicious circle. Tax administration—as well as industrial restructuring (see below)—is handicapped by absence of consistent and workable bankruptcy regulations. Widespread arrears and barter obstruct the diagnosis of bankruptcy; lack of adequate markets for industrial and commercial assets undermines its rationale; and judicial corruption makes the outcome of proceedings unreliable. In the later 1990s bankruptcy proceedings came to be employed as a weapon in struggles for corporate control precisely of profitable enterprises, rather than a means of liquidating insolvent ones. All this is part of the institutional weakness noted earlier.

At the same time there have been avoidable mistakes of tax administration. A whole set of problems concerns accountancy standards and the definition of the highly important corporate tax base. Not only has the definition and measurement of profits been questionable, but tax demands have been calculated with reference to estimated current profits rather than actual out-turns. Another error has been the theoretical imposition of unrealistic fines and penalties for late payment, alternating with periodic amnesties seeking to regularize matters. This sets up all the wrong incentives.

A disproportionate share of the arrears and non-payments had come to rest on the broad shoulders of the energy sector. Households, manufacturers, and public authorities alike delayed settlement of bills for heating and power, at the expense of the network of electricity companies, Gazprom (the national gas monopoly) and some coal and oil enterprises. The energy sector in turn, naturally, has been tardy in settling its tax bills. Again, the situation improved radically in 1999–2000.

One other remark must be made about barter. Besides immobilizing resources and raising transaction costs, it also has a debilitating effect on developments in the monetary economy. This is because it repeatedly puts goods into the hands of people or firms who do not want them, and who consequently engage in a permanent clearance sale of the items in question, depressing their cash price and making the enterprise which produces them even less able to sell its output at full cost.[15]

1.5. RESTRUCTURING

Restructuring means altering the composition of output and/or the techniques by which it is produced. It also includes relieving large enterprises of the burden of providing social welfare facilities (housing, creches, clinics, and so forth) for their employees. The purpose is to match changes in demand or in market opportunities, increase efficiency, and take up the slack in the country's productive potential. Russia (along with many other countries of the former Soviet Union) has been slow to do

---

[15] This point was emphasized to us by Patricia V. Isaeva in connection with a study of the Russian motor industry, 'Outlook and Perspectives of the Russian Car Market' (processed, Moscow, 1998).

this, for a number of clearly identifiable reasons. First, Russia is a highly industrialized and urbanized country, but with a manufacturing sector ossified by the combination of central planning (which gave overwhelming preference to creation of large enterprises) and gross overemphasis on military outputs (a memorial to Stalinism and to the Cold War). It is a far more pronounced feature in Russia than in the former COMECON countries of central Europe. It also renders irrelevant comparisons with China's recent economic performance. The starting-point of China's rapid growth in the last quarter of the twentieth century was a degree of industrialization and an urban/rural population split comparable to that of Russia at the time of the Bolshevik revolution.[16]

Secondly, Russia's manufacturing industry is dispersed and mislocated, with a considerable proportion in the Urals and Western Siberia (in part a legacy of the Second World War), while the main population centres are squarely in European Russia. Distances are huge and surface transport systems inadequate. Many smaller towns depend on one or two enterprises to sustain employment and welfare for the whole town. Immobility of the labour force is intensified by housing shortages and the unreliable character of the housing market.

Thirdly, the above considerations point to the need for vast capital investments as an indispensable component of restructuring and modernization. Yet industrial investment has been minimal since the onset of transition. A major reason must be the institutional weaknesses noted above, especially insecure property rights and undeveloped credit and capital markets. Profitable export enterprises, a potentially key source of capital funding, have preferred to accumulate assets overseas in the interests of both security and tax evasion. Such capital flight has amounted to many tens of billions of dollars.

Fourthly, social and cultural attitudes are unfavourable. The industrial manager class is still dominated in many areas by scientists and engineers, whose thinking focuses on technological attainment and the preservation of technological competence, rather than on profitability and wealth creation.[17] More broadly, there is reluctance to accept that

---

[16] Mau, *Russian Economic Reforms*, pp. 4ff. Mau prefers to liken China in the 1980s to Russia under the New Economic Policy of the 1920s. Along with the stage of industrialization and the population balance he emphasizes also China's low literacy rate and lack of comprehensive social security and welfare systems.

[17] A good case in point is the Russian aircraft industry, a sector where Russian competitiveness should be inherently strong. See Cooper, Julian, 'Consolidation and Restructuring in the Russian Aviation Industry', Paper prepared for the VI ICCEES World Congress, Tampere, Finland, July–August 2000, Birmingham: Centre for Russian and East European Studies.

economic advance may depend on eliminating productive facilities and skills for which demand has fallen away. In addition, personal enrichment is looked at askance. This is understandable given the extent of rent-seeking and corruption and the distasteful prominence of its leading practitioners, the so-called oligarchs. But it also reflects deep-seated negative egalitarianism: better that all be poor together than that some become wealthy at the imagined expense of others. Such attitudes are particularly tenacious in the agricultural sector,[18] along with the view that massive state subsidies are a God-given right for those who produce the nation's food.[19]

1.6. STANDARDS OF LIVING

Yet perhaps the most insidious obstacle to industrial restructuring is the fact that the country can get by without it—not prospering exactly, but certainly surviving. This is primarily because of the vast mineral resources which furnish the bulk of its exports. But manufacturing enterprises also play a role. Take, for instance, Russia's major producer of titanium metal at Verkhnyaya Salda in the Urals. By the latter part of the 1990s the firm (called VSMPO) had developed a sufficient export business with western customers such as Boeing and Airbus to sustain the town dependent upon it. Wages were low but generally paid without arrears. In the process the firm was utilizing no more than 10–15 per cent of its peak capacity—not surprisingly, since the plant was built with the USSR's Cold War military requirements in mind; but the idle 85 per cent is a vivid instance of the 'ossification' referred to above.

Although such cases involve an absence of *physical* restructuring, the refocusing on exports does constitute a perceptible *economic* restructuring. In consequence, the stylized facts about the Russian economy are that in the first decade or so of transition a 40 per cent decline in recorded GDP was accompanied by little net change in average living standards. This startling contrast was possible because, first, much of the output decline occurred in the defence and military-industrial sectors, which had contributed little to living standards previously. Secondly, the ratio to GDP of external trade in goods and services increased dramatically, and on the import side was concentrated on consumption goods, domestic fixed investment

---

[18] A well-known Russian anecdote explains the difference between western and Russian capitalism. In the west a farmer owning one cow will try to emulate his neighbour with two cows by acquiring a second one. In Russia he will plan to strangle his neighbour's second cow.

[19] Analogous perhaps to the average American's God-given right to cheap gasoline and electricity.

other than residential and office building being at a low ebb. Thirdly, Russia ceased to make unrequited resource transfers to other states of the former Soviet Union and eastern Europe, whether through the under-pricing of its fuel exports or through cash contributions to government budgets. Previously such policies were costing Russia 10 per cent or more of its GDP.[20] A possible fourth factor is that the net output decline may be overstated because of the relative growth of the 'grey' or shadow economy, whose full extent is not captured in the statistics. Although plausible, neither leg of this argument (relative growth and statistical capture) is wholly convincing; and the assessment does not greatly rely upon it.

The 'shortage' phenomenon of involuntary, or at least artificially high, household saving due to lack of attractions on offer disappeared after 1991; and on official Goskomstat figures the share of imports in consumer spending rose from 14 per cent in that year to nearly 50 per cent by 1994. Apart from the sheer volume of imports, the higher quality of many imported items was a benefit to living standards in Russia. And while the lack of business investment was regrettable, and a pointer to future pro-blems of worn-out and obsolete capital assets, the country could not be said to be living beyond its means: the current balance of payments was in sizeable surplus in every year except 1998, matched by the aforementioned outflow of capital, mostly into western financial institutions.

It should be noted in this context that official statistics of Russian household incomes and their utilization are not satisfactory. The matter has been usefully investigated by Sergei Nikolaenko of the Moscow Institute of World Economics, the Bureau of Economic Analysis, and the Russian European Centre for Economic Policy.[21] His researches are the source of the following remarks. Neither in the USSR nor in post-Soviet Russia has there been direct measurement of nominal household income or consumption expenditure. Instead the income picture is built up by

---

[20] See, *inter alia*, Tarr, D. G. (1994), 'The Terms-of-Trade Effects of Moving to World Prices on Countries of the Former Soviet Union', *Journal of Comparative Economics*, 18(1), 1–24; and International Monetary Fund (1994), *Economic Review: Financial Relations among Countries of the Former Soviet Union*, Washington DC: IMF.

    Cessation of these transfers meant some corresponding loss to the erstwhile recipi-ents—but also thereby encouraged them to reform their economies more speedily: see for instance Irina Starodubrovskaya's remarks about housing reforms in Kazakhstan (in chapter 14 below).

[21] Nikolaenko, S. (1998). 'Personal Consumption During the Transitional Period in Russia'. Moscow: RECEP. 1998. Incidentally, Nikolaenko's threefold institutional affilia-tion nicely exemplifies the operation (flexibility, restructuring) of the Russian labour mar-ket in the case of high-grade professionals.

Goskomstat from separate proxy estimates of the consumption component and the saving component, the latter with an adjustment for assumed tax deductions from income (mostly 12 per cent of registered wages in the 1990s). Consumption estimates are based on registered retail sales figures with some addition to allow for unregistered trade. Saving is calculated from financial data—as the sum of increases in holdings of bank deposits and other financial assets *plus* increases in the rouble note circulation *plus* gross purchases of convertible foreign exchange by residents.

If one is interested in living standards or economic welfare, then a further (positive) allowance must be made for items (mostly foodstuffs) produced and consumed by the same household, as well as for the social wage (health care, education, and other zero-priced services, whose value to the household sector is effectively indexed). By comparison with the Soviet era, the former has probably increased and the latter declined somewhat, with the decline largely made up by unregistered trade. But both remain important, the social wage critically so, since it continues to include the major item of housing, as well as secondary items such as free urban transport for pensioners and other designated groups.[22] In many poorer areas it also effectively includes household heating and lighting—whether through explicit subsidization by local government or through toleration of non-payment of bills.

In Nikolaenko's (persuasive) view, the most serious weakness in the core methodology is the over-estimation of saving. Goskomstat data show the household saving ratio in the 1990s as maintaining its pre-1992 level of around 25 per cent. This highly implausible finding can be attributed to the erroneous treatment of households' foreign currency purchases. Central bank data on currency transactions indicate that about half of these purchases are matched by household sales. In other words, dissaving by some matches saving by others. Taking gross purchases is like counting the inflow of deposits to a savings bank and ignoring withdrawals. In addition, a further 30–40 per cent of gross purchases are for financing two categories of imports: foreign tourism; and the purchase abroad of durable goods by small traders (the so-called shuttle traders), many of them doubtless unregistered. Altogether, only 20 per cent at most of households' gross foreign currency purchases should be attributed to saving.

[22] Privatization of formerly public housing (chiefly urban flats) means that, conceptually, the corresponding part of the social wage becomes imputed rent on owner-occupied dwellings.

This single correction yields a far more plausible saving ratio from 1994 onwards of 8–10 per cent. In other words, household savings have been 60 per cent lower than officially reported. The effect on estimated income is mitigated by the fact that individual tourist spending abroad (as distinct from packages paid for in Russia) is a previously omitted element of consumption, about 3 per cent of the total. So the estimate of personal money income ends up reduced by 12–15 per cent.

The main implication of the foregoing statistical discussion is that Russian households have lower stocks of liquid assets—whether as longer term savings or as a contingency reserve—than previously implied. While this subtracts from economic well-being, it does not alter the broad judgement that average living standards have undergone little net change in Russia's first decade of transition. The stylized average, however, conceals three major sources of variation: in the composition of the consumer basket; in the distribution of income across the population; and in year-to-year fluctuations within the decade. Some aspects of these variations are highlighted in later chapters.

As regards the consumer basket, the major shift was away from previously subsidized food and services (inter-city public transport, utility and welfare services) towards private cars, imported durable goods and foreign travel. The biggest single change was the increase in private car ownership, from 59 vehicles per 1,000 of the population in 1990 (itself double the 1980 figure) to over 100 from 1997 onwards.[23] The latter figure was still only one-quarter of the average in western industrial countries. Ownership of household durables (television and radio, washing machines, refrigerators, vacuum cleaners, etc.) was already at a high level in the 1980s; a slow upward trend was maintained after 1990, but here the main change was quality improvement associated with greater import penetration.

On the negative side, there was possibly some deterioration in medical services, though certainly not such as to account for the massive rise in male mortality in the first half of the decade, which went together with increased alcohol consumption.[24] Utility charges (for power, heating,

[23] This compares with 180 cars per 1,000 population in Poland. Russian car *production* peaked at 1.1 million in 1990, declined to 800,000 in 1994, and recovered to 982,000 in 1997. Production of trucks, in contrast, plunged from nearly 700,000 in 1990 to under 150,000 in 1996–7—another clear instance of excessive capacity and ossification bequeathed by the Soviet period. See Isaeva, 'Russian Car Market'; and Goskomstat Yearbooks for aggregate data.

[24] In the later 1990s the mortality rate fell back again almost as steeply, though it turned upwards once more in 1999–2000, suggesting a link with economic stress and hardship.

and telephones) were steeply increased, and in the cases of heat and power with little opportunity to economize other than by escaping with unpaid bills. Internal air, and to a lesser extent rail, travel was restrained by large price increases from absurdly low levels. Food consumption figures give some signs of deteriorating standards after 1991 (per capita declines in meat, fish, eggs, and dairy products), arguably reflecting hardship among lower income groups, a larger percentage of whose budget goes on food. However, the trend began not in 1991 but at least ten years earlier; so interpretation must be cautious.

A large increase in income inequality is none the less undeniable, and indeed was a predictable phenomenon of transition in view of the enforced compression of earnings under Communism. In Russia the standard index of inequality, the Gini coefficient, increased from 0.27 in 1990 to 0.48 in 1996 (the outer limits being 0 and 1).[25] Later figures are not available. Russia's inequalities have a strong regional dimension, which has probably become more marked. At the top end, Moscow and surroundings are appreciably more prosperous than other areas. At the bottom, many of the worst hit are in parts of the far north and east, dependent upon government outlays in one form or another.

The EBRD Transition Report for 1999 also cites 38 per cent of Russia's population as being 'in poverty'—a lower figure, incidentally, than in most other countries of the former Soviet Union, including the Baltic states. Much of this poverty, however, particularly in small towns and rural areas, reflects not deterioration since 1990 but standards little changed for a century or more. It is also doubtful whether the EBRD has adequately allowed for the fact that housing for most Russians remains to all intents and purposes zero-priced.[26]

As regards fluctuations over time, these have been largely a by-product of the liberalization process and of the ups and downs of financial stabilization policy. The final year or two of price controls without wage restrictions or output planning (1990–1) led to an unsustainable boom in real spending. This was followed by the price liberalization shock of

One reason for scepticism about a worsening of medical services is that their proclaimed reputation in the Soviet period was questionable. The number of doctors per head of population was high, but hospital standards were poor and treatments frequently out of date. For detailed discussion, see Christopher Davis in this volume.

[25] EBRD (1999), *Transition Report*, p. 260.

[26] This point certainly accounts for much of the perplexity and confusion in Simon Clarke (1999), 'Making Ends Meet in a Non-monetary Market Economy', Centre for Comparative Labour Studies, University of Warwick.

1992, which reduced real spending by half. The ensuing recovery was interrupted by the short-term rouble collapse in October 1994 and its aftermath, and by tighter monetary conditions in the first half of 1995. Renewed improvement in 1996–8 was brought to an abrupt halt by the devaluation of August 1998, which caused an immediate reduction of some 25 per cent in household real wages.

The Finance Ministry and the Central Bank remained commendably steadfast in the following twelve months, declining to permit a renewed wage–price spiral to develop. This underlined the long-term nature of the victory over inflation achieved by the authorities in 1995–6. It also enabled devaluation to yield real benefits in the form of enhanced competitiveness of import-competing enterprises, including small businesses in such sectors as building materials, electronics, and food-processing. Industrial production climbed about 10 per cent in the year following the 1998 devaluation. Of course the country, and especially tax revenues and the budget balance, also benefited greatly from the trebling of world oil prices in 1999–2000, which temporarily lifted Russia's current payments surplus to well above 10 per cent of GDP. The second decade of Russia's transition thus began on an upbeat note—even though only small inroads had been made into the country's deep-seated structural and institutional weaknesses.

2

The Political and Societal
Environment of Economic Policy

CHRISTOPHER GRANVILLE

2.1. INTRODUCTION

The Russian Federation began its existence as a new fully sovereign state on 31 December 1991. By then it had obtained international recognition as the continuing state of the former Soviet Union; and it had a government in place poised to carry out radical measures designed to transform on market lines the country's stricken centrally planned economy. These developments flowed directly from the failure of the coup attempt staged in Moscow in August 1991 by Party and KGB conservatives.

The coup plotters aimed to salvage the system that had already been fatally damaged by the effects of the political liberalization under Mikhail Gorbachev. Instead they precipitated the very outcome they wished to prevent. This made the coup at once futile in its own terms (it should go down as one of history's most counter-productive undertakings) but also revolutionary in its consequences. While the Soviet system may already have been doomed by the beginning of the decade, there were still many plausible ways and timescales in which the end of the system could have unfolded. The abortive *putsch* determined that the demise of the system would take the form of headlong collapse. The defeat of the coup led within days to the extinction of the Communist Party of the Soviet Union (CPSU), and hence of the order established by Lenin and his Bolshevik colleagues and successors after their seizure of power in October 1917. In a totalitarian system the removal of the linchpin (in this case, the CPSU) will logically cause general disintegration. So the CPSU, once defunct, could not be survived long by the centrally planned economy, or even (as the world discovered to its shock five months later) by the Soviet Union itself. The entire economy, like the empire, was 'bound up with and inseparable from the political system, and collapsed together with it'.[1]

The August coup attempt may therefore be taken as the most logical starting-point for the political and economic history of post-Soviet Russia. Thanks to the coup the decay characteristic of the Gorbachev period turned into dissolution, which in turn shaped the political conditions for the conduct of economic policy during the following years. But this shaping was contradictory. On the one hand, the collapse of the economic system made it possible for the first time to begin implementing serious economic reforms instead of merely talking about them.[2] On the other hand, the conduct of policies designed to establish competitive market capitalism was severely complicated and at times vitiated by the circumstances and effects of the systemic breakdown.

In short, economic reform was given its chance by the collapse of the system; but the collapse also undermined that chance, as efforts to form a free market competitive economy foundered in the ruins. Both effects of the political environment—positive in the short term for the launch of economic transformation, inimical to the success of that transformation in the medium to longer term—deserve close inspection.

2.2. THE POSITIVE EFFECTS OF SYSTEMIC COLLAPSE FOR ECONOMIC REFORM

The final discrediting of the central institutions (CPSU Central Committee, KGB, Council of Ministers) and their conservative leaderships did not remove the last political obstacle to the launch of real economic reform. Besides that, there had to be both alternative legitimate authorities in place, and broad public acceptance—especially in the ferment of the country's new-born democracy—for introducing policies which were necessarily radical and painful. Those two further conditions for economic reform to become politically possible were likewise met as a result of the collapse of the old system.

---

[1] Murrell (1997), p. 2.

[2] All talk and no action culminated in the blocking of the '500 Days' programme in autumn 1990 by the Soviet prime minister, Nikolai Ryzhkov, the most senior official in the state with direct responsibility for economic policy, who together with other conservatives still in a majority in the country's top leadership rightly saw that the programme's call for large-scale privatization spelled fundamental changes in state and society.

By 1991 even Muscovites had begun to experience the widespread shortages and rationing that had long been everyday reality for most people living outside the capital. Such hardships could be endured while they were stable, rather as lying in a tepid bath can be made tolerable by remaining completely still. But the relative attractions of what had become known as the Brezhnev 'period of stagnation' depended on there at least being something in the shops. When little or nothing could be got from 10-hour queues in freezing temperatures, or from bribing shop managers and staff (as even the black market experienced supply difficulties), then popular support was possible for previously unthinkable measures—beginning with the liberalization of prices. When the bath water temperature falls from tepid to cold the pain of movement (or reform) becomes preferable to continuing inaction.

Once the system could no longer guarantee a minimum level of subsistence, it forfeited its economic legitimacy, just as the products of *glasnost* (free speech, the exposure of Soviet lies and crimes, the unmasking of *nomenklatura* privilege) broke the spell of the Party's dictatorship. Usefully for the cause of economic reform, this delegitimization of CPSU rule preceded the final breakdown of the old economy, in the autumn of 1991. In those months after the coup it became apparent that the command system could no longer perform its most elementary functions, such as the centralized collection and distribution of grain and other agricultural products. Thus arose the threat of hunger in Moscow, St Petersburg, and other big cities during the coming winter. The alternative of importing vital foodstuffs was limited by depleted reserves, as heavy gold sales in the preceding year had exhausted that expedient. Continuing centralized imports of essential medicines became similarly unaffordable. The debacle culminated in December with the bankruptcy of the Soviet Vneshekonombank, including the unprecedented default on short-term trade debt which ruined the country's creditworthiness. This calamitous situation left no alternative to the previously unthinkable abandonment of administrative prices. In such circumstances the hardship from price liberalization could be perceived as the lesser evil, for which the public was braced.

Besides popular acceptance, the other precondition for radical economic action was political renewal. By the time that moment of truth for economic policymaking had been reached, the process of political change had advanced far enough for Russia to have already in place a determinedly anti-Soviet government under Boris Yeltsin. Yeltsin's victory in the RSFSR presidential election of June 1991 was the latest in a series of electoral successes born of popular revulsion against the discredited CPSU. Yeltsin had staked his pitch on leaving the system behind, rather than renewing it. With the economic emergency of the autumn and winter still in the future, Yeltsin's populist campaign could safely include economic policy slogans of painless reform. His promise at that time to 'lie down on the rails' to stop the 'locomotive' of price increases would later be used against him by his opponents. But the important point for the short term was that when faced with economic emergency a few months later, the Yeltsin administration had the political orientation and, above all, the political capital necessary to rise to the occasion.

This meant something more than the mere fact of deciding to free prices, a decision in any case dictated by the circumstances: it also allowed the administration to make a political virtue of that decision. Popular and legitimate, Yeltsin could tap the potential for public acceptance of price liberalization as the lesser evil. The crisis could be blamed on the hesitations and mistakes of the Gorbachev administration (and beyond that, on the seventy years of the Soviet system which Russia was now casting off). In his programme speech to the Fifth Congress of RSFSR People's Deputies on 28 October 1991 Yeltsin announced that economic reform would now begin for real: 'economic reform proposals which leave out price liberalization are so much empty talk'. Against that background, he could appeal for short-term sacrifices to win the future prize of 'normal life', by which was meant a society free from tyranny and the attainment of decent living standards comparable to the advanced western industrial democracies. These elementary political methods of sustaining painful reform policies depended on abundant political capital. We shall have to return to this theme of political capital formation as the key to understanding the dynamic of economic reform.

To summarize the positive impact of the Soviet 'meltdown' for embarking on policies designed to construct a new type of economy based on competitive market capitalism: the collapse itself created the essential political conditions for reform, in that entrenched élite opposition was (temporarily) removed, while the public could see that doing nothing was no longer an option. At the same time collapse immediately followed (rather than preceded) the emergence of a new legitimate authority in Russia, so there was a government already in place with the basic political equipment to implement that reform.

2.3. THE NEGATIVE EFFECTS OF SYSTEMIC COLLAPSE FOR ECONOMIC REFORM

That was only part of the political story, however. To be sure, the sequence of political followed by economic collapse greatly facilitated the initial implementation of radically new economic policies. But the minimum political construction for carrying through such policies was not yet in place. In legal and constitutional terms, Russia's break from the Soviet system had scarcely begun.

2.3.1. *The Soviet constitution*

The elected presidency had been grafted onto a Soviet political reality which would reassert itself with a vengeance after the economic reformers had spent what proved to be the briefest of political honeymoons. That reality was both conjunctural and systemic.

In terms of everyday politics, Russia's parliament had been elected for a five-year term in February 1990, when the CPSU still controlled the country. With the exception of the big cities, where the local Party organizations could no longer prevent genuinely independent democratic candidates standing (and almost always winning), the slate was fixed, and the result accordingly adjudged most satisfactory by the Politburo.[3] The systemic problem, however, was not the present composition of the parliament but rather its very nature as an institution. The RSFSR constitution in force at the moment of collapse in 1991 dated from 1977; and as was inevitable for a product of the Brezhnev era, enshrined the principles of the system established by Lenin. 'All power to the Soviets' remained the formal basis of the state; but this had always been a sham, given the reality of the total monopoly of power by the Party. After August 1991, however, the demise of the CPSU allowed that fiction of seventy-four years to become a reality. True, the constitution had been substantially amended. Following the example of the Congress of USSR People's Deputies in March 1990, its RSFSR counterpart had dropped the article in the constitution on the 'leading role' of the Communist Party. Then the referendum in March 1991 on the preservation of the union included an additional question in the RSFSR on introducing the

---

[3] A Politburo meeting chaired by Gorbachev in March 1990, the minutes of which were leaked to a liberal newspaper (*Kuranty*) in June 1993, congratulated itself on the record numbers of Party, KGB, and Interior Ministry personnel elected to the RSFSR Congress.

office of president elected by universal suffrage; and this constitutional amendment was approved by the necessary majority of over half the electoral roll. But such accretions could not change the fundamental principle enshrined in Article 104, that 'any matter for the Russian Federation falls within the competence of the Congress of People's Deputies'. The congress, and its standing parliament offshoot, the Supreme Soviet, on paper could decide whatever they liked—including, most importantly as events proved, the power to amend the constitution itself at will. In short, there was no separation of powers. Even the judges of the newly instituted Constitutional Court and other senior members of the judiciary were appointed solely by the congress. Standard checks and balances were non-existent.

Until a new constitution could be adopted, the systemic framework was a fundamentally Soviet one in the sense that there was a sole and supreme power to be struggled over, as opposed to a competition for power hedged by checks and balances. None of this would have mattered in a political environment where the struggle for power was conducted between parties and politicians united, despite rivalry and mutual animosity, behind a broad consensus on the country's identity, interests, and aspirations, and whose differences were not much wider than, say, those on taxation and public expenditure which typically divide major political parties in western democracies. In the revolutionary condition of Russia in the early nineties, by contrast, the substance of political struggle could hardly have been more fundamental.

At stake was the very direction of the country's development, and indeed the existence of the country. For mainstream opinion could not imagine the Russian state apart from the union, and more especially a Russia confined within the borders of what had been the RSFSR— a meaningless administrative demarcation inside the USSR, transformed overnight into a state frontier, beyond which lay not only former colonies but lands (such as in eastern and southern Ukraine, or northern Kazakhstan) inhabited by ethnic Russian or Russian-speaking populations, and difficult to think of as anything but Russian. The 'loss of the country', in the resonant phrase which became a favourite of the Communist and national Socialist opposition to the Yeltsin administration, was compounded by the reality of economic change. All this was not at all what had been bargained for by the *nomenklatura* of the Party, KGB, and state enterprises which formed the conservative majority of the Congress of People's Deputies, nor even by several prominent members of the 'Democratic Russia' grouping which formed the radical minority.

The ballast of the congress was formed by the second-tier *nomenklatura* which had always staffed the institutions of the RSFSR; so for the most part, the deputies were happy to join in the opportunistic political adventure led by Yeltsin against the senior Union Centre and Gorbachev, and to grant him majority support (albeit often a slim majority) in 1990–1.

This joint venture triumphed as Yeltsin and the RSFSR Supreme Soviet stood shoulder to shoulder in facing down the August 1991 coup. Looking back at the lost opportunity of using his unrivalled authority after the defeat of the coup to dissolve the congress/Supreme Soviet and secure a fully democratic parliament and new, post-Soviet constitution, Yeltsin wrote in his volume of memoirs published in 1994 that the successful political alliance with the deputies made such an emergency-type measure seem uncalled for. Besides, other matters seemed more pressing at the time, none more so than the launch of economic reform with the breakdown of the command economy. This calculation was apparently vindicated when the Fifth Congress in October acceded to Yeltsin's request for special decree powers for one year to launch economic reform. Amidst the general enthusiasm, the refusal of that otherwise benign Fourth Congress to adopt a new constitution was a warning signal that went unheeded. Within months a much larger majority was united in opposition to the policies of the Yeltsin administration, which it rightly saw as transforming beyond recognition the country and world it had known. This opposition denounced the hardship experienced by the whole population as price liberalization unleashed hitherto repressed inflation, laying bare the destruction of savings. The tribunes of the congress, led by its chairman, Ruslan Khasbulatov, and by Vice-President Alexander Rutskoi, declared that the people must be protected from mistaken reforms (while still paying lip-service to an undefined goal of reform: it was still too early for the outright nostalgia for the Soviet past which would grow by the middle of the decade into a powerful political factor). Yet as leaders of the opposition-dominated congress they showed little inclination to appeal directly to the voters. Instead they chose the safer battleground of using their power of constitutional amendment to try to reduce the presidency to the role of a decorative head of state. This would have neutralized Yeltsin and his hated reforms, leaving the congress leaders in complete control of all branches of power. Yeltsin's response, in the first great confrontation at the Seventh Congress in December 1992, was to say 'let the people decide'. He had no other way to assert his superior democratic legitimacy and by no means exhausted popularity against the impregnable Soviet constitutional legality wielded by the semi-democratically elected congress.

Here then was the first, and perhaps most immediate, of the negative ways in which the abruptness of the Soviet collapse shaped the political environment for economic reform. The RSFSR suddenly found itself a sovereign post-Soviet state, but still with a Soviet constitution. Piecemeal amendments had not changed the fundamental Soviet character of the constitution, which now became the legal basis of the state in more than the hitherto merely formal sense. With the Party dictatorship ended, constitutional legality entered the sphere of practical politics as the main weapon in the revanchist armoury.

Two other negative bequests of the systemic collapse to the causes of economic reform were more deep-seated. These bequests had to do with the élites, and with underlying social values.

2.3.2. *The Soviet élite*

If the Soviet constitutional legacy invited a debilitating struggle for total power, the systemic collapse ensured that this invitation would be taken up. The demise of the totalitarian order meant that the construction of a replacement would, accordingly, have to be total. As summarized by G. D. G. Murrell: 'Russia faced the task of building democratic institutions while transforming its economic system and trying to construct a new national identity.'[4] In the face of this enormity the élite was utterly disoriented. The opportunistic power grab from the union centre was a transient rallying point. It disappeared immediately after the RSFSR Supreme Soviet ratified in December 1991 the Belovezhskaya Pushcha Accord between Russia, Ukraine, and Belarus, by which the USSR was dissolved. The accord quickly became anathema to the bulk of the same political class which had voted it into law. In March 1996 the Communist-dominated State Duma denounced the 'Belovezhskaya conspiracy' and with it, the founding act of Russia's new sovereign statehood. There was thus no élite consensus on a national project, which would have allowed first a modern constitution to be quickly adopted and then a broadly stable policy agenda to emerge, with different political forces competing for the right to manage it in the framework of a stable set of rules defined by the new constitution.

---

[4] Murrell (1997), p. 2.

The lack of such a consensus continued to make itself acutely felt in economic policy difficulties throughout the decade, and most notably in the opposition of the political class to the fiscal adjustment measures designed to avert the financial debacle which, partly as a result of that opposition, duly came in August 1998. A chronic, but no less damaging, manifestation of this problem was the blockage on land reform. Denial of private land ownership, and still more of a free market in agricultural land, was an ideological shibboleth for the Communist and para-Communist segment of the political class, which had the voting power to block the relevant legislation in all the various parliaments during the decade. As a result, agricultural reform was stillborn.

An élite-led national consensus was key to economic advance in Poland and other successful 'transition' countries of central and eastern Europe. This consensus was based on the naturally unifying goal of national reconstruction after shedding the colonial yoke of Russia and the Soviet system. In Russia, by contrast, the task of total construction had to be undertaken in a climate of profound ambivalence; and more often, of élite hostility born of nostalgia for the lost order. That nostalgia was initially more pronounced among the former *nomenklatura* rather than the mass electorate. Ordinary people had less cause for immediate regret at the passing of the Soviet system; and while the death agony of that system remained fresh in the memory, they could hope for something better to emerge under the popular leadership of Yeltsin. At the same time, there were contradictory currents at work in what had been the *nomenklatura*. The truculent opposition, especially the new Russian Communist Party itself, was dominated by mainly middle-ranking career Party officials; others meanwhile, especially from the upper echelons of the old Party-state and economic apparatus were often astute enough to see, and energetic enough to exploit, the opportunities presented by the new circumstances, quietly enriching themselves. These contrasting élite reactions could often coexist in the same group, or even individual. Yuri Luzhkov's Moscow city government opposed and obstructed the mass voucher privatization campaign, while at the same time building a business empire based on partially privatized enterprises. More generally, enterprise directors used their political influence to agitate for the cost-free working capital they had enjoyed under central planning (often for good measure black-mailing the government with threats of worker unrest), while at the same time manipulating the privatization process to gain majority control of their enterprises and, in many cases, embezzling the enterprises' cash flow.[5] An equally good example were the directors of collective and state farms. Through the Agrarian Party (the rural offshoot of the CPRF), they led the campaign against land reform. At the same time, the inefficiency of their operations was no obstacle to many of them making personal fortunes from their control of the sales revenues.

To many observers, the way that the privileged élite of the old system so easily and completely exploited its collapse has seemed a particularly shocking aspect of Russia's transition. The least deserving were the greatest beneficiaries. Shocking perhaps, but hardly surprising. Once the end of the CPSU had removed the residual constraints of discipline and fear, there was every incentive and no serious obstacle to its former *nomenklatura* helping themselves to the material products and resources for which they had previously exercised a managerial responsibility already akin to ownership—at least relative to the unreality of the 'people's ownership' of official ideology.

Besides being unavoidable, this unedifying reality also had its desirable aspect. Any genuinely revolutionary situation such as the one in which Russia found itself in 1991, presents two alternatives as regards the privileged élite of the former regime. Either they are bribed to accept the new order, or else their resistance must be broken. The second course implies Bolshevik methods, or at least some sort of revolutionary coercion: but since the 1991 revolution was supported, on the ideological plane, by revulsion against a regime founded on purges and terror, this was not an alternative. There was certainly no alternative élite or opposition waiting in the wings. The CPSU 'was deliberately organized to exclude the possibility of any autonomous social unit, since it co-opted the ambitious in every walk of life'.[6]

Given the political realities of the time, however, there are no grounds for relief in the fact that the change of system in 1991 occurred without widespread revolutionary violence—which, as regards the former regime élites, tends to mean forced exile, enslavement, or murder. For there was no possibility of Russia's new rulers following in the footsteps of their Bolshevik predecessors in the years after 1917. As already noted, the prevailing ideological impulse at the time of the Soviet collapse was, by definition, hostile to the CPSU dictatorship and all its works. By the end of the 1990s the commitment to civilized political values of the

---

[5] Such looting became widespread after the State Enterprise Law of 1988 introduced the first relaxation of state control, and thus pre-dated mass privatization. At the same time privatization tended to make stealing even easier.   [6] Murrell (1997), p. 3.

leaders of 'Democratic Russia' who came to power in 1991, and especially of Boris Yeltsin himself, was widely seen as skin deep, if not hypocritical. Regardless of whether that stern judgement will stand the test of time and evidence,[7] there is no escaping the fact that the new Russian leadership was quite unlike the utopian and fanatical Boshevik revolutionaries in that it came from the heart of the old (in this case, CPSU) ruling caste, with the career of Yeltsin himself a much-cited case in point. This fact suffices to refute any hypothetical argument that the lack of an alternative élite was as true of 1917 as of 1991, and that the post-Soviet Russian authorities could therefore have imitated the Bolshevik example—while avoiding the worst Bolshevik methods—of pragmatic short-term exploitation of old regime specialists followed by their longer term exclusion and replacement with a new élite answering to new values. No such classic revolutionary programme, even in the form of the most pacific and orderly lustration, could be expected from the former CPSU officials who, whether from idealist conviction or opportunism, abandoned the Party and sought to lead Russia out of the Soviet system and into the mainstream of modern civilization.

It follows that in the Russian revolution of 1991 and its aftermath, the old élites would inevitably be accommodated rather than confronted. More precisely, the privileged could accommodate themselves. Self-enrichment was against the principles, or beyond the abilities, of the ideological diehards constituting that large part of the political class grouped by mid-decade around a revived Communist Party (now 'of the Russian Federation'—CPRF). Other, more opportunistic, hardliners combined discreet private business interests with the pursuit of the political dividends to be got from vehement public opposition to the declared liberal capitalist objectives of the Yeltsin administration. This hard political opposition was confronted by the new regime only in self-defence, as in the constitutional struggle culminating in the political violence of October 1993. As the decade progressed, however, ideological opposition became a minority pursuit for the old élites, which focused instead mostly on turning new circumstances to their advantage.

So it was that as regards the existing ruling class, Russia's change of political system was characterized more by accommodation and underlying

---

[7] Writing in *The World Today*, 55/6 in June 1999, Anna Matveeva leaves this question judiciously open: 'Reflecting on Yeltsin in decline, one might wonder how he will go into history. Was he ever bound by a sense of duty to his people? Did he feel responsible for them? Was he enthusiastic about anything apart from personal gain and what were his values, if any?'

continuity than by confrontation and repression. Just because this outcome was inevitable for Russia after 1991 does not necessarily make it less intrinsically preferable. After all, the alternative implies the political violence and terrorism of textbook revolutions. However, cases of the more humane path of transformation, as in Russia in the 1990s, pose the question of the price paid; or, put another way, of whether the underlying continuities were so strong as to compromise the goals of the transformation. For reasons that will become clear, this question bears not only on general historical value judgements about revolutions but also specifically on the subject of this chapter, which is the political context of economic reform efforts.

The answer is that the price was very high indeed. One might even say that the price could not have been higher: for the 'old-new Russians' took as much as they could, stopping at nothing. Gazprom serves as the emblem. By mid-decade, and as a result of a process devoid of any transparency, this monopoly extractor and transporter of the world's largest reserves of natural gas, and the economy's biggest wealth creator by far, had fallen under the effective control of its incumbent management with the State shareholding reduced to a minority (40 per cent). Anatoly Chubais, the architect of the mass voucher privatization, said in 1994 that the new business élite 'steal and steal. They are stealing absolutely everything and it is impossible to stop them. But let them steal and take their property. They will then become owners and decent administrators of this property.'[8] This sanguine vision was belied by events in the second half of the decade. Its realization would have required effective state action to make the new élite face up to their responsibilities as property owners on pain of insolvency procedures and loss of property. But the state was too weak for such action. In a process that became fully visible to the naked eye after the 1996 presidential election, and that has since been well described,[9] the business élite or new 'oligarchs'[10] not only used their political connections to obtain property in the first place (most notoriously in the rigged 'loans-for-shares' privatizations of 1995–7); but they also maintained those connections to ensure that they could do as they pleased with their property, often regardless of law or equity, while all the time appropriating further public assets and resources. This is the phenomenon which has

[8] This remark was made in a private conversation with Sergei Kovalyov, the leading human rights campaigner and former dissident.

[9] Notably by Anatol Lieven in ch. 4 of his *Chechenya: Tombstone of Russian Power* (1998).

[10] A term coined as pejorative in 1997 by First Deputy Prime Minister Boris Nemtsov, but since widely used as a descriptive shorthand, and even on occasion repeated with pride by the 'oligarchs' themselves.

become known as the 'privatization of the state'. In this context, political connections meant key decision-making officials being in the pay of 'oligarchs'. Indeed, by 1997, it seemed that large parts of the judiciary and federal government apparatus, including many ministers themselves, had been bought. The same applied *a fortiori* to the regional governments.

This state of affairs reached by the end of the 1990s might in hindsight appear a temporary aberration. The necessary political capital might yet be generated to dredge up the public service from this quagmire of corruption, and create a classic liberal state carrying out its circumscribed competences with strong impartial authority. Although Russia was a very long way from such achievements at the end of the first decade of transition, the alternative to the privatization of the state might have been an even worse version, namely a managerial (i.e. old élite) free-for-all under continuing nominal state ownership. This was the lot of Ukraine in the 1990s, and was indeed of Russia in the late Gorbachev period, when large-scale looting was triggered by the State Enterprise Law of 1988, which brought in the first relaxation of state control—but not, of course, privatization.[11] At least the formal private ownership of industry provided a foundation for the eventual emergence of an open and functional economy, however remote such a prospect may have seemed by the end of the 1990s. While these arguments go beyond the scope of this examination of the political environment of post-Soviet economic policy, they remain highly relevant to our subject in accounting for the evolution of the élites through the transition, given that élite interests will be the most powerful immediate determinant of economic policy.

Our conclusion at this point must be that the cause of economic reform in Russia found itself not merely deprived of a supportive élite-led national consensus on where the country should be headed, but actually placed in double jeopardy by élite concerns and interests. Not only was there the immediate and obvious resistance of ideological reactionaries to market-oriented economic policy (and associated 'pro-western' foreign policies). Secondly, less apparent at the outset, but more insidious and ultimately powerful, there was the influence of the new 'oligarchy' with its own interest in blocking further radical reform following the initial privatization.

[11] As Yeltsin himself put it in his great programme speech to the Fourth Congress in October 1991: 'For impermissibly long, we have discussed whether private property is necessary. In the meantime, the party-state élite have actively engaged in their personal privatization. The scale, the enterprise, and the hypocrisy are staggering. The privatization of Russia has gone on [for a long time], and often on a criminal basis.'

This double jeopardy was reflected most clearly, and perhaps also most importantly, in the behaviour of regional governors. Increasingly powerful in the second half of the decade, by which time they all held elected office as opposed to being Kremlin appointees, these men combined elements of both anti-reform strains in the élite. The rare exceptions were easily identifiable as those attracting foreign direct investment into their regions. As for the majority, the reality of day-to-day administration was incompatible with the more ideological nostalgia typical of the Communist parliamentarians in Moscow. But nostalgia with a practical bent was readily visible. In the political sphere, this took the form of media control and censorship, and occasional political repression.[12] As for economic management, conservatism manifested itself most obviously in resistance to enterprise restructuring. The social grounds invariably cited, while of course real enough, coincided conveniently with the benefits of continuing subsidies accruing directly to the enterprise manager-owners who were the natural associates, allies, and patrons of the governors. Governors' opposition to economic reform extended to most other important areas, notably fiscal policy. Here, moves by the central government to make regional finances transparent and barter-free in the context of a coherent framework of 'fiscal federalism' were not at all welcome to most governors attached to their off-budget funds, non-monetized and hence highly discretionary tax deals with local enterprises, and pocket banks. The common thread running through gubernatorial conservatism was an assumed continuity, and in several cases a direct personnel continuity, from the powerful old regional Party first secretaries. If anything, this continuity was enhanced in the conditions of the 1990s by the greater discretion of governors than in their previous life under the tutelage of the CPSU Central Committee, to run their territories as they wished.

Such retrograde conservatism blended easily with the distinct conservatism of the new economic élites. 'Oligarch' behaviour typical of governors included insider privatizations, sweetheart deals with local businessmen involving a cut for the regional government, and sometimes the construction of business empires held through the governor's relatives or members of his wider 'clan'.[13]

---

[12] Most notoriously in the far eastern region of Primorsky Krai under Governor Yevgeny Nazdratenko.

[13] The city of Moscow under Mayor Yuri Luzhkov is the most prominent and important case, but not untypical for that.

2.3.3. *Soviet values*

Understanding the damage done to the economic policy environment by élite interests also requires a wider view taking account of prevalent social values—or, rather, the lack of such values in the standard positive sense. This is the third fundamental factor which, arising from the Soviet collapse, undermined the socio-political platform for economic reform policies. Concerning as it does the morality of a society, this factor is the most difficult to treat. One is formulating generalizations about the causes and consequences of a disease based on the circumstantial evidence of its symptoms. But since these symptoms in the shape of corruption, theft, and nihilism (to name but three) were so evidently virulent, the generalizations ought not to be too controversial.

The weakness of the state and of society were two sides of the same coin. The ease with which the state could be privatized depended on the everyday venality of officials; and there were common roots to the rapacious greed of the new business leaders and the betrayal of the public interest by the officials and judges who took their shilling. In his excellent discussion of these matters, Anatol Lieven has pointed out the shortcomings of the fashionable analogy of the Russian 'oligarchs' of the 1990s with the late nineteenth-century 'robber barons' of the United States:

The robber barons never fully dominated US politics, let alone culture or morality; the country had old and strong representative and legal institutions and religious and moral traditions which combined to cut robber barons down to size.[14]

The contrast with contemporary Russia hardly needs labouring. Solzhenitsyn wrote in 1994 of 'a shattered society emerging from beneath the rubble of totalitarianism' while

at the same time, under the nascent savage non-producing capitalism, ugly new ulcers have surfaced from years of torment, ushering in such repulsive forms of behaviour and such plunder as the West has not known.[15]

These 'ulcers' were the product of decades of murder and confiscation by the Party-state. Society was atomized. Traditional morality, though not extinguished, survived only in the tight confines of family and close circles of friends who could be trusted. Beyond lay the law of the jungle.

---

[14] From 'History is not Bunk', in *Prospect* (October 1998).
[15] Solzhenitsyn (1994), p. 123.

By comparison with the CPSU and KGB, contemporary Russian organized crime and its enforcement gangs seem fragmented shadows. In such an environment, the concept of the public interest, let alone the interlocking rights and duties of the individual citizen, were meaningless. The most casual visitor to Russia is struck by the contrast between the hospitality, loyalty, and altruism typical of small circles, and the general incivility of wider society. Property was in practice ownerless.[16] A sense of duty to its official owner—society through the state—was absurd: the state was a bandit, and individuals and families were its victims out for redress. The morality of near universal pilfering from the workplace amounted to this: if you did not steal from the state, you stole from your family. There could likewise be no sense of shame in taking bribes. Theft and bribery were accordingly rife in the Soviet system. In the absence of moral restraints, people took whatever they could get away with. But that was not much compared to what followed in the 1990s, for CPSU rule maintained the powerful restraint of fear. The end of fear and repression led to the collapse of state power, which was thereby revealed to have no other basis—certainly not the legitimacy of public service, let alone a social contract. Once the cement of fear was removed, it is hardly surprising that a free-for-all ensued.

It is even less surprising in the light of what may be thought of as the positive side to Soviet civic morality. Ordinary people, and especially the educated, paid lip-service to the Party line and propaganda while internally ignoring them—at least in the context of everyday life, where such things as workplace slogans were meaningless.[17] Yet that was not the whole picture. The orderliness of the Soviet system, even if in large measure based on fear, nevertheless created a stable and predictable environment in which people could, however insensibly and vaguely, buy in to the values proclaimed by the state ideology. These values were all the more compelling for being universal. At the same time, their realization belonged to the 'shining future'—that utopia at the heart of the Bolshevik project which lay forever below the horizon, but whose attainment was depicted in propaganda as the objective of Communists' tireless struggle against external and internal enemies. All this gave official values some immunity from refutation by the obviously contrary facts of people's lives under real Socialism. In short, here was a true 'opium of the people'.

---

[16] *nicheynaya sobstvennost'*
[17] This well-remarked phenomenon of Soviet times was referred to by dissident writers as 'doublethink'.

The Soviet system left state and society unfit for a more demanding value system based on law, individual freedom and responsibility, and property. Thanks to the semi-clandestine liberal learning of the intelligentsia (along with technical education and high culture, one of the oases of civilization in the Soviet system), the 1990s saw skilled and sensitive home-grown drafting of the necessary legislation, including key economic laws such as the Civil Code. But the state was too weak to enforce the law, let alone ensure equality before it. Even if the state had miraculously performed better, citizens cast suddenly adrift from the Soviet system would have taken years to develop a reasonable level of trust. As it was, against the background of social amorality, even the official surface values were shattered. For no sooner had Marxist–Leninist doctrines been discredited than the new ideals were almost as thoroughly discredited in action, as savings were wiped out, wealth flowed to a few, living standards failed to improve, and laws were flouted by the strong at the expense of the weak. In this environment where all proclaimed values were exposed as hypocrisy or sham, there was nothing left for people to believe in, and therefore no restraints. Here was a situation of 'every man for himself'. The maxim could be realized on a wide spectrum, from predatory officials, looting factory managers, and violent gangster extortion, through to straightforward popular self-reliance—the latter representing a deep, albeit involuntary, shift from the old dependency culture, and as such capable of generating a stronger value basis for Russian society in the long run.

This last point underlines the need for all generalizations about social values to be severely qualified. Large numbers of individuals, associations, and enterprises adhered to and promoted firm civilized values. But the moral wilderness nevertheless advanced far and wide, withering trust, and so degrading the environment for effective economic policy. Popular willingness to consider the rouble a financial asset worth holding was an obvious casualty. The most damaging effect of all was capital flight, a fundamental brake on Russia's new market economy throughout the 1990s. Closely linked to capital flight, and a vivid example of the economic damage done by nihilism in society, was tax evasion. The popular assumption that there was nothing dishonest in evading the contradictory and punitive tax demands of a dishonest state was shared even by the would-be leaders of society at the top of the political class. A newspaper survey of leading politicians in early 1998 showed a variety of establishment figures, from the Communist speaker of the State Duma to the leader of the 'democratic opposition' Grigory Yavlinsky, supporting the view that it made no sense to pay tax to a corrupt state which would steal the money.[18] These artless admissions betrayed blindness to the implication: that a society prey to such total nihilism is 'in the most desperate trouble'.[19] The trouble was compounded by a vicious circle: corruption prevented a weak state performing key functions such as impartial law enforcement; and this fostered ever more corruption as society purchased the missing public goods by, for example, bribing policemen to ensure physical security, or bribing judges to protect contractual rights or deny those rights to counterparties, as the case may have been.

To summarize this survey of the determinants of the political environment of Russian economic policy in the 1990s, they all stemmed from the fact and effects of the way in which the CPSU dictatorship came to an end—that is, the precipitate collapse of the Soviet system. The resulting environment was initially positive in jump-starting market-oriented economic reform policies; but for the rest of the decade economic policy and performance suffered from the political and social toxins released by that collapse. The three key negative factors identified range from the specific to the general: the destabilizing anomalies of the constitutional legacy; the vulnerability of economic reform goals to the ex-Soviet élites; and the underlying amorality and nihilism of society at large.

2.4. POLITICAL DEVELOPMENTS DURING THE 1990s AND THEIR EFFECT ON ECONOMIC POLICY

To analyse a policy environment means setting things in perspective. But a final perspective must be gained by stepping back and recalling that the political environment of economic policy, while always influential and at times decisive, was by definition peripheral. The economic heart of the matter lay in the economic reality of Soviet central planning and the problem of constructing competitive market capitalism on its ruins. With that qualification, the political environment that emerged from the Soviet collapse remained stable through the 1990s in both its positive and more persistent negative influences. Few of the conspicuous fresh events occurring during the decade affected the environment for better or

---

[18] *Vlast'* (23 March 1998), pp. 4–5.
[19] The phrase is Anatol Lieven's (*Tombstone*, p. 159).

worse. A good example is the war in Chechnya, of 1994–6, which broke out afresh in 1999. Although the cost of military operations put additional pressure on the budget, the conduct of economic policy continued with no real change. If anything, the international opprobrium caused by these wars created a political incentive to demonstrate that reforms continued in the economic field. Thus both military campaigns coincided with more fruitful co-operation with the IMF than in the adjacent periods. The first successful macrostabilization was launched in January 1995 with the backing of an IMF stand-by arrangement: down in Chechnya, meanwhile, a mini-Stalingrad was being fought in Grozny. Similarly in the autumn of 1999, with Russian troops again attacking Grozny, the government accepted new demands which in unprecedented fashion had been added by the IMF to the conditionality of an already existing programme in response to the political pressures generated in the United States by revelations of large-scale flows of Russian flight capital through accounts in the Bank of New York.

Even leaving aside Chechnya, with all its calamities and atrocities, the political turbulence of the 1990s makes it all the more important to maintain a proper perspective. While the making and implementation of economic policy was bound to be affected by the vicissitudes of the months and years after the end of the Soviet Union, the political environment formed by the circumstances of the system change in 1991 nevertheless remained a powerful constant throughout the decade.

2.4.1. *The reform leaders*

The constant core was complemented by two other key factors, more closely linked to unfolding events than to the formative moment of the 1991 revolution. These two factors came respectively from above and below. The first was the motives and action of the leading reformers. The second stems from popular responses to reform policies and the shock of the new economic and social conditions. The thread linking the two factors was the formation of political capital, and the use to which it was put.

In 1991 there existed abundant political capital for economic change formed as a result of the systemic failure of central planning, and concentrated in the person of Boris Yeltsin, with his immense popularity and unique legitimacy. This proved the sole such opportunity of the decade. Accordingly, the single most important economic policy event of the 1990s was Yeltsin's decision to invest his political capital in the reform drive beginning with the liberalization of prices in January 1992.

That decision sparked the debate about the relative merits for Russia of 'shock therapy' as against a more gradualist approach to market-oriented reform. An associated debate exists on whether anything which might fairly be described as shock therapy was ever attempted in the first place. This is not the place to assess the various arguments. Here, rather, the initial 1992 reform drive needs examining as a political event. The term 'shock therapy' made sense at the time to both the Russian public and outside observers. Nor, at first, did Yeltsin's team challenge that characterization. This in turn gave rise to the criticism that the economic reform project was 'neo-Bolshevik', by which was meant that laboratory experiments were performed on the people by former economic institute researchers with no experience of administration and the real economy.[20] This jibe was aimed above all at the brilliant 34-year-old economist Yegor Gaidar, whom Yeltsin chose to run economic policy in November 1991, and promoted to the position of Acting prime minister in July 1992.[21] Gaidar in turn recruited several ministers with similar profiles to his own, largely self-taught in the principles of mainstream economics (such a training could not of course be had in the Soviet education system, although there were a very few shining exceptions such as Yevgeny Yasin at Moscow State University). The charge of Bolshevism referred not only to the imposition of alien theories (in this analogy, Milton Friedman and the Chicago School played the same role in relation to Gaidar as Marx and Engels to Lenin); the criticism was applied also to the revolutionary methods of 'shock therapy' with which the new precepts were implemented. The shock was deemed to have been insensitively administered, without proper measures to soften the blow for ordinary people, and all on the Bolshevik principle of means justifying ends.

As Gaidar never tired of pointing out afterwards, the discretionary element in the economic policy decisions taken at that time was close to zero. The Soviet centrally planned economy had melted down, and the choices left open to so-called economic policymakers were at most tactical ones, on how best to apply the forced emergency measures. Chief among these measures was the freeing of most prices and lifting of the state monopoly on foreign trade, to put some goods in the shops. The

[20] From the impeccable Soviet dissident intelligentsia perspective of Yevgeny Maximov or Andrei Sinaysky in 1992, to the dubious perspective of Boris Berezovsky in 1997.
[21] Gaidar had been brought to Yeltsin's attention by Gennady Burbulis, a former lecturer in Marxist–Leninist theory from Yekaterinburg, and in 1991 Yeltsin's closest adviser.

resulting inflation wiped out the real value of savings balances. In truth, the repressed inflation of the Ryzhkov government's combination of money printing and continued price controls had already destroyed the value of the increasing balances which virtually the entire population had had no choice but to leave in their Sberbank deposit accounts. There were no goods or assets available for people to purchase with their growing nominal money incomes. Meanwhile, the theoretical purchasing power of these forced Soviet rouble savings was lost, for goods could never again be available at the old official administrative prices. The result was a severe psychological shock to the entire population, especially older people who had given a lifetime of effort to a morally discredited and materially bankrupt system. More urgent still was the shock to living standards, again with pensioners on fixed incomes the worst affected in a near-hyperinflationary environment.[22] Gaidar (with Yeltsin, of course) was blamed for all this at the time, and remained a popular bogeyman for years after. But as he wrote in his memoirs, by the end of 1991, the time for careful incremental transition had long passed.[23]

Yet to the extent that the reformers had some small tactical room for manoeuvre, their choices were governed by a definite political project. This was revealed most clearly of all in perhaps the one fundamental voluntary (as opposed to merely reactive) policy decision of 1992, to privatize the industrial base by means (at least in part) of a mass voucher programme administered by Anatoly Chubais. The stated political aim was in the shortest time possible to make the exit from the Soviet system and centrally planned economy irreversible. Yet pragmatic calculation played a much larger part in this project than ideology. Gaidar, Chubais, and their colleagues spoke openly of themselves at the time of their appointment by President Yeltsin in November 1991 as a 'kamikaze' team. The suicide they envisaged was, of course, a political one. Faced with the task of building a market economy from scratch amidst the ruins of Soviet central planning, they expected to survive in office for no more than a few weeks, or at best months. The price liberalization, slashing of defence procurement, and other painful measures demanded by the emergency of that winter would, they imagined, trigger a social and political reaction which would soon enough cost them their jobs in government. But such forebodings were lightly born in comparison with

---

[22] In terms of comparative living standards, the universal shortages of the previous years were marginally more tolerable for pensioners, who had the leisure for hours'-long queues.

[23] Gaidar, *Dni porazheniy i pobed* (1997).

the perceived high historical stakes. Denying political ambition, the Gaidar group affirmed their readiness to make a political sacrifice of themselves in the cause of irreversibility.

In hindsight, this seems a rather facile rationalization. The failure and collapse of the Soviet system had not only created the economic necessity and hence political acceptability of radical policy; but had also made it possible for youthful outsiders to head the government formed to carry out such policy. It was easy enough at the outset to proclaim indifference to power when it had landed so improbably in their laps. In reality the exercise of power rapidly developed their taste for it, and desire to hold on to it. On the other hand, events bore out their guiding assumption, that the political opportunity would be fleeting. The backlash from the political class came in the fourth month of economic reform, with the Sixth Congress of People's Deputies held in April 1992. Thereafter the 'Gaidar' government was embattled, and its already limited room for policy manœuvre whittled away. When the deputies next met, at the revanchist Seventh Congress in December, they brought Gaidar down, in the teeth of Yeltsin's resistance. The new prime minister was Victor Chernomyrdin, the former head of the Soviet gas industry who had returned to the government as energy minister in the conservative reshuffle forced by the previous congress in April. His first step was to produce a draft order reinstating price controls. It seemed that the test of irreversibility had come exactly as the Gaidar group foresaw. There was nothing inevitable about the outcome. The experience of Belarus later in the decade showed that a bastard form of Soviet central planning could perfectly well be revived. If the economic policy vector survived December 1992, however, this was not fundamentally due to the anti-Soviet immunization programme underlying the previous year's policy efforts, important as those efforts were. The key reason was that the irreversibility test was sidestepped. Yeltsin's defeat at the Seventh Congress had not exhausted his political capital; and as that capital was depleted in the following years, its loss was offset by the extensive presidential powers he enjoyed under the new constitution adopted by referendum in December 1993. The real test came only much later, after the financial debacle of August 1998 had completed the political destruction of Yeltsin's presidency, at last allowing the Communists an opportunity to gain effective control over the government. The results showed that the point of no return had been passed.

So the reformers' basic political objective was attained. Ever since November 1991 they had been preparing for this test of the reversibility of economic policy. When the test finally came, in 1998, it was passed with flying colours. If this objective was defined by a pragmatic calculation, it still had an ideological motivation. The historic policy mission was to kill off the stricken system and replace it with normality and decency. By its nature, the project was susceptible to revolutionary excesses. As any inoculation means using the disease being combatted, so getting out of Soviet totalitarianism would entail the counter-revolutionary premises that smashing the old system was the top priority. This made the managers of the reform project vulnerable to the occupational hazard of allowing ends to justify means. Just as the Soviet regime achieved nothing that could not have been realized at a fraction of the cost (in human, economic, environmental, and practically all other terms), so a possible verdict on Russia's transition in the 1990s may be that, measured against its modest achievements, its human and social cost was excessive.

Full consideration of such a charge is beyond the scope of this chapter, and in any case, the perspective of many more years will be needed to pass convincing judgement on the first decade of post-Soviet Russian economic policy. The important point here is that the political methods of economic reform did indeed contain a revolutionary element of willingness to accept high short-term costs for the sake of the greater long-term goal. The most notable exponent of this approach was Anatoly Chubais.

The by now ineradicable designation of Chubais as the 'architect of privatization' is due mainly to his responsibility for the initial voucher campaign of 1992–4; but it may equally be applied to the 1995 'loans-for-shares' auctions in which controlling stakes in prime natural resource enterprises were sold to well-connected insiders for small sums (which in any case originated in good part from state money deposited in the fortunate buyers' banks).[24] Chubais admitted in hindsight that the auctions should not have been rigged; but he maintained that the exercise was worth while in advancing the paramount aim of establishing private property. He argued that the alternative of inaction would have meant a fatal loss of momentum in privatization, and further looting of enterprises nominally controlled by low-paid civil servants who could easily be bought off by incumbent managers in control of the cash flow.[25] In this same first of two stints as first deputy prime minister

---

[24] See the chapter in this volume by Moser and Oppenheimer.
[25] Interview in *Kommersant Daily* (5 March 1998). The argument was disingenuous inasmuch as Chubais himself was not, as it happens, the 'architect' of the 'loans-for-shares'.

with overall responsibility for economic policy, Chubais gambled a second time on attaining a strategic goal at a high price. This was the ending of high inflation by the substitution of T-bill ('GKO') issue for monetary financing of the budget deficit. The expedient of the GKOs in turn substituted for the essential, but politically much more difficult, policy of fiscal retrenchment which should have accompanied, and underpinned, the monetary stabilization. Both these ends-justifying-means choices of Chubais, whatever their effects on economic performance, carried heavy political costs for Chubais himself. Resuming responsibility for economic policy as First Deputy Premier in 1997, he reaped what he had sown. The priority now was fiscal adjustment: and improving tax revenues meant taking on powerful interests, above all those of the new 'oligarchs' created by Chubais's loans-for-shares scheme. The resulting battle was won by the 'oligarchs', who hounded Chubais out of the government; and the associated wider failure of fiscal adjustment was the underlying cause of the financial débâcle of August 1998. As already suggested, much greater distance in time will be required to attempt anything resembling a definitive cost and benefit analysis of this approach. By the end of the 1990s a negative verdict looked superficially more plausible; but unlike in Belarus or Ukraine, seeds had been planted—especially in the form of private property—which survived the decade's political trials, and had the potential to bear fruit.

No individual reformist minister influenced the politics of economic policy as strongly as Chubais: but even his influence paled, of course, besides that of Yeltsin himself. The most conspicuous part of Yeltsin's character as a politician was his tendency, especially in crisis or when confronted by his opponents, to respond with bold, sometimes impetuous, and invariably risky, moves. This in turn set the political tone for the action of reformers like Chubais. At such times Yeltsin could provide powerful leadership. Facing down the August 1991 coup plotters was his finest hour. The importance of his decision in late 1991 to throw his then huge political weight behind young radical reformers has already been noted. Even granted that the country's economic predicament forced decisive action, a more typical product of the CPSU *nomenklatura* than Yeltsin would still have balked—as did, for example,

---

If that title goes to anyone, it must be to Vladimir Potanin (head of Oneksimbank—later the Interros group—and for a short while also first deputy premier).

the newly elected president of Ukraine, Leonid Kravchuk, a former ideology secretary of the Ukrainian Party Central Committee. Another inescapable example of Yeltsin in this vein was the disastrous decision in December 1995 to send the army into Chechnya. After the humiliating failure of less drastic approaches to the separatist challenge from Chechnya, Yeltsin heard from his military advisers that a rapid military solution was possible. His decision to heed this flawed advice is easily explicable in terms of his political temperament: one bold stroke of the kind that had brought him such triumphs in the past would rid him of the headache of Chechnya. A further instance of Yeltsin 'going for broke', and this time successfully, was his decision to disregard the advice of Aleksandr Korzhakov (his influential bodyguard) to postpone the 1996 presidential election, thereby turning himself into a putschist; and his determination instead to aim for the prize of a legit-imate re-election.

With the glaring exception of Chechnya, all these momentous decisions were a forced response to drastic circumstances, and any alter-native course would have been more or less disastrous; though in each case, Yeltsin steeled himself to do the right thing.[26] Whatever his motives (of which the highest may have been a wish to go down in history as the father of a new democratic Russia),[27] they were often outweighed by other, contradictory elements in his character which were no less important in setting the political environment. Chief among these was a combination of inconstancy and caution.

Yeltsin was ready to take personal responsibility on the gravest matters with the highest stakes. But he was not a man to persevere on this lonely and arduous road. He frequently referred to the heavy burden of responsibility.[28] To illustrate this tension, one of the best examples once again is the initial reform drive of 1992. From October 1991 onwards Yeltsin repeatedly stated that the hardships would last a year, after which people would begin to feel an improvement. The significance of this lies in the personal signal, perhaps not made fully consciously, that such a

---

[26] In a television interview at the beginning of the presidential campaign, Yeltsin called the war in Chechnya 'the biggest disappointment of my presidency'.

[27] In the last phase of his presidency, his stated mission was to preside over a constitu-tional civilized handover of power to his successor—'not indifferent to the verdict of poste-rity', as his press secretary, Dmitry Yakushkin, said in a radio interview in September 1999.

[28] *'tyazhyolaya nosha'*: announcing to a gathering of newspaper editors in November 1993 that he would not run for a second term in 1996, he said 'there is only so much one man can bear'.

period was the longest for which Yeltsin felt ready to hold the shock. When it became evident that the transition to a growing market economy would take immeasurably longer, Yeltsin acted at times as if he reckoned he had done his bit, taking risks and responsibility, only to be let down by the economy. Alas 'the economy' could hardly be blamed for not keeping its side of a bargain whose terms had been unilaterally dictated by Yeltsin's temperament as a politician. A corollary of that temperament was that when confounded by economic or other events, or by his political opponents, he could lapse into melancholy or depression.[29] Conversely, the occasional success could trigger undignified euphoria. Such mood swings in both directions were accompanied by accusations, and more or less convincing evidence, of drunkenness—such as his tipsy conducting of a military band in the streets of Berlin in September 1994.

An even more typical manifestation of his inconstancy was a tendency simply to rest on his laurels. Immediately after his triumph of August 1991, with the fate of the country uncertain, he absented himself for two weeks' tennis and relaxation in Sochi leaving his advisers and supporters to squabble behind his back in Moscow on issues of the utmost seriousness, such as whether to try and preserve a single economic space in the soon-to-be former Soviet Union. An attractively plausible speculation is that in this, as in many other respects (such as partiality to drink), Yeltsin reflected deep traits in the national character. The great historian Klyuchevksy drew a generic portrait of the Russian peasant which can be read a century later as a remarkably precise character sketch of Yeltsin:

the Great Russian became accustomed to excessive short term exertion, to working quickly, feverishly and effectively, and then resting throughout the enforced autumn and winter inactivity. No other people in Europe is so capable of exertion over a short period as the Great Russian but no-one is as unaccustomed to even, measured and persistent work as the Great Russian. . . . uncertainty rouses his strength while success depletes it. It is easier for him to overcome an obstacle, danger, failure, than to sustain success with tact and dignity.[30]

This in turn would account for the strong popular identification with Yeltsin as 'one of us', clearly visible even as late as the presidential election

---

[29] As in his confrontation with the Seventh Congress in December 1992, when after suffering a humiliating setback at the hands of the deputies, he locked himself in the sauna in his *dacha*, and had to be extracted by the loyal Korzhakov, *Zapiski prezidenta*, p. 292.

[30] Klyuchevsky, V. O. (1990). I am grateful to Geoffrey Murrell, who spotted this striking coincidence, for drawing my attention to it.

campaign of 1996, by which time there was reason enough for disenchantment. However, the urge to relax may be explained in more convincing terms even than national characteristics. Most influential of all was the immediate social background. Anna Matveeva has summed this up best:

the leadership of the 1990s—including President Yeltsin—reflected its people. The President was also tired of sticking to the party line, party meetings, discipline, fear and responsibility. He wanted to relax and enjoy a bit of freedom rather than take up a huge political burden.[31]

Relaxation from the high road of reform also entailed the attractions of personal wealth and material comfort. Whatever is finally revealed by documentary evidence about the extent of personal corruption in Yeltsin's Kremlin, the atmosphere was far from the ascetic tone that would have been required to limit the growth of corruption endemic in the public service. As for the operational conduct of economic policy, the Yeltsin style could not ensure the close and sustained policy supervision necessary to work through the complicated and politically contentious structural reform agenda.

The problem was, of course, compounded by Yeltsin's deteriorating health. Barely three months after the setback of the December 1993 State Duma election from which Zhirinovsky's extreme nationalist 'liberal democrats' emerged as the largest party, and which resulted in the resignation of leading reformers from the Chernomyrdin government and a return to loose monetary policy, Yeltsin took sick leave and then retreated to Sochi for convalescence and vacation. It would be two years more before his heart condition became public knowledge: but the pattern was now set for the rest of his presidency.

On some occasions when economic reform policy suffered from Yeltsin's inconstancy, this reflected a political choice which, however questionable, was at least conscious. A good example is his decision in that parliamentary election campaign of autumn 1993 to refrain from explicit backing of the leading reformist party, 'Russia's Choice', in order to concentrate all his political firepower on the paramount goal of securing a 'yes' vote in the constitutional referendum—and so removing the conditions which had caused political confrontation culminating in the violent civil conflict the previous October. A further example came in October 1997, which marked a kind of high point in economic policy of the 1990s, with the

---

[31] Matveeva (1999).

economy beginning to grow for the first time. The frustrated Communists blocked the budget and triggered a confidence vote in the State Duma. Instead of taking advantage of his relative political strength to dissolve the Communist-dominated chamber and call elections for a new parliament capable of passing economic reform legislation, Yeltsin opted for a tactical compromise, abandoning a central tax reform proposal. He chose stability rather than submit the new constitutional order to the trial of a pre-term dissolution of parliament. The immediate result was yet another unrealistic budget which, as the 'Asian' crisis in global financial markets swept over Russia, contributed to the financial disaster of 1998.

The cause of radical economic reform prospered and faltered by turns as a result of simple rivalries for power and influence around Yeltsin. The reformers sometimes managed to mobilize Yeltsin's intermittent leadership qualities behind their programmes. Perhaps due to a paternalist streak, Yeltsin responded to young, energetic, and articulate ministers who served up a clear and coherent line for him to champion both at home and abroad, and held out the promise of delivering results which would bring glory to his presidency. This was true to an extent of Gaidar in 1992, and again in September–December 1993; but especially of Boris Nemtsov, who, together with Chubais, took control of government economic policy in March 1997. The head of government remained Victor Chernomyrdin, who completed over five years as prime minister before Yeltsin replaced him in March 1998 with Sergei Kirienko, another young reformist official. It was not, of course, paternalism that had induced Yeltsin to stick with Chernomyrdin for so long. Instead of youth and brilliance, Chernomydrin provided reassurance and stability. His solid, managerial, non-threatening style resembled that of the Soviet prime ministers of old. This resemblance made him acceptable to the anti-Yeltsin majority of the political class which dominated successive parliaments. He thus enabled Yeltsin both to avoid destabilizing prime ministerial confirmation battles with parliament, and also to promote the cause of reform by appointing 'young reformers' like Boris Fedorov (in January 1993) and Boris Nemstov (in March 1997) as deputy prime ministers—appointments which did not require parliamentary approval. Chernomyrdin lost his job only when he began to threaten Yeltsin's position by appearing and acting as the natural successor to the presidency.[32]

---

[32] I am grateful to Martin Nicholson for these insights.

A notable feature of the renewed reform drive after March 1997 was a series of weekly radio broadcasts by Yeltsin, devoted to explaining the point of current economic policy. In the earlier 'Gaidar' reform drive of 1992 no one thought of telling the public repeatedly and in some detail what the reforms were in aid of and why they were necessary in the first place.

Equally often, however, the Kremlin power game could turn against those implementing economic reform policy. The happier times of 1997 were brought to an end, even before the outbreak of the 'Asian' crisis, by jealousy of Chubais's ascendancy on the part of Boris Berezovsky and other 'oligarchs' with close ties to Kremlin insiders led by the chief of staff, Valentin Yumashev. They persuaded Yeltsin to act on a relatively minor impropriety by Chubais (concerning so-called book royalties), and by extension weakened Nemtsov.

Their success was almost certainly due to Yeltsin's inclination to preserve his power by remaining the decisive arbiter above his fractious magnates, whose rivalries therefore had to be kept in contending equilibrium, and any subject emerging as over-mighty accordingly cut down.[33] This 'byzantine' style, though often remarked on, does not provide the fundamental interpretative key to Yeltsin's rule. Clearly enough, an instinct for power was central. But this instinct operated on a deeper level than court intrigues, however much the old Party boss in Yeltsin relished the demonstrative power game of public praising and dressing down of Kremlin and government officials, leading respectively to their hiring or promotion and firing or demotion (treatment notoriously handed out in the last two years of his presidency not merely to ministers but also to a string of prime ministers). The deeper power instinct came down to there being limits on the risks to his own position that Yeltsin would take.

Events never forced a decisive trial of strength between Yeltsin's will to power and perhaps the only other fundamental motivation which could rival it: namely, his place in history. That test would have come only if Yeltsin had lost the 1996 presidential election to his Communist challenger, Gennady Zyuganov, and so been forced to choose between the two priorities. In other contexts, especially economic policy, all concessions made to reduce political risk could be presented as tactical and not compromising the historic mission. If any trait in Yeltsin's political character can fairly be called Bolshevik, then this is it—in any case far more

---

[33] The most recent and powerful account of this thesis has come from Shevtsova (1999).

fairly than the portrayal of the economic reform drive as a 'great leap forward'. In mid-1992, as he was trying to defend his position against the growing opposition to economic reform, Yeltsin remarked (referring to himself) that you do not close down large factories, or they might close you down.[34] This approach amounted to Lenin's NEP in reverse. Of course, there was no trace in the 1990s of the fanatical utopian project of the Bolsheviks, who as the 'vanguard of the proletariat' equated their clique's hold on power with the attainment of a new humanity. By contrast, Yeltsin's position amounted at most, and at worst, to saying not 'I/ we must hold power to achieve utopia', but rather 'I/we must hold power to avoid a return to dystopia'. None the less, of the additional political constraints on economic policy arising from the political process as it developed after 1991, and in particular as influenced by Yeltsin himself, this was the most powerful.

Yet even this 'Bolshevik' factor must be qualified. At times it could even favour economic reform. The most notable instance was the 27 per cent devaluation of the rouble on one day ('Black Tuesday') in October 1994. This episode resulted basically from large-scale money printing, which stoked up inflationary pressures and left nothing for the domestic financial system to do with abundant rouble liquidity than make a one-way bet against the rouble. No other asset could begin to match the risk-adjusted return offered by the US dollar. This shock nearly cost prime minister Chernomyrdin his job; and made him realize (or perhaps clinched an already dawning realization) that lack of reform endangered his hold on power as much as, if not more than, reform.[35] The balance of political risk was in favour of setting about serious stabilization at last. Yeltsin concurred; and Chubais was promoted to the rank of first deputy premier with orders to get the job done.

All Yeltsin's qualities and failings were on display in the great political crisis of his presidency, which was the constitutional power struggle with the Congress of People's Deputies and Supreme Soviet in 1992–3. This ultimately tragic episode began this chapter's survey of the pollutants of the political environment created by the systemic collapse. Without adding a detailed narrative assessment, it is enough to underline that a new constitution with some separation of powers was essential for Russia, and no less so for the fact that Yeltsin himself also needed it to protect his own power. The goal could have been reached at lower cost

---

[34] Quoted by G. D. G. Murrell in *Russia's Transition*, p. 107, aptly adding: 'a revealing comment'.   [35] See Granville (1995).

(that is, without the bloodshed in Moscow of September–October 1993) had Yeltsin used the clear mandate from his remarkable referendum victory in April 1993 to dissolve the Soviet parliament on the spot. Here again, his caution got the better of his decisiveness.

Although expensively won, Yeltsin's victory over Soviet power in October 1993, and the adoption of the new constitution by popular referendum in December, was decisive in half normalizing the political environment. It would be years before the Communists in particular, but also other segments of the political class, would recognize the December 1993 constitution as legitimate. Yet from the beginning they played by the clear rules of the game that it laid down. As a result, Russian politics began to resemble those of any country with a constitutional law-based system, in being a constant struggle for power *within* the system, as opposed to a struggle about what kind of system the country should have in the first place. Thus the new constitution laid the basis for systemic stability, without which the normal conduct of economic or any other kind of policy is impossible. In this light, the introduction of the new constitution, and subsequent respect for its key provisions must go down as Yeltsin's major political achievement post-1991—as he himself seems to have recognized at the time.[36]

2.4.2. *The constitutional settlement*

This judgement may sit oddly with the constant criticism to which the 'Yeltsin constitution' has been subjected ever since its adoption. The focus of the criticism has of course been the extensive presidential powers. These powers are hardly greater on paper than those of the president of the fifth French republic, and would have been weaker if Yeltsin's opponents had accepted the reasonable compromise he offered in the summer of 1993. For the rest of the 1990s Russian politicians with nothing to offer in the sphere of economic policy proposed constitutional reform as the answer to the country's problems, by which was meant specific shifts of control over the government and ministerial appointments from the presidency to the State Duma, the lower house of the federal parliament. While a good case can of course be made for this, as for several other possible amendments, the issue remains marginal. The basic model of a mildly authoritarian plebiscital order with, however, some real separation of powers not only stabilized the new Russian state in the first

[36] 'My Political Life's Work Completed', *Izvestiya* (31 December 1993).

decade of its existence—notably in defining its federal structure—but it also stands a good chance of being more comprehensively vindicated over time. As the political culture of Russian society matures, in particular with the emergence of genuine political parties besides the Communists, the federal parliament should be able to take on new powers. Even before any formal constitutional amendments had been adopted, the parliament increased its power simply by passing laws, thereby reducing the scope for legislation by presidential decree.

None of that, however, cancelled out the drawbacks of the new constitutional system for economic reform. First of all, there were conjunctural costs arising from the course and consequences of the constitutional struggle itself. Especially after it entered its climactic phase from December 1992 to October 1993, the all-engrossing struggle relegated economic reform to a secondary priority. Specifically, it prevented the reforming ministers in the government from influencing the loose monetary policy being conducted by the Central Bank, which was subordinated to the Supreme Soviet. More serious still, the struggle consumed much of the remainder of the start-up political capital of Yeltsin's presidency. The image of the burning Moscow 'White House', which Yeltsin had defended against the CPSU putschists two years earlier, but which was now being shelled by his own troops, shocked the country and the world. The violence clearly shook Yeltsin himself.[37] Already after the April 1993 referendum his mistaken hesitation mentioned above seems to have been due to the shock of a May Day street fight by 'red/brown' demonstrators which left one policeman dead (the autumn death toll would be 147). After 1993 Yeltsin again and again chose caution to protect the fragile new constitution and prevent a recurrence of the 1993 tragedy. One significant episode, avoiding confrontation with the Communist-dominated State Duma in October 1997, has also been covered above. More generally, Yeltsin searched endlessly in these years for civil accord and reconciliation in society— beginning with a grand Kremlin signing of a formal 'civic accord' agreement in April 1994. But for the purposes of winning the political battles necessary to implement sound economic policy, any such accord was illusory.

Besides such conjunctural losses, the new constitution also had systemic drawbacks affecting economic policy in particular. The constitution made policy highly dependent on the president, which meant

---

[37] Emotional television address to the nation on 6 October 1993.

all the characteristics of Yeltsin sketched above. The factor which needs stressing again in this context is Yeltsin's deteriorating health, and consequent rise of a Kremlin cabal with an agenda of protecting its power and wealth, and the influence to block any systematic economic policy that cut across its interests. But economic policy was no less vulnerable to the parliament. While weak relative to the presidency, the federal parliament could not be ignored by the government's economic policymakers, especially in what became the all-important sphere of fiscal policy. For the new constitution reserved to the State Duma and Federation Council (the upper house) the classic and fundamental function of any parliament, which is to vote supply. If anyone doubted this reality of the separation of powers, they were disabused in the summer of 1998, when the State Duma threw out the Kirienko government's emergency fiscal adjustment programme. There was nothing that President Yeltsin or the executive branch as a whole could do against this obstructionism of the federal parliament within its exclusive sphere of constitutional competence. The deputies' stance helped to precipitate the financial débâcle of sovereign default announced on 17 August.

Any political opposition has the liberty of taking up populist positions, promising all things to all men, and most typically, lower taxes and higher public spending. The peculiar irresponsibility of the Russian political class, especially in the configuration of the CPRF-dominated State Duma of 1995–9, naturally reflected the society from which it sprang. A commentator writing in mid-1999 provided the following neat summary: 'People are still driven by contradictory aspirations: they want order, but also want to benefit from the present anarchy; they wish to have economic freedom—but without individual responsibility—while enjoying state paternalism.'[38] In the light of this, it is hardly surprising that the State Duma rejected a programme that included a shift of the tax burden from enterprises to indirect taxes on consumption by households, which was the relatively cash-rich heart of the unrecorded economy. In answer to deputies' criticisms that this programme would leave many people worse off, Finance Minister Zadornov replied that the alternative was a devaluation, triggering inflation which would impoverish the entire population. He was proved right within weeks.

[38] Matveeva (1999), p. 21.

2.4.3. *Political capital and popular attitudes*

Yet popular and, by extension parliamentary, resistance was not the most important reason for the failure of that final economic reform drive of the 1990s launched by the Kirienko government in May 1998. The fundamental cause lay in the shortage of political capital. Even if Yeltsin had been in rude health, and the Kremlin free of cabals intriguing against the government, the result would have been the same. Yeltsin dutifully signed on the dotted line every decree that the Kirienko team drafted. But without political capital, their efforts were vain. The necessary fiscal adjustment was quite unlike the successful monetary stabilization programme of 1995, which, resting as it did mainly on the substitution of T-bill issue for monetary deficit financing, could be accomplished by administrative decisions entirely within the competence of the federal executive branch (including the Central Bank). Kirienko's programme for fiscal recovery entailed genuine and radical structural reform. In the enterprise sector imposing financial discipline implied widespread bankruptcies. In the social sphere the indiscriminate benefits and subsidies of the Soviet welfare system would have to be scrapped. Carrying through such a programme would have required at least as much authority and popularity as Yeltsin enjoyed in 1991, if not more. By 1998 he no longer had the choice of whether to risk being 'closed down' politically by closed-down factories. The 'virtual economy' of enterprises producing goods which nobody wanted to buy, and subsisting in dense networks of barter, was thus immune from the attentions of economic reformers for the rest of the 1990s.

If by 1998 there was no political capital for economic reform available to Yeltsin or anyone else, this was the result of popular attitudes. In the constitutional democratic system that he had created, the primary means of political capital formation was elections, and above all, the plebiscital presidential election. But the amount of political capital available after each successive election was ever lower, despite the result of key elections being in Yeltsin's favour, and hence in favour of the continuation of market-oriented economic reform policy. The reason was that the basis of electoral majorities was no longer enthusiasm for change, as in 1991, but rather fear of a revanchist Communist alternative. The point was already visible in the April 1993 referendum result. This was ostensibly a great victory for Yeltsin. His opponents in the congress, as always shamelessly wielding their Soviet constitutional powers, had rigged the questions against him. As well as the question of confidence in the president, they added a second, asking whether people also supported the president's social and economic policies. They were shocked by the majority 'yes' vote in answer to both questions, and especially the second. In reality, however, the voters saw clearly enough the political game behind the questions, and voted against the Soviet cause accordingly. As soon as the fear of the alternative was taken away, as in the first Duma election eight months later, the protest vote that reflected many people's true feelings could safely be cast: and Zhirinovsky was the fortunate recipient.

The same effect was repeated in the next Duma election of December 1995, won by a resurgent CPRF. Again, the lesser importance of the Duma reduced the stakes in that election. In the crucial June 1996 presidential election, however, the fear factor worked for Yeltsin. For all that they may have disliked him, a majority of voters preferred him to the Communist alternative. But this greatly reduced the political capital generated in Yeltsin's new mandate. There was enough for him to launch the new economic reform drive associated with Chubais and Nemtsov after he had recovered from his heart by-pass surgery and returned to active politics in March 1997. But it was nothing like sufficient to see that programme through: and by the moment of truth for economic policy the following year, that capital had been exhausted.

The political effect of the financial debacle of August 1998 was to deprive the Yeltsin administration of control over the government for the first time since 1991, regardless of the president's constitutional powers. The power base of the new prime minister, Yevgeny Primakov, was the majority of the Communists and their allies in the State Duma. In these apparently radically changed circumstances, there soon emerged a reality of the utmost significance: the political environment for economic reform was unchanged.

Just as the failure of the Kirienko government reflected insufficient political capital to support strong structural reform policies, the Primakov government revealed the same effect in reverse, that is as regards reactionary policies. Primakov's new economic team, led by the moderate Communist Yuri Maslyukov, started out with some policy ambitions. They wanted to correct the 'mistakes of the liberal reformers'. There was talk of a partial re-nationalization of foreign trade and even suspending the internal convertibility of the rouble. Primakov had to go on television to reassure people that there was no threat to their cash dollar savings.[39]

---

[39] October 1998.

Popular protest was now palpable not against the reformers' policies but rather against attempts to reverse them—and in this case, one of the fundamental Gaidar reforms of 1992, which was the introduction in July that year of internal convertibility (i.e. rouble convertibility for Russian residents) based on a unified market exchange rate.

Nor was that the end of the story. Popular discontent was, of course, the result of hardship: and a major perceived cause of hardship was inflation.[40] Opinion polls duly revealed the public's fear of inflation and understanding that printing money would fuel inflation. Taking due note of this, the Primakov government cautiously decided to print only modest amounts of money. But the decision-makers apparently lacked understanding of money demand. Given people's reluctance to hold roubles, the CPI responded to money printing with scarcely any time lag: Central Bank loans to the government of around Rbs20 billion (10 per cent of the monetary base) in October–November 1998 caused the CPI to jump 20 per cent in November–December. With that, Primakov backed off this experiment with monetary financing: and inflation thereupon declined.

In these circumstances, Primakov could do nothing, and this he did very well. The political environment for economic reform remained one of total blockage until the end of the decade. Political capital was utterly lacking to support policy movement in any direction. A consensus that this was a time for a pause united public opinion and the political class.

2.5. AFTERWORD: POST-YELTSIN POLITICS

That pause would not have occurred at all had Yeltsin resigned immediately on becoming a lame duck after the financial collapse of August 1998. His aim in soldiering on was to ensure a satisfactory transition to a successor administration.

On one level that meant power changing hands by due constitutional process. The political system formed and consolidated under Yeltsin in the 1990s was well prepared by the end of the decade for the challenge of preserving constitutionality in the transition to a successor administration. But this could still not be taken for granted. The legacy of political upheavals of recent history (1987–93) combined with the country's long previous history of revolutions and dynastic coups made it natural to

---

[40] Granville, Shapiro, and Dynnikova (1996).

presume that any political stability was a mere remission until the next emergency, when the rules of the game would be arbitrarily rewritten or improvized once again. So whatever the costs in terms of policy paralysis, Yeltsin's decision to serve out his term after and despite the August 1998 events did help to cement further systemic stability by strengthening the contrary presumption that, come what may, the normal constitutional path should be followed.

The environment for economic policy was improved not only by the fact of systemic stability but also by the practical result of adhering to due electoral process as laid down in the constitution. This secured legitimacy and popularity for the incoming administration, or at least enabled it to enjoy a measure of popular trust. These are the components of political capital, without which there can be little prospect of implementing serious, and therefore painful, structural reform measures. The main operational goal of the last phase of Yeltsin's presidency was to preserve 'continuity'. This meant preventing power falling into the hands of either ideological or clan opponents (personified respectively by the Communist leader Zyuganov, and the mayor of Moscow, Luzhkov, with Primakov falling somewhere between the two); and the only way to block these opponents' paths to the Kremlin was to find a strong alternative candidate.

In preparing the way for a chosen successor, Yeltsin took full advantage of the opportunities presented from remaining in office. Chief among these was the economic recovery produced by the sharp rises in global commodity prices and the positive effect of the rouble devaluation on both the external side and domestic output. In this more favourable environment Yeltsin and his associates made effective use of means both foul and fair to ensure the right succession. These ranged from media campaigns denigrating undesirable successors (Luzhkov and Primakov) and crude political exploitation of renewed fighting in the north Caucasus, to legitimate political moves in the strict (constitutional) sense: installing the preferred successor, Vladimir Putin, into the premiership and then, after the election of a new State Duma in December 1999 had revealed strong popular support for Putin, Yeltsin's decision to resign on New Year's Eve. Besides clinching the task in hand of shortening and hence securing Putin's trajectory to supreme office, this inspired last act of Yeltsin's political career also summed up much of his character as a politician, combining as it did splendid intuition and a certain grandeur with a baser theatricality. Instead of the unremarkable routine exit that awaited him at the end of his term, in June 2000, he preferred to bow out with a decisive and unforeseen flourish.

The political turning-point of December 1999, duly consummated by Putin's comfortable victory in the presidential election that followed in March 2000, left the question of whether the start-up political capital enjoyed by his administration would be wisely invested and spent in the cause of implementing structural reform. The country's future hinged on this. Either Russia would emerge onto a recognizable 'transition' path, and begin to emulate the successful former Communist states of central Europe, or else it would end up as 'failed state'—which is to say a failure to overcome the Soviet failure encapsulated in the astute old jibe about the Soviet Union amounting to 'Upper Volta with rockets'.

In these circumstances, implementation capacity would be decisive. It was not enough to have the right policy ideas, although Putin began his term by embracing the structural reform agenda in a more comprehensive and radical form even than in the previous reform proclamations of 1997–8 by Nemtsov, Chubais, and Kirienko. The radical programme adopted by the new administration may be partly explained by the extent to which the agenda of necessary reforms had been assimilated over the preceding years by a cohort of officials, at least in the key federal agencies, which had built up a good grasp of policy detail and considerable operational experience of implementation. Here was one of the more positive aspects of Yeltsin's legacy, and a favourable contrast to the situation which he himself faced on coming to power nine years previously. He brought about this outcome by the simple length of his rule—maintaining, or at least promoting, the same reformist policy orientation for nearly a decade.

The three key determinants of implementation capacity would be popular tolerance for tough structural reforms, the attitude of the élites, and, given the construction of the political system around the leader, the character and performance of President Putin and his successors. In all three cases, there were influences pulling in different directions.

As regards popular attitudes, the task of implementing painful policies was facilitated by the effect of political renewal already noted. By its very existence, a newly elected administration would at least initially enjoy public confidence (a 'honeymoon period') based on people's hopes for a better life. On the other hand, the disappointments and hardship associated with the long Yeltsin years had bequeathed deep public disenchantment bordering on nihilism. So economic reform could no longer be underpinned by the same hope, let alone enthusiasm, that was born of the Soviet collapse.

As for the élites, there were many who stood to gain from continued policy paralysis. The 'failed state' trajectory, that is a state effectively privatized by 'oligarch' clans at both federal and regional levels, would preserve and enhance the wealth and power of the beneficiaries of the 1990s. However, in this scenario, wealth and power would increasingly be divorced from the attributes of standing and prestige in the eyes of both domestic and (especially) international opinion. For many influential individuals and groups, the pariah status evoked at the time of the Bank of New York 'money laundering' scandal in the autumn of 1999 was not an attractive prospect. For all their cynicism and ruthlessness, selfishness and greed, Russian élites potentially retained sufficient ambition and realism to lead the country through the long transition road ahead. This is another way of saying that Russia is not a provincial country. An important incentive remained the view of the outside world, especially the advanced western countries, despite the bitter humiliation for the Russian élite of NATO's enlargement to the east and its war against Yugoslavia. Ever since the Gorbachev period, when the CPSU ruling class abandoned the shibboleths of Marxist-Leninism, and in due course the Soviet empire and economic community of Soviet-style centrally planned systems, the élites have had nowhere else to turn for status and respectability than the counsels and clubs of the advanced world. The alternative of backwardness made contemptible by kleptocracy constitutes an incentive to support measures necessary to achieve the sustained economic growth which will produce both international respectability and increasing domestic security for élite gains, however ill-gotten.

This leaves the impact of the president. Succeeding Yeltsin, Putin presented a sharp contrast in character and temperament. Whereas Yeltsin came to power after four years of pure political activity as an opposition leader, Putin had been an able administrator with minimal experience as a public politician. These differing backgrounds suited the respective times. Yeltsin created and rode a popular tide of revulsion against the Soviet system. Putin's determination, background in the security services, and relative youth answered a different national craving for order and renewal. Perhaps the most striking characteristics which Putin displayed during his first months in office were lucidity and drive. In his 'state-of-the-nation'[41] and other public speeches, he spared no tender sensibilities in diagnosing the country's dire plight. At the same time he

---

[41] 8 July 2000.

set out to make the federal executive branch a more effective instrument of power by reining in 'oligarchs' and regional governors alike. He promised to restore order while preserving liberty. In short, he accepted all the political challenges of implementing serious economic policy, citing the principle of 'nothing ventured, nothing gained'.[42] Despite his inexperience as a politician, and considerable scepticism among western commentators about his motives and abilities, the new president seemed determined to use the powers of his office and his starting political capital to implement economic policies necessary to achieve sustained growth and national recovery.

REFERENCES

Gaidar, Y. T. (1997). *Dni porazheniy i pobed*, Moscow: Vagrus.

Granville, B. (1995). *The Success of Russian Economic Reforms*, London: The Royal Institute of International affairs, distributed by Brookings.

Granville, B., Shapiro, J., and Dynnikova, O. (1996). 'Less Inflation, Less Poverty. First Results for Russia', *Discussion Paper No. 68*, London: The Royal Institute of International Affairs.

Klyuchevsky, V. O. (1999). 'Ethnographic Consequences of the Russian Colonisation of the Upper Volga . . . Influence of the Upper Volga Environment on the Economy of Great Russia and on the Tribal Character of the Great Russian', in *Istoricheskie Portrety*, Moscow: Pravda Publishing House.

Kommersant Daily, 14 April 1998.

Lieven, A. (1998a). 'History is Not Bunk', *Prospect*, October, pp. 22–6.

—— (1998b). *Checheniya: Tombstone of Russian Power*, New Haven and London: Yale University Press.

Matveeva, A. (1999). 'In Search of Enthusiasts', *The World Today*, 55/6 (June), pp. 19–21.

Murrell, G. D. G. (1997). *Russia's Transition to Democracy: An Internal Political History 1992–1995*, Brighton: Sussex Academic Press.

Shevtsova, L. (1999). *Yeltsin's Russia: Myths and Realities*, Washington, DC: Brookings Institution Press.

---

[42] Interview in *Izvestiya*, 14 July 2000: 'one could always sit and do nothing, not expend political resources, avoid confrontation, be liked by everyone. But I think that would be wrong. In that case, there would be no point being in the Kremlin, it would be better to do something else . . . Inaction for the sake of preserving political innocence? What on earth would be the point? If in doubt about something, I like to pause and check; but if I am convinced that a course of action is right, then I will act vigorously. Take economic policy: for years it has been clear what needs to be done, all that has been lacking is the will to do it . . .'.

Solzhenitsyn, A. I. (1994). *The Russian Question in the Twentieth Century*, London: Harvill Press.

Vlast', 23 March 1998, pp. 4–5.

Yeltsin, B. N. (1993). 'My Political Life's Work Completed', *Izvestiya*, 31 December.

—— (1994). *Zapiski prezidenta*. Moscow.

3

Dimensions of Transition

BARRY W. ICKES

3.1. INTRODUCTION

In the heady days after the failure of the coup in August 1991 many observers believed that transition from the planned to the market economy would be a straightforward process. Once the fetters of central planning were eliminated, the market economy would spring up. Of course, there were certain key steps that had to be implemented: liberalization of prices, stabilization, and privatization. But once these steps were taken reform would be achieved. With hindsight this consensus seems naïve. Transition has proved to be more complex than was anticipated. Successes have been achieved, but the prices paid were not insubstantial.

This chapter explores the dimensions of transition in Russia. To understand the rocky road that transition has taken, it is crucial to understand the initial conditions under which the journey began. This is because the Soviet-type economy had its own inner logic, which permeated the entire system and conditioned the behaviour of agents. And to understand fully the logic of the Soviet economy, it is necessary to examine not only the formal structure of the system but its informal structure as well.

The institutional structure of the command economy developed from two imperatives: control and growth. Maintaining central control of all aspects of the economy was an imperative of the Soviet system. In principle, it is possible to organize an economy without private property in a decentralized fashion. In practice, central control was a political imperative. To satisfy this constraint, the planning system developed its characteristic features and, as this system crystallized, reforms that challenged central control were rejected by the system.

The second imperative was the need rapidly to industrialize an underdeveloped economy. The Russia inherited by the Bolsheviks was a predominantly rural underdeveloped country, surrounded by potential enemies. Once the possibility of global revolutions receded, the Soviet leadership pursued the path of 'socialism in one country', and this led to an emphasis on growth and industrialization to meet potential threats.

3.1.1. *Dimensions of transition*

The nature of the transition in Russia is governed by the economic distance that must be travelled from central planning to the market economy. There are two types of legacies that determine this distance. First, *systemic* legacies complicate transition because of the differences between planning and the market. Critical institutions that are common to any market economy, *market infrastructure*,[1] are underdeveloped or non-existent. Transition requires the development of these institutions. Other features of the planned economy, such as the incentive system within enterprises, the operation of the foreign trade monopoly, and the Soviet system of pricing created legacies that have to be overcome in transition. The centrally planned economy de-emphasized the role of money and the banking system, for example, so that the very act of making a payment becomes complicated in transition. Most important, of course, Russia lacked the institution of private property on the production side of the economy. Privatization requires much more than a transfer of ownership. It requires a system of corporate governance, and this in turn depends on the legal system.

Second there are *structural* legacies. The operation of the planning system distorted the economy and especially the industrial structure. Soviet growth policy favoured heavy industry over light industry, investment goods over consumption goods, and defence over everything. The system was biased in favour of industry because this was believed to be critical to economic growth, and in favour of giant firms because a small number of organizations facilitated control and because economies of scale were overrated. Agriculture suffered from chronically low productivity. Services were underdeveloped.

In addition to the legacies of Communism, Russia has special features due to its size and its own historical legacy. This is especially important

---

[1] Market infrastructure refers to financial, distribution, and contractual institutions that support economic transactions in market economies. They are usually taken for granted due to their omnipresence in such economies.

with respect to the legal system, which was underdeveloped even under the tsar.

Finally, the break-up of the Soviet economy into separate national economies complicated transition by fragmenting what was a common economic space.

3.2. BASIC FEATURES OF THE SOVIET-TYPE ECONOMY (STE)

The basic features of the STE are state ownership of the means of production and centralized control by means of an administered system of planning *in physical terms.*[2] The system replaces the market with a set of directives from the centre to the production units throughout the economy. These directives are *commands*, not suggestions. They have the force of law, and subordinates are responsible for fulfilling them, even if the plans are not feasible.

During the New Economic Policy (NEP) in the early 1920s Lenin emphasized state control of the 'commanding heights' of industry. But in the mature command economy the state owned not only the 'commanding heights' but the foothills, the prairies, and the valleys as well. In the Soviet Union the state and collective sectors accounted for some 88 per cent of the value added in agriculture, controlled 98 per cent of retail trade, and owned 75 per cent of urban housing space (Ericson, 1991; Hay, Shleifer, and Vishny, 1996). The industrial sector was exclusively state owned. In 1985 91 per cent of employment was in state enterprises, and another 6 per cent in *kolkhozy*,[3] which have been essentially state farms since the mid-1950s.

It is misleading, however, to focus too heavily on state ownership. Many economies have some degree of state ownership. The central distinguishing characteristic of the STE is hierarchical control. The system was designed to implement the directives of the leadership.

Information in the planned economy flows only in the vertical direction: upwards from production units to the central planners, primarily in the form of reports on plan fulfilment; and downwards from the planners to the enterprises in the form of plan directives. There are, *formally*, no

---

[2] This is, necessarily, a cursory review. See Hewett (1990) or Nove (1986) for detailed descriptions of the Soviet economic system.

[3] *Kolkhozy*, or collective farms, differed from state farms (*sovkhozy*) in Stalin's time. Workers in state farms received wages, while peasants in collective farms split what was left after the state took its share of output. Of course, in both cases actions were centrally directed. But this made collective farmers residual claimants, and during tough times, peasants suffered. Under Khruschev the difference between the two essentially disappeared.

horizontal flows of information.[4] This means that only at the top of the hierarchy can opportunity costs be assessed. At lower levels agents lack the means to assess the trade-offs between different activities. This is because prices in the planned economy are set administratively and do not reflect marginal costs. Prices were typically set to reflect average cost of production, but this was usually estimated by *excluding* the least-efficient producers. The advantage of this, from the systematic perspective, is that it facilitates central control and the implementation of central priorities.

3.2.1. *The Soviet growth model*

The Soviet Growth Model (SGM) is a mechanism for extensive growth, that is, growth via the accumulation of inputs rather than through more efficient use of inputs. Resources, human and physical, are mobilized to that task.

With capital accumulation the problem is simple. The planners *decide* the proportions of output to be devoted to consumption and investment.[5] In a market economy high savings rates may require incentive to get households to save. In a planned economy, there is no need for incentives. Planners simply choose to produce levels of consumption goods consistent with their investment plans. This leaves the supply of consumption goods determined as a residual.[6]

It is useful to think of the SGM as if the Soviet economy were a single corporation: USSR Inc. The corporation owns a large stock of natural resources, has no outside shareholders (so that all 'profits' can be retained for investment), and hires labour. Moreover, as a monopsonist in the labour market, USSR Inc. can minimize the expenditure on labour. Transactions between enterprises are merely transfer prices between

---

[4] Informally, a parallel, or second, economy existed alongside the formal structure.

[5] There is, in fact, an important division of labour in decision-making. The decisions about how fast the economy should grow (this was deemed to be subject to Party control in the absence of 'wreckers') and the division of output between consumption and investment was a *political* decision, made at the highest levels of the Party. The planners' role was to implement these decisions in the form of plans that could direct the activity of ministries and enterprises.

[6] Notice that the plan determines the supply of consumption goods (independent of price) and the level of the wage bill which, in turn, determines aggregate demand, and the price level. Presumably they could set prices to clear the market for consumption goods. Typically, however, they do not. Setting prices below market-clearing levels facilitates bribe-taking. With goods in short supply it is possible to distribute rents without budgetary expenditure. It also means that queues and parallel market prices must rise to clear the market.

'divisions'. The exceptions are purchase of labour and engagement in foreign trade.

The objective for this firm is the maximization of government consumption (primarily defence), subject to the constraints that labour be supplied in proper quantities.[7] In order to obtain sufficient labour the state must produce consumer goods, including agricultural output, to induce this supply. We can think of the stock of consumption goods as the wage bill necessary to induce the target level of labour. Services are similarly viewed as input, not as value.[8]

Notice how this problem differs from a standard planners' problem. In the conventional model the planner is assumed to maximize the discounted value of household consumption. Here, however, household consumption is a constraint: the planners maximize the residual *net* of household consumption.[9] The economy is thus seen as a means of producing items for government consumption.[10] But the planning problem in the SGM is not a static one. The goal is to maximize not the current level of output but the discounted value of the path of government consumption. It is this objective which justifies depressing consumption to enhance capital accumulation,[11] and also producing heavy industrial goods, owing to the conception that to produce high growth emphasis must be placed on the machines that produce machines.[12]

---

[7] Notice that the state acts as a *monopsonist* in the labour market: there is no alternative avenue of employment. This means that the cost of labour to the government is less than the marginal product of labour. In other words, the state is able to squeeze out a larger share of national income by exploiting its monopoly power in the labour market.

[8] This accounts for much of the difference between Net Material Product (NMP) and GDP. NMP does not include services, except for freight associated with inputs.

[9] See Roberts and Rodriguez (1997), for example, for a related discussion.

[10] In practice this was primarily military production, but it could take other forms.

[11] Another way to think of this is that the discount rate that the planners use to discount future government consumption is smaller than the rate that the public uses to discount consumption.

[12] This is the essence of the Fel'dman–Mahalanobis model of economic growth. The economy is viewed as consisting of two sectors, machine producing (sector A) and goods producing (sector B). Both sectors rely on machines as an input. It is then argued that to maximize growth it is necessary to focus initially on the production of machines, expanding the capacity to produce goods in the future. The argument depends on the assumption that the key determinant of output in each sector is capital. The key conclusion is that the more capital that is retained in sector A, the higher the rate of growth of capacity, and hence of the economy. By postponing consumption the eventual capital stock in sector B can be higher, so higher future consumption can be attained. Now the point is not that Stalinist planners followed the formulas of the Fel'dman model but that their decisions were consistent with the model. The key issue was how much to postpone consumption in order to hasten industrialization.

The SGM was effective, ignoring the cost, at rapidly industrializing the Soviet economy. A predominantly agricultural economy became, in less than three generations, an industrial power, at least when measured by gross production of autos, cement, oil, and steel. Over time, however, the performance of the SGM began to decline. Growth rates of output per worker decreased from 5.8 per cent in 1950–9 to 2.1 per cent in the 1970s and 1.4 per cent in the 1990s (Easterly and Fischer 1995). Total factor productivity growth turned negative in the 1960s and remained so until the end of the regime.[13]

The key defect of the SGM is that output growth is pursued without regard for the opportunity cost of that growth. Consequently, resources are used beyond the point at which they make a positive net contribution to the economy. Because planners used resources to maximize the growth rate of production, it is perhaps not surprising that this led to ecological disaster. As Feschbach and Friendly (1992) argue:

> In the last decade of the 20th century, there are no leading industrial cities in the Soviet Union where air pollution is not shortening the life expectancy of adults and undermining the health of their children. The growth that made the USSR a superpower has been so ill-managed, so greedy in its exploitation of natural resources and so indifferent to the health of its people, that ecocide is inevitable.

Another fundamental defect of the SGM is that the return to capital is independent of other decisions. In particular, the model assumes that output is independent of labour's share.[14] Presumably, the amount of consumption will affect the supply (and quality) of labour effort. Any such feedback, however, is assumed away in the model. So the key to industrialization is seen in the growth of heavy industry. Now this model may have been effective when the level of terror was high. As Socialism develops, however, it becomes more and more difficult to maintain such forced industrialization. Consumption cannot be deferred. But when

---

[13] There is an important question of interpretation involved here. If one assumes that labour and capital could be freely substituted, then estimates of total factor productivity are as stated in the text. If one assumes, following Weitzman (1970), that such substitution is costly, then total factor productivity does not become negative. Rather the slowdown in Soviet growth is explained by more rapid growth of capital inputs compared with labour, resulting in reduced output growth due to the inability to substitute inputs. Much debate has centred on which interpretation is correct. (See Ofer (1987) and Easterly and Fischer (1995), for example), but both explanations are consistent with the defects we discuss.

[14] This is strictly true for the Fel'dman–Mahalanobis model, but not for the SGM where, as we have seen, labour supply is taken to depend on the supply of consumer goods.

growth is not achieved through forced industrialization it must be achieved through intensive means, primarily via technical change. This the Soviet economy was ill suited for; instead the SGM fell victim to the extensive growth trap.

The extensive growth trap arises because over time it becomes more and more difficult to mobilize resources. Extensive growth requires high input growth. In the early stages of industrialization high input growth can be achieved by shifting labour from traditional sectors, for example, the countryside, to the modern sector. High growth in the labour force can be achieved by moving people from agriculture to industry. But as this reserve is used up, labour force participation reaches an upper limit. After that, labour force growth is constrained by fertility. One can still accumulate capital at a high rate, but now the capital–labour ratio will rise, and if this causes the marginal product of capital to fall then the growth of output will lag.[15]

That the Soviet economy was stuck in the extensive growth trap was recognized by the leadership rather early. Discussions of how to accelerate technical progress, so that growth could be achieved *intensively*, was discussed often. In 1941 Georgii Malenkov reported to the 18th Congress of the Communist Party that '...highly valuable inventions and product improvements often lie around for years in the scientific research institutes, laboratories and enterprises, and are not introduced into products'. More than forty years later, at the 27th Party Congress, Mikhail Gorbachev complained that '...many scientific discoveries and important inventions lie around for years, and sometimes decades, without

---

[15] Ignoring technical progress (since we are considering extensive growth), *per capita* output growth can be written as

$$\frac{dy}{y} = F_k \frac{k}{y} \frac{dk}{k}$$

where y is per worker output, k is capital per worker, and F_k is the marginal product of capital. Because capital's share in national income $(F_k \frac{k}{y})$ is less than one, extensive growth necessarily means that the capital–output ratio must increase over time, as the capital stock must grow faster than output. The effect of this on output growth thus depends on what happens to the marginal product of capital, F_k. The key issue is whether the marginal product of capital decreases faster than the rate at which capital's share in income increases. If the elasticity of substitution between capital and labour is low, then the marginal product of capital will fall rapidly as capital is substituted for labour, and further extensive growth can only take place by devoting higher and higher proportions of income for investment. Thus the ratio of investment to output stood at around 14% in 1950, rising to 33 % by 1980. None the less growth rates of per capita income declined during this period (see Ofer 1987).

being introduced into practical applications' (cited in Dearden *et al.* 1990; p. 1,105). The problem is that the system was not designed to support innovation (for example, Berliner 1978; Dearden, Ickes, and Samuelson 1990). There are myriad reasons for this. Paramount is the emphasis endemic in planned economies on current plan fulfilment. The 'virtuous haste' that characterizes the Soviet planning system imposes costs on potential innovators who would sacrifice current production for future gains. This is critical because the gains from innovation are taxed away by the dynamic incentives problem that plagues these economies. In this environment innovation is deterred.

An important question is why it proved so difficult to escape the extensive growth trap. One explanation is that in an STE there is no self-correcting mechanism. In a market economy if investments are earning inadequate rates of return, investment goes elsewhere. In the STE, however, investment continues to go into activities where the rates of return are very low. This reflects the absence of a market for capital. One of the key points about Socialism was precisely to eliminate private ownership of capital.

One might also be tempted to ask why the elasticity of substitution was so low in the STE. To some extent it is due to the inability to substitute capital for labour in a functional sense. That is, the enterprise does not shed labour, it just under-employs it, as part of an over-employment system.[16] In the STEs the enterprise always wants to hoard as much labour as possible, as a reserve against taut plans. Moreover, it always wants to add capital to raise capacity. The capital stock was employed inefficiently due to lack of incentives to use inputs in a cost-minimizing manner. At the same time, there was a built-in input–output conservatism. Plans were based on previous plans. This tended to inhibit substitution as well.

A second explanation focuses on the absence of organizational innovation. Capital is simply poured into existing enterprises; there are no entrepreneurs who are able to reorganize the production process. In market economies an important source of productivity growth is the churning of firms as firms expand, contract, enter, and exit. This causes inputs to flow to higher value uses. In STEs enterprises enter but do not exit (Ickes and Ryterman 1994). Inefficient enterprises may contract but they do not cease operation.

---

[16] There is some question as to whether this was due to soft-budget constraints (Kornai) or a planning commitment to full employment (Granick).

In short, while STEs managed to invest increasingly greater shares of income,[17] the investments were of poor quality because of the informational problems in the economy and the lack of incentives for efficient investment. The public was forced to postpone consumption for the future, but these resources were invested so poorly that no positive return was earned.

The legacy of growth, without reallocation, is that Soviet industry was dominated by large, over-manned enterprises with inefficiently allocated capital. In transition economies the problem is that in order for capital to be reallocated there must be an owner. The absence of property rights makes it difficult to transfer capital assets.[18] Thus even after transition begins the capital stock is rather rigid.

Extensive growth also meant that enterprises used natural resources inefficiently. Energy was under-priced and over-utilized. The same is true for other primary commodities. The implication is that when prices are liberalized many industries are producing negative value added: the value of output is less than the aggregate value of the inputs used in production.[19] This is fundamentally a pricing problem. In particular, when the cost of capital is not accounted for, it will be invested in inefficient ways. We discuss the implications when we come to price liberalization.

3.2.2. *The price system*

An important feature of the planned economy was a pricing system unrelated to true costs.[20] Pricing under Soviet planning was an accounting device designed to measure enterprise performance, not a signal of terms of trade or of opportunity costs.[21] The price system was

---

[17] CIA calculations of Soviet national income show the capital–output ratio rising fourfold between 1928 and 1987, while official data show it almost tripling between 1958 and 1987. To accomplish this the Soviets had continually to increase the share of investment in national income; thus this share doubled between 1950 and 1975. See Ofer (1987) and Easterly and Fischer (1995).

[18] Notice that this is also true for leasing, especially of equipment. Clearly it would be advantageous to have leasing. It would allow capital to be reallocated without ownership change. The problem, however, is that without ownership leasing is impossible, since possession in this case is 100% of the deal. The absence of property rights makes the allocation of capital rigid.

[19] In 1935 Hayek had already noted that: 'The best tractor factory may not be an asset, and the capital invested in it is a sheer loss, if the labour which the tractor replaces is cheaper than the cost of the material and labour which goes to make a tractor, plus interest' (Hayek 1935).

[20] Hewett (1990) provides a good discussion of the principles of Soviet pricing.

[21] And correspondingly, money was neither sufficient, nor sometimes even necessary, to complete transactions. What was needed was the authority to purchase the goods.

designed to support the planning system, not the other way around. Prices for the same good differed based on the user.[22] Most important, perhaps, with pricing based on supply considerations, changes in demand did not result in changes in price. This means that costs measured at Soviet prices do not reflect actual values.[23] When prices were liberalized a new picture of the economy emerged. This laid important implications for the structural changes that were necessary.

Prices tended to remain fixed for long periods of time.[24] This is problematic because even if they had been initially set correctly cost conditions change, let alone demand, so after a few years prices become more distorted. The one exception to this is that new goods get new prices; hence, enterprises that wish to increase the price of their product (say because production costs have increased) try to convince the authorities that their product is really new. This leads to 'hidden inflation'.

Raw material inputs were under-priced in the Soviet economy. Their prices were based on the operating costs of extraction, ignoring rent; that is, the opportunity cost of using the resources now rather than in the future. No doubt this harmonized with the goal of increasing production today; scarcity pricing might have induced more conservation, which is inimical to current production.

This bias in raw material prices fed into the system of industrial prices. Heavy consumers of energy were, in effect, subsidized. So, too, were heavy users of capital, thanks to the absence of interest charges. Costs of production were thus calculated based on an incomplete enumeration of costs.

In addition to incomplete cost-based pricing, the system was biased towards certain users. The same commodity would carry a different price if it were used by heavy industry or light industry. This would then feed into the calculation of costs of production of these goods, so that high-priority sectors would *appear* to have lower costs of production than did low-priority sectors. This meant that the apparent distribution of productivities at the onset of transition was liable to mask the true picture;[25]

[22] Industrial prices can be divided into enterprise wholesale prices *received*; wholesale prices *paid* (which are the sum of received plus taxes and mark-ups); and settlement prices, which differ for each producer, used in branches such as mining, where costs vary widely among producers.

[23] Prices were set so that the branch would earn profits as a whole. Hence more productive enterprises would earn higher profits, rather than produce a larger share of production.

[24] Following the Soviet price reform in 1966–7 prices in industry were not changed until the price revision of 1982.

[25] See Ericson (1999) for an analysis of the implications of arbitrary pricing on the apparent and actual production of value added in the Soviet economy.

sectors that may have been thought to be productive may, in fact, have been highly inefficient.

The fact that the pricing system disguised the relative efficiency of various activities means that only with liberalization would the true viability of these activities become apparent. Many sectors that appeared to be productive of value turned out to be destructive of value once prices moved to reflect costs. The extent to which the Soviet economy produced the 'wrong things in the wrong way' could be gauged only after liberalization. The effect was magnified by the move to world prices. Many industrial enterprises could not cover costs once prices moved to market-clearing levels, rising prices led only to unsold output. Price liberalization revealed the extent to which value added in the Soviet economy was really created in the energy and raw materials sector, but it had the effect of making reform appear to be the destroyer of the manufacturing sector.

3.2.3. *The chronic seller's market*

Another important characteristic of the SGM was a chronic seller's market. The primary cause of this was the emphasis on growth at all costs. Fulfilling the output plan replaced other considerations, and became the criterion on which performance was judged at all levels. Plans were designed to be *taut*;[26] to press on possibilities. The hunt for 'hidden reserves' permeated the system.

The primacy of output over other considerations was associated with the phenomenon of *soft budget constraints*.[27] In order to ensure that enterprises fulfilled their plans it was essential that financial shortages did not hamper production. Hence, enterprises were subsidized, *ex post*, to cover any losses associated with plan fulfilment. The result of this was to eliminate any restraint on the part of enterprises in demanding resources needed for production. The absence of hard budget constraints combined with the pressure to fulfil plans implies that enterprises were always demanding resources. This led to chronic excess demand, which had several deleterious effects, most notably the priority for quantity over quality. When goods are in short supply customers will accept what they can get; they cannot afford to reject inferior quality goods.

---

[26] See Ickes (1986) for an analysis of the role of taut plans in Soviet planning.
[27] See Kornai(1992) for a comprehensive analysis of the phenomenon, by the originator of the term.

A perpetual seller's market also created an excess demand for labour. Enterprises could always find uses for more labour because output rather than profits or costs measured performance. Over-full employment planning eliminated the need to have an explicit policy for treating unemployment, which was considered to be a malady of capitalism.

At the same time excess demand meant chronic shortages of certain goods. Political control and distribution of these goods were used to enforce regime priorities. Privileged access to education, housing, careers, travel, and consumer goods were reserved for members of the *nomenklatura*. Moreover, such access allowed for the collection of bribe income. In this sense shortage was a necessity; without the items being in short supply no rents could be derived from positions of power.

While access to 'deficit goods' provided power and privilege, possession of money was of less importance. With goods in short supply it was not possession of money but rather access that made purchase possible. In the STE one could always find a way to pay for a good if one had access. But money without privilege was of much less value.

The combination of shortage and privileged access created a system where *personality* dominated. Allocation and reward were made on the basis of one's identity and position as opposed to the market ideal of anonymous rewards based on productivity. Of course, no social system has achieved complete anonymous rewards, but the Soviet system enhanced the role of personality to the greatest extent. An important consequence of this is the belief, most common among Russians, that those who succeed do so because of whom they know rather than what they have accomplished. This creates a cynicism that has plagued reform in Russia.[28]

3.2.4. *Dynamic incentives*

The Soviet economy provided material incentives to decision-makers based on performance relative to planned targets. This concentrated attention to the problem of fulfilling plan targets, linked, somehow, to measures of output.[29] The emphasis on growth led planners to base targets on previous achievements: 'planning from the achieved level.'

---

[28] To an important extent this belief predates the Soviet period, and has been prevalent in Russia, especially in villages, for centuries. The Soviet period merely enhanced it.

[29] At first targets were specified in physical units, usually gross output. Later these were converted to net output targets and then to value-based measures. See Nove (1986) for a discussion of the success indicator problem.

Thus, if an enterprise produced 100 tons of steel this year, its target for next year would be, say, 106 tons. This created a dynamic incentives problem,[30] undermining the power of static incentives. If an enterprise produces a high level of output today, its future bonuses will be jeopardized. To combat this, enterprises would limit the extent of current performance, to preserve a 'safety factor' which could be used against future uncertainty. Planners, however, recognized that enterprise directors engaged in such behaviour, so they made plan targets even more taut, and so on. Misinformation was intensified.

Under planning, the enterprise exploited its private information to increase its share of enterprise income in the form of bonuses or slack. The form that this behaviour took typically involved exaggerating current production and under-reporting true productive capacity. Of course, the planners were not ignorant of these activities, and set higher plan targets. The outcome was the familiar game played between planners and enterprise directors, where each side found it in its own interest to depart from the full-information signal.[31]

3.3. LEGACIES

As noted in the introductory section, it is useful to distinguish between *systemic* or *institutional* legacies of Communism and *structural*. We consider each in turn.

3.3.1. *Institutional legacies*

The most important institutional legacy was the absence of private property in the means of production. With the object of transition being to create a market economy, a process of privatization that would

---

[30] Sometimes termed the ratchet effect, in which agents under-perform this period because they know that the evaluation of their performance next period will depend on current performance.

[31] Thought of this way, the dissimulation that was the fundamental behaviour of central planning is analogous to tax evasion. Transition has changed the form of tax evasion. Enterprises reduce taxation by understating revenues. Considered in this way, it is hardly surprising that enterprise directors responded to corporatization by altering the form, but not the substance, of their use of private information. In order to survive the tumult of transition, and more generally to simply maximize net income, enterprise directors engage in activities to hide income from the tax authorities. And, just as under planning, the government responds by setting high, and a large number of, tax rates. Transition does not eliminate the game, it simply alters the form.

transform ownership was necessary. Such a process takes time to implement.[32] In the interim, ownership is ambiguous.

The primacy of planning in the Soviet system relegated *finance* to a secondary role. Financial flows were utilized as a form of monitoring; they did not motivate economic activity. The purpose of the Soviet financial system was not to intermediate between savers and investors; this task was accomplished directly through the state budget. Indeed, it was crucial that financial matters did not interfere with the dictates of the plan. To achieve this the Soviet economic system introduced the system of dual monetary circuits: cash (*nalichnye*); and non-cash (*beznalichnye*). The former was (still is) used by households: wages are received and goods purchased with cash money. Enterprises make transactions with non-cash, or book money. The rationale is easy to grasp if we think of the planning process.

Planners needed a system of measuring plan fulfilment. So enterprises had financial plans that mirrored the physical plans, and when goods were shipped, financial paper went in the opposite direction. If an enterprise had a deficit in its account then the planners knew it was not fulfilling its plan. But even if the enterprise had a deficit, *this could not be taken as a reason to prevent it from purchasing inputs*. The reason is clear. If an enterprise cannot purchase inputs it cannot fulfil its plan, and then other downstream plans, those of the users of the products from this enterprise, are jeopardized. So the banking system (*Gosbank*) would always extend credit to enterprises in deficit. But this explains why the money had to be non-cash. For cash money can be used to purchase consumer goods, and these were already in short supply. Hence, if credit is automatically extended to enterprises it must be a form that cannot *leak* back into the household sector of the economy.[33]

In this system enterprises do not borrow to invest or finance current production. Rather they accumulate debts when failure to do so would

---

[32] The Russian experience is one of the most rapid. Vouchers were distributed to the population in October 1992, and most of industry had been formally privatized by June 1994, probably a record speed when one considers the amount of assets involved.

[33] Of course, in practice such leakage did occur. The means were several. One was not to report when workers passed away, continue to argue for the same wage bill, and pocket the wages due to these 'dead souls'. Another was to raise the wages of workers and then take some of this back from them by agreement. The so-called co-operative movement under Gorbachev became a notorious sieve in these matters. An enterprise would enter a fictitious contract with a co-operative, say to paint a warehouse. Such a transaction would require a payment to the co-operative in cash. The enterprise and the co-operative would then split the cash.

jeopardize plan activities. Thus the banking system inherited from the Soviet period was hardly commercial in nature. Moreover, it was not very effective in the most fundamental aspect of exchange: making payments. The reason is that finance followed activity, so an order to pay for goods was issued when goods were to be shipped. There was no need for the payment to arrive before the goods were shipped:[34] after all, the same authority owned both enterprises. Hence, there was little need to invest in the payments system; especially in the speed of clearing. Payments used the surface mail, and often took weeks and even months to transit from one account to another. With the end of planning, the inadequacies of the payments system aggravated the problems that plagued Russia in 1992, and the inter-enterprise arrears crisis in particular (Ickes and Ryterman 1992).

Another critical institutional legacy from the Soviet period is the legal system. The nature of the legal system under planning was aptly summarized by Nikita Khruschev:

'Who's the Boss: we or the law? We are masters over the law, not the law over us—so we have to change the law; we have to see to it that it is possible to execute these speculators.' (Quoted in Simis 1982).

A system designed to maximize the scope for the leadership to govern events necessarily placed no restrictions on the type of interventions they could make. In Tsarist Russia, the rule of law had made very small inroads.[35] The structure of the Soviet system gave primacy to the Party over the rule of law. The plan that directed economic activity had the force of law, but was subject to change at the whim of Party officials. The predictability afforded by a system of contracts was inconsistent with the planners' perceived need to intervene to ensure plan fulfilment. Although the adverse consequences of such discretion were often recognized, and attempts to limit discretion embodied in reform

---

[34] In a market economy goods are often shipped before payment arrives, but in such cases an arrangement for payment has already been made.

[35] Witness the following remark of Count Witte: '[Russia] in one respect represents an exception to all the countries in the world . . . The exception consists in this, that the people have been systematically, over two generations brought up without a sense of property and legality . . . Under these conditions, I see one gigantic question mark: what is an empire with one hundred million peasants who have been educated neither in the concept of landed property nor that of the firmness of law in general?' (Quoted in Pipes 1990.) Witte refers here to two generations since the emancipation of the serfs, but there was clearly no such sense of property and legality developed prior to emancipation.

programmes,[36] they remained an endemic feature of the system. The costs of this were severe enough under planning, but the cost of this legacy for transition is even greater.

A rule of law is important to governments because it is critical to their ability to collect taxes and regulate the behaviour of firms in the event of market failure. But it is also critical to firms. Laws provide standards of behaviour, which can co-ordinate behaviour and reduce transaction costs. Under Soviet planning the rule of law was replaced by the rule of the plan and Party. Market activity unsupported by the legal system degenerates in major respects.

When legal institutions are ineffective parties must rely on informal contract enforcement mechanisms, most importantly a history of personal relations with particular individuals or enterprises. These mechanisms may be efficient for sustained relationships, but they make it very costly for firms to enter new relationships where no history exists.[37] Ineffective legal institutions can thus act as a barrier to entry, or in some cases, to changes in the boundaries and organization of firms in order to facilitate transactions.

The organization of foreign trade under planning is another institutional legacy. Foreign trade in the SGM was conducted through a centralized agency, the Ministry of Foreign Trade (MFT). This had several important consequences for the economy.

Most important, the MFT acted as an insulator, which allowed the divorce of domestic and world prices. The MFT purchased commodities from producers at domestic prices and exported them at world prices,[38] and vice versa for imports. The MFT, and thus the state budget, pocketed (absorbed in some cases) the difference between domestic and foreign prices. This insulation provided implicit protection for industrial producers whose costs exceeded those of producers elsewhere, and it allowed energy and other raw materials to trade domestically at prices far below world levels.

---

[36] Most notably, perhaps, in the Andropov experiment in the early 1980s, but also the *Shchekino* experiment in the 1970s. See Brada (1993) for an analysis of the costs of discretion under Soviet planning.

[37] Informal enforcement mechanisms are typically reputation based. These systems are rather effective when the parties expect to transact frequently. As they rely on informal, typically personal, relationships, however, they are difficult for outsiders to penetrate. This introduces a bias in favour of status quo relationships.

[38] This was true for exports to western economies. Trade within the Council for Mutual Economic Assistance (CMEA) was conducted in so-called *transferable rubles*, an accounting device that was used to create a third set of prices for this trade within the Socialist camp.

At the same time domestic producers had little incentive to produce for export, even when world prices were higher than domestic prices. This had a negative impact on the quality of domestic production; without the competitive pressure to produce for the world market, producers faced only a domestic seller's market. Moreover, many enterprises that produced value added at domestic prices were destroying valued added at world prices.[39] Such enterprises tended to become non-viable upon liberalization.

Another implication of the MFT system was currency convertibility, but of a specific form. Most countries with inconvertible currencies suffer from an exchange rate that is over-valued, creating an excess demand for foreign currency. In the Soviet economy the currency was institutionally inconvertible. Foreigners could purchase goods only through the MFT, which operated only in hard currencies. Hence, the foreign demand for Soviet roubles would be non-existent at any exchange rate.

Russia entered transition with an over-valued rouble; the impact effect of external liberalization was thus a significant nominal depreciation. This decline in the exchange value of the rouble reflected a flight from domestic assets due in part to inflationary expectations. The nominal depreciation had the effect of increasing the profitability of export sectors, mainly in energy and raw materials, and cushioning the extent of import competition on domestic producers. The initial nominal depreciation was followed, as in all transition economies, by a degree of real appreciation of the currency as domestic prices moved towards world market levels. This has been an important motor of the structural change accompanying transition.

3.3.2. *Structural legacies*

Structural legacies are the distortions in the economy that Russia inherited from the Soviet period. These legacies complicate the process of transition. The STE displayed a special industrial structure. Output and capital were skewed towards heavy industry and away from consumer goods. Industry was favoured over services. In 1980, for example, the services sector employed 37 per cent of the workforce in the Soviet

---

[39] As noted earlier, many producers were producing negative value added even at domestic prices.

Union, compared with 50 per cent in a sample of countries with similar GDPs.[40] The bias was determined by the emphasis on growth. It clearly does not reflect the preferences of Soviet society. Soviet-type economies focused on heavy industry because that was seen to be the key to growth. Investment was thus slanted towards industry, and industrial investment towards heavy industry.[41]

Table 3.1 shows the extent to which the Soviet Union's capital stock was skewed towards industry and agriculture. Whereas, however, the over-emphasis on industry was intentional, the large agricultural sector is more a reflection of low productivity. The ultimate irony of Soviet agricultural policy is that in the wake of collectivization, which was supposed to extract more resources from the countryside, Soviet planners continually had to increase investment in agriculture to produce even moderate growth.[42]

Apart from the nature of the SGM itself, a second reason why the country's industrial structure departed so dramatically from that of a normal market economy was the hyper-militarized state of the Soviet economy. It is indeed hard to over-emphasize the extent to which the Soviet economy was designed for, and around, military production. This holds for the Soviet Union more than for other Socialist economies and for Russia more than other former republics. Russia, with 51.8 per cent of the population of the Soviet Union, accounted for 71.2 per cent of defence-sector employment (Gaddy 1996). A hyper-militarized economy favours heavy industry over light because the former is required for defence production.

To gauge the importance of the military in the Soviet economy, consider one of the most important branches of industry, machine-building and metal-working (MBMW).[43] This is a key branch, the heart of heavy industry in the Soviet Union. According to official Soviet statistics, some

---

[40] The results for output shares are similar: 40% for the Soviet Union and 54% for the comparison group. The comparison group is from Chenery and Syrquin's work on patterns of structural change. Similar results hold for a comparison with European members of the OECD, where the employment service share for 1980 was 50%, and for output 57%. See Ofer (1987).

[41] Some estimates for the Soviet Union put the share of heavy industry in total industrial investment between 1917 and 1976 at 84% (Kornai 1992, p. 173).

[42] Perhaps the classic example of this is the substitution of the Machine Tractor Stations for livestock. The former was supposedly more scientific and therefore more productive. Its main function, however, was increased control over the affairs of the countryside.

[43] This and the next paragraphs follow Gaddy (1996).

Table 3.1. *Sectoral distribution of capital stocks, 1987 (per cent)*

	Agriculture	Industry	Dwellings	Other
Soviet Union	14.2	32.2	18.6	35.0
Industrial market economies	5.0	23.4	35.9	35.6
United States	2.8	22.4	45.6	29.2
Finland	7.5	19.9	33.8	38.8
Federal Republic of Germany	3.6	20.1	44.2	32.1

Source: Ofer (1987).

30 per cent of production in this sector went for arms, 20 per cent was consumer goods (cars, televisions, refrigerators, etc.), and the remaining 50 per cent was investment goods. But this calculation was based on official prices, and understates the true magnitude of defence orientation.[44] The reason is that production for defence output appears less burdensome to the economy than it actually was. The key point, however, is clear. The Soviet economy was highly militarized; it was a hyper-militarized economy.

It is difficult to provide a precise assessment of the size of the defence sector, VPK (*Voyenno-promyshlennaya kompleks*), compared to the rest of the economy. The reason is not so much secrecy but the absence of proper prices. In all economies it is difficult to value military production because there is no market, or only a partial market, for the output.[45] But in the Soviet-type economy there is the added (and more difficult) problem of the pricing of inputs. In the STE the price of inputs differs according to the *user*. Inputs to enterprises in the military sector are priced lower than the same inputs to the civilian sector.

---

[44] Suppose that we converted all MBMW output to world prices, a quite difficult task given the thousands of major products in the sector. Economists at the Institute for Forecasting tried to do this for 1998, and found that at world prices only about 5–6% of production was consumer goods, investment goods accounted for 32%, and the military took the remaining 60%. Of course, even this calculation probably understates the importance of the military in the economy because the investment goods are presumably used to produce output, and it is not clear how much of that is used to produce output for the military.

[45] Excluding arms sales, but these are often made for political reasons, and hence the prices often do not reflect costs.

Such pricing policies have two important effects. First, the defence sector will appear to be more productive than civilian enterprises, owing simply to pricing. Why? Because the same accounting value of material inputs implies larger quantities for defence enterprises. Of course, this superiority is an illusion due to pricing, but the belief that there was a real productivity difference had important implications for the operation of the system, and for transition.

The second effect of 'unequal pricing' is that the cost of producing military output is under-estimated. The lower price that VPK enterprises pay for material inputs is like a hidden tax on the rest of the economy. The opportunity cost of producing military output is understated because of the lower accounting price for defence. Think of how the United States would measure the cost of producing a hundred Stealth fighters if Congress passed legislation that required aluminium producers to supply the Pentagon at half the market price. The budgetary cost of producing Stealth fighters would be reduced. But a portion of the economic cost would be shifted on to non-military uses of aluminium (and from there to the rest of the economy). To assess the true cost of the Stealth fighters we should have to know the extent to which non-military aluminium prices were increased to compensate for the below-cost deliveries to the government.

Now, in the case of the Soviet economy we must multiply the number of pricing distortions by many orders of magnitude. For it is not just aluminium but almost all inputs that are priced differently in the two sectors. Moreover, prices in the civilian sector are not reflective of opportunity cost either. So, even though we know that costs are shifted from the VPK to the civilian sector, we are unable to measure them until we can value civilian production at market prices.

Another reason why it is hard to estimate the size of the VPK is that a good deal of civilian production took place in this sector. All aluminium production, for example, was produced in the VPK, as was a very large share of consumer electronics, such as sewing machines (100 per cent of total production), radios (100 per cent), televisions (100 per cent), video-cassette recorders (100 per cent), cameras (100 per cent), chainsaws (100 per cent), freezers (93 per cent), vacuum cleaners (69 per cent), washing machines (66 per cent), refrigerators (40 per cent), and the like (Gaddy 1996). This was not the result of a strategic decision to diversify production, as might be the case with a western defence manufacturer. Rather it was a means of augmenting the capacity of the military in the case of war, since civilian production facilities could be mobilized for military purposes at low cost. The reason is that civilian production used the same inputs,[46] and often similar specifications, as military output. This is why Russian trucks are typically too big for small commercial use and too small for inter-city freight hauling; their specifications are those for military use. The question is how to classify this production. Is it civilian or military?

The legacy of hyper-militarization was a defence burden that could not be maintained in a liberalized economy. The cost of maintaining the structure was simply too high. But this left a large segment of industry producing goods for which no effective demand could be found, and is at the heart of the problem of industrial restructuring in Russia. This cost is magnified by the location of many defence enterprises in cities where they are often the dominant or sole employers, making the social cost of cutting defence expenditures even greater. Defence conversion is always a difficult task. For Russia, defence conversion and industrial restructuring are almost the same thing due to the overwhelming importance of this sector.

Industrial Concentration

Apart from the military emphasis, the enterprise structure Russia inherited from the Soviet system has important characteristics that affect transition: an emphasis on size and an absence of small enterprises. Stalinist planners emphasized gigantic plants.[47] By the same token, Soviet enterprises tended to be located in a single area, or perhaps two locations, whereas large western companies tend to have numerous plants geographically dispersed. The Russian economy is much more regionally specialized than western economies, including the United States.

While the extent to which Soviet enterprises were excessive in size has frequently been exaggerated in the literature,[48] what is critical is that

---

[46] Although often not of the same quality. The military had first claim to inputs. Those rejected for military use would go for civilian production. For example transistors, as reported to Hedrick Smith by a worker in a plant: 'Military officers sit in each factory—in the big factories, these are generals—and they operate with strict military discipline. They are empowered to reject *brak* [junk or substandard items], and they reject great quantities of *brak*, often at great expense . . . I have seen how they make transistors. They would make 100 and the military representative would select only one or two. Some would be thrown out as defective and the rest would go to the [civilian] market (Smith 1976, p. 291).

[47] As Wiles noted: 'There is something "socialist" and "progressive" about mere size, even if unaccompanied by lower costs. Gigantomania as such, then, reinforces the view that, large capital expenditures are a good thing, even where smaller ones will do '(Wiles 1962, p. 304.)

[48] See Brown, Ickes, and Ryterman (1994) for a comparison of the size distribution of Soviet enterprises with other countries.

small enterprises were missing from the Soviet landscape. It is interesting to compare the size distribution of industry in Russia with that of the Unites States.[49] In the latter most employment is concentrated in small firms (less than 250 workers) or in very large firms (greater than 10,000 workers). These two groups comprised two-thirds of industrial employment in the United States compared with only 25 per cent in Russia. Russia has both fewer extra large firms and fewer small firms. Most striking is the difference with respect to small firms. In Russia 91.5 per cent of civilian employment and an estimated 94.5 per cent of manufacturing (including defence) employment is provided by enterprises with at least 250 employees, while in US manufacturing only 73.1 per cent of employment is provided by such firms. The lack of small enterprises in the Soviet economy no doubt was an important factor inhibiting innovation and technical change.

In addition to the absence of small firms in the Soviet economy it is commonly asserted that Russia suffers from a monopoly problem. Interestingly, Russian industry is not that highly concentrated.[50] Its concentrated branches tend to be small and account for a small proportion of employment. However, potential competition is inhibited by poor transport infrastructure.[51] Russia is, after all, a very large country, and the transport and distribution system inherited from the Soviet period was not designed to create national markets. Moreover, the underdevelopment of the financial and legal system serves as an entry barrier. These shortcomings in distribution, finance, law, and transport may be more important to developing competition than technological barriers (that is, economies of scale).

Summary

The upshot of these structural legacies is that at the onset of transition the Russian economy was dominated by large numbers of enterprises that

[49] This section follows Brown, Ickes, and Ryterman (1994). The comparison is made using the 1987 census of manufacturing for the US, and the 1989 Soviet census of industry for Russia.

[50] Where highly concentrated is taken, for example, to be a four-firm concentration ratio in excess of 60%. On the question of Russian industrial concentration, see Brown, Ickes, and Ryterman (1994).

[51] As the authors of the IMF–World Bank–OECD–EBRD joint study on the Soviet economy argued: 'Even where more than one enterprise exists, the national aggregates hide a high degree of regional monopoly power that is protected by generally poor communications and transportation and by administered marketing channels which, in turn, are insulated from one another by ministerial lines of responsibility' (IMF 1991, p. 16).

produced goods at costs that could not be recovered in the market. The Soviet industrial system was an edifice built up on the basis of natural resources, and the value added that appeared to be produced in manufacturing was simply transferred from other sectors though the pricing system.

With liberalization the magnitude of the distortions in the economy became manifest. With the cost of energy and other raw materials moving towards world prices large numbers of enterprises could not cover their costs. In an attempt to remedy this, enterprises raised the price of output, but there were no buyers at these prices.

The key factor that conditions the structural adjustments caused by liberalization is Russia's position as a raw materials exporter. The legacy of the Soviet period is a high-cost industrial sector financed by abundant endowments of raw materials, especially energy. Soviet industry used energy and raw materials much more intensively than market economies (see Table 3.2), using more inputs to produce a dollar of GDP than was the case in large western industrialized countries. When price liberalization raised the opportunity costs of material inputs the existing structure of production was not competitive. In many cases it is simply cheaper to export the inputs. This implies that as Russia moved towards more efficient use of inputs in production, some decline in industrial production was to be expected,[52] since the same value of GDP could be produced with fewer inputs. Indeed, a shift of resources towards other sectors could be possible with no decline in value added.

3.4. A LEGACY OF NEVER-ENDING REFORM

The last thirty years of the Soviet system were marked by a succession of attempts to reform the economy. A short-list would include Khruschev's creation of regional ministries (*sovnarkhoz*), the Kosygin reforms of the mid-1960s, the Brezhnev reforms in the late 1970s and the Andropov reforms in 1983, finally ending with Gorbachev's *perestroika*. The characteristic feature of all these reforms was the attempt to improve the system of planning rather than to replace it. Thus they are all characterized as *partial* reforms.[53] An important legacy for transition of the Soviet

---

[52] Unless the residual could be shifted to exports which, in the case of armaments was, at any rate, partly possible.

[53] See Hewett (1990) for an analysis of this experience. See Litwack (1991) for an analysis of how frequent reforms and discretionary policymaking affects the ability of policymakers to make commitments.

Barry W. Ickes

Table 3.2. *Indicators of raw materials and energy consumption, 1988*

	USSR	**USA**	**Germany**	**Japan**
Crude steel production (millions of metric tons)	280	19	11	34
Ratio USSR to		14.7	25.5	8.2
Refined copper production (thousands of metric tons)	11.73	381	114	307
Ratio USSR to		4.5	15	5.6
Primary aluminium production (thousands of metric tons)	4.116	809	200	11
Ratio USSR to		5.1	20.6	374.2
Synthetic rubber production (thousands of metric tons)	4.262	477	132	418
Ratio USSR to		8.9	32.3	10.2
Primary energy consumption (millions of bbls/day oil equivalent)	46	8	1	2
Ratio USSR to		5.8	46	23

Source: Handbook of Economic Statistics, CIA (1989), IFS, IMF; and the *Economist*.

reform experience is the expectation on the part of people that reforms issued from above are not likely to be persistent or to make much difference. A history of reforms that were frequently reversed (or amounted to very little) makes it hard for future reforms to be *credible*. People come to lack faith in announcements of new policies. Instead, they search for ways to get around the reforms and to protect themselves against reversal. Even a sensible plan of sequenced reforms may then fall victim to pessimistic expectations.

3.5. COLLAPSE AND TRANSITION

The collapse of the Soviet system set the stage for transition. The process by which the Soviet economy imploded is multi-faceted, and the full story cannot be told here. Several features are worth highlighting, however.

As STEs struggled to cope with declining performance they experimented with reforms that altered the mechanism without changing the fundamental nature of the system. One important feature was the weakening of central control. To a large extent this began with 'Brezhnev-Communism', aptly described as Stalinism without the terror.[54] Interestingly, the key element was stability in the bureaucracy. The result of this was an institutionalization of the system of bribes and payoffs to the *nomenklatura*. Stalin had implicitly recognized that without regular purges of the bureaucracy officials would turn the system to their own interest.[55] Terror is the instrument by which the command economy deters the exploitation of rents by executants. Abolition of terror gives executants the capacity to siphon off the rents attributable to their positions. In effect, the cost to the planners of achieving a given level of profits is increased by the rents that must be paid to subordinates.[56] Another way to put this is that the associated decline in revenues accruing to the Centre led to increasing budgetary shortfalls, just as larger resources were needed to finance modernization and accumulation for growth.

Perestroika, and related reforms in the east European economies, saw greater elements of decentralization introduced.[57] The idea of such reforms was to give discretion to managers who had greater information about what goes on in the enterprise, and to give them greater scope to use initiative. Yet as a whole the system was not fundamentally altered.

One important consequence was supply diversion (Murphy, Shleifer, and Vishny 1992) as enterprises used their increased discretion to capture the rents associated with non-market allocation. Not all supply diversion goes to more efficient uses. The reason, of course, is that the diverter acquires the resources at below opportunity cost, and plan prices may not reflect social value. None the less, the planning system depends on

---

[54] The Brezhnev period is usually referred to now as the period of *zastoi* (stagnation).

[55] Notice that as shortage becomes universal access to goods is the source of privilege. This provides an incentive for the élite to maintain the system of shortage. Moreover, distributing benefits in this way makes them opaque; the public cannot see the inequity built into the system.

[56] A related problem is that only the Centre has economy-wide information, so the increased discretion by agents lower in the hierarchy leads to less effective allocation of resources.

[57] Most important, in this context, is Gorbachev's Law on State Enterprise (1987), which introduced the system of state orders, *goszakhazy*. Under this system, enterprises were required to fulfil state orders and were allowed to make contracts for above-plan output.

deliveries that support the plan. Hence, the production sector can be starved of key inputs as goods are diverted to other uses.

Supply diversion not only caused a deterioration in performance it also led to the *pseudo-privatization* of profits. Enterprise directors and other agents used their added discretion to secure rents that were present in a system where prices did not clear markets. As long as the Centre could limit discretion, agents were limited in their attempts to siphon rents. With decentralization, however, enterprise directors were presented with far wider opportunities to divert resources to their own benefit. Besides reducing budget revenues, this created a growing public recognition of the inequities in the system.

Decentralization also led to less control over wages. As power shifted from the Centre to the enterprises the latter used this to increase wages. But prices did not rise, and as there was no acceleration in production, this led to more repressed inflation: the monetary overhang. Wage increases were financed by larger infusions of central bank credit, but this only worsened the imbalance between supply and demand. Of course, in parallel markets prices rose. This accelerated the emptying of shelves in official markets. Hence, increasing shortages and lengthening of queues marked the last stages of Socialism.

We can summarize the ultimate crisis of the command economy in three parts. Production declined and shortage intensified, as goods were increasingly diverted. The implosion in the economy led to a decline in budgetary revenues. And the collapse in budgetary revenues caused a crisis in the system of central control and state orders.

The basic problem facing Russian reformers in the fall of 1991 was that while the fundamental aspects of reform involved institutional changes such as privatization and liberalization of the economy, the reform *environment* was that of macroeconomic crisis, namely monetary overhang and increased monetary financing of budget deficits. This meant that stabilization would necessarily take centre stage. Towards the end of the Soviet period (in the early 1990s) monetary financing of the budget deficit approached 20 per cent of GDP.[58] With price fixed in official markets this led to aggravated shortages in state stores while prices rose steeply in unofficial markets. As wage pressure increased and production deteriorated the monetary disequilibrium grew. Inability to collect taxes

---

[58] See Ofer (1990) for an analysis of Soviet budget problems, and see Cochrane and Ickes (1995) and Granville (1995) for a discussion of the macroeconomic problems experienced by Russian reformers in the attempt to stabilize the economy.

increased the pressure to monetize deficits and magnified the monetary overhang.

When price liberalization was implemented in 1992 inflation became open and dramatic. Of course, the key Soviet pricing problem was distorted *relative prices*, and price liberalization was essential to remedy this. However, monetary disequilibrium meant that the costs of adjustment would be exacerbated by high inflation. Much of the debate and effort in the early years of Russian economic reform were devoted to monetary stabilization, leaving the more fundamental aspects of reform to a later date.[59]

REFERENCES

Berliner, Joseph (1978). *The Innovation Decision in Soviet Industry*, MIT Press.

Brada, Josef (1993). 'The Transformation from Communism to Capitalism: How Far? How Fast?', *Post-Soviet Affairs*, 9/2: 87–110.

Brown, Annette, Ickes, Barry W., and Ryterman, Randi (1994). 'The Myth of Monopoly: A New View of Industrial Structure in Russia', World Bank Policy Research Paper.

Cochrane, J. H., and Ickes, B. W. (1995). 'Macroeconomics in Russia', in E. Lazear (ed.), *Economic Transition in Eastern Europe and Russia: Realities of Reform*, Hoover Institution Press.

Dearden, James, Ickes, Barry W., and Samuelson, Larry (1990). 'To Innovate or Not to Innovate: Incentives for Innovation in Hierarchies', *American Economic Review*, 80/5, December.

Easterly, W., and Fischer, S. (1995) 'The Soviet Economic Decline', *World Bank Economic Review*, 9/3: 341–71.

Ericson, Richard (1991). 'The Classical Soviet-Type Economy: Nature of the System and Implications for Reform', *Journal of Economic Perspectives*, Fall.

—— (1999). 'The Structural Barrier to Transition Hidden in Input–Output Tables of Centrally Planned Economies', *Economic Systems*, 23/3: 199–224.

Feschbach, Murray, and Friendly, A. (1992). *Ecocide in the USSR*, Basic Books.

Gaddy, Clifford (1996). *The Price of the Past: Russia's Struggle with the Legacy of a Militarized Economy*, Brookings.

Goldberg, Linda, Ickes, Barry W., and Ryterman, Randi (1994). 'Departures from the Ruble Zone: The Implications of Adopting Independent Currencies', *The World Economy*, 17/3, May.

Granville, Brigitte (1995). *The Success of Russian Economic Reform*, London: The Royal Institute of International Affairs, distributed by Brookings.

---

[59] Against this, one could argue that the attention drawn to fighting inflation made it easier to implement privatization. The argument is that without this diversion greater political opposition to privatization may have developed.

Hay, Jonathon R., Shleifer, Andrei, and Vishny, Robert (1996). 'Toward a Theory of Legal Reform', *European Economic Review*, 40: 559–67.

Hayek, F. A. (1935). *Collectivist Economic Planning: Critical Studies on the Possibilities of Socialism*, by N. G. Pierson, Ludwig von Mises, George Halm, and Enrico Barone edited, with an introduction and a concluding essay, by F. A. von Hayek, London: G. Routledge & Sons Ltd.

Hewett, A. (ed.) (1990). *Reforming the Soviet Economy: Equity and Efficiency*, Brookings.

Ickes, B. W. (1986). 'On the Economics of Taut Plans', *Journal of Comparative Economics*, 10/4, December.

——, and Ryterman, Randi (1994). 'From Enterprise to Firm: Notes for a Theory of the Enterprise in Transition', in Robert W. Campbell (ed.), *The Post-communist Economic Transformation: Essays in Honor of Gregory Grossman*, Westview Press, 83–104.

—— —— (1992). 'The Interenterprise Arrears Crisis in Russia', *Post-Soviet Affairs (formerly Soviet Economy)*, 8/4 (October–December): 331–61.

—— —— (1994). 'Exit Without Entry: Industrial Dynamics Under Planning', Pennsylvania State University, Working Paper.

International Monetary Fund, The World Bank, Organization for Economic Cooperation and Development, and European Bank for Reconstruction and Development (1991). *A Study of the Soviet Economy*, vol. 2. Paris.

Kornai, Janos (1992). *The Socialist System: The Political Economy of Communism*, Princeton University Press.

Litwack, John (1990). 'Ratcheting and Economic Reform in the Soviet Union', *Journal of Comparative Economics*, 14/2, June.

—— (1991). 'Legality and Market Reform in Soviet Type Economies', *Journal of Economic Perspectives*, Fall.

Murphy, Kevin, Shleifer, Andrei, and Vishny, Robert (1992). 'The Transition to a Market Economy: Pitfalls of Partial Reform', *Quarterly Journal of Economics*, August.

Nove, Alec (1986). *The Soviet Economic System*, 3rd edn. London: Allen and Unwin.

OECD (1995). *Russian Economic Survey*, Paris.

Ofer, Gur (1987). 'Soviet Economic Growth: 1928–1985', *Journal of Economic Literature*, December.

—— (1990). 'Macroeconomic Issues of Soviet Reforms', in O. J. Blanchard and S. Fischer (eds.), *NBER Macroeconomics Annual*, vol. 5, 297–334.

Pipes (1990). *The Russian Revolution*, Knopf.

Roberts, Bryan W., and Rodgriguez, Alvaro (1997). 'Economic Growth Under a Self-Interested Central Planner', *Journal of Comparative Economics*, 24/2, April: 121–39.

Rutland, Peter (1994). 'Privatization in Russia: One Step Forward: Two Steps Back', *Europe–Asia Studies* (formerly Soviet Studies), 46/7: 1,109–32.

Simis, Konstantin (1992). *USSR: The Corrupt Society: The Secret World of Soviet Capitalism*, New York: Simon and Schuster.

Smith, Hedrick (1976). *The Russians*, London: Sphere Books.

Weitzman, Martin (1970). 'Soviet Postwar Economic Growth and Capital–Labor Substitution', *American Economic Review*, 60/4, September.

Wiles, P. J. D. (1962). *The Political Economy of Communism*, Oxford: Basil Blackwell.

4

The Problem of
Monetary Stabilization

BRIGITTE GRANVILLE

4.1. INTRODUCTION

The Russian financial crisis of 1998 was a bitter setback to stabilization
efforts after nearly three years of low inflation (crowned by a redenomin-
ation of the rouble on 1 January 1998 with the division of money values
by 1,000). Events were precipitated by the international situation. The
East Asian financial turmoil combined with the large drop in oil prices
after early 1997 and high financial returns in the United States and
Europe created an explosive mixture which Russia was ill-prepared to
confront. There was also an element of self-fulfilling prophecy by
external investors, doubtless including many Russians with funds channelled through foreign institutions. Yet the crisis would not have erupted
without serious underlying weaknesses in the domestic financial situation. Experience from many countries, especially in Latin America, has
shown that inadequate macroeconomic policies and poor regulation of
commercial banks are common harbingers of currency crises (Otker and
Pazarbasioglu 1995).

The aim of this chapter is to examine the achievements of Russia's
macroeconomic policy both historically and analytically by focusing on
the balance sheet of the Central Bank of Russia (CBR). It will be shown
that for the whole period 1991–8 monetary policy was constrained by the

This chapter draws on material originally contained in 'problemy stabilisazii denechnovo
obrachenie v Roccii', in *Voprocii Economikii*, 1: 13–32, Moscow, Russian Federation, January
1999 and in 'L'Echec de la Stabilisation Monetaire en Russie', *Revue d'études comparatives
Est–Ouest* (CNRS), numéro 2, juin 1999; numero spécial: *Les economies post-socialistes: une
decennie de transformations*, Paris.

public finances. Ultimately the ability of the monetary authority to maintain the stability of the domestic currency has been and is limited by the size of the budget deficit, however financed.[1]

Section 2 looks at the legacy which first brought such inflationary pressures into the system. Section 3 divides the period after 1991 into two sub-periods to emphasize that, whether financed initially by money creation or by borrowing, the fiscal deficit has needed to be controlled. A sufficient condition for such control is a primary surplus equivalent to the initial public debt multiplied by the difference between the real interest rate and real GDP growth. If the public debt is large enough to begin with, the condition becomes necessary as well. Failing it the government will have no choice but to rely increasingly on money creation. As money grows, so does the price level. If, or as, inflation accelerates, a limit is imposed on government revenue from seignorage. As the public progressively abandons the domestic currency, the government finds it harder to finance the budget deficit through seigniorage revenue, making fiscal measures unavoidable if still possible. A currency crash becomes more likely, with its attendant risks of economic depression and/or political destabilization.

The 1998 Russian financial crisis is a variant of the so-called first generation balance of payments crisis modelled by Krugman (1979). The causal mechanism in this model is excessively expansionary fiscal and monetary policies, resulting in a persistent loss of international reserves that ultimately forces the authorities to abandon their exchange rate peg. In the case of Russia credit policy was not loose but fiscal policy was. The market simply did not believe that the Ministry of Finance would be able to redeem its mounting debt without printing money. The loss of international reserves was caused not by expansionary monetary policy but through capital outflows triggered by the fear of financial loss including devaluation. The monetary authorities tried to allay such fears by raising interest rates. They failed because the budgetary burden of extraordinarily high interest rates was itself a significant part of the problem. The tighter monetary policy, the worse the fiscal situation became, driving the whole Russian economy into a vicious circle undermining the stability of the rouble. In other words the conflict between monetary, fiscal, and exchange rate policy became acute.

---

[1] The issue of fiscal policy itself is not studied in this chapter and the reader should refer to Grafe and Richter for a thorough study on 'taxation and public expenditure' in this volume.

4.2. THE LEGACY

Before the reforms introduced in 1987–8, the functions of Gosbank (the state monobank) covered those both of a Central Bank proper and of commercial banks. It was both 'banker to the government and lender to the enterprise sector'.[2] There were exceptions: international reserves were managed by the bank for foreign trade (Vneshtorgbank); household savings by Sberbank (literally the Savings Bank); and construction by the building bank (Stroibank).

Financial flows were divided between households and firms according to the cash plan and the credit plan. This dichotomy also meant two forms of means of payment—cash for households and non-cash for enterprises. Credit allocation and the holding of deposits, as regards both enterprises and households, were likewise centralized under the control of the Gosbank. Monetary and fiscal policies were subordinated to physical planning of outputs. Central plans were executed by state enterprises under the supervision of sectoral branch ministries (representing 90 per cent of production).[3]

Significant reform of banking occurred in 1987 with the introduction of a two-tier system. Three specialized state banks were created to channel credits to enterprises in agriculture (Agroprombank), industry (Promstroibank), and social investment, namely, housing (Zhilsotsbank). In addition, the 1988 law on co-operatives permitted the creation of co-operative banks to support the newly created co-operative enterprises not serviced by the state banks. The number of such banks grew from a few dozen in 1988 to about 400 at the end of 1991.[4]

The Gosbank remained otherwise untouched until 1991. No market disciplines were attached to credit allocation (which was direct—controlled by administrative order from the centre). Interest rates remained low, and were themselves frequently reduced in various types of concessional lending. Gosbank was formally liquidated on 25 December 1991 and the Central Bank of Russia (CBR) took over its responsibilities. Initially, however, the CBR remained a passive institution charged with financing the budget deficit.

The deficit had started to get out of control in 1986, owing partly to the fall of world oil prices and partly to the increase in investment expenditures authorized under the policy of 'acceleration'—a series of

---

[2] IMF (1992*b*), p. 3.   [3] IMF (1992*a*), p. 3.   [4] Balino *et al.* (1997), p. 7.

Table 4.1. *Russia: nominal and real wages,*[a] *1987–1990*
(period average, roubles)

	Nominal wage % change	Nominal wage Rbs/m	Real wage % change	Real wage W/P	RPI\b
1987		216		100	1.6
1988	9	235	9	108.58	0.2
1989	10	259	8	116.86	2.4
1990	15	297	9	126.9	5.6

Notes: [a]Defined as the nominal wage deflated by the Retail Price index (RPI): W/P.
[b]State stores and consumer co-operatives index up to 1989, consolidated RPI for 1990.
Source: Goskomstat; Koen and Phillips (1993), table 6, p. 37.

reforms aimed at reviving growth.[5] Over the years 1985–9 the deficit rose from about 2 per cent of GNP to 9–10 per cent of GNP.[6] Of particular significance was the 1987 Law on State Enterprises,[7] which effectively gave managers freedom to increase wages. As shown in Table 4.1, by 1990 measured real wages were 27 per cent above their 1987 level. These increases were financed with soft loans from the banking system and subsidies from the state budget.

At first wage increases did not affect the Retail Price Index (RPI), as this index measured only the state retail trade where prices were controlled.[8] Only in 1990 did inflation start to show with a yearly rate of 5% (Table 4.2).[9]

Until 1990 the authorities were able to keep monetary financing of the budget deficit at a low level thanks to loans from international markets

[5] See Granville (1995); Ickes (1998) in this volume.
[6] Lin (1993), p. 369. These figures are similar to the estimates of McKinnon (1991), p. 62: 'from 1.8% of GNP in 1985 to an estimated 9.9% in 1989'.
[7] IMF et al. (1990), p. 4: This law 'replaced traditional mandatory output targets for enterprises with so-called state orders (namely centrally directed orders to firms to deliver specified quantities of goods). The law also permitted firms some latitude to negotiate with each other, and granted them greater autonomy in the allocation of their internally generated funds, in particular, in the payment of wages and bonuses.'
[8] Ibid., p. 4: 'From 1988, enterprises were allowed to negotiate "contract" prices for so-called new products, but these were still subject to official surveillance and, in any event, covered only a fraction of enterprise production.'
[9] Linz (1990), p. 1 reports for the same period that a black market flourished with prices higher by up to 500%.

Table 4.2. *USSR: Inflation, 1985–1991 (annual % changes)*

	1985	1986	1987	1988	1989	1990	1991
Wholesale industrial prices					1.2	3.9	138.1
Retail prices						5.6	90.4
Food	0.1	0.6	2.1	0.4	0.7	4.9	112.7
Alcoholic beverages	6.2	24.7	15.4			1.9	28.6
Non-food products	−0.9	−0.9	−1.1		3.1	6.5	100.7
Retail prices in:							
State and co-operate trade	0.5	2.2	1.6	0.2	2.4	5.2	89.5
Co-operative trade	1.2	3.4	2.4	0.6	0.5	14.1	111.7
Collective farms	5.2	1.1	3.7	2.5	7.4	34.3	132.1

Source: IMF (1992*a*), p. 63.

and governments.[10] This however raised the external debt from US$20 billion in 1985 to US$96.8 billion at the end of 1991.

The budget deficit in the fourth quarter of 1991 totalled about 30 per cent of GDP.[11] This was due to the increase in state subsidies to support administratively controlled prices including the exchange rate, the decline in measured output, and the lack of tax discipline consequent on the break-up of the USSR, with a conspicuous loss of revenue payments from the republics to the centre. At this time all credit worthiness

---

[10] The increase in foreign lending to the Soviet Union in the Gorbachev years reflected the country's excellent credit history, which stood out particularly against the background of the Latin American debt crisis. Many western enterprises were so confident of the Soviet payments record that they declined the services of their governmental export credit agencies (ECAs). This private uninsured debt, caught up in the general default with the collapse of the Soviet Vneshekonombank in December 1991, remained an unrestructed obligation in 1998. The rest of the loans were extended by ECAs and commercial banks, and by 1996 had been fully restructured in the Paris and London Clubs respectively. The majority of the funds were tied to suppliers to Soviet industry of capital goods manufactured in the lending country. This financing became essential to meet the investment targets of the Soviet central plan at a time (1988) when falling oil prices were reducing the country's foreign exchange receipts.   [11] See Grafe and Richter in this volume.

with the West was lost, and the only remaining means of budget finance was rapid increases in the money supply.

4.3. CONFLICT BETWEEN MONETARY, EXCHANGE RATE, AND BUDGET POLICY: 1992–5 AND 1995–8

When the new Russian government freed most prices on 2 January 1992 few anticipated that the task of monetary stabilization was going to be so enormous. The country's finances not only had to be consolidated (see Grafe and Richter in this volume) but financial institutions had to be adapted to the new environment or even created from zero as in the case of securities markets (see Willer in this volume).

The schematic form of the balance sheet of the Central Bank of Russia (CBR) helps us to visualize the inflationary pressures in the Russian economy during 1992–8 and their development (Table 4.3).

The Central Bank proximately determines the level of the monetary base (MB) or reserve money. This is defined as the sum of currency outside banks plus banks' cash and deposits at the CBR. In its narrow sense it includes (besides currency outside banks) only the minimum reserve requirements of commercial banks; in a broader sense it includes any excess reserves of the banks as well.

Variation in base money must be matched by changes in the asset side of the balance sheet, which is composed of net international reserves (NIR), net credit to the government (NCG), credits to commercial banks either gross or net (GCB or NCB depending on whether the monetary base is defined as including or excluding excess reserves), credits to former Soviet republics (NCFSR), and other items net (OIN) which are mainly the profit of the CBR.

$$\Delta MB = \Delta NIR + \Delta NCG + \Delta GCB + \Delta NCFSR + \Delta OIN$$

$$(1)$$

An overall surplus (deficit) in the balance of payments adds to (subtracts from) net international reserves of the monetary authorities and, other items unchanged, increases (decreases) base money. Similarly, when the Central Bank brings about a *ceteris paribus* increase (decrease) of its assets by buying (selling) government securities or altering the total of its loans to commercial banks, the increase (decrease) in these assets is accompanied by an increase (decrease) in base money.

Table 4.3. *Balance sheet of the Central Bank of Russia*

Assets	Liabilities
NIR: Net International Reserves	MB: Monetary Base
GIR: Gross International Reserves	Cash Issued
−GIL: Gross International Liabilities:	+ Required Reserves of the
	commercial banks
	+ Excess Reserves of the
	commercial banks
NDA: Net Domestic Assets	
NCG: Net Credit to Government[a]	
+GCB: Gross Credit to Commercial	
Banks	
+NCFSR: Net credit to	
Former Soviet Republics	
+ OIN: Other Items Net	
Total assets	Total liabilities

Notes:
[a]Net credit to government = credits to government minus government deposits.
Net international reserves (NIR) are calculated as the difference between gross international reserves (GIR) and gross international liabilities (GIL). GIR include gold of both Central Bank and government, Central Bank and government holdings of foreign exchange, SDRs and reserve position in the IMF; and claims on non-resident financial institutions denominated in convertible currencies. GIL include liabilities in convertible currencies to non-residents with an original maturity of up to one year, as well as all liabilities arising from balance-of-payments support borrowing from foreign banks, institutions, and government, irrespective of their maturity.
ΔNCG: Net credit to the government i.e. the monetary financing of the budget deficit.
ΔGCB: Gross credits to commercial banks. In 1993 the IMF advised the CBR to change its methodology and to count net credits to the banks (that is gross credits minus excess reserves) rather than gross.
ΔNCFSR: Net credit to Former Soviet Republics (FSRs).

Domestic credits, the change in net domestic assets, is calculated as

$$\Delta CE = \Delta NCG + \Delta GCB + \Delta NCFSR$$
$$= \Delta MB - \Delta NIR - \Delta OIN \quad (2)$$

The relation between the monetary base and the money supply M—in other words, the scope of the money multiplier—depends chiefly on the banks' reserve requirement ratio, on the amount of excess reserves held by the banks, and on interest rates.

When the Central Bank grants a credit to the government, the funds are initially deposited at the Central Bank. According to the categorization above, this has no immediate impact on the monetary base, since the net credit to the government (gross credits minus deposits of the government at the Central Bank) will be unchanged. But once the government spends part of these deposits (by transferring them to a commercial bank), net credit to the government rises, and so does the monetary base. Likewise Central Bank lending to the commercial banks means a rise both in the Central Bank's assets and in its liabilities which constitute the monetary base (in the form of an increase in excess reserves of the commercial banks).

Two sub-periods can be distinguished within the period 1992–8. While Figure 4.1 shows yearly inflation rates (end of year) computed from the consumer price index, Table 4.4 shows the behaviour of the monthly inflation rates. The table shows the mean, median, and standard deviation of the inflation rate from January 1992 to July 1995 and from August 1995 to July 1998–17 August 1998 marked clearly the end of the second period with the announcement by the government of the domestic debt default.

The average monthly inflation rate reached 41 per cent in 1992 (due to the price jump over 200 per cent in January 1992 following the price liberalization and 18 per cent without the January observation), 21 per cent in 1993, 10 per cent in 1994, 7 per cent in 1995. The year 1996 marked the first average monthly inflation rate below 2 per cent with

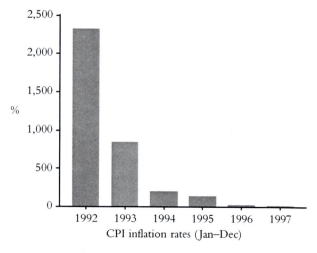

Figure 4.1. *CPI annual inflation rates*

Source: Goskomstat.

Table 4.4. *Descriptive statistics of monthly inflation, in per cent*

	Jan 1992–July 1995	Aug 1995–July 1998
Mean	21.6	1.6
Median	15.2	4.7
Maximum	296	4.7
Minimum	4.6	−0.3
Standard deviation	43.5	1.5

Source: calculated from Goskomstat.

1.7 per cent, followed in 1997 with a rate of 0.9 per cent and 0.6 per cent from January 1998 to July 1998.

From 1992 to 1995 Russia's large budget deficit, together with quasi-fiscal expenditures and credits to the rouble zone, was financed almost exclusively by money creation, leading to very high and volatile inflation.[12] At first the CBR had only direct monetary instruments at its disposal—directed credits and mandatory reserves. The market for short-term T-bills (GKOs) was started in May 1993. Demand for GKOs was at first very thin both because of high inflation (and the resulting capital flight) and because foreigners were denied access. Central Bank credit auctions designed to provide short-term liquidity to the banking system on market-related terms were begun in February 1994. In April 1995, with the adoption of the federal law on the Central Bank, the CBR became independent, allowing for the institutional separation of monetary and fiscal policy. This marks the beginning of the second sub-period. Money financing was to a large extent replaced by bond finance, and the public debt grew rapidly. In an effort to broaden the market for government debt and reduce interest rates, barriers to capital mobility were gradually dismantled from August 1996 onwards. The process was completed as far as T-bills are concerned in January 1998.

4.3.1. *January 1992–July 1995*

In the 1992–5 sub-period monetary base expansion reflected mainly the growth of net domestic assets (NDA). Only during the second quarter of

[12] See Granville (1995) for more details on the high inflation period of 1992–5.

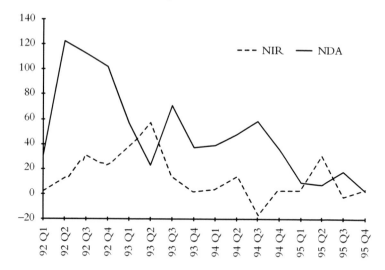

Figure 4.2. *Percentage change in base money generated by growth of domestic and external claims respectively, 1992–1995*

Source: calculated from Balino *et al.* (1997), table 3, pp. 15–16.

1993 and in 1995 was the leading role played by external reserves (NIR) (Figure 4.2).

Within NDA, the dominant influence lay until mid-1993 with the line called *credits to commercial banks*. These credits were designed not merely to provide liquidity to banks through the refinance rate; they also included quasi-fiscal outlays, that is subsidized credits channelled through the banking network to state enterprises. After mid-1993 credits to government became the main source of domestic asset growth (Figure 4.3).

In 1992 and 1993 there were also substantial increases in Net Credit to Former Soviet Republics. In the first quarter of 1994 inflation perform-ance improved, with the average monthly inflation rate (12 per cent) about half that of the equivalent period of 1993 (23 per cent). One of the reasons for this result was the end of the rouble zone[13] in the autumn of 1993. The rouble zone has been especially costly in 1992 with credits

---

[13] The 'rouble zone' is taken here to mean the fifteen former Soviet Republics (FSRs) which inherited a common (unconvertible) currency—the Soviet rouble—upon the break-up of the USSR in December 1991, and the succeeding months, those FSRs that con-tinued to use the same currency as Russia.

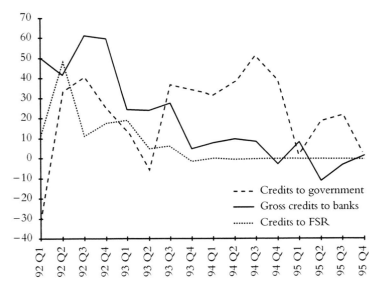

Figure 4.3. *Percentage change in base money generated by growth of various domestic claims, 1992–1995*

Source: calculated from Balino *et al.* (1997), table 3, pp. 15–16.

to FSRs reaching 8.5 per cent of Russian GDP if delivery of cash is excluded, and 11.6 per cent otherwise, in terms of Central Bank credits alone. The rouble zone owed its peculiarity to the monetary system inherited from the command economy mentioned earlier—namely the dichotomy between cash and non-cash.

Each republic had a branch of Gosbank on its territory. But when each FSR declared their independence/sovereignty (1990–1), they took over the Gosbank branch and made it the national central bank. However, they could issue only credits (the so-called non-cash roubles): the emission of cash roubles remained the privilege of the CBR. Russia was able physically to control all cash rouble emission because all Gosznak bank note printing plants were located on the territory of the former RSFSR.

The dichotomy between cash and non-cash roubles led to a situation where on one side there was a single currency—the cash rouble whose emission was controlled by the CBR—and on the other side there were as many non-cash roubles as independent central banks. The CBR provided both non-cash and cash credits to the countries of the 'near abroad' to allow their enterprises to continue trading with Russian partners.[14] The credits financed these countries' imports from Russia and thus had much the same effect as direct subsidies to Russian industries. At the same time Central Banks of the FSR were themselves able to issue rouble credits to be spent in Russia, thus further contributing to the growth of Russia's money supply and inflation.

In an attempt to restrain FSRs from issuing credits, Russia introduced a decree on 1 July[15] limiting the growth of corresponding accounts.[16] The national banks of the FSRs could only withdraw credits from correspondent accounts held at the CBR on condition that there existed deposits to cover transactions, and a new line of credits called 'technical credits' was opened for trade. These credits were subject to negotiations. However, the Central Banks of the FSRs kept issuing credits. This was possible because the lobby of Russian firms, which traded in the FSRs, was strong and wanted to be paid, and secondly because on 17 July 1992 Viktor Gerashchenko was appointed head of the CBR. He made no attempt to hide his policy of acceding to the requests of new credits with the professed aim of protecting commercial ties with these states and credit rocketed. The Central Bank was constitutionally subordinate to the Supreme Soviet, which itself opposed the government's policy of ending the rouble zone.

At the beginning of 1993 Boris Fedorov was appointed to the post of deputy prime minister. The fight against inflation became a major priority and credits to FSRs a major target. The incentive to limit the cost of the rouble zone for Russia was given by the negotiations with the IMF on a new credit line facility especially designed for Russia (the Systemic Transformation Facility—STF). By this time the IMF had recognized the necessity for each of the FSRs to introduce their own national currencies. Most technical credits had reached their limits and needed

---

[14] See Granville (1994) for a comprehensive account of the impact of the rouble zone on Russia's stabilization efforts.

[15] This followed the announcement by Ukraine on 12 June 1992 of a massive increase in credit approximately doubling its money supply to clear inter-enterprise arrears without consulting the Russian government.

[16] As of 1 January 1992 commercial banks were instructed to direct all transactions with FSRs through correspondent accounts at the CBR. The correspondent accounts of the Central Banks of the FSRs centralized the payment clearing system for inter-republican transactions. Payments were supposed to take place only on the basis of availability of funding. In fact, since traditionally the FSRs had a trade deficit with Russia, they were able to finance their deficits by money creation in Russia.

negotiations; it was therefore easy to not renew them. In April 1993 the government and Supreme Soviet of Russia in agreement with the IMF decided to abolish technical credits and all previous credits to FSRs accumulated over 1992–3 were transformed into state debts (denominated in US dollars and with an interest expressed in libor). The advantage of such a measure was that state debts were channelled through the budget. Therefore the Ministry of Finance (Fyodorov) was now in a position to have a direct control on the level of financial transfers to the FSRs.

With the unification and the declaration of a Russian exchange rate in July 1992 new style bank notes (with the Russian flags) were issued (Rbs 5,000 denomination). The new bank notes circulated in parallel with the old Soviet ones (depicting Lenin) but only Soviet notes were delivered to the FSRs. With the tightening of the credit policy to FSRs, the demand for cash increased dramatically and became the major source of transfer to the FSRs and the major threat for Russian inflation. The Lenin bank note therefore had to go. This was done on 24 July 1993. The CBR implemented a monetary reform aimed at isolating its cash circulation from the other FSRs. Old Soviet roubles pre-1993 were withdrawn and those countries in the rouble zone still using these notes found themselves in a situation where their money ceased to be legal tender in Russia.

The size of the budget deficit and its financing also affected the choice of exchange rate regime. As a strategy for ending high inflation, two alterative nominal anchors are advocated in the literature—money and the exchange rate.[17] Until 1995 Russia had in practice no option but to employ a money-based approach, that is targeting money and credit growth while maintaining a degree of exchange-rate flexibility.

In the spring of 1992 there was discussion of a possible fixed exchange-rate regime with the rate pegged at around Rbs 80 to the dollar, slightly lower than the average in trading on the Moscow Currency Exchange (MICEX),[18] which was Rbs125.26.[19] Monthly average inflation remained, however, in the range of 14 per cent in the second quarter of 1992. For an exchange-rate peg to succeed in halting it and thus prove sustainable would have required backing at the outset with substantial exchange reserves. Russia's own reserves at this time totalled no

[17] For a survey see Sahay and Vegh (1996).
[18] MICEX was created in April 1991 and operated through interbank transactions in foreign exchange.
[19] See Granville (1995) on the process of exchange-rate liberalization and unification and Lushin and Oppenheimer in this volume.

more than one month's imports and its routine access to external finance was very limited. With an eye to the Polish experience of two years earlier, there was discussion of an international assistance package from the IMF, the United States, and others totalling $24 billion. Including a so-called stabilization fund of $6 billion. The package never materialized.

Ultimately the effectiveness of a disinflationary programme depends on how the intermediate target—the exchange rate or money—is linked to the ultimate target—the price level. In Russia the money stock (M2) and the price level was clear from an early stage.[20] Not so the link between the exchange rate and the same price level, probably because of administrative controls on trade which were abolished only in 1995 and the thinness of the foreign currency markets.[21]

On the other hand, until the introduction of the exchange-rate band—the so-called corridor—in July 1995, the path of the exchange rate was itself heavily influenced by monetary conditions. The rate responded to the movement in rouble M2 with no more than a one month lag. Interventions by the CBR on the MICEX were substantial.[22]

Besides the problem of the public sector deficit, other factors also hampered the conduct and effectiveness of monetary policy. These included shortage of policy instruments, especially open market operations, which started only in the second half of 1995, and the unreliability of instruments such as required reserves, and finally the degree of dollarization of the economy. Moreover, the behaviour of the velocity of money was not stable. Such variability may be explained by the money demand function itself, changes in interest rates and inflation expectations. Rising velocity is a usual accompaniment of rapid inflation as the public seeks to minimize holdings of a rapidly depreciating asset. Increase/decrease in monetary velocity means that cumulative price increases are greater/ smaller than cumulative increases in M2. The higher the velocity, the higher is inflation (given nominal money growth and real GDP).

This reduces the seignorage which the government can obtain through creation of Central Bank money. As is shown in Figure 4.4, from 1992 to 1995 velocity of broad money varied widely.

---

[20] See Granville (1995).

[21] Easterly and Vieira da Cunha (1993), pp. 19–20. See also Lushin and Oppenheimer in this volume.

[22] According to Koen and Meyermans (1994), p. 7: 'Following exchange rate unification, the share of CBR intervention in total MICEX turnover remained large, averaging one third if measured by monthly net totals.'

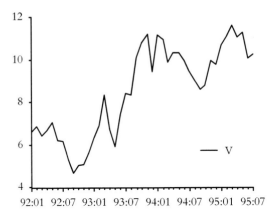

Figure 4.4. *Velocity of money*
V = Velocity of money defined as the yearly average GDP divided by M2. In other terms, velocity is the inverse of the ratio of M2 to GDP.

Source: calculated from Central Bank of Russia data and Goskomstat.

Still the money-based programme, despite its shortcomings, forced the authorities to decrease the budget deficit.'Black Tuesday' (11 October 1994), for instance, besides showing the power of the rapidly developing financial markets, demonstrated to the authorities that a nominal depreciation is no substitute for bringing monetary and fiscal policies under control. Black Tuesday was the result of the expansionary budget policy followed by the Russian government and the CBR after January 1994.[23] The 27 per cent fall in the exchange rate in a single day was the result of an excessive increase in M2 to finance the budget deficit, essentially to give more credits to the agriculture sector. From March to August 1994 M2 grew between 7 per cent and 18 per cent, while the rate of the exchange rate varied between 4 per cent and 6 per cent per month. Also the CBR lowered its refinance rate from 155 per cent per year to 130 per cent per year on 23 August 1994. Sberbank and the other commercial banks also lowered most of their deposit rates.

---

[23] Gaidar returned to the government on 24 September 1993. This led to a further liberalization of prices as to a limitation of subsidies financed by money creation. The result was a gradual decline in inflation until mid-1994 because of an approximate four months gap between money supply increase and price level change. But in the parliamentary election of December 1993 the Nationalists and the Communists gained about 40% of the seats in parliament. As a result of the December elections two out of the three leading reformers in the government, Boris Fedorov and Yegor Gaidar, resigned.

At the same time the public invested increasingly in bonds from May 1993 to August 1994. In this period the rouble fell dramatically and the government was able to outbid the dollar by offering 150 per cent interest on its paper. The market grew so quickly that the debt was serviced with the proceeds of new issues without the need to raise interest rates. After debt repayment, these bond issues generated net funds which could be used to cover part of the budget deficit. Since autumn 1994, however, investment in dollars has offered a higher return than bonds. To attract investors the government has been forced to offer very high yields to compete with the dollar, which has doubled its value against the rouble every six months. The market therefore stopped growing. New issues were barely sufficient to cover repayments of previous issues reaching maturity. Only about 10 per cent of new issues remained for the government to use. The interest cost of these bonds has become too high for this to be an effective means for financing the budget deficit.

Black Tuesday was the market response to the government's recent monetary and fiscal policies. The fall of the rouble exchange rate against the US dollar on this day sparked a political crisis and government reshuffle, leading to a strong renewed commitment by Chernomyrdin and his ministers to a pro-stabilization strategy. In this sense, the forces of financial markets had developed sufficiently over three years to exert a decisive influence on the government and impel it to resume its drive towards monetary stabilization. At the beginning of 1995, with the IMF programme signed on 26 March and the CBR independence in April, capital inflows started to pour into Russia which helped to put a successful halt to inflation but relaxed at the same time the constraint on fiscal policy.

4.3.2. *July 1995–1998*

The year 1995 saw the culmination of efforts to reduce the primary budget deficit. At the same time there was a shift from financing the budget deficit with Central Bank credits to treasury bills,[24] a major increase in the degree of independence of the Central Bank,[25] and, in the second half of the year, a new exchange-rate regime.

The new exchange-rate regime was initially introduced in July 1995 to curb the sharp appreciation in April–May 1995 (nominal as well as real) of the rouble brought about by the authorities' success in curbing the growth

---

[24] 1995 Federal Budget Law.   [25] The 'Central Bank Law' enacted in April 1995.

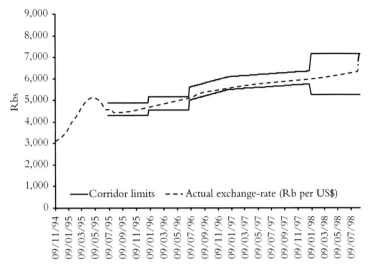

Figure 4.5. *Exchange rate regime, November 1994–August 1998*

Source: MICEX.

of domestic credit. The new arrangements consisted of an exchange-rate corridor or band whose outer limits were set for first three then six or twelve months at a time, allowing the rouble to fluctuate within a total range of about 12 per cent. The band itself was adjusted moderately downwards against the dollar in successive periods (Figure 4.5), in such a way as to allow the rouble exchange rate to remain approximately constant in real terms, i.e. to depreciate by the excess of Russia's inflation rate over the average inflation rate of the outside world.[26]

On 1 January 1998 (at the time of re-denomination of the rouble, equal to 1,000 previous roubles) exchange-rate policy was significantly modified to allow greater fluctuation in the rate at the same time as setting much longer term (three year) objectives. From 1998 to December 2000 there was to have been a targeted central rate of roubles 6.2 to the US dollar with a band of 15 per cent on either side (giving an upper limit of 5.25 and a lower limit of 7.15 to the dollar). The target for 1998 was an

[26] From July to December 1995 the limits of the corridor were 4,300–4,900 roubles to the US dollar. From 1 January to 30 June 1996 the limits were 4,550–5,150; and from 1 July 1996 to 31 December 1996 they were 5,500–6,100. For the year 1997 the limits moved from 5,500–6,100 on 1 January 1997 to 5,760–6,350 on 31 December 1997.

average rate of 6.1 for the dollar. On a day-to-day basis, the Central Bank
would set both a middle rate for the following day and a bid-offer spread
offer around that rate based on market quotations. The maximum deviation of the bid and offer rates from the central rate was to be 1.5 per cent.

In this system, two targets were set by the Central Bank: one for the
monetary base; and one for exchange-rate movement within the specified 'corridor'. Capital inflows and outflows, however, or more generally
the balance of payments position, threatened to create conflict between
these two targets.

Capital inflows facilitate government borrowing, but also encourage
exchange-rate appreciation. If the Central Bank reacts by accumulating
foreign reserves and thus expanding the monetary base, this is liable to
aggravate inflation and/or inflationary expectations. During the second
quarter of 1997, for instance, with the rouble maintained inside the band,
foreign portfolio inflows led to a rise in the money supply in excess
of Central Bank targets. Interest rates declined sharply (Figure 4.6). In
the event the demand for rouble balances also appeared to increase, so
inflation was not aggravated.

Capital outflows, on the other hand, may mean pressure on the
exchange rate to depreciate. By selling foreign reserves to support the
rate, the CBR reduces the monetary base. Interest rates tend to rise. This

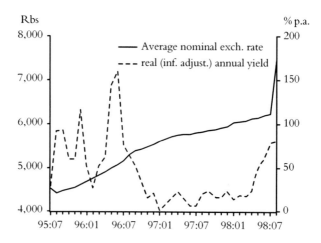

Figure 4.6. *Real annual percentage yield on GKOs and
nominal exchange rate*

Source: MICEX.

endangers the fiscal situation by raising debt service costs. The CBR may therefore intervene in the secondary securities market to re-expand base money and decrease interest rates. In so doing it is liable to renew the threat to the exchange-rate parity. The risk is that ultimately the CBR has to let either the interest rate or the exchange rate go. This is what happened towards the end of 1997. The Central Bank had to allow interest rates to move to whatever level was necessary for the exchange rate to be maintained within the band. Such high real interest rates, however, were fiscally unsustainable.

The focal point for this tension between exchange rate and monetary policy became the domestic market in rouble-denominated government debt. It was in this market, as restrictions on non-resident participation were gradually lifted (see below), that capital inflows and outflows were increasingly concentrated. This market became the main transmission mechanism by which confidence in the exchange-rate peg affected interest rates. By allowing yields to rise, the authorities aimed to demonstrate their commitment to holding the exchange-rate band, thus attracting new inflows and hence securing a decline in interest rates. For the calculation was that inflows would be attracted by the healthy real returns available from the combination of high nominal yields on rouble-denominated debt and the promise of a stable exchange rate. As things turned out, however, investors were less attracted by this future prospect than they were deterred by the present reality of ever higher interest rates, which created doubts that the government could afford the consequent rising debt service costs, hence the perception of increasing default risk. Put another way, the demonstration of commitment to the exchange-rate regime could not in itself ensure credibility in the face of the obstinate reality of loose fiscal policy.

By the time this tension between exchange rate and monetary policy came to a head in late 1997 the government rouble debt market in both short-term treasury bills (GKOs) and longer term paper (OFZs) had developed rapidly. By 1996 GKO/OFZ financing amounted to 5.7 per cent of GDP and 72 per cent of public-sector borrowing (Table 4.5). By the end of that year T-bills accounted for almost half of total Russian domestic public debt (Table 4.7). [27]

---

[27] Domestic indebtedness of the government consists of state treasury bills (GKOs), federal loan bonds (OFZs), rouble-denominated savings bonds (OGSZs), restructured domestic foreign currency debt of the USSR (OVVZs, known as Taiga bonds or MinFins), and securitized arrears on centralized credits to the agriculture sector and the northern regions.

Table 4.5. *Treasury bills and deficit financing*

	1993	1994	1995	1996	1997	Jan–June 1998
(1) GKO/OFZ financing as % of GDP	0.1	1	3.1	5.7	4.6	
(2) Federal deficit as % of GDP	15.6	10.6	5.3	7.9	6.5	4.8
Revenues as % of GDP	12.9	11.9	12	13.1	10.8	10.4
Expenditures as % of GDP	28.5	22.5	17.4	21	17.3	15.3
(1)/(2) GKO/OFZ financing as % of deficit	0.64	9.43	58.49	72.15	70.77	
Total GKOs outstanding as % of GDP	0.1	1.7	4.1	9.3	14.4	
Total domestic debt as % of GDP	26.2	18.9	14.8	20.4	28.4	
Interest payment as % of GDP	1.8	1.8	3	5.5	4.8	5.2
of which GKOs	—	0.2	1.5	4	3.3	
Primary deficit (−) or surplus (+) as % of GDP	−13.8	−8.8	−2.3	−2.4	−1.7	0.4
Memo						
Exchange rate, roubles/US$ end of period	1,247	3,550	4,640	5,555	5,863	6,225
GDP (trillion roubles)[a]	172	611	1,585	2,200	2,678	1,182
Real GDP growth (%)	−8.7	−12.6	−4.0	−3.5	0.8	−0.5

Note: [a]GDP revised in May 1998.

Source: Ministry of Finance and Goskomstat.

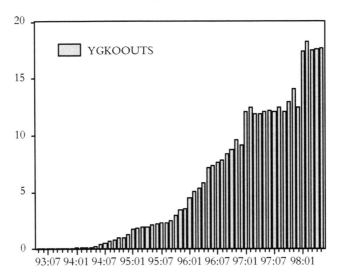

Figure 4.7. *Stock of outstanding GKOs as a percentage of annual GDP*
Source: MICEX.

But while considerable progress was made in terms of reducing the primary budget deficit, the ratios of debt service and domestic debt to GDP ratio were growing rapidly. Even by the outbreak of the financial crisis in late 1997, however, Russia's stock of public debt was not particularly high by international standards. The debt ratio at the end of 1997 was about 55 per cent of GDP, 26 per cent in foreign debt, and about 28.4 per cent in total domestic public debt (of which about 14 per cent in GKO/OFZ) (Figure 4.7).

This compares with a ratio of 70.4 per cent in the EU in 1996 and one of 63.1 per cent in the USA.[28] But while the stock of debt was still at a tolerable level by international standards, it was rising at an unsustainable rate. The rapid build-up of the GKO–OFZ market in 1995–7 coincided with record capital flows into emerging markets. This risk hunger was replaced by risk aversion after the outbreak of the 'Asian crisis' in 1997: and this change in market sentiment severely aggravated the problem which would have come to a head around this time anyway—namely, the explosive debt path.

[28] Dornbusch (1998), table 1.1, p. 4.

To reduce the growth of the debt to GDP ratio and so to turn market sentiment, the government should have either eliminated its budget deficit or else found a way (an alternative to the GKO–OFZ market during the global financial market crisis) of financing it at reasonable interest cost. The second solution was unrealistic. Given the low levels of domestic savings held inside the banking system (see below), the government depended on external financing. The vulnerability entailed by this dependence was aggravated by the fact that more than half the domestic debt was very short term, with a maturity of less than one year. Short-term debt at the end of June 1998 was nearly four times as large as official foreign exchange reserves.[29] And, given the short duration of domestic debt, a collapse of (international) investor confidence caused a liquidity crisis, which led inexorably to a solvency crisis. The only solution therefore was a rapid and sharp fiscal adjustment to stabilize the level of debt. To stop the debt ratio rising the government has to run a primary surplus equal to the public debt multiplied by the difference between the real interest rate and real GDP growth.

The dynamics of government debt are given by the following equation:

$$\Delta b = (r - n)b - d, \tag{3}$$

where

   $b =$ debt/GDP ratio

   $r =$ real rate of interest

   $n =$ rate of real GDP growth

   $d =$ primary deficit/surplus as a share of GDP.

Following the new IMF programme announced in mid-July 1998,[30] the revised 1998 budget assumed a real interest rate on both external and domestic debt of 22 per cent with a GDP growth rate of 0 per cent. The aim was to reach a primary budget surplus of 0.2 per cent. Inserting these figures into equation (3), the debt ratio in 1998 was projected to increase by about 11 per cent. To halve this rate of increase in 1999, assuming a slightly higher real GDP growth of 1.5 per cent as well as lower real interest rates at 15 per cent, would have required the primary surplus to

---

[29] In July 1998 Goldman Sachs arranged for one-tenth of outstanding treasury bills ($6.4 billion) to be exchanged for long term eurobonds.

[30] The IMF announced an additional financing of $11.2 billion.

reach 2.5 per cent of GDP, an extremely sharp fiscal adjustment. Russia's debt ratio would then have stabilized at around 60 per cent of GDP. Unfortunately, the high dependence of government revenues on corporate taxation, especially of the export sector, meant that revenues were hit by the fall in 1997–8 of the world prices of oil and other natural resources constituting the country's key exports. This further fiscal weakening aggravated financial market worries about the Russian government's capacity to service its debt. In the first half of 1998 the current account reached a deficit of 4 per cent of GDP from balance in 1997.

At the same time the Russian banking system failed to attract the necessary domestic saving into budget financing (Table 4.6).

Real interest rates turned positive at the beginning of 1995 (Table 4.7). Russian banks began to switch assets from foreign exchange to rouble treasury bills. At the same time, lacking a proper domestic deposit base, they began to build up foreign-exchange liabilities. About 80 per cent of all rouble household deposits were held with the majority state-owned Sberbank, the only bank enjoying a state guarantee on such deposits.

In addition, Russian household savings continued to be held largely in dollars despite the positive real interest rate. The share of household income used to purchase foreign currency showed signs of declining in 1995 but appeared to rise again in 1996–7. Some of the reversal may reflect increased foreign travel by Russian citizens (Figure 4.8).

Given this difficulty of attracting domestic savings into government debt instruments either directly or through the banking system, and despite high real yields, external financing was necessary to tide the authorities over while they sought to remove fiscal imbalances.

Despite the fact that accessing foreign demand was the only way to reduce the government's cost of borrowing, and hence interest rates in the economy as a whole, the Central Bank was at first reluctant to ease the restrictions on foreign investor participation in the government securities market. The main argument officially advanced in favour of caution was the danger of foreign 'hot money' attracted by abnormally high returns flowing out in the event of some shock as quickly as it had flowed in. Another unspoken concern underlying the Central Bank's hesitation was to protect the domestic banking system sector against a rapid fall in yields. Concern about the danger of 'hot money' might be considered to have been vindicated by events leading to the Russian government's default on its domestic debt in August 1998. Against that it may be argued

Table 4.6. *Deposits in the banking system (in million roubles and percentage of GDP)*

	Demand deposit	Time and saving deposits	Foreign currency deposits	Total deposits	%GDP	%GDP	%GDP	%GDP
1993	12,519	5015	12,086	29,620	7.3	2.9	7.0	17
1994	32,589	23,874	37,309	93,772	5.3	3.9	6.1	15
1995	69,332	69,241	55,256	193,829	4.4	4.4	3.5	12
1996	87,303	95,451	69,448	252,202	4.0	4.3	3.2	11
1997	133,672	104,308	85,022	323,002	5.0	3.9	3.2	12

Source: calculated from IMF, International Financial Statistics, March 1998.

Table 4.7. *Real (inflation-adjusted) interest rates on loans and deposits*

	Annualized inflation rate	Real lending rate % per annum	Real deposit rate % per annum	Net interest margin % per annum
94 III	97.05	204.55	84.25	120.30
94 IV	309.92	−12.62	−184.72	172.10
95 I	406.52	9.78	−263.62	273.40
95 II	165.26	213.24	−42.86	256.10
95 III	92.83	158.27	−19.93	178.20
95 IV	67.6	164.30	2.00	162.30
96 I	51.1	136.70	10.60	126.10
96 II	28.26	148.14	27.14	121.00
96 III	8.84	133.96	51.26	82.70
96 IV	12.94	67.26	30.06	37.20
97 I	21.13	42.77	7.97	34.80
97 II	17.12	31.48	1.08	30.40
97 III	7.40	31.00	3.60	27.40
97 IV	2.58	31.22	4.82	26.40

Source: calculated from International Financial Statistics, IMF, March 1998.

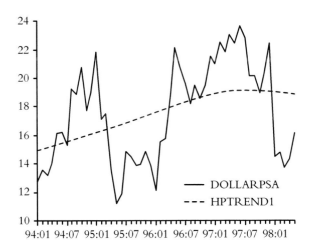

Figure 4.8. *Share of household nominal income devoted to purchase of foreign currency (percentage)*

Source: Goskomstat.

that the heavy borrowing begun in 1995–6 should never have been other than a temporary expedient to buy time for the fiscal adjustment necessary to set the public finances on a sustainable footing. In any event, whatever the merits of the general arguments for limiting capital flows into domestic emerging debt markets, this could never justify the high yield bonanza for the domestic banks. Such a massive transfer to the banks was economically harmful across the board, not least to the sound development of the Russian banking system itself.

The first, partial, relaxation of restrictions on foreign investment in the GKO–OFZ market was announced in August 1996. Foreign investors were allowed to enter the market by opening a specially created new category of accounts, known as 'S' accounts, in authorized Russian banks. The bank would then transfer the funds to its account at the MICEX, where it would buy and sell GKOs according to its foreign client's instructions. Foreigners investing in the GKO–OFZ market through 'S' accounts could thus trade freely in the secondary market. To prevent rapid outflows of foreign money, however, the Central Bank required foreign investors to tie up their investment for three months before repatriating their returns. At the beginning of this three-month period foreigners had to enter a forward contract with the Central Bank, with the rouble/dollar exchange rate being artificially set to ensure a fixed dollar return of 15 per cent.

An obvious drawback of the 'S' account scheme was that it required foreign investors to take not only Russian government default risk but also the counterparty risk of the Russian banks in which they had opened 'S' accounts. Despite that, the scheme attracted considerable inflows. Already by November 1996 foreign investors had bought $3.5 billion worth of GKOs through 'S' accounts increasing their total market share to 10–20 per cent, a significant fraction given that about 60 per cent of the GKO–OFZ market was taken by the CBR and its affiliates (Sberbank). In the following twelve months inflows increased rapidly, peaking at around $8 billion in the second and third quarters of 1997. By the time of the outbreak of the 'Asian crisis', in October 1997, foreign investors accounted for about 30 per cent of a market whose face value had grown to over $60 billion. That share of 30 per cent remained broadly stable through the subsequent decline of the market, culminating in the August 1998 default.[31]

---

[31] Central Bank of Russia.

As foreign inflows grew, so restrictions built into the 'S' account scheme were gradually relaxed. The compulsory 'lock-up' period was reduced by stages from three to two months, then from two months to one month, with the guaranteed dollar return from the Central Bank forward contract also gradually reduced in line with falling yields. Also, the Central Bank guaranteed a steadily smaller proportion of the forward, leaving the foreign investors free to hedge (or not) the remainder with their Russian bank counterparties. In January 1998, in line with an IMF programme commitment, all restrictions attached to the 'S' account scheme had been removed. This complete liberalization was complemented, from the foreign investor's point of view, by the addition of Russian subsidiaries of major western banks active in the GKO market to the list of banks authorized to offer 'S' account services.

Financing the budget deficit with foreign savings presupposes positive market sentiment towards the economic situation. Clearly in 1998 this disappeared. High real interest rates intensified investor worries, and the government's creditworthiness gradually crumbled. This, together with the reversal of the earlier speculative wave in favour of Russian equities,[32] led to capital outflows which were further reinforced by the growing probability of a substantial rouble devaluation. Whereas domestic T-bill holders may attach a liquidity factor to domestic debt, foreign holders in general do not. Therefore foreign investor demand is highly sensitive to expected net returns. At the same time government finances will be all the more sensitive to financial turmoil when the debt structure is dominated by short-term paper, as was the case in Russia.

The response of the CBR was to resist pressure on the rouble. Two reasons were given. First economic fundamentals did not warrant a devaluation. Secondly, devaluation would rekindle rapid inflation, because of the high import content of consumption.[33]

The main case for devaluation on the export side was the fiscal one that it would increase export value added in roubles and thereby contribute to improved tax revenues. But the volume of Russian oil exports[34] was limited by internal pipeline and sea port handling capacity, and thus cannot respond to devaluation in the short term. On the import side, devaluation should encourage some switch of expenditure by Russian consumers from imports to domestic products. On the other hand,

---

[32] See Willer in this volume.   [33] As high as 60% according to official estimates.
[34] Exports of oil and oil products in 1997 accounted for 21% of total exports. Russia accounts for about 8% of world oil supply.

experience in other emerging markets suggests that devaluation is not a reliable route to lowering real interest rates.

We have seen above that from 1995 onwards the CBR established itself as an institution striving for low inflation and exchange rate stability. In 1997–8, as in earlier episodes, it sought to defend the rouble by raising the refinance rate. This rate acted as an effective cap on the treasury bill yield and so signalled the level at which the CBR will support the yield. The refinancing rate was raised first from 21 to 28 per cent in mid-November 1997. In February 1998 it was increased to 42 per cent and in May 1998 to 150 per cent. The various Lombard rates[35] and the minimum reserve requirements on bank reserves were also increased. And until the default of 17 August 1998 and the subsequent change of government, these instruments were successful in defending the currency. Other factors contributed to the defence of the rouble at the time: notably the state presence in the banking sector— especially of Sberbank (as explained above, Sberbank had an effective monopoly over household deposits). This situation clearly facilitated the short-term defence of the currency. But more important was the lack of additional currency substitution by Russian households from the rouble and rouble-denominated instruments to the dollar facilitated the defence of the currency.

Another strong, but unavowed, disincentive to devaluation was the potentially fatal losses which a devaluation could inflict on the leading banks through their currency forward contracts. This danger was partly due to a supervisory oversight by the Central Bank, as it gradually withdrew from the system of fixed forwards for foreign investors in the GKO–OFZ market. The banks, for their part, rushed into the currency forward business, apparently tempted by the easy gains in defiance of ordinary prudential principles of risk management. By mid-1998 leading Russian banks had sold several billion 'forward' dollars to foreign counterparties hedging their GKO investments or other rouble exposures against a possible devaluation. To the extent that banks active in this field had troubled to make balancing purchases of 'forward' dollars from domestic counterparties, the devaluation when it came rendered the latter insolvent.

---

[35] The CBR would lend overnight money at the refinance rate. The Lombard rates were seen as a cap on money market yields.

Put another way, the devaluation ratified the insolvency of the banks by leaving them with dollar obligations on forward contracts many times greater than their capital. But the banks' earlier struggle against insolvency had itself precipitated that devaluation. Pressure on the rouble exchange rate had been intensified by a particular effect of the financial market crisis on leading Russian banks. Unable to attract large-scale retail deposits, the banks had funded themselves by using their portfolios of dollar-denominated Russian government securities for repurchase ('repo') operations with foreign counterparties. The progressive collapse of investor confidence in all types of Russian government debt triggered margin calls on those 'repos'. To meet these margin calls, the banks raised liquidity by selling their GKO holdings and other assets, and buying the necessary foreign exchange with the proceeds. Completing the vicious circle, the CBR responded by tightening money market lending in order to keep the rouble in its target band. Commercial banks reacted by cutting limits to each other and liquidating bonds and stocks to sustain liquidity.

In this environment, all demand, domestic and foreign, for new GKO issues disappeared. That meant that the government could no longer pay debt with debt. And redemption of weekly maturities averaging about roubles 9 billion had to be financed out of general taxation (plus last-ditch eurobond issues, which glutted the last segment of the debt market). Given the impossibility of sufficiently drastic cuts in non debt service expenditure, at least temporary default became unavoidable.

These interlinked and mutually reinforcing trends were reflected in the multiple decisions of the government and CBR of 17 August. First was the forced extension of GKO maturities: then a 90-day moratorium on debt servicing of private foreign credits of over 180 days maturity, as well as margin calls and currency contracts. Simultaneously the rouble target band was widened. The band was to range from 6 roubles to the dollar to 9.5 for a mean of 7.75 roubles. The internal day-to-day band of 1.5 per cent was abandoned.

The decisions marked the beginning of a new period. Rouble devaluation went out of control very quickly and at the beginning of September the rouble was already reaching 17.6 roubles for 1 US dollar, and the CBR officially abandoned its exchange rate target band. This, with the forced GKO restructuring and the foreign debt moratorium, resulted in a shattering blow to public confidence, additional public demand for foreign currency, and widespread expectation of a return to chronically rapid inflation.

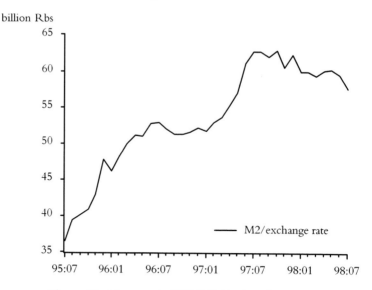

Figure 4.9. *Money supply (M2) divided by the exchange rate*
Source: CBR and MICEX.

The forced restructuring of T-bills affected the body of domestic banks badly (the leading banks, as we have seen, had in effect failed already). For government securities still dominated banking assets. Private loans represented only a fractional share of their activity. In 1998 private credit as a share of GDP was 10 per cent (of which only 3 per cent had a duration of over six months) compared to over 120 per cent, for instance, in Japan. The profitability of the majority of banks derived from the spread between deposit rates and government bond yields.[36] Part of the capital inflows in 1997 were channelled through the banking sector. For example, Figure 4.9 shows that M2 divided by the exchange rate almost doubled in the period 1995–7 even though real GDP decreased (with the exception of 1997). Just as shown by Calvo (1998) in the case of Mexico, as M2 rose, the CBR, which implicitly operated as lender of last resort,[37] acquired *de facto* short-term obligations.

[36] Central Bank data show that income on GKOs accounted for 41% of the earnings in the top 100 banks as of September 1997. Thanks to GKOs, Sberbank which held about 35% of the market scored pre-tax profits of $2 billion in 1996.

[37] The CBR established a special supervisory department ('OPERU 2') to monitor the largest national banks. Fourteen banks have been made subject to OPERU 2 supervision.

From this point, Russia headed into a deep recession. Inflation rose, household deposits were once again swept away, imports contracted, and the banking system collapsed into insolvency. The combination produced a severe decline in household real incomes and in the standard of living. All this threatened to destroy the central achievement of economic reform in recent years and the fundamental underpinning for the nascent economic recovery (Appendix 1).

4.4. CONCLUSION

In all countries debt and deficits of the public sector are at the heart of economic policy debate. In the developing world, the so-called emerging markets, debt has been associated with major financial crisis. The Mexican crisis followed by the currency turmoil in Asia led capital markets to monitor closely the maturity of the debt. And the speculative attack on the rouble in the summer of 1998 has made the Russian authorities fully aware that in a world of high capital mobility, Russia will be disciplined by the capital market. As President Boris Yeltsin said in a broadcast on 5 June 1998:

We ourselves share part of the blame for our difficulties, everyone should at last learn to live within their means . . . one of the causes of the [financial market] crisis is our inexperience of working in the conditions of an open economy. This we need to learn: and as it turns out, we need to learn more quickly. If we fail to learn, we will again see empty shelves in the shops, our lives will again be filled with the words 'shortages', 'queues', 'ration coupons'. We have had enough of those things. Entering the international economic community brings obvious advantages, but also quite a few dangers. The Government, Central Bank and other economic agencies, including in the private sector, must be ready to overcome these dangers, and in principle, take preventive steps so that they do not arise in the first place.[38]

Monetary and fiscal policy are strongly linked. Macroeconomic management in Russia in the 1990s was complicated, and ultimately undermined, by the tension between monetary and fiscal policy.

These fourteen banks represent 60–65% of Russia's banking assets (excluding assets of Vnesheconombank) and over 90% of Russia's bank deposits.

[38] President Boris Yeltsin, weekly radio address, 5 June 1998.

The problem started with the legacy of the former Soviet system which left the economy bankrupt. The final collapse of the Soviet regime and system in December 1991 saw the collapse of the Soviet Vneshekonombank and default on all debt, including short-term trade debt. From 1992 to 1995, while considerable progress was achieved in terms of fiscal consolidation and reduction of the primary deficit, the deficit was mainly financed by money creation and therefore led to a high rate of inflation. Starting in 1995, as a result of the failure to tighten further fiscal policy, revenue shortfalls were covered by issuing short-term debt. This was very attractive in the short run to the Russian government because there was no need to raise additional taxes or to finance the deficit by issuing money which would have caused the inflation rate to rise.

The replacement of a floating exchange rate with a (crawling) peg regime from mid-1995 made interest rates dependent on international investor sentiment. Adverse sentiment shifts could be external shocks in the sense of originating not from any serious deterioration in the fundamental macroeconomic-related risk factors in Russia itself, but rather from the contagion (intrinsic to a world of unimpeded cross-border capital flows) of financial market crises elsewhere—as it happened in East Asia. In a period of risk aversion in emerging financial markets interest rates would have to be allowed to rise to whatever level the market demanded if the exchange rate peg, or band, was to be held. At the same time punitive real interest rates increased the debt service burden, especially on short-term rouble-denominated debt, beyond the government's perceived capacity to bear. This perception in turn increased the risk of devaluation: for having let interest rates rise to defend the exchange rate, the government might be forced into letting the exchange rate go to prevent insolvency. So it was that this perceived devaluation risk completed the vicious circle that led in the end to both insolvency (default) and a massive devaluation. The problem was exacerbated by a fall in oil prices and a rise in imports which led to the first current account deficit since 1993. These high interest rates reflected the inconsistency between the fiscal and the exchange rate which lie at the heart of the failed stabilization plan. Ultimately the exchange rate policy needs to be consistent with fiscal policy.

To put the problem another way, the exposure to (sometimes arbitrary) global capital market disciplines was made that much more acute and immediate by the existence of a stock of government debt which was

(1) already large by the outbreak of the global financial crisis;
(2) growing at an unsustainable rate; and, above all
(3) of extremely short duration.

Amidst falling investor confidence, this short maturing debt could not be refinanced at tolerable yields, causing a liquidity crisis which contained within it the threat of insolvency.

The vulnerability to this threat could in principle have been reduced, or even eliminated, in three ways. First, the reversal of capital flight, especially of domestic currency substitution (cash dollar savings held 'under the mattress'), would have ensured sufficient domestic demand for government debt, so insulating that market from the vagaries of global capital flows. Secondly, the budget could have been balanced, so removing the need for new borrowing and reducing the cost of servicing existing debt. Both those goals call for consistency and perseverance in the application of policies bound to entail pain, and hence political unpopularity, in the short to medium term. The confidence necessary for capital flight repatriation can only be built, even with ideal policies, over several years.

The third possible solution, which seems easy by comparison, would have been simply a return to a floating exchange rate, allowing the interest rate to be controlled through domestic monetary policy. This approach might appear all the more attractive when it is recalled that the stabilization programme launched in January 1995, and which ultimately succeeded in ending high inflation, was based on monetary targets rather than an exchange rate anchor. In practice, however, the pegging of the exchange rate six months into that programme had a powerful stabilizing effect, which the authorities were afterwards reluctant to forgo. Any significant devaluation would cause a sharp increase in the CPI due to the predominance of imported goods in food and other consumer product markets. Over the longer term, moreover, exchange rate stability would assist the repatriation of flight capital, by making the rouble more credible as a financial asset worth holding. And until that effect had been achieved, with a normal level of domestic savings available for government and private sector financing needs, a stable real exchange rate would be essential for attracting into Russia the private voluntary international capital which, apart from the limited funds available from international financial institutions, was the only alternative financing source.

Thus there were compelling reasons, in terms of both short- and long-term priorities and goals, for attempting to defend the rouble exchange rate. Given that the exchange rate policy was itself an important part of the solution to the constraint of capital flight, the only way to resolve that tension was a decisive removal of fiscal imbalances.

In principle, and in contrast to the years needed to reverse capital flight, the necessary fiscal adjustment could have been achieved in time to prevent the collapse of August 1998. In practice, the attempt foundered on domestic political resistance. The wrecking power of political opposition in 1998 was increased by earlier government prevarication with fiscal reform. With hindsight, the favourable markets of 1996–7 should have been regarded as offering convenient bridging finance during a rapid fiscal adjustment. Instead, the Russian government took the rising bond prices for further opportunities to tap capital markets.[39] It was only in the emergency created by the 'Asian crisis' that the political will crystallized for decisive fiscal action. But by then there was too little time left to overcome all the obstacles, whether external (market confidence) or domestic (political opposition).

The reformist chapter in Russian economic policy which began after the bankruptcy of December 1991 ended thus in the bankruptcy of August 1998. Looking beyond the Yeltsin era, the final lesson is simple enough: such calamitous setbacks will recur unless the public finances are put in order through a genuine fiscal reform.[40]

---

[39] The agro-bond was developed in 1997, a financial instrument representing securitized debt of Russia's regions to the federal government. The agro-bond was followed by Energos, an instrument representing securitized debt in the power industry. Energos never caught on among investors.

[40] Macroeconomic developments have improved dramatically since early 1999: real GDP growth reached 7.7% in 2000. The macroeconomic performance reflects not only the large ruble depreciation in 1998 (40%), and the increase in oil prices, but also the strengthening of fiscal and monetary policies.

Appendix 1. **Russian Federation: Macroeconomic Indicators, 1996–2000**

	1996	1997	1998	1999	2000
					Programme
Production and prices (annual percentage changes)					
Real GDP	−3.5	0.9	−4.9	3.2	7
Change in consumer prices					
Annual average	47.6	14.7	27.7	85.9	18.6
12-month	21.8	10.9	84.5	36.7	16
Change in GDP deflator	43.9	16.5	12.4	63.3	32
Public sector[a] (in per cent of GDP)					
Federal government					
Overall balance	−7.9	−7.1	−5.9	−4.7	1.5
Primary balance	−2.2	−2.5	−1.3	1.6	6.1
Revenue	11.8	12.3	11.0	13.4	16.3
Of which: cash	9.2	10.0	9.0	13.4	16.3
Expenditure	19.9	19.4	16.9	18.1	14.8
Interest	5.9	4.7	4.5	6.3	4.6
Non-interest	14.0	14.8	12.3	11.8	10.1
External sector (in billion US dollars unless otherwise indicated)					
Total exports f.o.b	90.6	89	74.9	75.3	93.9
Total imports f.o.b	72.8	71.6	57.8	39.5	46.7
External current account (deficit−)	3.9	2.8	1	20.8	31.6
Federal government external debt service due	17.5	15.2	16.6	17.3	15.4
Stock of federal government external debt	136.1	134.6	152.4	147.6	149.8
As % of GDP	32.3	31.0	54.8	79.9	
Gross reserves coverage (months of imports of goods and services)[a]	2	2.9	2.8	2.9	4.7
Memorandun items (units as indicated)					
Nominal GDP (billions of roubles)	2,145.7	2,522.0	2,696.4	4,545.5	6,419

Appendix 1. *(continued)*

	1996	1997	1998	1999	2000
Exchange rate (roubles per US$ period average)	5.1	5.8	9.7	24.6	
Nominal GDP (billions of dollars)	420.7	434.8	278.0	184.8	

Note: [a]Revenues and expenditures on a cash basis, while primary balance and overall balance are on a commitment basis.

Sources: Russian authorities, and IMF staff estimates and projections quoted on the IMF web site.

REFERENCES

Balino, T., Hoelscher, D., and Horder, J. (1997). 'Evolution of Monetary Policy Instruments in Russia', IMF Working Paper 97/180, International Monetary Fund, December.

Calvo, G. A. (1998). 'Varieties of Capital-Market Crises', in G. Calvo, and M. King (eds.), *The Debt Burden and its Consequences for Monetary Policy*, Macmillan, pp. 181–202.

Calvo, S., and Reinhart, C. (1996). 'Capital Flows to Latin America: Is There Evidence of Contagion Effects?', in G. Calvo, M. Goldstein, and E. Hochreiter (eds.), *Private Capital Flows to Emerging Markets After the Mexican Crisis*, Washington, DC: Institute for International Economics, pp. 151–71.

Dornbusch, R. (1998). 'Debt and Monetary Policy: The Policy Issues', in G. Calvo, and M. King (eds.), *The Debt Burden and its Consequences for Monetary Policy*, Macmillan, pp. 3–22.

Easterly, W., and Vieira Da Cunha, P. (1993). 'Financing the Storm: Macro-economic Crisis in Russia, 1992–1993', mimeo, the World Bank.

Goldfajn, I., and Valdes, R. (1997). 'Are Currency Crises Predictable', IMF Working Paper 97/159, International Monetary Fund, December.

Goskomstat, R. F. (1992–8). 'Sotsial'no-Ekonomicheskoe Polozhenoe Rossiskoi Federatsii' (Socioeconomic Situation of Russia), various issues (January–December), in Russian.

—— (1992–8), 'Kratkosrochnye ekonomicheskie pokazeteli Rossiiskaya Federatsiya', (January–December).

Granville, B. (1994). 'So Farewell Then Rouble Zone', in A. Aslund (ed.), *Russian Economic Reform at Risk*, London and New York: Castle.

—— (1995). *The Success of Russian Economic Reforms*, London: The Royal Institute of International Affairs, distributed by Brookings.

International Monetary Fund (1992*a*). '*Economic Review: Russian Federation*', April.

—— (1992*b*). 'Money and Banking Statistics in Former Soviet Union (FSU) Economies', prepared by R. Calogero, W. Nahr, and T. R. Stillson, authorized for distribution by J. B, McLenaghan, WP/02/103, December.

—— (1995*a*). 'Russian Federation', *IMF Economic Reviews*, 16, March.

—— (1995*b*). 'Russian Federation—Statistical Appendix', IMF Staff Country Report 95/107, October.

International Monetary Fund, The World Bank, the OECD, and the EBRD, (1990). 'The Economy of the USSR, Summary and Recommendations', Washington, DC: The World Bank.

Kaminsky, G., Lizondo, S., and Reinhart, C. (1997).'Leading Indicators of Currency Crises', IMF Working Paper WP/97/79, International Monetary Fund, July.

Koen, V., and Meyermans, E. (1994). 'Exchange Rate Determinants in Russia: 1992–1993', IMF Working Paper 66, June.

——, and Phillips, S. (1993). 'Price Liberalisation in Russia, Behaviour of Prices, Household Incomes and Consumption During the First Year', IMF occasional paper 104, June.

Krugman, P. R. (1979). 'A model of Balance of Payments Crises', *Journal of Money, Credit and Banking*, 11 (August): 311–25.

Lin, S. (1993). 'A Monetary Model of a Shortage Economy', *IMF Staff Papers*, 40/2, (June): 369–94.

Linz, S. (1990). 'The Soviet Economy in Transition: A Resurgence of Reform, Econometrics and Economic Theory', paper 8901, Michigan State University.

McKinnon, R. (1991). 'Stabilising the Rouble: The Problem of Internal Currency Convertibility', in E. M. Claassen (ed.), *Exchange Rate Policies in Developing and Post-Socialist Countries*, San Francisco: International Center for Economic Growth Publication, ICS Press.

Obstfeld, M. (1994). 'The Logic of Currency Crises', NBER Working Paper 4640, Cambridge, Mass.: NBER, February.

—— (1996). 'Models of Currency Crisis with Self-Fulfilling Features', *European Economic Review*, 40, April: 1,037–47.

Otker, I., and Pazarbasioglu, C. (1995). 'Speculative Attacks and Currency Crisis: The Mexican Experience', Working Paper 112, November, Washington, DC: IMF.

Russian Economic Trends (1998).'Deficits, Debt and Financing', Working Centre For Economic Reform, Government of the Russian Federation and Russian Centre For European Policy (RECEP), March.

Sahay, R., and Vegh, C. (1996). 'Inflation and Stabilisation in Transition Economies: An Analytical Interpretation of the Evidence', *Policy Reform,* 1: 75–108.

Sachs, J., Tornell, A., and Velasco, A. (1996). 'Financial Crises in Emerging Markets: The Lessons from 1995', Brookings Paper on Economic Activity, 1, Washington, DC: Brookings Institution.

Sargent, T., and Wallace, N. (1981). 'Some Unpleasant Monetarist Arithmetic', Federal Reserve Bank of Minneapolis, *Quarterly Review*, 5/3: 1–17.

Tornell, A., and Velasco, A. (1995). 'Money-Based versus Exchange Rate-Based Stabilisation with Endogenous Fiscal Policy', NBER Working Paper 5300, October.

Vegh, C. (1992). 'Stopping High Inflation, An Analytical Overview', *IMF Staff Papers*, 39/3 (September): 626–95.

5

Taxation and Public Expenditure

CLEMENS GRAFE AND KASPAR RICHTER

5.1. INTRODUCTION

This chapter examines fiscal aspects of Russia's transition up to 1997, taking into account political and institutional factors[1] affecting the fiscal system. Section 2 describes the conditions underlying Russia's formation as a Federation. Progress in fiscal reforms was subject to political constraints, among them the substantial autonomy of Russian regions. Section 3 discusses conceptual problems of estimating the boundaries of the Russian public sector, and clarifies the choice of our data set. It then considers the changes in the size of the general government sector since the beginning of transition,[2] comparing it with other countries. Section 4 describes the reduction of the budget deficit. This chapter refrains from an analysis of the implications of the budget deficit and its financing for monetary policy and the stabilization. These issues are covered in depth in Brigitte Granville's chapter in this volume. Fiscal consolidation came about despite a continuous decline in government revenues. Sections 5 and 6 look at the causes of the revenue crisis, and assess the federal transfer system to the regions. Sections 7 and 8 consider the nature of the expenditure reductions, with particular emphasis on the adjustment in social programmes. The sections on revenues and expenditure relate the slow progress in fiscal reforms to economic characteristics of the transition process. A concluding section summarizes the main findings.

---

[1] For more details see the chapter by Christopher Granville in this volume.

[2] General government refers to the federal government, local and regional governments, extra-budgetary funds, and any other identified extra-budgetary expenditures. Consolidated government signifies the federal, local, and regional governments.

5.2. CREATION OF A NEW FEDERATION

The Soviet Union was a federation more in form than in substance.[3] Full subordination of the union republics and regions under the Central Committee of the Communist Party in Moscow was guaranteed by the principle of democratic centralism. Following guidelines issued by the Central Committee, the national Council of Ministers approved an annual aggregate all-union budget. It was composed of the budget plans of the different union republics, which in turn contained the regional budgets. The budget plans adopted at the level of the regions and union republics were based on instructions received from higher levels.[4] With the breakdown of the Soviet Union, the task was to safeguard the cohesion of Russia as a federation, while accommodating the demands of ethno-federal regions for greater autonomy.[5] The declaration of sovereignty by Russia in June 1990 led to similar declarations by seven national areas within Russia between July and September 1990, and to the independence declaration by Checheniya in October 1991.

The Russian Federation is a three-tiered federal state consisting of eighty-nine 'subjects' (krais, oblasts, okrugs, autonomous regions, national regions, metropolitan cities (Moscow, St Petersburg), and autonomous republics). Below this intermediate level are the municipal authorities and rayons. Republics are the traditional home of non-Russian ethnic groups recognized as having titular status. Oblasts are regions without special rights for non-Russian ethnic groups. Krais are generally larger than oblasts and historically contained ethnic minorities living in recognized ethnic homelands called okrugs (districts). These autonomous okrugs were granted full subject status in 1992.

The republics insisted that their preferential status relative to other regions ought to be maintained. Regions without republican status demanded an equal treatment of all eighty-nine 'subjects' of the Federation, and favoured a system of purely territorial federalism, as in (for instance) Germany. Some regions emphasized such demands by unilateral changes in status. Various autonomous oblasts declared themselves republics. Most of the autonomous okrugs, previously controlled by

---

[3] Schiffer (1989), pp. 85–6.   [4] See Sakwa (1996), p. 182.
[5] These territories are the Jewish Autonomous Oblast and ten autonomous okrugs, namely Aga Buryat AO, Komi-Permyak AO, Koryak AO, Nenets AO, Taimyr (Dolgan-Nenetsk) AO, Ust-Orda Buryat AO, Khanty-Mansi AO, Chukchi AO, Evenk AO, Yamal-Nenetsk AO. They comprise some 53% of Russia's territory, and account for about 17% of the total population.

some oblast or krai, proclaimed themselves independent subjects of the Federation.[6]

The outcome of accommodating such demands was a hybrid federalism, combining national and territorial elements of the ethno-federal legacy. Republics were granted greater rights towards cultural self-development. All regions and districts gained increased influence over their own economic affairs. At the same time the formation of a common political community within a single economic space was intended to weaken centrifugal tendencies in the regions.[7]

The legal form of the system was eventually determined by the constitution adopted in December 1993.[8] All subjects of the Federation (21 republics, 6 krais, 49 oblasts, 2 cities with regional status (Moscow and St Petersburg), and 11 autonomous okrugs) were declared equal (Article 5). Individual rather than collective ethnic rights were emphasized (Articles 19, 26, and 28/9), and the priority of federal laws was enshrined (Article 76). All governments, whether federal, regional, or local, have independent budgetary and administrative status (Articles 73 and 132).[9] The republics retained some preferential status (Articles 66 and 68). Subsequently, some republics and regions signed bilateral treaties with Moscow, which granted them special economic and fiscal rights (see section 6 below).

5.3. THE GENERAL GOVERNMENT SECTOR

Budget data of the Soviet Union and of Russia in the 1990s cannot be readily compared—the budget methodology having changed fundamentally—so the fiscal data presented here cover only the period since 1992. Given erratic accountancy procedures, the hybrid public–private nature of certain of the agencies and the different means of payments in which transactions occur (rouble, hard currency, in kind, veksels, etc.),

---

[6] Sakwa (1996), pp. 36, 184.

[7] Yegor Gaidar, the chief architect of the first wave of economic reforms during 1991–2, claimed that the development of a national market would create greater incentives for integration. See Sakwa (1996), p. 190.

[8] The regulations concerning the federal system were based on the Federal Treaty of March 1992 between Russia and its republics (with the exception of Tatarstan, which signed a separate bilateral treaty as sovereign state). However, strengthened by his victory in defeating the putsch in October 1993, Yeltsin reneged on parts of the Federal Treaty and weakened some elements of the asymmetric treatment of regions. See Sakwa (1996), p. 188.

[9] The same rights are granted in the law on budgetary rights of self-governments from June 1993.

the budget information provided by the Ministry of Finance cannot be relied upon to provide a fully comprehensive picture of public-sector expenditure and financing. For instance, roughly a third of the domestic government debt was purchased by Sberbank, the former sole savings bank. The state still holds a 51 per cent stake in it. Sberbank allegedly purchases government debt at below market yields and reduces thereby the budgeted interest expenditure of the state. Unorthodox government revenues such as 'charitable' expenses of enterprises and households is another item which makes the budgetary data misleading. For example, the reconstruction of the Cathedral of Christ the Saviour in the centre of Moscow was partly financed by contributions from the local business community, which were extracted by the Moscow city administration under the threat of withdrawing business licences.

In addition, official Russian budget data are normally compiled on a cash rather than an accruals basis. Finally, the government has built up financial obligations of a contingent nature by providing Ministry of Finance guarantees for commercial bank credits granted in the form of veksels. The total value of such guarantees in 1996 amounted to roughly 1 per cent of GDP.[10]

Another difficulty is that the classification rules for budgetary items used by the Russian Ministry of Finance differ from IMF definitions, and vary from one year to the next. The Minister of Finance adds privatization revenues and receipts from gold sales to non-tax revenues rather than to deficit financing. Various extra-budgetary funds were included in some years and not others. To avoid inconsistencies with international definitions and across years, the figures used in this chapter are based on IMF definitions.

Table 5.1 compares three different approaches to calculating budgetary data for the consolidated government in 1994–6. The expenditure data in all three approaches are defined on a cash basis, reducing the 1995 and 1996 expenditure shares by about 1 per cent and 2 per cent of GDP respectively, compared to the accrual basis. The first approach, the official picture, combines Ministry of Finance budgetary data and nominal GDP estimates from the official statistical office Goskomstat. The second concept adjusts the budgetary data for inconsistencies with international methodology, and the third approach replaces Goskomstat GDP data with IMF estimates, which are substantially higher.

The adjustment of budget data leads to lower revenue shares, and higher expenditure shares, relative to the official figures, while the GDP

---

[10] See Renaissance Capital (1997).

Table 5.1. *Budget data according to different methodologies (in %)*

	1994	1995	1996
Revenues/GDP			
MinFin/Goskomstat	28.2	26.8	24.9
IMF/Goskomstat	25.7	24.8	23.8
IMF/IMF	25.7	21.8	18.9
Expenditures/GDP			
MinFin/Goskomstat	37.7	29.8	28.9
IMF/Goskomstat	36.6	30.6	31.9
IMF/IMF	36.6	26.8	25.3
Deficit/GDP			
MinFin/Goskomstat	9.5	3.0	4.0
IMF/Goskomstat	10.9	5.7	8.1
IMF/IMF	10.9	5.0	6.5

adjustment reduces both these ratios. According to the IMF, revenues and expenditures are respectively 6 and 3.5 percentage points of GDP lower than according to government statistics. The budgetary data presented in the rest of the chapter follows the middle approach. Expenditures and revenues are categorized according to international convention, while the GDP figures are taken from Goskomstat. The Goskomstat GDP series is more widely used, better documented, far more detailed (monthly data, regional GDP), and compatible with other official national account data not recalculated by the IMF.

Table 5.2 analyses and compares with other transition economies the main developments of the general government budget. As a percentage of GDP, Russia's general government expenditures in 1996 were down by almost one-third and revenues by over one-fifth compared to 1992. With expenditures declining by more than revenues, the budget deficit dropped sharply to about 8.5 per cent of GDP.[11]

The contraction in expenditures was the result of the abolition of import subsidies and cuts in other federal expenditures. Regional spending and revenues rose both in relative terms and as a percentage of GDP. Even so, the federal government in 1996 accounted for over 50 per cent of all expenditures (including transfers), as against 38 per cent for regional budgets, 8 per cent of which was financed by transfers from the

---

[11] The World Bank has substantially higher estimates for general government spending for 1992, mostly due to the inclusion of estimates for quasi-fiscal spending by the Central Bank of Russia of over 20% of GDP. See World Bank (1996a), Annex A.1.

Table 5.2. *General government expenditures (Exp), revenues (Rev), and deficits (Def) in the FSU and eastern Europe (EE) as % of GDP*

	1995/1996					1992		
	Exp	Rev	Def	GDP	PPP GDP	Exp	Rev	Def
Russia	39.3	30.9	8.4	2,985	4480[b]	57.8	39.6	18.2
Armenia	26.9	14.2	12.7	361	2,260	12.3	4.2	8.1
Azerbaijan	24.5	19	5.5	368	1,665	46.3	49.1	−2.8
Belarus	46.3	43.7	2.6	1,001	4,220	56.6	54.7	1.9
Estonia	40.4	41.2	−0.8	3,000	4,431	34.9	34.6	0.3
Georgia	12.3	7.8	4.5	530	1,813	39	13.6	25.4
Kazakhstan	18.9	16	2.9	1,079	3,664	31.8	24.5	7.3
Kyrgyzstan	23.4	17	6.4	379	1,621[b]	33.9	16.5	17.4
Latvia	39.7	36.3	3.4	1,780	3,291	28.2	27.4	0.8
Lithuania	27	23.5	3.5	2,099	4,471	31.3	32.1	−0.8
Moldova	29.9	24.2	5.7	392	2,069	24.7	24.7	0
Tajikistan	17.6	12.3	5.3	177	920[b]	57.8	26.6	31.2
Turkmenistan	14	12.4	1.6	491	2,345	42.2	55.4	−13.2
Ukraine	42.7	37.8	4.9	723	2,400[b]	58.4	33	25.4
Uzbekistan	37.6	33.5	4.1	369	2,370[b]	43.4	25	18.4
			0					
Albania	34.3	24.3	10	745	1,305	43.9	21.9	22
Bulgaria	47.6	40.9	6.7	1,038	4,190	45.4	40.2	5.2

Croatia	47	46.5	0.5	3,992	3,828[a]	37	33	4
Czech Republic	50.2	47.8	2.4	4,814	9,770	41.9	39.2	2.7
FYR Macedonia	44.3	43.9	0.4	1,845	2,147	48.2	38.6	9.6
Hungary	50	46.5	3.5	4,357	6,410[a]	61.6	56.1	5.5
Poland	51.4	48.7	2.7	3,055	5,400	50.4	43.8	6.6
Romania	34.5	31.9	2.6	1,573	4,312	42	37.4	4.6
Slovak Republic	46	44.8	1.2	3,525	7,970	51	44	7
Slovenia	45.7	45.4	0.3	9,279	10,594[b]	45.8	46	− 0.2
			0					
			0					
Average	35.7	31.6	4.0	1,998.3	3,917.8	42.6	34.4	8.2
Aver(EE)	45.1	42.1	3.0	3,422.3	5,592.6	46.7	40.0	6.7
Aver(FSU)	29.4	24.7	4.7	1,048.9	2,801.3	39.9	30.7	9.2

Notes: The 1995–1996 data refers to 1996 for Russia, Kyrgyzstan, Tajikistan, Bulgaria, Croatia, Macedonia, Hungary, Slovak Republic, and Slovenia, for all others it refers to 1995.

GDP is defined as per capita GDP in dollar terms, PPP GDP refers to per capita GDP at purchasing power parity in dollar terms.

[a]PPP GDP refers to 1993.

[b]PPP GDP refers to 1995.

Sources: IMF, OECD, EBRD.

centre to the regions. Federal and regional budgets collected an equal share of 40 per cent of total revenues.[12]

Revenues to the extra-budgetary funds declined substantially.[13] Expenditures fell by less, and the share of these funds in general government spending increased from about 15 per cent to 20 per cent. Moreover their surplus position in 1992 had become a deficit by 1996.

By 1995–6, the transition economies displayed great variety in public sector sizes. The most successful reformers of central Europe had government expenditure shares of the same order as western European countries. Most CIS countries had substantially smaller government sectors. Russia was in a middle-ranking position between the CIS and the central European states.[14] Simple regression analysis suggests that the status of former Soviet republic (FSU) and the economic living standard have a strong effect on government sector size.[15] Allowing for less-advanced initial conditions in the FSU and the emergence of a large shadow economy, the level of government expenditure in Russia is the average observed in transition countries,[16] while the revenue level is below.[17]

---

[12] Expenditures are thus more centralized than revenues, in contrast to the pattern typical for developing countries. See Broadway *et al.* (1994), p. 23.

[13] The data refers to the consolidated balance of the main social extra-budgetary funds (pensions, employment, social insurance, and medical insurance). Other extra-budgetary funds include the three public funds (the federal and regional road funds, the ecological fund, and the technological development fund), the foreign exchange fund and around fifty industrial funds. The foreign exchange, and the federal road fund and the ecological fund were included in the federal budget in 1994 and 1995, respectively. See World Bank (1996a), p. 43.

[14] Three CIS countries, Belarus, Ukraine, and Uzbekistan, have higher revenue shares of GDP than Russia. In 1996 they were lagging behind in the transition process compared to Russia, and may still experience revenue contractions, once economic reforms advance. See Barbone and Polackova (1996), p. 18.

[15] The methodological concerns about calculating the size of the government sector become even more severe in the context of international comparisons. The regression results should therefore be treated with due caution.

[16] Russia's actual expenditure level exceeds the predicted level by 3.4% of GDP. Government expenditures (EXP) were regressed on a constant (CONST), the level (GDP) and the square of per capita GDP adjusted for purchasing power parity (GDPSQ), and a dummy for FSU countries (FSU). The regression statistics are as follows (t-statistics in brackets, adjusted R^2 equal to 0.54):

$$EXP = 24.9 * CONS + 0.007 * GDP - 5e - 07 * GDPSQ - 10.8 * FSU$$
$$\quad\ (3.5) \qquad\qquad (2.7) \qquad\qquad (-2.1) \qquad\qquad (-2.7)$$

[17] Russia's actual revenue level is 1.8 % of GDP lower than the estimated level. Government revenues (REV) were regressed on the same set of explanatory variables as expenditures. The results were as follows (adjusted R^2 equal to 0.59):

$$REV = 17 * CONS + 0.008 * GDP - 5e - 07 * GDPSQ - 11 * FSU$$
$$\quad\ (2.3) \qquad\qquad (3.0) \qquad\qquad (-2.3) \qquad\qquad (-2.6)$$

Table 5.3. *Russian Federation: general government budget (% of GDP)*

	1992	1993	1994	1995	1996	Change
Total revenues	39.6	36.2	34.6	32.0	30.9	− 8.7
Consolidated	28.6	27.8	25.7	24.8	23.8	− 4.9
Federal	16.7	13.7	11.8	12.1	11.9	− 4.8
Regional	13.5	16.7	18.0	14.2	14.5	1.0
Inter-governmental transfers[a]	1.6	2.6	4.1	1.5	2.7	1.1
Extra-budget	10.9	8.6	9.1	7.6	7.5	− 3.5
Federal transfers	0.0	0.2	0.1	0.5	0.3	0.3
Total expenditures	57.8	43.6	45.0	37.7	39.3	− 18.6
Consolidated	37.5	33.7	36.6	30.6	31.9	− 5.6
Federal	27.1	20.2	23.2	17.6	19.8	− 7.3
Regional	12.0	16.0	17.5	14.5	14.7	2.7
Extra-budget	8.3	8.0	8.6	7.6	7.7	− 0.6
Unbudgeted import subsidies	12.0	2.1	0.0	0.0	0.0	− 12.0
Deficit	18.2	7.3	10.4	5.7	8.4	− 9.9
Federal	10.4	6.5	11.4	5.4	7.9	− 2.5
Regional	− 1.6	− 0.6	− 0.5	0.3	0.2	1.8
Extra-budgetary	− 2.6	− 0.6	− 0.5	0.0	0.2	2.8
GDP in R trn	19	172	611	1,631	2,256	

Note: [a]From federal to regional budgets.

Source: IMF.

These results, however, teach us little about the desirable government sector size, just as comparisons with other emerging and industrial countries offer slight guidance for Russia's government sector reforms. The study of aggregated statistics is no substitute for a detailed analysis of the government revenue raising system and spending programme.

5.4. FISCAL CONSOLIDATION

The main achievement in the fiscal sphere was budgetary consolidation. This section concentrates on the implications of attempts to consolidate the budget rather than the implications of the deficit and its financing for the stabilization efforts.[18] The budget deficit in the fourth quarter of 1991 totalled about 30 per cent of GDP, and was being financed by rapid increases in the money supply. In 1992 the first attempt to curb the deficit failed because of lavish Central Bank (CBR) credits to enterprises and the continuation of the rouble zone on the post-Soviet territory.[19] In spring 1993 the government launched a serious fiscal adjustment programme, backed by an agreement with the CBR to reduce credits to the economy. The objectives were to eliminate monetary financing of the budget and to phase out the quasi-fiscal operations of the CBR. As part of the programme the rouble zone was abolished in the later part of 1993.

This second stabilization effort ended in mid-1994 with the re-adoption of an expansionary federal budget, combined with renewed acceleration of money printing by the CBR. A collapse of the rouble in October 1994 demonstrated the painful consequences of soft monetary policies, and efforts towards fiscal consolidation were taken up again at the end of 1994. The replacement of Gerashchenko as head of the CBR, and a new Central Bank Law forbidding direct credits from the CBR to the government (see Table 5.4), helped to bring about a rapid decline in inflation rates. With the decline in inflation rates, real interest rates turned positive, and the domestic capital market emerged as an important source of financing for the budget deficit. Despite heavy spending pressures in the run-up to the parliamentary election in December 1995, the general government deficit dropped to less than 6 per cent of GDP, partly helped by a significant under-estimation of inflation in the federal budget law.

In 1996 debt servicing costs rose quickly as annual interest rates reached more than 200 per cent before the presidential election in the summer. The share of foreign financing re-expanded when foreign credits became substantially cheaper than those obtainable on the domestic market. The budget deficit widened to over 8 per cent of GDP, even though substantial cuts in non-interest spending kept the primary deficit almost unchanged compared to 1995 in the face of an unforeseen decline in government revenue. In the following year, 1997, the budget deficit was held to 7.6 per cent of GDP during the first three quarters of 1997, including 4.8 per cent of GDP spent on interest payments.[20]

---

[18]　B. Granville's chapter in this volume discusses in depth the implications of the budget deficit and its financing for the stabilization efforts.

[19]　See Granville (1994) and B. Granville's chapter in this volume for more details.

[20]　For the role the deficit financing played for the Russian crisis of August 1998 see B. Granville in this volume and MacFarquhar (1998).

Table 5.4. *Sources of financing for the general budget*

	1992	1993	1994	1995	1996
Deficit (% of GDP)	18.2	7.3	10.4	5.7	8.4
Financing[a] *(in %)*	100	100	100	100	100
1. Net foreign financing	60.0	26.2	0.3	− 3.3	7.7
1.1. Foreign loan receipts	65.7	35.7	8.5	11.9	15.3
1.2. Principal repayment	− 5.7	− 9.5	− 8.3	− 15.2	− 7.6
2. Domestic financing	37.1	73.8	100.0	104.4	92.3
2.1. Domestic banking system	28.6	69.0	85.5	85.1	80.8
2.1.1. Monetary authorities	48.6	80.2	77.8	27.4	25.6
2.1.2. Rest of the banking system	− 20.0	− 11.1	7.7	57.7	55.1
2.2. Other financing	8.6	4.8	14.5	19.4	11.5
2.2.1. Privatization proceeds	2.9	3.2	1.1	5.0	0.8
2.2.2. Net proceeds from gold etc	5.7	7.9	6.1	11.1	9.7
2.2.3. Securities help by nonbank sector	.	− 4.8	8.7	− 1.2	− 1.6
2.2.4. Domestic principal repayment	0.0	− 3.2	− 1.4	− 0.6	− 0.3
2.2.5. Other	2.9	1.6	−	5.0	2.9

Note: [a]Shares do not always add up to 100 due to rounding.

Throughout the transition period, privatization receipts remained a minor source of financing.[21] Net proceeds from sales of gold, gems, and precious metals, on the other hand, accounted for 10 per cent of deficit financing during 1995–6.

5.4.1. *Regional budget deficits*

At the beginning of the transition process, the consolidated total of regional budgets was in surplus. Over time the federal government

[21] This reflected the widespread use of voucher rather than cash privatization, the heavy reliance on insider privatization, constraints on foreign participation, the volatile political environment, and inadequate regulatory practices (Cheasty and Davis 1996, pp. 6–8). The share of privatization receipts peaked in 1995 at 5% with the highly controversial 'loans for shares' auctions.

reduced its own budget deficit by shifting expenditures to the regional level without increasing regional revenue sources correspondingly. As a result, regional budgets went into deficit in 1995 and extra-budgetary funds in 1996. The funding needs of regional governments, together with the readiness of emerging market investors to hold regional debts, gave rise to the possibility of widespread sub-national borrowing. Investor interest was fuelled by a combination of declining interest rates on federal debt and increased awareness of the vast differences in regional economic and fiscal conditions. A presidential decree of April 1997 set limits on regional government borrowing: in any given year, total borrowing must not exceed 30 per cent of budget revenues. Interest payments on long-term debt must be less than 15 per cent of revenues.

5.5. REVENUE COLLECTION

Revenues of the consolidated budget as a percentage of GDP fell continuously from 1992 to 1997[22] (Tables 5.5 and 5.6). Part of the decline was due to tax reforms aimed at reducing the tax burden on the economy. These included narrowing of the profits tax base to a more reasonable definition of profits,[23] and the reduction in VAT rates.[24] But another part was due to the non-payment of taxes. Tax arrears to the consolidated budget grew from around 3.4 per cent of monthly GDP in January 1993 to some 80 per cent of monthly GDP by mid 1997. At the same time, the share of taxes collected in cash dropped sharply,[25] and tax evasion

---

[22]   The decline between 1994 and 1995 is under-estimated by about 1.2% of GDP due to the inclusion of budgetary and extra-budgetary funds in government revenues in 1995. During the first three quarters of 1997 revenues amounted to 22.7% of GDP.

[23]   The profits tax base included various business expenses which in western countries are tax-deductible. Depreciation allowances were also eroded due to high inflation in the first years of transition. As a result, Russia collected in 1993 almost 10% of GDP in profits taxes, compared to an OECD average of 2.9%. The profit tax system was adjusted in early 1996, when the excess wage tax element of the tax was abolished, amounting to about one-sixth of the profits tax base. The rule had been that monthly wage payments in excess of six times the minimum monthly wage were not deductible from corporate income liable to taxation.

[24]   VAT was introduced in January 1992 to replace turnover and sales taxes. In January 1993 the standard rate was reduced from 28% to 20% and the preferential rate from 15% to 10% and applied to an extended range of goods (World Bank 1996*b*, p. 18). The effective VAT rate dropped from around 17.8% in 1994 to 14.2% in 1996, as the so-called special tax, a VAT surcharge, was phased out.

[25]   The federal government share of cash revenues in total revenues dropped by almost 20 percentage points to 75% during 1994–6. While no equivalent figures are available for the regional governments, the ratio of cash revenues to overall revenues is likely to be still lower.

Table 5.5. *Revenues of the consolidated (Con), federal (Fed), and regional (Reg) budgets by sources (% of GDP)*

	1992			1993			1994			1995			1996		
	Fed	Reg	Con	Fed	Reg	Con	Fed	Reg	Con	Fed	Reg	Con	Fed	Reg	Con
Total revenues	16.8	13.7	28.9	13.7	16.6	27.7	11.8	18.0	26.0	12.1	14.2	24.8	11.9	14.5	23.8
1. Total direct taxes	3.7	6.8	10.5	3.2	9.2	12.4	2.8	8.0	10.9	2.7	6.7	9.4	1.8	5.1	6.9
Profit tax	3.7	4.7	8.4	3.2	6.6	9.8	2.8	5.2	8.0	2.5	4.6	7.2	1.5	2.8	4.4
Income tax	0.0	2.1	2.1	0.0	2.6	2.6	0.0	2.8	2.9	0.2	2.0	2.2	0.2	2.3	2.5
2. Total indirect taxes	12.1	4.2	16.3	8.3	3.2	11.5	7.6	3.5	11.1	7.5	4.0	11.5	8.7	4.5	13.2
2.1. Domestic indirect taxes	9.5	4.2	13.7	5.2	3.2	8.4	6.0	3.5	9.5	5.7	4.0	9.7	7.5	4.5	12.0
VAT	7.9	2.6	10.5	4.2	2.4	6.6	5.1	1.9	7.0	4.5	2.0	6.5	5.1	1.8	6.9
Excises	1.1	0.5	1.6	0.6	0.5	1.1	0.7	0.5	1.2	1.1	0.4	1.5	2.3	0.4	2.6
Nonenergy excise taxes	0.5	0.5	1.1	0.3	0.5	0.8	n.a.	0.5	n.a.	0.1	0.4	0.5	0.2	0.4	0.6
Energy excise taxes	0.5	0.0	0.5	0.3	0.0	0.3	n.a.	0.0	n.a.	0.9	0.0	0.9	2.0	0.0	2.0
Natural resource taxes	0.5	0.5	1.1	0.3	0.3	0.6	0.2	0.3	0.5	0.2	0.6	0.8	0.2	0.7	0.9
Property tax	0.0	0.0	0.0	0.0	0.0	0.0	0.0	0.8	0.8	0.0	1.0	1.0	0.0	1.6	1.6
2.2. Foreign economic activity	2.6	0.0	2.6	3.1	0.0	3.1	1.6	0.0	1.6	1.8	0.0	1.8	1.2	0.0	1.2
Export taxes	1.6	0.0	1.6	0.7	0.0	0.7	0.5	0.0	0.5	1.0	0.0	1.0	0.4	0.0	0.4
Import taxes	0.0	0.0	0.0	0.4	0.0	0.4	0.4	0.0	0.4	0.5	0.0	0.5	0.7	0.0	0.7
Other	0.5	0.0	0.5	2.0	0.0	2.0	0.6	0.0	0.6	0.3	0.0	0.3	0.2	0.0	0.2

Table 5.5. *(continued)*

	1992			1993			1994			1995			1996		
	Fed	Reg	Con	Fed	Reg	Con	Fed	Reg	Con	Fed	Reg	Con	Fed	Reg	Con
3. *Intergovernment transfers*	0.0	1.6	1.6	0.0	2.6	2.6	0.2	3.8	4.1	0.9	1.5	2.5	1.0	2.7	3.7
Other levels of government	0.0	1.6	1.6	0.0	2.6	2.6	0.2	3.8	4.1	0.0	1.5	1.5	0.0	2.7	2.7
Budg./Extrabudgetary funds	0.0	n.a.	n.a.	0.0	0.0	0.0	0.5	0.0	0.5	0.9	0.0	0.9	1.0	0.0	1.0
4. *Other*	0.5	1.1	1.6	2.2	1.7	3.8	0.9	2.3	3.2	0.9	2.0	2.9	0.4	2.3	2.6

Source: Ministry of Finance; World Bank.

Table 5.6. *Revenue crisis: federal and regional budget*

	1992	1993	1994	1995	1996
Federal budget					
Revenues (% of GDP)	16.7	13.7	11.8	12.1	11.9
Tax revenues	16.1	11.5	10.9	11.2	11.5
Cash tax revenues	n.a.	13.7	11.4	10.4	8.8
Direct taxes	3.6	3.2	2.8	2.7	1.8
Indirect taxes	12.0	8.3	7.6	7.5	8.7
Foreign trade taxes	n.a.	n.a.	3.4	2.5	2.6
% of total revenues					
Tax revenues	96.9	84.3	92.5	92.4	96.7
Cash tax revenues	n.a.	n.a.	96.5	85.3	73.9
Direct taxes	21.9	23.4	23.9	22.4	14.9
Indirect taxes	71.9	60.9	64.5	62.1	73.3
Trade taxes	n.a.	n.a.	29.0	20.9	22.2
Regional budget					
Revenues (% of GDP)	13.5	16.7	18.0	14.2	14.5
Tax revenues	10.9	12.4	11.5	10.7	9.6
Direct taxes	6.8	9.2	8.0	6.7	5.1
Indirect taxes	4.2	3.2	3.5	4.0	4.5
% of total revenues					
Tax revenues	80.8	74.5	64.1	75.1	66.1
Direct revenues	50.0	55.2	44.6	47.0	35.2
Indirect revenues	30.8	19.2	19.5	28.1	30.9

Source: Ministry of Finance, Moscow, Russia.

flourished through under-reporting of production, through use of barter transactions (estimated at up to 40 per cent of domestic economic transaction)[26] and, through capital flight.[27] According to the State Tax Service, about one third of all enterprises did not pay any taxes in 1996, and only 17 per cent of all enterprises regularly settled tax liabilities on time. The government tried, not very effectively to prop up revenues from other sources such as asset sales.

All in all, federal tax revenues failed to reach either the revenue targets in the federal budget or the tax revenue floor as stipulated in the 1996–7

[26] RET (1997), 4, p. 17. The share of non-monetary transactions of total sales grew to more than 50% by 1998, Pinto, Drebentsov, and Morozov (2000), Commander and Mummsen (1999).

[27] Pinto, Drebentsov, and Morozov (2000) estimate the costs to the budget of the growth of tax arrears and the use of tax offsets at 8–12% of GDP for 1996.

loan agreements with the IMF. The 1996 federal budget revenues, according to Ministry of Finance definitions, were about 15 per cent below the plan stated in the budget law, and 18 per cent short of the revenue target specified in the original IMF Extended Fund Facility. The IMF targets were subsequently lowered in September 1996, and then again in December, ensuring that the year-end revenue target was met. During the first three quarters of 1997 federal cash revenues were around 10 per cent below the IMF cash revenue floor and no less than 35 per cent below the figures in the 1997 Budget Law.[28]

The underlying causes of the revenue decline were a combination of a flawed tax system, institutional weaknesses, and policy failures.[29] The Soviet tax system relied heavily on the taxation of enterprises. Profits and turnover taxes, which were directly withdrawn from the accounts of state enterprises, contributed over 70 per cent of government tax revenues. In December 1991 a law on the basic principles of taxation set out the main structure of the new tax system.[30] Turnover tax was replaced by VAT, but in general the system was little changed from its Soviet predecessors. The tax burden remained concentrated on the traditional tax base, as newly formed enterprises were not included. Tax revenues fell as traditional tax bases contracted by more than GDP. Profits in large-scale enterprises in the industrial, construction, and transport sectors as a percentage of GDP declined by 65 per cent from 1995 to 1996. This accounted for most of the 45 per cent drop of profits tax revenue compared in 1996. Meanwhile the service sector, consisting mostly of small and medium enterprises, accounted in 1996–7 for half of total GDP, compared to 35 per cent in 1992, but its tax contribution remained modest. In particular, retail trade and catering together made up some 18 per cent of GDP, but their share of tax revenues was less than 7 per cent.

Russia is the world's second largest oil and gas producer. These sectors should be subject to royalties, to ensure an adequate fiscal benefit in return for the extraction of natural resources and their tax share should, accordingly, be higher than their share in GDP. Their actual tax share in 1994 was only 10 per cent against a GDP share of 15 per cent.[31] The situation improved over the subsequent two years. According to IMF estimates, the compliance rate on excisable oil and natural gas production

---

[28] RET (1997), 4, pp. 11, 18.
[29] For a discussion of the causes of the revenue decline in FSU countries, see Hemming *et al.* (1996).
[30] Wallich (1992), p. 27.
[31] See Gray (1995); Cheasty and Davis (1996), pp. 5–6; and World Bank (1996*b*), pp. 34–5.

rose from 50 per cent to 70 per cent. In 1997 the oil and gas sectors provided around 25 per cent of overall tax revenues.[32]

The tax base of major revenue earners was eroded by a proliferation of exemptions and shortcomings in tax design. At the end of 1996 total tax concessions was estimated to amount to 7 per cent of GDP.[33] According to IMF estimates, broad exemptions for VAT on imports and differential treatment of imports from CIS and non-CIS countries implied that in 1995–6 less than 40 per cent of recorded imports were subject to the full VAT rate. For 1995 the Ministry of Finance valued tax exemptions on import and excise taxes granted to the 'National Sports Foundation' for imports of alcohol at around 2 per cent of GDP.[34] Altogether, imports, while totalling in 1996 more than 15 per cent of GDP, contributed less than 1 per cent of GDP to the budget. The figure equals roughly the average of industrialized countries, but is far less than the 4.5 per cent of GDP which are commonly observed in countries with weak tax administration. The exploitation of loopholes in the profits tax law and its implementing instructions reduced profits tax revenues to 45 per cent of its potential yield. Income and payroll taxes were avoided by paying wages through subsidized credits, in-kind benefits, and deductions for employee insurance funds. Tax liabilities were not uniformly calculated on an accrual basis, as enterprises were given a choice between accrual and cash accounting. During the high inflation period time lags between the calculation and payment of tax liabilities severely reduced tax revenues. Against this, the erosion of depreciation allowances by inflation tended to increase revenue.[35]

With the transformation of the economy, the number of taxpayers increased sharply and incomes were earned from a greater variety of sources. For example, the tax authorities had to deal between 1992 and 1994 with an estimated additional 3.6 million profit tax returns and 10.8 million additional advance payments of profit tax.[36] The statistical share of wages in overall income declined from around 70 per cent in 1992 to 40 per cent in 1997, as individuals increasingly earned their living in the informal sector or were paid in the ways described above so as to avoid income tax. As a result, income tax receipts stayed at around 2.5 per cent of GDP, far below the levels typical in western countries. Contrary to the intentions at the beginning of the tax reforms, increasing reliance

---

[32] RET December 1997, Special Report.   [33] EBRD (1997), p. 121.
[34] See Aslund *et al.* (1996), p. 25.   [35] World Bank (1996b), p. 19.
[36] World Bank (1996b), p. 37.

on indirect taxes moved Russia away from tax structures observed in industrialized economies. A vicious circle arises. As the shadow economy spreads, the government needs to levy higher tax rates on the remaining formal economy to raise a given amount of revenue. This in turn induces further tax evasion.

The State Tax Service (STS), the federal agency in charge of administering taxes in the Russian Federation throughout its three-tiered (federal, regional, local) organizational structure,[37] has still to undergo a fundamental reform to obtain the administrative capacity required for a market-based tax system.[38] During the Soviet era, its officials verified the arithmetical correctness of bank transfers from state enterprises, but were not involved in any assessment, collection, or enforcement of taxes.[39] Despite a staff of over 160,000 (which is per head of population more than twice the number at the US Inland Revenue Service) the STS does not have the capacity to cope with its responsibilities owing to problems in organization, inadequate processing capacity, lack of training, and inadequate remuneration. In particular, local tax offices lack functional specialization and receive little instruction on the implementation of new tax decrees. The desk reviews of tax returns by tax inspectors are staff-intensive and ineffective in detecting under-reporting, payments are processed mostly manually, and little effort is directed towards informing taxpayers about their obligations. Co-ordination between the STS and other agencies responsible for tax and customs administration, including the Ministry of Finance, State Customs Committee,[40] and the tax policy is inadequate.

5.5.1. *Policy failure*

Countries like the Czech Republic, Hungary, and Poland had introduced western style tax systems by 1993 to the benefit of their general economic

---

[37] Before November 1991 the STS was integrated in the Ministry of Finance, and tax officers were accountable to the finance department of both local and federal authorities. According to Wallich (1992, p. 26), the regional administration remained responsible for providing housing and fringe benefits to tax officers. The dual subordination gave rise to potential conflicts of interest. However, according to our own experience from interviews with tax officers in different regions during 1997, tax officers regard themselves as fully accountable to the federal government. See also RET (1997), 4, p. 17.

[38] Dmitriev (1996), p. 19.   [39] Hemming *et al.* (1996).

[40] The State Customs Committee (SCC) is the federal agency which collects taxes and custom duties related to cross-border trade. The receipts accrue fully to the federal government.

performance,[41] while Russia by the end of 1997 still found itself in an intermediate stage of the reform of the tax system.[42] The failure to adopt a coherent reform strategy is evident from the frequent changes in legislation. The tax system is governed by around 2,000 legislative acts, leaving wide scope for arbitrary enforcement by the tax authorities. *Ad hoc* amendments to tax legislation were not only on the whole unsuccessful but also had negative repercussions for taxpayer compliance.[43]

The perception of an unjust tax system, the collapse in the availability and quality of government services (itself aggravated by revenue shortfalls), repeated tax amnesties,[44] and the widespread non-payment of taxes were all detrimental to general tax discipline. Enterprises could plausibly blame the government for their failure to pay taxes. The government itself was a large debtor to the enterprise sector (about 3 per cent of GDP),[45] and government regulation forbade some enterprises to halt supplies in face of non-payment by customers. Gazprom, for instance, until summer 1997 was prevented from cutting gas supplies to 'strategic customers' in spite of their non-payment of bills. Localities often depend on the fortunes of very few companies.[46] The social and political costs of enforcing bankruptcy on such enterprises in case of non-payment of

[41] Budina and van Wijnbergen (1997).

[42] In July 1995 the government attempted to pass a new law on the general principles of taxation, but the draft was rejected by the Federation Council. Meanwhile the government incorporated the draft law into the general part of the new tax code which was under discussion in the Duma during 1997. In November 1997 the head of the budget committee of the Duma and critic of the tax code, M. Zadornov, was appointed Finance Minister. He dismissed the deputy Finance Minister and 'father of the tax code', S. Shatalov. The government declared its intention to implement tax reform piece-wise by introducing tax laws separately rather than in a single reform package.

[43] An important part of such counterproductive initiatives was the acceleration of non-cash revenue schemes after 1995. In the first scheme, treasury promissory notes (KOs) issued in 1994 could be purchased at a discount in the secondary market and returned to the government to settle tax obligations. A subsequent scheme involved the offsetting of budgetary commitments against tax arrears using tax offset certificates (KNOs). Another scheme involved the mutual offsetting of government arrears and enterprise tax arrears with the help of short-term bank credit. A presidential decree in November 1997 outlawed all such schemes.

[44] Tax amnesties penalize those who complied with tax laws in the past, and undermine tax compliance as enterprises gamble on further tax amnesties. A poorly designed presidential decree of January 1996, which offered firms rescheduling of tax arrears in return for prompt settlement henceforth of current tax liabilities, failed to reduce tax arrears. Another tax debt restructuring plan in March 1997 was only marginally more successful. See RET (1997), 2, p. 110; RET (1997), 4, p. 19. [45] RET (1997), 4, p. 16.

[46] Gavrilenkov and Kuboniba (1997), p. 265.

taxes are potentially huge.[47] In some cases where the federal government pressed for initiation of bankruptcy procedures, the companies were still bailed out by regional government. Such conflicts of interest between the regional and federal governments further limit the effectiveness of the Emergency Tax Commission, established in late 1996, to compel the largest tax debtors to settle their liabilities—a critical issue given that a few dozen enterprises account for about 40 per cent of all outstanding tax arrears.[48]

5.6. REVENUE ALLOCATION BETWEEN FEDERAL AND REGIONAL BUDGETS AND INTER-GOVERNMENTAL TRANSFERS

While federal, regional, and local governments have budgetary autonomy, revenue-raising activities are subject to various legal regulations. The law on the basic principle of taxation adopted in December 1991 provides an exclusive list of taxes and fees available to the three government tiers.[49] Where revenues from specific taxes are shared between the federal and regional governments, the proportions are determined in the federal budget law.[50] Shared taxes are VAT on domestic goods and services, non-energy excises, profits tax, and personal income tax. In case

[47] The difficulties of the regional tax authorities in enforcing consistent tax discipline are well illustrated by the case of Western Siberian Railway, which is together with AO Novosibirsk Energo the largest tax debtor and (potentially) largest tax payer in the region. Following the presidential decree on tax arrears rescheduling from January 1996, Western Siberian Railway agreed a ten-year restructuring schedule. After initial compliance it soon failed to keep up with the schedule, resulting in fines of over 100 billion roubles to the State tax service. Additionally, it merged with Kemorovo Railways, thereby sharply increasing its tax arrears. The financial situation of the company worsened further, as the Russian government decided under pressure from the IMF to lower regional transport prices nationwide. Attempts to revise the rescheduling scheme in light of the changed circumstances were unsuccessful, as the company asked for a three months's delay in the implementation of any new scheme. Given the monopoly position of Western Siberian Railway, the importance of its services for the regional economy, and the large federal debts to the company, the tax authorities were essentially powerless to exert any credible threat on the company. Closure of the company would not only cause further damage to the economy but would also be highly unpopular and not supported by politicians in the region.

[48] RET December (1997), Special report.

[49] Only taxes listed in the law may be levied. For example, Yaroslavl oblast introduced at the beginning of 1997 a regional sales tax. Since such a tax is not foreseen in the list of regional taxes, Yaroslavl subsequently had to cancel the tax.

[50] A system of pure tax assignments, each tax contributing solely to either federal or regional governments' revenue, was envisaged in the law of December 1991 but was never adopted.

of non-compliance with tax-sharing agreements by regions, the Centre can impose sanctions.[51]

Despite these constraints, the regional governments maintained wide-ranging independence over revenue collection. Regions used the threat of splitting from the Federation to extract tax concessions from the Centre. For example, Tatarstan and Bashkortostan benefit from 'single channel' agreements. They retain all revenues from taxes collected on their territory and transfer a fixed amount to the federal budget.[52] In addition the bottom-up system of tax collection enables regions to withhold revenues from the centre. Revenues are collected by the STS, transferred to the finance departments at local and regional levels and shared up with the federal level. All taxes are shared on a derivation basis, meaning that the revenue raised is shared with the jurisdiction in which it is collected. During 1993 some thirty regions decided to determine uni-laterally the tax shares to be transferred to the centre.[53] The federal shares in VAT and personal income tax were in 1994–96 systematically below the shares stipulated in the budget laws.[54] Finally, regions can circumvent legal constraints on the introduction of new taxes to fund regional budgets by raising contributions to their local extra-budgetary funds.[55]

Not surprisingly in these circumstances, the decline in overall rev-enues was accompanied by an increase in the relative revenue share of sub-national budgets. Between 1992 and 1994 the regions increased their share in consolidated government revenues from 47 per cent to 70 per cent, marking the peak of decentralization (Table 5.7). The fiscal revenue system was somewhat re-centralized in 1995: the federal income tax share was increased and the level of federal transfers reduced. Transfers rose again in 1996,[56] and the regions' own revenue share increased fur-ther.[57] As a percentage of GDP, total regional tax revenues in 1996 were close to their level of 1992, while federal tax revenues had declined by about one-third. The regions benefited from higher general transfers

---

[51] Article 30 of the Federal Budget Law lists the range of sanctions available: stopping all central budgetary expenditure and investments in the territory, withholding export and import licences, denying Central Bank credit to the local banks, halting material supply from the central supply system, and withholding cash or currency.

[52] Wallich (1992), p. 24; World Bank (1996a), p. 17.

[53] World Bank (1996a), p. 15.

[54] 60%, 72%, and 66% respectively, rather than the 75% stipulated in the budget laws.

[55] World Bank (1996a), p. 15.

[56] This IMF statistic is not reflected in the Ministry of Finance figures, which show a constant level of federal transfers between 1995 and 1996.

[57] Regions' own revenues are defined as total revenues minus federal transfers and rev-enues from shared taxes.

Table 5.7. *Allocation of revenues*

	1992	1993	1994	1995	1996
% of GDP					
Federal revenues	16.7	13.7	11.8	12.1	11.9
Regional revenues	13.5	16.7	18.0	14.2	14.5
% of consolidated revenues[a]					
Federal	58.2	49.3	45.9	48.9	50.0
Regional	47.3	60.0	70.1	57.2	61.2
% of federal revenues					
Federal shared taxes[b]	71.9	57.0	57.9	32.5	34.0
Federal own revenues	28.1	43.0	42.1	67.5	66.0
% of regional revenues					
Regional shared taxes[b]	73.1	72.4	57.9	64.2	49.8
Federal transfers	11.5	15.4	22.8	10.7	18.4
Regional own revenues	15.4	12.2	19.3	25.1	31.8

Notes: [a] The shares of federal and regional revenues in consolidated revenues add up to more than 100% because federal transfers are included in both federal and local revenues.
[b] Shared taxes are VAT on domestic goods, non-energy excises, profits, and income taxes.
Source: Ministry of Finance, Moscow, Russia.

from changes in the sharing arrangement for VAT and profits tax after 1992 (even though the subsequent fall in profits tax revenues wiped out a large share of these gains) and from enhanced receipts of property taxes, and hotel or road taxes, which offset the reduction in revenues from shared taxes.

The substantial variation in the regional revenue share after 1992 indicates that the revenue allocation system was in a state of flux. The changes were only loosely related to modifications of expenditure responsibilities among government levels, signifying lack of a coherent approach towards designing the system of fiscal federalism. *De facto*, Russia moved more and more to a system of tax assignment, as each level's own revenue sources declined by less than the shared taxes.

Since there is a trade-off between raising revenues and reducing fiscal inequalities,[58] the tax allocation system has to be judged on whether it achieves an appropriate balance between the two objectives.[59] The Russian system has had ambiguous incentive effects on tax collection, yet fostered marked fiscal inequalities.

[58] Musgrave (1961).   [59] Shah (1994), p. 43.

The derivation system provides incentives to regions to improve tax collection, as each region benefits from the taxes collected in its own area. On the other hand, some revenues from the main taxes are shared with the federal government, which reduces the regions' incentive to collect these taxes.[60] In addition, the profits tax base is thought to be highly mobile across localities, which lowers the tax collection effort of regional authorities,[61] as does the design of the federal transfer system explained below.

As regards inequalities, the vast variation in resource endowments and population density, together with the Soviet legacy of economic specialization, gave rise to large economic inequalities among regions, once the transition process was under way.[62] There are corresponding differences in regional tax bases and revenue yields.

Property and natural resource taxes in particular,[63] whose tax bases differ more than those of other taxes, became more important for regional finances.

5.6.1. *Intergovernmental transfers*

In view of Russia's federal constitution, and the wide disparities of income and taxable capacity across regions, inter-governmental transfers could play an important equalising role. From an economic point of view, the standard objective is welfare equalization among individuals, not among regions. However, federal transfers to regions can be justified as a second-best solution in case effective inter-individual equalization mechanisms do not exist.[64] Furthermore, transfers to regions may be desired if the in-kind redistribution through health, education, and social services, as provided by the regions, is preferred to in-cash redistribution.[65] Indeed, most Federations have large federal transfer programmes, with federal transfers ranging from 4 per cent to 8 per cent of GDP in Germany, the USA, and Canada.[66] Federal transfers can

---

[60] Bahl (1994) finds no significant relationship in Russia between an index of tax effort and regional tax shares.

[61] Some regions waive parts of the regional tax burden for new investments, partly in response to tax competition from other regions.

[62] The coefficient of variation (i.e. the standard deviation normalized by the mean) of regional per capita GDP was 210% in 1994. See the chapter by Hanson in this volume.

[63] In 1996 property taxes accrued fully, and natural resource taxes about 80%, to regions.

[64] Musgrave (1971), p. 38.   [65] Shah (1994), p. 28.   [66] Ibid., pp. 36–7.

also support specific economic policies of sub-national governments, or subsidize regional programmes with benefits beyond the regional jurisdiction.[67]

The federal government provides transfers to the regions in various forms (subsidies to the far north, etc., short-term loans, mutual settlements, subventions, and transfers of the federal fund for financial support)[68] (Table 5.8). Until 1994 transfers were negotiated *ad hoc*. In July 1994 the government attempted to introduce a transparent, formula-based system by creating a unified federal Fund for Financial Support of the Territories (FFST).

Transfers are allocated according to the following procedure. The expenditure needs of regions are derived from regional budget expenses in 1991, reduced by capital expenditures, indexed for the growth in wage payments and material expenses, and corrected for additional spending functions due to changes in federal mandates in areas such as housing, child benefits, and police maintenance. Revenues are estimated from actual revenues in the previous year, adjusted for inflation and changes in tax legislation. Regions are divided into three groups according to economic and geographical criteria, which supposedly place regions with similar expenditure needs into the same group. Transfers are handed out through two windows. 'Needy' regions receive transfers if regional per capita revenues are less than 95 per cent of national per capita revenues. The transfers to a region are proportional to current expenditures, and are calculated starting from the difference between the region's per capita revenue RR and 95 per cent of the national average per capita revenue R. This difference is adjusted for the amount by which the average per capita expenditure EG in the region's group exceeds the national average per capita revenue R. EG is

---

[67] Federal transfers are sometimes justified as compensation for non-matching revenue-capacities and expenditure responsibilities between government levels (vertical imbalances) as opposed to horizontal—inter-regional—ones. However, as emphasized in Shah (1994, pp. 28–9), vertical fiscal imbalances should be addressed by a restructuring of the tax assignment system, unless the threat of regional tax competition is overriding, or administrative reasons favour a centralized tax collection system.

[68] Subsidies are granted to cities or areas in order to compensate for specific expenditure needs. Short-term loans are typically interest-free credits to guarantee the financing of 'protected' items in regional budgets at times of temporary revenue shortfalls. While these credits are supposed to be repaid within a year, they are often written off and included in mutual settlements. The latter refer mostly to transfers granted to cover expenses arising out of the implementation of presidential or governmental decrees. Subventions are general transfers, intended to reduce fiscal imbalances across regions.

Table 5.8. *Federal transfers (% of GDP)*

	1992	1993	1994	1995	1996
Federal transfers	1.6	2.5	3.5	2.1	2.1
Subventions	0.7	0.7	0.4	0.2	0.2
Equalization fund			0.4	1.2	1
Mutual settlements	0.8	1.8	2.7	0.7	0.8

Note: Subsidies and short-term loans are not included.
Source: Ministry of Finance, Moscow, Russia.

the expenditure net of capital investment. Thus the formula is

$$TN = (0.95^*R - RR)^*(0.95^*EG/R).$$

The total transfer to the needy region is the per capita transfer TN multiplied by the population of the region. 'Very needy' regions obtain additional transfers to cover any shortfall of revenues (including transfers received through the first window) to finance current expenditures. Finally, transfer entitlements are adjusted to bring them in line with the total resources available to the FFST. Since 1996 the equalization fund has been funded through 15 per cent of federal budget revenues, excluding the federal share of personal income tax and import duties.

In spite of the 1994 reform the transfer system has continued to suffer from a range of defects. It has at best been ineffective in reducing fiscal inequalities among regions,[69] partly because of the relatively low volume of federal transfers and partly due to insufficient targeting of transfers on poor regions. Regional tax effort was discouraged. Basing revenue predictions on actual budget receipts of a previous year reduces the longer term payoffs to regions from increasing their own tax collection. Also, regions had no incentives to eliminate extra-budgetary funds. Subsidies and short-term credits were given without conditionality.[70] They tended to preserve current expenditure patterns, and were not used in systematic fashion to promote national policy priorities.[71] Non-transparent forms

[69] The coefficient of variations of pre- and post-transfer regional revenues are almost equal between 1992 and 1995, even though transfers became more equalizing over the period. See Bogacheva (1996), pp. 80–1, Freinkman and Haney (1997), p. 11; Le Houerou and Rutkowski (1996), pp. 39–41; and Treisman (1996).

[70] As a first measure towards adopting a system of conditional transfers, the federal government introduced in 1997 targeted matching grants to those regions which implement systems of child allowances and social assistance following federal rules.

[71] Freinkman and Haney (1997, p. 23) argue that the federal government could successfully promote regional housing reforms. They find econometric evidence for the influence of federal transfers on regional spending on housing.

of transfers, such as mutual settlements, remained important. They appeared to be granted in discretionary fashion, raising suspicion of federal favouritism *vis-à-vis* some regions.[72] Transfer arrears were common. Regions received often a large share of their cash revenues through federal transfers.[73] Non-payment or delayed payment until the end of the year of these transfers led to the accumulation of regional government arrears to workers and enterprises.

Finally, the FFST has some flaws of its own. The grouping procedure appears too coarse to account for the large variety of fiscal situations in the regions. The calculation procedures for the FFST transfers are difficult to understand, and seem to give substantial leeway to the Ministry of Finance to fix the final sums arbitrarily. The expenditure pattern in 1991 had little relevance for subsequent expenditure needs. Finally, the transfer formula for both windows compensates for current but not for capital expenditures, and therefore biases regional expenditure patterns.

5.7. EXPENDITURE DYNAMICS

The persistent decline in revenues after 1990 imposed pressure to reduce government expenditures. Non-interest spending declined between 1992 and 1996 by almost 11 per cent of GDP. Expenditures were reduced under the headings of national economy (enterprise support programmes and investment), defence, net lending (mainly subsidies to the northern regions, agriculture, and industry), transfers to the regions, and other expenditures. The savings were partly offset by higher spending on social programmes, administration, and law and order. Most importantly, government debt servicing rose by over 3.5 per cent of GDP, because of real interest rate increases (Table 5.9). The expenditure reduction was in line with the shift of activities from the government to the private sector, and with reduced defence needs after the end of the Cold War. Yet the expenditure adjustments were *ad hoc*, resulted in underfunding of some important expenditure items,[74]

---

[72] Treisman (1996).

[73] Transfer arrears allowed the federal government to put pressure on sub-national governments. Regions were rewarded for opportune behaviour through the settling of transfer arrears.

[74] The World Bank developed an adjustment scenario on the basis of data from mid-1995. It suggested for 1996 revenues of 36% of GDP, and non-interest expenditures of 39.5% of GDP. The actual figures were 30.9 and 34.0% of GDP. See World Bank (1996*b*), p. 87.

Table 5.9. *Budgetary operation of the consolidated government (% of GDP)*

	1992	1993	1994	1995	1996
Total expenditure	37.5	33.6	36.6	30.6	31.9
Expenditure excluding debt service	37.0	31.6	34.6	27.3	26.3
1. National economy	11.1	9.5	10.4	8.3	6.4
1.1. Industry etc.[a]	n.a.	n.a.	6.2	4.3	2.4
1.2. Housing	n.a.	n.a.	4.2	4.1	4.0
2. Social programmes	7.7	8.6	9.1	8.0	8.5
2.1. Education	3.4	4.0	4.5	3.5	3.7
2.2. Health	2.7	3.1	3.2	2.6	2.7
2.3. Culture and mass media	0.8	0.6	0.8	0.6	0.5
2.4. Social policy	0.8	0.9	0.6	1.3	1.6
3. Administration and other functions	6.7	7.1	9.3	6.9	6.4
3.1. Administration, science and international activity	0.9	1.4	2.9	2.4	1.9
3.2. Law and order	1.1	1.5	1.8	1.6	1.7
3.3. Defence	4.7	4.1	4.6	2.9	2.8
4. Lending	3.9	2.2	2.8	1.8	1.0
5. Other expenditure	7.4	4.2	3.1	2.2	4.0
Government debt service	0.5	2.0	2.0	3.4	5.6

Note: [a]Industry, energy and construction, agriculture and fishing, transportation, and communication.

Source: Ministry of Finance, Moscow, Russia.

and failed to achieve a systematic restructuring of government outlays.[75]

The large government bureaucracy inherited from the Soviet era was further expanded during the transition period. In October 1995 Russia had seventy-three federal ministries, state committees and services, employing some 30,000 people. The president's office alone had a staff of 5,000 officials. Federal agencies in the regions employed 364,000

[75] These features are typical across the FSU countries. See Cheasty and Davis (1996), pp. 18–29.

Table 5.10. *Social spending of the general government sector (% of GDP)*

	1992	1993	1994	1995	1996
Budgetary programmes	7.7	8.6	9.1	8.0	8.5
Education	3.4	4.0	4.5	3.5	3.7
Health	2.7	3.1	3.2	2.6	2.7
Culture and mass media	0.8	0.6	0.8	0.6	0.5
Social policy	0.8	0.9	0.6	1.3	1.6
Extra-budgetary programmes	8.3	8.0	8.6	7.6	7.7
Total social spending	16.1	16.6	17.6	15.6	16.2

Source: Ministry of Finance, Moscow, Russia.

individuals, double the number for the USSR in 1990.[76] The resultant higher spending on administration as a percentage of GDP[77] did not improve the calibre of the bureaucracy. Staff face little competition in hiring and promotion, are inadequately trained, lack basic material equipment, and are susceptible to corruption.

In addition, Russia's public infrastructure and capital stock, already of poor quality at the beginning of transition,[78] decayed further after 1992, as government capital spending was successively reduced. Many infrastructure projects provide high social returns but can be carried out only to a limited degree by the private sector and are subject to deferral in the face of the public spending constraints.[79]

Spending on social programmes has remained roughly constant as a percentage of GDP since 1992 (Table 5.10).[80] While its resilience may seem surprising given the tight fiscal situation, budgetary spending on social protection was expected to increase during the transition process.[81] During Soviet times the government achieved redistribution mainly

[76] Sakwa (1996), pp. 154–5. It is difficult to draw international comparisons on the level of employment because the functions performed by federal agencies differ widely across countries. Nevertheless, it is illustrative that total employment in public administration in the more advanced transition countries, Poland, Hungary, and Czech Republic, remained constant over the same period, see European Commission (1995).

[77] World Bank (1996b), p. 23.   [78] Easterly and Fischer (1995).

[79] According to IMF estimates, capital expenditure by the federal government in 1996 fell to about 1.5% of GDP.

[80] Spending by the general government on social programmes remained constant between 1992 and 1996 at around 16% of GDP.

[81] Cheasty and Davis (1996), pp. 10–11.

through direct regulation, like the guarantee of full employment in the state sector, and control over food and energy prices. With the liberalization of prices, such interventions had to be done through the budget. Furthermore, divestiture of social assets, such as kindergartens, hospitals, and housing facilities, from enterprises to governments was an important element in promoting the restructuring of enterprises.[82] The process is by no means completed. The share of social benefits in the total wage bill in 1996 was estimated to be more than 20 per cent, compared to 10 per cent in eastern Europe and advanced western economies.[83] Even if the ultimate objective was the comprehensive privatization of such services, immediate implementation was considered politically and socially unacceptable.[84] Finally, the social safety net had to be extended for the unemployed.[85]

In view of the greater role for social spending by government in post-Communist society, and the unexpectedly large social costs of the transition process, spending on social programmes has been inadequate and inefficient, despite the relative stability of its overall level. The inherited health and education systems relied on provision of excessive physical capacity and employment, much of which were inefficiently used. Furthermore, employment levels tended to increase at the expense of outlays on maintenance and materials, such as medicine and textbook procurement, which were already at depressed levels due to sharp price rises.[86] The social safety net is neither cost-effective nor comprehensive. Some of the most needy do not receive any, or insufficient, benefits.[87] Targeted cash transfers play a small role in the social safety net, while non-targeted consumer subsidies, in particular for housing and public utilities, remain high.[88]

---

[82] State enterprises had been regarded not simply as producers of goods, but rather as a focus for the socialization of citizens. More trivially, linking social benefits to employment in state enterprises and state agencies ensured political loyalty. See Milanovic (1995), pp. 2–3.

[83] Commander and Schankermann (1997); IMF (1997).

[84] Freinkman and Starodubrovskaya (1996), p. 2.

[85] Rutkowski (1995), pp. 21–6.

[86] See Horton (1996), p. 4. Also IMF (1996); World Bank (1996b), p. 22.

[87] See Klugman and Marnie in this volume.

[88] As argued in Cheasty and Davis (1996, p. 27), the high levels of housing and household energy subsidies had adverse consequences at the macroeconomic level. They slowed down housing privatization and the development of a housing market, which in turn hindered labour mobility and sectoral adjustment. Low receipts from the household sector caused utility companies to accumulate arrears to other enterprises and the government. See Starodubrovskaya in this volume.

5.7.1. *The budgetary process and expenditure adjustments*

Idiosyncratic institutional arrangements governing the budgetary process have been important in impeding the structural transformation of government spending.[89]

Major areas of expenditure remain outside the political budget process. Outlays by extra budgetary funds amounted in 1996–7 to about 8 per cent of GDP or 20 per cent of general government expenditures. Social extra-budgetary funds are financed mainly through earmarked payroll taxes. In 1996 the combined payroll tax rate was 39 per cent, of which 29 per cent was allocated to the pension fund, 5.4 per cent to the social insurance fund, 1.5 per cent to the employment fund, and the remainder to federal and regional medical insurance funds. The largest fund is the pension fund. At the end of 1996 some 38 million individuals were entitled to payments from the fund, including 29 million old-age pensioners, 3.8 million disability pensioners, and 1.1 million social pensioners. The replacement rate (ratio of the average pension to the average wage) in 1994–6 was in the range 35–8 per cent. Arrears accumulated on pension payments after 1995 (and amounting to more than 2 per cent of GDP) were settled in July 1997.

Extra-budgetary funds are subject to little scrutiny by parliament, even though they have direct implications for government finance. While it is common practice to have social insurance funds outside the normal budgeting process, regular reporting to parliament would not only increase accountability but would also boost the transparency of all branches of government activity. Surpluses in the balance of extra-budgetary funds were routinely absorbed by the federal budget, while more recently (in 1997) federal government borrowing was increased in order to eliminate the payment arrears of these funds.

Before 1995 the budget classification system was not in line with the internationally accepted functional classification. Data on the economic classification of government spending were still lacking in 1997. The macroeconomic parameters underlying government spending projections were usually *ad hoc* and over-optimistic. Projections of budgetary expenditure levels on the basis of unrealistically low inflation estimates, as in the federal budget in 1995, was one unorthodox way to control the budget deficit. While cash spending commitments were fulfilled, real expenditures were kept below expected levels. The federal government

---

[89] For a thorough discussion of these aspects, see World Bank (1996*a*), chs. 3–5.

introduced medium-run macroeconomic and fiscal forecasts as part of the presentation of the 1997 budget.

Conflicting legislation on government expenditure commitments compounded the problem caused by unrealistic budgeting. The Duma routinely passed laws which increased government spending obligations beyond the figures stipulated in the Budget Law. Examples include increases in social benefits and the minimum wage and compensation for holders of accounts in Sberbank (the government saving bank) for losses incurred during the rapid inflation in 1992. While the Budget Law overrides any other legislation with financial implications, it caused confusion about the actual entitlements and increased the distrust of the public in government.[90]

The federal Budget Law is drafted by the Ministry of Finance, approved by the Duma and the Federation council, and signed by the president. The adoption procedures provide ample scope for significant delays in case of disagreements between the executive and the legislature, which throughout the transition period was dominated by the opposition. As a result, the 1996 budget was the only one passed in time for the start of the new fiscal year.[91]

Faced with revenues below target, the government resorted to sequestration and cash budgeting in order to contain the size of the budget deficit. According to official statistics, government arrears of wage payments, settling of state orders, and pension payments amounted to about 2 per cent of GDP in 1996.

The lack of a fully developed treasury system implied that the Ministry of Finance lacked full control over all stages of the spending process (commitment, verification, and payment). This invited misuse of budgetary funds at both federal and local level. Sequestration and weak control over spending by government agencies added to the arrears problem in the economy as a whole, and had a destructive effect on tax discipline. The government's failure to pay enterprises made it impossible for some of them to pay their workers and suppliers, and to settle tax liabilities, which in turn worsened the revenue crisis. For other enterprises, it offered a convenient pretext to run up wage and tax arrears and to put the blame on the government.

[90] Cheasty and Davis (1996), p. 20.

[91] The 1996 budget was passed by the Duma in December 1995. The annual budget for 1993 became law only after the dissolution of the Supreme Soviet in September 1993. The 1994 budget was adopted in June 1994, the 1995 budget in March 1995, and the 1997 budget in February 1997. The 1998 budget was adopted in March 1998.

Sequestration put strain on relationships between the federal government and regions. In 1996 federal transfers fell 15 per cent short of the level stipulated in the Budget Law, and most of them were paid out only at the end of the year. In anticipation of delayed and reduced transfer payments, regions withheld tax revenues from the federal government, emphasizing the dilution of federal government control. Similarly, government spending agencies reacted to sequestration by building up precautionary balances to ensure the financing of their top-priority programmes which might later fail to obtain funding. The federal government took measures to stop such erosion of central control over government expenditures. In January 1997 the treasury within the Ministry of Finance began processing the expenditures of all agencies except the defence and interior ministries. The funds of the defence ministry came under treasury control in January 1998.[92]

Auditing of government spending is still not an integral part of the budget process.[93] The government only started in the later 1990s to conduct strategic reviews of public expenditures, based on an evaluation of the economic impact of government spending.[94] Government investments, mostly undertaken as transfers to the production sector, are made without any cost-benefit analysis.[95] Projects are started without identified financing for the expected lifetime of the project.

Weak budgetary procedures offered advantages both to politicians and the administration. The government ensured the adoption of the budget by parliament without endangering the fiscal consolidation programme. Parliament voted in favour of large spending programmes, and later put the blame on the government for violating the Budget Law. The administration gained influence because bureaucrats in the Ministry of Finance, rather than members of the Duma, determined the actual spending pattern. Yet the social and political cost of sequestration, under-budgeting, and lack of coherent spending control was considerable. The resurgence of the Communist vote in the parliamentary election in December 1995 and the strong backing for the Communist candidate, G. Zyuganov, in

---

[92] See Cheasty and Davis (1996), p. 22.

[93] The creation of the Accounts Chamber with accountability exclusively to the Duma in January 1995 was an important improvement.

[94] The government developed a restructuring plan for the coal industry with the financial and technical support of the World Bank. In 1997 it launched an initiative to reduce housing subsidies, and announced plans for military reform. See RET (1997), 4, p. 14.

[95] On the case of agriculture, see Galbi (1995).

the presidential elections in June–July 1996 were widely interpreted as one consequence.[96]

The new budget code adopted in December 1996 addressed some of the deficiencies. It incorporated the various pieces of legislation regulating the budgetary process into one law, improving transparency and consistency. It shifted responsibility for the administrative aspects of execution of the budget from the Ministry of Finance to the treasury, depoliticizing the process of implementation. And it limited the discretionary powers of the Ministry of Finance. In case of a revenue shortfall of more than 10 per cent compared to projections in the Budget Law, the Budget Law had to be amended by the legislature, as promptly happened during 1997.

5.8. EXPENDITURE DISTRIBUTION BETWEEN THE FEDERAL AND REGIONAL BUDGETS

At the outset of the reforms, Russia inherited the Soviet spending structure across the different layers of government.[97] As shown in Table 5.11, around one-third of all consolidated expenditures was undertaken at sub-national level. The expenditure assignment was roughly in line with the benefit-area principle, which states that expenditure responsibilities should be determined by the geographical distribution of benefits from these expenditures. The decentralization at the first stage of the economic reform process resulted in further downward shifting of expenditure items. Despite a sharp contraction in federal transfers after 1994, the regional share in non-interest expenditures continued to increase in 1995–6, because the federal government cut down its own expenditures even more. By 1996 the share of regional and local budgets in consolidated non-interest expenditures had increased to over one-half. About 75 per cent of spending on industry, agriculture, and other production activities, and over 80 per cent of that on social programmes, were at sub-national levels.

Decentralization of government spending was facilitated by the fact that expenditure responsibilities of the different government levels were not prescribed by law. The federal government was thus able 'unilaterally' to unburden itself of expenditures without violating any expenditure

---

[96] Cheasty and Davis (1996), p. 21; Sakwa (1996), p. 112.
[97] The federal government took on expenditure responsibilities formerly assigned to the Union level. See Wallich (1992), p. 37.

Table 5.11. *Regional expenditure as a percentage of consolidated expenditure*

	1992	1993	1994	1995	1996
Expenditure	32.1	47.7	47.8	47.4	46.0
Expenditure excluding *debt sevice*	32.5	50.7	50.5	53.2	55.9
1. National economy	47.6	72.5	71.2	75.2	75.4
1.1. Industry etc[a]	n.a.	n.a.	72.7	53.5	35.8
1.2. Housing	n.a.	n.a.	98.5	98.0	97.8
2. Social programmes	66.0	83.8	81.1	83.8	83.5
2.1. Education	69.2	81.2	80.0	84.9	86.4
2.2. Health	80.6	90.6	88.4	86.3	86.3
2.3. Culture and mass media	36.2	70.2	63.7	71.4	80.7
2.4. Social Policy	33.3	81.0	71.1	81.8	73.1
3. Administration and other functions	6.1	8.8	6.6	13.1	13.6
3.1. Administration, science and intern act	40.3	35.1	20.0	20.1	24.6
3.2. Law and order	2.4	4.4	1.4	26.7	24.1
3.3. Defence	0.0	0.0	0.0	0.0	0.0
4. Government debt service	0.0	0.0	0.0	0.0	0.0
5. Lending	4.8	17.0	17.9	22.7	14.3
6. Other expenditure	14.3	21.7	52.9	9.4	44.4

Note: [a]Industry, energy and construction, agriculture and fishing, tranportation and communication.

Source: Ministry of Finance, Moscow, Russia.

code.[98] In addition, legal arrangements specified by the federal government over enterprise privatization meant that social assets from enterprises were transferred mostly to local governments.[99]

[98] In 1992 financing responsibility for most social expenditures, including consumer price subsidies and income maintenance programmes, was transferred to the sub-national level. The expenditures were previously administered by oblasts, but financed with transfers from the federal government amounting to about 5% of GDP. Additionally, the financing and implementation of major national investment projects were shifted downwards from the federal level. In 1994 sub-national governments became responsible for financing vocational technical schools. See World Bank (1996a), p. 23.

[99] According to estimates by Freinkman and Starodubrovskaya (1996, p. 24), the associated fiscal burden on local budgets will amount to 2% of GDP, some 60% of the level reported by enterprises according to official statistics.

While the economic literature typically emphasizes the advantages of decision-taking at lower levels,[100] most economists argue that Russia's decentralization was harmful both to equity and efficiency objectives.[101] Equity concerns originate from mismatches between regional revenue yields and expenditure needs. The big differences in regional revenues implied corresponding variations in the provision of public services and protection of the needy.[102] Following the trend in regional revenues, the disparities have grown over time.[103] Regions with large social and infrastructure needs tended to have insufficient financing, while affluent regions faced little pressure to cut down on wasteful projects.[104] The mismatch contributed to the sharp rise in regional inequality observed since 1991, and the lack of convergence in economic performance across regions.[105] The variation in regional incomes compounds the ineffectiveness of regional-level redistribution mechanisms to achieve equity objectives.

As regards efficiency of public services, decentralization may in principle help in a number of ways.[106] Since regional politicians are accountable to their constituencies, the selection of public programmes should be tailored more towards regional demand.[107] 'Voting with one's feet', or migration of dissatisfied citizens into other jurisdictions, can bring public spending further into line with public preferences. Regions can use their superior knowledge of the local economy to extract an

---

[100]   Boadway *et al.* (1994), p. 61, World Development Report (1997), p. 110.

[101]   Lavrov (1996); World Bank (1996*a*), pp. 31–2; World Development Report (1996), p. 126.

[102]   Expenditures on social programmes were less variable than spending on the national economy, since social spending items were more protected against changes in regional budget finances. See Freinkman and Haney (1997); Rutkowski (1996); and Stewart (1996).

[103]   The coefficient of variation of regional per capita expenditures increased from 1992 to 1996 by 55%.

[104]   Richer regions spend more on social and national economy programmes. The correlation coefficients of per capita regional GDP and per capita spending on social programmes and national economy came to 0.50 and 0.54, respectively, during 1994–5. Regions tended to absorb federal transfers through expenditure increases rather than to pass them on to their constituents via tax cuts, regardless of their fiscal situation. The phenomena, found in most federations, is known in the fiscal federalism literature as tax 'flypaper effect'. See Oates (1990), pp. 49–50.

[105]   Hanson in this volume; and Richter (1997).

[106]   Efficiency arguments also indicate possible disadvantages of decentralization arising from economies of scale and regional spillover.

[107]   Musgrave (1958), pp. 3–4.

information rent when implementing public programmes.[108] Finally, competition among governments can be a source of innovation and stimulate reform.[109] However, political and economic conditions in Russia have hitherto limited the relevance of such arguments. Most heads of regional administrations lacked any democratic legitimization, beyond being directly appointed by President Yeltsin.[110] The reform of public administration at regional level proceeded even more slowly than at federal level. Capacity for sound budgetary management remains underdeveloped. At the same time migration has been severely constrained by the lack of housing and real estate markets.[111] Not surprisingly, regional self-determination resulted in wide variations in economic policies across regions rather than a uniform promotion of reformist policies. Some regions, like Nizhny Novgorod or Tomsk, quickly adopted market-based policies, while others, like the agrarian regions of the Communist red belt, used their autonomy to curtail economic transformation.[112] Regions used their autonomy to protect vested interests, and to resist unpopular reforms (for example, housing subsidies) demanded by the federal government. This, of course, hampered fiscal consolidation of the government sector as a whole.

The potential benefits of decentralization may, however, become more tangible in the future. A series of local and regional elections from 1996 onwards boosted the accountability of local politicians.[113] The tight fiscal situation forced many regions to cut inefficient spending. Finally, the need to raise capital from investors in Moscow and abroad puts pressure on regions to adopt more transparent budgetary practices and remove impediments to entrepreneurial activity.

5.9. CONCLUSION

After six years of transition, Russia's economy and government sector have changed beyond recognition compared to the Soviet era. Yet, while

---

[108] The literature is reviewed in Gilbert (1996, pp. 349–50).

[109] The literature is reviewed in Favardin (1996).

[110] Sakwa (1996), pp. 220–3.

[111] Analysing internal migration in Russia, Brown (1996) finds evidence that immigration flows depend positively on apartment privatization.

[112] The variety of economic and political conditions in regions is described in Lavrov (1997).

[113] Warner (1996) uncovers econometric evidence that regional governments pursuing reform-oriented policies perform well in elections. See Aslund *et al.* (1996) for similar results from a cross-transition-country analysis.

economic reforms proceeded quickly in some areas, such as the privatization of state enterprises or price liberalization, progress in fiscal reforms was slow, despite the transformation in the economic role of government. The most important achievement was the fiscal consolidation. Once the CBR stopped providing direct credits, government spending had to be brought more into line with revenues. The persistent decline in revenues required repeated downscaling of government expenditures in order to contain the budget deficit. Tight finances accelerated the contraction of wasteful expenditures, such as enterprise, but absence of centralized control over government spending made it difficult to impose fiscal discipline. Revenue projections in budgetary legislation lacked realism, and, fiscal consolidation therefore, came at the cost of *ad hoc* sequestration and government arrears.

Crisis management of a fiscal system unsuited to an emerging market economy became the government's chief preoccupation, rather than wide-ranging fiscal reform. The introduction of a new tax code, on the political agenda from summer 1995 onwards, had still not been achieved by the spring of 1998. The adoption of a fully fledged treasury system, which should enable the Ministry of Finance to exert proper control over the spending process of the federal government, was itself completed only in 1998. Structural reviews of expenditure items such as education, health, housing, administration, and defence were begun in 1996–7, but had little immediate impact on actual spending patterns.

The revenue shortfall also had implications for the relationship between the Centre and regional governments, which gained budgetary autonomy in the new federation. The federal authorities shed expenditure obligations by transferring spending programmes to lower level governments. The decline in tax revenues from shared taxes, together with the reduction in federal transfers to the regions after 1994, resulted in growing financial independence of sub-national governments, which had to rely increasingly on its own revenue sources. The federal government was unable to enforce a uniform tax allocation system across the federation, as some regions were granted special fiscal arrangements.

The fiscal difficulties had detrimental effects on the economy, delaying financial stabilization, crowding out private investment through high interest rates, and exposing the economy to risks of withdrawal of foreign capital. High tax rates distorted incentives, encouraged a large shadow economy, and had a regressive impact on income distribution. Revenue shortfalls undermined the government's ability to maintain the public infrastructure, or to respond effectively to the deterioration in health, education, and other social indicators. The degree of decentralization of the government sector resulted in large differences in the provision of public services across regions, compounding inequalities in regional living standards and slowing down the overall fiscal consolidation process.

For all these negative impacts of slow fiscal reform, faster progress may well have been impossible given the dire economic situation at the beginning of the reform process, and the new political environment of post-Communist Russia. Reform-oriented politicians faced strong internal opposition within both the government and its bureaucracy, had to overcome resistance from the legislature, and needed to ensure success in parliamentary and presidential elections. The fiscal decentralization was unavoidable given the demands by regions for greater autonomy, and the imposition of uniform fiscal rules across all regions was unattainable because of the ethno-federal legacy from the Soviet era. In view of these constraints, the consistent commitment to economic and fiscal reforms throughout the transition process, the fiscal consolidation and the progress across a range of fiscal reforms after the middle of the decade, including the settlement of pension arrears, can be considered a major achievement and contributed significantly to the preservation of Russia as a federation (aside from the serious exception of Checheniya).

What are the prospects for government sector reforms in the future? In the short term government spending will continue to be primarily a reflection of the authorities' ability to raise revenues and find cheap sources of deficit financing. Until the revenue decline is halted, the government will have no choice but to continue cutting expenditure. In the medium run further fiscal reforms will remain a priority. The government should focus on securing basic public goods, notably macroeconomic stability, property rights, law and order, public health, and protection of the poor. Only when the public sector has learned to use its resources effectively, and the population has regained trust in the state administration, can a widening of government activity, if desired by the electorate, be justifiable. Visible progress in these areas will remove a lingering threat to Russia's economic and political cohesion.

REFERENCES

Aslund, A. (1995). *How Russia Became a Market Economy*, Washington, DC: The Brookings Institution.

Aslund, A., Boone, P., and Johnson, S. (1996). *How to Stabilise: Lessons from Post-Communist Countries*, Brookings Papers on Economic Activity, 1: 217–313.

Bahl, R. (1994). *Revenues and Revenue Assignment: Intergovernmental Fiscal Relations in the Russian Federation*, in C. Wallich (ed.), *Russia and the Challenge of Fiscal Federalism*, Washington, D.C.: The World Bank.

—— and Wallich, C. (1994). *Intergovernmental Fiscal Relations in the Russian Federation*, in C. Wallich (ed.), *Russia and the Challenge of Fiscal Federalism*, Washington, DC: The World Bank, pp. 321–79.

Barbone, L., and Polackova H. (1996). *Public Finances and Economic Transition*, World Bank Policy Research Working Paper 1585.

Blanchard, O., Boycko, M., Dabrowski, M., Dornbusch, R., Layard, R., and Shleifer, A. (1993). *Post-Communist reform—Pain and Progress*, Cambridge, Mass.: MIT Press.

Boadway, R., Roberts, S., and Shah, A. (1994). *The Reform of Fiscal Systems in Developing and Emerging Market Economies*, World Bank Policy Research Working Paper 1259.

Bogacheva, O. (1996). *Forming the Russian Model of Fiscal Federalism*, *Problems of Economic Transition*, 39/1: 69–82.

Boycko, M., Shleifer, A., and Vishny, R. (1995). *Privatising Russia*, Cambridge, Mass.: MIT Press.

Brown, A. (1996). 'The Economic Determinants of Internal Migration in Russia During Transition', Western Michigan University, mimeo.

Budina, N., and van Wijnbergen, S. (1997). 'Fiscal Policies in Eastern Europe', *Oxford Review of Economic Policy*, 13: 47–64.

Cheasty, A., and Davis, J. (1996). *Fiscal Transition in Countries of the Former Soviet Union: An Interim Assessment*, IMF Working Paper 96/61.

Commander, S., and Mummsen, C. (1999). *Understanding Barter in Russia*, EBRD Working Paper 37.

—— and Schankermann, M. (1997). 'Enterprise Restructuring and Social Benefits', *Economics of Transition*, 5/1: 1–24.

—— Tolstopiatenko, A., and Yemtsov, R. (1997). 'Channels of Redistribution: *Inequality and Poverty in Russian Transition*', World Bank, mimeo.

Coricelli, F. (1996). *Fiscal Constraints, Reform Strategies, and the Speed of Transition: The Case of Central-Eastern Europe*, Centre for Economic Policy Research Discussion Paper 1339, London.

Cornia, G. (1996). *Labour Market Shocks, Psychological Stress and the Transition's Mortality Crisis*, Research in Progress, 4, Helsinki.

De Melo, M., Denizer, C., and Gelb, A. (1996): *From Plan to Market: Patterns of Transition*, World Bank Economic Review, 10/3: 397–424.

Dmitriev, M. (1996). 'Russian Reforms and State Revenue Policy', *Problems of Economic Transition*, 39/1: 56–68.

Easterly, W., and Fischer, S. (1994). 'The Soviet Economic Decline', *The World Bank Economic Review*, 9/3: 341–71.

EBRD (1996). *Transition Report 1996*, London: European Bank for Reconstruction and Development.

—— (1997). *Transition Report 1997*, London: European Bank for Reconstruction and Development.

Eichengreen, B., and Wyplosz, C. (1996). *Contagious Currency Crises*, London: Centre for Economic Policy Research Discussion Paper 1453.

European Commission (1995). *Employment Observatory Central and Eastern Europe* 8, Brussels: The European Commission, p. 35.

Favardin, P. (1996). 'Concurrence entre collectivites locales', *Revue Economique*, 47/2, 365–81.

Ferreira, F. (1997). *Economic Transition and the Distribution of Income and Wealth*, World Bank Policy Research Paper 1808.

Freinkman, L., and Haney, M. (1997). 'What Affects the Propensity to Subsidise: Determinants of Budget Subsidies and Transfers Financed by the Russian Regional Governments in 1992–1995', The World Bank, mimeo.

—— and Starodubrovskaya, I. (1996). *Restructuring of Enterprise Social Assets in Russia*, World Bank Policy Research Working Paper 1635.

Frye, T., and Shleifer, A. (1997). 'The Invisible Hand and the Grabbing Hand', *American Economic Review, Papers and Proceedings*, 87/2: 354–8.

Gaidar, Y. (1997). 'The IMF and Russia', *American Economic Review, Papers and Proceedings*, 87/2: 13–6.

Galbi, D. (1995). *The Significance of Credits and Subsidies in Russian Agricultural Reform*, World Bank Policy Research Paper 1441.

Gavrilenkov, E., and Koen, V. (1994). *How Large was the Output Collapse in Russia?*, IMF Working paper 94/154.

—— and Kuboniwa, M. (1997). *Development of Capitalism in Russia: The Second Challenge*, Tokyo: Maruzen.

Gilbert, G. (1996). 'Le federalisme financier: perspectives de microeconomie spatiale', *Revue Economique*, 47/2: 311–63.

Granville, B. (1994). 'So Farewell then Rouble Zone', in A. Aslund (ed.), *Russian Economic Reform at Risk*, London and New York: Castle.

—— (1995). *The success of Russian economic reforms*, The Royal Institute of Economic Affairs, London, distributed by Brookings.

Gray, D. (1995). *Reforming the Energy Sector in Transition Economies: Selected Experience and Lessons*, Washington, DC: The World Bank.

Hemming, R., Cheasty, A., and Lahiri A. (1996). 'The Revenue Decline', in D. Citrin and A. Lahiri (ed.), *Policy Experiences and Issues in the Baltics, Russia, and Other Countries of the Soviet Union*, Washington, DC: IMF, pp. 76–92.

Hernandez-Cata, E. (1994). *Russia and the IMF: The Political Economy of Macro-Stabilisation*, IMF Paper on Policy Analysis and Assessment 94/20.

Horton, M. (1996). *Health and Education Expenditures in Russia, the Baltic States and the Other Countries of the Former Soviet Union*, IMF Working Paper 96/126.

IMF (1995). *Social Safety Nets for Economic Transition: Options and Recent Experiences*, IMF Paper on Policy Analysis and Assessment, 95/3.

—— (1997). *World Economic Outlook*, Washington, D.C.: IMF.

Lavrov, A. (1996). 'Fiscal Federalism and Financial Stabilisation', *Problems of Economic Transition*, 39/1: 83–94.

—— (1997). *Entrepreneurial Climate in Russia's Regions*, Moscow: Natschala-Press.

Le Houerou, P., and Rutkowski, M. (1996). 'Federal Transfers in Russia: Their Impact on Regional Revenues and Incomes', *Comparative Economic Studies*, 38: 2/3, 21–44.

Lloyd, J. (1998). *The Rebirth of a Nation—An Anatomy of Russia*, London: Michael Johnson.

MacFarquhar, R. (1998). 'The Russian Crisis', in *Transition Report*, EBRD, pp. 12–19.

McLure, C., Wallich, C., and Litvack, J. (1994). 'Special Issues in Russian Federal Finance: Ethnic Separatism and Natural Resources', in C. Wallich (ed.), *Russia and the Challenge of Fiscal Federalism*, Washingon, D.C.: The World Bank, pp. 379–404.

Milanovic, B. (1995). *Poverty, Inequality, and Social Policy in Transition Economies*, World Bank Policy Research Working Paper 1530.

Musgrave, R. (1958). *The Theory of Public Finance*, New York: McGraw Hill.

—— (1961). 'Approaches to a Fiscal Theory of Political Federalism', in *National Bureau of Economic Research, Public Finances, Needs, Sources and Utilisation*, Princeton: Princeton University Press.

—— (1971). 'Economics of Fiscal Federalism', *Nebraska Journal of Economics and Business*, 10.

Oates, W. (1990). 'Decentralization, Local Governments, and Markets', in D. Bennett, *Decentralization of the Public Sector: An Overview*, Oxford: Oxford University Press, pp. 43–58.

Pinto, B., Drebentsov, V., and Morozov, A. (2000). 'Give Growth and Macro Stability in Russia a Chance: Harden Budgets by Dismantling Nonpayments', World Bank, mimeo.

Renaissance Capital (1997). 'Veksels—Interim Opportunity as a Russian Corporate Debt Market Emerges', Moscow, mimeo.

RET (1997a), *Russian Economic Trends*, 1997–4, London: Whurr Publishers Ltd., London.

—— (1997b). *Russian Economic Trends*, 1997–2, London: Whurr Publishers Ltd.

—— (1997c). *Russian Economic Trends—Monthly Update December 1997*.

Richter, K. (1997). 'Economic Mobility of Regions in Russia', Russian European Centre of Economic Policy, mimeo.

RLMS (1997). *Monitoring Economic Conditions in the Russian Federation*, Chapel Hill, NC: University of North Carolina.

Rubinfeld, D. (1987). 'The Economics of the Local Public Sector', *Handbook of Public Economics*, II, pp. 571–645.

Rutkowski, M. (1995). *Workers in Transition*, World Bank Policy Research Working Paper 1556.

—— (1996). 'Federal Transfers in Russia and their Impact on Regional Revenues and Income,' World Bank, mimeo.

Sachs, J. (1996). 'Economic Transition and the Exchange-rate Regime', *American Economic Review Papers and Proceedings*, 86/2: 147–52.

Sakwa, R. (1996). *Russian Politics and Society*, London: Routledge.

Schiffer, J. (1989). *Soviet Regional Economic Policy*, Houndsmills: Macmillan.

Shah, A. (1994). *The Reform of Intergovernmental Fiscal Relations in Developing and Emerging Market Economies*, Washington, D.C.: The World Bank.

Stewart, K. (1996), 'The Impact of Fiscal Decentralisation on Social Expenditures in the Regions of the Russian Federation', The World Bank, mimeo.

Stiglitz, J. (1996). *Whither Socialism*, Cambridge, Mass.: MIT Press.

Ter-Minassian, T. (1996). *Borrowing by Subnational Governments: Issues and Selected International Experiences*, IMF Paper on Policy Analysis and Assessment 96/4.

Treisman, D. (1996). 'The Politics of Intergovernmental Transfers in post-Soviet Russia', *British Journal of Political Science*, 26: 299–335.

Wallich, C. (1992). *Fiscal Decentralisation: Intergovernmental Relations in Russia*, Washington, D.C.: The World Bank.

Warner, A. (1996). 'Is Economic Reform Popular at the Polls?', Harvard Institute for International Development, mimeo.

World Bank (1996a). *Fiscal Management in Russia*, Washington, D.C.: The World Bank.

—— (1996b). *Russian Federation—Toward Medium Term Viability*, Washington, D.C.: The World Bank.

—— (1997). *World Development Report 1997*, Washington, DC: The World Bank.

6

Privatization and the Structure of Enterprise Ownership

JOHN S. EARLE AND SAUL ESTRIN

6.1. INTRODUCTION

Russia's mass privatization has yielded a new ownership structure with important implications for Russia's transition to a market economy. The rapidity of the privatization programme has been extraordinary, changing the ownership type of around 122,000 enterprises since 1992 (Goskomstat 1996). In this chapter, we consider who owns Russian firms, and whether there are systematic patterns to these ownership structures by sector, region, size, and privatization method. Since various types of insider ownership are hypothesized to be less effective than outsider ownership (Frydman, Gray, and Rapaczynski 1996), our findings are relevant to expectations about the broader effects of Russian privatization on company performance.

Four categories of owners are distinguished (the state, workers, managers and outside investors) and two approaches are used to characterize influence by owners over enterprise decision-making. In the first, the bargaining power of a group of owners depends upon its ownership stake, relative to the stakes of others. In the second, we classify firms according to their control by a dominant group, presumed able to assert their control over enterprise decisions. Our original results are based on a survey of 439 industrial enterprises conducted in July 1994, just after the conclusion of the voucher privatization programme. We also report on some more recent findings.

The remainder of the chapter is organized as follows. In the next section, we summarize the key categories to be employed in our empirical work, and describe the data set. The empirical analysis of the structure of enterprise ownership in Russia is presented in the third section, while the relationship between methods of privatization and the resulting owner-ship structure is explored systematically in the fourth. Conclusions are drawn in the fifth section.

6.2. FRAMEWORK AND DATA

Privatization entails the transfer of ownership from the state to private agents.[1] In the West, this bipartite division is usually viewed as adequate to encompass the key conceptual and empirical differences in enterprise behaviour (see Vickers and Yarrow 1988 for a conceptual framework, and Boardman and Vining 1989 for an empirical application). However, in Russia, the relevant groups of private owners are not homogenous profit maximizers operating against a background of well-developed capital markets. The bulk of people who received ownership rights in Russia's mass privatization were insiders—both workers and managers (Blasi 1994; Blasi and Shleifer 1996). The 'outsider' category is also hetero-geneous, ranging from relatives of workers through company suppliers to investment funds and foreign corporations. Moreover, the state has retained a significant shareholding, even in nominally 'privatized' firms. Figure 6.1 shows our categorization of owners.

These distinctions are important in predicting likely future enterprise behaviour and performance because different categories of owners have different objectives. The state, for instance, may be interested in employ-ment, supplies, or votes in addition to profits. Insiders are likely to be interested in returns other than profits: managers are concerned with the size of the firm or managerial benefits, while workers are interested in wages and employment. Therefore inside owners may not be superior to the state for enterprise restructuring to raise productivity. But in Russia even outsider owners may not be motivated or able to play an effective role in corporate governance, because of the illiquidity and thinness of capital markets. This problem will be exacerbated if outsiders also have special interests other than profits which they seek to exploit from their ownership stake, for example control over the prices set by suppliers.

But ownership in Russia post-privatization is typically mixed—part insider, part outsider, part state. We therefore need to consider how best to analyse the data to categorize alternative ownership forms. We use

---

[1] This section builds on our previous analysis of Russian ownership structure (Earle, Estrin, and Leschenko 1996).

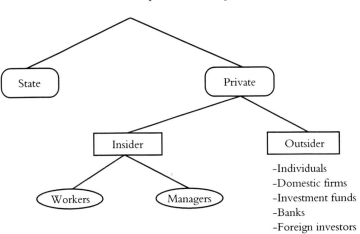

Figure 6.1. *Classification of share owners*

two approaches. In the first, the distribution of shareholdings is viewed as the determinant of relative bargaining power across ownership types. Groups of owners are presumed to influence enterprise decision-making according to the extent of their shareholding relative to other groups. It is assumed that the objectives of managers and workers are 'more similar' than those of banks, investment funds, and foreign owners, so that the former can be grouped together as 'insiders' and the latter as 'outsiders'. It is possible that instead coalitions are formed in a different way—for instance, that managers and state bureaucrats are allies, that insiders team up with the state to oppose restructuring proposed by outsiders, or that managers and some outside investors work hand in hand. Although anecdotal evidence of these is available, their prevalence in the overall pattern is harder to identify. In the empirical work which follows, we always report more disaggregated as well as the aggregated groupings so readers can form their own judgement.

Our second approach is to categorize firms by 'dominant owner', reflecting the fact that many Russian firms are substantially controlled by a single type of owner: the state, workers, managers, or outsiders. We also distinguish firms for which it appears that no owner is clearly dominant, and classify these separately. Figure 6.2 summarizes this approach. We first divide firms into 'old' and 'new', depending on whether they existed as state enterprises prior to the beginning of economic liberalization or

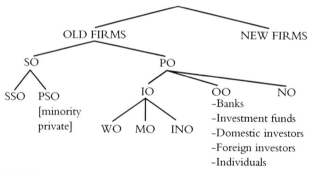

Definitions:

Old Firms—firms, which already existed before reform

New Firms—*de novo* firms

SO—dominated by state

PO—dominated by private owner

SSO—100% state-owned

PSO—partially privatized

IO—dominated by inside-owners

OO—dominated by outside-owners

NO—PO, but not clear dominant inside or outside owners

WO—dominated by workers

MO—dominated by managers

INO—IO, but not clear dominant worker or managerial owners

Figure 6.2. *Classification of dominant owner type*

are recently created entities.[2] Our focus on the manufacturing sector, however, limits practical importance of this distinction given the expected low incidence of new private firms in activities which are for the most part already over-developed and declining, as well as highly capital intensive.[3] For most purposes we shall restrict our attention to the medium and large firms emerging from the state sector.

---

[2] This distinction is not always clear, as new legal entities may be continuing the activities of state organizations, carrying over their structures, equipment, personnel, and ways of operating. However, prior empirical work on both Russia and east European countries has found enormous differences—in size, industry, and behaviour—between firms classified as *de novo* (DNs) and those which existed in the pre-reform period. See, e.g. Earle and Estrin (1996) on Poland; and Earle, Estrin, and Leshchenko (1996) and Richter and Schaffer (1996) on Russia.

[3] The poor quality of statistics on new start-up companies preclude strong statements about the proportion of new private firms in manufacturing or elsewhere, but all partial indicators support the contention that entrepreneurs have formed new companies predominantly in the service sector.

Among 'old' firms, we divide types of owners into state (SO) and private (PO). SOs are divided into firms which have been partially, but not majority, privatized (PSO), and those which remain 100 per cent state (SSO). Wholly privatized firms in turn are classified, into insider- and outsider-dominated entities (IO and OO), and IOs into worker and manager-dominated (WO and MO). In both divisions, we also distinguish a group of firms that cannot be clearly classified. NO refers to firms which are PO but are not clearly either IO or OO, while INO refers to firms which are IO but not clearly either WO or MO. Finally, institutional owners compromise banks, investment funds, domestic firms, and foreign investors.

We analyse these aspects of the ownership structure using a survey organized by the World Bank and conducted by VTsIOM (the All Russia Centre for Research on Public Opinion) in 439 companies during June and July 1994; 394 firms were randomly selected from a complete list of the population of manufacturing firms in Russia with at least fifteen employees in 1991, stratified by industry and region to ensure representativeness. In addition to this sample, which includes both state-owned and privatized enterprises, an additional 45 manufacturing firms in the new private sector were interviewed based on regional lists of all companies. As far as we know, this data set is the largest and most representative source containing detailed ownership and other information on industrial firms in Russia. More information about the survey and sampling can be found in Lee (1996).

To examine representativeness, Table 6.1 shows the composition of the World Bank sample of 'old firms' (the 394 state-owned and privatized companies, excluding the 45 firms in the new private sector) by groupings of industry, region, and size. The configuration of the population of 10,582 firms from which the sample was drawn is also shown. Although sample selection was stratified by industry and region, some non-representativeness in the number of enterprises crept in. The machine-building sector (both heavy and light), fuel and energy, and metals and chemicals are over-represented, while wood and construction materials and consumer goods are under-represented. When weighted by 1994 employment, however, the discrepancy is much less: for instance, 40.7 per cent of Russian industrial employment was in machine-building, while the corresponding sample percentage is 44.7 per cent (Commander, Dhar, and Yemtsov 1996). The survey exhibits bias towards large firms, but regional discrepancies between sample and population appear to be small.

Table 6.1. *Composition of sample and population*

	Sample Survey		Goskomstat Registry	De Novo Sample	
	Count	%	%	Count	%
Industry categories					
Fuel and energy	24	5	2	0	0
Metals and chemicals	50	11	5	5	11
Heavy machinery	66	15	8	4	9
Light machinery	125	28	17	11	24
Wood and construction materials	62	14	21	14	31
Consumer goods	90	21	40	9	20
Other	22	5	9	2	4
Region categories					
North	58	13	13	4	9
Volga-Vyatka	26	6	6	3	7
Povolzhski	56	13	11	4	9
North Caucasus	40	9	10	4	9
Urals	67	15	14	6	13
W. Siberia	52	12	13	2	4
E. Siberia	34	8	8	6	13
Moscow	55	13	9	7	16
Centre	51	12	18	9	20
Total	439	100	100	45	100
Size Categories (1991 employment)					
< 200	61	17	44	34	93
200–1,000	102	29	37	3	7
1,000–10,000	165	47	17	0	0
> 10,000	26	7	2	0	0
Total	354	100	100	37	100

Note: Industry groups were constructed by the authors on the basis of Goskomstat categories. 'Metals & chemicals' includes ferrous and non-ferrous metallurgy. 'Heavy Machinery' includes electro-technical industry, defence industry, shipbuilding industry, and heavy machine-building. 'Light machinery' includes machine tools, computers, automobiles, agricultural machinery, radio industry, communication and electronics, metal constructions, and machinery repair. 'Wood & construction materials' includes lumber, woodworking industry, and construction materials. 'Consumer Goods' includes textiles, clothing industry, food processing, and meat and milk industry. Regions use Goskomstat grouping except that we distinguish Moscow and include Far East in 'East Siberia' and both Northern and North-western region in 'North'. For the *de novo* sample the employment categories were computed using 1994 employment figures.

Sources: Columns 1, 2, 4, and 5 are authors' calculations from sample. Column 3 is from Lee (1996), based on Goskomstat registry of 10,582 industrial firms in Russia in 1991.

Table 6.1 also shows the composition of the *de novo* sample. The biggest difference between new and old firms is in size: 93 per cent of new firms had fewer than 200 employees in 1994, while only 7 per cent were in the 200–1,000 range. The regional distribution is also somewhat different, with disproportionate numbers of new firms in Moscow and east Siberia, and disproportionately few in west Siberia and the northern region, although the small sample size precludes strong inferences. The industrial distribution of new and old firms is rather similar, with the exception of the greater prevalence of *de novos* in wood and construction materials and their complete absence in fuel and energy.

6.3. THE STRUCTURE OF OWNERSHIP IN RUSSIAN INDUSTRY

In this section we apply our ownership categories to the enterprise survey data in order to examine the ownership structure in 1994. We first outline the findings of other studies, before reporting the distribution of shares among different types of owner for 'old' and *de novo* firms. We go on to consider the variation in ownership structure by industry, region, and size, as well as expectations concerning continued state ownership. We conclude with a discussion of selection effects in the Russian privatization process.

6.3.1. *Findings from previous studies*

The State Property Committee (GKI) released data on the numbers of privatizations, including some of their characteristics, but rather little on the actual ownership results. Table 6.2 shows the information available from Goskomstat (1996) on the ownership of industrial firms. The only published classification divides firms into 'state', 'mixed', and 'private', although these categories are not defined.[4]

Several surveys offer more information. Pistor (1994) reports, based on a sample of 36 privatized firms in 6 regions (Moscow, Novgorod, Yaroslav, Ivanovo, Perm, Sverdlovsk), that in 1993 all employees together (workers and managers are not reported separately) owned an average of 62 per cent of all shares, outsiders an average of 19 per cent, and the state retained 19 per cent. Webster *et al.* (1994) report on 92 privatized firms in Moskovskaya and Vladimirskaya oblasts in October 1993 that total employee ownership averaged 61 per cent, of which managers held

---

[4] We conjecture that 'state' implies 100% state ownership, 'private' implies 100% private ownership, and 'mixed' contains firms that are partially state and partially privately owned.

Table 6.2. *Ownership classification of industrial enterprises in 1994: Goskomstat data*

Per cent	Goskomstat classification					
	'State'	'Municipal'	'Public Institutions'	'Private'	'Mixed without Foreigners'	'Mixed with Foreigners'
Total number of enterprises	5.3	2.7	0.8	72.6	16.3	2.3
Total number of production workers	16.0	1.4	0.7	25.0	55.3	1.6
Total volume of output	9.4	1.0	0.2	18.8	69.6	3.0

Source: Goskomstat (1996). Classifications are explained in the text.

17 per cent; the size of the other holdings are unclear. Radygin (1996) reports 52 per cent ownership by workers, 14 per cent by management, 19.5 per cent by outsiders, and 14 per cent by the state, although the sampling and coverage of this study is unclear. The best information comes from surveys organized and reported by Blasi (1994, 1995, and 1996), and Blasi and Shleifer (1996). A survey of 127 privatized firms in 1993 showed insiders holding on average 65 per cent of the shares in 1993, of which 9 per cent was held by top managers. Outsiders held only 22 per cent, while the state accounted for the remaining 13 per cent.

However, the existing sources of information have several drawbacks. The sample sizes are small and sample selection was non random. With the exception of Webster *et al.* (1994), it appears that all data pertain only to enterprises privatized through the State Privatization Programme, omitting enterprises privatized through leasing arrangements. To omit leased enterprises is to omit an important part of Russian corporate structure. Goskomstat (1996) reports over 25 per cent of completed privatizations of enterprises as lease buy-outs over the years 1993–5, a result consistent with our survey data.[5]

Previous research has also omitted any analysis of firms remaining 100 per cent state owned. For instance, in an otherwise fairly detailed study of state ownership after privatization, Pistor and Turkewitz (1996) provide

---

[5] The percentage of firms privatized through lease buy-outs was 29.5, 20.8, and 29.8 of a total of 42,924, 21,905, and 10,152 firms privatized in 1993, 1994, and 1995, respectively according to Goskomstat (1996). Webster *et al.* find that leased enterprises were 50% more numerous than those in the state programme in the two oblasts they studied, but this appears to be an over-estimate of the importance of leased firms on a national basis.

no indication of the proportion of firms that had not been privatized. Yet both because some firms were prohibited from privatizing (in the military-industrial complex, for instance) and because the managers of others may have been reluctant to do so, the numbers remaining in state hands are large. As shown in Table 6.2, Goskomstat (1994) reports that 9 per cent of industrial enterprises and 16 per cent of industrial employment were in the state, municipal, or public institution categories.

6.3.2. *The findings from our survey*

In Table 6.3, we report the ownership composition of our enterprise sample. Of the 430 firms, 86 were 100 per cent state-owned, 299 had undergone some, at least partial, privatization (listed as 'privatized'), and 45 were newly created private enterprises.[6] Goskomstat (1996) does not distinguish new private firms from privatized enterprises formerly owned by the state. None the less, it is apparent that our sample under-represents new private firms in terms of number and possibly also in terms of employment and sales.[7] Concerning the division of 'old' enterprises, those that are or were state-owned, the results are quite consistent with Goskomstat (Table 6.2). Roughly one-quarter of old firms remained 100 per cent state-owned in 1994, while about three-quarters have been privatized, at least partially.

We go on to consider the share ownership structure resulting from this privatization process: first as to shareholding by ownership type[8] (Table 6.4) and then by dominant owner[9] (Table 6.5).

---

[6] Having 'undergone privatization' here means that a formerly state-owned enterprise was either bought out through a leasing arrangement or that it participated in the State Privatization Programme, but not necessarily, as the table demonstrates, that state ownership is zero. Indeed, we shall show that some 'privatised' firms remained, at the conclusion of voucher privatization in July 1994, overwhelmingly owned by the state.

[7] It is difficult to know how representative our *de novo* sample is. The state and privatized firms, on one hand, and the new private companies, on the other, were drawn from two different population lists. Incomplete reporting, and the difficulty of visiting a strictly proportional number of new private firms, resulted in the new private sector probably being under-represented in terms of numbers and over-represented in terms of employment. *De novo* firms are discussed further below.

[8] A small proportion of owners could not be classified into these groups. The main problem was with outsiders, some of whom could be disguised as insiders and others might be state organizations. We discarded observations where we could not determine whether an 'important owner' (more than 10% shares) was state or private.

[9] The results are shown for all old enterprises and newly created firms, including firms which have 'undergone privatization'. On these definitions, the data set contained ownership information on 345 firms, 246 privatized, 86 not privatized, and 24 *de novo*.

Table 6.3. *Ownership composition of enterprise sample*

	Ownership status		
	100 % State	**Privatized firms**	*de novo*
Number of enterprises			
Count	86	299	45
Row %	20.0	69.5	10.5
Employment 1994 (ths)			
Sum	130.3	565.1	1.2
Row %	19.0	81.0	0.2
Sales 1994 in billion roubles			
Sum	1,404.4	7,656.0	21.9
Row %	15.4	84.4	0.2

Source: Authors' calculations from sample survey data (July 1994). 'Privatized' firms in this table are former state enterprises with less than 100% state ownership.

In companies which had participated in some form of privatization, we find that, on average, insiders had 66.1 per cent of all shares, distributed between workers (non-managerial employees) with 46.2 per cent and managers with 19.6. Outsiders held 18.9 per cent and the remaining 15 per cent of shares were still held by the state. The nearly two-thirds concentration of shares in the hands of insiders provides strong confirmation of the view that employees, especially non-managerial workers, have been the biggest beneficiaries of Russian privatization policies. However, as our survey reveals, outsiders' shareholdings are not negligible, and they are distributed across companies unevenly enough to give outsiders dominant ownership in a substantial number of companies. The most important outsider owners are investment funds, other domestic firms, and individuals. The latter group is quite dispersed, since individuals acquired their stakes mostly by bidding for their vouchers singly in public auctions. The shareholdings of banks and foreigners are tiny.

When the 100 per cent state-owned enterprises are included (all 'old' firms grouped together), the pattern shifts significantly in favour of the state. An average manufacturing firm remains 38 per cent in state hands, while combined private shareholdings are reduced accordingly. Moreover, the state shareholding in privatized firms tends to be much greater in bigger firms. Weighting by 1994 employment (shown in columns 'weighted' in Table 6.4) produces an estimate that the state held 25 per cent of shares in 'privatized' manufacturing industry and 41.9 per cent in

Table 6.4. *Ownership structure in privatized, all old, and de novo firms*

Shareholding	Privatized firms (unweighted)	Privatized firms (weighted)	All old firms (unweighted)	All old firms (weighted)	De novo firms (unweighted)	De novo firms (weighted)
Total state	15.0	25.0	38.0	41.9	1.4	0.5
Total private	85.0	75.0	62.0	58.1	98.6	99.5
All insiders	66.1	54.2	48.2	42.0	71.4	62.4
Workers	46.2	39.9	33.5	30.6	6.5	4.0
Managers	19.6	14.3	14.3	11.0	63.6	57.2
All outsiders	18.9	20.8	13.8	16.1	27.1	37.1
Banks	1.0	0.7	0.7	0.5	0.0	0.0
Investment funds	4.5	8.6	3.3	6.6	0.0	0.0
Other domestic firms	6.7	4.5	4.8	3.4	7.6	2.0
Foreigners	0.4	0.7	0.3	0.5	0.0	0.0
Individuals	5.9	6.2	4.3	4.8	16.2	30.7
Valid N	235	235	319	319	24	24

Note: The category 'All old firms' includes enterprises that were partially or fully privatized and enterprises that had not begun privatization and were still held by state. 1994 employment was used to weight firms in the columns labelled 'weighted'.

Table 6.5. *Dominant owner type*

Dominant owner type	Privatized firms (unweighted)	Privatized firms (weighted)	All old firms (unweighted)	All old firms (weighted)
SO				
column %	8.3	20.3	32.5	38.1
PO				
column %	91.7	79.7	67.5	61.9
IO				
column %	76.7	58.7	56.4	45.6
WO				
column %	50.4	44.5	37.1	34.6
MO				
column %	14.6	8.3	10.7	6.5
INO				
column %	10.0	4.7	7.4	3.7
OO				
column %	8.8	12.1	6.4	9.4
NO				
column %	5.8	8.8	4.3	6.9
N	24	241	327	327

Note: The category 'All old firms' includes enterprises that were partially or fully privatized and enterprises that had not begun privatization and were still held by state. 1994 employment was used to weight firms in the columns labelled 'weighted'. SO = state-dominated, PO = private-dominated, IO = insider-dominated, WO = worker-dominated, MO = manager-dominated, INO = insider-dominated, but not clearly by workers or managers, OO = outsider-dominated, NO = private-dominated, but unclear whether by insiders or outsiders. See text for precise definitions.

all Russian manufacturing in 1994. Outsiders also tend to have more shares in larger firms: among privatized firms, they hold a weighted average of 20.8 per cent. Insiders' stakes, especially those of managers, tend to be larger in smaller firms. Their weighted average holding in all old firms comes down to 42 per cent of shares, divided into 31 per cent for workers and 11 per cent for managers. Viewed in this way, outsiders acquired about twice as much as managers, and all insiders together have well under 50 per cent of corporate shareholdings in 1994.

Our survey is for July 1994, and to evaluate our findings we need to know how shareholdings have evolved, especially since the state has begun to privatize its remaining holdings and employees may have begun to sell their shares (Earle and Estrin 1996). However, it appears that there were relatively few sales of shares by employees in the immediate years after privatization. According to Blasi and Shleifer (1996) zero sales by workers and voucher funds was the median change of ownership across all firms. The average sales of shares represented 4 per cent and 1 per cent of the total, respectively. This suggests that the share structure has hardly changed at all in most companies in Russia since privatization. Moreover, any expectations of a quick and dramatic sell-off by employees to outsiders, such as occurred in Japan in the post-war period (Aoki and Kim 1995), were contradicted by the results reported by Blasi *et al.* (1997) for the year 1996, when employee ownership, both that of managers and of workers, actually rose slightly compared to the previous year. Buck *et al.* (1996) do find some decline in the state shareholding, however, a corresponding increase in that of 'other organisations' in a small enterprise panel between 1994 and 1995–6, but they find no downward trend in insider equity holdings over the period. Finally, Buck *et al.* (1998) survey the evidence on ownership shares between 1994 and 1997. While the evidence is somewhat contradictory, most studies point to a modest fall in inside holdings over the period, primarily those of workers not managers. The state holding is also found to have fallen somewhat, while outsiders' shareholdings have increased commensurably.

The *de novo* category of firms in Table 6.4 was determined by examining several survey questions to identify firms which consistently reported that they started up with no legal predecessors, and that they were not spin-offs or privatized units of a state organization. Only twenty-four of the *de novo* firms (DNs) provide ownership information, but a clear (and not terribly surprising) difference arises in ownership; the DNs show hardly any state shareholdings whatsoever, and nearly two-thirds of all shares are managerially owned. It appears that these firms are entrepreneurships; workers own less than 7 per cent of shares on average. Only non-financial firms and Russian individuals are represented among outsider owners of *de novo* enterprises.

Table 6.5 reports our analysis of ownership based on dominant owners. All private DNs are excluded, and an enterprise is listed as 'state-owned' (SO) if and only if the state holds at least 50 per cent of its shares. Among privately owned firms (POs), a firm is 'insider-owned' (IO) if all insiders have more than 40 per cent of shares and if they own at least as much as all outsiders.[10] The firm is 'outside-owned' (OO) if outsiders hold more

---

[10] The 40% threshold is arbitrary but dominant owners in most cases have shareholdings well above 50%; Hence, the results for the classification of firms by dominant owner type are relatively robust to changes in the threshold.

than 40 per cent and more than the insiders. We classify a firm as having 'no clear owner' (NO) if neither outsiders nor insiders hold more than 40 per cent, and as INO if the firm is an IO but neither managers nor workers dominates in the sense of owning more than 40 per cent of all shares. Thus, the number of POs should equal the sum of the numbers of IOs, OOs, and NOs.[11]

Commencing with the privatized firms, 92 per cent are majority POs; on our definitions the state still dominates in 8 per cent of 'privatized' firms. Just over half of privatized firms are worker dominated WOs, while 15 per cent are MOs, 9 per cent OOs, 6 per cent NOs, and 10 per cent INOs. For manufacturing firms as a whole (including non-privatized ones), the state still dominates in one-third or, because the state shareholding tends to be greater in bigger companies, in 35 per cent when we weight by employment. Although the average shareholding of outsiders is small, there is none the less a substantial proportion of privatized firms—9 per cent unweighted, 12 per cent weighted—where outsiders dominate. Given the modest changes in insider versus outsider shareholdings in the first years after privatization, it seems unlikely that these proportions of dominant owner have altered substantially.

Table 6.6 shows that the classification system leaves few marginal cases. On average, the state owns 91.5 per cent in an SO, private owners own 88.6 per cent in a PO, insiders own 76 per cent in an IO, workers own 67.5 per cent in a WO, managers own 68.6 per cent in an MO, and outside investors own 63.5 per cent in an OO. By construction, the INOs and NOs have no group with over 40 per cent. The fact that average invest-ment fund ownership in OOs is 9.5 per cent may be due to the legal limitations imposed on investment fund portfolios; other outside invest-ors were not subject to this limitation. Possibly as a result investment fund ownership is more evenly spread than other institutional investors across dominant owner types.

Table 6.6 also shows some interesting associations of different types of owners. Among the WO, MO, and OO types, state ownership tends to be highest in MO, but it is still higher in the INO and particularly the NO types. On the other hand, both worker and outside owners are more likely to be found as minority owners with each other as the dominant owner, than as the junior partner of managers in MOs: worker owner-ship is about 50 per cent larger in OOs, and outside ownership 50 per cent larger in WOs, than either of these types of owner in MOs. This supports

[11] Note that there is sufficient information to classify four firms.

Table 6.6. *Ownership structure by dominant owner in all old firms*

	Dominant ownership categories							
	SO	PO	IO	WO	MO	INO	OO	NO
Total state	91.5	11.4	9.7	8.0	11.9	16.1	10.4	36.9
Total private	8.5	88.6	90.3	92.0	88.1	83.9	89.6	63.1
All insiders	7.4	68.6	76.0	78.7	80.8	53.8	26.0	36.3
Workers	5.9	47.7	52.4	67.5	12.2	33.3	18.7	29.6
Managers	1.5	20.6	23.3	11.2	68.6	20.5	6.7	6.6
All outsiders	1.1	20.0	14.3	13.3	7.3	30.2	63.5	26.8
Banks	0.0	1.0	0.9	0.8	0.8	1.2	3.2	0.0
Investment funds	0.6	4.7	3.8	3.6	1.5	8.4	9.5	8.7
Foreigners	0.0	0.5	0.1	0.1	0.0	0.0	2.9	1.5
Domestic firms	0.0	7.0	4.6	4.2	1.4	11.0	26.0	8.8
Individuals	0.4	6.4	4.3	3.8	2.2	9.6	22.1	7.8

Note: See text and previous table note for definitions.

the notion of workers and managers as distinct groups, rather than being lumped together as 'all employees'.[12]

6.3.3. *Retained state holdings*

An important feature of the Russian privatization process is the large proportion of shares retained by the state[13] in the first years of privatization: about 42 per cent of all shares in old manufacturing enterprises as of July 1994 when weighted by 1994 employment. The state has since sold some of its holdings but the changes are not great (see Buck *et al.* (1998)). The large initial state shareholding reflects the incompleteness of the first phases of the privatization process for those firms that did undergo some

---

[12] One reason for the apparent affinity between worker and outside ownership could be the greater ease for outsiders, facing a given level of total insider share ownership, to control a firm with more worker ownership and less managerial ownership, because of higher concentration and organization among managers relative to workers. An analysis of this should consider what we might call the 'substitutability' or 'complementarity' of different types of owners. According to one hypothesis, for instance, there might be similarities in terms of corporate governance between concentrated insiders (usually managers) and concentrated outsiders (usually institutional investors)—the two may be substitutes for one another.

[13] Russia is hardly unique in this respect; see Frydman *et al.* (1993*a* and *b*); or Pistor and Turkewitz (1996) for discussions of others countries. But because of the character and speed of Russia's mass privatization, this point is more likely to be overlooked compared to countries following slower routes of privatization such as in Hungary, Poland and Romania.

form of privatization, the fact that a significant number of firms failed to be privatized whatsoever, and the initial tendency of the state to retain significant stakes in large or 'strategic' companies. Despite the 'loans for shares' scheme, in 1995–7 most indications point to slow rate of government disinvestment across all firms after July 1994. The 'investment sales', the privatization vehicle for which 20 per cent of shares in most companies had been reserved, appears to have gone slowly too.

Table 6.7 shows the distribution in our 1994 sample of state shares for privatized and all old firms, unweighted and weighted by employment. We find that 6.7 per cent of all firms that have undergone some privatization process remained at least 50 per cent state-owned; we term these firms PSOs. When firms are weighted by their 1994 employment levels, 17.3 per cent were still majority state-owned. The state retained at least 10 per cent of the shares in almost two-thirds of privatized firms (weighted) in 1994. Similar figures are shown for all old firms, including those still 100 per cent state-owned. From this perspective, the state remains present at an ownership level of at least 10 per cent in more than half of Russian industrial firms, and when weighted the figure rises to 71.7 per cent. We calculate (in the bottom row, labelled 'O') that 48.5 per cent of enterprises that have undergone privatization, and 35.4 per cent of all old firms have been 100 per cent privatized (so that the state share is zero); but the completely privatized firms are relatively small, so that the percentage of 'old' firms with zero state holdings drops to 15.5 when weighted by 1994 employment. At the other extreme, just over a third (33.4 per cent) of all 'old' firms, when weighted, have the state as the majority owner. The percentage of firms with the largest state shares (60 per cent and over) is greater on an unweighted than weighted basis, because the 100 per cent state-owned firms (SSOs) tend to be small relative to privatized firms that have a large state stake (although the SSOs are larger than completely privatized firms).

Even in enterprises that are majority privately owned, the state was able to retain control through 'golden shares' permitted for firms in the State Privatization Programme under the Russian privatization law. Such shares, which could be issued only on the authority of the government of Russia or the State Committee on Administration of State Property (GKI),[14] carried veto rights over major company

---

[14] Legally that is. Pistor and Turkewitz (1996) note that 'exceeding their authority, regional GKIs or regional property funds have frequently decided to . . . issue a golden share. This practice forced the national GKI to adopt a special resolution that explicitly prohibited such activity.' They provide no estimate of the prevalence of golden shares.

Table 6.7. *Distribution of state shareholding across firms (per cent)*

	Privatized (unweighted)	Privatized (weighted)	All old (unweighted)	All old (weighted)
P100	0.0	0.0	22.5	19.5
P90	0.0	0.0	22.5	19.5
P80	0.0	0.0	22.5	19.5
P70	0.0	0.0	22.5	19.5
P60	2.9	5.1	24.3	23.1
P50	8.2	20.0	27.7	33.4
P40	13.9	24.0	31.3	36.2
P30	22.1	36.9	36.6	45.1
P20	36.5	52.8	45.7	56.1
P10	45.5	75.2	51.4	71.7
0	48.5	20.0	35.4	15.5
N	233	233	319	319

Note: The table shows the percentage of firms where the state shareholding is greater than or equal to x, with the corresponding row designated Px. The second-to-last row, labelled 'O' shows the percentage of firms where state ownership is zero. The weighting variable is Employment 1994.

decisions—amendments to the company charter, liquidation, reorganizations, etc.—initially for a three-year period. The only information that appears to be available on the extent to which golden shares were issued is Goskomstat (1996), which reports 204, 792, and 429 such cases in 1993, 1994, and 1995, respectively. This represents in total about 5 per cent of the joint-stock companies established through privatization during those three years.

An example of the evolution of governmental shareholdings is the Russian oil industry.[15] The sector was considered to be of 'strategic importance' and the government retained 38 per cent of ordinary shares, giving it 51 per cent of voting shares, during the initial privatization of the oil industry enterprises (subsidiaries) in 1992–3. These stakes were used as the basis of newly created holding companies. At the outset the government intended to retain a corresponding level of ownership in the holding companies for three years at least. However, in the loans for shares scheme of 1995–7, the government sold off in their entirety the shareholdings in most of the largest holding companies, for example, Yukos, Sidanco, Sibneft, and Surgut Holding. Moreover,

[15] The authors would like to thank Nat Moser for assisting with the discussion.

Table 6.8. *Expectation of privatization in unprivatized firms (SSOs)*

	Privatization not planned	Privatization delayed	Privatization planned within 12–18 months
Unweighted			
Count	41	19	17
%	53.2	24.7	22.1
Weighted by 1994 Employment			
%	40.3	12.0	47.7

Note: Sample was restricted to old firms that had not undergone privatization as of July 1994. The table shows enterprise managers' responses to a question on their expectation or plans concerning the future privatization of their firm.

the pressure to raise revenue has been such that the government intends to sell off its remaining stakes as soon as possible, in Lukoil, Tyumen Oil Company, and Rosneft, for example. Sales have, however, been inhibited by the sharp downturn in Russian share prices from the last quarter of 1997. The gas industry represents a sharp contrast to oil; the government retains a 40 per cent share in Gazprom and appears to have no plans to reduce it.

6.3.4. *Ownership sector: region and size*

In Table 6.9 we report how the ownership structure, in terms of shareholdings by ownership groups and of dominant owner, varies by industry group (branch as defined for Table 6.1) for all old firms. Ownership differs significantly across industries, with the state retaining large stakes in the fuel and energy, light machinery, and 'other' sectors, and the lowest stakes in metals, chemicals, and consumer goods. Among private owners, insiders—both workers and managers—are more commonly found in consumer goods, while outsiders are concentrated in the machinery sector. Among outside institutional investors, investment funds are concentrated in the fuel, energy, metals, and chemical sectors, while domestic firms have invested in both heavy and light machinery as well as metals and chemicals. Individual investors, most of whom would have received shares through the voucher programme, are fairly evenly distributed across sectors, although with some proclivity towards heavy machinery.

Table 6.9. *Ownership structure by industry group*

Shareholding (per cent of shares)	Groups of branches of industry							Total
	Fuel and energy	Metals and chemicals	Heavy machinery	Light machinery	Wood and construction materials	Consumer goods	Other	
Total state	52.4	22.2	37.2	47.2	45.4	22.7	59.2	38.0
Total private	47.6	77.8	62.8	52.8	54.6	77.3	40.8	62.0
All insiders	35.2	58.7	47.4	37.2	44.0	66.2	33.0	48.2
Workers	22.8	38.2	32.6	29.5	31.0	42.8	25.6	33.5
Managers	12.4	20.5	13.8	7.7	13.0	22.7	7.3	14.3
All outsiders	12.4	19.1	15.4	15.6	10.6	11.1	7.8	13.8
Banks	0.6	1.6	0.4	0.6	1.3	0.5	0.0	0.7
Investment funds	5.6	6.1	2.2	3.5	3.7	2.0	1.9	3.3
Domestic firms	0.6	6.8	5.8	5.3	2.4	4.8	4.3	4.8
Foreigners	0.0	0.0	0.7	0.6	0.3	0.0	0.0	0.3
Individuals	4.4	4.5	6.1	5.1	2.9	3.3	1.5	4.3

Table 6.9. *(continued)*

Shareholding (per cent of shares)	Groups of branches of industry							Total
	Fuel and energy	Metals and chemicals	Heavy machinery	Light machinery	Wood and construction materials	Consumer goods	Other	
Dominant owner type (per cent of firms)	%	%	%	%	%	%	%	%
SO	57.9	18.2	25.0	40.4	41.7	19.7	50.0	32.5
SSO	26.3	9.1	19.2	35.1	38.9	18.4	43.8	26.4
PSO	31.6	9.1	5.8	5.3	2.8	1.3	6.3	6.1
PO	42.1	81.8	75.0	59.6	58.3	80.3	50.0	67.5
IO	36.8	72.7	57.7	41.5	52.8	77.6	37.5	56.4
WO	10.5	48.5	36.5	31.9	33.3	48.7	31.3	37.1
MO	10.5	12.1	9.6	5.3	11.1	18.4	6.3	10.7
INO	15.8	12.1	9.6	4.3	8.3	6.6	0.0	7.4
OO	0.0	6.1	7.7	11.7	5.6	1.3	6.3	6.4
NO	5.3	3.0	9.6	6.4	0.0	0.0	6.3	4.3
Total number	No. 19	No. 33	No. 52	No. 94	No. 36	No. 76	No. 16	No. 326

Note: Sample is all old firms. See notes to Table 6.3 for definition of industry groups.

The percentage distribution in 1994 of firms by dominant ownership type within each industry group is shown in the panel at the bottom of Table 6.9. The probability of remaining state-owned varies widely, being highest in machinery and in the miscellaneous 'other' types of manufacturing. As noted above, the state had in 1994 a major shareholding in the fuel and energy sector, and a majority stake in more than 40 per cent of all firms in light machinery, wood and construction materials, and 'other' sectors. The pattern of insider dominance parallels that of shareholdings: managers have the highest incidence of dominating consumer goods factories, while worker dominance is also found in metals and chemicals. Outsiders dominate most commonly in light machinery, secondarily in heavy machinery. Fuel and energy has a fairly high rate (16 per cent) of INOs, and NOs have the highest incidence in heavy machinery.

Table 6.10 presents the ownership structure, both shareholdings and dominant owner types, by region (as defined in Table 6.1). By far the highest rate of privatization is in the north Caucasus and the lowest in Moscow and Povolzhski region. Outsiders have had a particular lack of success in Moscow. The story appears somewhat different when viewed in terms of dominant ownership type: outsiders, for instance, dominate in no firms in the north Caucasus, and in very few in Povolzhski and western Siberia.

Table 6.11 reports the 1994 ownership structure, in terms of shares and dominant types, by size category (where size is measured by number of employees in 1991). The relation between 1991 size and 1994 state shareholding is complex, the state share being largest at the extremes of the distribution: in the smallest size category (up to 200 employees) 42.7 per cent of shares are state-owned and 35.8 per cent of firms are SOs, while 48.5 per cent of shares are state-owned and 50 per cent of firms are state-dominated in the largest category (over 5,000 employees). This group shows particularly high incidence of partially privatized PSOs. Insider ownership is most pronounced in medium-sized companies, with a low incidence of IOs, especially MOs, in the largest category.

6.3.5. *The determinants of Russian ownership structures in 1994*

The observed variations along industry, region, and size dimension suggest that there may have been important selection effects in the Russian privatization process. Regarding the probability of privatization, the

Table 6.10. *Ownership structure by region*

Shareholding (per cent of shares)	Regions								
	North	Volga-Vyatka	Povolzhski	North Caucasus	Urals	West Siberia	East Siberia	Moscow	Centre
Total state	43.5	38.8	47.8	6.9	47.5	30.4	34.7	49.7	30.0
Total private	56.5	61.2	52.2	93.1	52.5	69.6	65.4	50.3	70.0
All insiders	40.7	44.6	42.1	76.5	39.0	56.0	50.8	41.9	52.7
Workers	28.5	35.6	30.8	56.7	25.6	39.9	25.8	26.4	38.6
Managers	12.2	9.0	11.3	19.8	13.4	14.8	25.0	15.5	12.3
All outsiders	15.8	16.6	10.1	16.6	13.5	13.6	14.6	8.4	17.3
Banks	1.3	0.0	0.2	0.0	0.3	1.1	0.3	0.7	1.8
Investment funds	4.2	5.9	3.1	2.7	3.7	2.6	0.1	1.6	5.2
Firms	4.1	1.9	4.0	8.0	4.2	5.9	6.5	4.0	4.9
Foreigners	0.8	0.0	0.0	0.5	0.0	0.0	1.5	0.3	0.0
Individuals	5.4	8.8	1.9	4.3	4.5	4.0	6.2	1.8	5.2

Dominant owner type
(per cent of firms)

	%	%	%	%	%	%	%	%	%
SO	34.7	33.3	44.4	3.1	44.7	25.6	28.6	43.2	23.7
SSO	30.6	22.2	35.6	3.1	34.0	20.5	19.0	43.2	15.8
PSO	4.1	11.1	8.9	0.0	10.6	5.1	9.5	0.0	7.9
PO	65.3	66.7	55.6	96.9	55.3	74.4	71.4	56.8	76.3
IO	44.9	55.6	51.1	93.8	42.6	69.2	57.1	45.9	60.5
WO	28.6	38.9	37.8	71.9	21.3	51.3	23.8	24.3	42.1
MO	10.2	5.6	8.9	12.5	8.5	7.7	28.6	13.5	7.9
INO	6.1	11.1	4.4	9.4	12.8	5.1	4.8	8.1	5.3
OO	16.3	11.1	2.2	0.0	6.4	2.6	9.5	5.4	5.3
NO	2.0	0.0	2.2	3.1	6.4	2.6	4.8	5.4	10.5
Total number	No. 49	No. 18	No. 45	No. 32	No. 47	No. 39	No. 21	No. 37	No. 38

Note: Sample is all old firms. See notes to Table 6.3 for definition of regions.

Table 6.11. *Ownership structure by size (1991 employment)*

Shareholding (per cent of shares)	1991 Employment						Total
	< 201	201–500	501–1,000	1,001–2,000	2,001–5,000	> 5000	
Total state	36.9	36.8	27.4	34.9	33.5	51.8	36.6
Total private	63.1	63.2	72.6	65.1	66.5	48.2	63.4
All insiders	49.1	55.3	58.7	50.1	49.2	34.5	49.6
Workers	34.0	37.9	38.9	35.2	35.0	27.3	34.8
Managers	15.0	17.3	18.3	14.9	14.2	5.5	14.3
All outsiders	14.0	7.9	13.9	15.0	17.3	13.8	13.9
Banks	0.6	0.5	0.2	0.7	1.8	0.3	0.7
Investment and funds	2.1	0.9	2.6	3.5	6.9	5.5	3.7
Domestic firm	4.9	2.4	8.6	4.5	5.0	3.0	4.8
Foreigners	1.0	0.0	0.0	0.4	0.3	0.5	0.3
Individuals	4.5	4.2	2.5	4.6	3.3	4.2	3.9

Dominant owner type (per cent of firms)

	%	%	%	%	%	%	%
SO	32.6	33.3	23.9	26.8	24.1	46.5	30.6
SSO	30.2	31.0	21.7	23.2	19.0	27.9	25.0
PSO	2.3	2.4	2.2	3.6	5.2	18.6	5.6
PO	67.4	66.7	76.1	73.2	75.9	53.5	69.4
IO	58.1	59.5	65.2	64.3	67.2	32.6	58.7
WO	34.9	40.5	41.3	41.1	46.6	25.6	38.9
MO	16.3	11.9	13.0	10.7	12.1	2.3	11.1
INO	4.7	7.1	6.5	12.5	8.6	2.3	7.3
OO	9.3	0.0	8.7	3.6	5.2	11.6	6.3
NO	0.0	7.1	2.2	3.6	3.4	9.3	4.2
Total number	No. 69	No. 60	No. 53	No. 41	No. 42	No. 24	No. 289

Note: Sample is all old firms.

objectives both of the state and of enterprises no doubt had some influence. The state, or some politicians or bureaucrats, would have attempted to prevent, and in some cases actually prohibited, enterprises in 'strategic sectors' and/or those with the greatest political sensitivity from privatizing. The legal regulations on leasing were rather murky and contained neither prohibited nor target lists of enterprises for privatization, so that the influence of the state on the process was only implicit; but the State Privatization Programme explicitly divided firms into those slated for 'mandatory privatisation' those able to privatize 'voluntarily' (with either GKI or cabinet approval), and those prohibited from privatization (Frydman *et al.* 1993*b*, or Boycko *et al.* 1995). The first category covered consumer services and light manufacturing. Voluntary privatization with GKI approval was the rule for heavy manufacturing, as cabinet approval was for the natural resource sector and most of the military-industrial complex. Privatization was prohibited in railways, health, and education.

The initiative for corporatization and privatization thus rested with the insiders of each firm, the formal decision being taken by the workers' collective in both the leasing arrangements and the state programme. One may hypothesize that the objectives of insiders would focus upon the expected profitability and riskiness of the company, the advantages to be gained from control (such as ensuring jobs and social benefits), and the expected support from the state. There was anxiety that subsidies might be cut off to enterprises once privatized; to allay this, Yeltsin issued a decree in late 1992 promising continued 'non-discriminatory' support for privatizing and privatized companies. Though the state tried to keep control of the privatization process in some firms, in most cases insider interests probably predominated. Outsiders could only participate in the early days through insider-controlled voucher auctions (or in a few cases, cash auctions), or later by buying shares from insiders on secondary markets. Outsiders' objectives largely would have concerned profitability, but customer and supplier companies (including banks) could have had other motives as well.

To take this analysis further we report in Table 6.12 the results from estimating regressions to explain the probability of an 'old' enterprise being privatized. In Table 6.13 we use regression analysis to explain the actual shareholdings by category of ownership, for example, private ownership shareholdings, etc. The regressions have a broader significance because it seems likely that for both insiders and outsiders the performance of firms before privatization might influence their willingness to bid for or accept shares. If 'good' or 'bad' performance persisted from the pre- to the post-privatization period, what might appear to be a correlation between, for example, insider ownership and 'good' enterprise performance might in fact reflect no more than the fact that insiders were able to gain control over the best firms. This selection problem might make it hard to interpret the effects of ownership regime on company performance.

Table 6.12 shows the result of estimating a logistic function, in which the dependent variable takes a value of 1 if the firm has been at least partially privatized (Non-SSO) and 0 otherwise, with the sample restricted to all old firms. The independent variables in this equation are dummies for industrial sectors, regions, and employment sizes. Overall, the model is highly significant (the chi-squared statistic is significant at the 99 per cent level of probability). Probably due to multi-collinearity among the characteristics, there are few individually significant coefficients. However, the bottom of the table reports the results of the Wald test of the joint significance of each group of variables: the set of industry dummies is significant at the 0.07 level, the regional dummies at the 0.02 level, and the size dummies only at 0.49. Thus, the probability of a firm being privatized by 1994 is significantly influenced by regional and sectoral factors but not by firm size.

Table 6.13 contains similar results from the least squares (OLS) estimation of functions of private shareholding (PSH), insider shareholding (ISH), worker shareholding (WSH), managerial shareholding (MSH), and outsider shareholding (OSH) as dependent variables, with the same groups of industry, region, and size effects as possible explanatory factors. F-statistics to evaluate the joint significance of the industry, regional, and size dummies respectively are shown at the bottom of each equation. As above, both industry and region effects are highly significant (at the 0.01 level) for all private shareholding together, with size significant only at the 0.10 level. Turning to the more disaggregated dominant groups, we find industry, region, and size are all highly significant in explaining insider shareholdings, but none is significant in the outsider equation. Among insiders, geographical region has more explanatory power for workers' shareholdings, while industry is more important in explaining the pattern of managerial dominance. However, the adjusted R^2 is not very high for any equation and is extremely low (0.0004) in the outsider equation.

These results confirm that there were selection effects in Russian privatization, with the probability of a firm being privatized being

Table 6.12. *Estimating the impact of industry, region, and size on privatization status*

Dependent variable = NON-SSO

Independent variable	Estimated coefficient	Estimated standard error
Constant	0.41	0.66
FUEL-EN	0.11	0.70
METAL-CH	0.78	0.74
L-MACH	-0.42	0.46
WOOD-CM	-0.65	0.57
CONGOODS	0.50	0.53
OTHER	-1.18^a	0.68
VOLGA-V	0.41	0.72
POVOLZH	-0.13	0.53
N-CAUCAS	2.42^b	1.09
URALS	-0.23	0.52
WSIB	0.89	0.62
ESIB	0.56	0.76
MOSCOW	-0.87	0.54
CENTRE	0.88	0.60
E < 500	0.30	0.53
E < 1000	0.85	0.55
E < 2000	0.79	0.54
E < 5000	0.98^a	0.55
E > 5000	0.66	0.56
Model Chi-squared	40.89	
Significance	0.0025	
N	291	

[a] statistically significant at 10% level
[b] statistically significant at 5% level

Wald test of 6 linear restrictions (Industry)
Chi-squared = 11.82, Sig. level = 0.07
Wald test of 8 linear restrictions (Region)
Chi-squared = 18.25, Sig. level = 0.02
Wald test of 5 linear restrictions (Size)
Chi-squared = 4.42, Sig. level = 0.49

Note: Logistic function estimates. Sample includes all old firms. Dependent variable (NON-SSO) equals 1 if the firm is at least partially privatized, and 0 if the firm is still owned 100 per cent by the state. Definitions of industry, region, and size dummies may be found in tables 6.9, 6.10, and 6.11. The omitted categories are as follows: Heavy Machinery for the group of industry dummies, North for the group of region dummies, and the smallest category of employment in 1991 (less than or equal to 200 employees) for the last group of size dummies.

Table 6.13. *Estimating the impact of industry, region, and size on ownership structure*

Independent variables	PSH B	SE B	ISH B	SE B	WSH B	SE B	MSH B	SE B	OSH B	SE B
FUEL-EN	-2.3	11.0	-1.8	9.7	-2.6	8.8	2.2	6.2	-0.6	5.6
METAL-CH	13.6	9.2	11.0	8.2	5.0	7.4	7.4	5.2	2.6	4.7
L-MACH	-3.2	7.2	-5.9	6.4	-1.0	5.8	-3.6	4.1	2.7	3.7
WOOD-CM	-4.8	9.2	-2.4	8.1	-1.5	7.3	0.2	5.2	-2.4	4.7
CONGOODS	20.1[b]	7.8	24.3[c]	6.9	13.6[b]	6.3	11.6[b]	4.4	-4.2	4.0
OTHER	-19.2[a]	11.8	-13.2	10.4	-9.4	9.5	-2.2	6.7	-6.0	6.0
VOLGA-V	3.7	11.4	3.7	10.1	5.4	9.1	-1.8	6.4	0.0	5.8
POVOLZH	-1.1	8.5	2.4	7.5	3.3	6.8	-0.8	4.8	-3.5	4.3
N-CAUCAS	27.4[c]	9.4	25.6[c]	8.3	22.8[c]	7.5	2.5	5.3	1.8	4.8
URALS	-2.4	8.6	-2.8	7.6	-3.5	6.8	0.6	4.8	0.4	4.4
WSIB	14.0	9.2	11.9	8.2	8.7	7.5	1.2	5.3	2.1	4.7
ESIB	5.9	11.5	2.9	10.1	-9.1	9.2	11.8[a]	6.5	3.0	5.8
MOSCOW	-12.4	9.3	-2.7	8.2	-1.8	7.4	-1.1	5.2	-9.8[b]	4.7
CENTRE	11.0	8.9	13.0[a]	7.8	12.7[a]	7.3	-0.2	5.1	-2.0	4.5

Table 6.13. *(continued)*

Independent variables	PSH B	PSH SE B	ISH B	ISH SE B	WSH B	WSH SE B	MSH B	MSH SE B	OSH B	OSH SE B
E < 250	20.2	13.2	18.0[a]	11.6	11.1	10.5	6.8	7.4	2.2	6.7
E < 500	28.0	13.4	30.7[a]	11.9	16.2	10.7	14.5[b]	7.6	-2.7	6.8
E < 1000	31.7[a]	13.0	28.4	11.5	16.0	10.4	11.7[a]	7.4	3.3	6.6
E < 5000	29.1	12.5	24.6	11.1	14.7	10.0	9.7	7.0	4.5	6.4
E > 5000	16.8	13.4	15.0	11.8	10.0	10.8	3.3	7.6	1.9	6.8
(Constant)	30.1	14.6	17.1	12.9	14.4	11.6	2.2	8.2	13.1	7.4
Adjusted R-squared	0.14		0.17		0.08		0.06		0.0004	
N	280		280		276		276		280	

[a] statistically significant at 10% level
[b] statistically significant at 5% level
[c] statistically significant at 1% level

F-statistics:

	PSH	ISH	WSH	MSH	OSH
Industry	3.73, Prob = 0.0014	5.72, P = 0.0000	1.97, P = 0.0703	3.12, P = 0.0053	1.03, P = 0.4046
Region	2.72, Prob = 0.0067	2.36, P = 0.0183	2.69, P = 0.0073	0.62, P = 0.7610	1.03, P = 0.4046
Size	1.89, Prob = 0.0959	2.20, P = 0.0553	0.69, P = 0.6308	1.56, P = 0.1722	0.70, P = 0.62

Note: OLS estimates. Sample includes all old firms. Dependent variable is the percentage shareholding of all private, all inside, worker, manager, and all outside owners, respectively. Definitions of industry, region, and size dummies may be found in Tables 6.9, 6.10, and 6.11. The omitted categories are as follows: Heavy Machinery for the first group of industry dummies, North for the group of region dummies, and the smallest category of employment in 1994 (less than or equal 100 employees) for the last group of size dummies.

systematically influenced by characteristics of the firm. The fact that firm characteristics influence the pattern of insider control, but not of outsider control, is consistent with the view that the privatization process was insider dominated.

6.4. PRIVATIZATION SCHEMES AND THE IMPLICATIONS FOR OWNERSHIP STRUCTURE

Some authors, for instance Blasi (1996), have contended that all methods of privatization in Russia have led to the same result. In this section we test this view by exploring whether the share ownership structure varies according to the method of privatization which was employed.

The results for share ownership and dominant owner are shown in Tables 6.14 and 6.15 respectively. The four main methods by which large enterprises were privatized were: options 1, 2, and 3 of the State Privatization Programme, which was implemented from late 1992 until mid-1994, and lease buy-out, whereby assets were originally leased, mostly in 1990–2, and subsequently acquired. The most common method is option 2 of the state programme, whereby 51 per cent of all shares were sold to the employees at a price of 1.7 times the July 1992 book value of the company (during a period of near hyperinflation). Nonetheless this accounts for less than half of all privatizations.[16] The main reason for the discrepancy between these and other figures (for example, Boycko, Shleifer, and Vishny (1995); or McFaul (1996)) is that we include lease buy-outs.[17]

Unsurprisingly, the highest proportion of insider ownership is among lease buy-outs, which have 90.6 per cent of all shares insider-owned and 95.5 per cent of companies classified as insider-dominated (IO). Two-thirds of the insider shares in lease buy-outs belong to workers, while on average outsiders have only 8 per cent, and the state only 1.4 per cent. Only 2 of 66 observations on lease buy-outs are OOs and only one is an

[16] The distribution of the 51% of shares among employees under option 2 was done on the basis of applications (with deposits) to the Privatization Committee set up for each enterprise (including representatives of the administration, work collective, and local government), with each applicant receiving one share and the rest of the shares divided pro-rata among all applications.

[17] While our data suggest that about 60% of enterprises in the State Privatization Programme selected option 2, Boycko, Shleifer, and Vishny (1995) cite a figure of 73%. All sources agree on the negligible importance of option 3, which was a kind of management buy-out conditioned on fulfilling a performance contract.

Table 6.14. *Ownership structure by method of privatization*

Shareholding	Method of privatization				Total
	Option 1	Option 2	Option 3	Lease buy-out	
Total state	25.0	17.9	8.3	1.4	15.0
Total private	75.0	82.1	91.7	98.6	85.0
All insiders	54.1	57.3	68.4	90.6	66.1
Workers	41.8	38.9	41.7	61.6	46.1
Managers	12.3	18.3	26.8	28.7	19.7
All outsiders	20.9	24.8	23.2	8.0	19.0
Banks	0.2	1.7	0.0	0.7	1.0
Foreigners	0.7	0.6	0.0	0.0	0.4
Investment funds	7.9	4.4	5.5	1.7	4.6
Other domestic firms	7.5	9.4	4.4	1.8	6.6
Individuals	4.2	8.4	13.3	3.7	6.0
N	61	102	3	66	232

Note: Sample is all firms that have undergone (at least partial) privatization. Options 1, 2, and 3 refer to enterprises included in the State Privatization Programme, while 'Lease buy-out' refers to firms whose assets were bought by lessees.

SO. Thus, the inclusion of leased buy-outs indicates even more insider domination than implied by information taken from the State Privatization Programme alone.

The differences between our results and those of others is smaller when we consider the three options in the state programme. Option 1, the method by which 25 per cent of shares were given to employees free of charge and an additional 10 per cent to workers and 5 per cent to managers at nominal prices, yielded smaller private shareholdings: on average 75 per cent compared to 82.1 per cent for option 2.[18] Option 1 favoured

[18] Both the free 25% and the discounted 10% under option 1 had some restrictions. Regarding the former, no employee could receive free shares worth more (in book value terms) than 20 minimum monthly salaries; regarding the latter, the discount applied only to shares worth up to 6 times the minimum monthly salary. The 5% reserved for managers could be worth no more than 2,000 minimum salaries per person. These limitations probably explain why we find some companies privatized under option 1 that have insider ownership less than 25%. Incidentally, the management (members of the company administration) were also members of the work collective, therefore also eligible to benefit from the free 25% and the discounted 10% in addition to the discounted 5% reserved for them. The distribution of shares under option 1 was determined by the work collective.

Table 6.15. *Dominant ownership by method of privatization*

Dominant owner type	Method of privatization				Total
	Option 1	Option 2	Option 3	Lease buy-out	
SO					
Cases	14	4	0	1	19
Column %	21.5	3.8	0.0	1.5	8.0
PO					
Cases	51	100	3	65	219
Column %	78.5	96.2	100.0	98.5	92.0
IO					
Cases	33	84	3	63	183
Column %	50.8	80.8	100.0	95.5	76.9
WO					
Cases	22	51	1	47	121
Column %	33.8	49.0	33.3	71.2	50.8
MO					
Cases	5	16	0	14	35
Column %	7.7	15.4	0.0	21.2	14.7
INO					
Cases	6	16	2	0	24
Column %	9.2	15.4	66.7	0.0	10.1
OO					
Cases	8	11	0	2	21
Column %	12.3	10.6	0.0	3.0	8.8
NO					
Cases	9	5	0	0	14
Column %	13.8	4.8	0.0	0.0	5.9
Total					
Count	65	104	3	66	238

Note: Sample is all firms that have undergone (at least partial) privatization. 'Options 1, 2, and 3' refer to the State Privatization Programme, while 'Lease buy-out' refers to firms whose assets were bought by lessees.

workers slightly, with an average of 41.8 per cent compared to 38.9 under option 2. Managers and most outsiders did rather better with option 2: 18.3 per cent and 24.8 per cent, respectively, compared to 12.3 and 20.9 under option 1 on average. Only the voucher investment funds, which were subject to a legal limit of no more than 10 per cent in any one firm being privatized, fared better under option 1 than 2, with 7.9 per cent in the former case and 4.4 per cent in the latter.

The pattern of dominant ownership, however, is somewhat different. Among the firms privatized through the State Programme, option 1 still shows the greatest shareholdings by the state (21.5 per cent of firms categorized as SOs). But IOs account for the majority of option 2 firms (approximately 80 per cent as against 50 per cent under option 1), and WOs are also more common with option 2 (49 per cent compared to 34 per cent), even though the average worker shareholding is larger in option 1. Moreover, MOs are nearly twice as common with option 2, while OOs are less common even though outsiders have larger shareholdings compared to option 1.

To test whether these patterns were statistically significant, we ran a regression linking the proportion of shares held by any owner Y (YSH) to the three privatization options and controls for industry, size, and region. The results are reported in Tables 6.16a, 6.16b, and 6.16c, and confirm that differences in the ownership outcomes from the various privatization methods are statistically significant.

Starting with private shareholdings (PSH) in Table 6.16a, lease buy-out is associated with 12 per cent more private ownership, and option 1 with 5 per cent less shares, compared with option 2. Option 3 firms show no significant difference in this or any of the other equations, although this could be due to the small number of firms in using option 3 (and therefore of observations in this category).

The coefficients on the privatization methods variables in the ISH and OSH regressions sum to the coefficients in the PSH equation so the effects of different methods on PSH can be decomposed between ISH and OSH.[19] Thus, we confirm that the inclusion of lease buy-outs increases both private shareholdings and insider stakes. Lease buy-outs have a significant positive effect on private ownership overall and in the decomposition the large (significant) positive impact on insider holdings more than offsets the negative (significant) effect from outsider shareholdings.

[19] This is because PSH = ISH + OSH and ordinary least squares estimation preserves additivity.

Table 6.16a. *Estimating the impact of privatization method on ownership structure*

Independent variables	Dependent variables: private shareholdings					
	PSH		ISH		OSH	
	all	voting	all	voting	all	voting
Option 1	−5.3[b]	−10.1[c]	−2.7	−16.0[c]	−2.6	5.9[*]
	(2.5)	(2.3)	(3.2)	(3.5)	(3.256)	(3.6)
Option 3	−0.1	−2.2	−0.5	−2.3	0.4	0.1
	(0.8)	(8.5)	(11.3)	(2.6)	(11.6)	(12.7)
Lease	11.8[c]	9.7[c]	28.2[c]	26.1[c]	−16.4[c]	−16.5[c]
buy-out	(2.5)	(2.4)	(3.2)	(3.6)	(3.3)	(3.6)
Adj R^2	0.382	0.436	0.486	0.506	0.125	0.167
N	206	206	206	206	206	206

Note: Sample includes all privatized firms. 'Option 2' is the omitted category. Covariates include 3 region dummies (Moscow−St. Petersburg, European Russia, Asian Russia (Siberia, Far East, and Urals)), 7 industry dummies, and 3 employment size dummies. Shares are expressed in percentages.

[a] statistically significant at 10% level
[b] statistically significant at 5% level
[c] statistically significant at 1% level

Table 6.16b. *Privatization method and insider shareholdings*

Independent variables	Dependent variables: inside shareholdings			
	WSH		MSH	
	all	voting	all	voting
Option 1	3.0	− 7.8[a]	− 5.8	− 8.3 [b]
	(4.4)	(4.6)	(3.9)	(4.0)
Option 3	−0.7	−2.0	−0.1	−0.5
	(15.6)	(16.2)	(14.0)	(14.2)
Lease	22.2[c]	20.6[c]	5.5	5.0
buy-out	(4.5)	(4.7)	(4.0)	(4.1)
Adj R^2	0.147	0.188	0.073	0.084
N	202	202	202	202

Note: Sample includes all privatized firms. 'Option 2' is the omitted category. Covariates include 3 region dummies (Moscow−St. Petersburg, European Russia, Asian Russia (Siberia, Far East, and Urals)), 7 industry dummies, and 3 employment size dummies. Shares are expressed in percentages.

Table 6.16c. *Effects of alternative privatization methods on outsider shareholdings*

Independent variables	Dependent variables: outside shareholdings									
	Banks		Investment funds		Domestic firms		Foreigners		Individuals	
	all	voting	all	voting	all	voting	all	voting	all	voting
Option 1	-1.6[b]	-1.6[a]	3.6[b]	7.3[c]	-1.1	1.6	-0.1	0.2	-3.4[b]	-1.7
	(0.8)	(0.8)	(1.6)	(1.9)	(2.4)	(2.6)	(0.5)	(9.6)	(1.6)	(1.8)
Option 3	-3.2	-3.2	0.3	-0.1	-2.5	-2.7	-1.5	-1.9	7.8	8.4
	(2.9)	(2.9)	(5.7)	(6.8)	(8.3)	(9.3)	(1.9)	(2.3)	(5.6)	(6.2)
Lease buy-out	-0.8	-0.9	-2.2	-2.0	-7.4[c]	-7.6[c]	-0.8	-0.9	-4.5[c]	-4.5[c]
	(0.8)	(0.8)	(1.6)	(1.9)	(2.4)	(2.7)	(0.6)	(0.7)	(1.6)	(1.8)
Adj R^2	0.009	0.007	0.100	0.149	0.042	0.056	0.012	0.021	0.079	0.074
N	201	201	201	201	201	201	201	201	201	201

Note: Sample includes all privatized firms. 'Option 2' is the omitted category. Covariates include 3 region dummies (Moscow–St. Petersburg, European Russia, Asian Russia (Siberia, Far East, and Urals)), 7 industry dummies, and 3 employment size dummies. Shares are expressed in percentages.

[a] statistically significant at 10% level
[b] statistically significant at 5% level
[c] statistically significant at 1% level

The choice of option 1 reduces private shareholdings; the coefficient is statistically significant and negative in the insider and outsider shareholding equations.

We study the impact of different privatization methods on insider shareholdings in Table 6.16b. The large positive effect of lease buy-out on private and insider ownership in Table 6.16a turns out to be almost entirely via worker shareholdings. The coefficient on managerial shareholding equation is insignificant (although positive). The negative impact of option 1 on insider holdings is found to operate separately on worker and manager shareholdings.

The effects of the alternative privatization methods on outsider shareholdings are explored in Table 6.16c. The impact of using option 1 are heterogeneous. The insignificant coefficient of -2.6 in the outsider equation can be decomposed into significant negative coefficients on all categories except investment funds. The large negative effects of using a lease buy-out method for outsider shareholdings are accounted for almost entirely by the effects on domestic firms and individuals.[20]

The results reveal a tendency for investment funds to behave differently from the other domestic institutional investors: banks and firms. The investment funds are the only type that tend to have larger shareholdings under option 1, and this may reflect a greater aversion on the part of these funds to insider power. Banks and firms are liable to be closely connected to insiders and therefore may be less likely to avoid firms where insiders have a majority. If so, investment funds could become agents for more active corporate governance.

6.5. CONCLUSION

We have presented evidence in this chapter on the Russian ownership structure emerging as a consequence of the lease buy-out and privatization programme of the early 1990s. We offer two ways to categorize the new ownership structures; according to shareholdings by the main groups of actions in the economy and according to dominant shareholder. We also provide information pertaining to all state enterprises prior to economic liberalization and to *de novo* firms, as well as to the group of privatized firms which have been the focus of attention in previous studies.

---

[20] It is predictable that outside individuals have relatively little opportunity to acquire shares in lease buy-outs, but it is less clear why institutional investors (other than domestic firms) show no significant difference compared to option 2 of the State Programme.

We confirm the findings that insiders in July 1994 held around two-thirds of shares, and that about the same proportion of firms was dominated by insiders. Around 70 per cent of insider-dominated firms were majority 'worker owned'; the remainder were dominated by managers or managers and workers combined. Of course, dominant ownership does not necessarily yield control and with worker shareholdings probably being more dispersed than those of managers, these figures understate the scale of managerial influence over company decisions.

While outsider average shareholdings in 1994 were modest (less than 20 per cent), they were concentrated, giving outsiders a dominant voice in some 10 per cent of Russian enterprises. The study also highlights the significance of state ownership in Russian firms even after privatization was concluded. The state shareholding in 1994 was on average 38 per cent in Russian industry, and even larger when firms are weighted by employment. The state retained at least 10 per cent holding in more than half of Russian industry, and this does not take into account 'golden shares'. This shareholding has been going down in some sectors more recently; however, the available evidence suggests that the grip of insiders (and especially managers) on shares has if anything been becoming more entrenched since 1994 (see for example, Buck *et al.* (1998)).

Finally, we have presented evidence that the presence of outsiders and other aspects of corporate ownership structure in 1994 were related to sector, size, and region, and to the different methods of privatization that have been applied to Russia. In particular the choice of privatization method, which must include the lease buy-out programme, has been shown to have significant implications for the extent of privatization and for the relative shareholding of different ownership groups.

REFERENCES

Akamatsu, N. (1995).'Enterprise Governance and Investment Funds in Russian Privatization,' in M. Aoki and H. K. Kim (eds.), *Corporate Governance in Transitional Economics: Insider Control and the Role of Banks*, Washington, DC: The World Bank.

Aoki, M., and Kim, H. K. (1995) (eds.), *Corporate Governance in Transitional Economies: Insider Control and the Role of Banks*. Washington, DC: The World Bank.

Belyanova, E., and Rozinsky, I. (1995).'Evolution of Commercial in Russia and the Implications for Corporate Governance', in M. Aoki and H. K. Kim (eds.), *Corporate Governance in Transitional Economics: Insider Control and the Role of Banks*, Washington, DC: The World Bank.

Blasi, J. R. (1994). 'Russian Privatization: Ownership, Governance, and Restructuring', Rutgers University School of Management and Labor Relations, unpublished manuscript.

—— (1995). 'Russian Enterprises After Privatization', Paper presented at the Association for Comparative Economic Studies Meeting, San Francisco, January.

—— (1996). 'Corporate Ownership and Corporate Governance in the Russian Federation', Research Report of the Federal Commission on the Capital Market, May.

—— Kroumova, M., and Kruse D. (1997). *Kremlin Capitalism: Privatizing the Russian Economy*, Ithaca: Cornell University Press.

—— and Shleifer, A. (1996). 'Corporate Governance in Russia: An Initial Look', in R. Frydman, *et al.* (eds.), *Corporate Governance in Central Europe and Russia, 2. Insiders and the State*, Budapest: CEU Press.

Boardman, A., and Vining, A. (1989). 'Ownership and Performance in Competitive Environment: A Comparison of the Performance of Private, Mixed, and State-Owned Enterprises', *Journal of Law and Economics*, 32: 1–33.

Boycko, M., Shleifer, A., and Vishny, R. (1995). *Privatizing Russia*, Cambridge, Mass.: MIT Press.

Buck, T., Filatotchev, I., Wright, M., and Zhukov, V. (1998). 'Corporate Governance and Employee Ownership in an Economic Crisis: Enterprise Strategies in the Former USSR', Paper presented at CISME Conference on Corporate Governance in Russia London Business School, 30 June.

Commander, S., Dhar, S., and Yemtsov, R. (1996). 'How Russian Firms Make Their Wage and Employment Decisions', in S. Commander *et al.* (eds.), *Enterprise Restructuring and Economic Policy in Russia*, Washington, DC: Economic Development Institute, The World Bank.

—— Fan, Q., and Schaffer, M. (eds.), (1996). *Enterprise Restructuring and Economic Policy in Russia*, Washington, DC: Economic Development Institute, The World Bank.

Dittus, P., and Prowse, S. (1996). 'Corporate Control in Central Europe and Russia: Should Banks Own Shares?' in R. Frydman *et al.* (eds.), *Corporate Governance in Central Europe and Russia 2*, Budapest: CEU Press.

Earle, J. S., and Estrin, S. (1996). 'Employee Ownership in Transition', in R. Frydman *et al.* (eds.), *Corporate Governance in Central Europe and Russia*, Budapest: CEU Press.

—— Estrin, S., and Leshchenko, L. (1996). 'Ownership Structures, Patterns of Control, and Enterprise Behavior in Russia', in Commander *et al.* (eds.) 1996.

Filatotchev, I., Bleaney, M., and Wright, M. (1999). 'Insider-controlled Firms in Russia', *Economics of Planning*, 32: 129–51.

Frydman, R., Gray, C., and Rapaczynski A. (eds.), (1996). *Corporate Governance in Central Europe and Russia. Volume 2: Insiders and the State*, Budapest: CEU Press.

Frydman, R., Phelps E., Rapaczynski, A., and Shleifer A. (1993). 'Needed Mechanisms of Corporate Governance and Finance in Eastern Europe', *Economics of Transition*, 1/2.

—— Rapaczynski, A., and Earle J. S. *et al.* (1993a). *The Privatization Process in Central Europe*, Budapest: CEU Press.

—— —— *et al.* (1993b). *The Privatization Process in Russia, Ukraine, and the Baltic States*, Budapest: CEU Press.

Goskomstat (1996). *Russia in Figures.*

Lee, U. J. (1996). 'Appendix: The World Bank Survey of Industrial Enterprises', in Commander *et al.* (eds.), *Enterprise Restructuring and Economic Policy in Russia*, Washington, DC: Economic Development Institute, The World Bank.

Litwack, J. M. (1995). 'Corporate Governance, Banks, and Fiscal Reform in Russia', in M. Aoki and H. K. Kim (eds.), *Corporate Governance in Transitional Economies.*

McFaul, M. (1996). 'The Allocation of Property Rights in Russia: The First Round', *Communist and Post-Communist Studies*, 29/3.

Pistor, K. (1995). 'Privatization and Corporate Governance in Russia: An Empirical Study', in M. McFaul and T. Perlmutter (eds.), *Privatization, Conversion, and Enterprise Reform in Russia*, Boulder, Col.: Westview Press.

——, and Turkewitz, J. (1996). 'Coping with Hydra—State Ownership After Privatization', in R. Frydman, C. Gray, and A. Rapaczynski (eds.), *Corporate Governance in Central Europe and Russia.*

Radygin, A. (1996). 'Privatization in Russia: Hard Choice, First Results, New Targets', Institute for Economy in Transition, unpublished manuscript, Institute for Economy in Transition, Moscow.

Richter, A., and Schaffer, M. E. (1996). 'The Performance of De Novo Private Firms in Russian Manufacturing', in S. Commander *et al.* (eds.), *Enterprise Restructuring and Economic Policy in Russia.*

Shleifer, A., and Vasiliev, D. (1996). 'Management Ownership and Russian Privatization', in R. Frydman *et al.* (eds.), 1996.

Vickers, J., and Yarrow, G. (1988). *Privatization*, Cambridge, Mass.: MIT Press.

Webster, L., Franz, J., Artimov, I., and Wackman, H. (1994). 'Newly Privatized Russian Enterprises', World Bank Technical Paper 241, Washington, DC.

7

The Banking Sector

MIKHAIL DMITRIEV, MIKHAIL MATOVNIKOV,
LEONID MIKHAILOV, LUDMILA SYCHEVA,
AND EUGENE TIMOFEYEV

7.1. INTRODUCTION

At the end of the 1980s the Soviet Union had barely emerged from the monobank system of the Communist era, when effectively one single banking institution—Gosbank—handled the full range of banking services required in the command-administrative system. In the subsequent decade the banking sector followed a turbulent and unpredictable path, remote from the broad infrastructural position characteristic of banking in stable market economies. In line with its Soviet ancestry, however, it continued to play an important part in relation to public-sector budgets, both in channelling government expenditure and in assisting tax collection.

Section 2 outlines the development of banking institutions and, especially for the period up to 1995, the sources of growth of banking business. Many new institutions were created, some of them short-lived. Regulation was virtually absent. Speculation, especially in foreign-exchange positions, was rife.

A minor crisis in the sector in August 1995 triggered a shift of direction. As outlined in section 3, monetary stabilization required the banks to introduce radical changes in the character of their operations, develop different instruments, and move into new segments of the financial market. After 1995 financing of the government budget deficit came to the fore in various ways, ranging from routine placement of household

This chapter has been adapted by the editors, with assistance from Nat Moser and Taras Sobolev.

deposits at the majority-state-owned Savings Bank (Sberbank) in government debt instruments, to the notorious one-off 'loans for shares' scheme in 1995–7, which transferred key shareholdings in major Russian export enterprises (oil and metals) to a handful of private, oligarch-controlled institutions.[1]

Following the government debt default and abrupt currency devaluation of August 1998, large parts of the sector ceased to be viable (section 4). Major banks were insolvent and, despite official declarations of intent about bank restructuring, a lengthy period of inaction ensued. The fact that this could be tolerated reflected the very limited role that the banking sector played in Russia's private-sector economic activity in the first decade of transition. Households relied overwhelmingly as a vehicle for liquid-asset holdings on US dollar currency and on the Sberbank. The business sector, too, especially the important part of it involved in international trade, preferred when possible to use foreign banking institutions rather than Russian ones. The authorities did their best to discourage this. Major banks that formed part of the leading financial industrial groups (FIGs) were in any case more akin to being financial offices of their parent enterprise than institutions at the service of the economy at large.

7.2. SPONTANEOUS PRIVATIZATION AND THE FORMATION OF COMMERCIAL BANKS

Until 1987 the Soviet Banking system was organized as a 'monobank' with the State bank (Gosbank) the agent of the government. Reform of the system started with the 1988 Law on Co-operatives, which permitted the creation of co-operative banks to service those newly created co-operative (that is, private) enterprises that did not wish to rely wholly on the state apparatus.

At the beginning of 1988 there were just four, state-owned commercial banks, the so-called *spetsbanks*: Vneshekonombank handled foreign trade and payments; while the three domestically oriented institutions were supposed to focus respectively on agriculture (Agroprombank), industry (Promstroibank), and housing (Zhilsotsbank). Over the next two years about 150 new banks were created. Then in 1990 many regional offices of the state banks became independent, bringing a further 800

---

[1] See chapter in this volume on the oil industry by Moser and Oppenheimer.

separate banks into existence on the basis of the former state network, especially of the former Agroprombank, Many of these newly spawned institutions were short lived. By 1993 most of them had been absorbed as branches of independent private institutions created from 1992 onwards and unconnected with the former state banks.

The new banks were a spontaneous by-product of the privatization of non-bank entities. Industrial companies, agricultural marketing bodies, and other business organizations wanted to keep control of their revenue and cash flows—both to facilitate misappropriation and to protect against misappropriation by others—by setting up their own 'pocket' banks to handle them. Acquisition of the former state-owned banks that had emerged from the fragmentation of the three domestically focused *spetsbanks* was facilitated by the swift depreciation of the state-owned banks' capital in the face of inflation.

By 1995 there were well over 2,000 commercial banks in existence across the country, about one-third of them based or with major offices in Moscow. Most of them were small, with average assets at the beginning of 1995 of a mere $36 million equivalent. Moscow-based banks accounted for most of the decade for around 70 per cent of commercial bank assets, with half of this total in the five largest banks.[2]

Banks' ownership structure reflected their origins. In mid-1996, according to a Central Bank survey, a mere 16 per cent of shareholders or co-proprietors[3] were individuals, the other 84 per cent being corporate bodies. Among the latter by far the largest category, accounting for two-thirds of the 84 per cent, were privatized limited companies, the other one-third comprising a mixture of credit institutions, state-owned enterprises, federal and local governments, and non-commercial organizations. In rare cases a dominant shareholding was in the hands of a local authority. This general pattern changed little over the succeeding two or three years, except that the founding and controlling shareholders tended to strengthen their grip by acquiring additional shares from outsiders. At the same time the number of functioning credit institutions declined steadily, to 2,000 in March 1997, 1,700 at the end of 1997, 1,600 in June 1998, 1,500 in November 1998, and 1,400 in mid-1999. At the end of 1999 the figure was down to 1,349. While there was some consolidation of

---

[2] OECD (1997), p. 94 ff.; and (2000), p. 73 ff.
[3] The distinction between shareholders and co-proprietors reflects two varieties of shared ownership recognized in Russian law.

small institutions, the main reason for the drop in numbers was insolvency and the revocation of bank licences by the Central Bank (CBR). In the wake of the August 1998 débâcle the banks which lost their licences had accounted before the crisis for almost one-quarter of the privatized banking system's assets.[4]

The above statistical picture, however, omits the huge continuing role of public-sector institutions in Russian banking. Above all, the Savings Bank (Sberbank) occupies a dominant position. Sberbank's history goes back to 1842. In its current form, following the enactment of Russia's law on Banks and Banking Activities in December 1990, it regained its separate status as a joint stock bank in March 1991, with the Central Bank of Russia as majority (50 per cent plus 1) shareholder. Its present-day dominance of the banking sector reflects several factors. One is the government-guaranteed status of Sberbank's household deposit liabilities, though such a guarantee arguably carries less weight than in western industrial countries. Apart from Sberbank, there is no deposit insurance in Russia. Another factor is its vast branch and agency network—over 34,000 outlets even after April 1996, when the number was reduced by 4,000. The largest branch network recorded for a (mainly) private bank (SBS—Agro in 1997) was 1,250.[5] A third factor is the restriction imposed by the authorities from mid-1996 onwards on collection of household deposits by private banks: the ratio of such deposits to a bank's net worth was limited to 100 per cent, while the ratio for Sberbank was set at 730 per cent.[6]

Sberbank's share of total household deposits rose from a low of about 40 per cent in mid-1994—when deposits in private banks appeared relatively attractive—to no less than 85 per cent in 1999.[7] This includes deposits in foreign currency as well as in roubles. Making due allowance for the fact that Sberbank collects only a small proportion of non-household (enterprise, etc.) deposits, and that households probably account for somewhat less than half of total rouble deposits, Sberbank may be estimated to hold about half the liabilities of the entire Russian banking system outside the Central Bank. At the same time more than half of its assets comprise Russian government rouble debt, and it has relatively small foreign currency claims; so it was severely affected by the August 1998 upheaval.

---

[4] Central Bank of Russia, various issues.   [5] Kryuchkova (1997), p. 8.
[6] Ibid.   [7] *Savings Bank of Russia* (1997–9).

Aside from Sberbank, state-owned banks include those servicing foreign economic relations (Vneshekonombank, Vneshtorgbank, and Roseximbank) as well as specialized institutions such as the Russian Financial Corporation and *Bank Razvitiya Predprinimatelstvo* (designed to promote new enterprises). In addition, there are forty-eight banks established with participation of the Russian Federation Pension Fund and its regional branches.

For most of the period since 1990 the commercial banks' main sources of deposits have been enterprises and the government sector. Households played a prominent role only for a brief spell from late 1993 to early 1995. It was at that time that Sberbank's share of total household deposits experienced its short-lived fall to below 50 per cent. This reflected, however, not a shift of existing deposits out of Sberbank but rather a rapid growth of the aggregate deposit total from a low base. During 1994 aggregate bank time and savings deposits in roubles rose from 5 trillion to 25 trillion, an approximate doubling at constant prices. Demand deposits rose from 12 trillion to 33 trillion.

Collection of household deposits was not at that time subject to Central Bank licensing or regulation, and the banks' main competitors for funds were a variety of unregulated 'savings businesses' which used colourful advertising, wild interest rates, and implausible sounding instruments (from certificates of deposit to 'agreements for joint investment in real property') to lure customers.[8] While rouble interest rates of 200 per cent or more might look plausible in a climate of high inflation, rates of up to 30 per cent per annum *in US dollars*, such as were commonly advertised in 1993–4 even on the Moscow metro, pointed clearly to fraudulent operations, especially pyramiding or 'Ponzi finance'. The most notorious instance was the MMM investment fund, whose organizer Sergei Mavrodi subsequently gained release from prison by getting himself briefly elected to the Duma. By early 1995 non-bank savings companies had largely disappeared, either bankrupted or in a few cases converted into (marginally more respectable) banks. Estimates of the number of depositors who lost money ranged from 20 million to 50 million.[9]

[8] Kryuchkova (1997), p. 10 f. Kryuchkova notes that 1993–4 saw the peak of financial advertising in Russia, with the financial services industry the lead spender in all the media. Based on the cost of television time, the ten biggest TV advertisers included four financial companies, all of which failed during 1995. Thereafter financial advertising by banks and investment funds was essentially confined to 'image-building'. [9] Ibid.

This colourful episode notwithstanding, interest-bearing deposits never accounted for more that one-quarter of commercial banks' liabilities, a far lower figure than is typical in western market economies. The central reason is that nearly all the deposits of the enterprise sector and of government bodies remained non-interest bearing. In the case of the enterprise sector, this partly reflected the symbiosis between 'pocket' banks and their associated businesses. But the more important explanation is the mass of varying state regulation which restricted companies' freedom of action both in managing bank accounts and in switching between bank deposits and cash.

Such regulation reflects a continuation of the Soviet system of using banks as the means of exercising financial control over enterprises (*kontrol' rublem*—control by the rouble).[10] The system rests on twin foundations. On the one hand, all settlements between enterprises, and between enterprises and public authorities, are required to be made through bank transfers. Cash may be drawn only to pay wages and pensions. On the other hand, the opening and maintenance of bank accounts by enterprises is subject to a complicated registration process involving (among others) the fiscal authorities. The latter, moreover, may draw money from a firm's account on their own initiative—a kind of state-enforced direct debit mechanism—in order to settle tax or other public obligations (such as statutory contributions to off-budget funds for health or employment insurance).

In the early 1990s the operation of the system was motivated mainly by the struggle for monetary stabilization. Cash shortages—rather than tight money—were employed as an anti-inflation instrument acting for the most part on wage payments. A special aspect in 1992–3 was the attempt to limit money creation within the still unified rouble zone (broadly, the former Soviet Union) by central banks other than that of the Russian Federation. While these other central banks could create non-cash roubles, the Russian Central Bank maintained its monopoly on cash (banknotes). From 1994 onwards, however, the focus shifted increasingly to the fiscal side, bank-account regulations playing a central role in efforts to increase revenue and diminish tax evasion.

Evasion sooner or later involves either unauthorized employment of cash or, for enterprises engaged in foreign trade, illegal accumulation of

---

[10] See Thompson (1997), and the literature there cited, especially Prill (1995).

funds abroad. Since individuals are freely entitled to use cash, transfers between firms and persons play a considerable role in the evasion process. As with any scheme of tax evasion, additional costs and inefficiencies arise. Official regulations fluctuate, as the authorities seek to close loopholes and counter new evasionary devices. Sometimes they are obliged to retreat from excessively draconian or unrealistic measures. From May 1994 to March 1995 enterprises were limited to the use of a single registered rouble account for settlement purposes. In August 1996 there was a short-lived attempt (by presidential decree) to subject every transaction on an individual's bank account to income tax.[11] Special restrictions on the use of funds apply to enterprises in arrears with their tax payments or extra-budgetary dues, including a decree dating from 1996 requiring such enterprises to establish a special tax-debtor's account into which they are obliged to pay all funds received and not designated for the payment of wages or current taxes or the financing of current government budgetary outlays. An initial executive attempt to give payment of tax arrears priority even over wages was halted by the Supreme Court as impermissible under the Civil Code.

The relationship between the banks' liabilities and their role as agents of government has changed over time, and is linked with parallel developments on the assets side of their balance sheets. In the early 1990s, and to a reduced extent in 1993–4, the banks were of great importance as channels for the delivery of directed (namely, government-subsidized) credits to enterprises at hugely negative real interest rates. According to World Bank estimates such credits amounted in 1992 to nearly 19 per cent of GDP.[12] The greater part of the funds involved were furnished to the banks through refinance by the Central Bank.[13] From 1995 onwards, however, subsidized credits with Central Bank refinance were a minor element—and the quantitative significance of banks in the economy declined correspondingly (see section 3).[14]

---

[11] Thompson (1997), p. 1165. This move appears to have stemmed from the investigations of a special inter-departmental commission set up in 1995 to devise measures against the illicit use of cash.

[12] World Bank (1996), p. 54. Subsidized credits were a major element in a huge web of subsidies totalling on some estimates more than 50% of GDP.

[13] Monetary authorities' credits to commercial banks in 1992 totalled 15% of GDP and carried a negative real interest rate averaging more than 12% per month.

[14] Federal subsidies and Central Bank credits to commercial banks both fell to little over 1% of GDP in 1995. However, non-federal budgetary expenditure on subsidies remained in the region of 7% of GDP. Thompson (1997), p. 1172, citing Halligan *et al.* (1996).

At the same time, however, financial transfers to and from the public sector at both federal and regional levels—taxes on the one hand and expenditures on the other—have since 1993 been channelled very largely through authorized (*upolnomochennye*) commercial banks.[15] The associated bank liabilities are not only interest free, but are subject to profitable abuse by the banks in the form of delayed transfer to the designated recipients for weeks or even months at a time. Such abuse has been an aggravating (though not initiating) factor in the general phenomenon of payments arrears. Appointment as an authorized bank, especially at federal level, has since 1995 been increasingly subject to criteria of capital adequacy and specified areas of operation. This will have reduced though scarcely eliminated the political influence and corruption factor. At the time of the first Chechen War in 1994–5 government outlays on the campaign were rumoured to be channelled largely through one Moscow bank, whose oligarch president duly became a senior member of the government.[16]

Probably the mainstay of commercial banks' profits in 1993–4 was their holdings of foreign currency balances in correspondent banks abroad, amounting to 40 per cent or more of their assets. With the great bulk of their liabilities in roubles and bearing zero nominal interest despite inflation running at 200 per cent per year, the mere retention of hard-currency balances was sufficient to ensure a disproportionate return on capital as the rouble depreciated month by month. The market in inter-bank deposits served to bring about a certain diffusion of profits to banks lacking direct access to foreign exchange.

7.3. THE SEE-SAW OF STABILIZATION, 1995–1998

Initial moves to lower the growth rates of money and the price level had begun in 1994.[17] Two main lines of attack were pursued to restrain the growth of bank balance sheets. One was a further reduction in directed credits to enterprises. The other was a shift in financing the federal

---

[15] Previously, central government outlays (other than directed credits) were effected through Sberbank, Promstroybank, and Agroprombank only.

[16] In January 1997 a Commission on financial, credit and monetary policy chaired by First Deputy prime minister Vladimir Potanin cut the number of fully authorized ('universal agent') banks from 85 to 16; the number of federally authorized banks was reduced to 54. In January 1998 it was announced that the institution of authorized banks would be gradually abolished, but in practice no great changes were made over the following two years.

[17] See the chapter by Brigitte Granville.

budget deficit from Central Bank credit ('money printing') to issuance of interest-bearing government debt. Rouble treasury bills (GKOs)—zero coupon instruments with three-month or six-month currency—had been introduced in 1993. In addition, issues of domestic bonds denominated in foreign currency (so-called MinFins or Taiga bonds) were expanded. Somewhat longer term rouble bonds (OFZs), with a quarterly coupon linked to GKO yields, followed later, from mid-1995 onwards.[18] Incidentally, the issuing procedures for GKOs in particular were another profit source for authorized institutions. The primary issuing agents for the government consisted initially of 19 commercial banks and six brokerage houses.

Although tight money was not pursued with full consistency in 1994, interest rates still rose sharply and at the year end were strongly positive in real terms. The policy strategy was pressed home in the first half of 1995. Directed credits faded, and bank credit to the non-financial sector dropped from 20 per cent of GDP in 1993–4 to 12 per cent. Federal government borrowing from the Central Bank virtually ceased, and government debt issues accelerated correspondingly. This set of policies kept real interest rates high, but very largely because it was effective in bringing down inflation from around 15 per cent to around 3 per cent per month. The exchange rate was the key transmission mechanism, thanks to a turnaround in net capital flows through the balance of payments. In the second quarter the rouble stopped declining and appreciated by over 10 per cent in nominal terms, implying an appreciation in real terms of about 50 per cent. The rapid movement was halted in July by the authorities introducing the exchange rate 'corridor' or broad-band peg.[19] While nominal depreciation of the rouble resumed shortly thereafter, it was kept slow enough to ensure continuing real appreciation up to the first quarter of 1996.

The 1995 exchange-rate developments had a traumatic effect upon banks relying on rouble depreciation as the mainstay of their business. Moreover, hugely positive real interest rates meant that borrowing from other banks to plug gaps in the balance sheet tended to aggravate the situation in anything but the very short term. Such borrowing constituted in effect a gamble on the resumption of faster inflation and rouble depreciation. When the gamble did not swiftly pay off there was

---

[18] There were also small amounts of other rouble instruments, mainly governments savings bonds(GKSZ) and treasury obligations of the Ministry of Finance (KO).

[19] See the chapter by Andrei Lushin and Peter Oppenheimer.

no alternative but to renew it and on a larger scale corresponding to the accrued interest. In late August 1995 the situation exploded. Creditor banks began to take fright and cut short their commitments. Interest rates on the inter-bank market soared and funds became unavailable. The Central Bank gave limited support through secured credits and some open-market purchases. The number of bank failures in the succeeding days and weeks reached well into three figures and included two relatively large institutions—Natsionalnyi Kredit and Tveruniversalbank—which were brought down by the volume of their uncollectable claims on the inter-bank market.

This episode and the change in Russia's financial climate led to a reversal of commercial banks' asset/liability preferences. The instinct was now to look to domestic (rouble) assets rather than to foreign-exchange holdings as the basic source of profits. The most flamboyant manifestation of this, initiated only a few months after the August upheaval, was the loans-for-shares scheme referred to above. In the guise of meeting urgent short-term financing needs of the government, and with the unstated interim purpose of forming an election war chest to ensure Boris Yeltsin's re-election as president in 1996, a handful of politically influential Moscow banks (the two most prominent being Uneximbank and Menatep) acquired control in 1995–7 of major export enterprises in the oil sector and elsewhere. This created a handful of conspicuous FIGs, an arrangement periodically promoted by the authorities as a means of bringing about industrial restructuring.

The enterprises became a crucial source of wealth for the controlling banks, who appropriated by one route or another not merely profit but total revenue streams of the enterprises in question, leaving them indebted to employees, suppliers, and the authorities, and sometimes with balance sheets stripped of their principal assets. The strategy was not riskless for the exploiting banks. Tax debts could lead to an enterprise being dismembered or seized as bankrupt on the initiative of regional fiscal authorities, who tended to act in consort with some rival corporate entities anxious to gain control of the exploited company. There were both successful and unsuccessful instances of such attempts at seizure. In short, there emerged a grotesquely distorted form of competitive struggle for corporate control, involving among other things blatant abuse of bankruptcy laws and of judicial processes.

These activities, although important enough to be harmful for the economy's development, were none the less confined to a small number of major players and were not a model that others could readily follow.

Commercial banks at large continued to register more orthodox-looking claims on the general run of domestic companies. Two points must be emphasized, however. First, relative to GDP the aggregate value of these claims remained low by comparison both with other transition and market economies and with Russia itself in the early 1990s when directed credits were still extensive (Tables 7.1 and 7.2).

Secondly, the nature and soundness of the banks' claims was generally far from transparent. Company attitudes to bank and other debt still reflected the Soviet-era mentality of 'soft' budget constraints. Interest and amortization schedules were often not taken seriously, especially where a company was also living on arrears to other creditors—though to be sure such arrears were for the most part a much cheaper credit channel than commercial bank loans. Banks for their part lacked reliable

Table 7.1. *The evolution of Russian banking, end-year, unless otherwise stated*

	1992	1993	1994	1995	1996
Number of operating credit organizations[a]	1,713	2,019	2,517	2,295	2,030
Licences withdrawn (number, cumulative)		13	78	303	592
Charter capital requirement for new banks (thousand US$)	214.4	70.6	1,244.7	1,291.5	3,648.9
Real monthly refinance rate of CBR[b]	−12.2	−6.9	4.4	7.6	6.5
Percentage shares of GDP					
Credit from monetary authorities to commercial banks	15	5.1	2.4	1.1	0.6
Bank credit to the non-financial sector	33.6	20.4	19.6	12	10
Interbank credit received		3.2	4.9	3.9	3.1
Gross assets of the banking sector	88	54	56	36	36
Households deposits	1.9	2.4	4.2	4.3	5.3
Households deposits outside of Sberbank	0.3	0.9	1.7	1.5	1.4

Notes: [a]1,360 at end 1991. [b]Yearly average of real monthly rates; for 1992 February–December (so as to exclude the January price jump).

Source: CBR, IMF, OECD. Published in OECD Economic Surveys (1997).

Table 7.2. *Commercial bank credit in selected central and eastern European countries: Credit to the non-financial sector as a percentage of GDP*

	1993	1994	1995	1996
Russian Federation	20.4	19.6	12	10.4
Poland	21.3	19.8	19.7	22.1
Hungary	28.4	26.5	23	22.9
Czech Republic	73.1	72.9	63.8	61.1
Slovakia	71.5	60.4	59.2	62.4
Romania	24.4	19	22.7	24.6
Slovenia	22.2	22.9	27.5	28.7
Bulgaria	67.8	51	41.3	69.5

Sources: CBR; National Banks of Poland, Hungary, Czech Republic, Bulgaria, Slovenia, Statistical Office of the Slovak Republic; Romanian National Commission for Statistics; IMF. Published in OECD (1997).

means of enforcing credit terms. The bankruptcy laws were an uncertain weapon, and if invoked on any scale might well bring down the bank itself instead of, or before, its miscreant clients. At the same time, accounting standards, particularly as regards provision for bad debts, were far less stringent than in western countries. It was easy, when compounding unpaid debt service back on to the originating loan, to pretend that the situation was healthy and the loan still earning good profits for the bank. Probable defaults tended to be acknowledged only on a scale small enough to be outweighed by supposed continuing interest earnings on other items. Thus a bank's loan portfolio might remain 'profitable' up to the moment of insolvency.[20]

Optimistic accounting practices are arguably more justified when commercial credits are guaranteed by the state. Such guarantees were extensively employed by both federal and local (*oblast* and municipal) governments as a means of financing deficits. In other words, instead of payment from public authorities, suppliers might receive state-guaranteed bank credit. This was attractive to the authorities in as much as budgetary appearances were improved in the short term, without depriving government creditors of funds. On the other hand, it was bad for payments discipline, since the enterprise receiving the credit had a positive incentive not to service it—unless the authorities happened to

---

[20] A technical point of interest is that under Russian accounting rules provisions are treated as a liability rather than as a diminution of assets, thus by western standards inflating the balance sheet at the very least. See Kryuchkova (1997), p. 28.

have some independent sanction over the enterprise, such as a threatened loss of orders or prosecution for tax offences. For this reason, banks granting credits of this type typically deducted 'up front' any interest and fees due to them and not covered by the guarantee.

State guarantees also had a negative effect on informational transparency. Not only was there ambiguity over the identity of bank debtors and, no doubt, inconsistency in banks' accounting practices in the presence of guarantees, but the total volume of guarantees outstanding at any moment appears not to have been reliably known. Finance ministry estimates reported by the OECD of the volume of state guarantees issued to commercial banks in the course of 1998 for the payment of federal government obligations alone ranged from 30 trillion to 55 trillion roubles ($5 billion to $10 billion). These figures were more than double those of 1995.[21] The larger total equalled about one-eighth of the year's federal government spending, and more than one-fifth of the broadly defined rouble money stock.

A key credit instrument for the banks, both on their own account and for incorporating state guarantees, were so-called *veksels*, or commercial bills.[22] It should be emphasized that this instrument constitutes only one segment, albeit an important one, of a much wider network of financial relations in Russia. The network has been characterized by extensive improvization, and is linked in turn to the fluctuating pattern of arrears and barter that has been a feature of the country's post-Communist economy. The issue of *veksels* was given legal sanction by a decree of the RSFSR parliament in mid-1991, before the break-up of the Soviet Union, but their proliferation dates from a presidential decree of October 1993 which sought to ease the problem of inter-enterprise arrears by encouraging their securitization and secondary trading.[23] Since then they have been issued not only by (large) enterprises but also by banks and by public authorities, especially at regional and municipal level.

At federal level a larger role was played by the guarantees to banks mentioned above, at any rate until such guarantees were formally forbidden by a presidential decree of May 1997. Prior to that the Central Bank reported that during 1996 some 18 trillion roubles' worth of *veksel'* credits with federal government guarantees were issued by twenty-six

---

[21] OECD (1997), p. 96.

[22] The Russian word *veksel'* is a straightforward transliteration of the German, indicating the origin of Russian financial institutions in Tsarist times.

[23] OECD (1997) ibid and 'Annex II: Money Surrogates', pp. 178 ff. This publication also reports the data on *veksel'*s cited below.

correspondingly authorized banks. This formed a significant proportion of the above-mentioned 20–55 trillion estimated range of aggregate Federal guarantees in that year.

Many *veksel'* and other bank credits were, of course, issued without guarantees. In the case of a *veksel'* credit, the bank lends its client a short-term negotiable obligation of the bank (that is, a money surrogate) in circumstances affording the bank specific assurances of being able to redeem this obligation on maturity. Either the initial borrower pays off his debt in cash on or before the maturity of the *veksel'*, or else the final holder of the *veksel'* has himself a debt to the bank at least equal in amount to the *veksel'*s redemption face value. The stated assurances are obtained at the outset by the lending bank informing itself of the sequence of transactions in which the borrower is engaged, and hence approving the list of successive holders of the *veksel'*. Financial penalties may be imposed (where feasible) in the event of the *veksel'* being transferred to an unauthorized holder. Arrangements of this kind obviously represent an attempt by the bank—or by the enterprise whose associated or 'pocket' bank it is—to overcome the risks and uncertainties of interfirm dealings in the Russian context.

Bank prescription of the identity of its *veksel'* holders is in principle inconsistent with the legal nature of *veksels* as freely transferable claims. In practice *veksels* vary widely in their risk and tradability status on the financial market, and formal restrictions on transferability may be seen as giving rise to one particular risk factor among many, especially bearing in mind that banks are far from being the only issuers of *veksels*. Moreover, banks issue *veksels* not only as part of their lending activity, but also to raise cash. In this case the *veksel'* functions like a certificate of deposit or bank promissory note, with formally unrestricted marketability.

The efficiency of *veksels* as a money surrogate depends on the risk characteristics of the *veksel'* in each case, especially the identity of its original issuer and of subsequent holders (each of whom has, in accordance with universal legal usage, to add his name to the list of the bill's guarantors when tranferring it). Even, therefore, if the precise volume of *veksels* outstanding at any given moment were known, its quantitative significance as a supplement to the money stock would vary with quality weighting. As it happens, statistics of the non-bank total in particular are very broad-brush, because of partial data collection. In the early part of 1997 commercial bank *veksels* outstanding totalled some 30 trillion roubles, but the total outstanding from all sources was perhaps ten times this amount, which would be the same order of magnitude as the broadly defined rouble money supply. Thus, there is no doubt that non-bank *veksels* have been an important substitute for bank facilities in Russian industry and commerce. One's confidence in this judgement is strengthened by the fact that in by-passing bank accounts *veksels* are another mechanism facilitating tax evasion and circumventing officially imposed payment restrictions occasioned by tax arrears.

The most conspicuous source of commercial bank earnings between the two crisis landmarks of 1995 and 1998 was the holding of GKOs and other related government paper. This was true even though statistically speaking the GKO market was dominated by Sberbank, which typically held over 40 per cent of the outstanding stock, accounting for significantly more than half its assets. Since around two-thirds of Sberbank's liabilities consisted of household deposits (its overwhelming preponderance in this area was noted earlier), one may reasonably say that during this period Sberbank acted simply as a conduit for channelling housing liquid assets into government debt. By contrast with Sberbank, commercial banks—especially the larger ones in Moscow—relied for their build-up of GKO holdings on the profitability of GKOs themselves and on various forms of foreign borrowing (credits from foreign correspondents, euro-market issues, and so forth). The balance-sheet position which thereby developed was to some extent a mirror image of that which prevailed in the period up to mid-1995: instead of foreign currency holdings matched by (mainly interest-free) rouble liabilities, there were now rapidly growing GKO holdings matched by (low-interest—if one ignored the exchange-rate risk) foreign currency liabilities.

The yield on GKOs fluctuated widely with the electoral and general political climate, ranging in real terms (that is, after adjusting for current inflation) from near zero to almost 200 per cent per annum; the latter was an absurd figure recorded in the second quarter of 1996 in the face of doubts about President Yeltsin's re-election. For no length of time, however, did real yields fall below 20 per cent, a level plainly unsustainable in the longer term, given that economic activity was still stagnant or declining. As a proportion of federal government spending interest on GKOs rose from 1 per cent to 20 per cent in two years (1994–6).

The exorbitant level of GKO yields was partly a result of protectionism. In the earlier stages especially politicians were nervous about opening the market to foreigners and were an easy prey to lobbying by greedy banks. Foreigners were prevented from acquiring GKOs just as from bidding in the loans-for-shares auctions. In 1996–7, however, there was considerable liberalization, policymakers being concerned about the rising cost of debt service and having discovered that the Russian banking and financial systems were not rendered stable by keeping foreigners out. A system of special non-resident bank accounts ('S' accounts) was enforced, to limit the profitability of the GKO market for foreigners by regulating the forward exchange rate at which they could reconvert roubles into dollars. Russian banks were drawn into making large-scale forward sales of dollars to foreigners, in disregard of any major exchange risk.

Unfortunately international financial conditions took a turn for the worse with the onset of the Asian crisis in autumn 1997. The withdrawal of foreign funds from Russia over the succeeding six months mainly affected the equity market. But foreign borrowing terms for Russian banks also hardened, and there was a serious indirect effect via the fall in world oil prices, which pushed Russia's current balance of payments into deficit and, more important, caused a sharp drop in federal tax receipts because of the profit squeeze in the oil export sector.

The tax position could have been ameliorated, and the 1998 federal debt default at least postponed, through timely devaluation of the currency, which would have raised export-sector profits in rouble although not in dollar terms. But this would not have avoided the collapse of the banking system, given its exposure to devaluation because of hefty borrowing and forward-market commitments in foreign currency. The banks therefore lobbied first of all against devaluation. Their arguments were strengthened by political fears that a large devaluation could not be prevented from re-starting the earlier spiral of rapid inflation. The immediate impact, however, of maintaining the exchange rate was to aggravate the deterioration in the public finances and government debt market, without diminishing the ultimate likelihood of devaluation. Nobody in government seems to have thought of attempting to boost confidence in the government's debt servicing capacity by enforcing a drastic administrative cut in GKO yields as a *quid pro quo* to the banks for maintaining the exchange rate.

When in mid-August devaluation was felt to be no longer postponable, its magnitude proved difficult to control and was eventually much larger than the government had hoped. This in itself was enough to render most of the large commercial banks insolvent because of their foreign-exchange liabilities. But, in addition, the GKO market collapsed and the federal government defaulted on (initially) all of its debts. At that point government paper appears to have constituted about 20 per cent of commercial bank assets. Financial market turmoils had, however, begun in late July, with banks switching from domestic to foreign currency assets. The Central Bank had endeavoured to stem the tide and sustain confidence in both the rouble and the banking system through selective market support, including long-term credits to two large banks. The only noticeable result was a bigger loss of foreign exchange reserves—though doubtless a few banks succeeded in mitigating the scale of their subsequent insolvency. At a late stage about one-third of household deposits with commercial banks—60 billion new roubles or 60 trillion pre-1998 roubles—were withdrawn.

Subsequently the Central Bank reported that in the nine months from 1 August 1998 to 1 May 1999 aggregate capital of the commercial banking sector shrank by 50 per cent in nominal terms (from 102 billion new roubles to 46 billion) and thus by 80 per cent in real terms. The real value of the sector's balance sheet reportedly fell by a smaller amount—about 25 per cent—mainly because of the presence of foreign currency assets, including cash balances. The status of foreign-currency claims other than cash, however, was questionable, especially where the debtor was an enterprise with little or no export revenue. From February 1999 onwards the Central Bank insisted on a minimum 40 per cent provision rate for the banks' foreign currency loans.

7.4. AFTERMATH

While Russia's banking débâcle of 1998 had its parallel at various times in other transition economies, it nevertheless represented a tremendous failure for policymakers who had for several years been attempting to put the banking system upon a sounder footing. The policymakers in question included both Russian domestic authorities, chiefly the Central Bank, and international institutions advising them, notably the World Bank and the European Bank for Reconstruction and Development (EBRD). The 1998 crash showed their policies to have been at best quantitatively insufficient, at worst irrelevant because they addressed the wrong targets.

Under Russian legislation[24] the CBR has—along with its monetary policy duties—sole responsibility for the issue and revocation of banking licences and for the prudential supervision of commercial banks and maintenance of banking stability. In the early 1990s prudential regulations were virtually non-existent. In 1994 the CBR initiated a policy of

---

[24] Cf. the 1990 Laws on the CBR and on Bank and Banking Activity respectively, together with subsequent amendments, notably a 1995 amendment of the CBR Law.

successive increases in minimum charter capital requirements for new banks: at first from $100–200 thousand to $1 million, then in 1996 to $2.5 million and in January 1997 to $3.5 million, with further increases in 1999.[25] These figures applied to banks seeking general licences for universal banking including foreign-exchange operations. Somewhat lower requirements applied in relation to licensing for domestic (rouble) operations only. All the figures, however, were tiny. Their declared rationale was to encourage consolidation of the smallest banks and thereby to reduce the total number of banking institutions. The urgency of this was debatable. Small banks have not been an important source of Russia's banking weakness.

Prudential regulation took a more serious turn in the wake of the 1995 inter-bank market crisis. In 1996 the CBR set up a special regulatory division for the monitoring of large banks that could pose a systemic risk. At the same time minimum capital adequacy ratios were established at 5 per cent, rising to 8 per cent by 1999, with the value of claims subject to this ratio set according to western (Basle)-style criteria. Separate regulations were issued governing open foreign-exchange positions and ceilings on the amount of a bank's *veksel*s outstanding—the latter not to exceed 200 per cent of a bank's own funds, which figure was halved to 100 per cent in April 1999. The CBR's sanction was, in principle, its power to revoke banks' licences.

Such revocations first took place in significant number in the wake of the 1995 episode—nearly 600 up to the end of 1996. None the less an overall impact on banking standards is hard to discern. Admittedly no practical system of prudential regulation can be proof against wholesale debt default by the government.

Aside from this, however, Russian banks in the current phase of their and the Russian economy's development could not be expected to have much patience or understanding for such a system. Prudential regulation is a sophisticated matter, a dynamic blend of consensus-based guidelines and legal compulsion, in which banks recognize that it is in their general interest to submit to restrictions on their commercial behaviour while also manœuvring to minimize the impact of such restrictions on their own competitive position. Russian banks were (and are) not yet into such subtleties. The permissive nature of Russian accounting practices made it

---

[25] See Bank of Russian Instruction No. 586-U, dated 24 June 1999, 'On Minimum Authorised Capital for Newly-Created Credit Institutions and Minimum Own Funds (Capital) for Banks Applying for a General Banking Licence'.

relatively easy to disguise infringement of prudential ratios. Major Moscow banks that were part of FIGs could routinely manipulate their accounts—whether just for reporting purposes or for more substantive reasons—by shifting assets and liabilities of different types between themselves and their affiliates. They could also exercise political influence to deter officials from over-zealous investigations. At times of acute speculative fever rules on such matters as open foreign-exchange positions were simply ignored: better to prosper with excuses than go bankrupt with a halo.

As it happens, none of the top Russian banks was transparently under-capitalized in the period preceding the 1998 crash. Table 7.3, taken from *The Banker* (July 1998), gives figures for mid-1997 on those Russian banks, twelve in number, which at that date were in the list of the world's thousand largest banks ranked by tier-one capital. (The latter is a multiple of Russian banks' charter capital.) The biggest strictly commercial institution among the Russians was Uneximbank, number 346 in the world ranking. The item in the table which catches the eye is Tokobank on account of its lack of reported profits; it was subsequently identified as bankrupt well before the general crash, and in due course had its licence revoked.

All this suggests that what Russian commercial banking stands most in need of is not external regulation but internal reshaping of objectives and

Table 7.3. *Russia's largest banks, end-1997*

World Rank	Name of bank	Capital ($ million)	Assets ($ million)	Annual profits ($ million)
134	Sberbank	2,752	29,764	759
279	Vneshtorgbank	1,023	3,126	97
346	Uneximbank	826	3,779	72
536	SBS-Agro	466	5,201	56
670	MFK	320	1,299	115
683	Rossiiskiy Kredit	314	2,135	60
697	Menatep	305	3,433	41
720	Tokobank	287	1,219	2
761	Inkombank	261	5,102	115
852	Imperial	210	1,110	65
919	Mosbusinessbank	183	1,509	62
993	Promstroibank	155	1,196	26

Source: The Banker, July 1998.

behaviour. The point has been amply recognized by knowledgeable western observers. In 1995 the World Bank, together with the EBRD and the European Union's Tacis programme, set up a Financial Institutions Development Project (FIDP) with the purpose of 'assisting Russian banks to adopt western standards'. In the following years the FIDP worked through the Federal Government's Foundation for Enterprise Restructuring (FRP) with several dozen Russian banks, in some cases organizing 'twinning' arrangements with western counterparts. Issues tackled included accounting standards and principles of banking supervision. A Banking Review Unit (BRU) within the FIDP undertook monitoring of Russian bank operations and identification of possible 'problem' banks.

A lesson of the 1998 crash was that the FIDP efforts had as yet borne insufficient fruit, whether because they were on too limited a scale or because of insufficient time (or both). But the aftermath of the crash also showed how critically necessary were the reforms promoted by the FIDP, and how they were obstructed both by corrupt bank managements and by infighting among policymaking institutions, with corruption doubtless at work there as well. What was wanted, had it been feasible, was an immediate and comprehensive strategy towards the commercial banking sector as a whole. The bulk of the sector was insolvent, and not just a few individual banks. Moreover, for what the figures were worth, large banks reported deepening losses on current businesses.[26] As a practical matter, however, policy measures were piecemeal, selective, inconsistent, and slow to emerge. More than a year after the crash there had been no firm action to re-establish the banking system on a proper footing. As is explained below, plausible looking legislation was at last in place and conflicts among policymaking institutions had been diminished. But former bank owners and management remained in control, their surviving assets disguised or transferred beyond the reach of outside creditors.

The creditors included few depositors. Following the crash, the CBR had managed to move promptly on one or two matters. The six large commercial banks with a significant fraction of household deposits in their liabilities (Inkombank, SBS–Agro, Promstroibank, Mostbank, Menatep, and Mosbusinessbank) were ordered to freeze

---

[26] The thirty largest banks turned loss-making in August 1998; a year later their reported net losses were running at 20% of capital (presumably on an annual basis). See OECD (2000), p. 78.

the funds in question and to agree with the CBR arrangements allowing depositors (if they wished) to transfer their deposits to Sberbank. The arrangement proved acceptable for rouble deposits. In respect of foreign-currency deposits holders were offered only a counterpart in roubles converted at much less than market rates; the majority elected to retain their currency claims on the various commercial banks in the hope of eventual full repayment. In addition, the CBR organized a central clearing system for payments and allowed banks temporary access to reserve balances with itself on a scale sufficient to permit continuance of ordinary businesses dealings.[27]

On the more far-reaching issue of bank restructuring, there was controversy and paralysis. The Russian government and CBR, in a document published in November 1998, outlined a policy with both selective and general aspects. A limited list of banks deserving of rehabilitation was to be identified. At the same time a new body, the Agency for the Restructuring of Credit Organizations (ARKO), was to have general but unspecified responsibility for restructuring the system. Problem banks not singled out for rehabilitation (yet presumably identified?) were to be swiftly merged (with whom?) or liquidated.

The dual approach in part reflected the promptings of international bodies (World Bank, EBRD) who were keen to apply unspent assistance monies to the tasks of bank restructuring and training ARKO staff. But it also suited the different Russian authorities, who could smell opportunities for enhanced political influence and favouring their friends. In fact, at the moment when the policy document was published, the FIDP in collaboration with the CBR, and assisted by western auditors, was already conducting a review of eighteen banks. Most of them had been involved with the FIDP's earlier programme. About half had been nominated for the review exercise by the CBR. The findings of the review were not published, and are not known to have led to any specific policy actions.

ARKO was mooted for half a year, and finally established in March 1999 as a joint stock company with a charter capital of 10 billion roubles (about US\$ 400 million). The figure was much too small to constitute serious financial muscle in relation to bank restructuring—compare the capitalization figures in Table 7.3. This suited both the Duma and the CBR, who wanted to retain their own leverage in the area and not be sidelined by ARKO or others. The international agencies for their part

---

[27] Ibid., p. 75

were reluctant to fund ARKO so long as it remained dependent on the CBR for personnel and information.

The CBR was under a cloud for two reasons. The more scandalous one was that its management and senior staff had come to be suspected of large-scale financial misappropriation. The charge stemmed first and foremost—though by no means exclusively—from the existence and activities of FIMACO, a Jersey company to which in the years 1993–8 the CBR had delegated the placement of up to US$ 50 billion of its foreign-exchange reserves. The presumption was that commissions paid to FIMACO ended up in the pockets of (unnamed) CBR officials. The circumstance was brought to light by Prosecutor General Skuratov on the eve of his resignation in February 1999.

Months earlier, however, the CBR had already begun to attract criticism on account of its capricious and untransparent policy towards the banking industry following the August events. It propounded no general principles or objectives; undertook only occasional and indecisive actions towards individual banks; and adopted a permissive attitude to home-made restructuring by major institutions, even when this was clearly suspect and designed to prevent creditors from asserting claims against incumbent managers and owners.

In October 1998 the CBR sought to make a scapegoat of Inkombank and its head, Vladimir Vinogradov, by revoking its licence, while a court initiated bankruptcy proceedings and imposed a temporary administration. Many months later the courts overturned the CBR's action. An even more chequered history is that of SBS–Agro. The CBR initially favoured it with a soft line of credit. Subsequently its licence was revoked, but later reinstated by court decision. Its future remained in doubt at the end of 1999.

As regards home-made restructuring, shortly after the August collapse three of the big names—Oneksimbank (Potanin), Menatep (Khodorkovsky), and Mostbank (Gusinsky)—announced a forthcoming merger to create a new giant, Rosbank. The motive was presumably one of mutual support in a crisis, especially with a view to extracting concessions from the authorities. In the event the merger was not carried through, but Rosbank remained in being as the successor of Uneximbank, exploiting its owners' political connections (becoming, for instance, in February 1999 one of a handful of banks entrusted with the distribution of soft credits to agriculture) but leaving their unpayable liabilities behind. Menatep for its part moved its principal assets into its St Petersburg subsidiary, whose ownership was then transferred to the Rosprom holding company (Menatep's FIG partner). Again the original Menatep was left with nothing but liabilities, while the public face of the bank was re-labelled 'Menatep St Petersburg'. In other, more straightforward, instances Unikombank was absorbed into Gutabank (part of the business empire associated with Moscow mayor Yuri Lushkov); the troubled Mosbusinessbank moved assets into the Bank of Moscow; and Impexbank merged with Rossiiskiy Kredit. Thus when the CBR in 1999 withdrew the banking licences of Uneximbank, Menatep, Unikombank, and Mosbusinessbank, this appeared as a mere cynical gesture, with no implications for future business standards.

Other licence revocations had more substance, though not necessarily of a legitimate kind: for example, that of Promstroibank at end of June 1999. This appeared to be an act of rivalry with the ARKO agency, which only a week earlier had announced that it would be helping to rehabilitate both Promstroibank and the newly enlarged Rossiiskiy Kredit. In previous months ARKO's restructuring initiatives had been limited to smaller regional banks, namely Investbank of Kaliningrad, three banks from the coal-mining region of Kemerovo and Avtovaz bank of Samara.

The last named was of wider significance because of its former association with the business oligarch Boris Berezovsky. Other activities of ARKO likewise pointed to political and personal influences. In April 1999 it purchased 2.5 billion roubles' worth ($100 million) of Finance Ministry bonds, part of a placement of government paper with domestic institutions in the absence of a properly restored government debt market. This was of doubtful consistency with ARKO's declared purpose. Still more striking, in late June ARKO announced a billion rouble ($40 million) credit to Alfabank to help expand the bank's branch network into new regions. This objective hardly constituted urgent bank restructuring, and in any case Alfabank was one of the few clearly solvent Russian banks of any size thanks to its fortunate switch away from government debt and into foreign exchange in the weeks before the 1998 crash. The ARKO credit was rumoured to reflect personal ties between the heads of the two institutions (Pyotr Aven—former foreign trade minister—of Alfabank and Alexander Turbanov of ARKO).

A step forward, not least towards co-operation rather than competition between ARKO and the CBR, was the enactment in July 1999 of the Law on Restructuring of Credit Organizations, complementing the February Law on Insolvency of Credit Organizations. The law required the CBR to place under temporary administration, and to submit to

ARKO as candidates for restructuring, banks meeting stated criteria of financial distress. Candidates found unacceptable by ARKO after inspection must lose their licences and be liquidated. Candidates accepted for rehabilitation must transfer a controlling shareholding (normally 75 per cent) to ARKO, which also has authority to write down or to expand the bank's capital and to nullify illegitimate deals undertaken by the bank's management in the previous three years (a provision almost certainly promising more than it can deliver). In addition the bank is granted a temporary moratorium on the service of its liabilities (i.e. realities are acknowledged). The CBR further announced that it would henceforth confine refinancing facilities to banks that either were clearly solvent or were engaged in an ARKO-approved restructuring programme.

By early autumn 1999 ARKO was working with no more than a dozen banks—including however a major institution in Rossiiskiy Kredit—and had disbursed less than 4 billion roubles on its task. It was intended that its resources should be augmented with contributions from the CBR, the state budget and international organizations, and conceivably from its own bond issues.[28]

While bank restructuring thus proceeded at a snail's pace, to which the population was indifferent, Russia's economic performance showed a distinct turn for the better. Industrial production increased, particularly among small and medium-sized enterprises; likewise federal tax receipts. This was partly due to higher world oil prices and partly to rouble devaluation, the latter maintained in real terms by the effective containment of inflation through fiscal and monetary restraint. In this respect the impotent condition of the banking system was a help. In all other respects the banks' irrelevance for the time being to Russia's economic fortunes was conspicuous.

This, however, is a temporary phase. Sooner or later Russia will need somehow to acquire a banking system appropriate to a modern market economy. The history of the past decade means that creation of confidence in Russian banks will be a long and difficult task—even on the assumption (which is not self-evident) that Russian bankers themselves regard it as an important objective.

Progress could be speeded up, if and only if major foreign banks were brought in, since the population would see them as trustworthy in the same way as dollar bills. Foreign banks would need to operate in their

---

[28] Ibid.

own name as branches or wholly owned affiliates of the parent, and not as subordinate or hidden partners of Russian institutions. Opportunities to move this forward arise from the unresolved issue of foreign bank creditors of Russian banks in the aftermath of the 1998 crash. Equity/ debt swaps and similar modes of acquisitions offer foreign institutions the prospect (probably the only prospect) of recovering their claims.

Such moves would certainly give an impetus and a new air of respectability to the bank restructuring process. They were rumored to be favoured by the CBR under Governor Gerashchenko. However, the CBR in June 1999 revoked the license of Mezhkombank just after it had become the first Russian bank to conclude a restructuring deal with foreign creditors and shareholders. Moreover, some Russian bankers and leaders of FIGs would obviously see their interests and position threatened by greater foreign participation in Russian banking and would lobby against it, finding allies among protection-minded and xenophobic elements in the Duma and elsewhere. An existing law already imposes a limit of 12 per cent on foreign participation in the capital of the banking sector. This would have to be relaxed to enable foreign banks to bring about decisive improvements in Russian banking practices in the foreseeable future. The chances of such a development are at best mediocre.

REFERENCES

The Banker (July 1998).

Central Bank of Russia, *Bulletin of Banking Statistics*, various issues.

Halligan, L. *et al.* (1996). *Russian Economic Trends*, 5/1, London: Whurr.

Kryuchkova, P. (1997). 'Households Deposits and Financial Intermediation in Russia', RECEP Working Paper No 1997/3 (TACIS).

OECD Economic Surveys (1997). *Russian Federation*, Paris.

—— (2000). *Russian Federation*, Paris.

Prill, O. (1995). 'Financial Sector Reform in the Soviet Union/Russia since 1987: Options and Consequences', D. Phil thesis, Oxford University.

Savings Bank of Russia (1997–9). Moscow, processed.

Thompson, W. (1997). 'Old Habits Die Hard: Fiscal Imperatives, State Regulation and the Role of Russia's Banks', *Europe–Asia Studies*, 49/7, Glasgow.

World Bank (1996). *The Russian Federation: Towards Medium-Term Viability*, Washington, DC.

8

Financial Markets

DIRK WILLER

8.1. INTRODUCTION

One of the features of the centrally planned economies was the conspicuous absence of (legal) financial markets. There were neither markets for foreign exchange nor for debt or equity. While the optimal timing of the introduction and liberalization of such markets is controversial, it is nearly universally accepted that the final outcome of the reform project had to provide for such markets. Consequently, one of the first steps of the Russian reformers was to create (or rather allow the creation of) financial markets. These markets have developed rapidly and were of constantly increasing sophistication up to the crash in August 1998. Since the domestic government debt market turned out to be the crucial link that translated worldwide emerging market pressures to Russia and caused the collapse, the authorities reacted to the crash by re-introducing controls over these markets, stopping the earlier process of increasing liberalization dead in its tracks. As the crash also led to significant changes in government, the strategy towards the creation of financial markets changed. After the crash the authorities proceeded much more carefully in the re-opening process of the financial markets. Just before the emerging markets crisis spread in earnest to Russia, at the end of 1997, the market for internal rouble-denominated government debt was worth about US$ 60 billion or 13 per cent of GDP. Similarly, the equity market, which comprised 100 firms (excluding banks) was in December 1997 worth about US$ 90 billion, after a dizzying rally with returns of more than 100 per cent in 1996 and another 100 per cent during the first half of 1997, followed by a very sharp correction in the wake of the emerging markets crisis in Q4 1997. Spreads, as quoted on the Russian Trading System (RTS), had come down to below 0.5 per cent for the most liquid stocks. There has also been a bout of issue activity on the international markets, as well by the government, as by corporates, mostly in the form of American Depository Receipts (ADRs). Only the corporate debt market had been slow to get off the ground.

This chapter describes the development of these markets up to beginning of the crisis, working out what the driving forces and the main impediments have been. Section 1 takes a look at the development of the equity market and its link to the real economy. In section 2 the debt market is analysed and reasons for the disappointing development of the corporate debt market are presented. Section 3 briefly discusses the crash of August 1998.

8.2. THE EQUITY MARKET

8.2.1. *Privatization*

The disappearance of share surrogates linked to pyramid schemes has been one important success for the Russian government in this area. Such shares, the most famous of which was called MMM, had promised huge dividends and had dominated the Russian security market until 1994. It was only towards the end of 1994 that the new civil code, followed by a federal law on the securities market was introduced. These laws called for stringent licensing procedure for brokers as well as for issues of new securities and led to the closure of such pyramid schemes. These closures have been achieved with surprisingly little turmoil in spite of the lack of major fiscal expenditures to compensate victims of such schemes.

Abstracting from such schemes, the privatization process, started by Anatoly Chubais in late 1991, laid the foundation for the development of the equity market in two respects. First, it created the supply of shares, that is the raw material for the trading to take place. Second, the privatization procedure supplied a training ground for brokers and dealers. While under the first heading the privatization process left something to be desired, under the second respect it succeeded beyond expectations. Most of today's successful Russian financial entrepreneurs learned their business trading vouchers. Between October 1992 and January 1993 vouchers were distributed to every eligible Russian citizen for a small fee. These vouchers could then be used to make a bid for shares of a certain company. Vouchers could also be freely traded. Financial entrepreneurs started to buy up vouchers from the population in order to acquire shares in companies that they believed to be of particular value and where demand in the auction could be expected not to be too large, so that the shares would be rather cheap. In other words, the first securities traders started to make money by investing into firms they expected to be undervalued in the primary auction.[1] Shortly after vouchers had been distributed to the population, voucher trading moved to the Moscow Interbank Currency Exchange (MICEX), where rouble trading had started in at the end of 1991. It is noteworthy that the fluctuations in the value of the voucher did correspond to political events that were perceived to alter the likelihood that valuable enterprises were actually going to be sold off—just in the way a Western type of market would react. For example, when President Yeltsin in November 1993 disbanded the Communist-dominated Duma and called for new elections, the voucher price more than doubled. This is the evidence that human capital in the financial sphere was accumulated very quickly (see Boycko *et al.* 1993).

However, the privatization process left something to be desired because the supply of shares was actually fairly limited. In the majority of firms, 50 per cent of the shares were allocated to insiders, namely to management and workers. Only 27 per cent were on average allocated to the population through the so-called voucher auctions. The rest was initially kept with the Federal Property Committee (Goskomimuchestvo, GKI). As management was keen to keep control of the firm, it often tried successfully to prevent its workers from selling their shares to outsiders. This limited the supply of shares on the market to the shares that were sold by the population at large. And the population did not sell immediately. This meant that the freefloat (the ration of shares that could actually be bought on the market) remained very low. Even at the end of 1996 it was much below 20 per cent of the market capitalization for most of the largest 100 firms (see Blasi *et al.* 1997).

8.2.2. *Corporate governance*

The combination of large residual state ownership and insider dominance not only reduced the supply of shares, but also led to severe corporate governance problems. In particular, the most important mechanism for changing management in the absence of large outside shareholders are take-overs, or at least the threat thereof. Yet, given the ownership structure resulting from privatization, take-overs were all but

---

[1] For a description of the early stages of the privatization process, see Frydman *et al.* (1996).

ruled out. This is likely to have cost the Russian economy dearly. Because Soviet style management needed completely different skills from management in today's Russian environment, a high turnover of management was in principle very important. Secondly, given that the industrial structure had not been created according to market principles, there should have been considerable Merger and Acquisition (M&A) activity to rectify some of the resulting inefficiencies. Since outsiders were in no position to press for such changes, little happened in this respect.

The situation started to improve slowly as the state very gradually divested its remaining shareholdings in the so-called second stage of privatization. This second stage excluded controlling stakes in many 'strategic' enterprises, for example shares of firms in the defence industries. In spite of such exclusions, it is noteworthy that even in the oil-extracting industry, which is by many developing countries around the world considered to be of strategic importance, substantial progress with respect to privatization had been achieved. While some of the sell-offs had been achieved through the highly criticized shares-for-loans auctions, which essentially granted share packages to well-connected Russian banks in exchange for loans to the budget, there had also been significant cash auctions for blocks of shares in Russian oil firms. Furthermore, the state has by now sold off most of its shares in other industries, such as light manufacturing or food processing. It is therefore not surprising that the only public take-over attempt prior to the crash occurred in that industry. In July 1995 Bank Menatep attempted to take over the Red October Chocolate Factory. While the bid failed in the end, Menatep did manage to appoint several directors to the board of Red October. This has so far been an isolated case. More take-overs may have been handled behind closed doors, presumably to the detriment of small minority investors.

In spite of the modest freefloat, which prevented more intensive take-over activity, the supply of shares on the market has been sufficiently large to generate outside blockholders (outsiders holding more than 5 per cent of the firm) in some firms. In early 1996 the average outside blockholding in the largest 140 firms that were actively traded was 30 per cent. While this includes the holding companies, for which ownership data is not always available and which might well be characterized by substantial inside ownership, a conservative estimate of the average outside block-holding excluding holding companies is just below 20 per cent (see Willer 1997; and for a sample of smaller firms, Blasi *et al.* 1996). To the extent that shareholder rights are honoured, such outside blockholders are likely to mitigate the corporate governance problem. In this sense the stock market had helped to re-allocate ownership such that more efficient ownership patterns are emerging.

8.2.3. *Valuation of corporate assets*

Another noteworthy feature of the privatization process were the very low prices for which the enterprises were sold. Even as late as in February 1995 Russian equity was by most comparisons hugely under-valued. For example, the market capitalization per unit of oil produced by Russian oil firms was only one-twentieth of that of a typical western firm (see Willer and Nash 1996). These low valuations were attributable to three factors: low quality of assets, macroeconomic risk, and the risk of expropriation of shareholders by the state or by management. Leaving aside the quality of assets, the perceived threat posed by the other factors greatly diminished over 1996 and 1997. This promoted a boom in Russian equity prices, which was only brought to an end by the emerging market crisis starting in Q4 1997, which led to a re-pricing of (emerging market) risk across countries (Figure 8.1).

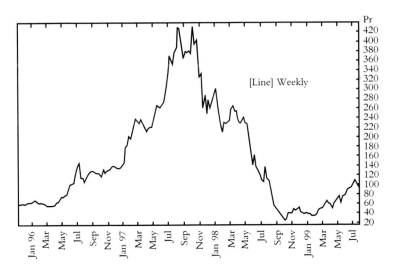

Figure 8.1. *The Moscow Times Index (US$) 09 Nov 95–28 Jul 99*

Source: Reuters.

The equity boom until Q3 1997 was been driven by a number of factors, as for instance the positive changes in the macroeconomic picture (see the chapter by B. Granville in this volume). In particular, the fact that for the first time GDP actually grew in 1997, if only by 0.4 per cent, is likely to have led to increased sales (or at least increased expectations of future sales) on the firm level and raised the value of many firms. Over 1996 and 1997 the risk of expropriation by the state has also been diminished from late 1994, when Mr Polevanov, former head of the GKI, could still threaten to re-nationalize Russian industry and was taken seriously. Although the Duma has not formally concluded its debates on the legality of privatization and possible re-nationalization, the election of President Yeltsin in 1996 and the subsequent installation of a highly reformist economic policy team all but removed the threat of re-nationalization from equity prices in mid-1997. In particular, the re-election campaign of President Yeltsin in 1996 showed that existing business interests are likely to do everything in their power to prevent the election of a presidential candidate who would re-examine the question of the legality of ownership rights transferred during privatization.

It is noteworthy, though, that in spite of the investor friendliness of the upper echelons of the government, there always were issues where the interests of the state clash with those of investors. For example, a presidential decree of May 1995 reduced the share of the privatization revenues that goes to the firm (and not to the federal budget) from 51 per cent to 14 per cent, which significantly decreased the value of the firms whose shares were still to be sold by the state. Another example was the attempt by the government to move the oil producer Purneft from the partly privatized holding company Sidanko to the still state-owned company Rosneft. Sidanko reacted by initiating court action, but consequently an agreement has apparently been found, allocating Purneft to Rosneft.

Yet a further example was the Potanin plan, approved in early 1997. This plan provided that firms failing to pay off their tax arrears were to securitize such arrears by issuing new shares to the state. This amounts to a *de facto* re-nationalization of parts of the enterprises and would dilute the control rights of existing owners. While the idea was that the state would subsequently sell such shares to outside blockholders, this would not have been automatic and to the extent that the mechanism of such sales remained unspecified investors were rightly worried. By the end of 1997 tax arrears have been securitized only in a handful of cases. Furthermore, this has been done only by bond issues, not by equity issues. Summarizing, for the market as a whole the perceived risk of expropriation by the state had decreased over 1996 and 1997. However, for specific cases, the risk has remained very real.

Lastly, and most interestingly, the risk of expropriation by management has also decreased, but maybe not by as much as has been the case for the other factors. This risk consists of a number of potential adverse actions by management. First, management has at times been able to strike investors out of the share-registry, or refuse to register shareholders in the first place. This is of considerable significance because in Russia share-registries are the only proof of ownership of shares. One example is the Krasnoyarsk Aluminium Smelter, where in the summer of 1995 management deleted the shareholdings of TransWorld, a British trading firm. Since those days, the risk has greatly diminished. In 1995 a presidential decree obliged firms with more than 1,000 employees to use independent share-registries. However, this rule has been widely ignored. Also, many 'independent' registries were on inspection not genuinely independent after all. Therefore, in 1996 the Federal Securities Commission (FSC), the securities watchdog created by presidential decree in 1995, began to license share registries. Also, the EBRD, in co-operation with the Bank of America, launched a share-registry in order to offer the market greater reliability and security. As a result, the problem of expropriating shareholders in this crude way lost much of its acuteness. Another policy adopted to protect outside investors was to prescribe the use of cumulative voting for elections to the board of directors, again introduced by presidential decree in 1995. Under this procedure each shareholder obtains as many votes as there are seats to be filled on the board of directors. Because the different votes can be cumulated on one particular candidate, this procedure helps minority shareholders to get a candidate on the board of directors. While this decree has certainly not been fully implemented, it is nevertheless clear that the law has helped outside investors in their struggle with management.

The court case launched by outside shareholders of the Novolipetsk Metalurgical Kombinat in 1997 also focused on the rights of outsiders to propose candidates for the board of directors. The fact that the court ruled in favour of the outside investors illustrates that laws to protect outside shareholders have begun to make a difference.

Another way in which management was traditionally able to expropriate shareholder rights was to restrict the dissemination of information. Without information management cannot be monitored. Again, this problem has been mitigated as more and more firms now produce western style accounts. This positive development is partly due to policy changes, as there can be certain tax exemptions once western style accounts are introduced. However, it seems that willingness to provide more information is more closely linked to the need to attract investors in order to upgrade the capital stock of the firms (Willer 1998).

Lastly, management can engage in dilutive share-issues, that is, selling equity to itself at less than market prices. This has happened in a handful of cases only. Komi-Neft, one of Russia's largest oil producers, issued additional shares to some of its shareholders much below market price, in May 1994. A more recent example is Surgutneftegaz, which in October 1996 diluted outside shareholders. New shares representing 10 per cent of outstanding chartered capital were issued to management-friendly investors well below market price. In both cases the reformist government decided to intervene. In the case of Surgut the intervention was initiated by the FSC. The outcome of that investigation was half a victory for the FSC. Surgut agreed to pay a higher price for the shares, but still below market value. Summarizing, the threat of expropriation through management had decreased as shareholder rights had become a more meaningful concept in Russia. From a statistical point of view, the reduction in risk is reflected in a reduction of the volatility of the MT index. The thirty-day volatility of the MT index for Q2 and Q3 of 1997 was half the volatility of Q2 and Q3 1996.

However, the quick rise between Q1 and Q3 1997 was followed by a sharp fall of the equity market in Q4. During this period the USD Moscow Times index fell by 24 per cent, similar as many of the Asian countries (Hong Kong −29 per cent, Indonesia −25 per cent, Thailand −66 per cent, Malaysia −25 per cent) but more severely than the emerging countries of Latin America (Brazil −13 per cent, Mexico −5 per cent). The crash in asset prices in Q4 therefore was initially largely not Russia-specific, although Russian assets were more severely affected than the ones of Latin American countries.

8.2.4. *The primary market*

But even before the crash the perceived reduction in risk and the accompanying rise in prices did not lead to a boom in new share issues. While it is clear that higher prices during mid-1997 made managers more willing to issue new shares, there were by end 1997 only a small number of (public) share-issues to raise new capital. The point is slightly obscured by the fact that all firms engage periodically in share issues without raising new capital. Every year the Ministry of Finance determines a factor by which the charter capital of all firms needs to be increased in order to account for inflation in that year. This increase in charter capital is then reflected in new shares that are issued free to existing shareholders. As the firm does not obtain any new capital, these issues have no impact on the financing of the firm. Public share issues which raise new finance are rare. One example is the Red October Factory, which in 1995 launched a share-issue to attract retail investors. But demand was very low. Subsequently this firm became the target of a take-over bid—maybe not surprisingly so: the share issue increased the available shares. Another example of a public share issues is that of Khlebniy Dom of St Petersburg, which also was aimed at the retail market. However, it is likely that there have been a multitude of private placements. As there seem to have been only a few cases of complaints of minority shareholders against such private placements (as discussed above), it seems likely that most of such private share issues did not entail an expropriation of minority shareholders, that is, were taking place at market prices.

Even in the absence of new share-issues, there are two ways in which higher share prices have affected firms. First, for some time the privatization procedure resulted in direct gains. Between May 1995 and September 1996 14 per cent of privatization revenues went to the firm and therefore higher prices have resulted in more financing from this source (see *Russian Economic Trends*, 5/3). Second, and more importantly, firms have used shares that were held in its treasuries to back American Depository Receipts (ADRs) or Global Depository Receipts (GDRs).

8.2.5. *American depository receipts*

ADRs are securities traded at foreign exchanges and backed by the underlying Russian shares. While the risk that is inherent in the performance of the firms is the same in the ADRs as in the shares, the settlement and depository procedures are much simplified. Furthermore, there are some type of funds which are legally prohibited from investing their money in Russia, but are allowed to invest in ADRs listed on western exchanges. ADRs are therefore an efficient instrument for Russian firms to tap the world's capital markets. Up to the end of 1997 all but one ADR issue has been a 'level 1'ADR. This means that the shares used to back the ADR already existed prior to the ADR issue. In that narrow sense, these

Table 8.1. *Percentage shares of ADRs in firms*

Firm	% shares in ADRs
Oil and gas	
Gazprom	2
LUKOil	22.7
Surgutneftegaz	0.3
Tatneft	13.9
Chernogorneft	10.9
Utilities	
Mosenergo	28
Retail	
GUM	20.9
Metal	
Seversky Tube	16.6

ADR issues do not represent 'new capital'. In practice, the shares used to back the ADRs had been previously held by the firms' treasuries and were either allocated to the firm in the privatization procedure or were bought back by the firms in the initial stages of the market development at low prices. In that sense, the ADR issues brought major cash inflows, even though a firm's charter capital did not change. By February 1997 eleven Russian firms had issued ADRs and ADRs were estimated to be worth about US$ 4 billion. The following firms had ADRs outstanding on 1 January 1997 (see Table 8.1).

Partly as the firms issuing ADRs provided simpler access for foreign investors and improved information on the firms, their shares tended to outperform the rest of the market. The return of equity of firms which had issued ADRs over 1996 were up to 250 per cent (including some very limited dividend payments), compared with the average return of the total market of just above 100 per cent.

Apart from transaction costs and liquidity considerations, ADRs tended to outperform the rest of the market because the sale of ADRs could signal that management is less likely to violate shareholder rights (Willer 1997). The argument behind this is the following. Once ADRs have been issued, the investor base contains large foreign institutions. Therefore, the international financial community will watch these firms much more closely. In the words of the Surgut management (*Moscow Times*, 16 November 1996): 'Of course, we had to dilute outside shareholders before launching our ADR. Such actions become much more cumbersome afterwards. Good analysts should have expected this to happen.'

Furthermore, violations of shareholder rights by ADR-issuing firms are likely to have strong spillover effects damaging the reputation of Russian firms and borrowers as a whole. The government has an incentive to crack down on such firms to mitigate these wider consequences. To summarize, ADRs had been the main way for Russian firms to raise new finance. And the process has been cumulatively reinforcing: higher share prices made it profitable for firms to issue ADRs and issuance of ADRs increased share prices.

Up to the end of 1997 the only ADR which was a 'level 3' ADR was issued by Vimpelcom, a Russian communications firm in early 1996. 'Level 3' ADRs are ADRs where the shares used to back the ADRs are new shares, i.e. where the charter capital is increased by the ADR issue. New York Stock Exchange (NYSE) regulations applicable to such ADR are stricter than for level 1 ADRs. Nevertheless, it is to be expected that more Russian firms are going to issue ADRs of level 1 as well as of level 3.

8.2.6. *Foreign investors*

In addition to ADRs, share-issues generally have become easier as the investor base for Russian equity has widened. In particular foreign capital—including Russian firms capital previously placed abroad—was during 1996–7 more likely to flow into Russian equity, as a result of the reduction of all types of risk discussed above. By the end of 1996 foreign funds held more than 15 per cent of equity in the top fifty firms (Barber 1997). However, there is likely to have been an outflow during Q4 1997. This outflow was most likely small, as the equity market quickly became highly illiquid as the crisis hit. Few transactions took place and it was mostly brokers marking down prices without any trades taking place. Also, there are no indications that foreign sellers of Russian equity sold to Russian investors as opposed to other foreign investors.

Overall, the Russian share-market was driven by foreign flows. This is illustrated by the correlation of changes in the MT index with the equity markets of Asia and Latin America. While the importance of foreign investors (including Russian money returning in disguise) seems to be more than a short-term feature of the Russian equity market, the type of foreign investor has changed over time. In 1992–3 it was mainly some hedge funds, later to be followed by dedicated

Russia funds. Only in 1996 did large pension funds become active investors. These were the main investors that lost considerable money in Q4 1997, as they had partly been buying shortly before the peak of the market.

Even before the sharp correction of asset prices in Q4 1997 the overall financial flows to enterprises from share-issues have been rather limited. Most of the financing of Russian firms has at this stage came from internal sources. Furthermore, even after the huge increases of 1996 and H1 1997, the share market was still relatively small when compared with western countries. At the end of 1997 the market capitalization of US$ 90 billion as a percentage of GDP was a mere 19 per cent in Russia, much lower than in the OECD economies. This indicates that the stock market at this stage of development still has a much less prominent role than in the typical western country.

8.2.7. *Preference shares*

The privatization process in Russia allowed for three different methods of privatizing a firm, which differ in the amount and type of shares allocated to insiders. Preference shares are shares that have been issued free to employees by firms that chose method 1 of privatization (which roughly 25 per cent of firms did). These shares total up to 25 per cent of charter capital. They carry no voting rights but are in general guaranteed preferential treatment with respect to dividend payments. The details of this preferential treatment vary across firms and are laid down in the corporate charters. Most of these charters state that either 10 per cent of after tax profits or the equivalent to the dividend on ordinaries, whichever is greater, have to be paid out as dividends to shareholders of preferred shares. Thus, preference shares are superior in terms of cash flows, but inferior in terms of control rights. In Russia there has always been a large premium on ordinary shares over preference shares. For example, the premium in the case of LUKOil at the end of 1997 has been about 45 per cent. This is much higher than the corresponding figure for the USA (5 per cent), but roughly on a par with that in Israel (31 per cent) and Italy (45 per cent). Such high premia imply that a share's voting rights are highly valued, presumably because private benefits to running the company are very large. This, in turn, is the case because outside investor protection is relatively weak in these countries which allows insiders to subtract substantial benefits for themselves.

8.3. **THE DEBT MARKETS**

8.3.1. *Corporate debt*

Before discussing the market for government debt prior to the crash, we note the under-development of the market for corporate debt. Up to the end of 1997 there had been only a handful of (domestic) public issues of a corporate bond. There have been issues of promissory notes (financial *veksels*), but these are very short-term instruments, issued mainly by banks and not by corporates. The vast majority of corporate *veksels* are non-financial as they are redeemable in kind. They represent therefore a type of trade finance, which is not well suited to finance longer term investment. Of course, this low development of the bond market has to be seen in the context of very limited financing of all corporate investment and is not specific to bond financing. Bank lending to Russian corporates has also been very limited and very short term. In December 1997 total outstanding bank loans to the private non-financial sector amounted only to Russian roubles 246 trillion, or 9.2 per cent of GDP, of which about 95 per cent was with a maturity of less than three months. In other words, banks did provide some short-term working capital to firms, but did in general not finance long-term investments (although there might well be implicit agreements to roll over the short-term debt). And it has been noted above that share-issues have been fairly limited. At the same time both bank lending and the equity market enjoy certain advantages over bond markets. First, banks are likely to have an informational advantage in today's Russia. If a bank succeeds in forcing a firm to which it lends money to keep most of its accounts with that particular bank, than the bank is likely to have better information on that company than do the securities markets. The short maturity of bank lending means that the need for management to roll over the debt becomes a way of enforcing the pay-back discipline of management (Jensen 1986).

Second, a handicap for debt versus equity comes in the Russian bankruptcy procedure, which is fraught with even more problems than those inherent in protecting shareholder rights. Although the Federal Bankruptcy Agency (FBA) had slowly been getting more effective in forcing bankrupt companies to restructure, the FBA is responsible only for firms with large debts to the federal budget and for firms where the state still holds more than 25 per cent of the equity. To declare any firm not belonging to these two groups bankrupt is the responsibility of the arbitration courts. Even under the pre-crash reformist government investors could not rely on these courts—as was demonstrated by the fact that even the government had not been able to put several of the largest tax debtors into bankruptcy—in spite of a dire financial situation and continued tax arrears. Moreover, the Russian bankruptcy code states that debts to the budget and debts to employees have to be paid off first. Given the large tax and wage arrears, it is unlikely that private creditors would try to solve their problems by pushing their debtors into bankruptcy. Tax debts are, of course, a prior claim everywhere. But wage arrears do not exist outside the transition economies. Taking this feature to the extreme, a firm could even build up wage arrears on purpose to prevent outside creditors from pushing it into bankruptcy.

These problems pose a severe impediment to industrial restructuring in Russia, and the policy focus on shareholder rights instead of creditor rights may have been overdone. In particular, there is one reason to prefer debt over equity as a way of financing for many Russian firms. Debt-issues allow management to remain in control, unless the firm performs so badly that it is threatened by bankruptcy. And casual observation suggests that remaining in control of the firm is one of the key objectives of management. This is accomplished, if necessary, even by resorting to illegal or semi-legal measures. This implies that management prefer debt-issues over equity-issues.[2] But investors are unwilling to buy such issues in the absence of a functioning bankruptcy procedure.

One can wonder why management seems so keen to remain in control. After all, one expects that management would be willing to give up control in case it was paid sufficiently well for transferring control to a possibly more-efficient owner. However, the difficulties that investors seem to face in bribing management out of their jobs is due to two (and possibly related) reasons: first, management enjoys significant private benefits from being in control of the company (as is implied by the discount preference shares trade at); second, management has the poten-tial to divert profits. To the extent that a new investor would not be able (or willing) to divert such profits (which also reduces taxes), the investor is not able to pay management enough for a transfer of control, possibly even though the new investor might be able to run the firm more efficiently.

A small number of firms have issued eurobonds on the international capital markets. Most of them are banks, with the notable exception of

---

[2] For a more detailed discussion of the different agency costs of debt and equity in transi-tion, see Berglöf (1995).

LUKOil which issued a convertible bond. Such bonds are governed by international law and are therefore not affected by the shortcomings of the Russian bankruptcy code. While there is the issue of enforcing rulings of foreign courts in Russia, the problems involved are easier to overcome for exporters like LUKOil in 1996. After all, creditors would be able to block export receipts in case LUKOil was unwilling to pay back its debt. Why international bond-issues developed less quickly than ADR issues is puzzling. It may be linked to institutional issues. If, for instance, it was the case that equity investors are less risk-averse than debt investors, then it makes sense for Russian firms to tap the equity markets first.

8.3.2. *Government debt*

The government debt market had been the fastest growing market in Russia in 1996 and 1997. While initially applauded for its ability to offer non-inflationary (or not immediately inflationary) financing of the budget deficit, it also turned out to be the mechanism that transmitted the emerging markets crisis to Russia. It was precisely the 'success' of this market (leading to relatively high amounts of foreign capital inflows, followed by sudden outflows) that would subsequently trigger default. The mid-nineties saw government debt markets grow quickly: on the international side, Russia completed its third eurobond issue in mid-1997, thus raising in aggregate more than US$ 4 billion in 1996–7; on the domestic side, there were two types of government debt instruments, both launched in 1993—rouble-denominated debt and US dollar-denominated debt. The US dollar denominated bonds are commonly referred to as MinFin bonds. They were issued to compensate clients of the Soviet Bank for Foreign Economic Activities (Vneshekonombank) for losses occasioned by the freezing of all hard currency accounts in 1991. Since the MinFin bonds were a one-off issue, it is more interesting to analyse rouble-denominated debt, which consists of GKOs (T-Bills) and OFZs (federal bonds). GKOs are public short-term zero-coupon bonds, issued by the Central Bank of Russia as the agent for the Russian Ministry of Finance. The maturity is below one year. OFZs were introduced in June 1995. They are medium-term bonds with a coupon that can either be fixed or floating. For floating interest rate OFZs the coupon, payable quarterly, is indexed to the previous month's GKO yields. Broadly speaking, the development of the market for GKOs and OFZs can be

Figure 8.2. *Index of GKO yields versus re-financing rates* *
*Weights of individual GKO issues according to size of issue outstanding.

characterized by the interest rate, the average maturity, and the out-standing stock of debt.

In the initial stages of the market, real interest rates were negative due to a burst in (unanticipated) inflation: in 1993 it averaged −290 per cent. As stabilization measures reduced inflation from 215 per cent in 1994 to 22 per cent in 1996 without an immediate matching reduction in infla-tionary expectations, real yields shot up to an average of 28 per cent in 1995 and, reinforced by the political uncertainty at the time of the pre-sidential election in 1996, to 62 per cent in 1996. Only as confidence in the reform programme and political stability increased after the victory of President Yeltsin did real yields come down to 6 per cent in September 1997. However, this downward trend of real yields was upset by the emerging markets crisis in Q4 1997. After some initial hesitation, the CBR defended the rouble by allowing interest rates to rise. Backward-looking real yields in December 1997 therefore shot up back to about 19 per cent. Figure 8.2 shows the index of GKO yields versus the re-finance rates from April 1995 to December 1997.

Average maturities tended to go hand in hand with the yields. At times when yields fell the government managed in general to lengthen the maturity of the debt portfolio, most notably in the first quarter of 1997. The average duration at the end of June 1997 was 207 days, up from 149 days at the end of 1996. Although the average duration had slightly fallen in Q4 1997 due to the difficulties of placing long-term debt during the emerging markets crisis, it was nevertheless still about 300 days.

While the general course of events is understandable, it is somewhat surprising that rates are taking so long to come down to sustainable levels. Experience in Poland, for example, was that real rates in 1994–5 were barely positive. This reflects the slower progress of financial stabilization in Russia, but there is also another important reason. Access for foreigners to the GKO market was fairly restricted until mid-1996. Even then, the Central Bank of Russia forced foreign investors under the so-called 'S-account' scheme to purchase dollars forward at artificial prices in order to cap the covered GKO yields. This procedure limited foreign interest in the market to some extent and kept yields higher than they would have been in a fully liberalized market.

The main reason for such policies has been the perceived need to subsidize the Russian banking system. The Russian banking system, which since 1992–3 had consisted of more than 2,000 banks, had mostly made its profits by taking deposits at very low nominal interest rates, i.e. paying a negative real interest on its deposits. These easy profits disappeared as inflation decreased. The main new source of income for banks was the government securities. At the end of 1996 25 per cent of the assets of banks comprised such securities. If interest rates on this paper had decreased too quickly, it might have put some banks close to bankruptcy, and in any case would have sharply lowered profitability, especially where bank portfolios contained many non-performing loans. Nevertheless, the question must be asked why the authorities subsidized the banking system in such an inefficient way. It would have been much cheaper to re-capitalize certain large banks that failed (maybe changing their management at the same time) than to shower money over all banks that had access to buying T-Bills. The (*ex-post*) more important reason to limit access for foreigners was the fear of a Mexico scenario, where sudden outflows could destabilize the debt as well as the currency market. Although this is exactly what happened in 1998, Russian policymakers were arguably more influenced by the political clout of the Russian banking system—certainly in the early stages of the stabilization in 1995–6, where those markets were still much too small to endanger macroeconomic stability. Ironically, it was precisely the fear by the CBR that the high real rates would endanger macroeconomic stability that caused the CBR to increase access for foreign investors to the T-Bill market. Following the introduction of the S-account scheme in August 1996, real interest rates fell from 60 per cent per annum to about 6 per cent in September 1997.

The high yields through most of 1995 and 1996 led to a quick build-up of the stock of outstanding domestic (rouble-denominated) debt. At the

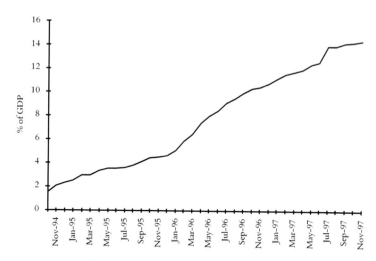

Figure 8.3. *Outstanding stock of GKOs/OFZs*

Source: Russian Economic Trends.

end of 1997 the outstanding stock of domestic rouble-denominated debt was US$ 60 billion, or 13 per cent of GDP, up from 4 per cent in January 1996 and 1.5 per cent in January 1995 (Figure 8.3). Most of that growth was the result of the high interest rates that had to be paid on the debt. Net financing to the federal budget was worth only 1.5 per cent of GDP in 1995, 1.7 per cent of GDP in 1996, and −0.3 per cent in 1997.

While the stock of internal debt was still small in Russia when compared to western countries (federal government debt in Germany was more than 20 per cent of GDP in 1995 and in the USA almost 40 per cent), the fact that real interest rates in Russia remained much higher than in western countries caused investors to worry about the sustainability of the debt market. In particular, the fact that the maturity profile was much shorter than in OECD countries meant that the focus on the size of the debt stock understated potential risks for holders of that debt, since the cash flow needs in any period were quite high.

Apart from the obvious damage to macroeconomic stabilization, there was also a negative impact on company finance. The budget deficit crowded out private investment by raising interest rates. The expected return on many potential projects in the real economy fell short of the rates paid on T-Bills. At the same time, T-Bills were more liquid than real investments and in the event of a crisis were thought to be correspondingly safer.

Another piece of evidence for the negative impact of high GKO yields on investment is the negative correlation between tax arrears and such yields (Grafe, Kirsanova, and Wyplosz 1995). The implication is that many firms preferred to invest in GKOs instead of paying their taxes. In these circumstances, it is plausible that these firms also preferred to invest in GKOs to investing in the real economy. However, it seems clear that the key for the very high real interest rates and the corresponding difficulties for Russian firms to finance themselves are less the growth of the GKO market but more the very substantial capital flight due to political uncertainty and the desire of Russian asset holders to diversify themselves.

There are also some other government debt instruments issued of limited importance. In 1995 the government introduced treasury notes, so called KOs, securitizing debt from the federal budget to enterprises. These KOs were rouble-denominated with a maturity of up to one year. This makes them similar to the corporate *veksel* market discussed above. An unusual feature of KOs was that early redemption was possible once they had been used a certain number of times to effect transactions between industrial enterprises. They could also be used in lieu of cash payments for taxes to the federal budget. As a result, KOs became a form of quasi-money, presumably with a higher velocity than cash. The possible inflationary impact and the associated pressure from the IMF caused the government to discontinue such practices in 1996. Lastly, there have been a variety of municipal bond issues. Over thirty regions and cities have issued such bonds, but the volumes were always very limited, apart from St Petersburg, the City of Moscow, and Omsk region. The most interesting feature of these debt markets was that the pricing did not always reflect the additional credit risk inherent in these regions. In particular, bonds issued by the City of St Petersburg at times failed to carry a yield premium over GKOs, which is most likely to reflect buying from investors with close links to the city administration.

8.4. THE 1998 CRASH

The emerging markets crisis of 1997–8, which had started with the devaluation of the Thai bath in 1997, increased risk-aversion of the international investors. Funds that lost money in Asia faced redemptions, and banks, which had been trading emerging market assets, cut the risk lines available for such trades. This reduction of capital that was willing to finance emerging markets also affected Russia and led to outflows of foreign funds from the by then quite large GKO market (as well as from the other Russian debt and equity markets). This caused GKO yields to go up and—due to the short maturity of the outstanding debt stock—caused bankers to draw up cash-flow analysis that would not only show that the debt stock would spiral out of control, but that also would show the number of weeks left before the cash flow deficit would have to cause a default on government debt—if nothing were done to address the problems. The first reaction of the government was to negotiate an anti-crisis package with the IMF. Initially this seemed to calm fears of investors, many of which had invested in Russia precisely because of the widely shared perception that the IMF would not let Russia go under, but would be willing to use substantial funds to avoid a default—the ultimate moral hazard trade. However, the IMF under-estimated the extent of capital outflows from the private sector (which was meant to slow down as a result of the IMF endorsement). The balance sheet contraction in international banking was just too large to allow sufficient funding of emerging markets borrowers. Private sector outflows continued, and the size of the public funds committed through the IMF package was seen as too small. In this situation, the government decided that the only option to avoid default would be to restructure the GKO market entirely, by converting this short-term domestic debt into long-term external (and US dollar-denominated debt). The argument was basically, that first, the stock of external debt was still relatively small; and secondly, that the interest rate was much less and the maturity much longer on external debt since there was no risk of a rouble devaluation priced in. Therefore, if the government was right and a rouble devaluation could be avoided, it would be much cheaper to have external debt than domestic debt (Willer 1997). At the same time the longer maturity profile of external debt would mean that the government could make amortization payments in several years time, when the real economy had hopefully stabilized. Since time was running out, the government decided against selling more external debt in a piecemeal fashion in order to use these funds to retire domestic debt. In any case, small offerings of external debt were more and more difficult to sell (even at a steadily rising interest rate) since such offerings were not perceived to alter the likelihood of a domestic debt default, which, it was feared, would also increase the likelihood of an external debt default. The chosen strategy was therefore to have a one-off transaction, where GKO investors could swap their GKOs at a premium to the current market value for a portion of cash and external US dollar-denominated debt. In theory, this transaction could have significantly reduced the stock of outstanding GKOs, removing the most obvious pressure-point and therefore—at the very least—buying the government more time to bring its fiscal house in order. However, as it turned out, this transaction was not successful, largely as the so-called prisoner's dilemma problem kicked in. Basically, investors figured that if enough of the other investors tendered their GKOs, this would mean that macroeconomic stability would return. In that case, the price of GKOs would rise significantly, because of the reduced default risk but also due to the much lower supply of such instruments. At the same time the price of the external debt that would be issued would presumably fall, given that the type of investor that would participate in the swap was unlikely to be willing to hold an instrument that he never intended to buy in the first place. In spite of the fact that there was a cheap hedge available against the fall in the price of external debt, the participation in the debt swap was disappointing, as investors were unwilling to give up their GKOs. Therefore, the last ditch attempt to remove the key threat to macroeconomic stability, the GKO market, had failed. And it is rather surprising that investors did not foresee that all the other investors faced incentives similar to themselves, which should have caused them to swap at least 50 per cent of their GKO holdings. In any case, capital outflows continued, and eventually the government was forced to declare default on its internal debt market and had to put administrative controls on the currency market.

REFERENCES

Barber, S. (1997). Comments on 'Corporate Governance and Shareholder Rights in Russia', in 'Investment Prospects in Russia', CEP conference volume.

Berglöf, E. (1995). 'Corporate Governance in Transition Economies: The Theory and its Policy Implications', in M. Aoki, and H.-K. Kim (eds.), 'Corporate Governance in Transitional Economies', *Economic Development Institute Development Studies*, The World Bank.

Blasi, J., Kroumova, M., and Kruse, D. (1997). *Kremlin Capitalism*, Cornell University Press.

—— and Shleifer, A. (1996). 'Corporate Ownership and Corporate Governance in the Russian Federation', Research Report for the Federal Commission on the Capital Market.

Boycko, M., Shleifer, A., and Vishny R. (1993). 'Privatizing Russia', *Brookings Papers on Economic Activity*, No. 2.

Frydman, R., Pistor, K., and Rapaczynski A. (1996). 'Investing in Insider Dominated Firms—A Study of Russian Voucher Privatization Funds', in

R. Frydman, C. Grey, and A. Rapaczynski (eds.), *Corporate Governance in Central Europe and Russia*, vol. 1, Central European University Press.

Grafe, C., Kirsanova, T., and Wyplosz, C. (1995). 'What Causes Arrears', RECEP Working Paper.

Jensen, M. (1986). 'Agency Costs of Free Cash Flow, Corporate Finance and Takeovers', *American Economic Review*, 76: 323–9.

Russian Economic Trends, various issues.

Willer, D. (1997). 'Corporate Governance and Shareholder Rights in Russia', CEP Discussion Paper 343.

—— (1998). *The Development of Equity Capital Markets in Transition Economies: Privatization and Shareholder Rights*, Physica-Verlag.

Willer, D., and Nash, R. (1996). 'Why Russian Shares are Undervalued', *Economics of Transition*, 4/2: 449–57.

9

External Trade and Payments

ANDREI LUSHIN AND PETER OPPENHEIMER

Foreign trade has been a highly visible and important sector of Russia's economy. It might be supposed that the collapse of Communism would have a lesser impact in this respect upon Russia than upon the economies of central Europe, whose natural commercial linkages with western Europe had been denied them by Soviet domination. Russia's vast land mass and large (150 million) and well-educated population make it a stronger looking candidate for self-sufficiency. The supposition is, however, mistaken. The reason lies not in the globalization of markets that is affecting long-established capitalist economies, though Russian consumers are, of course, influenced by demonstration effects emanating from western countries. Rather, it lies in certain other hitherto deeply rooted characteristics of Russia's economy and society.

Since tsarist times Russian manufacturing industry has been heavily controlled by government and disproportionately focused upon military ends. The Stalin era and the Cold War further magnified these tendencies. By contrast, production of sophisticated consumer manufactures lagged behind. Many of them, electrical and electronic articles particularly, were produced by the defence industries as lower priority items. Following the collapse of Communism, consumers switched enthusiastically to imports. Like the rest of the world, they wanted Japanese video recorders and hi-fi equipment, Italian washing machines, and German motor vehicles. Where competing products were available from Russian industry, they were seen as hopelessly inferior in terms of design, quality, and reliability. To compete on price alone was in many cases impractical.

In a few areas of industry—armaments and aircraft, for example—Russian producers are internationally competitive or nearly so. How to extend this status within a reasonable timespan to a wider range of industrial sectors is an issue that goes to the heart of Russia's economic prospects. The same applies to agriculture, together with food processing, distribution, and marketing. Meanwhile the marginal import propensity of Russian households has been extraordinarily high, albeit exaggerated—and its reliable measurement hampered—by the continued under-pricing of urban housing and of various utilities.

The total value of imports has none the less been far outweighed by Russia's exports, comprising mainly minerals (especially oil and gas) and semi-manufactures. Much of the raw materials come from Siberia. Russia has run a sizeable current payments surplus, matched to a great extent by illegal capital exports on the part of exporting enterprises. From mid-1995 to early 1998 accumulated net capital exports were reduced by some return flow of funds into Russia from western countries, chiefly for portfolio investment in both government securities and company shares. Numerous western companies have set up offices in Russia, but the associated volume of direct investment has not been great.

Large inflows of portfolio capital in 1996–7 were attracted mainly by the exceptional (and obviously unsustainable) level of real interest rates on rouble treasury bills. At the same time, the Russian government was also able to issue foreign-currency debt abroad on reasonable terms. The debt default of August 1998 delivered a critical blow to the process of financial-sector reform. In other sectors likewise the building, or rebuilding, of mutual confidence between Russian and foreign businessmen will be a slow process. An officially declared policy objective is to expand the share of manufactures in Russia's exports. But for the time being Russia's export capacity in raw and semi-processed materials is such that the balance of payments factor exercises no great pressure in favour of the speedy transformation of the country's manufacturing industries.

9.1. DATA PROBLEMS

Russian external trade statistics date from Russia's emergence as an independent state. Before that statistics were compiled only for the USSR as a whole, without any breakdown by different republics. All data on Russian foreign trade prior to 1992 are thus derived from the USSR statistics and should be regarded as estimates, whose accuracy decreases as one moves backward from 1992.

In 1992–3 Goskomstat generally retained the methodology of trade data collection and processing that had been used in the USSR under conditions of state monopoly of foreign trade. The reporting system assembled information not (as in western countries) from the customs authorities but from large foreign trade organizations reporting through regional statistical offices. The reliability of such information was poor. First, not all trading units were registered by local statistical organizations, especially after the state monopoly of trade was eliminated in late 1991. Second, reporting discipline was low. Third, a new type of economic activity appeared, in the form of imports and exports by private individuals (the so-called 'shuttle' trade),[1] which could not be properly registered. For all these reasons, initial Goskomstat data on trade were substantial under-estimates, especially on the import side. The figures were later adjusted jointly by Goskomstat, the Ministry for Foreign Economic Relations (MFER), and the State Customs Committee (SCC) to take into account customs data, statistics published by Russia's trade partners, and estimates of shuttle trade.

From 1994 trade statistics were gradually transferred to customs-based reporting. Some problems remain, notably the incomplete frontier coverage by customs controls, especially in the case of imports. In general, two bodies now compile Russian trade figures: the SCC and Goskomstat.[2] The SCC produces 'officially registered' figures of the quantity and value of merchandise trade. On the basis of these figures Goskomstat estimates total trade, which adds non-registered flows, basically the shuttle trade activity of individuals. The adjustment for shuttle trade is based on counterpart statistics of Russia's trade partners and various expert judgements. It is given only as an overall figure and not allocated among commodities. The gap between official and total figures is considerably larger for imports than for exports (Table 9.1).

9.2. MERCHANDISE TRADE

9.2.1. *Trade and GDP*

With the break-up of the Soviet Union, Russia's foreign trade showed substantial statistical expansion, as previous inter-republican trade became external trade. In this section, however, we describe mostly the

---

[1] Goods exported and imported in small lots by individual traders, exploiting the exemption from customs duties of their imports below a certain value threshold ($5,000 in 1993, $2,000 in 1994–5, $1,000 in 1996–7). Shuttle imports became subject to import tariffs from April 1998.

[2] The Central Bank also produces its estimates of exports and imports consistent with the balance of payments methodology. However, inputs for these calculations are data provided by customs and SCC.

Table 9.1. *Russia's external trade, 1994–1998*

	Exports (US$ billion)			Imports (US$ billion)		
	Officially Registered	Adjusted for non-registered trade	Shuttle trade as % of total trade	Officially registered	Adjusted for non-registered trade	Shuttle trade as % of total trade
1994						
Total	66.9	67.5	1.0	38.7	50.5	23.5
Non-CIS	53.0	53.0	0.0	28.3	37.0	23.3
CIS	13.9	14.5	4.7	10.3	13.6	23.9
1995						
Total	79.9	81.1	1.5	46.7	60.9	23.4
Non-CIS	65.6	65.6	0.0	33.1	44.1	24.9
CIS	14.3	15.5	7.9	13.6	16.8	19.3
1996						
Total	86.9	88.6	1.9	47.4	68.8	31.2
Non-CIS	71.0	71.0	0.0	32.8	49.1	33.2
CIS	15.9	17.6	9.7	14.6	19.7	26.0
1997						
Total	86.6	88.3	1.9	53.6	73.6	27.2
Non-CIS	70.0	70.0	0.0	39.4	55.9	29.5
CIS	16.7	18.4	9.3	14.2	17.8	20.0
1998						
Total	72.6	74.2	2.2	44.0	58.9	25.4
Non-CIS	58.9	58.9	0.0	32.7	45.4	28.0
CIS	13.7	15.3	10.5	11.3	13.5	16.5

Source: Goskomstat, State Customs Committee.

traditional trade with non-CIS countries (or 'far abroad').[3] The latter category includes trade both with western countries and with former communist (mostly CMEA) states.

Russian trade with non-CIS countries reached a peak in 1989–90, exports at $75 billion in 1989 and imports one year later at $82 billion. In 1990 exports fell by 5 per cent, but the real collapse of trade happened in 1991, when exports dropped by 28 per cent and imports by 46 per cent. This drastic reduction followed the decision to abolish the 'transferable

[3] The Baltic states, although part of the former Soviet Union (FSU), are also non-CIS.

rouble' for CMEA trade and conduct all trade in hard currency and at world prices. Moreover, the disintegration of the Soviet Union had already started and the administrative system of trade regulation was considerably weakened, while market stimuli to trade expansion were lacking. The more pronounced fall in imports than in exports reflected the shrinkage of trade credits accorded to the Soviet Union during the last year of its existence.

In 1992, when economic reforms started in earnest, chaotic regulatory conditions (the systems of quotas and licensing changing continuously during the year) as well as general economic recession caused both non-CIS exports and imports to decline by 17 per cent (Table 9.2), similar to the 16 per cent fall in GDP. In the following year export values began to expand and by 1996 had risen 67% compared to 1992. Import growth began a year later: in 1993 a further fall of 11 per cent was due partly to cuts in so-called 'centralized' imports, which were subsidized from the federal budget, and partly to the extraordinarily low level of the rouble (see the Exchange-rate section below), which made imports very expensive.

The share of consolidated (non-CIS and CIS) merchandise trade in GDP almost doubled between 1992 and 1998, to about 13 per cent for exports and 10 per cent for imports (Table 9.2). These figures value the GDP in dollars at the official PPP exchange rate. If the market exchange rate is used, the corresponding shares in 1998 are about twice as high: 26 per cent for exports and 21 per cent for imports. Table 9.3 shows the share of output exported for nine separate commodity groups which together account for nearly 60 per cent of total exports.

Goskomstat does not provide separate indices of price and volume changes for exports and imports. Such data are important as world prices for many Russian tradable goods are subject to considerable fluctuation. According to VNIKI estimates (Table 9.4), in 1993 and 1994 growth of export values largely reflected increased physical supplies, while in 1995–7 changes in value were chiefly due to price volatility. Import expansion from 1993 at first reflected higher import prices, while volume fell. In 1995 import prices rose by another 19 per cent. In general this means that the terms of trade moved against Russia in 1993–5. The country had to export a greater physical volume of exports to obtain a given unit of imports. Substantial growth of import volume was recorded only in 1996 and 1997, when the rouble was broadly judged as over-valued. Maybe for the same reason, export volumes stagnated during these years.

Table 9.2. *Russian merchandise trade—dollar values and percentage of GDP (1990–1998)*

	1990	1991	1992	1993	1994	1995	1996	1997	1998
Values (US$ billion)[a]									
Exports	88.5	66.8	53.6	59.6	67.5	81.1	88.6	88.3	74.2
Non-CIS	71.1	50.9	42.4	44.3	53.0	65.6	71.0	70.0	58.9
CIS[b]	17.3	15.9	11.2	15.3	14.5	15.5	17.6	18.4	15.3
Imports	94.8	55.1	43.0	44.3	50.5	60.9	68.8	73.6	58.9
Non-CIS	81.8	44.5	37.0	32.8	37.0	44.1	49.1	55.9	45.4
CIS[b]	13.1	10.6	6.0	11.5	13.6	16.8	19.7	17.8	13.5
As % of GDP									
Exports	8.8	7.0	6.9	8.1	10.2	13.2	14.9	14.9	13.0
Non-CIS	7.1	5.4	5.5	6.0	8.0	10.7	11.9	11.8	10.3
CIS	1.7	1.7	1.4	2.1	2.2	2.5	3.0	3.1	2.7
Imports	9.5	5.8	5.5	6.0	7.6	9.9	11.6	12.4	10.3
Non-CIS	8.2	4.7	4.8	4.5	5.6	7.2	8.3	9.4	8.0
CIS	1.3	1.1	0.8	1.6	2.0	2.7	3.3	3.0	2.4
GDP ($ billion)[c]	1,000	950	776	735	662	614	594	593	571

Notes: [a] From 1993—including non-registered shuttle trade.
[b] Figures for CIS trade in 1990 and 1991 are from VNIKI (1996).
[c] GDP values in dollars are obtained on the basis of the official PPP exchange rate calculated and published by Goskomstat. Figures for 1990–1 are estimates.

Source: Goskomstat.

Table 9.3. *Share of output exported (including exports to CIS countries), selected commodities (per cent)*

	1992	1993	1994	1995	1996	1997	1998
Crude oil	34.5	34.6	41.4	41.0	42.9	42.8	46.7
Petroleum products	21.4	25.5	29.1	32.6	40.2	42.9	41.6
Natural gas	29.5	27.7	30.4	32.3	33.1	35.2	34.5
Coal	11.7	14.7	13.0	17.1	15.8	14.5	15.7
Pig iron	5.4	6.2	9.2	7.2	5.7	6.7	7.6
Rolled steel	na	na	na	53.1	59.7	58.6	63.5
Mineral fertilizers	69.3	72.0	75.2	77.5	78.7	71.6	79.1
Timber	10.3	10.8	17.1	20.3	23.2	29.3	34.1
Cars	49.0	34.3	29.6	25.4	17.4	10.7	9.6

Source: Goskomstat.

Table 9.4. *Indices of trade value, volume, and unit value in 1991–1998 (in per cent of the previous year)*[a]

	1991	1992	1993	1994	1995	1996	1997	1998
Exports								
Value index	75.5	80.2	111.3	113.2	120.1	109.3	99.7	84.0
Volume index	94.6	92.0	119.6	110.6	103.8	100.6	101.6	99.7
Unit value index	79.8	87.2	93.0	102.4	115.7	108.6	98.1	84.2
Imports								
Value index	58.1	78.0	103.1	114.0	120.6	112.9	107.0	80.1
Volume index	86.3	95.0	86.6	91.5	101.2	112.7	112.8	86.7
Unit value index	67.3	82.1	119.1	124.6	119.2	100.2	94.8	92.3
Terms of trade index	118.6	106.2	78.1	82.2	97.1	108.4	103.5	91.2

Note: [a]Including trade with the CIS countries.

Source: VNIKI (1996–8).

9.2.2. *Geographical structure of trade*

A striking feature of the collapse both of Socialism and of national output in eastern Europe and then in the USSR was the shift of trading patterns away from mutual trade among the former Socialist countries. The previous pattern of intra-CMEA trade, when Russian fuels and other industrial materials were exchanged for low-quality manufactured goods, could not survive in the free market environment. At the same time a new pattern based on existing comparative advantage and geographical proximity could not quickly emerge. In their efforts to obtain closer integration with the EU, central and east European countries all concentrated on promoting trade in the 'western' direction, while ignoring possible means of co-operation with each other and with the CIS countries.

Between 1990 and 1994 the value of Russia's exports to the former CMEA countries dropped from $31 billion to $7 billion, and their share of Russia's total exports from 35 per cent to 10 per cent (Table 9.5). In 1995–6 there was a modest recovery—to $10–11 billion, or about 12 per cent of the total. Imports from CMEA countries fell even more, from $36 billion in 1990 to a mere $3 billion in 1994, and their share of total imports from 38 per cent to 8 per cent. In 1998 this share fell even further—to only 7 per cent (Table 9.6).

In line with the general tendency, Russia's trade with developed industrial countries—basically the OECD economies—expanded in 1990–7. Exports grew from $26 billion to $40 billion, and the OECD share from 29 per cent to 47 per cent (Table 9.5). The share of imports from OECD states remained at around 50 per cent in 1994–8 (Table 9.6). The bulk of trade with industrial countries involved European states, chiefly Germany, Switzerland, Italy, Finland, Netherlands, and the UK. Russia's exports to developed market economies have grown considerably faster than its imports. Its trade surplus with these countries increased from $1.7 billion in 1992 to $13 billion in 1998.

Trade with developing countries likewise expanded and shifted away from former political allies (North Korea, Mongolia, Syria) towards new partners among the industrializing economies of the Third World, notably the Asian 'tigers' (Hong Kong SAR, South Korea, Singapore, Taiwan) and China.

At the same time, a significant share of Russia's external trade has, not surprisingly, been with its neighbours in the CIS. This trade suffered in 1991–2, mainly from the disruption of established technological links between enterprises and of payments arrangements. Following the collapse of the rouble zone, trade in 1992 derived largely from inter-governmental agreements based on barter or bilateral clearing. When payment in local currencies became more widespread and a system

Table 9.5. *Geographical composition of Russia's exports (per cent)*[a]

	1992	1993	1994	1995	1996	1997	1998
Total (US$ billion)	53.6	59.6	66.9	79.9	86.9	86.6	72.6
Total (per cent)	100.0	100.0	100.0	100.0	100.0	100.0	100.0
Industrial countries	46.0	43.3	51.9	48.1	46.0	46.8	48.2
EU	38.8	32.9	35.9	32.8	31.3	33.0	32.8
Germany	11.1	8.5	9.5	7.6	7.7	7.9	8.3
USA	1.4	3.3	5.3	5.7	5.8	5.5	7.4
Japan	3.2	3.4	4.2	4.5	3.9	3.6	3.1
Developing countries	16.9	17.4	14.3	18.9	20.1	18.2	17.7
China	5.3	5.1	4.3	4.3	5.5	4.6	4.4
India	1.1	0.8	0.6	1.2	0.9	1.1	0.8
Turkey	1.2	1.8	1.5	2.1	1.9	2.3	2.7
NIS[b]	1.2	1.9	2.2	2.8	3.1	2.0	1.2
Former CMEA members	15.2	12.6	10.4	12.3	12.5	12.2	12.2
CEE[c]	14.3	12.0	9.9	11.4	11.6	11.3	10.5
Others[d]	0.9	0.6	0.5	0.9	0.9	0.9	1.7
Former USSR	21.9	26.7	23.3	20.6	21.4	22.8	21.9
CIS	20.9	25.7	20.7	17.9	18.3	19.2	18.8
Ukraine	na	na	10.3	8.7	8.7	8.4	7.7
Baltic states	0.9	0.9	2.6	2.8	3.1	3.6	3.1

Notes: [a]Excluding non-organized shuttle trade.
[b]Hong Kong SAR, Republic of Korea, Singapore, and Taiwan Province of China.
[c]Central and eastern European countries (Bulgaria, Hungary, Poland, Romania, Slovakia, Czech Republic).
[d]Cuba, Vietnam, Mongolia.
Source: Goskomstat and Direction of Trade Statistics (IMF).

of correspondent accounts of Russian banks with those in the 'near abroad' was established, trade values started to recover.

The export share falling upon the CIS countries fluctuated around 20 per cent in 1992–8,[4] while the import share was around 30 per cent starting from 1993. Russia's trade balance with the CIS countries turned negative in 1995–6 (Figure 9.1), reflecting a reduction in net credits from Russia to CIS countries, as well as the effect of the (somewhat inchoate)

---

[4] Russian exports to CIS states were not always paid for. The largest trade debtor to Russia for oil and gas supplies has been the Ukraine.

Table 9.6. *Geographical composition of Russia's imports (per cent)*[a]

	1992	1993	1994	1995	1996	1997	1998
Total (US$ billion)	42.9	38.3	38.7	46.7	47.4	53.6	44.0
Total (per cent)	100.0	100.0	100.0	100.0	100.0	100.0	100.0
Industrial countries	53.7	41.9	51.0	48.6	47.1	49.7	50.3
EU	38.5	29.3	39.8	38.4	35.7	37.1	36.3
Germany	16.4	13.4	14.7	13.9	12.2	12.6	12.7
USA	6.8	6.0	5.4	5.7	6.2	7.7	9.5
Japan	4.0	3.6	2.9	1.6	2.1	1.9	1.9
Developing countries	18.8	20.1	12.2	12.0	13.5	14.1	15.2
China	4.2	6.1	2.5	1.9	2.1	2.4	2.6
India	2.0	1.7	1.5	1.3	1.3	1.5	1.5
Turkey	1.1	1.7	1.0	1.2	1.3	1.5	1.2
NIS[b]	3.8	3.1	2.3	2.0	2.6	2.4	2.8
Former CMEA members	13.1	7.5	8.4	8.1	7.4	7.7	7.3
CEE[c]	10.7	5.7	7.3	7.5	6.3	6.8	6.1
Others[d]	2.4	1.8	1.1	0.6	1.1	0.9	1.2
Former USSR	14.4	30.5	28.4	31.3	32.1	28.4	27.2
CIS	14.0	30.0	26.7	29.1	30.8	26.5	25.6
Ukraine	na	na	11.4	14.2	13.3	7.3	7.4
Baltic states	0.5	0.4	1.7	2.2	1.3	1.9	1.5

Notes: [a]Excluding non-organized shuttle trade.
[b]Hong Kong SAR, Republic of Korea, Singapore, and Taiwan Province of China.
[c]Central and eastern European countries (Bulgaria, Hungary, Poland, Romania, Slovakia, Czech Republic).
[d]Cuba, Vietnam, Mongolia.

Source: Goskomstat and Direction of Trade Statistics (IMF).

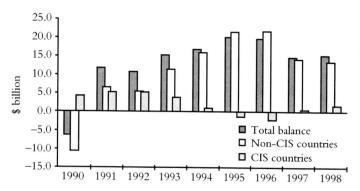

Figure 9.1. *Trade balance with CIS and non-CIS countries, 1990–1998*[a]

Note: [a] including non-organized shuttle trade

customs union between Russia, Belarus, and Kazakhstan. Booming imports from the CIS countries to Russia in 1995–6 may be a statistical artefact, since the elimination of the customs border with Belarus makes it more difficult to detect the country of origin of imported goods. Western imports may be wrongly reported as originating from the CIS, with importers utilizing the Belorussian tax-free corridor for evading customs duties.

9.2.3. *Commodity composition of trade*

Exports

Russian exports are concentrated, with the largest single contribution coming from oil and gas (Table 9.7). In 1997 within overall exports (that is, including to CIS states), the top three commodities (crude oil, natural gas, and ferrous metals) accounted for 49 per cent; the top five commodities (the above plus aluminium and petroleum products) for 62 per cent; and the top ten (adding fertilizers, timber, rough diamonds, copper, and nickel) for nearly 72 per cent. In 1998 this figure increased further to 75 per cent.

Exports of machinery and equipment performed poorly during the years of reform, their share declining from 18 per cent in 1990 to only 8 per cent in 1994, before recovering somewhat thanks in part to arms sales. In 1995 Russia was the second arms exporter in the world after the USA. The current value of Russia's arms exports is still small compared to the former USSR (Table 9.8), which in an average year had sales of $14 billion and peaked at $31 billion in 1987.[5]

Russian (non-military) machinery exports have consisted mainly of material- and energy-intensive items whose cheapness offset low technical standards. The real appreciation of the rouble in the mid-1990s largely wiped out this advantage. In general, Russia has been exporting an increasing share of semi-manufactures (Table 9.9), including those where production involves significant environmental costs, such as base metals, chemicals, cellulose, and paper products, whose combined share in exports rose from 18 to 31 per cent between 1992 and 1997. It is a reasonable supposition that if polluting enterprises such as paper mills

---

[5] However, Soviet arms deliveries were provided largely on credit, while Russia's are mostly for cash.

Table 9.7. *Commodity structure of Russian trade (per cent)*[a]

	1992	1993	1994	1995	1996	1997	1998
Exports							
Foodstuffs and agricultural raw materials	3.9	3.8	4.2	3.3	3.7	2.8	3.0
Oil, gas, and other mineral fuels	52.1	46.7	45.1	42.0	47.3	47.8	42.3
Chemical products, rubber	6.1	6.0	8.2	9.9	8.5	8.3	8.5
Leather, furskins and articles thereof	0.2	0.2	0.6	0.4	0.4	0.5	0.5
Timber, paper, cellulose	3.7	4.2	3.9	5.6	4.2	4.3	4.8
Textiles, footwear	0.6	0.4	2.0	1.5	1.1	1.1	1.2
Metals, precious stones	16.4	23.2	26.4	26.1	23.5	24.0	27.5
Machinery & equipment, means of transportation	8.9	6.5	8.3	9.9	9.8	10.3	11.3
Other products	8.1	9.0	1.3	1.3	1.5	1	0.9
Total	100.0	100.0	100.0	100.0	100.0	100.1	100.0
($ billion)	42.4	44.3	66.9	79.9	86.9	86.7	72.5
Imports							
Foodstuffs and agricultural raw materials	26.0	22.2	27.7	28.2	25.3	25.1	24.6
Oil, gas, and other mineral fuels	2.7	4.0	6.5	6.4	6.4	5.8	5.4
Chemical products, rubber	9.3	6.2	10.0	10.9	14.4	14.4	15.0
Leather, furskins and articles thereof	1.9	2.6	0.5	0.4	0.4	0.3	0.3
Timber, paper, cellulose	1.2	0.5	1.5	2.4	3.3	3.6	3.8
Textiles, footwear	12.2	13.9	7.9	5.5	4.7	4.5	4.0
Metals, precious stones	3.3	3.5	6.7	8.4	9.8	7.1	7.1
Machinery & equipment, means of transportation	37.7	33.8	35.2	33.7	32.0	35.3	36.2
Other products	5.7	13.3	4.0	4.1	3.7	3.9	3.6
Total	100.0	100.0	100.0	100.0	100.0	100.0	100.0
($ billion)	37.0	26.8	38.7	46.7	47.4	53.5	44.0

Note: [a] Excluding non-organized shuttle trade. 1992–3—trade with non-CIS countries only.
Source: Goskomstat.

Table 9.8. *Russia's arms exports to non-FSU countries ($ billion)*

	1987	1989	1990	1991	1992	1993	1994	1995	1996	1997
Arms exports	31.2[a]	21.8[a]	16.3[a]	7.1[a]	2.3	2.5	2.9	3.7	3.6	2.5

[a] USSR.

Source: *Financial Times*, 23 October 1998.

Table 9.9. *Russia's exports to non-CIS countries by major industry and commodity type (per cent)*

	1992	1993	1994	1995	1996	1997
Produce of agriculture, forestry, fisheries, and mining, of which	50.4	46.1	45.1	41.1	45.1	45.6
Crude oil and natural gas	37.8	35.7	34.2	30.7	33.3	34.2
Manufactures, of which	49.6	53.9	54.9	58.9	54.9	54.3
Semi-finished goods, of which	33.6	40.9	46.2	48.9	43.8	43.4
(a) environment-intensive (basic metals and chemicals, cellulose, paper products)	18.3	23.5	29.1	33.8	29.4	31.3
(b) resource-intensive (petroleum products and wood products)	11.1	9.4	8.0	8.1	11.1	11.0
Finished goods, of which	16.0	13.0	8.7	9.9	11.1	10.9
machinery and transport equipment	8.9	6.5	6.0	8.1	7.7	8.1

Source: VNIKI (various issues).

or metallurgical giants like Norilsk Nickel had to cover the costs of environmental protection or rehabilitation according to western standards, they would have lost a lot of their price competitiveness on world markets.

Imports

The commodity structure of officially registered imports (Table 9.7) shows the share of food rising from 20 per cent in 1990 to above 25 per cent starting from 1994. That of machinery and equipment dropped sharply in 1991 and recovered only fractionally in succeeding years. Machinery and transport equipment for investment has traditionally constituted a significant part of Russia's imports from non-CIS countries. By the mid-1990s, however, more than half of this category consisted of consumer goods in the form of electric and electronic machinery (TV sets, video-recorders, computers, etc.) and motor vehicles. Moreover, the figures exclude shuttle imports, which are entirely consumer goods and amounted in 1994–8 to almost one-quarter of total imports—see Table 9.1.

Import penetration in domestic consumption exceeded 50 per cent from 1995 onwards.[6] Imported consumer electronics have taken 80–90 per cent of the Russian domestic market, imports of apparel and footwear 78 per cent and 82 per cent respectively. The proportion of imports in food consumption is estimated by the Association of Agricultural Producers at one-third, though levels for individual commodities may vary considerably. This degree of import penetration led to growing pressure on the government for protectionist measures. In 1995–7 trade policy (see below) became much more restrictive than before with respect to imports.

9.2.4. *Barter trade*

Barter transactions continued to play a role in Russia's trade, amounting to approximately 3 per cent of exports and imports *vis-à-vis* non-CIS countries in 1995–7 (Table 9.10). Barter trade means that exporters receive in exchange for the delivered goods some amount of commodities from their foreign partner instead of payment in cash. These goods are not

---

[6] See VNIKI (1996). This includes shuttle imports.

Table 9.10. *Russia's barter trade with non-CIS and CIS countries*

	Non-CIS countries						CIS countries			
	1992	1993	1994	1995	1996	1997	1994	1995	1996	1997
Total exports ($ billion)	42.4	44.3	53.0	65.6	71.9	69.5	14.5	15.5	17.2	17.9
of which barter	13.0	5.2	2.7	2.2	2.4	2.1	1.4	2.7	3.2	3.4
Barter as % of total exports	30.7	11.7	5.1	3.4	3.3	3.0	9.7	17.4	18.6	19.0
Total imports ($ billion)	37.0	32.8	37.0	44.1	44.0	50.1	13.6	16.8	18.3	17.5
of which barter	9.1	2.8	1.6	1.1	1.2	1.3	2.3	3.3	3.1	3.0
Barter as % of total imports	24.6	8.5	4.3	2.5	2.7	2.6	16.9	19.6	16.9	17.1

Source: Goskomstat and State Customs Committee.

usually consumed by the exporter, but are sold on the domestic market for money. The peak of barter deals with non-CIS countries was in 1992. Several factors contributed, including the avoidance of foreign exchange constraints and the exploitation of differences between domestic and world prices. Although the share of barter in non-CIS trade has much diminished, it still poses a problem because of the non-equivalence of exchange. By definition, barter exports and imports should balance in value, but in the case of Russia's trade with non-CIS countries the value of exports measured in world prices is usually higher than the value of corresponding imports. Because of this, barter transactions with western industrial countries may be viewed as a concealed means of capital flight. The government has sought to reduce the amount of barter trade. In 1992–3 it imposed higher export taxes on barter than on regular transactions. In November 1996 currency controls were extended to barter deals (see Appendix 1 for details). The main idea is to force import values to equality with barter export values, thus closing loopholes for capital flight. The main partner country in Russian barter trade outside the CIS has been China, followed by Germany and Finland. Metals account for about half of barter exports. The largest commodity groups in barter imports are foodstuffs and machinery.

In contrast to trade with the 'far abroad', barter trade with the CIS states expanded in 1995–7, and in some years Russia even ran a deficit, thus receiving capital inflows from the rest of the CIS, chiefly the Ukraine, Kazakhstan, and Uzbekistan.

9.3. TRADE IN SERVICES

Russia's trade in non-factor services with non-CIS countries has been in growing deficit (Table 9.11). Expenditures abroad on tourism and travel rose to almost $10 billion in 1995–7, reflecting the prosperity of 'new Russians' and, of course, the relaxation of the visa regime with the

Table 9.11. *Russia's trade in non-factor services*[a]

	1992	1993	1994	1995	1996	1997	1998
Exports	3,893	6,437	8,950	12,446	12,945	13,519	12,937
(US$ billion)							
Total (per cent)	100.0	100.0	100.0	100.0	100.0	100.0	100.0
Transport	na	42.3	53.0	49.4	26.3	25.5	24.4
Travel	na	39.5	26.9	34.6	53.1	51.0	50.3
Construction	na	3.8	1.5	0.8	0.7	0.7	1.1
Financial services	na	0.0	1.0	0.5	0.6	0.9	0.8
Other	na	14.4	17.6	14.5	19.3	21.9	23.4
Imports	−6,270	−8,970	−15,444	−20,536	−18,660	−18,717	−16,087
(US$ billion)							
Total (per cent)	100.0	100.0	100.0	100.0	100.0	100.0	100.0
Transport	na	29.4	24.7	20.0	13.3	16.6	15.8
Travel	na	44.2	45.9	56.5	55.0	54.0	53.9
Construction	na	11.7	12.0	8.1	5.8	4.2	3.3
Financial services	na	0.0	0.4	0.3	0.5	1.0	1.5
Other	na	14.7	16.9	15.0	25.4	24.2	25.6
Balance	−2,377	−2,533	−6,494	−8,090	−5,715	−5,198	−3,150
(US$ billion)							

Note: [a]1992–3—for non-CIS countries only.

Source: The Central Bank of Russia (CBR).

end of the Cold War. The balance on transport services turned positive from 1993, whilst construction services were in growing deficit, as foreign firms obtained construction contracts in Moscow and elsewhere. Trade in financial services remains tiny.

9.4. TRADE POLICY

After the preliminary liberalization of Russia's foreign trade by presidential decree in November 1991 Russian trade policy started with a very open import regime but heavily regulated exports. By the end of 1996 the pattern had been reversed to the more usual one of almost complete liberalization of exports but significant protection on imports.

This sequence reflected the developing situation in the domestic economy. At the outset of the transition process Russia was still in the throes of market shortages, huge differences between domestic and world prices, and a greatly under-valued exchange rate. In order to prevent a drain of resources from the country, drastic measures were implemented to control exports. These measures prolonged the distortions in domestic prices (in particular, low energy prices), stimulated depreciation of the rouble, and generated rent-seeking and corruption because of the high profitability of export sales. By the middle of the decade an appreciating real exchange rate had substantially closed the gap between domestic and world prices, and practically all export restrictions (both tariff and non-tariff) were removed by the end of 1996. (However, in January 1999 temporary export duties were re-introduced for some commodities, including crude oil and non-ferrous metals. This reflected the difficult fiscal position of the government and also a recovery in world commodity prices.) Future policy with regard to exports is likely to concentrate on export promotion and quality-enhancement schemes in order to realize Russia's potential in areas other than natural resources, especially high-tech products.

By contrast, imports were practically unregulated at the outset of economic reforms. Import expansion was welcomed as a short-term remedy for shortages. Moreover, the under-valued rouble protected import-competing producers. For the same reasons that export regulation was eased (chiefly the narrowing gap between domestic and world prices as the rouble appreciated in real terms), import policy became more restrictive in 1994–7 in response to protectionist pressures from industrial lobbies. Import subsidies were replaced by differentiated import tariffs, whose average level rose progressively. Many of the industries thus protected produce low-quality or outdated goods. The question is whether any of the industries—and which ones—will actually use the opportunity afforded by tariff protection to modernize and become genuinely competitive. A separate matter is the revenue argument for tariffs. Given the problem of the Russian budget, a moderate uniform tariff of 5–10 per cent could be an optimum source of revenue. Details of trade policy measures are presented in Appendix 1.

One needs to be cautious in inferring the range and extent of Russian industrial comparative advantage from data on actual exports. This is because breakthroughs by exporters to new industrial markets are liable to elicit a protectionist response from the importing country. At the time of writing Russia had not yet been admitted to any global or regional trade organizations that would preclude such a response. A list of EU 'anti-dumping' measures against Russia in force at end-1995 is given in Appendix 3. Russia applied in 1995 for membership of WTO, but had not been admitted by 2000. Accession to WTO will entitle Russia to most favoured nation treatment, including elimination of discriminatory trade barriers in the form of differential surcharges and anti-dumping procedures. Russia also signed an Interim Agreement on Trade and Trade Related Matters with the EU, which came into force on 1 February 1996. It is especially important for Russia that the Interim Agreement stipulates more equitable terms for conducting anti-dumping investigations, which will take into account the 'natural competitive advantages' of Russian industry.

9.5. THE ROUBLE EXCHANGE RATE

The development of Russia's trade policy was influenced by the dynamics of the exchange rate. In the early stages of economic reform the rouble was tremendously under-valued. At the average 1992 exchange rate and Russian prices the whole of Russia's GDP was estimated at $86 billion, yet the annual output of crude oil and natural gas alone measured at world prices was more than $100 billion. From a low level prevailing in 1992, the rouble appreciated strongly in real terms during 1993–5 (see Table 9.12 and Figure 9.2). Although such real appreciation has been typical for most transition economies, its magnitude in Russia (by almost 600 per cent) was remarkable. From 1996 the real exchange rate more or less stabilized following the introduction of the band ('corridor') for the

Table 9.12. *Exchange rate indicators, 1992–1998*

	Nominal exchange rate[a] (R/US$)	PPP[b] (R/US$)	PPP exchange rate as % of nominal rate	Real exchange rate[c] (1992 = 100)	Real rouble appreciation (%) (year on year)	Average wage (US$ per month)
1992	222	24	11	100	60.0	27
1993	933	231	25	229	129.1	63
1994	2,205	922	42	387	69.0	100
1995	4,562	2,508	55	509	31.5	104
1996	5,126	3,611	70	652	28.1	154
1997[d]	5,785	4,250	73	680	4.3	164
1998[d]	9.7	4.7	48	448	−34.0	108

Notes: [a]year average.
[b]PPP—Purchasing power parity reported by Goskomstat.
[c]Real exchange rate index calculated on a CPI basis.
[d]Estimate.

Source: Russian Economic Trends, various issues; Goskomstat.

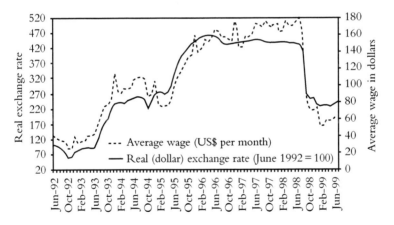

Figure 9.2. *Average wage in dollars and real dollar exchange rate of the rouble*

nominal rate from mid-1995 (see Appendix 2). This lasted until the financial collapse of August 1998, when both the nominal and the real exchange rate plummeted.

Different phases of nominal exchange rate behaviour reflect shifts in economic conditions and in official policy. Starting from 169 R/$ at the end of 1991, the market rate fell to 224 R/$ in February 1992 as part

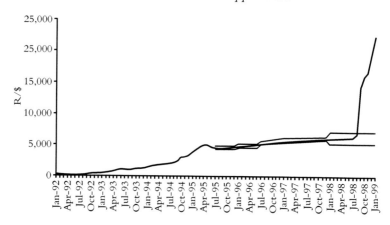

Figure 9.3. *The nominal exchange rate and the exchange-rate band*

of the price liberalization shock. The Central Bank then began to intervene massively in an attempt to stabilize the currency. The highest level reached as a result of these efforts was 112.3 R/$, in mid-June 1992. Following the switch from multiple rates to a single exchange rate on 1 July, depreciation resumed. The goal of the Central Bank was now to avoid sharp fluctuations and if possible to keep rouble depreciation slightly behind inflation. For almost a year the price of foreign exchange rose virtually at the same rate as the money stock. Then, from mid-June 1993 the exchange rate stabilized at around 1000 R/$, as restrictions on money supply expansion led to a turnround in real interest rates.

Between October 1993 and February 1994 political turmoil (military struggle between president and parliament, elections, and then a government reshuffle in early 1994) occasioned a renewed slide to around 1600 R/$. Thereafter, from March to June 1994 depreciation was smoother and slower than inflation. The calm was interrupted in August-September, with nominal depreciation up to 5 per cent in August and 11 per cent in September. Market psychology, for the first time playing a significant role in Russian financial developments, reacted adversely, evidently in fear that the CBR under Governor Gerashchenko was abandoning the struggle against inflation. In a fit of panic speculation, the exchange rate soared from 2633 R/$ at the end of September to 3926 R/$ on 11 October ('Black Tuesday'). Thereafter the joint efforts of the Central Bank and the government brought a recovery to around 3000 R/$ at the end of October (Figure 9.3).

From January to April 1995 the exchange rate depreciated more or less in line with inflation, reaching about 5,000 R/$. In May the rate began to strengthen, reaching a ceiling of 4405 R/$ in the first half of August. This nominal appreciation of the rouble, despite still relatively high domestic inflation, was due to tighter monetary conditions in Russia, resulting from the restrictive monetary policy initiated in the first quarter of 1995 and the higher bank reserve requirements introduced by the CBR from May. The urgent wish to prevent excessive strengthening of the rouble led the authorities to announce the exchange rate band on 5 July. The move was successful in dampening speculation, and from September 1995 the rouble started to depreciate again by 1–2 per cent per month. Steady depreciation at this rate with appropriate adaptation of the corridor continued until the end of 1996. In 1997 the slope of the corridor was somewhat reduced and depreciation of the rouble continued at a slower pace. From January 1998 until collapse in August 1998 the currency fluctuated within a narrow band around a peg of 6.2 R/$ (the rouble was rebased by a factor of 1,000 from 1 January 1998).

The package of emergency measures introduced on 17 August 1998 included a decision to extend the exchange-rate band to 6.0–9.5 R/$. However, all efforts to defend the peg failed and from 2 September 1998 the rouble was allowed to float freely. This resulted in a substantial depreciation and by the end of 1998 the rouble stood at 21 against the dollar. In 1999 both higher oil prices and a drastic drop of imports led to substantial recovery of the balance of payments. The Central Bank managed to keep the exchange rate under control (it was 27 R/$ by year-end), and also restored its depleted foreign exchange reserves.

9.6. THE BALANCE OF PAYMENTS

Table 9.13 shows consolidated balance of payments statistics (with both CIS and non-CIS countries) for 1994–8. Capital and financial items are structured according to IMF methodology. Balances of payments for 1992–3 are available only for non-CIS countries and were compiled by the CBR on a different basis. For these reasons, they are not directly comparable with those for 1994–7. They are presented in Appendix 4.

Table 9.13. *Russia's consolidated balance of payments, 1994–1998 ($ billion)*

		1994	1995	1996	1997[a]	1998
1	Exports (fob)	67.8	82.7	90.6	89.0	74.8
2	Imports (fob)	−50.2	−62.2	−67.6	−71.6	−57.4
3	*Trade balance*	*17.7*	*20.5*	*22.9*	*17.4*	*17.3*
4	Non-factor services, net	−6.7	−9.4	−5.7	−4.7	−3.2
5	Labour income net	−0.1	−0.3	−0.4	−0.3	−0.2
6	Investment income net	−1.7	−3.1	−4.9	−8.1	−11.2
7	*Services and factor incomes, net*	*−8.5*	*−12.8*	*−11.1*	*−13.1*	*−14.5*
8	*Net current transfers*	*−0.3*	*0.1*	*0.1*	*−0.3*	*−0.4*
9	**Current account**	**8.9**	**7.8**	**12.0**	**4.1**	**2.4**
10	*Net capital transfers*	*2.4*	*−0.3*	*−0.5*	*−0.8*	*−0.4*
11	*Direct investment, net*	*0.5*	*1.7*	*1.7*	*3.6*	*1.2*
12	*Portfolio investment, net*	*0.0*	*−2.4*	*8.8*	*17.6*	*7.8*
13	*Other capital flows—assets*	*−17.7*	*5.0*	*−29.1*	*−26.6*	*−16.1*
14	Foreign currency in cash and bank deposits	−5.6	4.5	−9.7	−12.5	1.9
15	Foreign currency	−5.7	0.1	−8.7	−13.4	0.9
16	Bank accounts and deposits	0.2	4.3	−1.0	1.0	1.0
17	Trade credits and advances granted	−3.7	8.0	−9.5	−6.8	−6.8
18	Other credits and loans granted	9.5	8.6	9.5	7.0	5.3
19	Arrears on debt payments to Russia	−12.8	−10.6	−9.5	−3.0	−7.4
20	Non-repatriated export revenue	−3.9	−4.9	−9.8	−11.5	−8.6
21	Other assets	−1.3	−0.6	−0.1	0.1	−0.5
22	*Other capital flows—liabilities*	*−13.4*	*−15.8*	*−4.7*	*−1.5*	*−5.9*
23	National currency in cash and bank deposits	1.4	2.9	1.3	−4.7	−2.8
24	Trade credits and advances received	−1.0	−8.1	−0.8	−0.1	0.3
25	Private credits received	1.2	1.3	5.1	10.1	0.6
26	Amortization of official credits falling due	−15.3	−12.8	−11.2	−7.3	−3.3
27	Other liabilities	0.3	0.9	0.9	0.5	−0.7
28	**Capital account**	**−28.1**	**−11.9**	**−23.8**	**−7.7**	**−13.4**
29	**Errors and omissions**	**−0.3**	**−7.8**	**−8.6**	**−7.8**	**−7.9**

Table 9.13. *(continued)*

		1994	1995	1996	1997[a]	1998
30	Adjustment[b]	−1.8	1.1	−1.5	0.0	−0.1
31	**Overall balance to be financed**	**−21.4**	**−10.8**	**−21.9**	**−11.5**	**−19.0**
32	**Total Financing**	**21.4**	**10.8**	**21.9**	**11.5**	**19.0**
33	*Reserve assets*	1.9	−10.4	2.8	−1.9	5.3
34	*Exceptional Financing*	*19.5*	*21.2*	*19.1*	*13.4*	*13.7*
35	Debts formally rescheduled	12.4	12.1	8.4	3.1	2.1
36	Accumulated external arrears	3.2	1.1	2.7	3.5	5.1
37	Credits from international institutions	1.9	6.3	4.2	4.3	6.4
38	of which IMF	1.5	5.5	3.2	1.5	5.2
39	other international institutions	0.4	0.9	1.0	2.7	1.2
40	Bilateral official credits	2.1	1.7	3.7	2.5	0.0

Notes: [a]Figures for 1997 do not show the conversion of $28 billion of debt to the London Club into bonds.
[b]To remove double counting of official reserves in transactions with local banks.

Source: Central Bank of Russia.

Broadly speaking, up to 1998 the trade balance showed a large surplus, while invisibles were in deficit because of Russian tourist outlays and interest payments. The current account surplus was not sufficient to put Russia into a comfortable external payments position and the country had a deficit on the overall balance, especially large in 1996—$22 billion. This was for several reasons, notably the substantial outflow, much of it illegal, of private Russian capital, far exceeding inflows of direct and portfolio investment funds to Russia from abroad. Other factors were the foreign currency debt inherited by Russia from the final years of the Soviet Union, and largely falling due for repayment in the first half of the 1990s, and the substantial volume of trade credit connected with Russian exports, especially in 1996–8. Moreover, large amounts due to Russia from foreign debtors (around $10 billion a year in 1994–6) provided no consolation, as Russia's debtors stopped virtually all payments on credits previously granted by the USSR (see also below, section 8).

Foreign direct investment in Russia rose by a factor of 7 between 1994 and 1997 although its amount was still small compared with the size of the economy. Up to 1995 the inflow of portfolio investment to Russia was negligible. From 1996 a new mechanism for attracting foreign capital into domestic government securities was introduced and, in addition, the government started placing eurobond issues. Foreign investment in Russian treasury bills (GKOs) reached almost $6 billion in 1996 and $11 billion in 1997. At the same time eurobond issues raised $1 billion and $3.5 billion respectively. Subsequently, the burden of servicing the soaring domestic debt exceeded the capacity of the Russian government and it effectively defaulted on GKOs in August 1998.

The increase in foreign currency holdings by the non-banking sector peaked in 1997 (about $3 billion). In 1995, when a degree of de-dollarization was observed, there was practically no increase in cash dollar holdings by households. At the same time, residents withdrew some $4.3 billion from bank accounts abroad for conversion into roubles and placement in Russian government treasury bills and other securities. In 1996 political uncertainty ahead of the presidential elections led to renewed growth of almost $9 billion in foreign currency holdings outside the banking sector. In 1998, when the dollar became prohibitively expensive after the crisis and people had to spend some of their dollar savings for everyday needs, these holdings decreased by almost $1 billion.

The overall payments deficit was financed through postponement and rescheduling of debts, together with official external borrowing, chiefly from the IMF. Between 1992 and 1998 the fund provided Russia with net credits of $19.4 billion and the World Bank granted loans totalling over $6 billion.

9.7. CAPITAL OUTFLOW

The key factor underlying capital outflows from Russia is the redistribution of property rights and revenues from foreign economic activity, previously a state monopoly, among private economic agents. This has enabled some firms and individuals to acquire huge sums in a short period of time, not always legally. Political prospects and uncertainties in Russia influence the consequent disposition of these sums. Motives of tax avoidance and evasion loom large. So does the insecurity, or vulnerability, of business property rights in Russia. Other things being equal (that is, no changes in perception of political or fiscal risk), capital flows respond to the adjusted interest-rate differential, that is, the difference between interest rates on rouble and on dollar deposits abroad less the expected depreciation of the rouble.

Our estimates of capital outflows from Russia use an extended version of methodology devised by M. Sarafanov.[7] Two main types of outflow are distinguished. *Legal* capital movements comprise changes in foreign assets of Russian commercial banks and in foreign currency assets of Russian non-bank residents. The relevant data can be taken directly from the BoP statistics—lines 15–16 of Table 9.13. *Illegal* capital flows are more varied and much more difficult to measure. Some types of these flows are by their nature not measurable (smuggling, offshore operations, etc.). Therefore, our exercise deals with only a limited number of such flows and in some cases uses rather arbitrary assumptions. Hence our estimates represent a broad order of magnitude only. Specifically, the illegal flows considered include:

- unrepatriated export earnings
- payments under fictitious import contracts (for both goods and services)
- price manipulations under barter transactions
- underpricing of exports.

Data for the period 1992–8 are presented in Table 9.14. Illegal capital flows reflected in the BoP fall under unrepatriated export earnings and false import invoicing (line 20 of Table 9.13), errors and omissions, and adjustment to barter. Errors and omissions are thought to include non-repatriated export earnings and payments under fictitious import contracts explicitly not recorded in the BoP, and also under-reported imports. The first two items are assumed to constitute 50 per cent of the errors and omissions total.

Adjustment to barter is the difference between the value of barter exports and barter imports, derived from trade statistics (see Table 9.10). We assume that 20 per cent of this difference is acquired by Russian residents and left abroad illegally. The remaining 80 per cent is taken to be 'lost profit', or the cost to Russia's terms of trade of engaging in barter.

Capital flows not recorded in the BoP correspond mainly to under-valuation of exports. With control over export prices becoming stricter

[7] M. Sarafanov (1995), 'Russia's actual and potential role in international capital flows', in Janos Gacs and Merton Peck (eds.) *International Trade Issues of the Russian Federation*, Laxenburg IIASA.

Table 9.14. *Estimates of capital flight from Russia, 1992–1998 ($ billion)*

	1992	1993	1994	1995	1996	1997	1998
A. Legal capital flows	**-4.03**	**-3.27**	**-5.58**	**4.46**	**-9.67**	**-12.47**	**1.92**
1. Changes in Russian commercial banks' foreign assets	-4.03	-1.07	0.16	4.33	-1.00	0.98	0.97
2. Recorded inflow of foreign currency (net)	na	-2.20	-5.74	0.13	-8.67	-13.44	0.95
B. Illegal capital flows	**-19.71**	**-15.29**	**-10.88**	**-15.96**	**-21.85**	**-22.98**	**-20.46**
I. Recorded in the BoP or trade statistics	*-12.63*	*-8.79*	*-5.13*	*-9.92*	*-15.29*	*-16.17*	*-13.18*
(1) Export earnings not transferred from abroad	-6.41	-5.13	-3.86	-4.93	-5.47	-4.59	-4.40
(2) Advance import payments without delivery	na	na	na	na	-4.30	-6.87	-4.23
(3) Fraction of 'errors and omissions'[a]	-2.31	-1.26	-0.17	-3.89	-4.32	-3.91	-3.96
(4) Barter exports less barter imports, of which	-3.90	-2.40	-1.10	-1.10	-1.20	-0.80	-0.60
(a) assets of Russian residents (20%)	-0.78	-0.48	-0.22	-0.22	-0.24	-0.16	-0.12
(b) gains of foreign partners (lost profit—80%)	-3.12	-1.92	-0.88	-0.88	-0.96	-0.64	-0.48
II. Not recorded	*-7.08*	*-6.50*	*-5.75*	*-6.04*	*-6.56*	*-6.81*	*-7.28*
(1) Undervaluation of exports, of which	-6.36	-5.32	-4.24	-3.94	-3.55	-2.80	-2.36
(a) assets of Russian residents (20%)	-1.27	-1.06	-0.85	-0.79	-0.71	-0.56	-0.47
(b) gains of foreign partners (lost profit—80%)	-5.09	-4.25	-3.39	-3.15	-2.84	-2.24	-1.88
(2) Interest on illegal external assets (5% per annum)	-0.73	-1.18	-1.51	-2.11	-3.01	-4.02	-4.92
Total illegal outflows (I + II), of which	**-19.71**	**-15.29**	**-10.88**	**-15.96**	**-21.85**	**-22.98**	**-20.46**
(1) explicit capital flight (assets of Russian residents)	-11.50	-9.12	-6.61	-11.93	-18.05	-20.10	-18.09
(2) lost profit (gains of foreign partners)	-8.21	-6.17	-4.27	-4.03	-3.80	-2.88	-2.36
Total capital flows (A + B)	**-23.74**	**-18.56**	**-16.46**	**-11.50**	**-31.52**	**-35.45**	**-18.54**

[a] It is assumed that 50% of 'errors and omissions' represent capital flight.

Sources: Goskomstat, Central Bank of Russia, own estimates.

Table 9.15. *Stock of Russian private external assets ($ billion, end of period)*

	1992	1993	1994	1995	1996	1997	1998
A. Legal external assets	14.03	17.30	22.88	18.42	28.09	40.56	38.64
of which	9.03	10.10	9.94	5.61	6.61	5.64	4.66
I. Accounts and deposits (end of 1991 = $5 billion)							
II. Hard currency in cash in domestic non-banking sector (end of 1991 = 5 billion)[a]	5.00	7.20	12.94	12.81	21.48	34.92	33.97
B. Illegal external assets							
I. Stock (end of 1991 = 3 billion)[b]	14.50	23.62	30.23	42.16	60.21	80.31	98.40
Total (A + B)	**28.54**	**40.92**	**53.11**	**60.58**	**88.30**	**120.87**	**137.04**

Notes: [a]Brought in by commercial banks only.
[b]Accumulated illegal capital outflows (excluding lost profit, but including interest yield).
Source: Table 9.14.

from the mid-nineties, we estimate the total amount of these flows as a share of total exports falling from 15 per cent in 1992 to 4 per cent in 1998. As with barter trade, we assume that 20 per cent of these totals is obtained by Russian exporters in cash as their personal gain, the remaining 80 per cent being again 'lost profit' obtained by foreign importers.

A further heading not recorded in the BoP is interest and dividend payments received by Russian residents on their illegal external assets (see note 6 to Table 9.15). In principle these sums should be included in Russia's current invisible receipts (and in its GNP), matched by a corresponding addition to payments (capital outflows or errors and omissions). In practice the Russian authorities have not accorded such treatment to this controversial item.[8]

Estimates of the stock of Russian private capital abroad are shown in Table 9.15. The end-of-year levels reflect outflows during the year (Table 9.14), with an allowance made for the initial position at end-1991. Our calculations put the stock of Russian private capital abroad at the end

[8] Russian external assets also include any capital gains (such as appreciation of real estate or share values) accruing on external holdings. To the extent that the total annual return (i.e. interest and capital gains together) exceeds 5%, it is omitted from item B in Table 9.15. Other countries' data on external assets are as a rule similarly deficient.

of 1998 at approximately $140 billion, of which about $100 billion stemmed from illegal transfers.

9.8. FOREIGN DEBT AND INTERNATIONAL RESERVES

An overview of Russia's external balance sheet must take account not only of private assets but also of official debts and reserves. Russia's official foreign debt (Table 9.16) consists of debts taken over from the former USSR, as well as foreign borrowings made by Russia after the disintegration of the USSR at end-1991. The broad groups of creditors are:

- foreign states ('official creditors')
- international financial organizations (the IMF, World Bank, EBRD, EU)
- private commercial banks and firms.

The greater part of the debt was acquired during the last few years of the USSR, which saw chaotic and large-scale borrowing abroad. As a rule, credits were granted for short periods and at high rates of interest. This left Russia with large amounts of debt service in the 1990s. The severity of the burden was acknowledged in long-term rescheduling agreements concluded with the Paris and London clubs of creditors. At the same time, during 1992–8 Russia accumulated its own debt of about $55 billion, which was not subject to any rescheduling.

The most important debt restructuring agreement prior to the August 1998 default was in April 1996, when the Paris club of official creditors agreed to reschedule its former Soviet debt of nearly $40 billion over twenty-five years. The decision was greatly aided by that of the IMF to provide the EFF loan starting in March 1996. The debt was to be repaid between 2002 and 2020. Moreover, during the six-year grace period Russia had to pay only part of the interest due. The overall agreement with the Paris club was incorporated in bilateral agreements with each of the eighteen member countries. A framework agreement with the London club of commercial creditors had actually been signed earlier, in November 1995, along similar lines. Western commercial banks agreed to reschedule the principal over twenty-five years. Repayments were to start in 2002, with interest at LIBOR + 13/16 per cent. Meanwhile,

Table 9.16. *Russia's official foreign debt, 1993–1998 ($ billion, end of period)*

	1993	1994	1995	1996	1997	1998
1. Inherited from the USSR						
Official creditors	67.8	69.9	62.6	61.9	56.9	59.5
of which Paris club	34.8	39.6	41.6	42.3	37.6	40.0
CMEA	29.0	25.7	16.6	15.4	14.9	14.7
Commercial banks and firms	36.1	36.0	38.3	37.8	33.9	35.2
of which London club	28.3	31.1	33.0	32.5	29.7	31.2
Other	na	10.3	9.7	8.7	8.2	8.1
USSR: subtotal	103.9	116.2	110.6	108.4	99.0	102.8
2. Borrowings by Russia (from 1992)						
Official creditors	5.3	5.9	6.0	7.9	7.6	9.7
Commercial banks and firms	0.0	0.0	0.0	0.0	1.3	0.2
International financial institutions	3.5	5.4	11.4	15.3	18.7	26.0
of which IMF	2.5	4.2	9.6	12.5	13.2	19.4
World Bank	0.4	0.6	1.5	2.6	5.3	6.4
Eurobonds	0.0	0.0	0.0	1.0	4.5	16.0
Minfin bonds	0.0	0.0	0.0	3.5	3.5	3.5
Russia: subtotal	8.8	11.3	17.4	27.7	35.6	55.4
Total Russian Debt	112.7	127.5	128.0	136.1	134.6	158.2
Total (excluding CMEA debt)	83.7	101.8	111.4	120.7	119.7	143.5

Source: IMF.

Russia was supposed to pay only current interest and partly overdue interest. In 1997 the debt to the London club was converted into $28 billion of Vnesheconombank bonds.

These agreements with both the Paris club and the London club proved to be short lived. After the August 1998 crisis Russia defaulted on payments to both clubs and initiated a new round of negotiations. The Paris club provided flow rescheduling for two years, but negotiations on another stock rescheduling made little progress during 2000. Negotiations with the London club, on the other hand, reached a mutually acceptable solution in February 2000. The creditors agreed to write-off about a third of the outstanding debt stock and provided Russia with a seven-year grace period. In return, Russia agreed to convert the defaulted debt into eurobonds with cross-default clauses that put them on a par with the existing stock of Russia's sovereign debt. Estimates suggest that the conditions of the new agreement provide Russia with a total London club debt reduction of about 50 per cent in net present value terms.

In discussions with the Paris club it was important for Russia not only to reschedule former USSR debt but also to confirm her status as a creditor, as she inherited from the USSR an enormous volume of claims on developing countries. These claims are estimated at not less than $130 billion, which almost equates to Russia's total external debt. In September 1997 Russia joined the Paris club as a creditor country, which made it possible to justify the legal status of these claims. However, this joining was not without a price—Russia agreed to provide up-front discounts on her claims in the range of 35–80 per cent.

Russia's external debt service up to 1998 is shown in Table 9.17. The amount paid each year was approximately equal to the amount borrowed abroad during the same year. In other words, Russia was not attracting new loans over this period, but rolling over old debts which had not been restructured. With foreigners increasingly permitted from 1996 onwards to hold rouble 'treasury bonds' (see section 6), aggregate debt service payments to non-residents rose during 1996–7 above those related to foreign currency borrowings. Even without hindsight this was ominous and pointed to the need for a decisive fall in interest rates on rouble debt if the situation were to remain manageable.

Russia's official international reserves are shown in Table 9.18. Foreign exchange reserves include Russia's Reserve Position in the IMF and also

Table 9.17. *Russia's debt service of official external debts, 1993–1998 (including former USSR debt)*

	1993	1994	1995	1996	1997	1998
Payments falling due ($ billion)	20.7	20.2	20.2	18.7	14.2	14.6
Payments made ($ billion)	3.6	4.6	7.1	7.7	7.7	9.1
Debt service ratio (%)[a]						
due	34.4	26.8	22.1	18.1	13.8	16.7
actual	6.0	6.1	7.8	7.5	7.5	10.4
Official borrowings abroad ($ billion)	3.4	4.0	8.0	7.8	7.6	10.5

[a]Ratio of debt service to exports of goods and non-factor services.

Source: Central Bank of Russia.

SDRs. Foreign liabilities come mostly from IMF credits. The monetary authorities succeeded in gradually increasing the level of gross international reserves from $4.5 billion at end-1992 to $19.2 billion in the first quarter of 1996. Especially noteworthy was the $10 billion increase in 1995, when the CBR was actively buying dollars in order to limit appreciation of the rouble. By the second quarter of 1997 gross reserves had reached $24.5 billion as a result of a massive inflow of

Table 9.18. *Russia's international reserves ($ million, end of period)*

	Foreign exchange reserves [1]	Gold[a] [2]	Gross international reserves [3 = 1 + 2]	Gross foreign liabilities[b] [4]	Net International Reserves [5 = 3−4]
1992					
Q4	1,954	2,578	4,532	1,517	3,015
1993					
Q1	2,798	2,471	5,269	1,159	4,110
Q2	4,396	2,737	7,133	1,088	6,045
Q3	6,157	2,927	9,084	2,598	6,486
Q4	5,835	3,059	8,894	2,519	6,375
1994					
Q1	4,602	3,040	7,642	2,555	5,087
Q2	8,048	2,463	10,511	4,179	6,332
Q3	4,161	2,584	6,745	4,220	2,525
Q4	3,980	2,525	6,505	4,210	2,295
1995					
Q1	4,148	2,404	6,552	4,487	2,065
Q2	10,086	2,327	12,413	6,203	6,210
Q3	11,154	2,467	13,621	7,580	6,041
Q4	14,383	2,824	17,207	9,617	7,590
1996					
Q1	16,331	2,917	19,248	10,714	8,534
Q2	12,792	3,085	15,877	11,465	4,412
Q3	11,398	3,677	15,075	11,977	3,098
Q4	11,276	4,047	15,323	12,508	2,815
1997					
Q1	12,429	4,066	16,495	12,587	3,908
Q2	20,396	4,153	24,549	13,170	11,379
Q3	18,737	4,363	23,100	13,510	9,590
Q4	13,018	4,889	17,907	13,231	4,676

Table 9.18. *(continued)*

	Foreign exchange reserves [1]	Gold[a] [2]	Gross international reserves [3 = 1 + 2]	Gross foreign liabilities[b] [4]	Net International Reserves [5 = 3 − 4]
1998					
Q1	11,911	4,948	16,859	13,648	3,212
Q2	11,161	5,009	16,169	14,269	1,900
Q3	8,840	3,869	12,709	19,324	−6,615
Q4	7,801	4,422	12,223	19,335	−7,112
1999					
Q1	6,679	4,086	10,765	17,914	−7,149
Q2	8,190	3,964	12,154	16,784	−4,630
Q3	6,634	4,579	11,213	16,748	−5,535
Q4	8,457	3,998	12,455	15,238	−2,783

Notes: [a]Gold is valued at $300 per troy ounce.
[b]IMF credit and loans outstanding.
Source: Central Bank of Russia, International Financial Statistics (IMF).

external funds to the GKO market. In the fifteen months the reserves halved and net reserves turned sharply negative, as the Central Bank spent huge sums in a futile attempt to defend the exchange rate of the rouble. In 1999 gross reserves stabilized at about $11–12 billion, with inflows from the current account surplus financing debt service payments by the Central Bank.

Appendix 1. **Principal Measures of Trade Policy, 1992–1997**

1. *Export Controls*

1.1. *Non-tariff measures*
Export quotas and licences were introduced at the beginning of 1992. The quota list included twenty-three commodity groups (fuels, ferrous and non-ferrous metals, basic chemicals, and others) and covered about 70 per cent of Russia's exports to non-CIS countries. The rationale was to meet domestic demand before 'surplus' production was exported; also to keep basic commodity prices (especially fuels) below the world level. In 1993 the quota list was reduced to seventeen items, and subsequent revisions continued this trend. From 1 July 1994

all export quotas were abolished except those on oil and refined oil products, which were maintained until 1 January 1995.

From 1 July 1992 the institution of 'special exporters' (registered by the Ministry of Foreign Economic Relations) was established, as well as a list of so-called 'strategically important commodities' (SIC), practically identical to the list of goods subject to quotas. Special exporters were the only organizations authorized to export commodities on the SIC list. The purpose was to avoid income losses for the country at large and the state budget in particular from under-pricing of export goods, and also to secure the repatriation of export earnings. The system was eliminated in March 1995.

1.2. *Tariff measures*
Export tariffs also were introduced in January 1992. In 1992–3 they covered about 75 per cent of Russia's exports. They were highest on items where the prior gap between domestic and world prices was largest, notably fuels. Among finished industrial goods, tariffs were applied only to aircraft and arms. Export tariffs on items other than on crude oil were abolished from 1 April 1996; on crude oil from 1 July 1996.

Starting January 1999 temporary export taxes on a number of commodities were introduced. A 10 per cent duty was levied on some varieties of seeds, skins and leather, timber, and non-ferrous scrap metals. Five per cent duty was levied on coal, oil, natural gas, petroleum products, and non-ferrous metals and products. Later the level of tariffs on crude oil and petroleum products was determined as a fraction of the world price.

2. **Import Controls**

2.1. *Non-tariff measures*
Import limitations in the form of licensing were not significant in 1992–7, relating only to special products (pesticides, medicines, industrial wastes, arms, nuclear materials, precious metals and stones). There were no import quotas. From 1 January 1997 imports of pure alcohol and vodka became subject to licence, largely to close fiscal loopholes.

Existing legislation permits non-tariff measures against imports if they are regarded as liable to damage Russian producers of similar or directly competing commodities. Measures may be introduced only in line with WTO rules: a special investigation is to be carried out and its results approved by the Government Commission on Defensive Measures in Trade.

2.2. *Tariff and tax measures*
Import tariffs were first introduced on 1 July 1992. The rate was 5 per cent for most goods. Foodstuffs and medicines were exempt. The rate was raised to 15 per cent on 1 September.

More differentiated tariffs came into force on 1 April 1993. Exempt items included foodstuffs, medicines, medical equipment, children's clothes, and other 'socially significant' goods. For other goods, the rate varied from 5 per cent (intermediate goods, metals, transport equipment) to 15 per cent (capital goods, consumer durables). The highest rate was applied to pure alcohol (150 per cent). The weighted average tariff level was about 9 per cent. After 1993 import tariffs were revised annually (in July 1994 and 1995, and March 1996), generally increasing with each revision. In 1996 the average tariff level was 14–15 per cent. The biggest single change was that foodstuffs, which had been duty free, were subjected to rates of 5 per cent to 30 per cent from 1996.

From 1 February 1993 all imported goods were subject to VAT and excise duty where applicable (luxury goods, tobacco, cars, and alcoholic beverages).

In June 1998 the 30 per cent tariff rate was cut to 20 per cent and the number of items subject to it from 857 to 557.

3. *Centralized Trade*

Direct state involvement in trade continued to be significant in 1992–4 in the form of centralized exports and imports. Centralized exports were based on quotas for state needs, which allowed the state purchasing agent (Roscontract) to buy exportable goods (mainly fuels and raw materials) on the domestic market and sell them abroad to collect the difference between domestic and world prices. The earnings from centralized exports were initially used to finance centralized imports, which were strongly subsidized (see below); after import subsidies were removed at the end of 1993, state earnings from trade were used as budget revenue and to service external debt. As the gap between domestic and world prices narrowed, the share of centralized exports in total exports fell from 33 per cent in 1992 to 15 per cent in 1994. In 1995, following the elimination of export quotas, centralized exports were limited to sales of arms, precious metals and stones, and also to implementation of Russia's international agreements (for example, supply of crude oil to some eastern European countries).

The system of centralized imports was used to provide domestic consumers with imported goods at a price lower than the world market price expressed in roubles at the current exchange rate. The price difference was a subsidy paid by the government. Centralized imports covered 'socially important' consumer goods (mainly foodstuffs and medicines) as well as investment goods and industrial inputs. Different commodities had different subsidy coefficients, which varied in 1993 from 56 per cent on food products to 80 per cent on investment goods. By 1993 the ongoing depreciation of the rouble had made import subsidies too large to be supported by the budget. They were first reduced and then abolished on 1 January 1994.

4. *Foreign Exchange Control of Trade Operations*

From 1992 Russian exporters were obliged to sell 50 per cent of their export earnings for roubles. Details are given in Appendix 2 below.

In order to establish proper supervision over repatriation of foreign exchange earnings and to diminish capital flight, the Central Bank together with the State Customs Committee introduced a system of foreign exchange control over exporters' hard currency revenues from 1 March 1994. The aim is to detect any difference between the announced value of the contract and actual revenues obtained by exporters. Every export transaction must be recorded in a special registration document ('passport'), including all details of the deal (volume, price, terms of delivery, date of payment). Using this document, information on actual shipments (according to customs declarations) and also bank data on payments transferred to exporters' accounts, the Customs Committee compares export earnings with the value of goods delivered, thus identifying non-repatriated export earnings. When goods delivered are not paid for in due time, the authorities initiate a special investigation that may lead to fines on the exporter or his bank. In cases where the normal time period between export shipment and payment exceeds 180 days, the exporter has to have a special licence from the Central Bank.

From 1 January 1996 the authorities extended the same type of control to imports, to halt capital flight through false import contracts (payment without delivery).

From 1 November 1996 controls were extended to barter trade, in order to enforce equivalency of exchange. The 'passport' of the barter deal must specify prices and volumes of exports and imports and also the terms of delivery. If the exporter and customs authorities disagree on contract prices, the customs authorities are empowered to fix prices at world level independently of the exporter. As in the case of ordinary import transactions, exporters must ensure the delivery of imported goods (or payment in cash) within 180 days of the export shipment.

Appendix 2. **Foreign Exchange Regulations and the Exchange Rate Regime**

1. *Multiple Exchange Rate System (January–June 1992)*

In the initial months of economic reform in 1992 the multiplicity of exchange rates characteristic of the pre-reform period was retained. The only genuine market rate was that determined in the dollar auctions of the Moscow Inter-Bank Currency Exchange (MICEX), the successor to the currency exchange of the

USSR State Bank. From January to March 1992 auctions at the MICEX took place weekly; from April onwards twice a week. The auctions were conducted under the supervision of the Central Bank, which used its hard currency reserves to influence the exchange rate through interventions.

Until June 1992 exporters were allowed to retain 50 per cent of hard currency revenues; of the rest, 40 per cent was to be sold to a Republic Hard Currency Reserve at a fixed ('special commercial') rate of 55 R/S and 10 per cent to the Central Bank of Russia (CBR) at the 'official market' rate (which was 110 R/S in January and 85 R/S in June 1992). Importers could purchase foreign exchange at the MICEX, or obtain it from the government at a subsidized rate (mainly for grain and other food imports and medicines).

2. *Floating Exchange Rate (July 1992–June 1995)*

On 1 July 1992 foreign exchange regulation was radically changed. Exchange rates for current account transactions were unified and the rate was allowed to float and was determined at the bi-weekly MICEX auctions. Exporters still had to sell 50 per cent of their hard currency earnings, but not to the government at an artificially high rate. Instead, they were to sell 20 per cent at inter-bank exchanges (primarily the MICEX) through authorized banks where their hard currency accounts were kept, and a further 30 per cent to the Central Bank, all at the market rate.

Multiple exchange rates were partially re-introduced in September 1992 in the form of subsidies for centralized imports (foodstuffs, medicines, industrial raw materials, and equipment) through special 'exchange rate coefficients'. These coefficients were expressed as a share of the market exchange rate and differed for different commodities within a range of 0.2–0.8. The margin between the market exchange rate and a coefficient was paid to importing organizations from the off-budget hard currency fund of the government. This system existed for more than a year until it was eliminated at the end of 1993.

From 1 June 1993 MICEX traded dollars on a daily basis. Also from that date commercial banks were obliged to observe limits on open positions in convertible currency. From 1 July exporters were to sell 50 per cent of export receipts directly to the inter-bank foreign exchanges through commercial banks (rather than 30 per cent to the Central Bank and 20 per cent to currency exchanges). Also non-residents were allowed to open rouble accounts in Russian banks and to buy and sell hard currency on the MICEX.

3. *Fixed Exchange Rate Corridor (July 1995–June 1996)*

On 5 July 1995 the government and the CBR announced a commitment to maintain the exchange rate within a corridor of 4,300–4,900 R/S until October, subsequently extended until the end of 1995. In November modified limits for the corridor were announced for the first half of 1996, specifying a range of 4,450–5,150 R/S (see Figure 9.3 in the main text).

Russia accepted the obligations of Article VIII of the IMF Articles of Agreement from 1 June 1996, which meant the introduction of full current account convertibility for the rouble, including relaxation of restrictions on the use of rouble accounts by non-residents. Non-residents must be able to buy roubles in order to pay for current items and to convert their rouble holdings into foreign currency for the purpose of profit repatriation.

4. *Crawling Exchange Rate Corridor (July 1996–December 1997)*

In mid-May 1996 the CBR announced a modified exchange rate system for the second half of 1996. On 1 July the corridor shifted to R5,000–5,600 per dollar. From then until the end of 1996 the band was depreciated on a daily basis at a pre-announced rate of about 1.5 per cent a month, maintaining its R600 width. At the end of the year it stood at R5,500–6,100. Also from 17 May the official exchange rate was no longer the MICEX rate. Instead the CBR started to announce its own daily buying and selling rates for dollars, with a spread of not more than 1.5 per cent. The official rate was defined as the average of buying and selling rates of the CBR (effective the next banking day for accounting purposes).

The CBR was successful in keeping the exchange within the crawling corridor. From January 1997 the corridor's slope was somewhat reduced (to an average monthly depreciation of 0.7 per cent compared with 1.5 per cent previously) and the targeted exchange rate band for end-1997 was set at R5,750–6,350. The idea was to adjust the exchange rate path to inflation and thus to keep the real exchange rate in 1997 broadly unchanged. In 1998 the CBR switched to a band around a fixed exchange rate of R6,200 with a margin of ±15 percent (or 5,270–7,130 R/S). Despite a formally wide range of possible fluctuation, a narrower daily intervention band remained in operation until the August 1998 crisis, when the band was removed (2 September) and the exchange rate depreciated massively.

5. *Floating Exchange Rate (from September 1998)*

Two significant measures were introduced in the course of 1999 in an attempt to inhibit capital flight.

First, the export surrender requirement was raised to 75 per cent and the period within which the surrender must be effected shortened from 14 days to 7. Second, a 100 per cent deposit requirement at the CBR was imposed on all purchases of foreign exchange relating to the prepayment of imports.

Appendix 3. **Anti-dumping Measures Taken by the European Union against Russia, in Force on 31 December 1995**

1991

23.9.91 UREA, duties imposed on Russia and Venezuela

1992 (None)

1993

13.9.93 ARTIFICIAL CORUNDUM, duties imposed on Russia with Ukraine

28.9.93 FERROCHROME (LOW CARBON) duties imposed on Russia with Ukraine and Kazakhstan

2.12.93 FERROSILICON, duties imposed on Russia, Ukraine, Kazakhstan, Brazil, and Venezuela

1994

29.3.94 ISOBUTOL, duties imposed on Russia. (Market share increased from 13.5% in 1988 to 23.2%; EC prices fell by 31%)

16.4.94 PIG IRON (HAEMATITE), duties imposed on Russia with Ukraine, Brazil, and Poland. (Market share of imports from all countries increased from 30% in 1987 to 50%, undercutting EC prices by 12.3%)

21.3.94 POTASSIUM CHLORIDE, duties imposed on Russia with Belarus and Ukraine. (Market share increased from 5% in 1986 to 11% in 1990)

12.4.94 SILICON CARBIDE, duties imposed on Russia with Ukraine, Poland, and China

19.10.94 CALCIUM METAL, duties imposed on Russia and China (Market share increased from 35% in 1989 to 53% in 1992; EC prices undercut by 24%)

1995

16.8.95 AMMONIUM NITRATE FERTILISER, duties imposed on Russia and Lithuania. (Market share increased from 0.3% in 1990–91 to 7.3%)

6.10.95 FERRO-SILICO-MANGANESE, duties imposed on Russia with Ukraine, Brazil and South Africa. (Market share increased from 15.4% to 29.7%)

19.10.95 GRAIN ORIENTED ELECTRICAL STEEL SHEET, provisional duties on Russia imposed during investigations. (Market share increased from 0.7% in 1990 to 7.4% in 1993, undercutting EC prices by 28%.) Product used in defence industry. Duty 43.2%

20.12.95 UNWROUGHT MAGNESIUM, provisional duties imposed on Russia during investigations. (Market share increased from 4% in 1991 to 20%; prices cut on EC market by 30–40%)

9.6.95 UNWROUGHT UNALLOYED ZINC, investigation initiated. (Increased market share hit sales, prices and financial position of EC producers)

Source: Emerson (1996).

Appendix 4. **Russia's Balance of Payments with Non-CIS Countries in 1992–1993 ($ billion)**

	1992	1993
Exports	42.4	43.7
Imports	−36.9	−33.0
Adjustment for non-equivalent barter	−6.4	−1.2
Trade balance	*5.5*	*10.8*
Non-factor services, net	−2.4	−2.5
Investment income	−2.0	−2.9
receipts	3.5	2.5
payments	−5.5	−5.4
Transfers	*3.0*	*2.3*
Current account	**−2.2**	**6.4**
Medium- and long-term capital (net)	*9.1*	*−0.4*
Official credits	9.9	9.9
Other credits	0.8	−8.2
Trade credits	0.0	−1.8
Direct investment	−0.1	0.7
Portfolio investment	0.2	0.1
Other long-term	−1.6	−1.0
Short-term capital (net)	*−4.1*	*−7.3*
Monetization of gold	*0.0*	*0.5*
Total capital account	**5.0**	**−7.7**
Errors and omissions	**−4.6**	**−2.5**
Adjustments[a]	0.6	1.6
Overall balance	**−1.2**	**−2.3**
Net international reserves	−0.7	−3.4
Postponement of debt service (net)	2.0	5.7

[a] Adjustment to international reserves.

Source: Goskomstat.

REFERENCES

Brenton, P. (1995). *External Liberalisation and Russian Trade*, Brussels: Centre for European Policy Studies.

Drebentsov, V. (1995). 'Russia's Commercial Policy from 1992 to 1994', in J. Gacs and M. Peck (eds.), *International Trade Issues of the Russian Federation*, Laxenburg, Austria: IIASA.

Emerson, M. (1996). 'The Three Horses of Russia's Foreign Trade Troika: Globalism, Regionalism and Protection', paper presented at a Workshop on Business Prospects in Russia, LSE, November.

Granville, B. (1995). *The Success of Russian Economic Reforms*, London: The Royal Institute of International Affairs, distributed by Brookings.

Koen, V., and Meyermans, E. (1994). 'Exchange Rate Determinants in Russia: 1992–93', IMF Working Paper 66, June.

Konovalov, V. (1994). 'Russian Trade Policy', in C. Michalopoulos and D. G. Tarr (eds.), *Trade in the New Independent States*, Washington, DC: The World Bank.

Lushin, A. (1994). 'Foreign Trade of the Russian Federation in 1992–1994', in *Economic Bulletin for Europe*, 46, Geneva: UN.

—— (1996*a*). 'Foreign Exchange Policy and the Exchange Rate Performance', *Russia: Foreign Economic Relations. Trends and Prospects*, *Quarterly Review*, 1, Moscow: VNIKI.

—— (1996*b*). 'Estimates of Capital Flight from Russia in 1992–95', Discussion Paper, Moscow: *Russian European Centre for Economic Policy*.

Michalopoulos, C., and Tarr, D. G. (1992). *Trade and Payments Arrangements for the States of the Former USSR*, Washington, DC: The World Bank.

'Russia: Joining the World Economy' (1993). *The World Bank Report*, July, Washington, DC.

Sarafanov, M. (1995). 'Russia's Actual and Potential Role in International Capital Flows', in J. Gacs and M. Peck (eds.), *International Trade Issues of the Russian Federation*, Laxenburg, Austria: IIASA.

Smith, A. (1996). *Russian Foreign Trade in the Transition*, London: RIIA.

VNIKI, *Russia: Foreign Economic Relations. Trends and Prospects*, *Quarterly Review*, Moscow, various issues.

10

The Oil Industry: Structural Transformation and Corporate Governance

NAT MOSER AND PETER OPPENHEIMER

10.1. INTRODUCTION

Oil, together with gas, was arguably the most important sector of the Russian economy in the 1990s, providing a key direct support to the domestic economy as well as a substantial proportion of both export earnings and of government tax revenue.[1] Whereas the gas industry remained a monolith under a single company, Gazprom, in which the state was the major shareholder,[2] the oil industry underwent far more extensive change in structure and ownership. Indeed, the post-Soviet struggle for control over the oil industry and its lucrative export revenue streams was fierce.

When the Soviet Union broke up, at the end of 1991, all oil industry enterprises in Russia were 100 per cent state-owned and reported directly to the Ministry of Fuel and Energy. By 1995 most oil-producing associations and refineries were incorporated into ten large joint stock companies (combining state and private ownership, and vertically integrated to a greater or lesser extent); four autonomous republic companies;

The authors are grateful to Ivan Mazalov and Nick Halliwell for their help. Any mistakes are the responsibility of the authors alone.

[1] In 1997 oil and gas accounted for an estimated 30% of Russia's GDP, and 40–50% of federal tax revenues (*Russia Review*, 14 August 1998). In 1997 Russia's share of global oil production was 8.8% (making it the 3rd largest producer in the world after Saudi Arabia and the USA), its share of global proven crude oil reserves was 4.7% and of global oil consumption was 3.8%. The Former Soviet Union accounted for 8.5% of global oil exports in 1997 (British Petroleum, 1998).

[2] Gazprom was privatized by a secretive arrangement in 1992 that left the government owning 40% and management and unspecified other interests the rest.

and one state-owned holding company. In 1997 a number of these oil companies became fully privatized. They were bought either by the existing managements or a new force, bankers. Several oil companies then became major components in the emerging industrial empires, or financial-industrial groups (FIGs), of a small number of powerful, politically well-connected individuals. Figure 10.1 shows the structure of the oil industry in 1999.

Privatization of oil resulted as much from *ad hoc* manœuvres as from strategic plans. In the creation of the vertically integrated companies between 1992 and 1995 the independent actions of the 'oil generals', the former general directors of the production associations, played as important a role as government decrees. Similarly, the loans-for-shares scheme of 1995–7, which dramatically changed the nature of ownership within the sector, resulted from government short-term financial needs on one side and the bankers' search for power and profit on the other.

This chapter examines changes in the corporate structure and governance of the Russian oil industry. It describes and analyses the different phases of transformation through the 1990s: privatization, 1992–5; the loans-for-shares scheme, 1995–7; and consolidation, 1997–9. It then specifically discusses the role of government ownership and foreign participation in the sector.

The background to these changes was a near halving of Russian oil production and refinery throughput during the decade 1987 to 1997.[3] This dramatic decline resulted from the interplay of technical factors in the industry and national economic developments. Technical factors included a Soviet legacy of faulty field development techniques (which led to high costs,[4] huge working capital requirements, and damaged reservoirs), low-tech refineries yielding the wrong products, and pipeline and port capacity constraints (which limited exports). On the national economy front it was a question of the collapse of solvent domestic demand and of government funding. Despite the presence of vast proven reserves, new capital was reluctant to enter an industry suffering from severe tax burdens (a system that focused on taxing revenue and production rather than profits), uncertain legal terms, and often

---

[3] Oil (crude and condensate) production in 1987 was 591.4 million tons (mt); in 1998 it was 303.3mt. Refinery output in 1986 was 263.8 mt; in 1996 it was 142.5mt (Energy Intelligence Group, 1999).

[4] Tyumen Oil Company (TNK) reported per barrel US$ production costs of $12.50 in February 1998 falling to $3.50 in March 1999 with the depreciation of the ruble (MFK-Renaissance, *Daily Monitor* (26 March 1999)).

Figure 10.1. *Russian oil industry structure, 1999*

	Integrated Companies									Autonomous Republic Companies				Independent Companies		
	LUKoil	Yukos (including VNK)	Surgut Holding	Sidanco	Sibneft	Tyumen Oil Company (TNK)	Rosneft	ONACO	Slavneft	Tatneft	Komi-TEK	Bashkiria Petrochemical & Bashneft	Yunko	Sibur	Norsi-Oil	East Siberian Oil & Gas
HOLDING																
PRODUCTION	LangepasNG, UraiNG, KogalymNG, PokachyovNG, KalianagrafanoeNG, NizhnevolzhskneftNG, Permneft, AstrakhanNG	YugankNG, SamaraNG, Tomskneft (VNK)	SurgutNG	ChernogorneftNG, Kondpetroleum, Udmurtneft, NovosibirskNG, SaratovNG, VaryoganNG, Varyoganneft	NoyabrskNG	NizhnevartovskNG, TyumenNG, SamotlorNG	PurNG, SakhalinmorNG, Dagneft, KrasnodarNG, StavropolNG, Termneft, YugNG	Orenburgneft	MegionNG	Tatneft	Komineft	Bashneft, Ishimbaineft	Grozneft			
EXPLORATION		TomskNG-geologiya (VNK)			NoyabrskNG geofizika	ObNG-geologiya	Arkhangelsk-geoldobycha	Orenburg-geologiya	MegionNG-geologiya			Bashneft geofizika, Geofizika				Yeniseri geofizika, YeniseiNG-geologiya
REFINING	Perm, Volgograd	Kuibyshev, Novokuibyshev, Syzran, Achinsk (VNK), Tomsk Petro-chemical (VNK)	Kinef (Kirishi)	Angarsk, Khabarovsk, Saratov (Kreking)	Omsk	Ryazan	Komsomolsk, Krasnodar, Moscow Lubricant Factory, MoscowNP Plant, Tuapse	Orsk, Orenburg Lubricant Factory	Mozyr (Belarus), Yaroslavl, Yaroslavl (Mendeleyev)		Ukhta	Kauchuk Petrochemical, Novoufa, Salavat, Ufa Refinery, Ufaorekhim, Ufaorgsintez	Grozny	Perm GPP, SibNG-pererabotka, Sorbent	Norsi	

Key: NG: neftegaz. NP: nefteprodukt. VNK (Eastern Oil Company)—a majority stake was purchased by Rosprom–Yukos in 1997. Until then it had been an integrated company in its own right; components are indicated.

Note: This table does not include distribution and retail companies, Joint Ventures (JVs) with foreigners, and small private oil companies.

indecipherable ownership structure. As a result, the industry was starved of working capital, let alone new investment funds. Inter-enterprise arrears and state tax debts accumulated and a large proportion of transactions was conducted in barter.[5] Cash sales, and hence supply efforts, shifted—so far as pipeline constraints would permit—from the domestic market and CIS (or near abroad) to the far abroad.

10.2. PRIVATIZATION, 1992–5

Decentralization of the oil industry began in the last years of the Soviet Union, as part of Mikhail Gorbachev's economic reforms. The power of enterprise directors was increased as a result of the Law on State Enterprises of January 1988 and the reorganization of the government's executive branch in June 1989, both of which aimed to break the ministries' power to dictate to local managers. Though the success of these measures according to their original aims—to revive the Soviet economic system—was limited, they nevertheless gave enterprise directors their first taste of real autonomy.

The official documented view of the privatization of the Russian oil industry emphasizes various presidential decrees that 'created' the vertically integrated oil companies (VIOCs). However, this does not necessarily provide an accurate explanation of events. In fact, the general directors of the former Soviet oil enterprises were in many instances the prime movers in the establishment of the VIOCs, with the government essentially in a passive role of simply sanctioning the changes.

The leading role played by Vagit Alekperov, the first and, up to 2000, continuing president of LUKoil, needs to be highlighted. At the expiry of the Soviet Union in 1991 Alekperov was the general director of Kogalymneftegaz, one of many production associations (*NGDUs*, by their Russian initials) as well as a first deputy oil minister in the government. At that time the situation was one of uncertainty and a power vacuum. A number of powerful former Soviet institutions, including the Ministries of Oil and Geology, were jockeying for position. Competing proposals were on the table and the prospect of a unified national oil company, on the lines of Gazprom in the gas industry, was not out of the question. The government improvized by designating Rosneftegaz (Russian State Oil and Gas Corporation) to oversee the sector. All oil-producing

---

[5] Cash collection on domestic sales in the late 1990s was as low as 25% of reported transaction value. (MFK-Renaissance, *Oil & Gas Monthly Review*, January 1999).

associations were to be part of this loosely organized corporation. However, Alekperov opposed this, and in 1991–2 convinced two other general directors of production associations to stay out of Rosneftegaz and to join with him in forming the holding company LUKoil, in principle modelling this new entity on a western company.

The timing of Alekperov's initiative was important. The economy was in chaos and central political control had been drastically weakened. Large volumes of oil were being illicitly exported (as energy prices had not been freed in 1992 the imbalance between domestic and export prices was enormous). In this uncertain situation the government saw in Alekperov's action a possible way forward, and used his company as a template which official policy could follow. The fact that the new VIOCs would resemble western majors was viewed as a definite advantage.

The official founding document for the reform of the oil industry was Presidential Decree No. 1403 of 17 November 1992. Its main features were:

(1) reorganization of all enterprises involved in oil production, refining, and marketing into joint stock companies;
(2) establishment of the first three VIOCs—LUKoil, Surgut Holding, and Yukos;
(3) establishment of the state enterprise Rosneft to manage in trust for a period of three years the majority of shares of oil enterprises which were not members of the original three VIOCs;
(4) as the industry was considered to be of strategic importance, a controlling interest in each of the newly independent joint-stock companies was to be retained by the state for at least three years;
(5) foreign ownership of Russian oil companies was restricted to 15 per cent.

The VIOCs themselves were organized into two tiers, comprising holding and subsidiary (operating) companies. Corporatization, followed by privatization, took place at both levels (see share ownership structure, below). The creation of a new level of ownership (the holding companies) provided a means of consolidating the government's controlling shareholdings in partially privatized oil subsidiaries, and would later also allow the government effectively to sell the same assets twice over.

In May 1994 another four VIOCs—Sidanco, Slavneft, VNK (Eastern Oil Company), and ONACO—were created by government Ordinance No. 452. On 1 April 1995, Presidential Decree no. 327 created the eighth and ninth VIOCs. These two, Rosneft and TNK (Tyumen Oil Company), swept up the remaining state-owned oil production, refining, and geological enterprises that had not been included in any of the existing holding companies. Rosneft's transformation into a VIOC replaced the government's original intention of dissolving it after three years.

In August 1995, as a result of pressure on the government from the authorities in western Siberia to form a powerful regional oil company, Sibneft was established as a further VIOC. This was allocated certain components from Rosneft (Noyabrskneftegaz and Omsk refinery). In return, Purneftegaz, which was originally going to be part of Sidanco, was given back to Rosneft by a government bill in the same year.

Particular decisions regarding which subsidiary enterprises—in production and refining—were to form which VIOCs were based less on commercial or economic rationality than on personal connections and power plays, among general directors themselves and between them and the state. By 1995, apart from Alekperov (LUKoil), the leading players to emerge included Vladimir Bogdanov (Surgut Holding), Sergei Muravlenko (Yukos), and Anatoly Sivak (Sidanco). In several cases general directors were reluctant to take a subordinate role to another 'general', thereby effectively being demoted. For this reason Victor Gorodilov (Noyabrskneftegaz) and Victor Ageyev (Purneftegaz) both objected to working under Victor Paliy (Nizhnevartovskneftegaz/TNK) and Sivak (Sidanco), respectively. Similarly, neither wanted to have to report to Alexander Putilov (Rosneft). The result was that the geographical spread of different upstream or downstream components within many VIOCs was considerable and that some companies were more integrated, from well to gas station, than others. TNK, for instance, for a long time lacked a refinery, which would obviously be expected to be part of a 'true' vertically integrated company.

10.3. SHARE OWNERSHIP STRUCTURE, 1992–5

Shares in the oil companies were issued both at the operating or subsidiary level and at the vertically integrated company or holding level. The initial government stake in the subsidiary companies was typically 51 per cent of ordinary (voting) shares, which amounted to 38 per cent of total shares.[6] The plan for the remainder of the subsidiary enterprise shares, in

---

[6] Total shares also include preference shares. Except when the dividend on them is not paid, these are non-voting.

accordance with the mass privatization schemes of 1992–4, was for them to be divided among management, employees, and members of the general public (in exchange for privatization vouchers). However, the nature of the privatization scheme—the different variants which it allowed the management to choose—and the fact that enterprises often organized closed auctions, selling only to people authorized by them, meant that the bulk of these shares ended up in the hands of the managers and employees. The managers then frequently bought them off the employees after a short interval, in some cases applying pressure on employees to sell. Alternatively, management exerted pressure on employee voting patterns. The insider nature of oil company privatization closely resembled simultaneous developments in other sectors of the economy and as such was not unique (see the chapter by Earle and Estrin in this volume).

The government stakes in the subsidiary companies were used to form the holding companies. The government aimed at the outset to repeat the pattern of the subsidiary level in retaining a controlling share of these companies (51 per cent of ordinary [voting] shares) for three years. For the rest, around 30 per cent were to be distributed via privatization vouchers, 15 per cent sold at auctions, and 5 per cent to go to employees of the VIOCs themselves. The government shareholdings were to remain under the joint management of the State Property Committee (GKI), the Ministry of Fuel and Energy and the Anti-Monopoly Committee.[7] After three years they would be sold at auction. For LUKoil, Surgut Holding, and Yukos the three-year term expired in late 1995.

In fact, there were considerable delays in reducing the state's fraction of holding company shares through voucher and auction distributions, with the result that the percentage of government ownership in 1995 remained generally higher than had been planned. This applied particularly to LUKoil (60 per cent) and Yukos (no less than 84 per cent).[8] Although at the end of 1995 the government shareholding in Surgut Holding conformed with the privatization plan (45 per cent), shares were acquired (as in the case of subsidiary company shares) not by the general population but by company insiders. Overall, at the end of 1995 the government clearly still had a controlling interest in the VIOCs.

---

[7] The State Property Committee (GKI), established in 1992 as a temporary body to transfer shares of privatized enterprises to their employees and the Russian population, acted as depository for the government shares, while the corresponding shareholder rights were exercised by sector ministries, in the case of the oil industry primarily the Ministry of Fuel and Energy.

[8] Petroleum Advisory Forum and Boston Consulting Group (1995).

10.4. THE LOANS-FOR-SHARES SCHEME, 1995–7

According to the initial privatization rules the sale of the state's controlling share in the holding companies should have begun in late 1995 and continued through 1996. Although the sale of shares went ahead towards the end of 1995, it was not in the manner first envisaged, that is, to management, employees, and the general population via voucher sales. This was a consequence of the government's pressing need for fiscal revenue, increasingly critical as the 1996 presidential elections approached.

A loans-for-shares scheme was first put forward by a consortium of Russian bankers led by Vladimir Potanin, the chairman of Oneksimbank, in early 1995, and was approved by the government in a revised form in September of that year. The government proposed to auction off the right to manage its stake in state companies in exchange for bank loans (phase 1). The conditions stated that if, by 1 September 1996, the government failed to repay a particular loan, the lending bank would be permitted to arrange a sale of the shares, dividing any capital gains 70 per cent to the government, 30 per cent to itself (phase 2). The auction technique was meant to ensure that the government received loans close to the market value of the shares as well as a large fraction of any subsequent increase in market value.

The scheme involved the following VIOCs: Yukos, Surgut Holding, Sidanco, LUKoil, and Sibneft. With the exception of LUKoil (5 per cent), the government pledged between 40 per cent and 51 per cent of the stock of these companies. Though the oil companies were the chief participants, the scheme also included a number of state firms in the metallurgical and maritime shipping industries.

10.4.1. *Phase 1*

By the time the original auctions for the right to manage the shares were conducted in late 1995 several important developments had affected the character of the scheme. The firms on the auction block lobbied for, and received, special terms and restrictions, most notably a complete exclusion on foreigners. In addition, obligations imposed on the trustee (the lending institution) to pay companies' federal tax bills or to carry out investment programmes blurred the value of the shares, and made it very difficult for outsiders without close connections to the companies in question to participate. Finally, the banks themselves, accustomed to operating in conditions of rapid inflation and continuous currency depreciation, were hit by the sudden stabilization of the rouble in the third quarter of 1995, and caught in a liquidity crisis (see the chapter in this volume by Dmitriev *et al.*).

The result was a series of deals in which state shares were acquired by financial organizations with close links to the managements of the oil companies concerned. There was little competition and most purchases were at far less than market prices. The government received considerably less revenue than hoped for.

10.4.2. *Phase 2*

In September 1996, three months after President Yeltsin's successful re-election, the government (in particular Security Council Secretary Alexander Lebed and First Deputy Prime Minister Vladimir Potanin[9]) confirmed that the winners of the 1995 loans-for-shares auctions would have the right to sell the shares to third parties. Between December 1996 and June 1997 the stakes were sold off in a series of government-regulated auctions. A basic pattern emerged for the auctions which broadly reflected the array of restrictions and special deals established in 1995. The inadequacy of revenue receipts was carried forward correspondingly.

10.5. ANALYSIS OF THE LOANS-FOR-SHARES SCHEME

As indicated in Figure 10.2 the following characteristics of the loans-for-shares scheme in both its phases can be identified. First, the shares were acquired by insiders. The initial auctions essentially comprised a series of agreements between the lenders and the management of the companies involved, or even *de facto* management buy-outs by enterprise bosses using banks set up to handle their own company's revenue. In the cases of Surgut Holding and LUKoil the management of the oil companies themselves won the auctions. In the cases of Yukos and Sidanco, the winners were the financial organizations that organized the auctions— Menatep (controlled by Mikhail Khodorkovsky) and Oneksimbank, respectively. In the second series of auctions, the direct or indirect winner of the stake in every case was the company that provided the original loan in 1995.

---

[9] Deputy PM in charge of the economy from August 1996 until March 1997.

Oil Company	Size of stake under auction %	Loan provided by auction winner to government, 1995 ($m)	Bank which organized auction, 1995-7	Auction winner, 1995	Guarantee issuer, 1995	Minimum sale price, 1996-7 ($m)	Price paid by auction winner, 1996-7 ($m)	Auction winner, 1996-7	Amount raised by government in 1996-7 as a result of sales (in addition to original loans)[1] ($m)
Yukos	45[2]	159	Menatep Bank	Laguna (Menatep affiliated)	Menatep, Stolichny Savings Bank, Tokobank	160	160.1	Monblan (Menatep affiliated)	0.77
Surgut Holding	40.12	88.40	Uneximbank	Surgutneftegaz Pension Fund	Uneximbank	74	73.5	Surgutfondinvest (linked to Surgut)	0
Sidanco	51	130	Uneximbank	MFK (Part of Uneximbank Group)	Uneximbank	129	129.8	Interros-Oil (part of Uneximbank Group)	0
LUKoil	5	35.01	Imperial Bank	LUKoil, Imperial Bank	Slaviansky Bank	43	43.6	LUKoil-Reserve-Invest (linked to LUKoil)	6.013
Sibneft	51	100.3	Menatep Bank	NFK, Stolichny Savings Bank	Menatep Bank	101	110	FNK (an offshoot of NFK, linked to SBS-Agro)	6.79

Figure 10.2. *Russian oil industry and the loans-for-shares scheme, 1995–1997*

Notes: [1] 70% of sale profit (above value of original loan) accrued to government.
[2] An additional issue of shares in 1996—an approximate 36% share capital increase—to repay the debt of the companies' subsidiaries reduced the 45% of Yukos's shares pledged by the government to Menatep under the loans-for-shares scheme to 33%. Menatep purchased 80% of the additional emission of shares.

Second, proxy companies, often previously unknown and with undeclared ownership, were used as bidding vehicles. The Yukos auctions were won by ZAO Laguna and ZAO Monblan, both Menatep affiliated companies, the latter previously unknown. Oneksimbank used its affiliates MFK and Interros-Oil in winning Sidanco. The winner of the second auction for the stake in Surgut Holding was Surgutfondinvest, while LUKoil-Reserve-Invest won the second auction for the shares in LUKoil. Both were insider companies, previously unknown, and their ownership was undeclared at the time. A consortium of investors led by Boris Berezovsky, a financial/industrial magnate whose wealth originally was derived from control of the LogoVAZ car retail network, used a range of companies to purchase Sibneft, including NFK, FNK, Sins, and Rifle Oil. He repeatedly denied any connection to them.

Third, auction requirements prevented outsider bidders. A number of tender conditions in the initial or concluding auctions, or indeed in both, made it impossible for outsiders to compete. In several cases requirements involved intra-company asset transfers which only the actual oil companies or winners of the initial auctions would have been able to achieve. With Surgut Holding, the winner was required to transfer 5 per cent of Surgut Holding's main operating company, AO Surgutneftegaz, to the holding company. With Sidanco, bidders were required to transfer a major stake in the Angarsk refinery to Sidanco. The Interros group had such a stake in Angarsk but other companies did not—and they would have been hard pressed to buy one between the announcement of the auction and the deadline for the bids. Other conditions involved complicated investment requirements. In the second LUKoil auction (May 1997), the winner had to supply $20 million worth of modern high-tech drilling equipment to LUKoil by the end of December 1997, something that only the company itself could realistically achieve.

Fourth, procedural obstacles were employed to prevent successful outsider bids. In the initial auction for Surgut Holding (November 1995), the only bidder for the shares, apart from the company itself, was Rosneft. The bidding commission—composed of Tyumen vice-governor Gennady Burtsev, Surgut Holding general director Vladimir Bogdanov, Bogdanov's deputy, and an official from the Tyumen regional property committee—ruled the Rosneft bid out of order for 'failing to comply with the established procedure'. The procedures they cited concerned signatures. First, Promstroibank's guarantee of Rosneft's ability to pay off Surgutneftegaz's R1-trillion ($228 million) debt to the federal budget was signed by Promstroibank's deputy chairman, rather than its chairman. Second, the annual balance sheet which Rosneft submitted to the bidding commission was signed not by its general director, but by his deputy. Finally, to make sure that there were no other hostile bids, the Surgut airport was closed on the auction day, to prevent bidders from arriving.[10]

In the second auction for Sibneft (May 1997), KM Invest, representing Vladimir Potanin's Oneksimbank, transferred the sizeable deposit required for participation in the auction—more than $100 million—into the organizer's account with SBS-Agro, the bank managing the auction deposits, on the appointed day before the tender. However, part of the deposit was immediately returned for 'technical reasons'—the necessary accompanying documents had apparently not been received—leaving the candidate with no time to remedy the situation. SBS-Agro thus disqualified Oneksimbank's bid.

Fifth, and finally, the amounts paid for the state's holdings were far below their true value as assessed by such criteria as production, reserves, or asset value. This takes into account the auction requirements (even though it is anyway questionable when, and to what extent, these requirements will ever be fulfilled), and the fact that it would have been difficult to have placed so many shares on the market at one time. The original loans provided in 1995 fell far short of the intrinsic value of the collateral. The prices paid by the auction winners in 1997 were at or only just above the original size of the loans and only just above the required minimum bids. The result was a major loss of revenue to the government. This is indicated by the following examples.

Share market values for June 1997 suggested that the government could have raised $400 million from the sale of a 5 per cent stake in LUKoil, whereas it actually raised only $6 million. Shares with a market value of $608 million were sold for $43.6 million, against an original loan of $35.01 million. The government received 70 per cent of the capital gain, $6.01 million.[11]

For the other oil companies, such a calculation is not as simple because they had not yet been consolidated into a single share issue. However, the value of the stakes sold in individual production associations—whose

[10] Lloyd (1998).

[11] On 20 June 1997, when the government sold the 5% stake in LUKoil, LUKoil ordinary shares were quoted at $17.025. The market value of the stake at this time was $608.3 million, or $573.29 million more than the original loan of $35.01 million. The government's share of the gain would have been $401.31 million.

shares were quoted—provides a comparable indication. On 26 February 1997 Surgutfondinvest paid $73.5 million for a 40.12 per cent stake in Surgut Holding. According to stock market values on 17 February, the corresponding fraction of Surgut Holding's stake in Surgutneftegaz (the company's production association) alone was worth $591 million, $517.5 million more than the sale price.[12] Another example is Uneximbank's purchase of 51 per cent of Sidanco in January 1997 for just $130 million. In November 1997, by comparison, British Petroleum paid Uneximbank $571 million for a 10 per cent stake in Sidanco.

Simultaneously with the loans-for-shares scheme various other government share sales enabled Financial Industrial Groups (FIGs) to acquire complete ownership of the holding companies. In January 1996 Menatep purchased 33 per cent of Yukos stock from the state; in March 1996 it bought a further 7.6 per cent. In September 1996 Interros-Oil, part of the Interros financial-industrial group built around Uneximbank, won an investment tender for a 34 per cent stake in Sidanco. Various auctions of shares in Sibneft took place in 1996 (14 per cent in January, 19 per cent in September, and 15 per cent in October), all of which were won by companies connected to Boris Berezovsky. These investment tenders followed the pattern of the loans-for-shares deals in that they were won by insiders, at low prices, and with contrived auction requirements preventing competitive (hostile) bids.

Via a 'swap' deal with the government in January 1996, Menatep also acquired a package of shares in six oil companies (including 9 per cent of TNK, 3.87 per cent of Sidanco, and 4 per cent of KomiTEK) while the government received a stake in Menatep worth, according to the bank's own figures, only $2.5 million. The 9 per cent stake in TNK was later acquired by Victor Paliy, the general director of Nizhnevartovskneftegaz, TNK's production association, at an unknown price. He sold it on to Alfa Group for an alleged $300 million.

In July 1997 the government sold a 40 per cent stake in TNK to Alfa Group for $820 million. This sale also lacked transparency and competition. However, intense scrutiny of the tender in the aftermath of the now notorious loans-for-shares fix was heightened by the opposition of Victor Paliy. He refused to come to an agreement with Alfa Bank and protested at the fixing of the sale of TNK in their favour. This resulted in the price of the stake being pushed up to a level which much more closely

---

[12] Surgutneftegaz's market capitalization was $3,877 million and Surgut Holding owned 38% of Surgutneftegaz, worth $1,473 million, of which 40.12% equals $591 million.

reflected its market value. This sale was followed in December 1997 by the government's sale of a 45 per cent stake in VNK (Eastern Oil Company) to Menatep for $800 million, a value that even more closely reflected the market price. Menatep thereupon owned 54 per cent of VNK as it had earlier bought 9 per cent of the company's shares on the open market.

10.6. CONSOLIDATION AND MANIPULATION, 1997–9

The various manœuvres described above resulted in controlling stakes in the holding companies being concentrated in the hands of single entities or individual business magnates in the case of Yukos, Sidanco, Sibneft, and TNK; and former production association directors in the case of LUKoil and Surgut Holding. For Yukos, Surgut Holding, Sidanco, and Sibneft these controlling shareholdings were in excess of 80 per cent. The holding companies in turn held majority voting share stakes in the subsidiaries. Even so, these forces did not always control the decisions of subsidiary managers regarding production, distribution, and sales. A striking instance was the inability of Alfa Group, the owners of a majority stake (51 per cent) of the holding company TNK, to control the aforementioned Victor Paliy. He overtly operated TNK's main production subsidiary without regard to the holding company.

To increase their control the holding company owners first aimed to augment their presence in subsidiary boardrooms. Once this was achieved, they were in a position to pursue their real aims, which were, first, to centralize (and appropriate) cash flows; and, second, to abolish the separate listing of the subsidiaries and create a single consolidated company share.

Decree no. 327 of 1 April 1995 (besides creating Rosneft and TNK, see above) permitted VIOCs to issue additional stock to be swapped for shares of their affiliates, which would thus become wholly owned subsidiaries with a single stock issue representing the entire company. LUKoil started the process shortly afterwards, when it announced plans to unify shares of its Langespasneftegaz, Uraineftegaz, and Kogalymneftegaz subsidiaries into a single LUKoil share. Up to the end of 1999 LUKoil remained the only company to have completed the process, though Surgut Holding and Sibneft were close.

Under normal western practice the holding companies, following shareholder approval, would be expected to acquire shares of subsidiaries in return for their own shares at a rate corresponding to the relative market prices of the shares, or alternatively to the relative net asset values of the different entities. The higher the market price of a subsidiary, and the lower the price of the holding company, the bigger the cost incurred by the holding company (in terms of its own capitalization) in the process of a swap.

Thus, in Russia, in order to achieve advantageous merger terms (swap ratios) it was in the financial and control interest of the holding to maximize its own market value and minimize that of the subsidiary. Therefore, in the run-up to a possible consolidation the holding companies employed a variety of devices to undermine the value of the subsidiary companies and drive down their share prices. The devices included share dilution, transfer pricing, asset stripping, and biased corporate restructuring.

Share dilution involves an issue of new shares by the subsiduary, preceded if necessary by an increase in its authorized capital. The new shares are then placed (often at below market prices) with favoured shareholders, that is, the holding company management or preferred companies closely connected with them. Such issues occurred at Surgutneftegaz, the main production association of Surgut Holding, in October 1996[13] and Noyabrskneftegaz, the main production association of Sibneft, in September 1997. Minority shareholders in the subsidiaries were liable to lose not only income and/or capital from entitlements, but also the ability to form a blocking vote. Under joint Stock Company Law, at least 75 per cent of a subsidiary's shareholders need to approve a holding/subsidiary consolidation.[14] The 1997 issue of shares by Noyabrskneftegaz—a more than doubling of the company capitalization—reduced the minority interest from over 25 per cent to under 12 per cent.

In December 1997 Uneximbank attempted to achieve the same end via a different route. It sought to triple Sidanco's charter capital through the

---

[13] The Federal Securities Commission (FSC) later forced Surgut Holding to buy out the issue at a higher price (some argued still below market price), though the dilution remained.

[14] Since holding companies proposed merger terms for subsequent approval by subsidiary shareholders, the holding company had the initiative in the decision-making process. Outside shareholders in the subsidiary had protection only if there were enough of them to block inadequate terms. As the holding companies already typically controlled 38% of a subsidiary's charter capital and 51% of the votes, and the employees voted in favour of most proposals, disadvantageous terms could be blocked only if a 25% minority was in the hands of allied foreign and domestic portfolio investors. Even if this blocking vote existed, there was a multitude of ways in which shareholders were prevented from voting (though not necessarily permanently). These included proxies that were deemed unacceptable, or voting slips mailed to the wrong address or without sufficient time for response.

issue of convertible bonds (at one-tenth of market price) which only two Oneksimbank affiliates (Kantupan Holdings and MFK investment bank) were allowed to buy. The bonds would have been swapped for Sidanco subsidiaries' stock in order to increase Sidanco's (and therefore also Oneksimbank's) control of the subsidiaries to more than 75 per cent. After considerable protest by minority shareholders in the holding company who faced dilution, the Federal Securities Commission (FSC) forced Sidanco to cancel the issue and come to an agreement with minority shareholders.

Intra-company transfer pricing involves the exploitation by the holding of its subsidiaries as 'cost centres'. The output of the subsidiaries is sold to the holding or its affiliates at below-market prices, while operating costs and debts (including unpaid tax debts) are left with the subsidiaries. Profit is thereby shifted to the holding companies. Yukos, Sibneft, and Sidanco all engaged in this practice. Thus, in 1996 Yukos holding recorded an after-tax profit of $91.5 million in its consolidated accounts, while the subsidiary minority interests (Yuganskneftegaz and Samaraneftegaz) lost $345 million.[15] In 1996 Yuganskneftegaz alone lost an estimated $195 million through transfer pricing.[16] As long as a holding company could get away with this, corporate consolidation was arguably irrelevant as the subsidiaries' shares were simply being rendered valueless. On the other hand, as long as minority shareholders remained on the scene, prepared potentially to conduct a legal and political fight against holding company abuses, some motivation for consolidation remained.

Biased corporate restructuring involves the transfer of assets from a subsidiary to the holding (or newly formed companies under the control of the holding) without any or adequate compensation. Yuganskneftegaz's 1996 sales of its stakes in Yuganskfracmaster (a joint venture with Canadian Fracmaster) and Tokobank to Yukos at prices well below market values are both clear examples of this.[17]

In the light of these practices, and in anticipation of the biased consolidation terms that would not reflect true economic value, the Russian stock market during 1997 revalued the relative prices of holding and subsidiary companies. In the twelve-month period ended 30 January 1998 the price of Yuganskneftegaz and Samaraneftegaz shares fell by 30 per cent and 47 per cent, respectively, while Yukos shares rose by 185 per cent.

---

[15] Price Waterhouse (1997*a*).   [16] Moser and Oppenheimer (1998).
[17] Price Waterhouse (1997*b*).

In March 1999, in a series of extraordinary general shareholder meetings (EGMs) of the subsidiaries Yuganskneftegaz, Samaraneftegaz, and Tomskneft, the holding company Yukos attempted to push through a triple blow of share dilution, asset stripping, and transfer pricing both against minority shareholders in the subsidiaries and against creditors (bondholders) of the holding company itself. The proposed dilutive share issues were to be bought in a closed subscription by Yukos affiliated offshore entities, and moreover were to be paid for with the debt (*veksels*) of one of the other Yukos subsidiaries. In a series of court battles, Yukos succeeded in having the shares of minority shareholders arrested, thus preventing them from exercising their 25 per cent veto. The minority shareholders then sought to have the FSC prevented through court action from registering the newly issued shares. However, by November 1999 Yukos had succeeded in both registering the dilutions of Yuganskneftegaz and Samaraneftegaz shares and in transferring the greater part of its own shareholdings in its operating subsidiaries to offshore entities out of reach of West Merchant, Daiwa, and Standard Bank of South Africa, its creditors. In December 1999 Dart Management, the major external investor in the operating subsidiaries, agreed to sell its shareholdings to Yukos for a reported sum of $120 million, representing a presumably partial but none the less significant salvaging of the original investment. This was only achieved after a long and acrimonious media and legal campaign against Yukos.

10.7. GOVERNMENT OWNERSHIP

In 1999 of the six largest integrated majors—LUKoil, Surgut Holding, Yukos, Sidanco, Sibneft, and TNK—the federal government still had a significant stake only in LUKoil (16.6 per cent) and TNK (49.87 per cent). Elsewhere, the government retained holdings of more than 38 per cent in a number of the smaller integrated companies, namely Rosneft (100 per cent), VNK (36.76 per cent), Slavneft (77.1 per cent), and Onaco (85 per cent).[18] In order to raise budget finance, authorities had intended to pursue progressive sell-offs of these holdings. However, in the aftermath of the August 1998 financial crisis and a succession of aborted sell-offs (TNK, VNK, Rosneft) it was unclear when they would be able to achieve this.

At the same time, the government retained considerable influence within the industry through taxation, export licences, and its control

[18]   Energy Intelligence Group (1999).

over Transneft, the oil transportation company. In conditions of a short-age of export pipeline capacity, the government was able to use the threat of reduced access to export pipelines as a lever against the oil companies. However, this was not always successful, failing for instance in 1998 to get companies to meet their taxation obligations. Furthermore, besides encouraging corruption, the fact that preferential government treatment in the form of tax exemptions or increased export allocation could be more fruitful to a company than its own internal restructuring efforts was not conducive to improvements in operating efficiency.

A specific problem facing oil companies still in the state sector was that frequent changes in government administrations were accompanied by changes of management and a resulting lack of consistent direction. Moreover, corruption meant that profit streams were commonly diver-ted away from the state (and minority shareholders) to the pockets of the managers and their associates. Thus, during the corporate presidency of Yuri Bespalov, who was close to Boris Berezovsky, at Rosneft in 1997–8, its main production association Purneftegaz supplied oil to Omsk refin-ery (part of Sibneft, controlled by Berezovsky) at artificially low prices, thereby enriching Berezovsky at the expense of the state. Other man-œuvres saw state assets stripped or sold off on the cheap. A particularly daring attempt at this also involved Purneftegaz. In February 1998 cred-itors of Rosneft sought via court action to get control of Purneftegaz (which had an estimated market value of several hundred million dollars) after Rosneft failed to pay back outstanding loans totalling $7 million. Although the identity of the predators was not clear, LUKoil and Alexander Putilov, a former president of Rosneft, were the most likely candidates. When their attempts were frustrated and overturned by fed-eral government action in late 1998, they apparently tried to enlist the local authorities in Yamal-Nenets on their side and urged them to press home bankruptcy proceedings against the subsidary (due to unpaid taxes the regional authority was a major Purneftegaz creditor), as another way of getting control.

After acquisition of the oil companies in 1996–7, the owners of the FIGs (also known as the 'oligarchs') practised a policy of plundering export cash flows, while honouring as few as possible of their corporate obligations, such as wages for workers, federal and regional taxes, debt service, and profit attribution to shareholders. While the federal govern-ment tolerated this behaviour, and foreign investors and minority share-holders proved powerless to stop it, regional authorities began in the latter half of 1998 to stand up against it. Their chosen approach as reluctant creditors, namely bankruptcy proceedings, posed a serious threat to the integrity of the oligarchs' oil holding companies.

In the face of unpaid tax bills, regional authorities initiated bankruptcy proceedings in November 1998 against two Sidanco subsidiaries: Angarsk refinery and the production unit Kondpetroleum. This was followed by proceedings against Chernogorneft in December and Udmurtneft in January 1999 (regional authorities were also involved in the attempt to bankrupt Purneftegaz in the latter half of 1998—mentioned above—and in a struggle with Yukos for control of Tomskneft in 1998–9). The bankruptcy proceedings resulted in a loss of control for Sidanco over the subsidiaries in question, with temporary outside management appointed by the courts. This undermined the revenue flow of the holding company itself and led to the announcement in January 1999 of the commencement of bankruptcy proceedings against it.

10.8. FOREIGN PARTICIPATION

As well as being inhibited by an uncertain political situation and an insecure fiscal regime, foreign equity investment in the Russian oil industry was limited by legal restrictions. Foreigners were excluded from the 'mass privatization' of 1992–4 and were not invited to participate in the second phase of privatization (loans-for-shares scheme) in 1995–7. The 15 per cent company cap imposed by presidential decree in November 1992 was lifted only on 5 November 1997.

However, where there was some secondary market activity in shares, foreign equity investment took place. This was generally at the subsidiary rather than at the holding level, as sales in the latter were, at least initially, tightly controlled. The exceptions were ARKO's purchase of 8 per cent of LUKoil in September 1995 and BP's 10 per cent of Sidanco in November 1997. The minority status of all foreign shareholders meant that they were hard pressed to counter the decisions of Russian managements of the companies in which they held interests. There were numerous instances of rights being infringed and dividends not paid. Irregular voting procedures or sweeping delegation of powers to management were a feature at both company shareholder and board meetings. The practices described above of share dilution, transfer pricing, and asset stripping effectively robbed most foreign (and other minority) shareholders of their entitlements and left them with huge losses on their investments. In 1998, anxious not to reveal the extent of their malpractice, Yukos and Sidanco successfully resisted independent audits of subsidiary oil companies which were to be paid for by western minority investors.

Despite intermittent action by the Federal Securities Commission (FSC) against shareholder abuses, considerable action is still needed to safeguard the rights of minority shareholders. A lack of legal clarity with, for instance, contradictions between the Civil Code and the Joint Stock Company Law, needs to be addressed before progress can be made. Even where proper laws exist on paper, there remains great potential for manipulation. Thus, when Navaromco, a minority shareholder in Noyabrskneftegaz, appealed against a share dilution in September 1997 by the holding company Sibneft, a court in Yamal-Nenets Autonomous District rejected the appeal (24 August 1998) on the flimsy grounds that the signature on the appeal document appeared to differ from the signature on the original complaint.

Partly to avoid such problems, several billion dollars' worth of foreign investment in the Russian oil industry in the 1990s took the form of joint ventures (JVs) and production-sharing agreements (PSAs), which allow participating companies to circumvent many of the revenue taxes in Russia, rather than equity investment. But here also investment was impeded by the lack of a properly overhauled taxation system and the reluctance of the State Duma to approve the law on PSAs. Russia's perceived investor unfriendliness—combined with high production costs and poor infrastructure—meant that foreign investment post-1991 was more attracted to other FSU states, notably Azerbaijan, Kazakhstan, and Turkmenistan, and other energy-producing regions in general.

British Petroleum's experience in Russia in the 1990s is instructive of the difficulties facing foreign investors. After a failed venture with Purneftegaz in the early 1990s, BP came to an agreement in November 1997 with Vladimir Potanin, the head of the Interros FIG, and purchased a 10 per cent stake in the holding company Sidanco for $571 million. They were subsequently caught up in the conflict noted above between Sidanco subsidiaries and regional authorities over unpaid taxes. In February 1999 BP-Amoco wrote down the value of its investment in Sidanco by $200 million as an interim measure. In the last quarter of 1999 its attempts to rescue and refinance Sidanco were frustrated by the controversial sales of Kondpetroleum and Chernogorneft. These key Sidanco subsidiaries were sold in bankruptcy auctions to TNK in October and November 1999. The sales proceeded despite BP-Amoco and other major Sidanco shareholders claiming that the bankruptcy process had been manipulated, that the sales violated the law, and that

Chernogorneft in particular was still viable. In December 1999, following political negotiation and the suspension of a US Eximbank credit to TNK, an agreement was announced whereby TNK would return Chernogorneft to Sidanco in return for a 25 per cent blocking stake in Sidanco. How such an agreement would work out in practice, especially in terms of effective management, was wholly unclear.[19]

10.9. CONCLUSION

Up to 1995 insiders were the beneficiaries of oil industry privatization. As in other sectors of the economy, privatization involved recognizing and legitimizing the *de facto* control of existing enterprise directors, the strongest stakeholders. With respect to corporate governance, a company- and shareholder-based system was meant to replace state control. However, the mechanisms to control the managers were new and untested, and because management had succeeded in restricting the distribution or sale of shares to outsiders, in practice very weak or non-existent. Oil company executives, as they gained autonomy from the state, were therefore not subject to effective external supervision. Guarantees of good management were lacking and prospects of attracting external finance, much needed for restructuring, were poor.

In 1995–7 a number of these enterprise directors had their new-found autonomy undermined by the loans-for-shares scheme, which gave control of several oil holding companies to outsiders. The scheme reflected the political strength of certain banks, especially Menatep and Oneksimbank, and entrepreneurs, notably Boris Berezovsky, as well as the political influence of the banking sector in general over other sectors of the economy, including the oil industry. Although the scheme took place with the agreement and co-operation of the existing oil company managers (or they were pressured to accept it), the new business and banking interests clearly dominated the resultant financial industrial groups (FIGs). The oil companies were divided between them. Yukos (Menatep), Sidanco (Oneksimbank), Sibneft (Berezovsky), and TNK (Alfa) were all included in one of the new FIGs. The exceptions were LUKoil and Surgut Holding, which were strong enough to remain independent, with LUKoil powerful enough itself to be considered

---

[19] BP-Amoco also withdrew in March 1999 from an earlier (Amoco) commitment to join with Yukos in developing the major Priobskoye field in western Siberia. This decision was presumably influenced at least in part by Yukos' treatment of other foreign investors.

a FIG. Good connections in central government were the crucial factor in determining ownership during this period. Oil generals without access to the highest level of state structures lost out.

Contrary to the argument of many analysts and economists that outsider management would be a crucial advance for the industry, the existing insider managers or established oil men of LUKoil and Surgut Holding proved better and more responsible than the new banker entrants. While the insiders had at least some long-term vision for their companies, the outsiders exploited the companies for short-term gain. The exception was TNK, where the new management, in contrast with the abuses practised by Victor Paliy as general director of Nizhne-vartovskneftegaz, was an improvement over the old.

The bankers' haste to plunder the oil companies' resources stemmed partly from the lack of clarity regarding ownership and shareholder rights. An adversarial relationship between holding and subsidiary companies resulted from the government's sale of the oil companies at two levels, with the holding companies being sold at absurdly low prices. No one understood better than the new banker owners of the holding companies the danger of losing newly acquired assets, for instance after a change in government. Their response was to initiate a policy of plundering the revenue (not just the profit) streams of the companies. To achieve advantageous consolidation terms, a strategy of undermining the financial performance of subsidiary companies, rather than effective restructuring and investing in the companies' futures, was devised.

The Russian oil industry illustrates many of the problems that Russia faces in its transition from a command to a market economy. It demonstrates how Russians have proved themselves adept at distorting and manipulating basic elements of the market system such as share ownership or bankruptcy proceedings, in furtherance of corrupt or otherwise unethical practices. As a result analysts and economists have come to appreciate more fully the importance of governance and institutional factors in a properly functioning market economy, and are less focused on price mechanism and privatization alone.

In terms of corporate governance, a number of key elements remain undeveloped in Russia. These include the fiduciary responsibility of managements to shareholders, and the nature of creditors' priority claims upon defaulting companies. Even basic western concepts of 'ownership' and 'property' remain in doubt. In the absence of a properly functioning legal system, law-based control of assets has been shown to be far less important than power-based control of revenue flows. This makes all the more regrettable the tendency for western advisers, auditors, brokers, and consultants in pursuit of fees and commissions to overlook questionable aspects of Russian enterprises whom they are endeavouring to 'sell' to western investors. A central need for real investment in the oil sector remains. Without this the spoils over which the different groups are fighting will simply get smaller and smaller. Where this investment will come from is unclear. The profits which the sector generates are seldom ploughed back and frequently end up in foreign bank accounts. Global investment is going elsewhere. If this pattern persists, the Russian oil industry, although continuing to provide riches for a privileged few and somewhat erratic revenue support for the fragile public sector budget, will not make the contribution of which it is capable to Russia's prosperity at large.

REFERENCES

British Petroleum (1998). *BP Statistical Review of World Energy*, London, June.

Brunswick Brokerage (1997). *The Russian Oil Industry—Merger Risk Remains the Major Obstacle to Investment*, Moscow, 13 June.

Credit Suisse First Boston (1997). *Share Swap Risk and Russian Oils*, London, 12 September.

Dienes, L., Dobozi, I., and Radetzki, M. (1994). *Energy and Economic Reform in the Former Soviet Union*, New York.

Energy Intelligence Group (1998–1999). *The Almanac of Russian Petroleum 1998 & 1999*, New York.

Gustafson, T. (1989). *Crisis Amid Plenty—The Politics of Soviet Energy under Brezhnev and Gorbachev*, Princeton.

International Finance Corporation (IFC) Library, Moscow (1992–5). *Russian Federation Laws 1992–5 Relating to the Oil and Gas Sectors*, Moscow.

Lloyd, J. (1998). *Rebirth of a Nation, An Anatomy of Russia*, London.

MC-BBL–MC Securities Ltd. (1997). *Russian Oil: Financial Analysis*, London, 26 February.

MC Securities Ltd. (1996). *Siberian Oil Company: New Kid on the Block*, London, 13 May.

Moser, N. (1996). 'The Privatization of the Russian Oil Industry 1992–1995: Façade or Reality?', M. Phil. thesis, University of Oxford.

—— and Oppenheimer, P. (1998). *Yukos, Yuganskneftegaz and Samaranefugaz: 1996 Exports, Export and Domestic Market Pricing, and Intra-Company Transfer Pricing*, processed, Moscow, 7 September.

NatWest Securities (1997). *Diamonds & Rust—Exposing Value Amongst the Russian Oils*, London, October.

Paribas–United Financial Group (1997). *Russian Oil Holdings*, Moscow, 19 March.

Petroleum Advisory Forum and Boston Consulting Group (1995). *Developing an Equity Market for Russian Oil Companies*, New York.

Price Waterhouse AO (1997*a*). *OAO NK Yukos Consolidated Financial Statements as of 31 December 1996*, Moscow.

—— (1997*b*). *OAO Yuganskneftegaz Consolidated Financial Statements as of 31 December 1996*, Moscow.

Newspapers and periodicals, including: *The Economist* (London); *Expert* (Moscow); *The Financial Times* (London); *Johnson's Russia List* (Washington, DC); *Moscow Times* (Moscow); *Neft i Kapital* (Moscow); *Nefte Compass* (Moscow); *Renaissance Capital* Morning/Weekly/Monthly Monitors (Moscow); *Russia Review* (Moscow); *Russian Petroleum Investor* (Moscow and Los Angeles).

11

The Labour Market

SIMON COMMANDER AND ANDREI TOLSTOPIATENKO

11.1. INTRODUCTION

A distinguishing feature of the transition in east and central Europe
(ECE) and Russia by comparison with the former Soviet Union (FSU)
has been the behaviour of the labour market, especially unemployment.
The contrast is particularly pronounced when using registrations data.
Seven and more years into their respective transitions, unemployment
in ECE averaged over 10 per cent of the labour force as against under
3 per cent in Russia. Part of this discrepancy is rightly attributed to
measurement error. Some official estimates of unemployment based
supposedly on labour force survey data suggest a far smaller gap; unemployment in Russia, for example, exceeded 11 per cent at end-1998, rather
than the 2.5 per cent rate shown by registrations data. However, the first is
more an estimate than a robust measure and even if correct, given the size
of shocks to output and the speed at which privatization was carried out,
Russian unemployment still remains low relative to east and central
Europe (ECE), as can be observed in Figure 11.1.

The variation across these groups of countries is not confined to the
level of unemployment. Available data indicate large gross flows in
employment and large flows in and out of unemployment in Russia. In
recent years over 10 per cent of regular employees in medium and large
firms have changed jobs and over 90 per cent have been quits. The characterization of unemployment as a somewhat stagnant pool, that appears
to hold in ECE, does not seem appropriate to Russia or other former

Thanks to Mark Schankerman and Zafiris Tzannatos for suggestions and insights at various
points along the way. The editors have also made very helpful comments on an earlier
version.

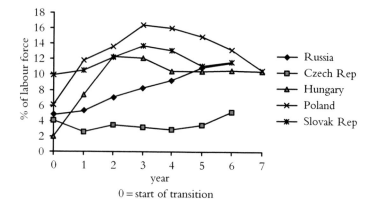

Figure 11.1. *Unemployment in ECE*

Sources: Registration data for eastern and central Europe; LFS for Russia, EBRD.

states of the Soviet Union.[1] Part of this is probably attributable to the different generosities and durations of unemployment benefits and social assistance available to workers. In Russia, the replacement rate for unemployment benefits has barely exceeded 0.1. By contrast, in ECE the average replacement rate has ranged between 0.3 and 0.4. Moreover, while involuntary flows to unemployment from the firm sector have remained small and have—somewhat surprisingly—been accompanied by significant accessions, there is also evidence that firms in Russia and other parts of the FSU have commonly adjusted hours more significantly than employment. Short-time working has been widely reported across large parts of the Russian economy. Official estimates indicate that nearly 20 per cent of the labour force was subject to short-time work or involuntary leave in 1997–8. Wage arrears have also become endemic; by 1998 their magnitude amounted to over 2 per cent of national income, with over a third of employees owed some part of their wage.[2]

This unwillingness to induce large-scale separations and hence to sanction larger unemployment has complex roots—political and economic. The consequences have, however, been significant, not least in

---

[1] See Boeri (1994).

[2] Thanks to Elaine Buckberg for providing the available data. Grogan (1998) finds that unpaid leave is best explained in terms of firm or sector specific shocks with a somewhat higher incidence among the low paid, unskilled, and female workers.

understanding some of the reasons for the Russian crisis of August 1998. Superficially, the crisis was prompted by the government's default on its treasury bonds and an underlying fiscal impasse. This unsustainable fiscal path was obviously a product of many factors, but a key ingredient has been the inability of the state to maintain its tax base. Part of this is an enforcement issue, but a greater part is the result of a declining production and tax base—despite large-scale privatization—alongside an informal sector, largely operating outside the tax net.

Behind this fiscal trap has been the very limited degree to which Russian firms have engaged in restructuring, including reductions in employment. Continued and chronic over-manning has largely remained the norm. Not that all these hoarded staff necessarily receive wages. Many do not. But they have not been separated and exist instead in a world of multiple jobs with much of their time given to working in the informal economy. The simple reality is that the Russian government has refused to let substantial parts of its moribund economy actually fail.

The overall impression that emerges is of a firm sector reluctant to impose involuntary separations and preferring to absorb shocks primarily through adjustments to wages and hours of work. Surveys of the unemployed indicate that many of those registering as unemployed remain attached to firms, even while receiving low or absent monetary compensation.[3] These features and the underlying model of adjustment appears radically different from that adopted in ECE; which raises the obvious question 'why'?

This chapter attempts to answer this question. First, it briefly chronicles the response of firms to shocks, the emerging distribution of employment over formal and unofficial sectors and the size and characteristics of the unemployment that has been generated. Second, it takes a look at the factors explaining the response. Third, having isolated the role of soft finance, the structure of compensation, and the control regime of firms as the major factors, it sets up a model of labour allocation across two sectors. It then looks at the implications of a change in the financing regime—namely, a cut in subsidies—on firm level choices over wages and employment. The chapter concludes by assessing the costs and benefits of this adjustment path.

---

[3] For a closer look at the characteristics of the unemployed, see Commander, Tolstopiatenko, and Yemtsov (1999).

11.2. OUTPUT AND ITS COMPOSITION

Russia started the transition with negligible unemployment, substantial labour hoarding, and a vigorous but restricted unofficial economy. Shocks to output have subsequently been large and persistent. This can be attributed to the combined effects of the break-up of nations, trade networks, and disorganization associated with the collapse of the Soviet Union.[4] Official data suggest that by end 1998 Russian GDP was less than half the level attained in 1989. However, the change in employment relative to output was quite differently signed. Employment relative to output in industry increased by over 50 per cent in the same period; a clear contrast with ECE, where employment commonly adjusted faster than output. An apparently sluggish response of employment to output changes could, of course, also be consistent with smaller actual changes to output than reported. Clearly, reporting procedures have failed to keep up with changes in the structure of the economy, leading to under-estimation of output.

In accounting for the size of the unofficial economy, one approach has been to use energy consumption as a cross-check. The cumulative drop in electricity consumption between 1989 and 1995 was under half the reported decline in GDP.[5] This discrepancy is largely absent in east and central Europe. Based on this gap, and assuming an output elasticity of electricity consumption of 1.15—in other words of declining energy efficiency—Kaufmann and Kaliberda (1996) estimated that actual Russian GDP was roughly 50 per cent higher by end 1995 than official figures estimate.

Figure 11.2 plots the size of the unofficial economy across a range of countries, using the estimates based on energy consumption. It can be seen that the size of the unofficial economy in Russia has generally remained significantly larger than in ECE. Indeed, by these measures the Russian unofficial economy expanded from around 12 per cent to over 40 per cent of aggregate output between 1989 and 1995. This probably over-estimates the rate of increase. Most estimates of the size of the unofficial economy at the end of the Soviet period range between 17 per cent and 35 per cent of GDP.[6] Even so, the size and persistence of the unofficial economy relative to most ECE economies is evident.

---

[4] See, for example, Blanchard and Kremer (1997).   [5] EBRD (1995), p. 182.
[6] See the discussion and references in Alexeev and Gaddy (1993). The GDP figure for 1989 for Russia (573 billion roubles) is taken from EBRD (1995).

Size of Informal Sector

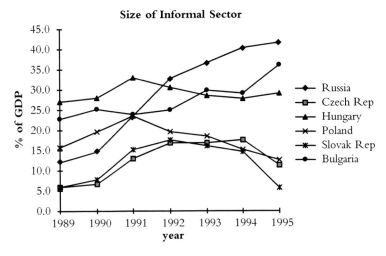

Figure 11.2. *Size of informal sector in ECE*
Source: Johnson, Kaufmann, and Schleifer (1997), table 1.

The initial conditions cannot account for the bulk of the story. It has been argued that high, punitive rates of taxation on labour and capital income have driven agents into the unofficial economy.[7]

While taxation is clearly central to the problem, there are a number of problems with emphasizing only this channel. In the first place, although it is true that tax rates have varied more widely and been subject to greater innovation and uncertainty—including at regional and local levels—in Russia than in most of ECE, average and marginal tax rates on labour and personal income have not been very significantly higher in the former. Second, what is striking in Russia is the way in which the unofficial economy has coexisted beside the formal economy. Rather than thinking of agents picking to be in one or other sector, a more appropriate characterization appears to be involving the contemporanous assignation to both sectors.[8] Further, if multiple job-holding in both formal and informal sectors has been permitted, this raises the question

---

[7] See Johnson, Kaufmann, and Schleifer (1997). Note, the way they define the economy in their set-up makes the system over-determined with knife-edge properties.

[8] In the set-up of Johnson *et al.* (1997) the choice is whether to be in one or other sector. Yet household data show widespread contemporaneous involvement in both sectors.

of what set of firm control regimes and decision-making rules have permitted such multiple job-holding.

11.3. FIRM RESPONSES TO SHOCKS

Firm level data provide an important cross-check on the blurred picture emerging from aggregate numbers.[9] In order to get a sense of the way in which shocks have been distributed over both employment and wages, Tables 11.1 and 11.2 report the results of a simple set of exercises on a large panel of Russian firm data.[10] What is reported are two regressions relating the change in the logarithm of employment and wages to the change in the logarithm of sales—as a proxy for output—and to a vector of characteristics, including profitability, price controls, firm size, ownership at end of period, receipt of government transfers, and branch dummies over two periods, 1994–90 and 1994–3. The objective is to get a better sense of the way in which Russian firms have responded in terms of wage and employment changes to shocks to output.

In the employment equation the coefficients on the sales terms are significant, positive, and small. Over the longer period, the employment elasticity was no larger than 0.09; significantly smaller than that reported for firms in central Europe.[11] Location in a major city, profitability, and the size dummy exerted a positive effect, while receiving government transfers exerted a predictably negative influence. It is striking that, relative to state firms, privatized or privatizing firms had negatively signed coefficients on the sales term, pointing to a weak impact of privatization or its prospect on firm's employment behaviour. By contrast, *de novo* private firm status had a positive and significant effect. In sum, there is evidence of only a weak association of employment and sales changes at firm level.

With regard to the responsiveness of wages to firm-specific financial characteristics, Table 11.2 shows the coefficient on the sales variable in the long panel to be small at 0.08. There is some sign of increasing responsiveness over time; the coefficient on the 1994–3 regression rises to 0.1. In wage determination, being profitable was consistently negatively signed. In the long panel, firms receiving financial transfers from government had lower wage-to-productivity elasticities, but this effect had washed

---

[9] This section is based on Commander, Dhar, and Yemtsov (1996).
[10] The survey comprised 439 industrial firms and was administered in 1994. For full details of sampling and for a more complete set of findings, see Commander, Fan, and Schaffer (1996).   [11] See Commander (1998).

Table 11.1. *Regression of the change in employment*

Dependent variable	Change in employment (log)	
	1994–90/91	**1994–93**
Independent variables		
Change in sales (log)		
1994–90	0.092^c	
1994–2		0.031^c
Dummy variables		
Profit maker	0.002	0.043
Price control	0.165^b	0.038^b
Size (> 3,500)	0.172^c	0.043^a
Moscow/St Petersburg	0.102	0.037
Government support in 1994	−0.057	$−0.036^a$
Privatized	$−0.326^c$	$−0.122^c$
Delayed Privatizer	$−0.292^c$	$−0.099^c$
To be privatized within 18 months	−0.209	$−0.104^b$
Private	0.025	0.155^c
n	196	252
adjusted R^2	0.4	0.27

Notes:
Dummies for industrial branches included.
[a]Significant at 10%.
[b]Significant at 5%.
[c]Significant at 1%.
Source: World Bank Survey.

out by 1994–3. Being located in the major urban areas exerted a positive effect. Of interest is the fact that, in the long panel, non-state status at the end of the period had a very significant and negative effect. The sign is reversed in 1994–3, but the ownership dummies are generally insignificant. The overall picture is that by end-1994 there was yet little to differentiate non-state from state firms in their employment and wage responses. However, despite small elasticities across ownership types, firms have generally been quite effectively constrained in their wage setting by their revenues; wages per worker have largely been set within the size of the per worker distributable surplus. Available evidence after 1994 suggests relatively little change in the behaviour of Russian firms, even those that have been privatized.[12]

[12] See, for example, Blasi et al. (1997).

Table 11.2. *Regression of the change in wage rate*

Dependent variable	Change in wage rate (log)	
	1994–90/91	1994–93
Independent variables		
Change in sales per worker (log)		
1994–90	0.083[c]	
1994–2		0.102[c]
Dummy variables		
Profit maker	− 0.418[c]	− 0.137
Price control	− 0.237[c]	0.169
Size	− 0.047	− 0.381[c]
Moscow/St Petersburg	0.133	0.173[a]
Government support in 1994	− 0.226[a]	0.090
Privatized	− 1.234[c]	0.017
Delayed privatizer	− 1.220[c]	0.158
To be privatized within 18 months	− 1.122[c]	− 0.140
Private	− 1.021[b]	− 0.455[a]
n	172	215
adjusted R^2	0.8	0.34

Notes:
Dummies for industrial branches included.
[a]Significant at 10%.
[b]Significant at 5%.
[c]Significant at 1%.

Source: World Bank Survey.

In summary, firm level data indicate that insiders—workers and managers—have been able to choose high employment and low money wages as the dominant response to a deterioration in the product market. This has had obvious consequences for unemployment. Workers have combined continuing attachment to state firms with growing involvement in informal activity.

11.4. UNEMPLOYMENT: SCALE AND CHARACTERISTICS

We have already seen that there are major imprecisions in the measures of unemployment that are commonly cited. One useful source that provides a better measure is the Russia Longitudinal Monitoring Survey; in particular the three rounds implemented between 1994 and end-1996. Grogan (1998) estimates that in 1994 unemployment was 6.5 per cent, rising to around 8 per cent by end-1996. These numbers are lower—by around 1 percentage point—than those reported in the official series for these points in time. The mean duration of unemployment was also found to be low, at no more than 6.5 months, although there is evidence of a growing share of long term in total unemployment. Aside from confirming low aggregate unemployment levels, this household survey dataset suggests that the highest risk of unemployment appears to be among the young but that there remains surprisingly little variation across education levels.

As to the character of unemployment and the characteristics of the unemployed, a pair of surveys implemented in 1994 and covering 2,000–3,000 individuals provides a more refined sense of the nature of the employment problem.[13] In particular, it allows for discrimination over individuals without work and those with informal or secondary employment. Based on questions about job search and hours worked, those without work yet searching could be separated from those with other, non-primary, employment. What emerged was that while all those subject to employment loss as well as hours adjustment accounted for over 10 per cent of the sample, the 'true' unemployed actually accounted for no more than 3.5 per cent of the sample. That share rose no higher than 5 per cent if workers experiencing very substantial downward adjustment to hours worked were also included.

With respect to characteristics, probit estimates for the true unemployed found that there was a negative, but insignificant, association with age, being female, and the extent of education. Location variables did not vary, although subsequently there has been significant divergence in regional unemployment rates. It was also the case that being involuntarily separated was, unsurprisingly, positively associated with being true unemployed. However, consistent with the aggregate data, relatively small numbers of individuals were involuntarily separated. A significant share of the unemployed could be traced to new entrants or re-entrants to the labour force as well as to those who had quit their previous employment.

In short, the limited information that is available on the unemployed continues to support the view that not only have they remained relatively few in number but that a significant share of workers has been subject to hours adjustment, leading in some instances to multiple job-holding and moonlighting. Anecdotal evidence suggests that multiple job holding has tended to be more common in the larger urban centres and among the more educated.

---

[13] See Commander, Tolstopiatenko and Yemtsov (1999).

11.5. CONTROL, BENEVOLENCE, AND SOFT BUDGETS

Why have Russian firms maintained high employment given shocks? One factor has clearly been the governance regime and, in particular, the evidence that the controlling agents continue to place a large weight on objectives that are much broader than profit maximization. Firms behave as if they have important social responsibilities which cause them to act with benevolence. Privatization has as yet failed to snap this behaviour.[14]

Another key factor, and one that may ultimately explain a significant part of this apparent benevolence, has been the continuing flow of subsidies to firms. While subsidies to firms from the federal budget dwindled from around 30 per cent of GDP in 1992 to under 2 per cent by 1995, and explicit transfers to firms from regional budgets have hovered around 1 per cent of GDP throughout this period, these figures are major underestimates of the soft financing available to firms. This is not only because of measurement error but because of the multiplicity of channels by which subsidies reach the firm sector. The available evidence suggests that soft financing originates not only from the various levels of government, public utilities, and the tax administration, but also from the financial system. In recent years, a principal channel for subsidy has been barter and the use of non-monetary transactions. As such, the pressure to release labour coming from the budget constraint has been weaker than in ECE.

While the budget constraint is an important part of the story, it is incomplete without thinking more specifically about the reasons why workers choose to stay in state and privatized firms and indeed why firms allow those workers to stay in, despite major, and not easily reversible, shocks to demand for their products. This brings us to the issue of worker compensation and its components.

11.6. THE STRUCTURE OF COMPENSATION

One important inheritance of the Soviet system was that firms commonly provided a wide range of social benefits, including housing, child and health care, to their workers. This was particularly true in the larger firms, as measured by employment, and ensured that access to benefits was explicitly linked to the site of employment.[15] Indeed, the planners

---

[14]   Blasi *et al.* (1997).

[15]   An empirical overview is provided in Commander, Lee, and Tolstopiatenko (1996).

had aimed to raise attachment and lower labour turnover precisely by the use of such firm-specific components of compensation. Associated with this was a relatively low monetary wage. Survey evidence suggests that near the start of transition in 1992 benefits comprised as much as 30 per cent of total labour costs in Russia, with enterprise spending on social assets in the range of 4 per cent of GDP. By 1994 survey data for Russian manufacturing firms gave an estimate of mean benefits comprising around 16 per cent of total compensation.[16] Nevertheless, the same survey showed that changes in the scope of provision since 1990 had been relatively limited and that in larger firms—as measured by employment—the change in scale was also quite restrained. A 1998 survey of 350 Russian firms likewise confirmed that while benefits provision had indeed been declining, a significant number of firms—primarily in manufacturing—provided substantial social benefits for their employees.[17] It is also evident that many firms—particularly the larger firms—have received compensating finance for benefits provision from various levels of government. Regional and local governments have tended to subsidize or extend *ad hoc* tax exemptions to firms that have maintained large stocks of social assets.[18] Indeed, indirect subsidies to households for housing and utility—many of which were, however, channelled through the firm—have comprised between 4 per cent and 5 per cent of GDP between 1995 and 1997.

In sum, Russian workers have continued to have access to benefits—including merit goods, like health and child care—through the firm. There has been some limited movement towards higher cost recovery,[19] but the costs of benefits provision by the firm have generally continued to be offset by subsidy from government. The structure of compensation has duly had implications for workers' labour-market decisions. We now formalize this argument with a view to understanding the factors determining the allocation of employment across state and private sectors, including part-time work.

11.7. A MODEL OF LABOUR ALLOCATION

Our framework has the economy composed of two sectors; a state and private sector. The full model is set out in Appendix 1. Being in the

---

[16] See Commander and Schankerman (1997).
[17] Commander and Mummsen (1999).   [18] See Le Houerou (1995).
[19] See Commander and Schankerman (1997).

state sector ensures compensation that comprises not only monetary wages but also social benefits, such as health care. Recent empirical work suggests that such benefits tend to be subsidized, commonly by government.

We first characterize the state sector. Here, firms are assumed to be controlled by insiders, defined as the coalitions of managers and workers. Because of the structure of control and decision-making we assume that not only are wages set consistent with average product but also that insiders can allocate their time over work in the state firm as well as in private activity. Multiple job-holding is permissible, subject to a minimum work requirement in the original state firm. The private sector can use both full- and part-time labour, depending on a variety of factors, including differences in wages, benefits, and hours.

The model offers some insights into the way in which informal private employment can be propagated and the relative incentives for the parties involved. In the first place, the allocation of employment in the informal sector depends importantly on the control regime of the state firm. Such firms are controlled by insiders; they can respond to product market shocks not only by picking employment and wage combinations but also by adjusting hours. As such, and subject to a minimum hours commitment, workers can participate in private sector activity. The extent that they choose to work in the private sector will depend on the relative returns. The private sector maximizes profit. The key factor determining its choice of full- or part-time workers will be the relation between returns to full- and part-time work. However, private firms will need to compensate full-time workers to a level at least commensurate with full-time employment in the state sector. As is apparent, this will imply either offering workers a monetary wage equivalent to the benefits share or else offering comparable benefits. In other words, an important factor in maintaining the attachment to state firms has been the compensation regime. We now look at the implications of a change in that regime and more particularly a change in the way benefits—an important component of compensation—are financed.

11.7.1. *Shocks to benefits: exogenous case*

The representative state firm is assumed to be controlled by insiders who maximize their utility;

$$U = N(w + b - x),$$

where w is monetary wage, b is benefits, x is the outside opportunity, all subject to a zero profit constraint,

$$\pi_1 = pY(t) - (w + b(1 - s))N = 0$$

where s is the subsidy related specifically to benefits provision.
  Limiting to one factor of production, labour, we have;

$$Y = F(N) = (N)^\beta, \quad \text{where } 0 < \beta < 1$$

From the zero profit constraint we find

$$c = w + b = \frac{pY}{N} + s$$

where $c =$ total compensation. Substituting into the utility function we get:

$$U = N(w + b - x) = N\left(\frac{pY}{N} + s - x\right) = pY - N(x - s).$$

Subsidies, s, and hence benefits, b, are exogenously given.
  The first order condition for maximization of utility is:

$$x - s = pY' = \beta\frac{pY}{N}$$

Combining it with the constraint we get compensation;

$$c = w + b = \frac{pY}{N} + s = \beta^{-1}x - (1 - \beta)\beta^{-1}s$$

and from

$$\frac{pY}{N} = \beta^{-1}x - \beta^{-1}s$$

we get employment,

$$N = \left(\frac{\beta p}{x - s}\right)^{1/(1-\beta)} > N_0 = \left(\frac{\beta p}{x}\right)^{1/(1-\beta)}$$

where N_0 is the case of no subsidies.

In other words, with subsidies, employment is larger and compensation smaller than without subsidies. Subsidies influence employment and compensation through both the utility maximization and the constraint. Subsidies shift the average product curve upwards and allow for larger employment and/or compensation. But they also shift the relationship between inside and outside opportunities (x to $x - s$), which will increase employment. Given the production function and the fact that $\beta < 1$, this channel acts more strongly on compensation, resulting in lower compensation and larger employment than in the case without subsidies.

We now look at what happens if subsidies are cut. In the short run employment will decrease and compensation (or wages if social benefits are fixed) will increase. If we also introduce an adverse output price or demand shock ($p(t) < p(0)$) we will have the same increase in total compensation and a larger decrease in employment. Therefore, a price or demand shock only influences employment and leads to its decline.

11.7.2. *Endogenous benefits*

In the case discussed above we could not say anything about how benefits change when cutting subsidies because we considered them as exogenous and only looked at changes in total compensation. To separate out the consequences for both wages and benefits it is necessary to endogenize benefits. For this purpose the set-up can be slightly modified to allow for wages and benefits not being perfect substitutes. Assuming for simplicity a separable utility function:

$$u(w, b, x) = \alpha_w \ln(w) + \alpha_b \ln(b) - \alpha_x \ln(x)$$

the utility of those working in the firm—insiders—will be:

$$U = N(u(w) + u(b) - u(x))$$

In this case we can find the maximum of utility over the set of three variables (N, w, b) (if $s < 1$). The first order conditions for the case $s < 1$ will be:

$$MRS_{wb} \equiv -\frac{dw}{db} = \frac{u'(b)}{u'(w)} = 1 - s(t)$$

$$u(w) + u(b) - u(x) = (1 - \beta(Y))u'(w)(w + (1 - s)b)$$

which we must solve together with the zero profit constraint

$$pY - (w + b(1 - s))N = 0$$

In the case of the simple utility function written above in logarithmic form and with Cobb-Douglas technology ($\beta < 1$), we get from the first-order conditions;

$$w = \frac{\alpha_w}{\alpha_b}(1 - s(t))b$$

$$N = \left(\frac{\alpha_b p}{(\alpha_b + \alpha_w)(1 - s)b}\right)^{1/(1-\beta)}$$

$$b = e^{1-\beta}x^{\alpha_x/(\alpha_b+\alpha_w)}\left(\frac{\alpha_b}{\alpha_w(1 - s)}\right)^{\alpha_w/(\alpha_b+\alpha_w)}$$

Substituting b into w and N,

$$w = \frac{\alpha_w}{\alpha_b}(1 - s(t))b = e^{1-\beta}x^{\alpha_x/(\alpha_b+\alpha_w)}\left(\frac{\alpha_w(1 - s)}{\alpha_b}\right)^{\alpha_b/(\alpha_b+\alpha_w)}$$

$$N = \left(\frac{\alpha_b p}{(\alpha_b + \alpha_w)(1 - s)b}\right)^{1/(1-\beta)}$$

$$= \left(\frac{\alpha_w p}{(\alpha_b + \alpha_w)e^{1-\beta}x^{\alpha_x/(\alpha_b+\alpha_w)}}\right)^{1/(1-\beta)}$$

$$\times \left(\frac{\alpha_b}{\alpha_w(1 - s)}\right)^{(\alpha_b/(\alpha_b+\alpha_w))\cdot(1/(1-\beta))}$$

When cutting subsidies, we now get a decrease in benefits, an increase in wages, and a decrease in employment. Therefore, the only qualitative difference from the previous set-up with risk-neutral individuals and exogenous benefits is that wages and benefits move in opposite directions when cutting subsidies on benefits. At the same time the elasticities of wages and employment with respect to subsidies will depend on the preferences of workers (α_b/α_w), as well as on the elasticity of output, β.

11.8. CONCLUSION AND POLICY IMPLICATIONS

The Russian transition has been notably different than that observed in much of ECE. Employment both in state and privatized firms has tended to stay high, labour hoarding has remained significant, and unemployment has remained at relatively low levels. At the same time, the private sector's growth—though far from trivial—has been quite distinct from ECE. In the latter, *de novo* firms appeared early in the transition, initially in services, and then expanded into other sectors. By contrast, in Russia and the FSU the private sector has tended to be closely linked to existing state or privatized firms and to have been widely dependent on part-time, informal labour. By retaining attachment to the formal sector workers have not been excluded from access to public goods and social assets through participation in the unofficial economy. At the same time, the informal sector has not only grown substantially but has remained largely outside the tax net. This, of course, has had serious and negative implications for fiscal revenues and ultimately for the supply of public goods. In addition, the proliferation of an unofficial economy has tended to raise the level of corruption in the economy and lowered the ability to enforce contracts and binding agreements. In this regard, the growth of the unofficial economy is just as likely to have been a factor helping to perpetuate the absence of a stable context for transactions as an outcome of such absence.

These differences in the respective labour market responses of Russia and ECE can be attributed to a variety of factors, not least the continuation of soft budget constraints in the former. But there are several specific features that have exacerbated the outcome. Primary among these has been the legacy of social protection in the firm and the associated structure of compensation. Workers have continued to receive a significant share of compensation in non-monetary form. Firms have cut hours and monetary wages but have proven remarkably averse to imposing involuntary separations. Aside from adjustment costs, this also reflects the structure of internal control and the coalitions that have been formed among insiders. It can also be traced to pressures on firms from government—local and federal—to limit the flow of workers into unemployment.

Given this structure of control by insiders, we have concentrated on the resulting implications for the allocation of employment across formal and informal sectors. For the formal sector, we found that there would be a strong incentive for workers to stay in those firms but allocate effort in part-time or moonlighting activity in the private sector. This result, of course, is accentuated when benefits provision is subsidized by government. We then went on to look at the implications of a loss of subsidy for the compensation and employment decisions of insider-dominated firms. We show that, under certain conditions, such firms will tend to scale down benefits provision and employment. In general, there are good reasons for thinking that lower subsidies and associated measures aimed at reducing the degree of social protection offered by firms will be associated with accelerated restructuring.

What policy conclusions can be drawn from this analysis? The barebones of the situation are as follows: the Russian government has refused to let substantial parts of its moribund economy actually fail. Privatization has done nothing to address this, because the basic underlying compact—to maintain employment—has remained largely in place. The consequences—not least a fiscal morass—have been severe and adverse. However, a significant number of Russians now raise a part of their income from informal sector work, particularly in urban areas. In many cases, the shells of state and privatized firms provide relatively small parts of total compensation. Moving to enforce separations, as well as the incentive for workers to move voluntarily, should be less difficult now than earlier, although the problem remains huge in those parts of Russia where the local economy remains dominated by a few, large, and failing enterprises.

In short, the starting-point must be to accelerate the process of exit for non-viable firms and banks. Fiscal and quasi-fiscal supports to failing firms—as from the utilities—must cease. This will shrink the market for promissory notes and other rapidly proliferating forms of non-monetary transactions, such as barter, and will undoubtedly lead to a chain of bankruptcies and firm failures. Where, for whatever reasons, firms are not to be allowed to fail, then subsidies for their support should be made explicit and time-bound. But in the majority of cases, exit has to be actively encouraged. When that happens, however, those who lose their jobs must be provided with a more adequate set of fallbacks—unemployment benefits are currently less than 10 per cent of the average wage—and these fallbacks must be set up outside the firm. Maintaining social protection in the firm has proved an impediment to restructuring.

Accelerating restructuring among state and privatized firms must be coupled to better incentives for entry and for the cross-over of existing informal sector firms into the taxed economy. Aside from institutional barriers to entry, a key area for reform is obviously the tax system, where, after years of chronic evasion and complicity, any solution must be simple; for personal income tax, a tax code with few bands and low average rates; a scrapping of profit taxes and a shift to corporate taxation that again rewards investment and is initially pitched at low average rates. Tax holidays for new starts should be explicitly accepted—they already exist *de facto*—and encouragement offered to firms that switch from the lowly capitalized and artificially small informal firm sector into the lightly taxed economy. The benefits of crossing into the tax system have to be made very tangible. Years of artful evasion cannot be brushed aside; coercion will not work. This means that in the medium term direct tax revenues can recover but slowly. In the longer term changing the incentives against low investment, low productivity informal firms will unleash growth.

Appendix 1

1.1. *The State Sector*

For insiders in state firms, the utility function can most generally be represented as;

$$U(N, w) = N^{ss}(u(w^s + b^s + p^s) - v(h^s)) + N^{sp}(u(w^s + b^p + w^p)$$
$$- v(h_0^s + h_0^p)) + (M^s - N^{ss} - N^{sp})u(x)$$

This says that N^{ss} workers have a job only in the state sector where they allocate h^s hours, for which they receive compensation in both money and in kind, $(w^s + b^s + p^s)$. The monetary component of compensation comprises two parts, a base wage—w^s—conditional on allocating a minimum amount of hours and hence ensuring access to the non-monetary part of compensation—b^s—which denotes the value of social benefits per worker provided by the state firm. The second monetary component comprises—$p^s = \lambda^s(h^s - h_0^s)$—which is the additional monetary wage workers receive for allocating more than the minimum hours. In addition, N^{sp} workers have a primary job in the state sector where they allocate h_0^s hours and receive $(w^s + b^s)$. They also hold a secondary job in the private sector where at a minimum they allocate h_0^p hours and receive a wage—w^p. Their total compensation thus comprises $(w^s + b^s + w^p)$.

We assume constant elasticity of substitution (CES) technology in the state sector so that;

$$Y^s = C(\alpha(h^s N^{ss})^{-\rho} + (1 - \alpha)(h_0^s N^{sp})^{-\rho})^{-\beta/\rho}, \quad \text{where } 0 < \beta < 1,$$

The elasticity of substitution, $\varepsilon = \beta/(\beta + \rho)$, is between the products generated by full-time and multiple job workers allocating different hours.

Utility is maximized subject to a constraint given by zero profits. This flows from the idea that insiders appropriate all revenues accruing to the firm;

$$\pi^s = pF(N^{ss}, N^{sp}) - w^{ts}N^{ss} - w^{tp}N^{sp} = 0,$$

where, $w^{ts} = w^s + p^s + b^s$ and $w^{tp} = w^s + b^s \leq w^{ts}$.

Denoting χ as the marginal rate of substitution between workers with one and two jobs, we have:

$$\chi = \frac{u(w^s + b^s + w^p) - v(h_0^s + h_0^p) - u(x)}{u(w^s + b^s + p^s) - v(h^s) - u(x)}$$

$\psi = h_0^s/h^s \leq 1$ where ψ is the ratio of hours for part-time to full-time workers

$\gamma = w^{tp}/w^{ts} \leq 1$ where γ is the ratio of wages in the state and private sectors.

N^{ss} and N^{sp} are the only endogenous variables. The first order condition for maximization is;

$$\frac{pF'(\cdot)\rho(1-\alpha)h_0^s(h_0^s N^{ss})^{-\rho^{-1}} + w^{tp}}{pF'(\cdot)\rho\alpha h^s(h^s N^{ss})^{-\rho^{-1}} + w^{ts}} = \chi$$

Any increase in utility associated with a higher wage must at least compensate the disutility associated with the hours required when working in both sectors simultaneously. With some manipulation we get two equations for determining θ which denotes the ratio of workers with one and two jobs; viz; $\theta = N^{sp}/N^{ss}$;

$$\theta(\chi - \gamma)(\alpha\theta^\rho + (1-\alpha)\psi^{-\rho}) = \beta(1 + \gamma\theta)(\alpha\chi\theta^{1+\rho} - (1-\alpha)\psi^{-\rho})$$

and

$$N^{sp} = \frac{\theta^{1/(1-\beta)}}{(1+\gamma\theta)^{1/(1-\beta)}} \left(\frac{p(h^s)^\beta}{w^{ts}}\right)^{1/(1-\beta)} (\alpha\theta^\rho + (1-\alpha)\psi^{-\rho})^{-\beta/(1-\beta)\rho}$$

It follows from the first equation that

$$\theta = \frac{(1-\alpha)\beta - \alpha\theta^{1+\rho}\psi^\rho(\beta\chi - (\chi-\gamma))}{\alpha\theta^{1+\rho}\psi^\rho\beta\gamma\chi - (1-\alpha)(\chi - \gamma + \beta\gamma)}$$

For an interior solution to exist, θ must not be negative. It is easy to show that this is equivalent to the conditions:

$$(1-\alpha)\beta - \alpha\theta^{1+\rho}\psi^\rho(\beta\chi - (\chi - \gamma)) \geq 0$$

$\alpha\theta^{1+\rho}\psi^\rho\beta\gamma\chi - (1-\alpha)(\chi - \gamma + \beta\gamma) > 0$ and in addition $\psi \leq 1, \gamma \leq 1$, $\beta < 1, \alpha \leq 1$, by definition.

1.2. *The Private Sector*

The private sector is also assumed to be governed by CES technology with an elasticity of substitution, $\varepsilon = 1/(1 + \rho)$, between two types of labour ($\beta = 1$) or between the products generated by full-time and part-time workers ($\beta < 1$). Accordingly, with this function the private firm's maximization problem is;

$$\pi^p = p(\alpha(h^p N^{pp})^{-\beta\rho} + (1 - \alpha)(h_0^p N^{ps})^{-\beta\rho})^{-1/\rho} - (w^{pp})N^{pp} - w^{ps}N^{ps} \Rightarrow \max,$$

The first order conditions for profit maximization are;

$$pF'(\cdot)\alpha(h^p)^{-\beta\rho}(N^{pp})^{-\beta\rho-1} = w^{pp}$$

$$pF'(\cdot)\alpha(h_0^p)^{-\beta\rho}(N^{ps})^{-\beta\rho-1} = w^{ps}$$

The allocation of employment is obtained as follows;

$$\mu = \frac{N^{ps}}{N^{pp}} = \left(\frac{h_0^p}{h^p}\right)^{(\beta(\varepsilon-1))/(\beta+(1-\beta)\varepsilon)} \left(\frac{1-\alpha}{\alpha} \cdot \frac{w^p + p^p + b^p}{w^p}\right)^{\varepsilon/(\beta+(1-\beta)\varepsilon)}$$

Obviously, the number of workers of each type is determined by the ratio of compensation to hours (when $\varepsilon > 1$) and the degree of such dependence is proportional to the elasticity of substitution between the two types of labour. The sensitivity in the allocation of labour to differences in wages, benefits, and hours increases in step with the elasticity of substitution between the two types of labour. We have an implicit constraint on the number of full-time workers which should be at least greater than or equal to one. A smaller value for the number of full-time workers implies a corner solution.

REFERENCES

Alexeev, M. V., and Gaddy, C. G. (1993). 'Income Distribution in the USSR in the 1980s', *Review of Income and Wealth*, Series 39, pp. 23–36.

Blanchard, O., and Kremer, M. (1997). 'Disorganisation', *Quarterly Journal of Economics*, November, 112–14, 1091–1126.

Blasi, J., Kroumova, M., and Krusa, D. (1997). *Kremlin Capitalism: Privatizing the Russian Economy*, Ithaca: Cornell University Press.

Boeri, T. (1994). 'Transitional Unemployment', *Economies of Transition*, 2/1: 1–25.

Boycko, M., Schleifer, A., and Vishny, R. (1995). *Privatising Russia*, Cambridge, Mass.: MIT Press.

Cohen, D. (1995). 'Success and Failure in Russian Reforms', CEPREMAP, Paris, mimeo.

Commander, S. (1998). *Enterprise Restructuring and Unemployment in Models of Transition*, Economic Development Institute (EDI), Washington, DC: The World Bank.

—— and Mummsen, C. (1999). *Understanding Barter in Russia*, EBRD Working Paper 37.

—— Fan, Q., and Schaffer, M. (eds.) (1996). *Enterprise Restructuring and Economic Policy in Russia*, Economic Development Institute (EDI), Washington, DC: The World Bank.

—— Tolstopiatenko, A., and Yemtsov, R. (1999). 'Channels of Redistribution: Inequality in the Russian Transition', *Economies of Transition*, 7/2: 411–47.

—— Dhar, S., and Yemtsov, R. (1996). 'How Russian Firms Make their Wage and Employment Decisions', in S. Commander, Q. Fan, and Schaffer (eds.) (1996). *Enterprise Restructuring and Economic Policy in Russia*, Washington, DC: World Bank.

—— Lee U., and Tolstopiatenko, A. (1996). 'Social Benefits and the Russian Industrial Firm', in S. Commander, Q. Fan, and Schaffer (eds.) (1996).

—— and Schankerman, M. (1997). 'Enterprise Restructuring and Social Benefits', *Economics of Transition*, 5/1: 1–24.

Estrin, S., Earle, J., and Leshchenko, L. (1996). 'Privatisation and Corporate Governance in Russia', in S. Commander, Q. Fan, and Schaffer (eds.) (1996).

European Bank for Reconstruction and Development (1995). *Transition Report*, London.

Grogan, L. (1998). 'Worker Characteristics and Administrative Leave in the Russian Federation', Amsterdam: Tinbergen Institute, mimeo.

—— and van den Berg, G. (1998). 'The Duration of Unemployment in Russia', Amsterdam: Tinbergen Institute, mimeo.

Johnson, S., Kauffmann, D., and Schleifer, A. (1997). 'The Unofficial Economy in Transition', Brookings Papers on Economic Activity, 2.

Kauffman, D., and Kaliberda, A. (1996). 'Integrating the Unofficial Economy into the Dynamics of Post-Socialist Economies: A Framework of Analysis and Evidence', Policy Research Working Paper 1691, December, Washington, DC: The World Bank.

Lehmann, H., Wadsworth, J., and Acquisti, A. (1998). 'Grime and Punishment: Job Insecurity and Wage Arrears in the Russian Federation', Working Paper, Ann Arbor: William Davidson Institute.

Le Houerou, P. (1995). 'Fiscal Management in the Russian Federation', Washington, DC: The World Bank.

12

The Development of Small Enterprises

ANDERS ÅSLUND

An outstanding peculiarity of the Soviet economy was the dearth of small enterprises. Therefore, the development of small private enterprises is a *sine qua non* for the post-Communist economy becoming a normal market economy. The issues are both private ownership and size of enterprises. East–central Europe, notably the four Visegrad countries, saw a tremendous growth in small private enterprises with the transition to a market economy from 1990. In Russia, as in most of the former Soviet Union, however, the expansion of small enterprises has been subdued.

The purpose of this chapter is to investigate what has really happened to the small enterprise sector in Russia and why. Initially, we need to establish a standard. What is the state of small enterprises in ordinary market economies and what has been accomplished in east–central Europe? Second, what do statistics tell us about the situation of the small enterprise sector in Russia? Third, what is the qualitative state of small private enterprises in Russia and what problems do they encounter? Fourth, in order to find an explanation to our observations we need to scrutinize government policy and assess what it has actually amounted to. Finally, we shall discuss how the policy needs to change.

12.1. THE DEVELOPMENT OF SMALL ENTERPRISES IN OTHER POST-COMMUNIST COUNTRIES

International definitions of small enterprises vary, but essentially enterprises with less than 200 employees are implied, regardless of capital and orientation.

We are focusing on legally registered private enterprises rather than informal economic activities or the underground economy, because legality is an important borderline. Illicit status usually implies serious economic distortions. A legally registered enterprise can expand its activities, while most underground activities are very small; lawful enterprises dare to invest, unlike black enterprises, which fear detection and punishment; illegalities imply risk premia, which may be substantial, and they tend to be reflected in high earnings of those involved and poorly functioning markets, characterized by high mark-ups and large price differentials between different markets. Ultimately, legality signifies lower transaction costs and thus greater economic efficiency.

Small- and medium-sized enterprises are being given ever greater credit for economic development in the West, where they account for about two-thirds of employment, and not less than 50 per cent in any country. Small- and medium-sized enterprises have many advantages. First of all they are flexible. Therefore, they tend to be more innovative. They swiftly move into new markets and develop new products. In recent years, they have provided most new employment in the West.

In Russia, a current idea is that Russia has always been a country dominated by big enterprises, and that small enterprises cannot give much return in Russia. This is another version of the view that Russia is different and that worldwide experience for one reason or another does not apply to Russia. This idea is popular among the new Russian capitalists, who have made more money on the state than on the market—which indicates the problem with this view. On the contrary, considering that the post-Communist countries are facing a long period of intense restructuring, a large number of small enterprises seem even more important for them (EBRD 1995, pp. 139–42).

The Communist economies hardly had any small private enterprises to begin with. Before the end of Communism a significant number of legal enterprises existed only in three Soviet-bloc countries: Poland, the German Democratic Republic, and Hungary (Åslund 1985). Although private enterprise was formally legal, it was burdened by innumerable regulations, notably licensing and hostile tax legislation, as well as many restrictions on trade that was equated with speculation. In addition, market economic infrastructure, including transportation, wholesale trading facilities, financial services, and information, was largely missing.

As Communism collapsed in east–central Europe, there was an explosion of private enterprise throughout the region. Entrepreneurship turned out to be far more alive than hardly anybody had expected. The most remarkable increase occurred in Czechoslovakia, where there had been no legal private enterprises until the end of Communism in November 1989. Less than two years later their number had exceeded 1 million in a population of 15 million. By 1994 small- and medium-sized enterprises already employed about 40 per cent of the labour force in the two radical reform countries, Estonia and the Czech Republic. Poland and Hungary, with their more-established private sectors, also showed impressive rises (Johnson 1994, pp. 244–5, 250). Even relatively unsuccessful Bulgaria had 460,000 private enterprises registered by mid-1994, or one enterprise for every twenty citizens (EBRD 1995, p. 147).

However, the explosive development of small private enterprises has not been universal. In most of the former Soviet Union, only a few per cent of the labour force was employed in such enterprises; in Russia 10 per cent (EBRD 1995, p. 140). This is likely to impede the evolution of an ordinary market economy and thus economic growth and welfare, as the scarcity of small enterprises means little or no competition on a multitude of markets.

12.2. A STATISTICAL SURVEY OF SMALL ENTERPRISES IN RUSSIA

Let us first investigate what small enterprises look like in Russia. Like most post-Communist countries, Russia has very bad statistics on the evolution of small enterprises.[1] Until 1986 legally registered private enterprise did not exist in Russia, and until 1996 the country did not have aggregate statistics across all enterprises. Instead, various groups of enterprises were singled out in the political process and measured accordingly.

Russia has, however, had all along a large informal economy that was permitted, notably private agricultural plots and private sales of their produce. The number of private plots rose sharply from 1990 until 1993, and at the beginning of 1996 there were no less than 43.6 million private agricultural plots. Most of them, however, were very small—about one-fifth of an acre (Shmelev 1996, p. 127; Goskomstat 1997, pp. 265–6) and they essentially contribute to people's ability to cope with hardship rather

---

[1] In the Communist world, only Poland and the German Democratic Republic had more or less comprehensive statistics of all enterprises and their ownership. Not even Hungary had such statistics (Åslund 1985).

than to entrepreneurship. They do not appear to have played any major role for the evolution of business enterprises.

The Soviet Union always had a certain black or underground economy. Much has been written about it, but the most striking observation is how limited it actually was, only a few per cent of the urban value added (Ofer and Vinokur 1992). No doubt it has expanded as the crushing controls of the old system have been eased, but, as noted above, an illegal economy is of a distinctly different nature from an official economy, and if really subject to persecution it tends to be highly inefficient.

From November 1986 onwards 'individual labour activity' or self-employment was allowed and received some statistical attention. However, the self-employed were subjected to burdensome conditions, and their numbers soon stagnated. In 1989 only some 300,000 were involved in individual labour activity in the whole of the Soviet Union (Åslund 1991, pp. 163–7).

In May 1988 a surprisingly liberal law on 'co-operatives' was promulgated in the Soviet Union. In effect, the co-operatives were genuine private enterprises. They could be any kind of private enterprises with at least three owners. Until 1991 new co-operative enterprises were the dominant and most dynamic group of private enterprises (Åslund 1991, pp. 167–71). They have formed the base of small- and medium-sized businesses in Russia.

In 1990 private family farms were permitted. Their number rose fast until 1993, when there were 270,000, but then stagnated and dropped (Åslund 1995, p. 262). Joint ventures with foreign companies were allowed in 1987, but they have remained much less important than purely Russian private enterprises (Åslund 1991, p. 144). Finally, a Russian Law on Enterprises and Entrepreneurial Activity was adopted on 25 December 1990, and it allowed all kinds of enterprises. The boundaries between different private enterprises became less strict and relevant, and the basic principle was that all kinds of ownership would be given equal treatment (Åslund 1995, p. 224). In principle, this was a major ideological breakthrough, as the whole Marxist distinction of various forms of ownership was thrown overboard.

Statistical categories changed with the new enterprise law. On 18 July 1991 the Russian Council of Ministers adopted a decree 'On Measures to Support and Develop Small Enterprises in the RSFSR', which defined small enterprises as enterprises employing up to 200 people in industry and construction; up to 100 people in science; up to 50 in other productive activities; and up to 15 in trade and catering. This was a pretty narrow definition, and it was confusing that the definition varied by branch, with a few additional criteria also injected. The statistics are further confused by changes in the definition of small enterprises in 1993 and again in 1995, which mainly reduced the ceilings, notably to 100 employees in industry and construction (Belokonnaya and Plyshevsky 1995).

The statistics remain unsatisfactory. Curiously, Russian enterprises do not have only one tax and registration number but several. The tax authorities have their own registration number, and so does the Unified State Register of Enterprises and Organizations, as well as a few other authorities depending on branch of the economy. As a result, statistical presentations are neither complete nor comparable, and Goskomstat complements their measures with estimates of what they think they have missed.

The longest time series is that for 'small enterprises'. We can view them as private enterprises, since no less than 96 per cent of them are non-state owned (Belokonnaya and Plyshevsky 1995, p. 9). The first headcount refers to the end of 1991. Their number more than doubled in 1992 and grew by another 54 per cent in 1993, to reach 865,000. Since then, however, the number has stagnated, though the changes in definition of small enterprises in 1993 and 1995 make it difficult to establish whether there has been an actual decline (Table 12.1).

Curiously, the number of small enterprises grew most in the years when macroeconomic instability was greatest. We can immediately draw three important conclusions. First, high inflation has not been the key constraint on the development of small enterprises. Second, nor are inter-enterprise arrears a fundamental constraint: inter-enterprise

Table 12.1. *Number of small enterprises in Russia, 1991–1997*

	1991	1992	1993	1994	1995	1996	1997	1998
Total (thousand)	268.0	560.0	865.0	896.9	877.3	841.7	861.1	862
Change (per cent)	na	109	54	4	−2	−4	2	1

Notes: At the end of the year. The definition of 'small enterprise' changed in 1993 and 1995, reducing their number by several per cent.

Sources: Belokonnaya and Plyshevsky (1995), p. 8; Goskomstat Rossii (1996), p. 13; Goskomstat Rossii (1998b), p. 10.

arrears peaked in mid-1992, when small enterprises proliferated as never before or since. Third, bank credits do not appear essential for the development of small enterprises, because their availability has increased with the stagnation of the small enterprise sector (ISARP 1996). This corresponds well with experience in Poland, where the development of private enterprise was particularly buoyant in the period of high inflation in 1989 and 1990 (Johnson 1994, pp. 285–6). This is not to say that high inflation is good for small enterprises, though it does impede the functioning of government and its regulations. A plausible hypothesis is therefore that the fundamental problem of small enterprises is government regulation and harassment, which presumably was less effective at the height of inflation.

In the 1996 statistical yearbook, the total number of enterprises in Russia was published for two years—1995 and 1996—on the basis of the new Unified State Register of Enterprises and Organizations of all forms of ownership. The 1997 statistical yearbook added the two preceding years (see Table 12.2). Table 12.2 suggests a massive and continuous rise in the number of enterprises, while Table 12.1 shows a decline in the number of small enterprises from 1994 until 1996. However, the trend in Table 12.2 must be treated with great scepticism, as the Unified State Register was being established during these years, and the reported increase in the number of enterprises is probably only reflecting improved reporting. Yet, for further developments this register should be of relevance. Hence, both tables indicate an increase in 1997—by 8 per cent for all enterprises to 2.7 million, and by 2 per cent to 844,000 small enterprises. Still, the majority of enterprises is likely to be small, and it does not seem plausible that large enterprises increased so much more than small enterprises.

Even the higher figure, which includes all conceivable enterprises, implies a rather small number of enterprises—only one enterprise

Table 12.2. *Number of enterprises in Russia, 1993–1997*

	1993	1994	1995	1996	1997	1998	1999
Total (thousand)	1,245	1,946	2,250	2,505	2,727	2,901	3,087
Change (per cent)	na	56.3	15.6	11.3	8.9	6.4	6.4

Note: At the end of the year.

Sources: Goskomstat (1998*a*), p. 323; Goskomstat (1998*b*), p. 9.

per fifty-five Russians in 1997. By contrast, Poland, Hungary, and the West in general have about one enterprise per ten people, indicating a great shortage of enterprises in general and small ones in particular in Russia. The overall numbers for the small enterprise sector in Russia are that in 1995 it possessed 3.4 per cent of the fixed assets, employed 14 per cent of the occupied labour force, produced 12 per cent of GDP, accounted for 11 per cent of all capital investments in the Russian economy, and one-third of the profits (Vilensky 1996, p. 30; Goskomstat 1996, pp. 6–7). As we would expect, the small enterprise sector appears to use capital much more efficiently and reap larger profits than large enterprises. Yet it is surprising that it currently accounts for as large a share of investments as of GDP. In comparison with small enterprises under Communism (Åslund 1985), these numbers do not suggest an all too harassed sector.

The employment of the small enterprises is very flexible. In 1995 the average employment was 13.9 million, of whom 8.9 million worked full time. This means that about 19 per cent of the labour force worked at some time in the small enterprise sector, and the average employment per enterprise was eleven full time employees (Goskomstat 1996, pp. 6–7). In short, this sector is dominated by truly small enterprises, which change orientation and employment swiftly.

At first glance, the development of small enterprises appears distinct from privatization. By 1997 Russia had as large a private sector as east–central Europe if not larger, with 70–80 per cent of the GDP arising from private producers. However, much of the development of the new private sector in Poland arose from the sale of assets by state enterprises that were facing a hard budget constraint and therefore faced a real threat of bankruptcy (Pinto *et al.* 1993). Unlike Russian enterprises, Polish enterprises could not ignore paying wages and taxes. As a result of minimal fiscal discipline, barely half the large privatized state enterprises in Russia have undertaken any restructuring (Blasi *et al.* 1997).

Still, there is a clear positive correlation between privatization and private enterprise development in cross-country regressions. Notably, those post-Soviet countries that have not privatized much, such as Ukraine and Belarus, have very few new enterprises (Åslund *et al.* 1996). In Ukraine, there is only one legally registered enterprise per eighty people, according to the enterprise register of the tax authorities, which is the most complete.

If we look into the branch structure of the Russian small enterprise sector, moreover, we find a striking correspondence with the branch structure of the privatization. Three broad areas of the economy each

Anders Åslund

Table 12.3. *Branch structure of small enterprises, 1995*

	Number of enterprises	Full-time employment
Total	100.0	100.0
Industry	14.6	29.0
Agriculture	1.2	1.1
Transportation	2.0	2.1
Construction	13.8	29.3
Trade and commerce	55.4	30.2
Science	5.8	2.6
Others	7.2	5.7

Source: Goskomstat (1996), pp. 19–20, 43–4.

account for roughly 30 per cent of the employment in small enterprises, namely industry, construction, and commerce (Table 12.3). They are also the most privatized branches of the Russian economy, and almost half the enterprises in construction and commerce are small enterprises (Goskomstat 1996, p. 57).

The major anomalies are agriculture and transportation, which are typically dominated by small private enterprises in other countries—family farms and individual truck, bus, and taxi drivers. In Russia both sectors have remained highly socialized because of political resistance. As little as 1 per cent of the agricultural employment pertains to small enterprises, and only 4 per cent of the employment in transportation (Goskomstat 1996, p. 57). The failure of the development of legal private enterprise in these two branches is also reflected in a large number of 'black' taxis and private agricultural plots. Both phenomena are important coping mechanisms for the population to hold poverty at bay, but they do not promote economic efficiency.

To conclude, regardless of poor statistics, we can extract a pretty clear picture of the small private enterprise sector in Russia in the mid-to-late 1990s. Small enterprises account for slightly more than one-tenth of employment and GDP (whereas small- and medium-sized enterprises account for more than half of GDP in all western countries). The dominant branches in the small enterprise sector are industry, construction, and commerce, but even for these sectors there are too few small enterprises by international comparison (except possibly construction). Most small enterprises have evolved in those branches that have benefited from most privatization, and there is a striking lack of small private enterprises in agriculture and transportation. The shortcomings in the development of the small enterprise sector appear serious, although they are even worse in most other former Soviet republics. Russia has far too few small private enterprises, which limits competition and thus economic growth and development.

12.3. THE NATURE OF SMALL ENTERPRISES IN RUSSIA

This statistical overview needs to be complemented with a qualitative assessment. A fundamental difference between a market economy and a command economy is that it requires an effort to sell in a market economy, whereas it is hard to find supplies in a command economy. Conversely, commodities and services are in chronically short supply in a command economy, while money is scarce in a market economy.

Thanks to a large number of polls among entrepreneurs, we have a rather clear perception of small enterprises in Russia. The polls show unequivocally that the biggest problem of small enterprises in 1994 and 1995 was to sell, while supplies presented no serious problem. The top concerns of small as well as large industrial enterprises were inadequate purchasing power of customers, their own scarcity of money, and insufficient markets for their output. Only as a fourth problem came the scarcity of raw materials and other material inputs. (Goskomstat 1996, p. 95; Alimova *et al.* 1995*a*, pp. 16–17). In all these regards, large and small enterprises had the same priorities. There was a difference, however, with regard to interest rates and investments. Large enterprises were much more concerned by high interest rates and a shortage of investments. Most small enterprises could not get access to bank credits in any case, so they did not suffer directly from the very high real interest rates (ISARP 1996).

Enterprise adjustment may be either tactical and defensive or strategic and offensive. Russian small enterprises are quite good at defensive adjustment. They are far more flexible than larger enterprises. They readily cut their input stocks, showing that they know how to economize on resources, and they adjust relatively swiftly to demand. They tend to move between different branches, depending on where they can make money.

To date small enterprises have not shown themselves particularly aggressive. While their investment is almost average by Russian standards, current Russian standards are very low. Small enterprises do not enjoy sufficient security to be able to plan for the long term. Instead, they have to improvise and be prepared to encounter new difficulties raised by both the federal and local authorities.

In Poland in the early 1980s private entrepreneurs earned at a minimum three times the average wage (Åslund 1985). By contrast, a poll among 1,628 entrepreneurs in Russia in the second half of 1994 showed that wages of private enterprises were only marginally higher than the average wage in the region (Alimova *et al.* 1995*a*, p. 18). This suggests that the conditions of small enterprises, which are predominantly private, do not significantly differ from those of state-owned enterprises. They are not seriously discriminated against or subject to dreadful legal risks.

However, among small enterprises, there is a distinct difference between those that previously were state-owned or are still closely connected with state-owned enterprises and those that are new start-ups. The latter have higher incomes and are far more dynamic than those that derive directly from the state sector, which tallies with Johnson and Lovemen's (1995) findings from Poland.

Opinion polls point to several major problems of a systemic nature. First, entrepreneurs cite uncertainty about government policy as their prime anxiety. Second, an arbitrary tax system with high tax rates on enterprises is almost as great a concern, even if large enterprises are likely to suffer more from that than do small enterprises. Third, enterprises suffer badly from multiple and arbitrary inspections and penalties on the part of local authorities, and this is clearly a rising concern.

Crime, on the contrary, does not figure as a great problem. It is perceived as relatively significant in Moscow and St Petersburg and Magadan.[2] However, if we look at the geographical distribution of enterprises, it turns out that private enterprises are most frequent in Moscow, St Petersburg, Tiumen, Magadan, and Kamchatka (Table 12.4), approximately the same places that have the greatest crime problems. Admittedly, these are also among the richest regions of Russia. Even so, it is difficult to avoid the impression that Russian organized crime is far more predictable and reliable than the Russian government—at both federal and local level. Even if crime is bad for entrepreneurship, the Russian state is far more harmful.

One of the most surprising observations from a poll among managers of small Russian enterprises in 1994 was that an overwhelming majority of the managers had never had any recourse to courts. Effectively, the state had no legal system to offer them (Alimova 1995*b*, p. 74).

---

[2] Interview with Ludmila Khakhulina, deputy director of VTsIOM in October 1996; Buev 1996.

Table 12.4. *Geographical distribution of enterprises, 31 December 1995 (number of registered enterprises per 1,000 inhabitants in region)*

	Small enterprises	All enterprises
Moscow	20	50
St Petersburg	14	23
Tiumen	10	17
Magadan	9	30
Kamchatka	9	20
Volgograd	7	16
Mordovia	2	8
Ingushetia	2	10
Tambov	2	11

Sources: Goskomstat (1996), p. 5; Goskomstat (1997), pp. 215–16, 317–18.

12.4. GOVERNMENT POLICY TOWARDS SMALL ENTERPRISES

These statistical and quantitative observations of the small enterprise sector reflect Russian government policy towards the private sector as a whole. It has gone through three distinct stages in the last decade. First comes a period of the breakdown of the command economy and *nomenklatura* enrichment, which started in 1986. A second period was the brief but conceptually important spell of *laissez-faire* under Yegor Gaidar in early 1992. It was soon succeeded by a third phase of licensing, government control, and selective support of small enterprises.

In hindsight, we can consider the last Soviet period (1986–91) one of *nomenklatura* privatization and arbitrage between the state and private sector. The primary activity of 'private' enterprises was to seize state-owned assets at low state-controlled prices and sell them at free market prices at home or abroad. The most profitable economic activity was elementary arbitrage between state-controlled prices and free market prices. In particular, oil was 'purchased' by people with connections at about 1 per cent of the world market price and sold abroad at the going world market price. In order to carry out these transactions, a large number of trading co-operatives and associations were established. Often, some transfer of state property was involved as well, but that was of much less economic consequence.

Hence, the very aim of government policy appears to have been not to level the playing field but, on the contrary, to offer privileges to some in the name of the market, while the old regulations persisted for the country at large. The private farms were similarly set up as well-endowed units for people with connections. The prime purpose appears to have been to enhance privileges for the select few of the old economic *nomenklatura*, but this was done in the name of the market. The number of private enterprises did rise at great speed, but, as most prices remained strictly regulated, while the swiftly expanding money supply boosted all free prices and brought down the market exchange rate of the rouble, price distortions grew ever wider. One consequence was that the old command economy broke down, leaving little choice but to switch to a market economy. Another was that the select few became very rich, while many Russians started perceiving a market economy as a system of greater privilege than the old Communist system.

The policy of privilege to the old economic élite was followed by an attempt at *laissez-faire*. This period was augured by a couple of laws on privatization promulgated by the Russian Supreme Soviet in July 1991. On 18 July 1991 the Council of Ministers of the Russian Federation adopted a Decree 'On Measures for the Support and Development of Small Enterprises in the RSFSR' (Belokonnaya and Plyshevsky 1995). However, the concepts were still very confused. Real *laissez-faire* towards the private enterprise sector persisted for only three months—from February to April 1992. On 29 January 1992 Yegor Gaidar managed to get a presidential decree issued on the freedom of domestic trade. It read: 'Enterprises, regardless of their form of ownership, and citizens are granted the right to engage in trade, intermediary, and purchasing activities . . . without special permission . . . Enterprises and private citizens may sell things . . . in any place of their convenience.' For three months central streets and squares of big Russian cities were awash in free entrepreneurial activities. Unfortunately, existing state shops opposed the free competition; these spontaneous 'bazaars' also ran against the Soviet demand for 'order'. In particular, there was no way for the racketeers to control all the many temporary and unorganized traders. By the end of April 1992 the restrictive forces headed by Moscow mayor Yuri Luzhkov had got the upper hand and street trade was severely restricted. Hence, racketeering, regulation, and monopoly won the day, and Yegor Gaidar's heroic liberalism was defeated (Åslund 1995, pp. 142–3). Even so, in 1992 the number of small private enterprises more than doubled, and price regulation was not reintroduced. Interestingly, this massive expansion of the number of small private enterprises occurred even though 1992 saw near hyperinflation of 2,500 per cent price increases.

The restriction on street trade was the beginning of much more far-reaching regulation of domestic trade. In effect, local licensing persisted, although the Law on Enterprises and Entrepreneurial Activity of December 1990 had formally done away with restrictions on private enterprise. In May 1993 the government gave in to demands from local authorities to license all enterprises. It issued a decree that required regional authorities to license virtually all kinds of economic activity, and it has remained in force (Åslund 1995, pp. 144–5). Since then Russia has not had freedom of enterprise even on paper. Although little public criticism is directed against this form of licensing, it is obvious that it seriously restricts competition. It appears that local authorities throughout most of Russia intentionally limit competition, generating monopoly profits in the licensed enterprises, which to some extent are then skimmed off into 'donation funds' and other local extrabudgetary funds that the local rulers can exploit more or less freely to their own taste or benefit. Moreover, for local officials, licensing facilitates the extraction of bribes. In one poll, entrepreneurs were asked the question 'Do you agree that now it is impossible to solve most economic problems without bribes to civil servants?' No less than 70.8 per cent agreed (Blinov 1996, p. 45). However, for established entrepreneurs the limitation of competition is largely beneficial, even if it harbours the threat of their own licence being withdrawn. It is one reason for their high profits. Any visitor can notice that prices of western goods in Moscow are anything up to twice as high as in Germany, which is mainly the result of monopolistic trade practices. Similarly, price differentials within Russia are enormous, even at short distances, as local authorities use police posts to impede various forms of domestic trade. A scourge for all enterprises, moreover, are the ever more frequent inspections and certifications, which appear to have increased greatly as the old bureaucracy recovered and started harassing enterprises to a far greater extent than in the early days of transition. Such inspections can concern anything, and they appear to vary considerably by place. Tax inspections are by no means the key issue (Buev 1996).

In his first speech to the State Duma, prime minister Sergei Kirienko pointed out that in 1992–7 the administrative staff of the Russian government increased by no less than 1.2 million people—almost 2 per cent of the Russian labour force (Kirienko 1998).

While bureaucracy is a problem also in the West, it is the arbitrary powers of all kinds of officials that is the real scourge of the post-Soviet state. The key problem of Russian taxation, for instance, is not that tax rates are high but that Russia has no consistent tax system. In practice, taxation is a free negotiation between tax inspectors and taxpayers, and such disputes are usually settled on the basis of political leverage. Hence, big, powerful businessmen can get away with paying minute taxes, while many small businessmen are forced out of business by arbitrary and often exorbitant penalties without having recourse to legal process against the government.

At first glance, it might appear strange that increased licensing and inspection of enterprises have also been accompanied with an enhanced emphasis on the need for government support for small enterprises. On 11 May 1993, the Russian government adopted a decree 'On Priority Measures for the Development and State Support of Small Enterprises in the Russian Federation', and this decree was followed by a law promulgated by the State Duma in July 1995 'On State Support for Small Enterprises in the Russian Federation', which led to the creation of the State Committee for the Support and Development of Small Enterprises in Russia (Belokonnaya and Plyshevsky 1995). However, these legal acts were issued in the same spirit as the licensing was introduced, namely that local authorities should intervene in private enterprises in a discretionary fashion with both sticks and carrots, such as support for select small enterprises in the form of tax relief and subsidized credits. They also emphasized 'business-incubators', offering all kinds of infrastructure for select enterprises.

Thus, the licensing, inspections, and the 'state support' served the same purpose: to give regional and local authorities more discretionary power to interfere in private enterprises. Not surprisingly, the adoption of the law purportedly in support of small enterprises in 1995 did not benefit them, because the development of small enterprises is not facilitated by far-reaching and discretionary regulation.

A first attempt at a serious policy change was made at the end of October 1997, when the liberal deputy in the State Duma, Irina Khakamada, was appointed chair of the State Committee for the Support and Development of Small Enterprises. Khakamada immediately pointed out that the main government task was to simplify the tax system and reduce tax rates. A businessman usually had to pay about 10 per cent of his total sales to a criminal protector, and he accepted that, because he got certain services from his protector, notably protection from other criminals and the tax inspection. By comparison, the government was more expensive. Its tax demands varied arbitrarily, and its services were miserable. Khakamada wanted to start by offering a low and steady tax rate and then gradually improve the service provided by the state. While businessmen were usually rather content with their protectors, they were afraid of conflicts between different gangs, competing for turf. Therefore, they would ultimately prefer to pay taxes rather than racketeering fees.[3]

A federal programme for the support of small business in 1998–9 was drafted by Khakamada's state committee on these lines. Its main lever would be the new tax code, under consideration in the State Duma in the spring of 1998. It would provide simplified taxation and low tax rates. The goal of this federal programme would be to raise the contribution of small enterprises to the GDP to 15 per cent and double the number of Russians employed by small businesses from some 7.5 million to 15 million (Program, 1998). Yet, by April 1998 it had not been adopted.

12.5. POLICY SUGGESTIONS

In the late 1990s Russia has reached a crossroads. A new policy is long overdue. Regardless of what statistics are right, it is plain that the private enterprise sector is not at all as dynamic as it could be. Russia's small enterprise sector should be several times larger to form a truly dynamic market economy.

The evidence presented above shows that the big problems facing entrepreneurs are connected with the actions of both the federal and the local government. In some branches of the economy, notably transportation and agriculture, small private enterprises are given hardly any chance of legal existence. In commerce, construction, and industry, there are numerous small private enterprises, but both their actions and competition are seriously restricted. The obvious conclusion is that both federal and local authorities must grant entrepreneurs much greater peace and leeway. Several fundamental changes are needed. Together they would amount to a new liberal economic policy of equal treatment for small enterprises. Such enterprises should neither be discriminated against, nor benefit from, special privileges.

1. The concept of freedom of enterprise must be established. Therefore, licensing of enterprises should be abolished. Local authorities should be obligated to register new enterprises within a month or so and have no

---

[3] 'Irina Khakamada' (1997) and conversation with Khakamada in Davos on 29 January 1998.

right to refuse their registration as long as a few elementary formal requirements have been fulfilled. The adoption of a law on enterprise registration abolishing the current arduous red tape should do the trick.

2. The tax system must be fundamentally reformed. First, the arbitrary invention by local authorities of taxes that are more or less designed for particular enterprises must be abolished. A federal law should determine what taxes are allowed and their maximum rates. Second, the profit tax and the value-added tax (VAT) must be properly formulated so that they become consistent. At present, banks and agriculture are effectively exempt from most taxation, while industry pays 65 per cent of all taxes. Enterprises have great problems getting VAT refunds. Third, tax rates should be brought down, notably the payroll tax of officially 38 per cent, which is often higher locally. Fourth, taxpayers must be granted legal security against tax collectors. The current practice of rewarding the tax police with a commission on what they collect is disastrous for the legal security of honest taxpayers. Taxpayers must be able to take the tax authorities to court in an effective manner. Fifth, for very small enterprises, lump-sum taxes should be more widely used. They have many advantages. As long as such taxes are not very high, entrepreneurs have a clear incentive to pay and emerge from the underground economy, because that will guarantee them legal security and a predictable tax burden. For lump-sum taxes, no bookkeeping or accounts are needed. The government does get some revenues from taxpayers who would otherwise pay little or no tax. In addition, lump-sum taxes weaken the hand of organized crime that can no longer threaten small entrepreneurs with the tax authorities. Lump-sum taxes were part of the success of the expansion of private enterprise in Poland (Åslund 1985).

The draft tax code in the form discussed by the State Duma in the spring of 1998 after a first reading, foresees a far-reaching simplification of the taxation of small enterprises. They would be relieved from a score of taxes and only pay a flat profit tax of 18 per cent, but this is still only in the legislative process. The idea is that it would be cheaper for the businessmen to pay their taxes than to pay their protectors. The next step should be that the state also offered better services than the world of organized crime.

3. Not only the tax inspections but the whole Russian system of inspections and penalties must be revised. The number of inspectorates appears excessive, and they should be cut down to the most necessary. A multitude of absurd Soviet requirements that were never meant to be imposed in reality are still on the books and should be abolished or

amended. For instance, Soviet ecological legislation was very strict, with threshold levels often one-fifth or one-tenth of western levels of pollution. The intention was to boast about the Soviet legislation, but the strictness was never supposed to be enforced. Now these norms form a base for extortion by inspectors. Sometimes new norms are introduced, more or less designed for one enterprise, so that the local authorities or the inspectors themselves are able to extract more money from the target firm. Furthermore, inspectors can visit or harass an enterprise as often as they want. Limits must be set on their discretionary behaviour.

4. Although Russian privatization has been impressive, it is by no means complete. From the perspective of small enterprise development, the two key sectors are transportation and agriculture, which remained largely socialized in large enterprises. In particular, it is an urgent task at long last to break-up the large trucking companies and auction the trucks to individual drivers, as was done in Poland. In Russia, the old Ministry of Transportation has simply been too strong to allow that. Today, a far-reaching privatization should be possible, and the large, poorly functioning trucking companies should be broken up at the same time. A large number of individual truck companies would also provide Russia with a flexible infrastructure which could greatly enhance competition and efficiency in the whole economy. Excessive transportation tariffs would be subject to real competition, and the still great regional price differentials would come under pressure. The privatization of agriculture might be of less strategic importance to the economy, but it is a large sector, which in most parts of the world is dominated by family farms.

5. In order to promote a flourishing small enterprise sector it is not enough to focus only on the conditions of small enterprises. Large enterprises, state-owned or private, must be reigned in and become subject to hard budget constraints. The huge tax debts of many of Russia's largest companies show that the Russian government has so far not insisted on bankruptcy. In Poland, many of the new small enterprises were created on the basis of assets that state enterprises were forced to sell off because they faced hard budget constraints. This process has started in Russia, but far too little has been accomplished to date. As a consequence, disinterested and incompetent managers of formerly state-owned enterprises continue to tie up large resources—machinery, equipment, premises, and labour force—in large enterprises that do not really work. These resources need to be released, and much of it should logically be transferred to the small enterprise sector. In particular, small enterprises suffer badly from shortage of premises, while the large

enterprises have abundant premises that are not used. An important improvement is the introduction of a new stricter bankruptcy law from 1 March 1998.

6. The concept of government support through discretionary treatment of enterprises should be abandoned. All discretionary tax reliefs, subsidized credits, and other business support programmes should be abolished, as they harm rather than help enterprises. Discretionary government action is just an opportunity for rent-seeking. Instead, the government should focus on establishing a liberal and stable legal environment.

7. A normal legal system must be developed. Entrepreneurs must be able to take both one another and the state to competent and impartial courts, but it will unfortunately take a long time for such courts to evolve in Russia. In the meantime the best we can hope for is that the state will at least keep out of small enterprises as far as possible.

In conclusion, Russia has got a small private enterprise sector, which after all does embrace more than one-tenth of the economy, regardless of measurement. Still, this sector remains repressed and thus much less economically efficient that it could be. Considering the importance of the small enterprise sector in any modern economy, this means that the Russian economy shows far less flexibility, innovation and dynamism than could be the case. Therefore, it is vital that the Russian small enterprise sector be given better opportunities to develop. As is plain from this analysis, the main issue is to establish real freedom of enterprise in Russia and hinder government at all levels from discretionary interventions in the small enterprises. Russian small enterprises do not need government support, but freedom and a stable legal environment to develop.

REFERENCES

Alimova, T., Buev, V., Golikova, V., and Dolgopyatova, T. (1995*a*). 'Maly biznes Rossii: adaptatsiya k perekhodnym usloviyam', *Predprinimatelstvo Rossii*, 1/1: 15–22.

——— ——— ——— (1995*b*). 'Problems of Small Business Formation in the Transition Period', *Communist Economies and Economic Transformation*, 7/1: 67–82.

Åslund, A. (1985). *Private Enterprise in Eastern Europe: The Non-Agricultural Sector in Poland and the GDR*, London: Macmillan.

—— (1991). *Gorbachev's Struggle for Economic Reform*, 2nd edn. Ithaca: Cornell University Press.

—— (1995). *How Russia Became a Market Economy*, Washington, DC: Brookings.

—— Boone, P., and Johnson, S. (1996). 'How to Stabilize: Lessons from Post-Communist Countries', *Brookings Papers on Economic Activity*, 1, pp. 217–313.

Belokonnaya, L., and Plyshevsky, B. (1995). 'Razvitie malykh predpriyatii v Rossii', *Voprosy statistiki*, 9, pp. 3–13.

Blasi, J. R., Kroumova, M., and Kruse, D. (1997). *Kremlin Capitalism: Privatizing the Russian Economy*. Ithaca: Cornell University Press.

Blinov, A. (1996). 'Maloe predprinimatelstvo i bolshaya politika', *Voprosy ekonomiki*, 7, pp. 39–45.

Buev, V. (1996). 'Kak vyzhivaet malye predpriyatiya', *Predprinimatelstvo Rossii*, 2/4: 36–44.

European Bank for Reconstruction and Development (EBRD), *Transition Report 1995*, London: EBRD.

Goskomstat Rossii (1995). *Maloe predprinimatelstvo v Rossii v 1994 godu*, Moscow: Goskomstat.

—— (1996). *Maloe predprinimatelstvo v Rossii v 1995 godu*, Moscow: Goskomstat.

—— (1997). *Sotsialno-ekonomicheskoe polozhenie Rossii, 1996 g.*, Moscow: Goskomstat.

—— (1998*a*) *Rossiisky statestichesky yezhegodnik, 1997 g.*, Goskomstat, Moscow.

—— (1998*b*) *Sotsialno-ekonomicheskoe polozhenie Rossii, 1997 g.*, Moscow: Goskomstat.

Institut Strategicheskogo Analiza i Razvitiya Preprinimatelstva (ISARP) (1996). 'Sravnitelnoe issledovanie finansovykh uslug, dostupnykh dlya mikro- i malogo biznesa', mimeo, Moscow.

'Irina Khakamada: Managers Will Free Small Enterprises from Bureaucrats' (1997). *Izvestiya*, 5 November, p. 2.

Johnson, S. (1994). 'Private Business in Eastern Europe', in Olivier Jean Blanchard, Kenneth A. Froot, and Jeffrey D. Sachs (eds.), *The Transition in Eastern Europe*, 2, Chicago: University of Chicago Press, pp. 245–90.

Johnson, S., and Lovemen, G. W. (1995). *Starting Over in Eastern Europe: Entrepreneurship and Economic Renewal*, Cambridge, Mass: Harvard Business School.

Khakhulina, L. A., and Stevenson, S. A. (1996). 'Predprinimatelskaya aktivnost naseleniya: usloviya i perspektivy', *Ekonomicheskie i sotsialnye peremeny: monitoring obshchestvennogo mneniya*, 5, pp. 34–41.

Kirienko, S. V. (1998). 'Speech at the State Duma, April 10', Washington, DC: Federal News Service.

Kolesnikov, A., and Kolesnikova, L. (1996). 'Maly i sredni biznes: evolutsiya ponyatii i problema opredeleniya', *Voprosy ekonomiki*, 7, pp. 46–58.

Ofer, G., and Vinokur, A. (1992). *The Soviet Household under the Old Regime. Economic Conditions and Behaviour in the 1970s*, Cambridge: Cambridge University Press.

Pinto, B., Belka, M., and Krajewski, S. (1993). 'Transforming State Enterprises in Poland: Evidence on Adjustment by Manufacturing Firms', *Brookings Papers on Economic Activity*, 1, pp. 213–71.

'Program on Small Business Receives Preliminary Approval' (1998). Radio Liberty, *Newsline*, Pt 1, 27 February.

Shmelev, G. (1996). 'Individualnye formy vedeniya selskokhozyaistvennogo proizvodstva', *Voprosy ekonomiki*, 7, pp. 122–8.

Vilensky, A. (1996). 'Etapy razvitiya malogo predprinimatelstva v Rossii', *Voprosy ekonomiki*', 7, pp. 30–8.

13

The Reform of Agriculture

CAROL SCOTT LEONARD AND EUGENIA SEROVA

13.1. INTRODUCTION

Russian agriculture made only limited progress towards the market economy in the 1990s. Roughly 1,000 farm enterprises out of 26,900 were restructured.[1] Most farm managers were more concerned with state orders and volume of production rather than with economic efficiency and profits, a management style which was characterized by analysts as post-Communist 'survival' behaviour (Dolgopiatova and Evseeva-Boeva 1995; Leonard 1996). 'Survival' strategies included the retention of labour, reliance on subsidies and debt write-offs, and long-term contracting. Lack of government effort to eliminate this 'survival' behaviour by deep restructuring was the main policy failure of the transition reform of agriculture in Russia.[2]

The survival behaviour of firms was unanticipated by the Russian government as an outcome of transition policies, which had been modelled on the precedents set in central and eastern European countries. The key policies were price liberalization, privatization, and de-monopolization, which were designed to stimulate a market economy in agriculture. It was also thought that a leaner fiscal regime would encourage financial

The research for this paper was supported by a grant from the National Council for Eurasian and East European Research PN 98958.

[1] 170 farms in the 1990s were restructured by auctions of land and assets according to the Nizhnyi Novgorod model, discussed below. About 10 per cent of large farms have been restructured. This includes other less formal restructuring, by which small farms separated from large enterprises. The enterprises made contractual arrangements to supply these peasant farms with equipment and services. Such arrangements generally required small farmers to contribute labour and funds to support the social sphere on large farm enterprises, which diminished their real independence (Novikov 1996 and OECD 1998, p. 15).

[2] Deep restructuring is the term used in Aghion and Carlin (1997) to distinguish strategies based on marketing, the acquisition of new capital, and new kinds of labour management, from reactive restructuring, or 'survival' behaviour.

discipline in agricultural producer behaviour. Subsidies were reduced in a general fiscal tightening in order to control inflation and reduce the budget deficit. Output was anticipated to decline for a period of time and then slowly recover, as occurred elsewhere in central and eastern Europe.

However, output steadily dropped in Russia in the 1990s. Agriculture's share of GDP declined from 15.3 per cent in 1990 to 6.7 per cent in 1998 (ERS 2000). Land under crops fell by 17 per cent between 1985 and 1995 (*Bulletin No. 1*, 1995, p. 314). Following the crisis of 1998, by the end of 1999, cultivated land fell by another 3.5 per cent (Serova 2000). Livestock production halved in value between 1990 and 1996 (*SPR* 1997, p. 6). The removal of subsidies, the retreat from mechanization, the decline in fertilizer usage, and the drop in demand for forage caused cereal production to fall by 25 per cent between 1992 and 1995 (*Current Statistical Survey* 1995, p. 27; Liefert 1997). The share of the population engaged in agricultural production meanwhile remained roughly the same, putting pressure on wages and resulting in a sharp decline in per capita income. The wage of agricultural workers relative to the average wage in the economy fell from 95 per cent in 1990 to 50 per cent in 1995 (*SPR* 1997, p. 59).

This chapter describes the transition policies and their outcomes. After tracing the background of agricultural reform by the Communist government in section 2, it describes in section 3 the transition reforms and the stalemated situation, focusing on the contradictory government policies as well as farm enterprise behaviour that defeated reform efforts in the 1990s. Some aggregative statistics of performance are presented in section 4, and a brief conclusion in section 5.

13.2. THE DECLINE: CONTINUITY FROM CENTRAL PLANNING

Current difficulties in agricultural reform partly reflect a historical decline in rates of growth. The ills of the 1990s emerged not only from transition policies but also from the consequences of Soviet agricultural collectivism (*SPR* 1997, pp. 3–4), whose failure lay in the lack of producer incentives inherent in centralized allocation of resources. The incentive problem was of concern to post-Stalin leadership. After Stalin's death, in 1953, the concept of profit was introduced. Reform measures between the 1960s and the 1980s encouraged private plots and kolkhoz markets, eased taxation, improved investment, experimented with contract prices, and created a new accounting framework to stimulate a profit orientation. Decentralization was the centrepiece of reform under Gorbachev, but it did not generate significant improvement in productivity, despite extensive capital investment (Desai 1987). By the 1980s agriculture came to absorb roughly 20 per cent of total annual investment in the economy without improving on-farm efficiency (Brooks 1990, p. 463). This is in large part because government investment went towards equalizing conditions among regions, or supplementing resources of regions which were less productive rather than rewarding superior performance (Dmitrieva 1996). Redistribution led to the concealment of production figures and wasted resources. Doses of market stimuli, in other words, were defeated by the government's regional policy, which put emphasis on equity without equal regard for incentives favouring economic efficiency.

Evidence that Soviet farming performed less efficiently than market-based agriculture was provided in numerous studies done at the time. In the early 1980s Karen Brooks and D. Gale Johnson gathered statistical evidence for comparisons from a range of countries where soil and climate conditions matched various territories in the Soviet Union. They found that Soviet farms, using relatively greater amounts of fertilizer and about ten times more labour than in climatologically similar parts of the United States, were roughly half as efficient in total factor productivity (Brooks and Johnson 1983, p. 142). How expensive Soviet farming had become before the collapse of Communism was evident in budget figures for 1986 to 1990. The share of subsidies for food consumption in the total budget rose from 19.4 per cent to 33.9 per cent, during a period when total agricultural output declined by 4 per cent.[3]

Under Gorbachev, government concern with the weak performance of agriculture turned into open political debate. The need for markets was widely recognized, although a consensus was not easily achieved on how to introduce them (Serova 1998; Van Atta 1997). In 1989 the Supreme Soviet of the USSR adopted new legislation which introduced inheritable possession of land and a land tax, as well as a law providing for the lease of land. The principles used in the division of land into shares and their distribution to members of collectives, contained in this All-Union legislation, was fleshed out in the Peasant Farms Law (1990), confirming separate entitlements

(1) to an equal share of land (*uslovnaia zemel'naia dolia*); and
(2) non-land assets (*uslovnyi imushchestvennoy pai*), which were allocated by seniority.

---

[3] Data from the Ministry of Agriculture and Food Production, 1997.

This general land reform, adopted by the Supreme Soviet of the Russian Federation on 28 February 1990, guaranteed land ownership in Russia. Farm enterprises and individuals were allowed to lease the land from the state or hold it in inheritable tenure, although the purchase and sale of land (*kuplya/prodzhia*) was not allowed. It also amended the terms of the Constitution (Article 12) to eliminate distinctions between state farms (sovkhozy) and collective farms (kholkhozy), two separate forms of farming since collectivization in the late 1920s. The main concern of the Supreme Soviet in the law of 28 February 1990, however, was less with the actual ownership of the land and assets than with the autonomy of management by collective and state farm members. That is, reform was not intended to intervene in farm operations. This is the reason that reform did not impose restructuring nor require the land actually to be distributed to farm employees.

Following the passage of this law, independent reformers (mostly agricultural economists) and members of the Supreme Soviet pursued still more legislation to allow individuals and households to set up independent farms and to organize co-operatives to provide services. In 1990–1 the success of their efforts against opposition in the RSFSR Supreme Soviet was witnessed in a series of reforms, including the Russian Federation Land Code (25 April 1991), which significantly expanded the earlier agrarian reform.[4] The Land Code of 1991, passed with difficulty through the RSFSR Supreme Soviet, permitted the purchase and sale of land with the proviso, a clause added to the Federation Constitution in 1990, that land shares could be sold after a waiting period of ten years. After the moratorium expired, however, the disposition of arable land was securely governed by property rights that were put in place, and on 29 December 1991 'peasants'[5] became the owners of these rights to land and asset shares.[6] The redistribution of rights from the state

[4] There were three major laws in 1990 forming the basis of independent farming: 'On Peasant Farms' (20 November), 'On Land Reform' (27 December), and 'On Social Development of the Countryside', which launched other legislative initiatives.

[5] This term is no longer used in official Russian documents, except to denote independent farmers, where it does not imply characteristic features of a peasantry, such as subsistence farming, which would generally be inferred from its usage in western literature.

[6] The Russian Land Code gave extensive rights to local soviets on land reform; the abolition of the soviets after the abortive coup attempt meant the transfer of authority to other state agencies. On 29 December 1991 a presidential edict on land reform, 'On Reorganisation of the Kolkhozes and Sovkhozes', was promulgated, and on 1 January 1992 a further presidential decree, 'On Urgent Measures for Realization of Land Reform in the RSFSR', which guaranteed the purchase and sale of land.

to the farm members, therefore, was less far-reaching than the reforms initiated in the CEECs, but far more significant than the sheer formality of re-registration, a reform criticized at the time as a superficial measure (Serova 1998, p. 576). By the end of 1992 farm enterprises were under local management and independent farms were spreading.

13.3. AGRICULTURAL REFORM, 1992–2000

As indicated above, the government of the Russian Federation, while granting private ownership in the reorganization of farms, reaffirmed a collectivist principle in agriculture and did not promote thoroughgoing restructuring. Re-chartering of large farms confirmed their dominance in the agricultural sector mainly in a new form, that is, joint stock associations and co-operatives, although roughly 30 per cent of the total number of farms refused to be privatized and retained their status as state farms.

Over the next few years, due to the adversity of terms of trade for the agricultural sector, which burdened all farms equally, it was difficult to determine the impact of reform simply by looking at the form of enterprise. Neither state firms nor joint stock enterprises fared well. By 1998, 84.4 per cent of the new forms of farm were loss making (*Rossiiskii Statisticheskii Ezhegodnik* 1999, p. 507).

However, without an arable land market, prevented by the moratorium, due to the cumbersome process of disposing of land and other assets, the stagnation of the farm sector was not relieved by out-migration to other sectors. Indeed, although the market for agricultural land was blocked, markets for other kinds of land, for example, subsidiary plots, expanded rapidly, and small vegetable farming was encouraged. Such land could be sold, beginning in 1992. The levy of a new land tax required a pricing mechanism, which was done by a special assessment. It was the government's intention eventually to apply the pricing mechanism to arable land as well, and this occurred before ten years passed. In December 1993, approved by referendum, the moratorium was repealed, thus permitting the sale of agricultural land (*Doklad* 1995).[7] Between 1993 and 1994, despite the removal of the prohibition, there remained a limited market for agricultural land. The parcels of allotment land sold jumped during these two years by ten times, reaching a total in 1994 of 100,133, or 10,959 hectares (*Doklad* 1995, p. 86). But few farm employees withdrew from the collective to set up as independent farmers. Out of

[7] See *Doklad* (1995), pp. 85–7.

Table 13.1. *State support for the independent farming sector (federal and regional levels, in constant 1991 prices)*

Category	1991	1992	1993	1994	1995
Migrants assistance	52	220	174	5	2
Tax relief	0	22	33	19	11
Construction	459	88	97	130	42
Loan guarantees	418	723	258	84	5
Interest-rate subsidies	0	465	275	235	39
Budgetary loans	631	0	0	16	71
Other	0	0	5	10	24
Total	1,560	1,519	842	515	194

Source: Data of MARF.

10.5 million workers in agriculture, the number of individuals choosing to set up independent farms in 1991 was 4,400 (for a total of 17,000–20,000, including family members). Of these, 75 per cent were individuals from urban areas returning to the land. The number of independent farms grew to 270,000 by 1994 but only by another 10,000 in 1995 (Serova 1997).[8]

Writing in 1994 for a World Bank report, Douglas Galbi attributed the slow rise in numbers of farmers to a decline in support for independent farmers in the budget. For seasonal credit and additional land purchases, in the spring of 1991, the Russian government had provided 1 billion roubles (about £57 million at the average 1991 exchange rate) to AKKOR (the newly formed Association of Independent Peasant Farms and co-operatives) regional offices for credits to be distributed to farmers. These credits were reduced following concern over how these funds were distributed by AKKOR, however, and by 1994 the level of support in real terms dropped by a factor of ten (Galbi 1995).[9] In a sampled survey carried out in 1992 by Karen Brooks and Zvi Lerman for the World Bank, in 1992, only 6–7 per cent of independent farmers indicated that AKKOR supplied their short- or long-term credit (Brooks and Lerman 1994, p. 88). Table 13.1 is based on data supplied by the Ministry of Agriculture, showing the actual level of government support in subsidies and credit for private farms between 1991 and 1995.

[8] In 2000 there were 261,100 independent farms. *Rossiia v tsifrakh* 2000, p. 202.
[9] The drop in funding, on the part of the government, in part, reflected criticism of AKKOR's use of government resources.

In constant prices, the total amount allocated to independent farmers declined, therefore, by a factor of eight. Faced with insufficient resources and insecure rights, independent farmers did not on average expand their holdings, and their numbers stopped growing. The government's agricultural reform policy in transition was oriented almost entirely to production on large farm enterprises.

13.3.1. *Price policy*

Extensive liberalization of prices and of foreign trade and payments occurred in the early months of 1992. Although items such as bread and milk and a dozen other principal foodstuffs were initially still widely subject to regulation, price regulation was not long lasting. Federal regulation on consumer food prices lasted only until March 1992, apart from bread prices, which were regulated until autumn 1993. Regional governments intervened for much longer, with price support provided through procurement agencies.

Liberalization of prices, combined with an initial period of local regulation, produced a profit squeeze affecting agriculture in 1992–4, as input prices jumped and important farm gate prices were held back, partly by the limited purchasing power of the populace. Federal input cost compensation, leasing, and trading credit programmes also affected the level of related prices, often not in favour of farms. Energy prices were increased (although not freed) in May 1992. The effect of the price squeeze on farm profits was almost simultaneous with the effects of the removal of state subsidies, which put pressure on farm enterprises to reduce costly inputs and release labour.

As output continued to decline, the government re-assessed levels of budgetary expenditures on agriculture, increasing some direct producer subsidies and compensation for livestock, fertilizer, machinery, pesticides, pedigree breeds, and élite seeds. The subsidies that were restored amounted to direct intervention in the production process. For example, compensation of up to 30 per cent was provided for purchases by farm enterprises of mineral fertilizer. [10] Cuts in funds for livestock at the federal

---

[10] Annual domestic use of fertilizer dropped from 14 million tons to 3 million tons between 1993 and 1994. Less compensation was actually requested than was available: only up to half of available funds were used. Constrained in western markets, fertilizer producers continue to seek government resources for domestic producers. Murtazaev, E. (1995). 'Proizvoditeli mineralnykh udobrenii nadeiutsia na gospodderzhku sel'khozproizvoditelei', *Segodnia*, 14 November, p. 9.

Table 13.2. *Ratio of agricultural transfers to GDP, for selected countries (1992)*

Country	%
Australia	0.6
Austria	2.4
Canada	1.6
European Community	2.2
Finland	4.1
Japan	1.9
New Zealand	0.2
Norway	3.9
Sweden	1.4
Switzerland	2.4
United States	1.6

Source: OECD Secretariat estimates.

level were not restored, but there was an increase in regional livestock subsidies and regional intervention through procurement. Because of lack of transparency in regional budgets and failure by the government in 1995 to include debt write-off and tax credit on budget, the level of this new spending cannot be known for certain. The level of federal subsidies was considerably lower than before 1992, according to Douglas Galbi. The overall volume of federal transfers to the agro-industrial complex was reduced between 1992 and 1994 by a factor of more than four, falling to 2.9 per cent of GDP (Galbi 1995). Actual disbursements of federal funds fell still more. An *Izvestiia* investigation into agricultural finance reported disbursements through November 1994 as 1.3 per cent of GDP (Galbi 1995), which is comparable to general levels of subsidies for agriculture in other countries (Table 13.2).

The removal of subsidies, combined with the government's failure to provide new market infrastructure, put producers in a situation that called for knowledge and institutions, which they did not have.[11] Financing agriculture in a market economy requires accessible price information, commodity exchanges, and financial mechanisms. Producers had been accustomed to soft budget constraints, as the Soviet price policy was called, and they expected this policy to continue. Soft budget constraints

[11] In 1997 centralized soft credit was introduced again. See below.

were the equivalent of abundant long-term seasonal credit and debt write-offs, a principal means of price adjustment in central planning. In the Soviet era the government had made budgetary allocations to the Agprombank to cover the bank's losses, whenever producers could not repay loans. After removing subsidies in 1992 the government continued to write off debt by special *ad hoc* decrees. From 1994 to 1995, 20 trillion roubles to the agricultural sector had been written off (*Russian Economy*— 1996, p. 65). Crop insurance, another form of soft budget constraint, was also continued, despite moral hazard problems; it was common in the late 1980s, for example, for up to 85 per cent of producers to request compensation for crop loss.[12]

In 1992 and 1993 the government continued to subsidize farms by charging a negative real interest rate on loans, 28 per cent annually for large farm enterprises and 8 per cent for independent farmers (at a time when the CBR refinance rate was over 150 per cent). The use of authorized banks for transfers turned banks into cashiers. Banks were allotted 3 per cent profit margins (paid monthly) for servicing the loans. The cashier function gave banks an incentive to use the funds and hold back the credit. Subsidized directed credit was ended in October 1993. The intention of the government in ending interest-rate subsidies was to create new financial conditions by providing loans at commercial rates, but there was still some subsidy in that the government guaranteed long-term loans at a new rate at a time when three-month loans were all that was commercially available.

Having ended soft credit, the government none the less attempted in 1995 to ease credit conditions by introducing 'trading credit'. This was allocated to producers in the form of oil products and other input supplies, which suppliers gave to producers with reimbursement in the form of tax relief. The budget was reimbursed by suppliers in a form of procurement, which was done at a contract price agreed upon before the harvest (financed by an annualized preferential interest rate of 10 per cent) and supplied after the harvest.

Government procurement of farm produce had previously been carried out exclusively through procurement agencies. In 1995, with trading credit, the procurement process was reformed. Procurement prices in 1995 and 1996 were only about one-quarter to one-half of free market prices. Even with subsidized interest rates on trading credit, by which procurement was handled, this low contract price acted as a net tax

---

[12] Information provided by Rosgosstrakh.

Table 13.3. *Share of government procurement in farm sales volume, %*

	1992	1993	1994	1995	1996
Grain	56	56	29	35	33
Beet sugar	81	75	32	21	3
Sunflower seeds	65	32	—	19	3
Potatoes	57	47	33	14	8
Vegetables	70	67	54	47	31
Cattle and poultry, in liveweight	90	88	79	60	51
Milk and milk products	95	96	93	80	71
Eggs	86	92	85	87	79

Sources: Kratkosrochnye ekonomicheskie pokazateli, Rossiiskaia Federatsiia 1996 (1997). Moscow: Goskomstat, p. 55; data from annual reports of agricultural enterprises.

on producers. Food sales shifted measurably into the shadow economy (*Russian Economy*—1996, p. 64) and amounts procured by the government declined correspondingly (Table 13.3).[13]

In 1995 bread prices in Moscow rose by about 10 per cent per month, over twice the rate of monthly inflation. The government favoured rural interests before parliamentary elections scheduled for December 1995, in contrast to the usual preference of government, which requires the urban electorate to be favoured by keeping food prices low. In 1994 and 1995 trading credit debt was restructured and plans were made to increase budgetary support for 1996. In addition, funds were allocated to seasonal credit and import tariffs were imposed, averaging a moderate 15 per cent for most items, except sugar (Table 13.4).[14]

In 1996 the government, in an important decision regarding the Agprombank, which had begun to falter, rejected the idea of re-nationalization and merged the bank with the Stolichnyi Savings Bank under the new name of SBS-Agro. This step, creating an apex structure for pooling resources of local credit co-operatives and loans based

[13] It should be noted that the figures for meat and dairy procurement are inaccurate. Procurement is officially calculated as the output of those processing agencies authorized as state purchasers. Although privatized, these processors handle not only state but also private trade. Procurement is therefore exaggerated. These figures also fail to show much about the regional situation. In some regions, Nizhnyi Novgorod, for example, state procurement of meat and poultry has been eliminated (Serova 1997).

[14] 'O merakh po stabilizatsii ekonomicheskogo polozheniia PK RF v 1996 g.', No. 135, 7 February 1996.

Table 13.4. *Tariffs on agricultural commodities, 1994–1996*

	1 July 1994	1 July 1995	15 May 1996
Import tariffs in %			
Meat, meat products	8	15	15 (not less than 0.15 ECU/kilo)
Poultry	20	25	30 (not less than 0.30 ECU/kilo)
Milk, milk products	15	10–20	10–20
Grain	1	1	5
Berries and fruit	1	5–10	5–10
Animal fat	15	20	20 (not less than 0.09 ECU/kilo)
Sunflower seed oil	0	15	15 (not less than 0.09 ECU/kilo)
Other seed oils	0	0	5
White sugar	20	25	25 (not less than 0.07 ECU/kilo)
	1 October 1993	**1 October 1994**	**1 September 1995**
Export Tariffs in %			
Meat, meat products	70	0	0
Milk, milk products	15	0	0
Grain	70	10–25	0
High protein wheat	0	0	17
Wheat	0	0	7
Corn	0	0	10
Berries	15	0	0
Flour	0	0	10
Beet sugar	0	15	0
Animal fat	15	0	0
Seed oils	70	0	0
Sugar, ECU/ton	70	60	0

Source: Regulatory acts.

primarily on savings deposits, was intended as a new start in rural finance. Commercialization, however, was undercut by restoration of preferential loan rates in a new fund created in 1997 for agricultural producers. This loan rate was 25 per cent, the same as the refinance rate of the Central Bank. In 2000, the government owned the majority of shares in the restructured agricultural bank.

To summarize, agricultural price policy between 1992 and 1994 generally favoured the development of market mechanisms. Fiscal tightening entailed a drastic reduction in subsidies. However, efforts made first to provide a form of trading credit through input suppliers, and then to develop formal credit institutions were not adequate. Trading credit led to the development of barter, and it also encouraged monopoly in supply networks.

13.3.2. *Privatization and de-monopolization*

Beginning in 1992 the government focused on de-monopolization and privatization of downstream activities, processing and distribution, as the motor of institutional transformation in agriculture. 'Roskhleboprodukt', the government grain processing and procurement agency, was privatized and broken up into separate regional procurement agencies. By 1997 (Table 13.5) 92 per cent of meat, dairy, flour, and flax processors were privatized. In effect, the state processing system had been gradually phased out.

Restructuring of the sector was a more difficult task than privatization. Continued government procurement and vertical integration

Table 13.5. *Privatization of food processing*

	Privatized firms (%)	Firms with government part ownership in the total number of privatized firms (%)	Privatized firms in which the controlling package of shares belongs to agricultural producers (%)
Processing, total	92	18	14
Including:			
Meat	92	16	9
Dairy	92	18	16
Flour	90	35	14
Flax	83	32	11

Source: Survey data from the Ministry of Agriculture of the Russian Federation from 72 regions of Russia, 1997.

in the agricultural sector as residuals of central planning inhibited transformation of processing. Processors had difficulty locating new supply outlets, and they found profit margins squeezed by anti-monopoly policy. The territorial anti-monopoly committees at the regional level fixed rates of profit and wage levels, which weakened incentives for investment in processing. The government aimed to solve the investment problem through greater producer involvement in ownership, and in 1994 required that processors emit new shares especially for producers. But producers resisted the offer to buy shares in the financially weak processing sector, and the emission never took place (Serova 1997).

Another difficulty was the weakness of infrastructure. The story of commodity exchanges is revealing. Exchanges for grain were set up in Saratov in 1991 and Rostov-on-Don in 1992. Grain contracts were computerized, helping to establish market prices in the south of Russia even for government procurements. Exchanges began to appear across the country. However, the government undermined the exchanges by temporarily (1992) raising procurement prices above market prices; as procurement agencies attracted grain, the exchanges declined in importance. Commodity exchanges faced other barriers, too. When procurement prices again fell (1994) with price regulation continually in effect, large grain producers generally preferred to sell directly to large wholesalers rather than at commodity exchanges, including some of the larger financial groups, Inkombank, Alfa capital, and Menatep, which purchased grain and sunflower seeds through their own regional organizations and oil companies, which also purchased grain through private channels directly from large producers. In short, the movement of grain was drawn into Russia's improvized barter network, rather than clearing markets for cash.

By 1996 many of the restrictive conditions in which producers were operating eased. Commodity markets in grain began to function again. In 1997, an agricultural futures market opened in Nizhnyi Novgorod, where thirty-two grain contracts were on offer for 320 tons of third-grade wheat from the 1997 harvest.

Vegetable markets have, from the onset of transition in 1992, been less constrained by government intervention than have grain markets. Commodity exchanges for vegetable production, supplied mainly by households and small-scale farms, spread rapidly, especially in the south of Russia. Trade on these exchanges tends to be conducted by independent traders, both firms and individuals.

13.3.3. *Farm privatization and restructuring*

On the farms themselves, the government's key policy move was privatization through re-registration of farm enterprises, as discussed above. Re-registration was highly successful in de-nationalizing over 85 per cent of the land. Shares became transferable to non-members as well as members of the former collective or state farm (Serova 1998). However, because opposition remains fierce to land markets, especially in parliament, operational restrictions on the sale of land remain, even though the right to own land is guaranteed by the constitution and by presidential decree, 'On the Regulation of Land Relations and the Development of Agrarian Reform in Russia' (27 October 1993).[15] The ambiguity of the situation is a disadvantage to those most interested in acquiring land, that is, independent farmers. They have not in practice been able to use land as collateral, obtain deeds to their plots, or easily acquire new land (Stephenson 1995).

The operational difficulty in selling agricultural land is in part a consequence of lack of popular support for reform (Leonard 1996). Between 1993 and 1998 there was a succession of draft new land codes, but the parliamentary and government positions diverged so significantly on the issue of land sales that there was no agreement. In 1996 the government recommended a draft which allowed severe restrictions on the transfer of land so as to exclude, for example, the right of 'physical persons' (that is, individuals as opposed to 'juridical entities') to buy land. Russia's Choice (the reformist party led by Yegor Gaidar) submitted another, more liberal, draft. Neither draft was accepted by parliament, which produced several drafts in 1997 and 1998, in which the term 'land ownership' remained, but land transfers were not allowed. Both parliamentary drafts were vetoed by the president, the last in 1998.[16]

---

[15] Russian law is code-based, and land regulations are determined by the land code passed in 1991. However, since that code contradicts many parts of the constitution of 1993, the president revoked by decree nearly 50 articles of the 1991 land code (although the code itself remains in force) and called for the development of a new land code not in contradiction with the constitution. The most prominent requirement is the right to private ownership of land, as guaranteed by the constitution, that is, the right for entities and individuals to purchase, sell, and mortgage agricultural lands.

[16] Both parliamentary drafts would have ended rights for private farmers and for agricultural entities to mortgage private plots. They envisioned leasing arrangements rather than ownership for those collective farms not yet fully privatized. Farmers who owned land, according to these drafts, would have been deprived of the right to sell it, being obliged to return it to state or municipal ownership on terms set when it was acquired.

Lacking parliamentary support for a new federal land code permitting land sales, government reformers nevertheless went forward at a regional level. The regional government of Nizhnyi Novgorod found international funds for a western-style experiment in land privatization, by which land and other assets were auctioned.[17] Publicly endorsed by Prime Minister Victor Chernomyrdin in 1994, the experiment was adopted by the federal government as its national programme. Over the following four years roughly 1,000 farms were restructured along the lines of the Nizhnyi Novgorod pilot project. This, however, still left 16,000 un-restructured joint stock companies, 6,000 kolkhoz- and 3,600 sovkhoz-type farms, which retain their former management structure and farm labour work force (Leonard 1996).

The survival of large farm enterprises inhibited countrywide productivity improvement on large farms as well as the development of small independent farming. As noted above, the government initially gave independent farms a package of privileges, including a five-year tax holiday and preferential credit. It also helped to organize a new farm credit system through the association of independent farmers (AKKOR). But by 1998 independent farms remained relatively few in number (278,600) and small (44 hectares on average), due in large part to the drop in government support by 1994 (see Table 13.6a). Arable land in Russia remains overwhelmingly the asset of large farms of up to 15,000 hectares (Brooks and Lerman 1994, p. 45; *RSE* 1996, p. 552). Independent farms had barely begun to make an impact on overall output (Table 13.6b).

Independent farms were, however, economically sustainable. The typical family farm was not a subsistence farm. Between 70 per cent and 80 per cent of sales were of crop products, by contrast with farm enterprises, which continued to sell mainly (over 40 per cent) livestock

[17] The scheme was roughly the same as in industry. Within the boundaries of one firm, an inventory of land and assets was taken, with all workers and pensioners receiving certificates of rights to assets and land shares. Evaluation took place with 'points' as units for hectares and rouble shares. The share received by an individual depended upon salary and seniority. Nominal owners became property holders in the course of an auction, where the mode of payment was the certificate of right of ownership. Certificates were good for buying plots, forming co-operatives or partnerships, or selling to a neighbour. The first land auction was 9 November 1993 at the farm Pravdinskii in Balakhninski raion. On an area of 3,600 hectares, 12 farms were set up. By 1995 29 similar experiments had been carried out using this model. Part of the difficulty in judging the success of this method is that most of the farms petitioning restructuring did so because of financial insolvency. Ishkova, E. (1995). 'Zemlya stanovitsia predmetov torgov, no eshche ne predmetom kupli-prodazhi', *Finansovye izvestiia*, 30 March.

Table 13.6a. *Number and size of peasant (independent) farms (based on data for the beginning of the year)*

Year	Number of farms	Average size of land allotment in hectares
1991	4.4	41
1992	49.0	42
1993	182.8	43
1994	270.0	42
1995	279.2	43
1996	280.1	43
1997	278.6	44

Source: SPR (1997), p. 107.

Table 13.6b. *Share of total agricultural output produced by independent farms, %*

	1991	1992	1993	1994	1995	1996
All	—	1	2	2	2	2
Grain	0.2	2.1	5.2	5.1	4.7	5.0
Sunflower seed	0.4	5.8	9.9	10.2	12.3	11.0
Beet sugar	0.03	2.0	3.9	3.5	3.8	3.0
Potatoes	0.3	0.8	1.0	0.9	0.9	0.9
Meat (live weight)	0.1	0.7	1.1	1.4	1.7	1.8
Milk	0.1	0.5	1.1	1.3	1.5	1.8

Sources: AKRF (1994), pp. 29–43; SEP (1997), pp. 50–6; *Osnovnyie pokazateli funktsionirovaniia APK v 1995 godu* (1996); *Statisticheskii biulleten'* No. 1 (APK) (1996), Moscow: Goskomstat, pp. 20–1.

products, despite reporting that livestock production was unproductive. These findings by Brooks and Lerman in 1992 were confirmed for later years by official government data published in 1997 by the Working Centre for Economic Reform (WCER) in Moscow. According to the WCER, the allocation to cash crops increased on independent farms from 61 per cent of arable land in 1991 to 71 per cent in 1996 (SPR 1997, p. 11). Crop yields, according to the Brooks–Lerman sample, were indistinguishable on private farms and farm enterprises, but milk yields achieved by private farmers were significantly higher than those achieved by collective farm enterprises (Brooks and Lerman 1994, pp. 77–89). Nearly all private farms were involved in joint activity for the use of services. However, of this co-operative activity, between 30 per cent and

Table 13.7. *Share of gross agricultural output produced by private plots, %*

	1991	1992	1994	1995	1996
Agricultural output	28.0	33.0	38.0	43.0	46.0
Grain	—	0.5	0.7	0.9	0.0
Beet sugar	—	0.2	0.7	0.0	1.0
Sunflower seed	—	1.2	1.6	2.0	2.0
Potatoes	72.0	78.0	88.1	89.9	90.0
Vegetables	46.0	54.7	67.0	73.0	77.0
Meat	31.0	35.3	42.9	47.8	51.0
Milk	26.0	31.4	38.7	41.7	45.0
Eggs	—	26.1	28.8	30.0	31.0

Sources: AKRF (1994), pp. 31–43; SEP 1996.

40 per cent involved co-operation with other private farmers for production, marketing and input supply, use of machinery, and supply or access to credit. All in all, there is little to indicate that independent farming was less successful at the farm level than collective farming in the 1990s, even though large increases in numbers of independent farms were not observed.

The private plot, or household subsidiary plot, inherited from the Soviet era, was also important for agriculture in the 1990s. Its overall contribution was up to half of agricultural output (Table 13.7). Labour and other resources were drawn away from the farm enterprise as farm members channelled them into their commercially oriented private plots (Tarasov 1996).

13.4. AGGREGATE PERFORMANCE

13.4.1. *Output decline and emerging markets*

By some measures, collective and state farm enterprises had made gains in productivity over the 1970s and 1980s, although even these were less than advances due to biotechnological applications during the same period in the USA and western Europe (Table 13.8).

More important, Russia's 'productivity gains' were in fact due to increased inputs, arguably the 61 per cent rise in use of electrical energy in agriculture, the 22 per cent increase in use of mineral fertilizers, and the 40 per cent rise in capital investment. Total output grew during this time by only 12 per cent (Serova 1997) and total factor productivity declined (Figure 13.1). Capital investment, in particular, was wasteful.

Table 13.8. *Agricultural productivity in selected countries*

	World	Western Europe	USA	Canada	USSR	RSFSR
Production potential of grains, in centners/hectare						
1970	17.8	27.9	31.6	21.1	15.7	13.7[a]
1989	26.5	45.8	44.8	21.2	18.9	16.1
1989 as % of 1970	149	164	142	100	120	118
1994	—	45.4	56.2	25.4	—	14.4
Annual average yield of milk per cow, kilos/year						
1970	1,932	3,269	4,423	3,256	2,110	2,328
1989	2,127	4,059	6,533	5,806	2,555	2,773
1989 as % of 1970	110	124	148	178	121	119
1994	—	4,831	7,277	6,077		2,162

Note: [a] Average for 1971–5.
Sources: Serova (1977) *RSM* (1996) pp. 288–90, 313–15; *Narodnoe khoziastvo SSSR v 1985* (Moscow 1986); *Narodnoe khoziastvo SSR v 1990 g.* (Moscow 1991); Financy I statistika 1986; *World agriculture/Trends and indicators/1970–1989* (1990). Washington, DC: USDA.

It was not unreasonable, therefore, for capital outlays on agriculture to decline in the transition (Table 13.9) as part of a drive for greater efficiency. However, the actual fall was excessive. Tractor and agricultural machine production fell by 41 per cent, mineral fertilizer production by 17 per cent, and herbicide production by 21 per cent (*Russian Economy in 1996*, 1997, p. 77). Decline in the use of these inputs also shows up in resource use data (Tables 13.10a and 13.10b).

The government's investment programme for farms aimed to be market-oriented. A scheme for leasing agricultural machinery was set up in 1994 in an effort to alleviate the shortage and deterioration of equipment, while encouraging production and sales. One trillion roubles were put into a leasing fund. The government ordered (mainly from its former state suppler, the newly privatized Rosagrosnab), large machinery for distribution to regional authorities, who in turn made decisions about which producers were to receive help. This assisted Rosagrosnab in obtaining a monopsony position. It charged a 5 per cent service fee for co-ordinating and marketing on behalf of machinery producers. Looking, by 1996, even more like central planning, 'leasing' funds were also used to distribute fertilizer, seeds, and pedigree cattle to large farms,

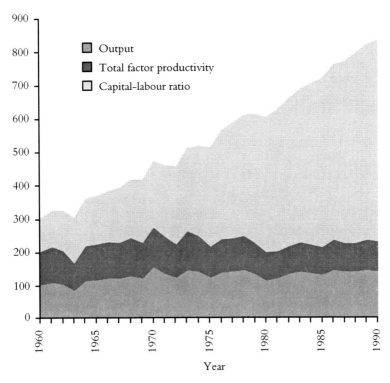

Figure 13.1 *Agricultural productivity measures, 1960–1990 (index: 1960 = 100)*

Table 13.9. *Government investment in agriculture*

	1991	1992	1993	1994	1995
Government capital investment in agriculture in constant prices, base year 1991 (billions of roubles)	37.4	13.0	8.1	3.9	na
Tractors supplied to agriculture (thousands)	131.4	65.4	39.5	22.1	9.7
Grain combines supplied to agriculture (thousands)	31.7	17.3	14.3	9.1	4.4

Source: *SR* (1995), pp. 34, 37.

Table 13.10a. *Fertilizer use in the agricultural sector (1985 = 100, in %)*

	1985	1990	1995	1996	1997
Use of mineral fertilizers, per hectare	100	97	20	20	21

Source: SR (1998), p. 45.

Table 13.10b. *Purchase of oil products by agricultural enterprises (millions of tons)*

	1985	1990	1995	1996	1997
Benzine for automobiles (total)	18.5	11.3	3.3	2.9	2.8
Including by direct trade	—	—	0.4	0.3	0.4
Diesel energy (total)	23.5	20	7.1	6.2	4.0
Including by direct trade	—	—	0.8	0.6	0.5

Source: SR (1998), p. 48.

crowding out competition in highly profitable upstream activities (Serova 1997).

As capital investment programmes, while limited in total amount, were not designed to change system features, output declined sharply. Between 1990 and 1997 Gross Agricultural Output (GAO) declined by 36 per cent (SR 1998, p. 32).

13.4.2. *Farm size and productivity*

Attempts to relate productivity data to performance by size of farm in transition Russia are hazardous. At first glance, statistics seem to show that large farm enterprises did not perform at a level that merited government support. By 1997 90 per cent of the large farm enterprises were in arrears in payment of wages (SPR 1997, p. 60). However, conditions in the agricultural sector in the 1990s combined with lack of reliable information make the judgement tentative. A closer look at trade and supply networks and the location of storage facilities on large farms, for example, points up potential advantages that large farms might have if they were technologically transformed and well run. They have the advantage of usable equipment in their inventory, which medium and small farms lack. The cost of buying all new equipment, of searching for suppliers, and of marketing small quantities may be prohibitive for medium- and small-sized farms. Large farms have the further advantage of political networks and access to preferential credit on a discriminatory basis.[18] It seems unlikely, in view of the well-organized political network of farm directors and strong path dependence that generally governs the use of agricultural technology, that reformers will succeed in generating favourable conditions in the Russian Federation for small and medium-scale farming (Ruttan and Hayami 1990; David 1988; Serova 1998). The well-being of large farms is viewed by the government as decisive in the recovery of key industries, particularly chemical fertilizer and farm machinery producers.[19] It is also viewed as decisive in resolving food security issues. The government has shown no inclination to stop supporting these heirs to the former Agro-Industrial Complex (APK), where vertically integrated production linked livestock and crop production, and facilitated flows of capital into upstream and downstream activities. This point was underscored in the late 1990s by a new legislative initiative permitting price intervention.[20]

13.5. CONCLUSION

Conditions are insufficiently transparent to hazard a clear statement about the prospects for Russian agriculture (Havlik 1996). On the supply side, poorly developed infrastructure and restraints on processing limited domestic sales (RE 1996). On the demand side, consumer preference for imports was clearly demonstrated in the mid-1990s, as Table 13.11 illustrates. Nevertheless, there were also positive indicators that the government was not retreating from reform and that market arrangements will strengthen in the years ahead. Transition effects by 1996 included the widening of private channels of trade; 80 per cent of grain marketed by 1996 was marketed by private channels, up from 66 per cent in 1995. Most vegetables produced were sold in 1996 through private channels rather than through state agencies (RE 1996, p. 61). The only sector in which private trade had not expanded by then was the livestock sector.

[18] The distribution to producers of trading credit, among other forms of support, is at the discretion of regional government authorities.

[19] As an example of the way in which machinery production has been affected, the factory 'Rostsel'mash' produced 85,000 grain combines a decade ago, and in 1995, 8300.

[20] Yeltsin in mid-1997 signed a new law on price parity for industrial and agricultural products and on agricultural subsidies and compensation from the federal budget, as well as state regulation of insurance in the agricultural sector. The law authorizes commodity price intervention (*Interfax* 23 July 1997).

Table 13.11. *Share of imports in average consumption of food products per person, %*

	1994	1995
Meat and meat products	12.8	18.7
Milk and cream	—	10.6
Fish and fish products	5.5	14.9
Oil	21	41.4
White sugar	—	28.9

Source: calculated by the Agrarian Policy Division at the Institute for the Study of the Economy in Transition (IET) from data provided by Goskomstat of the Russian Federation on foreign trade tariffs.

The crisis of 1998 did not significantly affect overall trends, although afterwards there was a greater tendency towards government price intervention, especially in regard to grains. Processing (except in the livestock and dairy sectors) benefited from the surge in investment following the devaluation of the rouble, which led to the substitution of domestic for imported food products as well as increased demand (Serova 2000).

In conclusion, the progress made in decentralizing the management of Russian agriculture was due to in large part to the ending of procurement and planning policies of the Soviet era. Federal government procurement dropped significantly and, although regional government procurement increased in some regions, the levels of support remained well below the EU average. Central planning-based regionalization broke down, and new market infrastructure emerged in some sectors, for example, vegetable production and marketing. Some nationwide wholesale markets for poultry and meat also began to function in the 1990s.[21] The progress can also be credited to the introduction of laws allowing private property in land, even though procedure for buying and selling still lack the necessary clarity. That the number of independent farms remained fairly steady in the period 1994–7, at 279,000–280,000, shows that private farming was accepted in rural areas. Independent farming was attractive and viable, despite the profit squeeze, since entries balanced exits and the average size of farms increased. Credit

---

[21] By 1997 the share of small wholesale markets in the aggregate volume of purchases by the population was 30 per cent for meat and poultry (*Russian Economy in 1996*, 1997, p. 85; Serova 1997).

co-operatives and other savings facilities for small producers made a start after 1995.[22]

These points support the common understanding among reformers and foreign observers that the agricultural sector is improving (Leonard 1997). Farm management is recognized as the priority issue. Technical advancement should be supported to serve as a catalyst to facilitate the substitution of power and machinery for labour on small and medium-size farms (Ruttan and Hayami 1990). However, without improved farm management, or deep farm restructuring, such improvement cannot be anticipated.

Also critical is further legal and regulatory reform. The passage of a new land code has been held back by controversy over provisions introduced in the parliamentary version to prevent the buying and selling of arable land, which means that implementation of presidential decrees confirming this right is not yet widespread. There is also considerable popular rejection of the idea of buying and selling arable land, which fuels parliamentary opposition. This opposition need not, however, be explained as adherence to traditional cultural values as much as to the setting up of independent farms under uncertainty about the costs of doing so, including retraining as well as start-up capital costs (Leonard 2000). So further measures might well diminish this opposition if they were directed towards providing subsidies for retraining, loss offsets, and other targeted, non-distortionary rural income support for those who undertake the move to private farming. If the numbers of independent farmers increased, then parliamentary support for buying and selling land might also increase, leading to an important development in a new land code permitting it.

By 1997 consumer price regulation in the major cities had been eliminated, even though it was not ended in some smaller cities in some regions. After the financial crisis, however, local authorities again raised trade barriers and imposed fixed prices. The shift in policies fuelled suspicion and resistance to the government decrees, a problem particularly important in regard to property rights in arable land. Lack of trust in government is part of the legacy of the collapse of Soviet-era governments across central and eastern Europe (Davidova and Buckwell, 1996, p. 8). This situation is in contrast to the process of agrarian reform in China, where the government focused on encouraging producer autonomy and private channels of trade from the beginning. In Russia, as in

---

[22] They numbered about 100 in 1996 (Ianbykh and Serova 1996).

Ukraine and other states of the FSU, government intervention—and the lack of clear regulations—has prevented the full realization of producer autonomy and thus also slowed down the effectiveness of agrarian reform.

REFERENCES

Aghion, P. and Carlin, W. (1997). 'Restructuring Outcomes and the Evolution of Ownership Patterns in Central and Eastern Europe', in Salvatore Zecchini (ed.), *Lessons from the Economic Transition*, Dordrecht: Kluwer Academic Publishers, pp. 241–62.

Agrarian Institute (1993). 'Agrarnaia Reforma v Rossii', *Zemlia Rossii*, No. 1.

Agricultural Policies, Markets and Trade in the Central and Eastern European Countries, Selected New Independent States, Mongolia and China, Monitoring and Outlook (1995). Paris: OECD.

Agropromyshlennyi kompleks Rossiiskoi Federatsii (AKRF) (1994). Moscow: Goskomstat.

Bates, R. (1990). 'Macropolitical Economy in the Field of Development', in J. E. Alt and K. A. Shepsle (eds.), *Perspectives on Positive Political Economy* NY: Cambridge University Press, pp. 31–56.

Bezrukov, S. (1995). 'Nizhegorodskaia model': ne panatseiia ot vsekh zol, a shans dlia rossiiskogo sela', *Nezavisimaia krestianskaia gazeta 'Rossiiskii fermer'*, 11 August.

Boiko, B. (1995). 'Russian Landownership—An Endless Story', *Kommersant-Daily*, 2 September, p. 2 (translated and condensed in *Commersant Daily* [CD], 47/37: 12–14).

Brooks, K. (1990). 'Agricultural Reform in the Soviet Union', in *Agricultural Development in the Third World*, pp. 459–79.

—— and Johnson, D. G. (1983). *Prospects for Soviet Agriculture in the 1980s*, Bloomington, Ind.: Indiana University Press.

—— and Lerman, Z. (1994). *Land Reform and Farm Restructuring in Russia*, World Bank Discussion Papers, No. 233, Washington, DC: World Bank.

Browning, L. (1995). 'Harvest Catastrophes Sow Seeds of Discord', *Moscow Times*, 21 November.

Chandavarkar, A. (1992). 'Of Finance and Development: Neglected and Unsettled Questions', *World Development*, 20/1: 133–42.

Cooper, R. N., and Gács, J. (1997). *Trade Growth in Transition Economies: Export Impediments for Central and Eastern Europe*, Cheltenham: Edward Elgar, for IIASA.

Current Statistical Survey (1995), 10. Moscow: Goskomstat.

Dasgupta, P. (1995). *An Inquiry into Well Being and Destitution*, Oxford: Clarendon Press.

David, P. (1988). 'Path Dependence: Putting the Past into the Future of Economics', Technical Report 533, The Economic Series, Institute for Mathematical Studies in the Social Sciences, Palo Alto, Cal: Stanford University.

Davidova, S., and Buckwell, A. (1996). 'Agricultural Reform', in *Privatisation of Agriculture in New Market Economies: Lessons from Bulgaria*, Boston, Mass.: Kluwer Academic Publishers, pp. 1–22.

Davis, E. Philip (1995). *Debt, Financial Fragility, and Systemic Risk*, Oxford: Clarendon Press.

Desai, P. (1987). *The Soviet Economy: Problems and Prospects*, Oxford: Blackwell.

Dmitrieva, O. (1996). *Regional Development: The USSR and After*, London: UCL Press.

Dolgopiatova, T., and Evseeva-Boeva, I. (1995). 'The Behaviour of Russian Industrial Enterprises Under Transformation', *Communist Economies and Economic Transformation*, 7/3, pp. 319–31.

Eicher, C., and Staatz, J. (eds.) (1990). *Agricultural Development in the Third World*, 2nd edn., Baltimore, Md.: The Johns Hopkins University Press.

ERS (www.ers.usda.gov/briefing/Russia/data_ataglance.htm) 14 March 2001.

Farm Restructuring and Land Tenure in Reforming Socialist Economies: A Comparative Analysis of Eastern and Central Europe (1995). World Bank Discussion Paper 238, Washington, DC: Euroconsult Centre for World Food Studies of the World Bank.

Fernandez, R., and Rodrik, D. (1994). 'Resistance to Reform: Status Quo Bias in the Presence of Individual-Specific Uncertainty', in *Monetary and Fiscal Policy*, pp. 371–86.

Food and Agricultural Policy Reforms in the Former USSR: An Agenda for the Transition (1992). Studies of Economies in Transformation, Paper 1, Washington, DC: The World Bank.

Galbi, D. (1995). 'The Significance of Credits and Subsidies in Russian Agricultural Reform', Policy Research Working Paper 1441, March, Washington, DC: The World Bank.

Gosudarstvennyi (Natsionalnyi) Doklad 'O Sostoianii i ispol'zovanii zemel' Rossiiskoi Federatsii za 1994' (1995). Moscow: Komitet Rossiiskoi Federatsii po zemel'nym resursam i zemleustroistvu, March (Doklad).

Havlik, P. (1996). 'Uncertain Recovery Prospects in Russia', *Economics of Transition*, 4/2: 459–69.

Hill, B. (1996). *Farm Incomes, Wealth and Agricultural Policy*, Avebury, UK: Ashgate Publishing Limited.

—— (1990). 'In Search of the Common Agricultural Policy's agricultural community', *Journal of Agricultural Economics*, 41/3: 316–26.

Ianbykh, R., and Serova, E. (1996). 'Sel'skokhozaistvennyi kredit: sostoianie i perspektivy razvitii', Working paper, Institute for the Economy in Transition.

Interfax Food and Agriculture Report (1997). FBIS Transcribed Text, FBIS-SOV-97-204 23. July.

Josling, T. E. (1974). 'Agricultural Policies in Developed Countries: A Review', *Journal of Agricultural Economics*, 25/3.

Komitet Rossiiskoi Federatsii po zemel'nym resursam i zemleustroitstvu (1995). *Gosudarstvennyi (natsional'nyi) doklad o sostoianii i ispol'zovanii zemel' rossiiskoi federatsii za 1944. [Doklad]*

Korbut, L., and Serova, E. (1995). 'Foreign Trade in Agricultural Produce and Foods in Russia', Moscow: Banking Business Center Concern, August.

Kuznetsov, V. V. (ed.) (1996). *Organizatsionno-ekonomichekie faktory razvitiia regional'nogo APK*, Rostov-on-Don: Vserossiiskii NII ekonomiki i normativii.

Land Privatisation and Farm Reorganisation in Russia, Annexes (1995). Washington, DC: International Finance Corporation.

Leonard, C. S. (1995). 'The Budget of the Russian Federation for the Agricultural Sector, 1995–1996', Memorandum presented to the Ministry of Finance, Department of Agriculture and Food Processing, July.

—— (1996). 'Farm Enterprise Survival Strategies in the Russian Transition', Paper presented at All Souls College, November.

—— (1997). 'Rural Poverty and Agrarian Policy in Transition Countries', Paper presented to a workshop organized by the United Nations Development Program, January 1998.

—— (2000). 'Rational Resistance to Land Privatisation in Russia: The Response of Rural Producers to Agrarian Reforms in Pre- and Post-Soviet Russia', *Post-Soviet Geography and Economics* 41/8, pp. 605–20.

—— and Serova, E. (1996) 'Braking and Entering: Transition to a Market Economy in Agriculture, 1992–1995', presented at the American Economics Association Meeting, San Francisco, 8 January.

Liefert, W. M. (1997). 'Grain Sector Reform and Food Security in the Countries of the FSU', in *Cereals Sector Reform*, pp. 93–107.

McKinnon, R. I. (1984). *Financial Repression and Economic Development*, Taipei: Academia Sinica.

—— (1993). *The Order of Economic Liberalisation: Financial Control in the Transition to a Market Economy*, 2nd edn., Baltimore, Md.: The Johns Hopkins University Press.

Meliukhina, O. (1994). 'Russian Agriculture and Agrarian Policy in 1994', Report prepared for the World Bank (Washington, DC: The World Bank).

—— (1995). 'Regionalizatsiia agrarnoi i prodovol'zstvennoi politiki Rossii v 1992–1994 godakh', *Predprinimatel'stvo v Rossii*, 3–4, pp. 26–9.

—— and Serova, E. (1996). 'Otsenka urovnia gosudarstvennoi podderzhki sel'skogo khoziastva: primenimost' standartnykh metodov v perekhodnoi ekonomike', *Voprosy ekonomiki*, 7 (1996), pp. 101–11.

Narodnoe khoziastvo SSSR v 1989 g. Statisticheskii ezhegodnik (1990). Moscow: 'Financy i Statistika'.

Nove, A. (1969). *An Economic History of the USSR*, Middlesex: Penguin Books.

Novikov, V. (1996). 'Institutional Transformations in Agriculture', *Moskovskii ekonomist*, 12 (December), pp. 69–75, FBIS Transcribed Text, FBIS-SOV-97-012.

Pack, H., and Westphal, L. E. (1986). 'Industrial Strategy and Technological Change: Theory Versus Reality', *Journal of Development Economics*, 22: 87–128.

Penny, D. H. (1983). 'Farm Credit Policy in the Early Stages of Agricultural Development', in *Rural Financial Markets in Developing Countries*, pp. 58–66.

Persson, T., and Tabellini, G. (1994). *Monetary and Fiscal Policy*, vol. 2, Cambridge, Mass.: MIT Press.

Pischke, J. D. Von, Adams, D. W., and Donald, G. (eds.) (1983). *Rural Financial Markets in Developing Countries*, Baltimore, MD.: The Johns Hopkins University Press.

Pitzer, J. S., and Baukol, A. P. (1971). 'Recent GNP and Productivity Trends', *Soviet Economy*, 7/1: 46–82.

Review of Agricultural Policies: Hungary (1994). Centre for Co-operation with the Economies in Transition, OECD [*OECD* 1994].

Review of Agriculture Policy and Trade Developments in Russia (15 September 1995). An Hoc Group on East/West Economic Relations in Agriculture, OECD.

Review of Agricultural Policies: Russian Federation (1998). Paris: Organization for Economic Co-operation and Development (OECD).

Rossiiskii Statisticheskii Ezhegodnik: statisticheskii sbornik (1996). State Committee for Statistics of the Russian Federation, Moscow: 'Logos' [*RSE*].

Rossiia i strany mira, Russia and Countries of the World (1996). Moscow: Goskomstat [*RSM*].

Rossiia v tsifrakh (2000). Moscow: Goskomstat.

Russian Economy—1996, Half Yearly Report, Trends and Perspectives (1996). Institute of Economy in Transition of the Russian Academy of Sciences, Academy of the National Economy—Government of the Russian Federation [*RE*].

Russian Economy in 1996, Trends and Outlooks (March 1997). Moscow: Institute for Economy in Transition.

Ruttan, V., and Hayami, Y. (1990). 'Induced Innovation Model of Agricultural Development', in *Agricultural Development in the Third World*, pp. 97–114.

Schultz, T. (1964). *Transforming Traditional Agriculture*, New Haven, Conn.: Yale University Press.

Sel'skoe khoziastvo v Rossii (1995, 1998). Moscow: Goskomstat [*SR*].

Sel'skokhozaistvennoe proizvodstvo Rossii: Dinamika i effektivnost' (1970–1996 gody) (SPR) (1997). Moscow: Tsentr ekonomicheskoi kon'iunktury pri Pravitel'stve Rossiiskoi Federatsii.

Serova, E. (1996a). 'Disparitet tsen v Agropromyshlennom Komplekse v perekhodnykh usloviiakh', Working Paper, Institute for the Economy in Transition.

394   *Carol Scott Leonard and Eugenia Serova*

Serova, E. (1996b).'Land in Russia's Agriculture',Working Paper, Institute for the Economy in Transition.

—— (1996c). 'Polozhenie v Agropromyshlennom Komplekse', Working Paper, Institute for the Economy in Transition.

—— (1996d). 'Otzyv na 'Analiz ekonomicheskikh posledstvii reorganizatsii sel'skokhozaistvennyi predpriatii Nizhegorodskoi oblasti', Working Paper, Institute for the Economy in Transition.

—— (1997). 'Institutsionnal'nye reformy v agropromyshlennom komplekse', Working Paper, Institute for the Economy in Transition.

—— (1998). 'Institutional reforms in the agro-industrial complex', *Ekonomika perekhodnogo period: Ocherki ekonomicheskoi politiki postkommunisticheskoi Rossii 1991–1997,* Moscow: Institut ekonomicheskikh problem perekhodnogo perioda, pp. 561–648.

—— (2000). 'Vlianie krizisi 1998', Gaidar Institute, February.

Schmitz, A., Moulton, K., Buckwell, A., and Davidova, S. (1994). *Privatisation of Agriculture in New Market Economies: Lessons from Bulgaria,* Boston, Mass.: Kluwer Academic Publishers.

Schuh, G. Edward (1990). 'The New Macroeconomics of Food and Agricultural Policy', in *Agricultural Development in the Third World*, pp. 140–153.

Smetanin, N. E., Tikhonov, V. A., Lemeshev, M. Ia., and Belov, M. I. (1980). *Narodnokhozaistvennyi agropromyshlennyi kompleks. Teoriia i praktika,* Moscow: Ekonomika.

Smith, L. D., and Spooner, N. (1997). *Cereals Sector Reform in the Former Soviet Union and Central and Eastern Europe,* Wallingford, Oxon: CAB INTER-NATIONAL .

Sotsial'noe ekonomicheskoe polozhenie Rossii v 1996 godu (SEP) (1997). Moscow: Goskomstat.

Statistical Report (1995). The Interstate Statistical Committee of the Common-wealth of Independent States (Interfax), Moscow: Interfax News Agency.

Statisticheskii Biulleten' No. 1 (APK), Osnovnye pokazateli funktsionirovaniia agropromyshlennogo kompleksa Rossiiskoi Federatsii v 1994 goda (1995). Moscow: Goskomstat Rossii.

Statisticheskii Biulleten' No. 10 (APK), Osnovnye pokazateli funktsionirovaniia agropromyshlennogo kompleksa Rossiiskoi Federatsii v ianvare-sentiabre 1995 goda (1995). Moscow: Goskomstat Rossii.

Stephenson, N. (1995). 'Private Farmer Enjoys Freedom', *The Moscow Tribune,* 17 October.

Swinnen, J. F. M. (1997). *Political Economy of Agrarian Reform in Central and Eastern Europe,* Aldershot, U.K.: Ashgate.

Tarasov, A. N. (1996). 'Problems of Financing in Russian Agriculture (based on materials from a sampled survey, June 1996, 'Sources of Financing Activities of Agricultural Firms in the Transition, Rostov oblast', designed by Renata Ianbykh).

Townsend, R. (1995). 'Consumption Insurance: An Evaluation of Risk-Bearing Systems in Low-Income Economies', *Journal of Economic Perspectives*, 9/3: 83–102.

Van Atta, D. (1997). 'Agrarian Reform in Post-Soviet Russia', in *Political Economy of Agrarian Reform*, pp. 321–37.

Wangwe, S. (1993). 'New Trade Theories and Developing Countries: Policy and Technological Implications', UNU/INTECH Working Paper 7, Laxenburg, Austria: IIASA.

Williams, C. (1996). 'Economic Reform and Political Change in Russia, 1991–1996', in C. Williams, V. Chuprov, and V. Staroverov (eds.), *Russian Society in Transition*, Aldershot, England: Dartmouth Publishing Company Limited, pp. 37–54.

14

Housing and Utility Services

IRINA STARODUBROVSKAYA

14.1. INTRODUCTION

From the beginning of reforms in post-Communist countries there has been continuous debate about the relative merits and demerits of two possible approaches to change: relatively slow and step-by-step; or radical and fast. The former has been termed 'gradualist'. The second is increasingly referred to as 'shock therapy', a term traditionally applied only to anti-inflation programmes in the macroeconomic sphere.

Perhaps the most conspicuous example of the gradualist approach in Russia has occurred in the housing and communal utilities sector. The sector comprises two major components: on the one hand, construction of new dwellings and development of the housing market; and on the other, maintenance of the housing stock and provision of utility services. The former has seen fairly rapid institutional changes. The latter has followed a much slower development, because of political sensitivities. For the same reason it forms the principal focus of this chapter.

Housing and utility services are consumed by the entire population and payment for these services is an influential factor in determining the subsistence minimum income, and family budgets in general. The reform process has been characterized by maintenance of distinct tariffs for businesses and households, with household tariffs adapted to household income rather than subjected to abrupt price liberalization.

Table 14.1 shows the ownership structure in housing at mid-1990. The state owned 67 per cent of the total housing stock, with the figure reaching 79 per cent in urban areas and between 80 per cent and 90 per cent in large cities such as Moscow, St Petersburg, Ekaterinburg, and

Table 14.1. *Ownership structure of housing stock, June 1990 (%)*

Housing stock	Russia	Rural zones	Urban zones	Moscow
State-owned *of which*:	67	37	79	90
Local government	25	2	35	70
Enterprises and organizations	42	35	44	20
Co-operative-owned *of which*:	7	9	6	10
Collectives: kolkhoz, sovkhoz	3	9	1	0
Building co-ops	4	0	5	10
Privately owned	26	54	15	0

Source: Struyck, R., and Kozareva, N. (1994), p. 9.

Novosibirsk.[1] The state housing stock was divided between local governments and so-called departmental authorities in the form of enterprises and other non-municipal bodies. The latter accounted for the greater share of the housing stock (more than 60 per cent). In many cities virtually all housing was departmental. Individual home ownership was largely concentrated in rural areas and small towns. For long periods private housing construction was prohibited in cities with more than 100,000 residents. Housing co-operatives formed a significant element only in large cities.

Administration of the housing stock was highly centralized, with a vertical chain of command running from the housing and utility sector ministry of the RSFR, through regional housing and utility sector directorates, to the municipal directorates. The Soviet system allowed the centre to regulate all basic processes in the housing sphere, even though the sector was theoretically run by local councils. Enterprises providing housing and utility services lacked independence, and either were not organized as local entities at all or else had been arbitrarily consolidated (for example, at various times it became fashionable to have one single multi-function housing and utilities enterprise per city). Services were provided on a monopolistic basis not only where there was technical

[1] Struyck, R., and Kozareva, N. (1994), p. 9: In Moscow, the state owned 89.5% of the housing stock; in St Petersburg 84.4%; in Ekaterinburg 87.3%; and in Novosibirsk 80.4%.

justification (as with heating and hot water from combined heat and power [CHP] plants), but also where there was clear potential for competition (as in maintenance of the housing stock). Like other parts of the economy, the housing and utility sector went through numerous organizational changes during the Soviet period. The ministry would be transformed into a committee, regional directorates into territorial production associations, and so forth. In reality, all these changes were without substance.

Housing and utility tariffs were kept at an absurdly low level, 80–90 per cent subsidized by the state. In 1990 households' expenditure on housing (rent plus utilities) amounted to 2.5 per cent of their cash income.[2] Low tariffs in this field were viewed as one of the most important social benefits provided to the population.

Technical decisions regarding residential construction and provision of utility services were determined primarily not by the objective of optimizing the use of resources but rather by convenience for local management. Regardless of economic efficiency, priority would be given to large and concentrated facilities such as CHP plants providing the bulk of a city's heating from a single source. The possible advantages of decentralized heating supply were not assessed or even considered. One consequence was vast losses from leakages in the urban heating network. A further 30 per cent of heating and up to 20 per cent of hot water was estimated to be lost in the buildings themselves. The design of buildings made the installation of separate metering for heat and water consumption in individual apartments either far too expensive or even technically impossible.

14.2. THE APPROACH TO REFORM OF THE HOUSING AND UTILITY SECTOR

Initial policy moves towards housing and domestic utilities after the ending of the communist regime was characterized by three key features.

First, on 27 December 1991 the Russian parliament adopted a resolution on the distribution of state property among various levels of government. Housing stock in the hands of local (regional) Soviets was transferred, together with its utility infrastructure and maintenance and repair units, to municipal ownership. Further legislation provided for the departmental housing stock to be similarly transferred from enterprises

---

[2] Ibid., p. 10.

undergoing privatization to municipal ownership. Housing became a municipal item and this created the basis for all decisions on housing to become a matter for local districts and cities.

The formerly centralized and vertical control of the sector was thus replaced by a patchwork of local management structures across the country. The pace of change was highly variable. In Volgograd years elapsed from the beginning of reforms before bodies responsible for housing services even became legal entities. At the other extreme, in Novocherkassk (Rostov *oblast*) the housing services company was privatized at the outset. In most cases a few large municipal housing service enterprises (housing trusts) were set up and weakly controlled by the city administration. These enterprises combined functions of both final customers and contractors: they determined maintenance and other work schedules, collected charges from the local population, received subsidies from the local budget, and were accountable to nobody in particular. In many areas a whole hierarchy of such bodies sprang up, with only vague division of responsibilities between the various levels.

As regards supplies of water and heating, municipal enterprises were usually formed, covering both production and distribution. The resulting structures were again cumbersome, multi-layered, and with an irrational distribution of functions between the various bodies. A high degree of (local) monopolization was preserved.

Secondly, at the time of the price liberalization of 2 January 1992, it was decided to leave residential tariffs on housing and utility services untouched. They thus remained fixed at the level of 1928, when the rental per square metre of living space was set at 13.2–16.5 kopecks a month ($0.0006 at the average 1992 exchange rate of 223 roubles to the dollar).[3] In other words, virtually zero. The opportunity was thereby missed to make consumer charges the basis for financing housing and utility services, which could have created an incentive for rapid institutional change and improved resource use in this area.

Thirdly, a further obstacle to rational reform of the sector was the method of housing privatization. The relevant legislation incorporated the (virtual) 'give-away' principle, with an indefinite timetable and with no compulsion upon the owners of privatized apartments to accept a portion of responsibility for management and maintenance of the

---

[3] See Malpezzi and Ball (1991). This study shows that among the countries or cities which engage in some form of rent control, only the least developed follow the rigid, undifferentiated, and costly type of rent control policies found in Russia.

building in which their apartments were situated. So long as the owners of privatized apartments declined to form condominiums and assume ownership of the common parts of their building, the latter remained in municipal ownership even if the majority of apartments within it had been privatized. Possible alternative methods of reshaping property relations in the existing housing stock were blocked by the permanent (indefinite) right of residents to privatize their apartments.

As a result, the privatization process affected mainly the formation of the housing market, and had little influence on the management and running of the housing stock. In principle it was possible for the provision and payments for housing and utility services in buildings where all the apartments had been privatized to be identical with those in which there was not a single privatized apartment.

Following various piecemeal items of legislation in the course of 1992, the underlying policy for the sector was defined by the December 1992 law 'On the Formation of Federal Housing Policy'. A number of subsidiary measures followed in 1993 and in 1995–6.[4]

The basic strategy regarding payments for housing and utility services was one of gradually increasing consumer charges. At the same time, a system of means-tested social support was envisaged for poor households. Eligibility for assistance would arise where payments for housing and utility services exceeded the established norm expressed as a percentage of family income, and taking account also of the norm for living space per person applicable in the relevant region.[5]

---

[4] The significant items in 1993 were: Presidential Decree n. 8 of 10 January 1993 'On the Use of Various Forms of Real Estate of Enterprises in the Course of Privatization'; Government Resolution n. 935 of 22 September 1993: 'On the Transition to a New System of Payments for Housing and Utility Services and Procedures for Providing Citizens with Subsidies for Housing and Utility Service Payments'; Presidential Decree n. 2275 of 23 September 1993: 'On the Provisional Status of Condominiums'; Government Resolution n. 1325 of 23 December 1993: 'On the Financing of Various Forms of Real Estate Transferred to Local Authorities upon the Privatization of Enterprises'; Government Resolution n. 1329 of 23 December 1993: 'On Additions to Government Resolution n. 935 of 22 September 1993'. And in 1995–6: Government Resolution n. 235 of 7 March 1995 on 'The Procedure for Transferring Various Forms of Real Estate from Federal Ownership to that of the Regions and Municipalities'; Presidential Decree n. 32 of 29 March 1996 on 'The Development of Competition in the Provision of Running and Repairs Services to Municipal Housing'; Law n. 2 of 15 June 1996: 'On Condominiums'; Government Resolution n. 707 of 18 June 1996: 'On the Regulation of Payment for Housing and Utility Service'.

[5] The set norm for living space per person in each region was based on the average supply of residential housing in that region.

In 1993 it was proposed that household charges should cover all costs fully by the end of a five-year transition period, as shown in Table 14.2. At the beginning of 1996 parliament decided to extend this period from five to ten years, which meant that households should cover all housing and utility services costs by 2003. In 1999 this period was prolonged up to 2008.

At the same time reforms were directed towards lowering unnecessary costs and raising the quality of services in the housing sector. The concept envisaged a reduction in the number of management layers, and a clear distinction between the roles of customer and contractor. A key element in the new structure was a procurement service established most commonly in the form of a municipal institution. This service was to be responsible for contracting on behalf of residents with various housing and utility sector enterprises, monitoring the quality of their work, and paying for the services in question with funds accruing partly from the residents themselves and partly from budget subsidies.

In those areas where it was technically feasible, above all in housing services and maintenance, the principle was established of putting contracts out to tender. In principle municipal and private enterprises were to participate in these tenders on equal terms, with discrimination against private firms prohibited at every stage.

The legislation of 1993 and 1996 likewise established the legal basis for creating condominiums. Such bodies were to be formed on a voluntary basis, although once a decision to establish a condominium

Table 14.2. *Planned household charges for housing and utility services as per government resolution of 22 September 1993*

Year	Proportion of costs to be covered by household charges, %	Maximum share of expenditure on housing and utility services as a proportion of household income, %
1994	15–20	10
1995	20–40	15
1996	40–60	15
1997	60–80	15
1998	100	20

Source: Institute of Urban Economics, Moscow.

had been taken, membership was compulsory for all owners of residential and non-residential premises in the building. As regards entitlement to subsidies from the local budget, condominiums were to be treated equally with municipal housing, so that establishment of a condominium did not entail major changes in the level of housing and utility payments levied on the residents of a building. At the same time a condominium could obtain additional revenue from the letting of non-residential premises; and this revenue could be used for general improvements to the building. Thus reform did incorporate incentives to create condominiums and thereby speed up ownership changes in the housing sector.

Reforms also focused specifically on the departmental housing stock, in the first instance housing belonging to enterprises which were being privatized. This housing could not pass into the fixed assets of a privatized enterprise and was to be transferred to municipal ownership within a maximum of six months from the date of privatization (presidential decree of January 1993). Until the moment of transfer such housing remained on enterprise balance sheets, which meant that enterprises retained responsibility for the running and financing of the housing, but could no longer take decisions on its use or sale.

Although various policy documents had different things to say about the finance of newly municipalized housing, only two genuine financing sources were created. First, cities were allowed to levy a turnover tax on enterprises of not more than 1.5 per cent to support the housing stock and other social infrastructure. Enterprises could offset against this liability current expenditure on housing remaining on their balance sheets. Enterprises which had already transferred all their social assets to the municipal authorities had to pay the tax in full. Secondly, federal budget transfers to help finance the transfer of housing from enterprises to municipalities were instituted.

In general it was reckoned that keeping housing and utility tariffs at a low level initially, and increasing them only gradually, would reduce social tension resulting from the implementation of radical reforms in other fields, thus forming a kind of social buffer. One early study of housing sector reform summarized as follows the reasons why the government 'rejected shock therapy in the increase of apartment charges':

Firstly, from a political point of view, it was quite impossible to pass a law providing for such major changes in housing policy. Secondly, potential for speeding up the process is limited by lack of information . . . no one knows the real cost of housing upkeep in today's Russia . . . Thirdly, the gradualist approach allows more time for household incomes to increase.[6]

14.3. IMPLEMENTATION: 1994–1997

The reform strategy outlined above was implemented without significant alteration over a period of years after 1993. This section assesses its realism and effectiveness.

Most immediately apparent are the deep differences in the pace and comprehensiveness of housing reforms pursued in different cities. The key factors in these differences were the level of understanding and commitment of the local authorities, rather than material factors such as the population size or financial situation.

Some cities and regions embarked on a serious programme of housing sector reform, viewing it as the spearhead of their economic policy. In such cases management structures in housing and utilities services were reorganized, a local authority housing fund was relatively swiftly established, the creation of condominiums was encouraged, and competitive tenders for housing maintenance made their appearance. These policies characterized a rather restricted group of leaders in housing sector reform. Many cities endeavoured to bring in particular strands of reform without adopting a comprehensive strategy for the sector and, it must be said, with no clear idea of ultimate objectives. Another large group of towns and regions made no efforts at all to initiate housing sector reforms at this stage. Finally, a few regions tried to carry through restructuring policies of their own making, sometimes diverging significantly from federal policies.

Even leaving aside the numerous cases of local authorities which completely neglected housing reforms and kept the old system unchanged, implementation of reform policies varied widely in both execution and outcome in different cities. Moreover, in cases where the official reform concept was not fully accepted or imperfectly understood, the outcome was liable to be entirely at variance with the underlying objectives of the reform. The most frequent instance of this occurred where a new-style management structure (for example, the procurement services and their branches) was established without abolishing the old organization that it was meant to replace (for example, housing trusts).

[6] Struyck and Kozareva (1994).

This resulted in housing management becoming more rather than less complex and expensive, while de-monopolization and consumer interests were ignored. Another example is the attempt to increase charges without providing for allowances to protect the poorest strata of the population. This typically resulted in reform programmes being aborted half-way, while the rationale of imposing realistic charges on residents was lost from view.

However, it would be wrong to base an overall assessment exclusively on such instances of poor implementation of official policy, when in many other cases reforms have been conducted, if not absolutely comprehensively at least without major distortion of the basic concept.

The first conclusion that appears from those cities where genuine reforms were carried out is that all aspects of the reform showed themselves to be realistic and practicable. As presented in Tables 14.3, 14.4, and 14.5, reforms were successfully introduced in cities of very different size, location, and administrative status. The data suggest that the most favourable conditions for housing reform were found in the capital cities of autonomous republics and *oblasts*. However, in small cities too (less than 100,000 population), and even in one company town, it was possible with sufficient effort to get reforms started.

Most of the concerns about the practicality of various aspects of housing reform proved groundless. Thus the claim that it was useless to introduce competition in housing services because private firms

Table 14.3. *Tenders for housing maintenance and services up to 1 January 1997*

Cities	Number of tenders	Number of lots tendered for	Companies winning tenders		Number of apartments serviced on a competitive basis
			Municipal	Non-municipal	
Moscow	41	55	3	48	358,945
Nizhny Novgorod	4	9	3	6	5,098
Novosibirsk	2	7	0	7	2,992
Orenburg	3	3	2	1	7,927
Petrozavodsk	2	5	1	2	12,718
Ryazan	5	10	5	4	16,269
Volkhov	2	3	0	2	2,255

Source: Institute of Urban Economics.

Table 14.4. *Number of condominiums in various Russian cities*

Cities	January 1996	December 1996	June 1997
Moscow	18	49	57
Nizhny Novgorod	16	44	61
Ryazan	29	38	49
Novocherkassk	6	21	28
Gus-Khroustalnyi	0	11	30
Orenburg	2	10	15
Novgorod	4	6	9
Petrozavodsk	0	2	5

Source: Institute of Urban Economics, Moscow.

Table 14.5. *Parameters of housing subsidy programme in various cities, 1997*

Cities	Charge for a standard apartment(1) (roubles)	Proportion of families receiving housing subsidies	Spending limit on housing and utility services as a proportion of family incomes
Moscow	148,890	11.4	12.5
Nizhny Novgorod	114,738	8.4	12.5
Ryazan	78,150	1.2	15
Novocherkassk	135,750	13	15
Novgorod	166,431	4.8	16
Petrozavodsk	148,194	18.5	5–10–15
Samara	218,547	32	10
Cherepovets	160,000	2	15
Orenburg	138,300	9.8	10

Note: ᵃA standard apartment means 54 m² for 3 persons, consuming 150 kwh of electricity per month.

Source: Institute of Urban Economics, Moscow.

were not interested in this sphere and would not take part in the tenders was not borne out. On the contrary, with properly conducted tenders and no discrimination, private firms were eager to enter this new market. Privatized and private repair and construction enterprises have been particularly active, as have private firms whose managers came from the old housing and utility service organizations and were ready to return to familiar territory, once earnings from other activities diminished. There have been cases of more than ten participants in tenders; five to seven participants is typical. In some cities the share of municipal dwellings serviced on a competitive basis rose to between one-third and one-half.

A shortage of qualified managers did not prove a serious obstacle to the creation of condominiums. In cities where the movement was supported by municipal authorities it developed rapidly. Table 14.4 shows the number of registered condominiums in selected towns at various dates. The number has continued to increase and in several cities had reached 100 or more by 1999.

Another concern was that increased residential tariffs would lead to social discontent. There were isolated incidents, including a short-lived demonstration in St Petersburg. By and large, however, careful work to prepare residents along with the newly launched mechanism of social support made it possible to revise tariffs fairly painlessly even where the increase was very substantial. For example, in Cheropovets residential tariffs were raised in 1994–5 by 160 per cent, and a further increase followed in August 1996, taking the proportion of housing costs covered by residents to 40 per cent. Similar figures were attained in Petrozavodsk and Orenburg. At present 50–60 per cent cost recovery from the population is considered an acceptable level in many regions across the country.

Another consequence of higher residential charges in some circumstances has been the growth of non-payments. At the prevailing level of charges one-third or more of households may fail to pay their bills on time. This is often used as an argument against further tariff increases. However, cities which have seriously tackled the problem of indebtedness show much better results, with current arrears of households no higher than 3–5 per cent.

Also groundless were anxieties about a sharp possible increase in the proportion of families entitled to housing allowances, which might have absorbed most of the budgetary savings expected from increased household charges. Even with charges covering 50–60 per cent of costs, the proportion of families receiving allowances seldom exceeded 15 per cent.

None the less, despite their successful introduction, the reforms did not speedily achieve their objective of rationalization and cost reduction. Housing and utility service costs grew faster than inflation in 1994–5, even in cities that were most thorough and scrupulous in pursuing the reform agenda. This was partly because the reform strategy focused chiefly on organization and provision of housing services, while the lion's share of expenditure in the sector is incurred by utility services, mainly heating and hot water. In this domain reform is difficult to implement fully at local level, since heating comes mainly from stations linked to the unified Russian power system (RAO UES), and regional energy commissions have an exclusive right to set tariffs. No satisfactory mechanism for regulating Russia's natural monopolies has yet been elaborated.

However, even in the management and running of the housing stock, which it was the first priority of the reform concept to rationalize, no serious reduction in cost was achieved. Tendering may have produced some reduction in running costs, but these were offset by other items, such as accounting and management overheads.

This raises once again the question of priorities in local policymaking. Outside observers invariably emphasize the desirability of lessening the budgetary burden of subsidies to housing and utilities, especially given the plight of other public services, such as health care and education. Local leaders, however, may have other considerations in mind. One is to retain broad political support. Housing charges affect the whole population, whereas local revenue shortfalls in the short term have consequences only for certain groups, chiefly public sector workers (wage arrears to teachers, doctors, and staff of the housing services). In these circumstances official decisions may well be determined by political rather than economic management considerations.

Furthermore, housing reform almost inevitably entails some conflict with elements of the local élite. Experience shows that restructuring the management system in the housing field, and in particular breaking up housing service trusts, may be a risky undertaking politically. Hence the desire either to avoid reforming housing management altogether, or else to ensure that former housing bosses are compensated with alternative appointments or other rewards. The same applies to tenders for housing services which result in former managers of housing enterprises losing their jobs.[7] All in all it is unsurprising that restructuring of housing and utility sector management has achieved a reduction in costs and in the number of employees only in isolated instances. An example is Novgorod, where in 1995–6 seventy-five staff were dismissed and administrative outlays cut by 13 per cent.

---

[7] In Cherepovets the tender process revealed the possibility of reducing housing service tariffs by more than 20%. However, many months passed before contracts were signed with the tender winner, and the results of the tender had no apparent effect on the general level of charges in the city.

The motivation of local authorities is not the only obstacle to managerial economies. Another factor has been a concept at the heart of the reforms themselves. This is the creation of the procurement service as a municipal body representing end-users, namely the population. Under the scheme control over the work of housing enterprises is not exercised by end-users themselves but rather is organized from above, with staff engaged to verify the quantity and quality of work performed by contractors and its conformity with contractual obligations. There has as yet been no assessment as to whether the extra expense of organizing such controls is justified.

But in any case that is not the end of the story. While various ways of structuring procurement services were envisaged, the model most widely followed has been the creation of a single service for a whole city (with neighbourhood branches as necessary) in the form of a municipal institution.[8] This means that management of the housing stock is concentrated in one centre, creating a new type of monopolist or rather monopsonist, arguably more powerful than those arising in the previous system of housing management. Being subject neither to competitive pressures nor to regulatory controls, such bodies, like any bureaucratic structure, begin to reorient themselves away from the goal of rationalizing the housing sector and improving the quality of its management towards strengthening and developing their own position: that is, simply working for themselves.[9] There is a lack of identity between the interests of the purchaser and of the consumer, which in turn influences the behaviour not only of the consumer but also of the contractor.

A crucial factor in the motivation of contractors is that they see themselves as working for the procurement service rather than for

---

[8] This occurred with the so-called Ryazan model when it was adapted in other cities. In Ryazan, with a population of 500,000, the procurement service employed some 300 people. It comprised a central office (with the status of a municipal department) and 11 branches. It disposed of considerable funds for payment of current housing costs (both budget subsidies and residential payments). Controlling the work of contractors involved regulatory checks carried out by technical inspectors in the branches. The checks determined the level of payment, and of fines levied on contractors for sub-standard work. Unfortunately imitations of the Ryazan model elsewhere have tended to lose the system's leanness and integrity, retaining instead the old top heavy and multi-layered management systems.

[9] Moreover, this need not happen only with the passage of time. In one of the leading cities in the housing reform field my request for a meeting with the head of the recently established procurement service was denied on the grounds that he was busy repairing the new service's office building.

the residents. This applies equally to municipally owned and to private contractors. The trend is reinforced by the tendering system because the interest of the procurement service is paramount in determining the results of the tender. For this reason, local authorities have become increasingly active in running such tenders. The procurement services sense that, far from being a threat to their power, tenders are an instrument for strengthening them.

Analogous issues have arisen in relation to condominiums. Conditions for the formation and functioning of condominiums are laid down mainly by municipal authorities for whom the spread of this institution implies a shrinkage of their own housing stock. Moreover, budget subsidies have to be allocated to the new associations on the same terms as to municipal housing. Not surprisingly, in many cities substantial budget arrears to condominiums are the norm. Furthermore, procurement services typically regard condominiums not only as competitors in the struggle for control and resources, but also as an unwelcome example of the possibility of more rational management; and so they do everything they can to block the formation and registration of these associations. Alternatively, they seek to affiliate condominiums to municipal enterprises, and so prevent the associations from taking independent decisions and running their own finances—which was the whole point of their creation in the first place. The result is that by no means all bodies formally known as condominiums are in fact self-standing non-municipal formations capable of seriously influencing housing management in cities.

Difficulties in local finance and the related problem of non-payments have not prevented implementation of housing reforms, but they have accentuated inconsistencies present in the reform programme from the beginning. Terms formally imposed on contractors are hard to enforce when municipalities (procurement services) are unable to pay for work carried out. The tendering process for housing services is distorted when purchaser and contractor alike recognize that fulfilment of obligations undertaken will be subject to the actual availability of finance. There is a likelihood of more favourable conditions being created for related municipal enterprises at the expense of 'alien' enterprises from the private sector. Condominiums are in a difficult situation as a result of not receiving the official finance due to them.

It is often the line of least resistance for municipal authorities not to make up payment shortfalls to housing enterprises and associations and not to seek actively for cost savings, all the more so as any savings are liable to be confiscated in the following year. Fiscal relations between regions and municipalities are still mainly based on the principle of actual spending; so that cost savings are effectively penalized in the next year's budget. The absence of a proper structure of fiscal federalism, and the extreme dependence of most municipalities, constitute one of the main obstacles to the rationalization of administration at municipal level. Thus the quality of housing and utility services has tended to decline, while popular resistance to rising charges has increased. By early 1997 the reform process had seized up practically everywhere, and in places went into reverse.

14.4. A NEW PHASE OF REFORM: 1997–1999

In April 1997 Presidential Decree no. 25, 'On Reforms of the Housing and Utility Sector in the Russian Federation' signalled a new phase of reform, with stronger federal control over local policies.

The new decree defined four federal standards in the housing field covering: normal living space; the cost of housing and utility services per square metre of living space; cost recovery for housing and utility services through charges on residents; and a ceiling on these charges as a proportion of family incomes. While regional and local authorities retained the right to set the basic parameters of the transition to a new system of housing payments, transfers from the federal budget were to be allocated on the basis of these federal standards. If regions considered it right to set softer conditions for residential housing payments, then the related cost would have to be borne from their own internal financial resources.

The federal standards were designed to bring about a gradual increase in the level of residential payments, thus effectively reproducing the policy of Government Resolution no. 935 of 22 September 1993, but with three modifications: the cost to be covered by residents now included capital repairs; the transition to 100 per cent cost coverage was extended to 2003; and there was provision for more flexibility in the ceiling on housing and utility services payments in family budgets.

The federal living space norm was adopted uniformly for the whole country at 18 square metres per person in families of three or more; 42 square metres for two-person households; and 33 square metres for those living alone. Federal standards of housing and utility service costs were set with differentiation by regions, ranging from 6,000 to nearly

Table 14.6. *Planned timetable for moving to the new system of residential housing and utility service payment as at April 1997*

Year	Proportion of costs to be covered by household charges (federal standard, %)	Maximum share of expenditure on housing and utility services as a proportion of household income (federal standard, %)
1997	35	16
1998	50	18
1999	60	19
2000	70	20
2001	80	22
2002	90	23
2003	100	25

17,000 roubles per square metre of general living space, with a national average of 8,200 roubles.[10]

The new programme also called for acceleration of institutional reforms, in particular de-monopolization and privatization. The share of the housing stock maintained on a competitive basis was to increase to 60 per cent by 1998 and to 100 per cent by 2000.

While confirming the earlier principles of support for the creation of condominiums, extension of contractual arrangements in the housing sector, and complete transfer of non-municipal housing stocks into municipal ownership, the 1997 programme called for some reshaping of relations between home owners, management organizations, procurement services, and firms engaged to service the housing stock and utility infrastructure facilities.

Russia's continued emphasis on gradualism in the housing sphere invites comparison with some other countries, Kazakhstan especially, where radical reforms were enforced in 1996.[11] It has to be said that even in the years 1992–5 housing reform had in several respects developed more swiftly in Kazakhstan than in Russia. The bulk of the non-municipal housing stock had been transferred out of enterprise ownership, and roughly 85 per cent of the state housing stock had been privatized.

---

[10] Government Resolution n. 621 of 26 May 1997 'On Federal Standards for Transition to a New Housing and Utility Services Payments System'.

[11] Several documents on housing reforms in Kazakhstan were kindly provided by Alexander Guzanov of the Institute of Municipal Economics.

However, there had been no comprehensive change in housing management or its financing. This began in the spring of 1996. At that point the position in Kazakhstan was broadly similar to that in Russia. Households paid an average of 30 per cent of the cost of housing and utility services, with wide regional variation. Heating charges varied between 3.3 per cent and 75 per cent of cost. Utility service subsidies, mainly for heating and hot water, took 10 per cent of regional budgets (considerably less than in Russia).

From then on transition to full residential cost recovery in Kazakhstan was completed in less than a year. Average residential tariffs for heating went up by more than 640 per cent; for hot water by 1440 per cent; for cold water by 640 per cent; and for gas by 30 per cent.[12] The increases were accompanied by a system of targeted housing benefit provision similar to that in Russia. However, the expenditure ceiling for housing and utility service payment in family budgets was set at almost twice the level in Russia (and also Ukraine), namely 30 per cent (which was similar to the figure in Estonia).

At the same time major institutional changes were initiated.[13] In Kazakhstan home owner co-operatives (HOCs) were equivalent to the condominiums in Russia. It was laid down that in all apartment blocs in which HOC had not already been created by 1996, such bodies were to be set up under management appointed by the local authorities. Thus the country's housing was effectively put onto a condominium footing, eliminating the gap between purchasers and consumers of housing maintenance services as consumers themselves were transformed into purchasers.

There was a parallel reform of enterprises providing housing and utility services. HOCs could provide own maintenance for their members. Tougher anti-monopoly controls were established over the tariffs of utility enterprises. This led to cuts in heating tariffs of between 5 per cent and 30 per cent. The process of privatizing utility enterprises was begun.

Implementation of the programme was not problem-free. Residential payment arrears in the course of 1996 increased more than threefold.[14] And the process of establishing HOC *en masse* was somewhat chaotic, its

---

[12] See Rudenko (1997), p. 13.
[13] Enactments included Kazakh Government Resolution n. 587 of 13 May 1996 'On the De-monopolisation of the Housing and Utility Sector and the Ordering of Payments for Housing and Utility Services' and n. 647 of 27 May 1996 'On Measures to Develop Home Owner Consumer Co-operatives'.
[14] From Tenge 1.2 billion, to Tenge 3.8 billion (Rudenko 1997).

rationale poorly understood by much of the population. None the less the experience showed that radical housing reforms can be introduced swiftly, though admittedly involving substantial administrative pressures. In countries where sharp increases in residential housing payments were combined with voluntary institutional changes, the latter developed at quite a moderate pace. In Estonia, for example, despite a full transition to unsubsidized housing and coverage of all costs by residents, only 12 per cent of possible condominiums had been registered by the middle of 1996.

As regards the further progress of housing reform in Russia, two kinds of difficulties remained to be overcome. The more tractable category may be labelled 'methodological' or 'technical', involving the application and adaptation of general principles to economic conditions and structures, both in the housing sector itself and in the economy at large. For example, federal standards for housing and related costs by regions do not take account of intra-regional variations connected with local peculiarities of the housing stock (prevalence of lifts, rubbish chutes, and other facilities) or with technical characteristics of heating and hot water systems; which can involve substantial cost differences impossible to align in the short term. Wages also vary between cities in the same region. In short, cost variations may be more substantial within regions than between them, so that a regional classification is not always the appropriate basis for differentiating federal standards of service costs.

A different issue is that Russian accounting systems are not uniform, and tariffs in various towns and regions incorporate differing cost schedules. A significant item in this context is expenditure on housing stock management which may be covered either out of service charges or directly from the local budget. The more advanced the reform of management structure, the more likely are management costs to be included in charges, which rise accordingly. As a result, the advancement of reforms can lead to unexpected financial penalties.

Also problematic is the introduction of a uniform scale of residential tariff increases, regardless of the capacity of the local economy to carry them. The fact is that there are feasible limits to tariff levels, which vary not only by regions but also from town to town. Experience shows that with similar levels of cost recovery the share of families receiving housing allowances can vary widely. For example, a 50 per cent cost-recovery figure resulted in 13 per cent of families receiving housing allowances in Orenburg and only about 5 per cent in Cherepovets. Although such variations can be quite serious, they are not fundamental. Correcting them is a matter of reasonable flexibility in realizing reforms whose basic intention is agreed. The same cannot be said of obstacles in the second category, which are conceptual or institutional in character.

In a word, there remained and remains a serious gap between the objectives of housing reform in Russia and the incentives or motivation driving those responsible for its implementation. The latter are essentially the municipal authorities. Despite the emphasis on competition in the management sphere, there has been no obstacle to the establishment and continuation of municipal procurement services which monopolize the housing management field and are linked to the political interests of the local authority. Further, although the reform strategy envisaged that by 2003 condominiums would become the prevailing form of management of residential apartment blocs, it was not clear how this transition would be carried out or which organized interests would wish to support it. There was a real danger that private firms entering the housing utility market would become just like the municipal enterprises in this field in terms of their motivations, the efficiency of their management, and the winning of tenders as a result of some special relationship with the local authority. In other words, there was no guarantee whatsoever that the new elements in the housing reform strategy would succeed in transforming the old institutional relations as opposed to being absorbed by them.

The experience of the later 1990s confirmed in significant measure the apprehensions felt by the advocates of strong housing reform. Two phases may be identified by the changing political climate relating to the sector. Until mid-1998 the federal authorities favoured a speeding-up of reforms and applied administrative pressures accordingly. This may indeed have brought some genuine progress in the sector. What it highlighted, however, was the superficial, formal aspects of reforms, and these did not necessarily reflect fundamental realities. A focus on simple, quantifiable indicators tended to overshadow the need for specific and detailed actions designed to achieve more efficient operation of housing and utility services.

In the subsequent second stage official interest in reform waned. There was talk of slowing down the restructuring process. Such talk eventuated in the decision of the Duma to approve a further lengthening—from 2003 to 2008—of the timetable for eliminating subsidies in the housing sector. The climate of reform was thus negatively affected by inconsistent signals from the federal level.

Another unfavourable background element was the lack of structure in inter-budgetary relations between the constituents ('subjects') of the Federation and the lower municipal tier of government. The federal authorities, in exercising general control over the pace of housing reform, applied financial stimuli and sanctions to subjects of the Federation. The reforms themselves, however, were carried out at municipal level. And the leaders of these reforms not only received no reward for economies achieved but typically found themselves penalized by a cut in their budgetary allocations, which regional governments distributed in accordance with perceived 'real' repayments.

At the same time there was no question of halting reforms altogether. The problem of local budget deficits, where housing and utilities accounted for up to 50 per cent of budgetary expenditure, simply would not allow this. Not, at any rate, in relation to items having a direct impact on the volume of subsidies—namely, the housing and other charges levied on households. This was indeed the area in which reforms made most progress. Cities and regions actively pursuing a reformist programme achieved a 50–60 per cent rate of cost recovery from consumer charges. Estimates suggest that the national average was 40–5 per cent. Considerable inter-regional variation obviously remained, with some areas still recovering less than 30 per cent of costs through new charges.

In other respects restructuring has made little real progress overall. A favourable picture emerges in some cities—such as Moscow, Nizhny-Novgorod, and Novcherkassk, where more than half the housing stock is maintained with the help of a competitive regime. In St Petersburg, Novocherkassk, and Novgorod the number of housing condominiums more than doubled in 1998–9; in Nizhny-Novgorod and Krasnoyarsk as well as Moscow and St Petersburg the number came to exceed 100.[15] These achievements, however, should not obscure the extent of problems remaining. For the country as a whole the central objective of bringing the housing sector fairly and squarely into the market economy has not been achieved.

There has been little substantive progress as regards proprietorship. Municipal authorities have amply demonstrated their inability to function as an effective proprietor of the bulk of the housing stock. Formation of condominiums is proceeding much more sluggishly than was envisaged in the reform programme. In the country as a whole less than 1 per cent of housing was covered by condominiums by 1998–9.

[15] Data from the Institute of Urban Economics.

Even in the case of new buildings condominiums are not always set up; and apartment blocks continue to be taken into municipal ownership, even where the municipality has a nil share of the apartments in question. Evidently condominiums are not going to resolve the issue of effective proprietorship in the housing sector in the foreseeable future.

In these circumstances particular importance attaches to the quality of management of the housing stock. In practice this retains an administrative character and is not viewed in business terms. Private organizations are almost invariably excluded and there is no mechanism of competition. Those in charge do not see the enhancement of efficiency or of the value of dwellings as a primary task. The indifference of owners and the bureaucratic approach of managers mean that there is no serious incentive to suppliers of housing and utility services to enhance the quality of their outputs.

Particularly glaring is the inadequacy of measures directed to the regulation of local monopolies. Instead of a proper regulatory system designed to take account of differing interests and of the balance of supply and demand in the separate regions and municipalities, there have been only isolated measures such as individual enterprise audits, with no clear objectives or consequences for housing policy.

The idea emerged, in response to mounting greed of monopoly suppliers and mounting payments arrears for water and heating services on the part of local budget authorities,[16] that there should be an administratively enforced reduction in utility tariffs come what may—which would, of course, undermine any economic rationale for the conduct of utility-sector enterprises. The absence of a normal regulatory system has prevented not only market but also administrative mechanisms from acting to raise the efficiency of enterprises. Regulatory bodies would at least require transparency in the conduct of firms and could be expected to influence their strategy and investment programmes and to facilitate the effective application of budgetary funds allocated to the sector.

In sum, full accomplishment of housing-sector reform requires three components. First, the system of user charges for housing occupancy and utilities provision must be carried to completion, removing dependence on subsidies, and enabling the sector to operate on a normal financial basis.

Secondly, management of the housing stock must be brought into the sphere of market relations and become a business matter, with effective forms of responsible proprietorship at its core.

---

[16] In some municipalities the amount of arrears was greater than the annual budget.

Thirdly, enterprises supplying utility services to households must be subjected to a regulatory regime which will oversee their economic performance, while also guaranteeing their autonomy and freedom from arbitrary political interference.

These three objectives are indispensable both for efficiency and healthy development of the housing sector and for eliminating the housing subsidies which have been the black hole of local government finances.

REFERENCES

Buckley, R., and Gurenko, E. (1997). 'Housing and Income Distribution in Russia: Zhivago's Legacy', *The World Bank Research Observer*, 12/1, February: 19–32.

Butler, S., and O'Leary, S. (1996). 'Programme for Freeing Russian Enterprises of Municipal Housing', Institute of Urban Economics, Moscow.

Malpezzi, S., and Ball, G. (1991). 'Rent Control in Developing Countries', World Bank Discussion Paper, 129, September.

Rudenko, I. (1997). 'The Transition to the Subsidy-Free Functioning of Enterprises in the Housing and Utility Sector', *Asia—Ekonomika i zhizn'*, 13, March.

Struyck, R., and Kozareva, N. (1994). *Reforms of the Russian Housing Sector, 1991–94*, Moscow.

15

Regional Income Differences

PHILIP HANSON

15.1. INTRODUCTION

Along with a decline in Russia's GDP and increased inequality of incomes, the fortunes of Russia's regions have diverged substantially. At one end of the scale, Moscow city has a booming economy and in the third quarter of 1997 recorded average incomes 9.0 times the locally costed 'subsistence minimum' (*prozhitochnyi minimum*).[1] Real income levels in Moscow are probably higher now than they have ever been before. At the other end of the scale, in Ingushetia, Dagestan, and Tyva, average incomes are reported to be below the subsistence level.

Regional income differences in Russia are now indeed very large and the scale of these differences matters. The inter-regional dispersion of personal incomes was much larger than, for example, the dispersion of per capita GDP across the 183 second-level regions of the European Union (of twelve countries) in 1993. There the range from poorest to richest was 1:5.5,[2] or less than half the apparent range across the seventy-seven main Russian regions recently.[3]

The project on which this paper is based is supported by the Economic and Social Research Council (grant R000 23 6398). I am indebted for comments on an earlier draft to Brigitte Granville, Peter Oppenheimer, and Douglas Sutherland. I am also grateful to Douglas Sutherland for his assistance.

[1] *Izvestiya*, 25 October 1997, p. 5.

[2] Voreio Aigaio in Greece to Hamburg in Germany; European Commission (1994).

[3] The 183 second-level EU regions of the EU12 (before EU enlargement to include Finland, Sweden, and Austria) had an average population of 1.9 million. This happens to be the same as the average population of the main 78 Russian regions—that is, *oblasti*, *kraya*, and republics, with the eleven autonomous *okrugs* not treated separately. In the data used in this chapter, Chechnya is always omitted, leaving a maximum number of regions of 77. For some years, data for particular regions are lacking, so the data-set in some years is slightly smaller—usually 74 or 75.

Such regional disparities are one reason for questioning whether Russia will become a well-functioning economy within the next decade.[4] Apart from income variations, Russia's eighty-nine 'federal subjects' differ widely in levels of urbanization; their populations exhibit large differences in ethnic composition; the infrastructure of transport and communications linking them is poor by western standards; and in the early and middle 1990s, at least, there were striking differences between them in the way in which new rules of the economic game developed.

One view that has been put forward is that the new Russian economy has a 'leopard-skin' pattern: that it is made up of regional patches that differ radically from one another (Sapir 1996). On this view, Russian regional differentiation is associated with a tendency for some regional economies to become or remain substantially un-monetized or barter-based, while others function as more or less 'normal' monetary economies.

If that is so, creation of a single economic space in which resources are mostly market-allocated across as well as within regions is not underway. This would not prevent market integration occurring across substantial chunks of Russian territory, but it would mean that other substantial chunks were being left out. It would also help to explain slow aggregate growth, with a slumbering hinterland weighing down what might be quite dynamic growth in some regions. That would resemble the recent situation in India.

This chapter is a preliminary assessment of regional disparities in terms of one variable: per capita real incomes of the population. I shall consider evidence about the dynamics of regional inequalities in 1992–7, evidence for 1995 that bears on the leopard-skin hypothesis, and also investigate some of the likely influences on regional disparities, again using mainly 1995 data, but with a few references to 1996 and 1997.

The chapter is organized as follows. The next section is a survey of the main economic processes affecting inter-regional income differences. The third section presents some statistical results, and the fourth section offers brief conclusions. The data and their limitations are set out in the appendix.

---

[4] Some other grounds, unrelated to regional issues, for doubting this are discussed in Hanson (1997*a*). The basis for judging that Russia has or has not become a well-functioning market economy is also discussed there; I suggest that sustained (say, average over five years) growth at above the trend level for the OECD countries would be a reasonable criterion, given Russia's low starting-point and relatively high level of human capital.

15.2. PROCESSES OF REGIONAL DIFFERENTIATION

Market integration began in European Russian regions as early as 1992–3 (Berkowitz 1994), following the January 1992 package of liberalization and stabilization measures. The data analysed in this chapter thus reflect around five years' adaptation. What we are examining is a continuing and incomplete process of radical adjustment to the reform programme launched at the start of 1992.

The possible origins of the present inter-regional economic differences are many. We distinguish between structural influences and policy or political influences on regional economic performance. The former comprise elements inherited from the previous economic regime, together with demographic and other factors affecting the capacity for spontaneous adaptation and transformation. The latter are divided into central government and regional government influences.

15.2.1. *Inherited structures*

Less-developed regions such as Dagestan or Tyva were poorer than regions like Moscow city or St Petersburg long before 1992. Pre-reform shortages and price controls, however, plus discontinuities and other deficiencies in the data, make any before-and-after quantification problematic. We therefore focus on developments from 1992 on.

The fall in real aggregate demand after 1989 and the partial liberalization of foreign trade and of domestic prices and production after 1991 changed costs and opportunities differentially across Russian regions. Broadly speaking, activities dependent on the domestic market suffered more than those that either were already oriented to export demand or could readily be shifted towards external markets. Activities newly vulnerable to import competition were especially likely to suffer. Domestic trades handling imported goods, however, prospered. Final demand for military production was particularly heavily cut at the start, when military hardware procurement was slashed by four-fifths in a year. Other things being equal, one would expect regional economies to be differentially affected by these changes, according to their initial production structure.

In practice, it has been hard to measure the impact convincingly. Individual regions are often cited as victims or beneficiaries of particular structural changes: Ivanovo *oblast'* hit by the competition of cheap imported textiles and clothing; the St Petersburg economy damaged by cuts in military spending; Tyumen' doing well out of oil and gas in both export and domestic markets; most agricultural regions probably suffering from the weakening of agriculture's terms of trade with the rest of the economy—due in part to the inflow of subsidized European Union surpluses; but a shift-share analysis of the regional impact of changes in structure within the industrial sector was unable to account for more than a small part of the variance in regional industrial rates of decline through 1994 (Sutherland and Hanson 1996).[5] Still, some such effect must have been occurring.

In addition, it is likely that the very large under-pricing of long-haul freight transport in the Soviet era, and the subsidizing in other ways of production in remote locations, will have handicapped some regions in adjusting to the market, regardless of initial changes in the pattern of demand. Adjustment by net out-migration is occurring from the far north and the far east, but it has not proceeded fast enough to prevent the position of those regions in the league table of regional real incomes from deteriorating.

On the positive side, a number of regional commercial and financial hubs have been developing outside Moscow, as economic decisions have become less centralized. These are identifiable from their foreign exchange inflows and institutional development—the early establishment of foreign-currency exchanges, the installation of online securities trading on the Russian trading system, the branching of Moscow banks, and so on. The leading examples are St Petersburg, Nizhny Novgorod, Samara, Sverdlovsk (the province containing Ekaterinburg), and Novosibirsk. Whether Primorskii krai should be added to that short-list is a matter of judgement (see Hanson 1997*b*).

What Moscow and the five listed regions have in common is that they comprise the largest urban agglomerations in Russia and are located at major road, rail, air, and pipeline junctions. Their advantages seem to be locational and based on urban scale rather than the possession of a particularly resilient inherited production structure. Some of the scale economies may arise from producer externalities. If so, these are likely to reflect proximity to know-how and general capabilities in many other activities (so-called Jacobs externalities)[6] rather than knowledge

---

[5] This may have been largely a data problem. The available branch breakdowns of industrial output and employment at regional level are highly aggregated.

[6] Named for the writer on architecture and cities, Jane Jacobs (especially Jacobs 1963) and the economists Marshall, Arrow, and Romer, respectively. See Callejon and Costa (1997).

spillovers generated by adjacent producers in the same line of business (nowadays labelled MAR—Marshall, Arrow, Romer—externalities after the eponymous economists). In those lines of economic activity where Russia has seen growth in the 1990s (retailing, wholesaling, and financial services, mainly) the influence on location of the advantages of closeness to firms in the same line of business is unlikely to have been as strong as that of the advantages of being in a large agglomeration of economic activity in general.

15.2.2. *Adaptability 'from below'*

It is possible that some Russian regions have fared less badly than others not because of inherited production patterns, nor because of policy influences, but because of superior grass-roots ability to adapt. If a region's population is particularly open to change, that might reasonably be expected to be an advantage. A young population, or one that was relatively highly educated, or both, might be favourable to more rapid adjustment to the market. In so far as big cities contain concentrations of young, educated, people, this sort of effect might be associated with urban agglomerations, and would shade into the 'Jacobs externalities' already described. It is possible that an inflow of migrants, who are likely to be geographically more mobile within a region than its long-term residents, and who are also quite likely to be relatively young, could also be a favourable ingredient in adaptability from below—although associated at the same time with additional pressure on housing and public services.

15.2.3. *Policy and political factors: central government*

The federal government in Moscow influences regional economies differentially in several ways. First, there is the influence of the pattern of federal spending—for example, on defence procurement or on subsidies to agriculture and coal-mining. Second, there is the legislation of special status for particular regions (like the duty-free status of Kaliningrad). Third, there are the idiosyncratic 'power-sharing' agreements between the centre and particular regions, which often leave a region with a special deal on its retention of tax collected on its territory. Less formal *ad hoc* deals may also give a region a special injection of funds for the sake of political fire-fighting. Finally, there are inter-regional transfers explicitly aimed, after 1993, at assisting the budgets of poorer regions: from the Fund for Federal Financial Assistance (*fond federal'noi finansovoi pomoshchi*, or FFFP).

The central authorities themselves reportedly do not have region-by-region information on the effects of the first of these influences (personal communication from Aleksei Lavrov 1996). Coal and farm subsidies apart, this influence may in fact have become quite small by the mid-1990s, as federal-government funding of investment fell to very low levels: 9.2 per cent of all gross fixed capital formation in 1996 (Goskomstat 1996*b*, p. 43).

Some of the dimensions of federal government policy should be visible in the balance of transfers in both directions between regional and federal budgets within a year. Lavrov (1996) provided data on these for 1995. Both Hanson and Kirkow (1997) and McAuley (1997) found that regional differences in per capita real income in 1994 had a statistically significant influence on the per capita size of those net transfers in 1995, with poorer regions tending to gain more than richer regions. Whatever the role of regional transfers then and earlier in buying off regional discontent or the belligerence of some regional leaders towards Moscow, in 1995 at least part of federal budgetary policy tended to be mildly equalizing in its effects between regions.

15.2.4. *Policy and political factors: regional governments*

Many Russian regional leaders are conspicuous in media coverage of the Russian political scene, and attract attention for, among other things, what is thought to be their influence on the economic and political fortunes of their particular patch of turf.

It is not surprising that they are often credited both inside and outside Russia with a capacity for such influence. Their administrative machinery retains much of the old, Soviet-era linkages with local large enterprises; at the same time the discipline imposed on their Soviet-era predecessors' (Party *obkom* first secretaries') activities by the Communist Party chain of command has disappeared. They are now in principle answerable to local voters rather than to the president. Even in 1991–5, however, before most of them were elected, they seem in practice to have been more responsive to local interest groups than to Moscow.

In other words, Russian regional leaders have had both opportunity and motive to pursue regional economic policies of their own. The chief constraints imposed from the centre have comprised macroeconomic policies and federal legislation on privatization, to the extent that this legislation was enforced in local courts.

Whether regional leaders make a difference is a tricky question. In Bradshaw and Hanson (1994) an attempt was made to measure a separate regional-leadership effect in regression analysis of regional outcomes. This was done by inserting a dummy variable indicating whether a region's leadership did or did not have a reformist reputation. There was a statistically significant effect in the expected direction. Other things being equal, a region did slightly better if its leadership had a reformist reputation than otherwise. But the basis for identifying regions as 'reformist' was dependent on media coverage, which in turn may label a local leadership reformist precisely *because* a region is (for example) attracting foreign investment in readily noticeable ways.

Specifying reformers and non-reformers among local leaders is not difficult in extreme cases. Boris Nemtsov in Nizhny Novgorod was an example of the former; Evgenii Nazdratenko in Primorskii Krai is an example of the latter. Between the two extremes, however, are the great bulk of regional leaderships, including successful teams headed by Mayor Luzhkov in Moscow and Governor Konstantin Titov in Samara, neither of whom, as an individual, is associated with vigorous reform initiatives *à la* Nemtsov.

At all events, economic policies can and do differ across Russian regions, and regional policy initiatives not largely determined by local circumstances may sometimes make a difference. A sustained reformist policy orientation at this level, however, might perhaps be expected to show measurable results in regional income levels only over quite a long period of time, since the main contribution that local leadership can make is to facilitate market-oriented institutional change and to stop putting impediments in the way of market entry and market exit.

From the foregoing overview of influences on regional differences in adaptation a great many hypotheses could be formulated. In what follows, two main lines of investigation will be pursued. One is an enquiry into the 'leopard-skin' hypothesis. Is the evidence of a clear division into monetized and (largely) un-monetized regions convincing, or are the patterns of regional differentiation compatible with the more-or-less inclusive (nationwide) process of market integration?

The second line of enquiry focuses directly on the differences in real household incomes across Russian regions. Are the posited effects of inherited economic structure and location really to be found? Do hub regions and other regions where producers are well placed to do business with the outside world (while the domestic economy has been depressed) show a clearly more favourable movement of real incomes? To the extent that such factors explain real-income differences, the scope for explanations from regional differences in human capital, or from central and regional policymaking, is correspondingly reduced.

The basic data used here are given in the appendix, along with a review of their limitations.

15.3. EXPERIMENTS WITH THE DATA

Sapir (1996) drew attention to the fact that savings rates varied across Russian regions in ways that did not seem to be well explained by differences in income levels. There were a number of regions where average income was well below the national average but where savings ratios were well above the national average. He assumed that, within a single country and a single short period of time, average propensity to save could be expected to rise with income. He argued that the existence of a number of poor regions with high savings rates suggested that households in those regions were behaving in ways that required some non-standard explanation. His hypothesis was that these were regions in which monetization was low and what Russians call a 'natural economy' (*natural'noe khozyaistvo*, that is, barter) predominated. A high proportion of money incomes was saved in those regions because money did not play a large role in most of the residents' daily lives.

Sapir did not, however, adjust the recorded regional per capita money incomes for the widely differing price levels of different Russian regions. It is real income, not nominal income, that should influence savings rates, so it is worth asking whether the variations in Russian regional savings rates look quite so odd when they are related to the variations in real incomes. (The latter, it is true, will be deflated money incomes only— 'real money incomes'—and not real incomes including subsistence production—'real real incomes'—but allowing for the large differences in regional price levels may still produce a somewhat different story.)

Figure 15.1. is a scattergram of regions' per capita real income (as defined in the appendix) against the APS index (Russian average = 1) for 1995. Some of the points on the outer edges of a rather dense mass of points are identified on the chart.

One can imagine, eyeballing the chart, a plausible regression line from bottom left to top right, going from very poor north Caucasus regions to Moscow city via St Petersburg. On the other hand, the points are not normally distributed around such a line and there are some

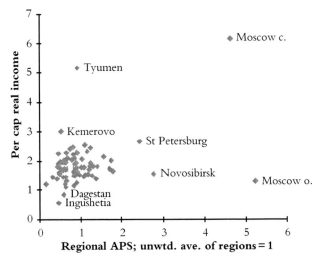

Figure 15.1. *RF Regions: per capita real incomes and savings indexes, 1995*

odd-looking outliers: Moscow region, in particular. The picture is certainly not a tidy one.

A simple linear regression of the APS index on per capita real income indicated a significant positive relationship between the two, at better than 1 per cent. However, the coefficient of determination was low (about one-eighth), so any relationship between the two variables is poorly specified.

A regression allowing for a non-linear relationship between savings ratios and real incomes, however, does capture a great deal more of the variation in the APS index and indicates quite a strong relationship between the two variables. Moscow *oblast'* is excluded as an outlier.

$$\text{APS95} = \underset{(2.664)}{9.408} - \underset{(-1.198)}{3.533} \text{ REAL Y 95} + \underset{(4.455)}{1.897} \text{ (REAL Y 95)}^2$$

$$n = 76 \qquad \text{DW} = 1.621 \qquad F = 33.767 \qquad \text{adj } R^2 = 0.466$$

The bracketed figures are *t* statistics. The coefficient for the square of real income is highly significant, the proportion of the variance in savings rates accounted for rises to almost a half, and the equation as a whole is satisfactory (the Durbin-Watson statistic is within the range that indicates that spatial auto-correlation is very unlikely to be present).

Therefore, by allowing for regional price differences and for the possibility that the relationship between savings rates and real incomes is not linear, we find that inter-regional differences in savings rates are not quite so mysterious in their relationship to income levels, after all.[7]

This suggests that variations in savings ratios across Russian regions are accounted for without resort to the notion of a strong divide between monetized and (largely) un-monetized regions. To that extent, this particular piece of evidence favours the view that cross-regional market integration is proceeding. There is no doubt considerable variation across regions in the extent to which households rely on barter. But it is not obvious that the resulting differences in behaviour are so large as to justify our thinking of Russian regions as falling into two radically different sorts of economic regime.

15.3.1. *The variations in regional real income levels*

According to Goskomstat, inequality in personal incomes in Russia as a whole grew from the start of the reforms through 1994 and then levelled off or slightly declined in 1995–6. The decile ratio (top 10 per cent of incomes to bottom 10 per cent) was officially reported at 13:1 for 1996, having been 14:1 in 1994 (OMRI *Daily Digest*, 15 January 1997). Whether these calculations for the national population take into account the very large regional differences in price levels is unclear.

Variability among regional-average real incomes (based on regional average incomes and regional costs of the nineteen-item food basket) continued to increase through 1995, and probably through 1997. Table 15.1 summarizes the evidence on regional variance in 1992–7.

What Table 15.1 portrays is a situation in which inter-regional variability increased during a period when, after the initial fall in real incomes between 1991 and 1992, the reported national average real income fluctuated, reaching a higher level in 1996 than in 1992. That apparent growth between the end-years has to be seen in context: between 1991 (annual average) and 1992 (annual average) food prices rose 21-fold and money incomes 7.5-fold, implying almost a two-thirds fall in statistical real income (from Goskomstat 1993, pp. 16, 45).

If one takes Goskomstat data at face value, then, average Russian real income (on our crude proxy measure of it) was in 1996 still well below the 1991 level. It is true that, given the extreme shortages of 1991 and the likelihood of growing official under-estimation of household incomes,

---

[7] I am indebted to my colleague Douglas Sutherland, who ran this regression.

Table 15.1. *Russia: Regional variation in real incomes, 1992–1997*

	1992	1993	1994	1995	1996[a]	1997
						III
Coefficient of variation (%)	30.6	26	32.2	39.5	42.3	49.8
Number of regions	74	74	77	77	76	77
Memorandum RF real y	2.54	3.79	2.38	2.3	2.2 [3.24]	

Note: [a] 1996 and 1997 data are for money incomes divided by the subsistence minimum, not the 19-item basket. The 1996 data are for November only and the 1997 data are for the third quarter. The bracketed Russian Federation real income figure for 1996 *is* comparable with those for earlier years. An inconsistency between the national and the regional figures is described in the appendix.

Sources: Calculated from Bradshaw and Palacin (1996); Goskomstat (1996a) and (1996b); *Izvestiya*, 25 October 1997, p. 5.

the true trajectory of average Russian material welfare must have been less grim than these numbers imply.[8] None the less, the growth of regional dispersion of real incomes has been occurring against a background of what has been at best a hesitant recovery from an initial sharp fall.

How much of the increased inequality in Russian personal incomes can be ascribed to growing regional differences? It is clear that there are large inequalities within regions. Goskomstat regularly publishes income distributions within regions, dividing the population into quintiles according to per capita household income. If one takes the quintile ratios (top 20 per cent to bottom 20 per cent), they are in most regions and most years somewhat smaller than the national-level quintile ratio (see Bradshaw and Palacin 1996 for a convenient assembly of 1992–4 data, and Goskomstat 1996a for 1995).

The exceptions appear to be the best-off regions. Thus, in 1995 the quintile ratio for Russia as a whole was 8.5. In almost all the regions it was less than this, but in Moscow it was 19.5 and in Tyumen' 10.5.[9]

[8] An early 1997 survey of 2,000 households across Russia by the Russian Market Research Company concluded that average incomes were twice those estimated by Goskomstat. *Financial Times*, 26 March 1997, p. 2.
[9] It should be borne in mind that the national-level quintile measure probably (a) blurs real and money income differences by not allowing for inter-regional price differences; and (b) is based on income data that are not comparable to those for the regions—see the previous section.

Part of the inequality that is now observable in Russian personal incomes generally, and probably part of its increase between the Soviet era and the mid-1990s, can be ascribed to the growing regional differentiation shown in Table 15.1. But how much of it? Plainly not all. We have seen that there is considerable inequality within as well as between regions. Still, can the degree of regional inequality be put in context as one of the elements in Russia's general inequality in the late 1990s?

As explained in the appendix, national and regional income data are not consistent. It is likely that national inequality measures such as decile ratios would be different (probably smaller) if all incomes were adjusted for local prices. It is possible, none the less, to arrive at an indirect indication of the scale of inter-regional differences in terms of the population as a whole.

This was done by identifying two groups of regions containing, respectively, around the richest tenth and the poorest tenth of the population, as grouped by their regional average incomes.

The following calculation was made for November 1996. A group of richest and a group of poorest regions, on the real-income proxy measure of regional average money income divided by regional subsistence minimum, were found, each of which contained close to 10 per cent of the total Russian population. These were: first, Moscow, Tyumen', and St Petersburg; and, second, a much larger number of mainly small regions that contained around the same number of people—in ascending order of real income, Ingushetia, Tyva, Marii-El, Chita, Kalmykia, Dagestan, Adygeya, North Ossetia, Penza, Karachaevo-Cherkessia, Novosibirsk, Mordova, and Chuvashia.

In fact, these groups of regions each contained approximately 11 per cent of the population: the nearest the regional boundaries allowed us to get to calculating a decile ratio. The three richest regions contained 11.2 per cent of the Russian population (at 1 January 1996), the fourteen poorest contained 10.8 per cent. The population-weighted average measure of real income in the three richest regions was 5.01 (that is, about five times the subsistence minimum, locally priced). The average income of the richest group was 4.4 times that of the poorest group.

If incomes within each region were all identical, in other words, the decile ratio for all Russian incomes would be less than 5:1. So inter-regional inequality, thus defined, accounts for something like 35–40 per cent of overall inter-household inequality.

Thus, inter-regional income inequalities have been growing (see Table 15.1), but are not the dominant source of inequality in Russia.

Moreover, the regional component in inequality, as measured here, is almost certainly over-stated. The proportion of rural residents in the group of poorest regions is higher than in the richest three regions, and the role of uncounted household food production in their real incomes is therefore higher (see the appendix).

That last statistical quibble reinforces the judgement that, if all real incomes could be accurately measured, inter-regional inequality, in the sense of differences between regional averages, though substantial, is not the major source of inequality among Russian households.

15.3.2. *Sources of regional inequality*

Even if inter-regional differences in average real incomes do not dominate other sources of inequality in Russia, they still matter. First, they are in themselves a substantial source of inter-personal inequality. Second, they appear to have continued to increase through 1997. Third, precisely because Russian administrative regions are sub-national political units and times are turbulent, material inequalities between them are capable of disturbing the domestic political scene. There are therefore practical reasons for trying to understand the forces that determine their evolution.

One simple starting-point is the observation that, in a country whose domestic demand has been shrinking, those regions in which there is a larger amount of business with a relatively buoyant world economy are likely to gain, relatively to regions that are overwhelmingly dependent on domestic trade, investment, and credit. Therefore the index of per capita forex inflows (see the appendix), as a measure of business links with the wider world, might help to explain regional differences in average real incomes.

The scattergram of per capita forex inflows against per capita real incomes (Figure 15.2) seems to confirm this point. As with Figure 15.1, there is not a conveniently tight grouping of points around a likely linear trend, but there is a suggestion of a positive association between the two variables.

In late 1997 Goskomstat made available gross regional product (GRP) data for the years 1994 and 1995 (see the appendix). In most countries of the world one would expect that regions with high per capita total output would tend to have high personal incomes. Substantial inter-regional financing of transfer incomes could weaken the link, but on the whole it would be surprising if such an association were not found.

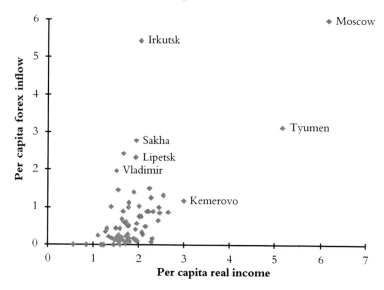

Figure 15.2. *RF regions: per capita real incomes and forex inflows, 1995*

Figure 15.3 suggests that in 1995 per capita GRP and per capita real incomes were indeed associated across Russian regions.

Per capita levels of gross regional product, forex inflows, and personal real incomes, are all quite well correlated with one another, at any rate for 1995. If it is the case, however, that the ability of a region's residents to gain foreign currency has been of special importance to regional income levels, one might expect that rates of forex inflow would help to account for differences in regional income levels.

There turns out to be a striking difference between 1994 and 1995. For both years, the index (Russian average = 1) of per capita personal income was taken as the dependent variable and corresponding indexes of per capita GRP and per capita forex inflows were tried as explanatory variables. The variables are labelled REALY, GRP, and HCPC below.

For 1994, with Moscow city and Altai krai taken out because they were outliers, per capita GRP does not have a significant effect on real income levels, given per capita forex inflows. The influence of forex inflows is weak but significant. This is the case whether the variables are left untransformed or put in log form. Leaving out the GRP variable and simply relating the index of income levels to that of forex inflows, one gets some support for the proposition that forex flows mattered—and

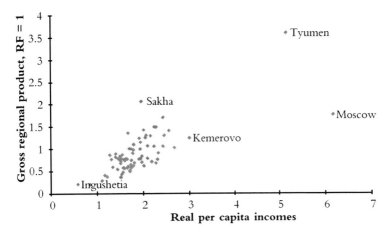

Figure 15.3. *Russian regions 1995: gross product and real personal income levels*

apparently mattered more than gross regional product levels. (The bracketed figures below are, as before, t statistics. The HCPC coefficient is significant at better than the 1 per cent level.) This sort of relationship was found earlier for the year 1993 as well (Hanson 1997*b*).

$$\text{REAL Y 94} = \underset{(29.54)}{0.919} + \underset{(3.19)}{0.057\,\text{HCPC94}}$$

$$n = 74 \qquad \text{adj } R^2 = 0.111 \qquad \text{DW} = 1.720 \qquad F = 10.155$$

With the numbers for 1995, the same exercise produces a quite different picture. It is the per capita forex inflow measure (HCPC) that shows up as not significant, while gross regional product displays a strong and significant influence. In this case putting the variables in log form worked best; indeed, in the regression for 1994 with per capita GRP and per capita foreign currency inflows as independent variables, the latter proved to be redundant. Moscow is again omitted as an outlier.

$$\ln\text{REAL Y 95} = \underset{(0.13)}{0.003} + \underset{(11.29)}{0.519\ln\text{GRP95}}$$

$$n = 75 \qquad \text{adj } R^2 = 0.631 \qquad \text{DW} = 1.684 \qquad F = 127.500$$

An alternative specification, in which Moscow is included with a dummy variable for Moscow/not-Moscow added, also works well. The coefficient on ln GRP does not change greatly; nor does its significance level. The coefficient for the Moscow dummy is predictably high: 0.862.

So forex inflows influence regional income levels in 1994 and regional gross output levels do not; in 1995 this conclusion is reversed. One explanation might simply be that the primary data are defective, and therefore tell us conflicting stories in successive years, none of which is reliable.

It is, however, quite possible that the turmoil of the past few years has produced rapid changes in the strength of different influences on regional outcomes. Recorded output in each region (GRP) under-represents *de novo* private-sector activity. Much of this activity has centred on trading in imported consumer goods. The importing of consumer goods and the subsequent wholesale distribution of them within Russia is likely to be concentrated in the new commercial and financial hub regions, one of whose characteristics is comparatively high per capita inflows of foreign currency.

It is often in those regions that industrial output has collapsed most precipitously (see appendix Table 1). One reason for this is that defence production was concentrated in the regions with the biggest urban agglomerations, and those have also tended to be the new hub regions. The gross regional product data reflect industrial decline better than the rise of new activities, and that is presumably why they show Moscow behind both Sakha and Tyumen in per capita GRP in both 1994 and 1995. But if industrial and other well-recorded activity is adjusting over time to the shock of the 1992 changes, one would expect more 'normal' relationships—including a strong correlation between recorded regional per capita output and regional per capita incomes—to begin to emerge.

This would be all the more likely if the growth of the under-recorded informal sector were slackening, as seems to be the case in Russia. Opportunities for profitable arbitrage between controlled and uncontrolled markets have shrunk as those (often local) controls that survived the initial liberalization have been eroded. The same is true of incomes from the simple disposal of inventories and other assets. The selling-off of the family silver is by definition a finite process.

The change between the two years could also reflect an increase in market integration across regions. There are now well-established markets for foreign currency in Russia. It is to be expected that foreign exchange that flows into bank accounts in one region of an integrated economy will be purchased by potential users in other regions, if the foreign exchange market encounters no regional barriers. There is no reason, in such a situation, for gains from trade to be captured only by certain regions, in the sense that firms and households in a region that generates exports would have some sort of exclusive right to use those proceeds to buy imports. Such integration of the foreign-exchange market may have developed by 1995, but not earlier.

In short, there are reasons for believing that the declining role of forex inflows and the rising role of gross regional product as determinants of regional income differences might reflect a decline in the importance of short-term emergency adjustments, against a background of diminishing turmoil. The change between the two years may also (or alternatively) signal increased integration of the internal Russian currency market.

Other possible explanatory variables were tried out, without improving the explanation of the variance in 1995 regional per capita real incomes. First, the notion that the fact that a region contained a large city might be a source of relative strength in market adaptation, separately from the strength of its business links with the outside world, was tested by adding a dummy variable for regions containing a city (or cities—Samara, uniquely, has two) of over 700,000 population. This did not improve the results, and the big-city dummy, though showing the expected sign, was not significant at 5 per cent. Second, a proxy measure of the strength of regional demand was tried, in the form of an index (Russian average = 1) of registered unemployment rates. This additional variable also did not assist the enquiry. In this case, the coefficient had the expected sign, but was nowhere near being significant.

The ability to win foreign exchange may be less important to a region's income levels now, but it does seem to have been of considerable importance in the immediate aftermath of the 1992 liberalization. Two kinds of region have been relatively rich in foreign exchange: a small number of commercial-hub regions; and a small number of regions that have inherited a strong export sector, usually based on natural resources. In so far as one can judge from the figures for 1995 (appendix Table 1), the former include Moscow city, Samara, and Novosibirsk. The latter include Tyumen' (oil and gas), Sakha (diamonds), and Lipetsk (quality steel from high-quality iron-ore deposits and 1970s-vintage imported German steel mills).

There are other regions with relatively high 1995 per capita inflows of foreign exchange where the local story behind the figure would need to be checked before the region was pigeon-holed in this way. And the classification into hubs and 'inherited export capabilities' is not always watertight: Samara benefits greatly, at present, from VAZ car exports from Togliatti—a prop that could prove more fragile than a decent oil field, for the VAZ works is in poor shape.

15.4. CONCLUSION

The idea that Russian regions are adapting to the post-Communist environment in radically different ways, with a substantial part of the country retreating into low monetization, is not supported by the evidence analysed here. When regional savings rates are compared with regional real income levels, and a non-linear relationship between them is allowed for, the regional differences in savings rates do not seem to require some sort of dual-economy explanation. To that extent, the notion that Russia is not becoming a single economic space is also not supported.

The same, comparatively hopeful, conclusion comes from an analysis of the determinants of regional income differences. The rates of foreign-exchange inflows were of some importance before 1995, and in 1994 did more to account for regional income differences than did regional output per head. In 1995, however, a more 'normal' situation could be observed: regional per capita output levels began to work better in explaining regional income differences, and, given those output levels, rates of inflow of foreign exchange no longer helped to account for regional differences. That might reflect *inter alia* a greater cross-regional integration of foreign-currency transactions.

At the same time, regional differentiation in real incomes has continued to increase through the third quarter of 1997. Inter-regional differences account for well under a half of inequality among Russian households in general. They may none the less be politically troublesome. The maintenance of national solidarity probably requires that they begin to be reduced before long. The process of market integration should in the long run help to reduce regional differences; but the quantitative evidence presented here is not strong enough to allow confident predictions that this will happen quickly.

In the third quarter of 1997 the highest real income levels were (in descending order) in Moscow city, Tyumen', St Petersburg, Perm'. Murmansk, Karelia, and Samara. The lowest (in ascending order) were in Ingushetia, Dagestan, Tyva, Chita, Buryatia, and Kalmykia. The large gaps between these two extreme groups are not likely to be closed in the foreseeable future. It is none the less desirable that regional inequalities begin soon to lessen. Despite the offsetting effects of migration and (perhaps) capital flows to cheap-labour regions, agglomeration advantages in the emerging hub regions may work quite powerfully to preserve the differences. In addition, Russia contains a number of regions that are very far from large markets: the far north and eastern Siberia, in particular. Subsidies to energy, transport, and food supplies to these regions assisted their over-development in the Soviet period; they now have to adjust to an economic order in which they have abruptly become peripheral. That adjustment seems certain to be costly.

The kinds of regions that are doing better than the national average are a small number that contain emerging commercial and financial hubs or are gateways to western countries, and another small contingent with strong inherited assets in the form of natural resource-based export capabilities. The future prospects of the former would seem to be dependent chiefly on the overall performance of the Russian economy. The future of the latter group of Russian regions will be sensitive to price changes on world markets and to natural resource depletion—perhaps also to the passing of control over natural resources to Moscow-based financial groups. (So far as the two leading regions are concerned, Moscow's advantage over Tyumen' already increased sharply between 1995 and 1997.)

None of the attempts made here at accounting for regional real-income differences is statistically so strong as to leave little scope for differences in policy (central or local) to have had an influence, too. But any exercise in assessing the 'performance' of regional leaders or the regional impact of specific federal policies needs to be undertaken with some caution. A region's inherited economic structure and location, and whether it does or does not contain a very large conurbation, are considerations that do seem to have affected the pattern of regional adjustment since 1992. These factors may well be considerably more important than anything that politicians do.

There are signs, in the evidence considered here, that market forces are doing something to integrate the economies of Russian regions. Obviously, however, they are not so far doing this fast enough to prevent a continuing divergence of income levels. Is there a role for federal policy here? We have mentioned evidence that the 1995 pattern of net intra-governmental budget transfers was very mildly equalizing. Beyond that, it is not obvious that the centre has the means and the information to do a great deal that would be helpful. The current campaign by the Ministry of Justice and the State Anti-Monopoly Committee to attack regional barriers to market entry (*Izvestiya*, 4 November 1997, p. 1) may well be as useful as anything else that can realistically be expected.

Appendix. **Regional data on household incomes**

Data problems and limitations

The data used here are all from Goskomstat. One series described as coming from the government's Centre for the Standard of Living, seems in fact to be of Goskomstat origin. Most of the data are for 1995, because full regional data for 1996 or 1997 were not published at late 1997. However, some 1996 and (third-quarter) 1997 data that were available have been used.

The regional values to be 'explained' are the real values, or purchasing power, of the reported average money incomes of each of seventy-six or seventy-seven regions (all *oblasti*, *kraya*, and republics, without Chechnya, with the autonomous *okruga* not treated separately but included within their main administrative regions). The money income data are preferable to the wage data in at least one respect: it is well established that wage payments are massively under-reported. Money income data should in principle include, for instance, interest on bank accounts—one of the forms of remuneration used by employers to minimize their tax bills.

The income figures should in general be treated with caution, but they should at least be capturing a large amount of personal income that is not reported as wages and salaries. They none the less have two clear defects.

First, they exclude income in kind. This matters because its relative importance is likely to vary across regions. Household subsistence food production has been claimed by one Russian source to be equivalent to an additional 20 per cent of reported money income for Russian households in general, and for an additional 100 per cent for rural households (Gurvich 1997). If this is true, real income levels will be systematically under-stated in the regions with a comparatively large rural population, relatively to other regions. This suggests that the wide apparent gap between income levels in Moscow and Dagestan (say) is an exaggeration of real differences in average material welfare.

Second, the ways in which the personal income data are derived may not be independent of consumption data. The large category 'income from entrepreneurial activity' may be derived simply as the residual when reported wages plus benefits are subtracted from the sum of reported consumer spending and saving (OECD 1995, p. 20). Whether this is done at regional levels is not clear.

To get a real income measure for regions, I have taken the regional money income and divided it by the reported regional cost of the nineteen-item consumer 'food basket'. That produces the 'real y 95' column in appendix Table 1.

This is an exceedingly crude regional real income measure. It conveys information only about the food-purchasing power of incomes. The food basket is priced only in the region's capital city, and the proportion of the population living outside the regional capital varies, as (probably) does the difference between capital-city and other-regional prices. Even so, this measure may be, for the

Appendix Table 1. *Russian regions: data series used in this chapter*

	APS 95	aps index	real y 95	GRP 95	HCPC 95	ind q 95/91	reg u/e index
Karelia Rep	7.6	0.745	2.429	1.071	0.64	0.523	1.63
Komi Rep	8.1	0.794	2.449	1.699	0.99	0.597	1.81
Arkhangel'sk oblast'	5.1	0.5	1.732	0.977	0.61	0.602	2.56
Vologda	4.7	0.461	2.245	1.494	1.49	0.757	0.91
Murmansk	11.1	1.088	2.541	1.420	1.32	0.584	1.91
St Petersburg	24.8	2.431	2.662	1.020	0.87	0.418	0.66
Leningrad	9.3	0.912	1.639	0.781	0.68	0.429	1.69
Novgorod	6	0.588	2.022	0.620	0.75	0.488	1.25
Pskov	8.5	0.833	1.656	0.579	0.12	0.262	2.88
Bryansk	6.9	0.677	1.729	0.551	0.07	0.362	1.56
Vladimir	8.7	0.853	1.507	0.678	0.16	0.361	2.81
Ivanovo	6.4	0.627	1.446	0.530	0.03	0.325	3.91
Kaluga	8.4	0.824	1.507	0.775	1.97	0.391	0.81
Kostroma	6.1	0.598	1.944	0.767	0.12	0.38	2.47
Moscow City	47.2	4.627	6.161	1.737	5.99	0.375	0.16
Moscow Oblast'	53.2	5.216	1.3	0.753	0.43	0.318	0.86
Orel	9.4	0.922	2.273	0.688	0.08	0.387	0.72
Ryazan	11	1.078	1.483	0.821	0.43	0.408	0.59
Smolensk	6.4	0.628	1.966	0.700	0.56	0.47	0.28
Tver	9.3	0.912	1.587	0.736	0.16	0.394	0.59
Tula	8.2	0.804	2.187	0.715	0.89	0.446	0.56
Yaroslavl	8.6	0.843	2.090	1.062	0.33	0.361	2.59
Marii-El	5.8	0.569	1.442	0.536	0.13	0.396	1.47
Mordova	4.7	0.461	1.593	0.547	0.01	0.396	2.06
Chuvashia	4.8	0.470	1.556	0.578	0.26	0.321	2.34
Kirov	4.7	0.461	1.910	0.750	0.16	0.458	2.31
Nizhnii Novgorod	13.3	1.304	1.790	0.985	0.5	0.573	0.88
Belgorod	11.8	1.157	2.319	0.899	0.89	0.783	0.31
Voronezh	14.4	1.412	1.802	0.690	0.08	0.387	0.62
Kursk	8.2	0.804	1.745	0.746	0.22	0.569	0.47
Lipetsk	9.2	0.902	1.935	1.154	2.34	0.725	0.38
Tambov	6.5	0.637	1.718	0.522	0.03	0.54	2.06
Kalmykia	6.5	0.637	1.109	0.291	0.25	0.308	2.56
Tatarstan	8.3	0.813	2.227	1.053	0.89	0.558	0.44
Astrakhan	6.1	0.598	1.739	0.585	0.1	0.613	1.38
Volgograd	9.1	0.892	1.579	0.761	0.43	0.434	0.41
Penza	9	0.882	1.720	0.500	0.05	0.52	1.78

Appendix Table 1. (*continued*)

	APS 95	aps index	real y 95	GRP 95	HCPC 95	ind q 95/91	reg u/e index
Samara	17.8	1.745	2.016	1.423	1.01	0.595	0.63
Saratov	8.4	0.824	1.618	0.780	0.21	0.429	1.06
Ul'yanovsk	9.2	0.902	2.299	0.749	0.16	0.653	1.03
Adygeya	9.9	0.971	1.530	0.427	0.08	0.38	0.73
Dagestan	6	0.588	0.842	0.208	0.01	0.24	2
Ingushetia	4.6	0.451	0.567	0.203	0	0.289	1.27
Kabardino-Balkaria	6.3	0.617	1.210	0.348	0.01	0.295	1
Karachaevo-Cherkess Republic	8.4	0.823	1.172	0.408	0.03	0.293	1.38
North Ossetia	11.4	1.118	1.515	0.369	0.08	0.236	1.22
Krasnodar	17.5	1.716	1.731	0.644	0.23	0.498	0.56
Stavropol	13.2	1.294	1.511	0.715	0.18	0.395	0.56
Rostov	12.6	1.235	1.794	0.622	0.17	0.428	0.38
Bashkortostan	9.2	0.902	1.759	1.009	0.5	0.624	0.72
Udmurtia	6.8	0.667	2.098	0.795	0.28	0.357	2.75
Kurgan	6.7	0.656	1.330	0.595	0.23	0.379	2.03
Orenburg	9.1	0.892	1.273	0.852	0.34	0.62	0.28
Perm'	10.5	1.029	2.066	1.285	0.74	0.55	1.47
Sverdlovsk	16	1.569	2.155	1.294	0.49	0.459	1.09
Chelyabinsk	10.3	1.010	1.768	0.938	0.28	0.462	0.81
Altai Rep	12.1	1.186	1.556	0.472	0.08	0.426	0.63
Altai Krai	8.4	0.823	1.591	0.578	0.13	0.376	0.91
Kemerovo	5.2	0.510	3.002	1.238	1.18	0.64	0.59
Novosibirsk	28.2	2.765	1.545	0.876	1.46	0.465	0.63
Omsk	12.8	1.255	1.933	0.997	0.4	0.478	0.78
Tomsk	8.7	0.853	1.910	1.244	1.4	0.532	1.25
Tyumen'	9.4	0.922	5.168	3.600	3.14	0.635	0.78
Buryatia	3.2	0.314	1.456	0.769	0.12	0.583	0.56
Tyva	1.7	0.167	1.213	0.368	0	0.507	0.81
Khakasia	4.5	0.441	1.772	0.910	1	0.637	1.06
Krasnoyarsk	6.6	0.647	2.268	1.482	1.25	0.658	0.97
Irkutsk	7.9	0.775	2.046	1.281	5.46	0.662	1
Chita	4.4	0.431	1.393	0.809	0.19	0.356	0.97
Sakha	5.6	0.549	1.957	2.066	2.77	0.773	0.25
Primorskii	14	1.373	1.394	0.891	1.01	0.556	0.94
Khabarovsk	12.4	1.216	1.697	0.998	0.58	0.335	1.66

Appendix Table 1. (*continued*)

	APS 95	aps index	real y 95	GRP 95	HCPC 95	ind q 95/91	reg u/e index
Amur	5.1	0.5	1.972	0.838	0.11	0.467	1.76
Kamchatka	5.8	0.569	1.667	1.357	2.43	0.443	1.44
Magadan	12.8	1.255	2.459	1.313	0.85	0.63	0.84
Sakhalin	11	1.078	1.791	1.097	1.11	0.527	1.69
Kaliningrad	18.1	1.775	1.663	0.592	0.9	0.366	1.81

Definitions: 95 denotes the year 1995; APS = recorded savings as proportion of money income; APS index = regional APS, where the unweighted average of all regions' APSs = 1; real y = region's average reported money income divided by the regional cost of the 19-item food basket; HCPC = index of per capita inflow of foreign currency into a region, where RF average = 1; ind q 95/91 = industrial output in 1995 as a proportion of industrial output in 1991, i.e. where 1991 = 1; reg u/e index = index of percentage registered unemployment, RF average = 1; big city: dummy variable, = 1 if the region contains a city with >700,000 inhabitants, 0 otherwise.

Sources: derived from Goskomstat data as given in Bradshaw and Palacin (1996) and Goskomstat RF (1996*a*), Tables 759, 775, 781–5, 823, 833. In the case of Ingushetia, 1995 unemployment rate and industrial output figures, not given in the source, were interpolated by the author as the unweighted averages of north Caucasus republics' equivalent figures.

period 1992–6, the best regional living-cost measure we have. (In 1997 it was replaced by a twenty-five-item basket.) There is also a 'subsistence minimum' (*prozhitochniy minimum*) measure for each region, which has been more heavily used by Goskomstat since 1994. But this is reported to be constructed somewhat differently—and in some cases tendentiously—in different regions (McAuley 1997). In the absence of regional cost of living indexes of a more comprehensive kind, the real y 95 measure is the best we can at present come up with.

One peculiarity of the resulting sets of regional real income data, whether calculated from the nineteen-item basket or from the subsistence minimum, is that they are not consistent with the overall figure for the country as a whole. Typically, when the national figure for personal income as a multiple of the food-basket cost or of the subsistence minimum is compared with the equivalent figures for the regions, the national figure is higher than those in all but a dozen or so regions. The regions that appear above the average typically contain only about one-sixth of the Russian population.

Either the money incomes figure for the country as a whole is calculated separately from those for the regions and something is included in it that is not included at regional level, or the various cost of living figures for the whole country are calculated in a way that does not give a population-weighted average of the regional figures. Or both. When I have calculated coefficients of variation for regional measures of real income, the mean that is used to divide the standard deviation is the unweighted arithmetic mean of the regional figures (see Table 15.1 in main text).

The figure for personal savings as a proportion of personal income (the APS 95 column in appendix Table 1) is reported saving. It is not clear to me whether the Goskomstat savings figures go beyond changes in reported accumulated rouble Savings Bank (Sberbank) and perhaps other bank personal accounts to include changes in rouble cash holdings and rouble foreign currency holdings. Goskomstat has at the national level treated the purchase of foreign exchange as a form of saving, despite the fact that a large proportion of such purchases goes into buying for the shuttle trade and is not savings at all (*Russian Economic Trends*, March and June 1997 monthly updates).

The APS series has been turned into an index, with the unweighted arithmetic mean of the regional numbers = 1 (APS index in appendix Table 1).

The remaining series in appendix Table 1 are more straightforward. The gross regional product (GRP) figures are only recently published, and were the subject of considerable debate before publication. They do not sum to Russian GDP; a 'federal contribution' to GDP of around 12 per cent is not allocated among regions. Exactly how that federal element is defined, and what it implies for the meaning of the GRP figures, is unclear. It is likely that the GRP numbers (possibly to a proportionally greater extent than the national GDP figure) under-state new private economic activity. Some calculations for unrecorded activity are apparently made only at the national level. That might explain why, for example, Moscow city's per capita GRP in 1995 was below that of both Tyumen' and Sakha.

HCPC 95 is an index (national average = 1) of the figures for 'inflow of foreign exchange' (*postuplenie valyuty*) into a region, divided by the population of the region. This inflow (forex inflow henceforth) represents flows during the year into bank accounts in a region. These flows are partly from export earnings and partly from foreign credits and foreign investment in financial form. They do not include all export proceeds of producers in a region, because part of export earnings is either spent or banked (legally or illegally) offshore (personal communications from Andrei Sizov of Sovekon in Moscow and the regional statistical office in Samara).

Subject to further information about the compilation of this data-series, it is a useful if very rough measure of a region's direct gains from business with the outside world. A large flow of export earnings that remains offshore (like most of the earnings, reportedly, of the fishing fleet based in Primorskii krai and some of the oil and gas earnings from Tyumen') would not be included. A region that attracts foreign credits and foreign direct investment (other than in kind) in substantial amounts but had only modest export earnings would with some justice look quite good on this indicator.

The measure of industrial output in 1995 as a proportion of 1991 probably under-states industrial output in 1995 (Kuboniwa 1996). It is also somewhat problematic because the base year is one that precedes price and output liberal-ization—though in 1991 there was already a partial breakdown of price control, and in 1992 shortages did not all disappear at the start of the year. What matters for the purposes of this chapter is whether the resulting distortion varies much across Russian regions. It would do so, given the variation in the industrial structure of regions, if there was systematic variation in this distortion across industrial branches. Beyond that, one can only hope that Alec Nove's Law of Equal Cheat-ing, postulated for Soviet-era time series, applies (more or less) to industrial cross-section data across post-Soviet Russian regions.

The unemployment measure used here is that for officially registered unem-ployment. The ILO-definition unemployment measure (from labour force sur-veys) is substantially higher, but across regions there is quite a strong correlation between them. For present purposes, therefore, it should not matter much which series is used.

REFERENCES

Berkowitz, D. (1994). 'Russia: Market Integration Against the Odds', Washington, DC: National Council for Soviet and East European Research.

Bradshaw, M. J., and Hanson, P. (1994). 'Regions, Local Power and Reform in Russia' in R. W. Campbell (ed.), *The Postcommunist Economic Transformation. Essays in Honor of Gregory Grossman*, Boulder, Col.: Westview, pp. 133–63.

—— and Palacin, J. (1996). *An Atlas of the Economic Performance of Russia's Regions*, Working Paper 2, Birmingham: Birmingham University Russian Regional Research Group.

Callejon, M., and Costa, M. T. (1997). 'Agglomeration Economies and the Loca-tion of Industry', Paper presented at the European Network for Industrial Policy International Conference on Industrial Policy for Europe, London, June.

European Commission (1994). *Competitiveness and Cohesion: Trends in the Regions*, Luxembourg: European Union.

Goskomstat (1993). *O razvitii ekonomicheskikh reform v Rossiiskoi Federatsii v 1992 godu*, Moscow.

—— (1996a). *Rossiiskii statisticheskii 1996*, Moscow.

—— (1996b). *Sotsial'no-ekonomicheskoe polozhenie Rossii 1996*, Moscow.

Gurvich, V. (1997). 'Bogatykh ne stalo bol'she, bednykh ne stalo men'she', *Delovoi ekspress*, 21 January, p. 16.

Hanson, P. (1997a). 'What Sort of Capitalism is developing in Russia?' *Communist Economies and Economic Transformation*, 9/1: 27–43.

—— (1997b). 'How Many Russias? Russia's Regions and Their Adjustment to Economic Change', *The International Spectator*, 32/1: 39–53.

—— and Kirkow, P. (1997). 'Tomsk: Federal-regional Relations', Paper presented at the OECD-Tomsk Regional Administration conference on Industrial Re-structuring in Tomsk Region, June.

Jacobs, J. (1963). *The Economy of Cities*, Harmondsworth: Penguin.

Kuboniwa, M. (1996). 'Russian Output Drop in Early Transition and Its Macro- and Micro-economic Implications', Hitotsubashi University Institute of Economic Research, Discussion Paper D96-11, November.

Lavrov, A. (1996). 'Pochemu dotatsionnye regiony golosuyut za kommunistov', *Rossiiskie vesti*, 10 April 1996, p. 3.

McAuley, M. (1997). 'The Determinants of Russian Federal-Regional Fiscal Relations: Equity or Political Influence?', *Europe–Asia Studies*, 49/3, May: 431–44.

OECD (1995). *OECD Economic Surveys. The Russian Federation 1995*, Paris: OECD.

Sapir, J. (1996). 'The "Washington Consensus" and Transition in Russia: History of a Failure', draft, Ecole des Hautes Etudes en Sciences Sociales.

Sutherland, D. J., and Hanson, P. (1996). 'Structural Change in the Economies of Russia's Regions', *Europe–Asia Studies*, 48/3: 367–92.

16

Poverty

JENI KLUGMAN AND SHEILA MARNIE

16.1. INTRODUCTION

Poverty in Russia is not a phenomenon which arrived with transition, but the economic reforms have been associated with steep rises in the levels and severity of poverty, and changes in the profile of poverty. This chapter reviews available evidence of these changes. We also look at evidence of increasing inequality, using available data on per capital income levels, and at growing inter-regional inequality in the country. We examine the main determinants of poverty in the 1990s, and look at the sections of the population most at risk. The impact of various social transfers on the incidence of poverty among different groups is also examined. The analysis draws together available official data together with the published and unpublished research on the topic that has proliferated since the transition began.

The chapter is organized as follows. The next section briefly reviews approaches to poverty measurement in the pre-reform period. Section 3 investigates what is known about trends in poverty and inequality during the transition, including the depth and duration as well as the incidence of poverty. Section 4 presents results relevant to the composition of poverty, highlighting the impact of labour market adjustment and the vulnerability of the old and young; while section 5 looks briefly at the regional dimension. Section 6 examines the impact of social protection policies, and section 7 concludes.

16.2. POVERTY IN THE PRE-REFORM PERIOD

In the Soviet period, there was officially no poverty. The right to work, and the system of state pensions and benefits, was supposed to ensure that everyone had a source of money income, and state subsidies for housing, utilities, basic foodstuffs, and transport meant that everyone could in principle be assured a minimum standard of living. In the 1960s, however, the term 'low-income' (*maloobespespechennye*) families was introduced to denote those falling below a semi-official minimum standard of living, and in 1975 a cash child support benefit was introduced for such families (Mozhina 1992; Atkinson and Micklewright 1992; Mikhalev 1997). In this section we review the approach taken to setting a 'poverty line', look at how household-level data was collected, and summarize the available evidence about the structure of poverty during the pre-reform period.

16.2.1. *Pre-reform poverty lines*

The setting of a poverty line usually entails a choice between an 'absolute' and a 'relative' approach. Either an 'absolute' level of income is defined, which is considered necessary in order to assure a minimum standard of living; or the poverty line is defined as 'relative' to the average income in the country, and will rise or fall with changes in the average level (Ravallion 1992). The minimum consumption budgets, constructed by Soviet research institutes from the 1950s,[1] contained aspects of both approaches. Although the methodology used to calculate the budget was essentially that used to obtain absolute poverty levels, the goal was to define a minimum acceptable standard of living for Soviet citizens, rather than an absolute (physiological) poverty level. Thus, the minimum consumption budget contained items which would not normally be considered necessary to achieve an absolute consumption minimum, including, for example, cultural and sporting activities, as well as tobacco and alcohol (Matthews 1986). Aspects of the relative approach were reflected not only in the composition of the consumption budget but also in the final choice of the rouble threshold, which was originally set at half of the national average per capita income. The Soviet consumer budget was criticized alternatively for being too generous (since the food basket included a higher proportion of fats and protein than would normally be considered essential for a healthy diet) and for being too austere (ignoring the fact that in a shortage economy goods could not always be bought at official state prices).

Thus, while there was officially no poverty in the Soviet Union, there was a tradition defining a minimum acceptable standard of living and, associated with that practice, some recognition by the authorities of the

---

[1] The most detailed information on these budgets was published in Sarkisyan and Kuznetsova (1967).

existence of relative poverty, even if the estimates of the consumption minimum were not officially published until the late 1980s. From the mid-1970s onwards there was also some attempt to help those households falling below the unofficial poverty line through the granting of cash benefits to low-income families.

The Gorbachev period saw greater openness in the discussion of poverty. In 1988 prime minister Ryzhkov announced, for the first time, that 41 million people in the USSR were living below the subsistence minimum. The State Statistical Committee reported that approximately 14 per cent of the population of the USSR and 11 per cent in Russia were living below the consumption minimum in 1989 (Goskomstat SSR 1991) and at the end of the *glasnost* period, Gorbachev issued a presidential decree requiring that the minimum subsistence level be calculated and published monthly.[2]

16.2.3. *Pre-reform data sources*

The Soviet State statistical committee (Goskomstat) derived information on household income and expenditure form the Family Budget Survey (FBS). It is useful to review the nature and problems associated with this survey, since up through 1997 the FBS has remained substantially unchanged, and has continued to be the primary source of official data on poverty and living standards in the Russian Federation. The survey was carried out regularly from the 1950s onwards, but over the years was strongly criticized both by Russian and western scholars (Shenfield 1983; Braithwaite and Heleniak 1989; Atkinson and Micklewright, 1992). Most criticism was directed at its sampling method, which differs significantly from the probability sampling methods usually employed for household budget surveys in the West, and which led to certain sampling biases. Families were selected by sampling individuals at their place of work. A quota sample was constructed on the basis of two main categories: state sector 'workers and employees'; and collective farmers.[3]

The sample size was quite large, but not representative of all territorial units. The last major sample increase occurred in 1988, when the

---

[2] A translation of the decree is given in Atkinson and Micklewright (1992).

[3] The sample of workers and employees was drawn according to the so-called 'territorial branch principle', by establishing quotas for each branch of the economy, and then branches of industry. A list of enterprises ranked according to average monthly wage was drawn up for each branch, and then, within the enterprises, a list of individual workers was drawn up, again ranked according to average monthly wage. Workers in each wage category were supposed to be proportionally represented. From 1988 onwards a quota of purely pensioner households (with no wage earners) was added.

number of households surveyed increased from 32,900 to 48,600 in Russia alone. According to Goskomstat, the sample then covered all regions, all branches of the economy, and most but not all branches of industry.[4] Individual workers, once selected, were asked to remain in the sample for an indefinite period; there was no planned rotation, but when families dropped out, they were replaced by the families of workers with the same skill and wage level.[5]

The sample was biased, mainly because families were encouraged to participate indefinitely. Thus workers who had relatively longer work records, and who tended, in the Soviet period at least, to have correspondingly higher wages, were more likely to be included. On the other hand, the section of the population which was not in employment or was self-employed was under-represented, since it could only be sampled indirectly, if by chance other members of the family were sampled through the place of work.[6] Moreover, the more working members in the family, the greater the probability there was of the family being selected and also the higher the likely per capita income. In the post-Soviet period, the unrepresentativeness of the sample has worsened since there is now much more scope for private entrepreneurial activity, and also growing numbers of unemployed.

Despite these criticisms, the FBS was considered by Goskomstat to be an adequate source of information on household budgets, as long as wages from the state and collective farm sectors were the primary source of income for almost all households, and as long as the Soviet state could ensure that illegal or unofficial (non-reported) sources of income were minimal. The survey was also considered adequate in a context where there was no tradition of, and no perceived need for, using household survey data for policymaking purposes or for academic research. There was, for example, no tradition of monitoring poverty dynamics through the exploitation of survey data.[7]

---

[4] More detailed investigation into the Uzbek FBS sample inherited from the Soviet era has shown that its sample was not representative even at this level, i.e. the quotas for each branch of the economy were not proportional to the numbers employed in these branches. It is difficult therefore to accept similar claims for Russia at face value. See Falkingham and Micklewright in Falkingham *et al.* (eds.) (1997).

[5] Natural rotation achieved in this way was claimed in 1994 to total annually 15–20% of the sample.

[6] In the late 1980s the share of the adult Russian population that was 'not employed' was about 7% according to Goskomstat estimates.

[7] Although the FBS was a panel survey, households did not have an identifying code, and the dynamics of living standards were not studied. Data were stored using software designed to produce a set of standard tables each quarter.

16.2.3. *Who were the Soviet poor?*

Soviet censorship made it difficult to carry out systematic studies of poverty. Not even the FBS data was available to research institutes. Only one institute attached to the Academy of Sciences (directed by Rimashevskaya) managed to carry out independent surveys of income levels in one industrial town, Taganrog, considered to be representative of western Russia. The Taganrog studies, and other western analyses based largely on surveys of emigrés (Ofer and Vinokur 1992) none the less permit the construction of a profile of poverty during the Soviet period.

These earlier studies identified the following groups as being particularly vulnerable. First, families with children under 18, particularly those with more than three children, and single-parent families, or households with only one wage-earner. Secondly, certain groups of pensioners, mainly those living alone and with no other source of income; and thirdly, those working in low-wage branches of the economy, or low-wage job categories. Fourthly, there was a small group of homeless and those recently released from prison who could be categorized as extremely poor.[8]

FBS data suggested that families with three or more children represented the most vulnerable group, and there is evidence that average family size in the lowest income quintile was significantly higher than that in the top quintile. The Taganrog studies suggested that it was the number of dependants in a family, both children and elderly (or the ratio of dependants to wage-earners) which was the main determinant of poverty, not just the number and presence of children (Braithwaite 1997). In sum, households which deviated from the 'norm' of two wage-earners and a maximum of two dependants were at risk, and those within the 'norm' were also slightly at risk if one or both wage-earners were employed in the jobs at the lower end of the tariff scale.

Pensioners as a whole were not considered a vulnerable group. Pension rates varied considerably, and not all pensioners relied on the pension as their sole source of income. Some continued to work and were entitled to both a wage and pension; others benefited from private transfers or from living with other family members who were wage-earners. There seems, however, to have been a consensus that pensioners living alone with no other source of income were a distinct category of the

---

[8] For more details, see Braithwaite in Klugman (ed.) (1997); Matthews (1986); and McAuley (1979).

poor, and that those who were entitled only to the minimum pension (14 per cent of all old-age pensioners in 1988) were definitely at risk.

There was also a gender dimension to poverty in the Soviet period, in that the lowest paid branches and jobs tended to be those employing predominantly female employees (McAuley 1979). Thus, the risk of poverty for female-headed households was considered greater (Braithwaite 1997). Lastly, the homeless and recently released prisoners were numerically the smallest group of poor, but were considered to be the most vulnerable.

16.3. THE POOR—HOW MANY IN THE 1990s?

New approaches to poverty measurement have been employed since the transition began. This allows us to review evidence about trends in the incidence, depth, and duration of poverty during the 1990s. Not only have there been steep increases in the incidence and depth of poverty, but overall high levels of poverty have persisted even after stabilization and signs of resumption of economic growth. Worsening trends in the distribution of income and expenditure have been an important contributing factor.

16.3.1. *The poverty line*

Reliance on the traditional Soviet approaches to poverty measurement raised major problems. First, according to estimates based on the minimum consumer budget and information from the FBS on per capita incomes, over 70 per cent of the population was living below the poverty line by early 1992. These results were not useful to policymakers, who had to decide how to identify the poorest in society and target scarce budget resources. Nor were the results politically palatable. The existing minimum consumer budget was therefore deemed to be an inappropriate tool for estimating how many and who were poor. A review of its composition was undertaken, with the aim of obtaining a measure closer to a concept of poverty rather than a socially desirable minimum.

External assistance provided in the early 1990s helped to address these problems. A new 'minimum subsistence income' (MSI) was calculated, using the methodology usually associated with absolute poverty levels (Popkin *et al.* 1992). The food component of the budget was redefined, and the non-food component is now given simply as the percentage of the overall budget not required for food purchases.

Separate MSIs are calculated for the adult working-age population, children, and pensioners, meaning that the MSI incorporates an implicit equivalence scale,[9] and the subsistence budget allows for an average of 68.3 per cent of income to be spent on food (83 per cent for pensioners).[10] The revised subsistence minimum was intended to reflect a more austere absolute minimum, consistent with the consumption patterns of the poor. The Ministry of Labour (MOL) remains responsible for calculating what is referred to below as the official poverty line or minimum subsistence level.[11]

The results reported below are based on the MOL's national poverty line, unless otherwise indicated. Ideally regional poverty lines should be used, given the significant regional variations in price levels (see section 5 below for more detail). These are now calculated by regional offices of the MOL, but have not always been available for the earlier analyses. Since our aim here is to identify trends, use of the MOL national poverty line allows us to compare results across data sources from various years.

16.3.2. *Data sources*

Redefining the poverty line was only one side of the problem. More reliable information on family incomes was also needed in order to carry out poverty analyses. This implied the need for a representative sample in the FBS, and also for better use to be made of the data derived from the survey. The FBS is still conducted regularly, but since 1992 several rounds of a large living standards survey (the RLMS) have been conducted parallel to it.

The Russian Longitudinal Monitoring Survey (the RLMS) was designed to collect regular information on the living standards of a

[9] The equivalence scale, however, affects only the relative shares of food and non-food components. The MSI does not explicitly allow for economies of scale associated with household size (and fixed household costs of consumption), as we discuss further below.
[10] See Frolova (1996) for a detailed description of the official methodology.
[11] There are alternative poverty lines which are also published regularly in Russia. The government Centre for Economic Analysis and Forecasting (*Tsek*) publishes two poverty lines: a physiological subsistence minimum and a higher subsistence minimum (see Mikhalev 1997; Klugman and Braithwaite 1998). Subjective poverty lines, based on sociological surveys carried out by the Russian Centre for Public Opinion Research (VtsIOM), are also available, which provide data on popular perceptions of the amount of income necessary to provide a subsistence minimum. These subjective poverty lines are generally significantly higher than the official threshold.

nationally representative sample.[12] At the time of writing there have been seven rounds of the RLMS, with rounds 1–4 being a panel survey based on the same sample, and the later rounds being based on a revised sample design.

In 1994 Goskomstat revised the questionnaire for the FBS, with the objective of collecting data needed to weight consumer price indices. The questionnaire was revised again in 1996, and in 1998 it is planned to redesign the sample completely, in order to create a probability sample derived from lists of households, which will be representative on a national and regional level. (Note that all of the Goskomstat data reported below are derived from the FBS before sample redesign.)

For the transition period in Russia, there are thus two basic sources available for estimating the incidence of poverty, that is, the numbers or share of the population living below the poverty line. Goskomstat publishes monthly, quarterly, and annual figures, based on the FBS data on per capita income. The RLMS is available for several points in time.[13] Among the advantages of the latter source, beyond better representatives of the population, is the availability of the microdata for empirical analysis. Most analysis using the RLMS data has drawn on household expenditure data, including the imputed value of goods and services produced at home or received from employers (World Bank 1995; Klugman and Braithwaite 1998; Kolev 1996). This allows a useful comparison with the Goskomstat income–based figures, since expenditure-based data can be expected to avoid the dangers of under-reported household income (although it is not without its own problems).

16.3.3. *How many poor in the 1990s?*

The adoption of a new, different, poverty line (the subsistence minimum) from 1992 onwards makes it difficult to compare post- and pre-reform poverty. As far as poverty trends go, however, available evidence consistently points to a large increase in the numbers of poor in

---

[12] The Russian Longitudinal Monitoring Survey (RLMS) has been carried out since 1992. At the time of writing there have been 7 'rounds'. Phase I (rounds 1–4) had a sample which was representative at a national level, but not representative at regional levels. The overall sample in Phase I was 7,200 households, and the initial response rate was 88%, falling to 76% by round 4. Phase II (rounds 5–7) has a smaller overall sample (4,000 households), and a response rate of over 80%.

[13] The rounds were carried out in (I) July–August 1992, (II) December 1992–February 1993, (III) May–June 1993, (IV) October–November 1993, (V) November 1994, (VI) October–November 1995, and (VII) October–November 1996.

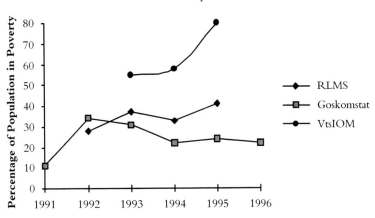

Figure 16.1. *Trends in poverty, 1991–1996: a comparison of alternative data sources*

Notes: All figures are relative to the official national poverty line except 1992. Goskomstat (based on the old Soviet social minimum), and the VtsIOM estimates that are based on a subjective poverty line.

Sources: Goskomstat 1996(*b*); Vserossiiskii . . . (1997); Braithwaite and Klugman (1997).

1992–3: from 11 per cent of the population in 1989 to over 30 per cent using Goskomstat figures and around 40 per cent using RLMS data by 1995 (see Figure 16.1). The share of the population which could be classified as 'very poor', having either per capita income or expenditure at below 50 per cent of poverty line, also rose significantly. Both the FBS and RLMS then indicate a gradual decline in the numbers below the poverty line from 1993 onwards. There is another slight rise in poverty in 1995 using both Goskomstat and RLMS derived data, but Goskomstat data for 1996 suggest a subsequent decline.[14] However, even if we take the more conservative Goskomstat estimates, the numbers living below the poverty line remain high (approximately 32 million, or 21.6 per cent of the population) in 1996.[15]

---

[14] Recent analyses carried out using RLMS data and regional poverty lines produce somewhat contradictory results. Thus Mroz and Popkin (1997) using rounds VI and VII argue that there has been another sharp increase in the incidence of poverty, of the order of 20%; while Commander *et al.* (1997) using rounds I–VI maintain that poverty levels have been declining. These analyses are not reported in greater detail here, since use of a different poverty line means that they are not easily comparable with the results reported above.

[15] Sensitivity analysis was carried out by the World Bank (1995) and Kolev (1996) using Rounds 1, 3, and 6 of the RLMS, to test the effect of slightly higher and lower national

Goskomstat publishes the subsistence minimum each month, which is adjusted monthly for inflation. Regional estimates of the subsistence minimum are also available. However, the monthly headcount figures that are published officially are unreliable in several respects besides the unrepresentative sample; since the FBS data are gathered only quarterly, the monthly headcounts are estimated using other economic indicators as a proxy for monthly income increases. The significant fluctuations in the monthly figures, which largely reflect seasonal changes in inflation rates during the year, are a further reminder of the caution needed in interpreting these figures. For example, the monthly figures have tended to be higher at the beginning of the year, when price increases occur, then to decrease in summer, and drop in December as wage arrears, annual bonuses, and interest payments are paid. The Goskomstat quarterly figures presented in Figure 16.2 provide some idea of the seasonal variations.

16.3.4. *How poor are the poor?*

The headcount figures reported above do not reveal the depth of poverty, in that they assign equal weight to those households whose income (or expenditure) is just below the poverty line and those with zero income. There are complementary measures to indicate changes in the depth of poverty. The Foster–Greer–Thorbecke P1 index measures the average shortfall of all individuals (households) below the poverty line. If Q is the group of poor, the average poverty gap is given by:

$$P1 = \frac{1}{n} \sum_{i \in Q} \frac{(Z_i - Y_i)}{Z_i},$$

poverty lines. Their results suggested that the distribution of the sample in terms of household expenditure was not particularly 'bunched' around the poverty line. In 1995 simulations using 10 and 20% higher poverty thresholds raised the poverty headcount by 3.8 and 8.4%, respectively; similarly, lowering the poverty line by the same proportions reduced the headcount by 5.2 and 9.8% (Kolev 1996, table 5). Standing apart from most other estimates, however, are the poverty headcounts based on subjective estimates of what should be the poverty threshold. These much higher thresholds naturally result in the share of the 'poor' in the population being much higher than either the RLMS or FBS-based measures suggest (Kovaleva and Zubova 1997). Moreover, the perceived level of poverty continued to rise at least through 1995. The best-known estimates of the share of the population in poverty, calculated by the All-Russian Centre for Public Opinion (VtsIOM) rose from 54% in 1994 to 80% in 1995 (see Mikhalev 1997).

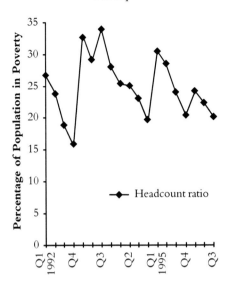

Figure 16.2. *Official estimates of poverty incidence, by quarter, 1992–1996*
Sources: Mikhalev 1997 (1992–3); and Vserossiiskii . . . 1996 (1994–6) (based on the FBS).

where n is the size of the sample population, Z is the poverty line, and Y is income (or expenditure) of the individual (or household).

The so-called 'P2' (or 'Severity') measure is a weighted average version such that the weight given to a household's poverty shortfall increases with the size of the shortfall:

$$P2 = \frac{1}{n}\sum_{i \in Q}\frac{(Z_i - Y_i)^2}{Z_i}$$

Available evidence derived from the RLMS data suggests that both depth and severity of poverty have increased sharply over the period 1992–5 (Table 16.1). However, the severity measure has abated since the peak of 1993.

The panel aspects of the two RLMS phases shed light on the dynamics of poverty. Foley (1997) shows that, at least in 1992–3 there was considerable movement in and out of poverty. For example, nearly half of those households that were very poor in the summer of 1992 had expenditures above the poverty line a year later, while one-quarter of non-poor households fell into poverty over the same period. It is striking that more

Table 16.1. *Trends in the depth and severity of poverty among households*

	1992	1993	1994	1995
Depth (P1 * 100)	9.8	13.6	11.7	13.2
Severity (P2 * 100)	5.4	8.0	7.2	6.9
Headcount for individuals (%)	26.8	26.9	30.9	41.1

Notes: See footnote 12 for specific dates in each year. The estimates are based on reported expenditures relative to the official minimum subsistence level.

Source: Kolev (1996) (RLMS).

than half of all households fell into poverty at some time between 1992 and 1994, but that there was a much smaller pocket of chronically poor. It has been estimated that the core of chronically poor households who have remained below minimum subsistence level since (at least) 1992 represent 8–12 per cent of households (Commander *et al.* 1997).

16.3.5. *Trends in inequality*

These increases in the level and severity of poverty have been accompanied by dramatic increases in income inequality. The Soviet economy was associated with a distribution of money income that was relatively compressed (Atkinson and Micklewright 1992)—even if access to goods and services in the face of pervasive shortages often depended as much on an individual's position and contacts as on disposable income. None the less, economic liberalization was expected to bring significant increases in the scale of inequality since prices and wages are no longer administratively controlled and 'levelled out' as the experience of eastern European countries in the late 1980s shows (see Milanovic 1995). Moreover, while the initial increases in poverty levels are expected to be a temporary phenomenon, an increase over pre-reform levels of inequality is partly viewed as an inevitable and permanent feature of the transition to a market economy. Of course, increasingly visible differences in personal living standards and the stark contrast between overt destitution and conspicuous consumption may well not be socially desirable nor politically tolerable.[16] Again we use Goskomstat and RLMS data to try to gauge the extent of the increase in equality, and to get an idea of the trends since 1991.

---

[16] See Tchernina (1996) for a review of the tensions and problems associated with growing inequality and worsening social exclusion in Russia, with a particular focus on Siberia.

The most frequently used measures of inequality are the Gini coefficient[17] and the decile ratio.[18] For the pre-reform period, Atkinson and Micklewright (1992) used the FBS to calculate levels of inequality of earnings in Russia of the order of 0.272. Goskomstat began to calculate Gini coefficients only in 1992, on the basis of income data from the FBS. These official figures tend to suggest lower levels of inequality than measures derived from RLMS data, which is not surprising since the FBS sample design can be assumed to under-represent both the lowest and highest income brackets (it does not capture the non-employed population, nor much of the private, entrepreneurial class, for example). Figure 16.3 presents inequality figures from the alternative sources, for the period 1989–96.

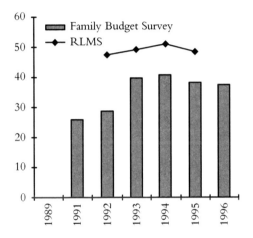

Figure 16.3. *Trends in inequality: reported Gini coefficients, 1989–1996*

Notes: RLMS measure is expenditure-based; FBS measure is income-based. See text for further details.

Sources: Goskomstat 1996a; Klugman and Braithwaite (1998); Kolev (1996); Atkinson and Micklewright (1992).

[17] The Gini coefficient lies between zero, where all incomes are equal, to one, when all incomes accrue to a single household (individual). Alternatively, suppose that two households are chosen at random. The expected value of the difference between their incomes as a proportion of the average income is twice the Gini coefficient. For example, a Gini of 0.40 means that the expected difference between the incomes of two randomly chosen households is 80% of the average income (Atkinson 1983).

[18] If we are interested in the extremes of the distribution, the decile ratio usefully portrays the average earnings of individuals in the ninetieth percentile over that of the first.

The available data suggest steep rises in the level of inequality in 1992–4, as measured by the Gini coefficients, which had decreased only slightly by 1996 and which were considerably higher than those experienced since transition by most central and eastern European countries (Klugman and Braithwaite 1998).

Analysis of the RLMS expenditure-based data suggests that the share of the top decile has been increasing, with the relative position of the 'middle' deciles showing the most marked deterioration. Thus, the top decile accounted for 33.3, 35.8, and 37 per cent of total household expenditure in 1992, 1993, and 1995, respectively; while the bottom five deciles increased their relative share slightly over the same period (Kolev 1996).

Goskomstat data present a somewhat different story. Despite the sampling problems described above, the FBS suggests that the widening of the income distribution has been even sharper. Goskomstat, which has generally published quintile rather than decile distribution, has reported over the period 1991–4 (Table 16.2) a steady deterioration in the relative position of the bottom three quintiles (especially the bottom 40 per cent), and a sharp increase in the share of the top quintile. The decile ratio reported in 1990 was 4.5, rising to 15.1 in 1994, and falling slightly to 13.5 in 1995 (Goskomstat 1996*a*).

To summarize, available evidence suggests that poverty levels peaked in 1993, and both numbers and severity have been decreasing slowly since then, although overall levels remain high. Analysts have identified considerable movement in and out of poverty, suggesting that there is a small group of chronically poor on which policymakers should be concentrating. We have observed significant increases in income inequality reported in various data sources. Coupled with the dramatic declines in national income, these trends have been associated with the overall increases in poverty reported above. The trends in income inequality

Table 16.2. *Percentage distribution of total household income by quintile*

Quintile	1980	1991	1992	1993	1994	1995
First	10.1	11.9	6.0	5.8	5.3	5.5
Second	14.8	15.8	11.6	11.1	10.2	10.2
Third	18.6	18.8	17.6	16.7	15.2	15.0
Fourth	23.1	22.8	26.5	24.8	23.0	22.4
Fifth	33.4	30.7	38.3	41.6	46.3	46.9
Decile ratio		4.5	8.0	11.2	15.1	13.5

Source: Goskomstat 1996*a*.

have been driven largely by changes in the structure of earning, as we discuss below.

16.4. WHO WAS POOR IN THE 1990s?

Despite divergent views about the scale of the increases in poverty during the 1990s, analysts using official and alternative data sources have drawn very similar profiles of poverty. There is agreement that, as during the Soviet period, the majority of the poor is composed of the working population and that families with children have a greater probability of being poor, this risk rising with the number of children. Other vulnerable categories include households headed by single parents, the unemployed, and households which rely solely on income from pensions, particularly pensioners living alone (World Bank 1995; Kolev 1996; Vserossiiskii . . . 1996). Table 16.3 uses data from round VI of the RLMS

Table 16.3. *Incidence of poverty by selected household characteristics, 1995 (percentage of group below the poverty line)*

Household characteristics	Poor	Of whom, very poor[a]
Household size		
One	20.6	7.1
Three	40.2	12.9
Five or more	56.1	19.9
Number of children		
One	23.4	6.4
Three	42.0	12.9
Five or more	66.9	26.5
Number of Pensioners		
None	40.9	9.6
One	31.3	13.8
Residence		
Urban	33.6	9.6
Rural	38.2	13.8
Employment Status of Head		
Employed	38	11.1
Unemployed	53	23.2
Retired	20.3	5.6

Note: [a]50% or worse below the poverty line.

Source: Kolev (1996), based on RLMS Round 6 using reported household expenditures and the national minimum subsistence level.

to present a basic profile of poverty by family type, area of residence, and employment status. This profile differs from the picture of poverty prior to reform mainly in the significantly higher incidence of poverty among the working population, and the emergence of open unemployment as an important risk factor. These descriptive statistics suggest, first, a large correlation between family size (number of children) and poverty incidence. Whereas households with one child have a poverty rate of about 23 per cent, more than two-thirds of households with five or more children are in poverty, of whom almost half have expenditures below 50 per cent of the household-specific poverty line. Second, and conversely, a higher number of pensioners in the households is associated with lower poverty incidence, 31 and 22 per cent for one and two or more pensioners respectively, compared to about 41 per cent for households without any pensioners. Hence, the incidence of poverty is lower among households headed by a retired person, relative to where the head is working and, especially, where the head is working-age unemployed.

Beyond simple cross-tabulations, multivariate analysis has been used to isolate those individual and household features that are most positively correlated with poverty.[19] These confirm that family size and in particular the presence of children under 18 has a significant effect on the likelihood of the family being poor, and that whereas the presence of additional adults increases the probability of being poor, the presence of additional pensioners or disabled members does not. The presence of an unemployed working-age member also has a clear impact on the probability of the household being poor. In the rest of this section we review each of these socio-economic groups in greater depth.

16.4.1. *The working poor*

In the Soviet period the average family was more or less protected from poverty through the earnings of two adults (female labour participation was high and open unemployment negligible) and extensive subsidies to ensure access to basic goods and services. We have seen that Soviet households were more vulnerable to poverty either if they had three or more children, and/or one of the working-age members was not in paid employment.[20] In the 1990s the 'average' family became

---

[19] The primary sources are the World Bank's poverty assessment for Russia (World Bank 1995) for 1992–3; Foley (1997); and Kolev (1996) for 1995.

[20] According to Goskomstat, only 7.5% of workers' families had three or more children in 1989.

more vulnerable, given the significant declines in the average real wage, pervasive wage arrears, and rising open unemployment.

There has been a dramatic erosion in the measured average real wage since the transition began. In December 1995 it stood at only about a third of its December 1991 level. Over the same period the ratio of the average wage to the adult minimum subsistence level narrowed considerably, from over five to less than two times. In late 1995 the legal minimum wage stood at only 16 per cent of the adult minimum subsistence level (Table 16.4).

Yet the official wage figures reported above are misleading to the extent that arrears in payment mean that employees receive their wages irregularly and often with two to three months' delay. According to RLMS data, more than half of working-age adults were owed wages in October 1996, compared to about 40 per cent in 1994 and 1995. These arrears average one month's expenditures for the average household (Mroz and Popkin 1997, p. 14). This has heightened the vulnerability of the employed population.

There have been significant shifts in the structure of relative wages, which mean that some have lost while others have gained. Measures of earnings dispersion have increased significantly, although different sources have reported increases that are quite different in scale. According to Goskomstat the decile ratio for earnings was 7.8 in 1991, 23.4 in 1994, and 26.4 in 1995 (Goskomstat 1996*b*). Hence, official data suggest that shifts in the wage distribution have been sharper than in the distribution of total household income.

Official data on average wage by branch indicate which branches of the economy and industry have gained and lost in the transition period (Figure 16.4). These changes in turn reflect sectoral changes in

Table 16.4. *Trends in the average and minimum wage, relative to the minimum subsistence income, 1991–1995*

	1991	1992	1993	1994	1995
Average wage ('000 roubles)	1.2	16.1	141.2	354.2	710.0
Average wage/MSI (%)	569	333.3	291.7	216.5	192.8
Minimum wage ('000 roubles)	0.18	0.9	14.6	20.5	60.5
Minimum wage/MSI (%)	85.7	18.6	30.2	12.5	16.4
Real wage	100	51.6	48.2	38.4	33.2
Memo: CPI (Dec./Dec.)	260.0	2610.0	939.8	314.7	231.6

Source: Ministry of Social Protection of the Russian Federation.

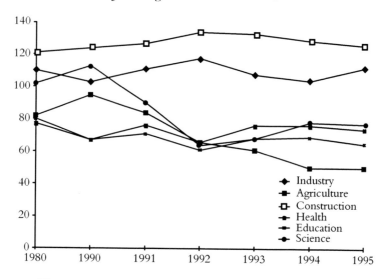

Figure 16.4. *Average wage as a percentage of the national average, selected sector, 1980–1995*

Source: Goskomstat 1996*a*.

productivity and profitability in the wake of liberalization and the withdrawal of most production subsidies. Agricultural workers' wages have fallen fairly dramatically in real terms, as have wages in the so-called 'budget sector', namely, those employed by the state (health, education, science, culture, etc.). The average wage in agriculture was 95 per cent of the national average in 1990, but only 50 per cent; in 1995. Not surprisingly, therefore, the RLMS shows that the incidence of poverty among households headed by skilled agricultural workers in 1995 was 64.7 per cent compared to a national poverty incidence of 35 per cent (Kolev 1996). Agriculture has also suffered severely from wage arrears, which amounted to 36 per cent of the monthly wage bill in 1993, 68 per cent in 1994, 102 per cent in 1995, and 189 per cent in the last quarter of 1996 (compared to figures for industry of 13 per cent, 31 per cent, 61 per cent, and 133 per cent, respectively, *Russian Economic Trends* 1997.1). Within industry, the fuel and extraction branches have been well protected, while machine building has lost its previous standing, and certain branches of light industry (notably the predominantly female textile industry) has a relative average wage that has declined to less than half of the average for industry as a whole.

16.4.2. *The unemployed*

The incidence of poverty among those households affected by unemployment is very high. According to RLMS data in 1993, about 63 per cent of households headed by an unemployed person were poor (Foley 1997). According to Goskomstat, in 1996 60–70 per cent of the families where one of the working-age members had no job had a per capita income below the poverty line. In some regions, all families in this category fell below the poverty line (Vserossiiskii . . . 1996). Unemployment benefits, limited in amount and duration, are available to the unemployed who register with the Federal Employment Service. However, only a minority of the unemployed in fact register, partly due to the low level of benefit, which provides little incentive to register. Table 16.6 below reveals that in late 1995, when about 13 per cent of poor households had an unemployed member, less than 3 per cent of the poor received unemployment benefits.

According to the RLMS, the proportion of the unemployed who are out of work for longer than three months went from about 51 per cent in 1993 to almost 80 per cent by the end of 1996. Fewer than 8 per cent of the unemployed reported job finds within four weeks.

16.4.3. *The young* . . .

In the early years of transition, 1992 and 1993, the composition of poverty was dominated by households with children. About 60 per cent of households with expenditures below the poverty line had one or more children (World Bank 1995). The incidence of poverty was especially high among larger families: in 1992, 85 per cent of households with three or more children under 6 years were poor. Later results did not modify this picture. Hence, while the RLMS-based poverty headcount index rose by 8 percentage points between 1994 and late 1995, the increase was more than 19 points for households with children under 6.[21] Data for 1996 show that in Russia as a whole 80 per cent of households with three or more children are poor (Vserossiiskii . . . 1996). Goskomstat has calculated the severity of poverty (the P2 index defined in section 3 above) for three types of households in 1995: households without children (7.95), households with children under 16 (18.8), and households

---

[21] In late 1995 the incidence of poverty was 57.6% among children under 6 and 52% for children under 18, compared with 41% for working age adults, and 26.7% for the elderly (Kolev 1996 (RLMS)).

comprising pensioners living alone (2.24) (Goskomstat 1996*b*; figures for January 1995 and available for other months). These estimates suggest not only that the incidence of poverty is much higher among households with children, but also that its severity is much worse than among either households without children or the elderly living alone. The state support provided to families with children has been seriously eroded during the transition. In December 1995 child allowance was equivalent to less than 0.13 of the child minimum subsistence level. The ratio of the child allowance to the average wage fell from 0.26 in 1991 to about 0.05 for the period 1993–5 (UNICEF 1997, Annex table E7).

16.4.4. *And the old*

The elderly defined in Russia by pensionable age (55 for women and 60 for men), are a large demographic group, comprising about 25 per cent of the population. The incidence of poverty among pensioner-headed households was about 20 per cent in 1995 (using RLMS data), compared to 38 per cent for a household where the head was employed.

There are a number of reasons why the incidence of poverty is evidently lower than average among pensioner households. Most important, perhaps, is the fact that average pensions have been relatively well protected from inflation, and maintained above the poverty line (see section 6 below). Given that pensioners generally have fewer dependants than working-age families, they are therefore on average relatively better placed.

Living standards of the elderly also benefit from the relatively low pension age; about one in five pensioners continue working without any diminution of their full benefit. For 1993 official Goskomstat data on the average structure of pensioner household money income revealed that social transfers accounted for about 73 per cent, and home production and 'other' sources the balance of retired workers' income. For retired farm workers, social transfers represent less than half of money income, an equivalent amount accruing from home production. Thus, pensions are not the sole source of income for many pensioners.

It should, however, be remembered that pensioners living only on pension income and those on a minimum pension constitute a clearly defined group of poor. There is also some evidence that pensioner households constitute an unproportionally high share of the chronically poor. Commander *et al.* (1997) use rounds I–VI of the RLMS[22] to build-up

---

[22] Commander *et al.* (1997). They use the two panels separately to give results for the period 1992–6.

a profile of the chronically poor, by looking at the characteristics of those households which were poor throughout the 1992–5 period. Pensioner households are found to be disproportionately (highly) represented among these households.

While the available data is consistent in portraying these relative advantages and disadvantages of families with children and those with pensioners, some methodological cautions are in order. First, the evidence presented does not capture economies of scale in household consumption. Thus, the greater apparent incidence of poverty among families, which rises with the number of children, may be due to the fact that economies of scale are being ignored. Foley (1997) found, based on analysis of the RLMS up through 1993, that the neglect of economies of scale did not significantly influence the incidence and profile of poverty in Russia. This is understandable so long as the share of food in household expenditure is high, and the fixed costs of the household (housing and utilities) remain relatively low. Secondly, the official subsistence minimum for the elderly is much lower than for a working adult or child, which obviously reduces the share of the elderly in the population deemed to be poor.[23]

16.5. REGIONAL INEQUALITIES

Poverty in the 1990s not only affected different social groups of the population; inhabitants of different regions have also been relatively better or less at risk of poverty. Such variations can be explained, at least in part, in terms of regional variations in economic endowment, the structure and distribution of production, and corresponding fiscal capacity, as well as demographic factors.

Official poverty headcount indices for each oblast are being published, based on the official minimum subsistence methodology calculated using the oblast prices.[24] In order to assess the scale of differences in poverty and living standards, we have constructed the following figures

---

[23] The elderly are assumed to have lower nutritional requirements; and in addition, their non-food requirements are only 17% of their minimum subsistence level, compared to approximately 30% for the able-bodied. Thus, in 1995, for example, the monthly minimum subsistence levels were 186, 214 and 297, 184 roubles for the elderly and adults, respectively (Frolova 1996).

[24] Some oblasts, notably Moscow, have adapted the MOL methodology on the grounds that certain items of expenditure, such as transport, are much more expensive than the national average, and thus the share of non-food expenditure should be greater.

with information on selected oblasts. Our selection is inevitably arbitrary. The aim is to draw attention to the extent and scale of regional variety in living standards.

Figure 16.5 gives the regional poverty rates for 1995 and decile ratios for selected regions in the last quarter of 1996. The twenty regions were chosen on the basis of the regional cost of the basket of twenty-five food products, which forms the basis for the calculation of the national and regional subsistence minimum. We have taken the nine regions where the cost of the basket was highest in December 1996 and the nine regions

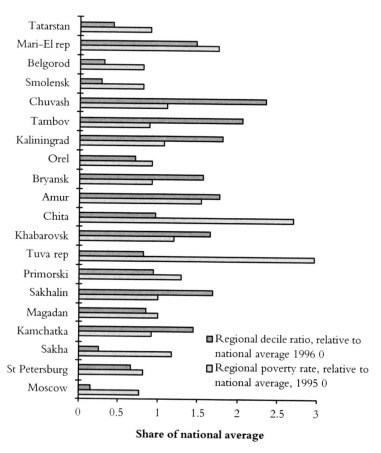

Figure 16.5. *Poverty and inequality measures, selected regions, 1995–1996*
Source: Goskomstat (1996a).

where it was lowest, plus Moscow and St Petersburg. In Figure 16.5 the nine regions beginning with Tatarstan are the 'cheapest', and the nine beginning with Amur are the most expensive.[25]

The Goskomstat figures reported in Figure 16.5 suggest not only that there is significant regional variation in poverty levels, but also that there is no straightforward correlation between the regional poverty rates and decile ratios. Tuva Republic, for example (an 'expensive' region), has a poverty rate which is almost three times that of the national average, but a decile ratio which is lower than the average. About half of the oblasts, both expensive and cheap, have a poverty rate which is lower than the average. Moscow has a surprisingly compressed income distribution; whereas Chuvash and Tambov, which have lower than average poverty rates, show greater intra-regional inequality.

Regional unemployment rates likewise varied (Commander and Yemtsov 1997). In 1995 officially registered unemployment ranged from 2.1 per cent in St Petersburg to 12.5 per cent in the oblast of Ivanovo, which is dominated by the textile industry. The high unemployment areas were primarily oblasts with concentrations of military firms, light industry, or both. Low unemployment areas are primary resource-rich regions in the east, or the major cities, including Moscow and St Petersburg. Chuvash, Tambov, and Dagestan, for example, have rates double the national average, while Moscow and four other regions have less than half the national average. Any reduction in these differences seems unlikely in the near future, given the low levels of labour mobility which are reinforced by continuing housing shortages (Commander and Yemtsov 1997, p. 146).

Goskomstat data point to significant regional differences in per capita money incomes and wages, but not in other living standards indicators such as consumption of food products, housing conditions, and property ownership. This may be a temporary phenomenon of the transition and regional inequalities seem likely to persist and worsen in the foreseeable future.

In the face of growing regional disparities in economic performance, the federal government has not pursued an effective redistributive policy. Indeed, the current decentralized financing responsibility for

---

[25] In the far eastern oblasts of Sakha, Kamchatka, and Magadan the cost of the basket of 25 food products was approximately twice that of the national average in December 1996. In the 'cheaper' oblasts, the cost is about 60–70% of the national average. For more details see *Russian Economic Trends* (1997) 2.

basic social services as well as for social assistance to the poor has probably exacerbated regional inequality in living standards. Empirical analysis suggests that existing systems of central fiscal transfers, including the transfer formula introduced in 1994, have failed to alleviate significant differences in public expenditure across the country. The volume of central transfers is small (in 1995 it amounted to only about 12 per cent of oblast budget revenue) and the net effect of central transfers has not been sufficient to offset differences in revenue (Le Houerou 1994; Stewart 1997).

16.6. THE IMPACT OF SOCIAL TRANSFERS

The Russian government in 1995 directed about 4.5 per cent of total consolidated budget expenditures towards social transfers the bulk of them provided by regional budgets. The real value of transfers has been seriously eroded as measured GDP has declined (as Table 16.6 illustrates for pensions). The average pension, which has hovered around half the level of late 1991, has nevertheless been relatively better protected than both the average wage and other benefits. The level of unemployment benefits, which we approximate by referring to the minimum wage,[26] suffered the worst erosion, standing in 1995 and 1996 at less than one-fifth of its late 1991 level. The minimum pension has also been badly affected, falling in 1995 and 1996 to around one-third of the level of late 1991.

The available data (discussed in section 4 above) suggest that most of the older population has been relatively less affected by the increases in poverty during the transition, while young children are particularly vulnerable. The same cannot be said of people dependent on the minimum pension, however, which has eroded to about half the elderly subsistence level (Table 16.5). Since 1990 trends in the ratio of the average pension to the average wage have favoured the former, rising from 0.34 to 0.38 in 1995, but the minimum pension relative to the average wage has fallen from 0.23 to 0.19 (UNICEF 1997, Annex table 6).

Pensions appear to be effective in keeping rates of poverty among the elderly below the national average poverty rate since 1992. For the

---

[26] Due to benefit calculation rules and the way past earnings are taken into account, during the high inflation years of 1992–4 the vast majority of those receiving unemployment benefits got only the minimum.

Table 16.5. *Average and minimum pension*

	1991	1992	1993	1994	1995
Average pension ('000 roubles)	0.31	3.65	43.1	119.2	233.4
Average pension/MSL	243.8	124.4	142.7	116.3	101.2
Minimum pension ('000 roubles)	0.29	2.25	26.3	54.1	110.5
Minimum pension/MSL	227.7	76.7	87.2	52.8	47.9
Average pension/ Average wage	26.1	22.7	30.5	33.7	32.9
Real pension (1991 = 100)	100	44.8	56.3	49.5	41.8

Source: Ministry of Social Protection of the Russian Federation.

majority of those receiving the pension who are not poor (Table 16.6), pensions represent more than half their income.[27]

According to the RLMS for the period from 1992 to late 1995 public transfers accounted for almost 30 per cent of total household income (Foley and Klugman 1997). As expected, the average contribution of transfers to the income of *recipient* households is higher: an estimated 42 per cent in late 1995. Important trends can be observed in the relative importance of different transfers. The major programmes are presented in Table 16.6, which shows the share of very poor, poor, and non-poor households receiving each benefit, and the contribution to household income, at two points in time, early 1994 and late 1995. While pensions remain the most widely received benefit, unemployment benefits have become increasingly important for the poor, especially for the very poor, as unemployment has risen. Coverage of family allowances has remained steady for the poor, but dropped for the non-poor (probably due to low take-up), and has also generally declined as a share of income, even of very poor households, given the erosion of their real value and payment arrears.

While coverage of public transfers across the population is fairly extensive, there are some perhaps unintended results. For example, Table 16.6 shows that local social assistance is much more frequently received by the non-poor than the poor. Moreover, a large number of households do not receive benefits at all (Table 16.7). More than three out

[27] This pattern mirrors that of an increasing number of OECD countries, where the public pension systems have helped significantly to reduce, and in some countries virtually eliminate, old age poverty (Scherer 1997).

Table 16.6. *Coverage and significance of public transfers, 1994 and 1995*

	Very Poor		Poor		Non-Poor	
	Receiving the benefit %	Share of recipient household income %	Receiving the benefit %	Share of recipient household income %	Receiving the benefit %	Share of recipient household income %
Family allowance						
1994	28.8	23.6	32.4	14.5	25.7	5.9
1995	29.3	16.3	32.3	13.1	17.2	7.1
Pension						
1994	40.3	75.0	41.0	66.9	48.7	58.4
1995	36.8	61.5	39.7	54.7	54.0	52.5
Unemployment benefit						
1994	0.8	21.7	0.4	17.8	0.3	9.8
1995	2.1	37.6	2.6	19.6	0.9	14.1
Local social assistance	10.4	9.6	10.4	9.6	14.5	8.1
Enterprise subsidy[a]	5.0	9.4	8.7	10.8	17.7	11.7
Housing subsidy[b]	3.3	7.5	3.6	7.5	6.4	5.2
Scholarship	5.2	17.8	6.2	18.2	6.7	5.2
All transfers						
1994	66.8	58.5	70.9	48.4	74.4	42.6
1995	61.6	43.3	67.7	40.3	70.0	43.3

Notes: All transfers includes those listed, except enterprise subsidies which are shown for comparative purposes only.
[a]Data on local social assistance and enterprise subsidies were not collected in 1995.
[b]Information on the housing benefit is for 1995.
For 1994 the period relates to the first quarter for 1995, December 1995, and January 1996.

Source: Foley and Klugman (1997); Kolev (1996).

Table 16.7. *Errors in targeting of public transfers, 1995 (percentage)*

	Among the Poor	Among the very poor	Among the non-poor
1. Not receiving	33.0	39.8	30.9
2. Ineligible	6.1	6.2	13.5
3. Not receiving although eligible (error of exclusion)	29.7	36.4	22.8
4. Receiving although ineligible (error of inclusion)	1.5	0.8	3.9

Note: Public transfers considered here are pensions, unemployment benefits, scholarships and family allowances.

Source: Kolev (1996) based on the RLMS.

of ten households classified as poor, and two in five of the very poor, did not report receipt of any transfers. Yet the majority—over two-thirds—of non-poor families do receive public transfers. The system's shortcomings appear to be partly administrative in that eligible households in all categories often fail to receive any state support. The problem is more pervasive among households in poverty, suggesting that inadequate information and lack of access may also be contributing to low take-up rates. Errors of inclusion—receipt of benefit by those who are not entitled—appear to be relatively limited. The RLMS data suggest that these overall patterns have persisted throughout the transition. In short, the stance of social protection policy helps to explain the observed trends in poverty. While pension indexation has assisted the elderly during the transition, families with children appear to have been relatively neglected. In particular, the evidence suggests that the persistence of traditional notions about the identity of the poor has been associated with large numbers of poor and very poor families being practically excluded from state assistance.

16.7. CONCLUSION

This chapter has pointed out that poverty was unofficially acknowledged in Russia before the transition period, and that there was a tradition of monitoring and calculating minimum living standards. The large increases in poverty in the initial transition years and the removal of social guarantees meant that poverty thresholds had to be redesigned, and household survey methods changed. The estimated magnitudes of poverty presented for the period 1992–6 are not beyond dispute, but none the less confirm an initial surge followed by continuing high levels of poverty since 1992–3. Poverty profiles drawing on different data sources point consistently to families with children being most at risk, with some types of pensioner households and those headed by an unemployed person or a single parent also having a high probability of being poor. We have also shown that the structure and size of social transfers have significantly influenced Russia's poverty profile in the 1990s. This point helps to explain why, for example, most pensioners have been relatively better protected from poverty than the unemployed or families with children. However, it is worth while once more drawing attention to the methodological underpinning of the results reported in this chapter. The poverty profile which we have drawn, as well as the poverty rates which we have reported, are obviously influenced by the poverty threshold, in this case, the official national MOL subsistence minimum. Our analysis showed how different data sets can affect our conclusions about poverty trends. Future analysis based on regional poverty lines, or thresholds which incorporate different assumptions about the equivalence scale, may produce different results again, both in terms of the numbers living in poverty and the composition of the poor population.

REFERENCES

Note: The word 'processed' describes informally reproduced works that may not be commonly available through library systems.

Atkinson, A. B. (1983). *The Economics of Inequality*, 2nd edn. Oxford: Clarendon Press.

—— and Micklewright, J. (1992). *Economic Transformation in Eastern Europe and Distribution of Income*, Cambridge: CUP.

Bradshaw, M. J., and Palacin, J. A. (1996). 'An Atlas of the Economic Performance of Russia's Regions', University of Birmingham, Russian Regional Research Group, School of Geography and CREES Working Paper 2.

Braithwaite, J. (1997). 'The Old and New Poor in Russia', in J. Klugman (ed.), *Poverty in Russia During Transition*, Washington, DC: The World Bank.

—— and Heleniak, T. (1989). 'Social Welfare in the USSR: The Income Recipient Distribution', Center for International Research, US Bureau of the Census, processed.

Commander, S. (1997). 'Characteristics of the Unemployed', in J. Klugman (ed.), *Poverty in Russia During Transition*, Washington, DC: The World Bank.

—— and Yemtsov, R. (1997). 'Russian Unemployment: Its Magnitude, Characteristics and Regional Dimensions', in J. Klugman (ed.), *Poverty in Russia During Transition,* Washington, DC.

—— Tolstopiatenko, A., and Yemtsov, R. (1997). 'Channels of Redistribution: Inequalty and Poverty in the Russian Transition', Working Paper 42, The William Davidson Institute, University of Michegan Business School.

Falkingham, J., Klugman, J., Marnie, S., and Micklewright, J. (eds.) (1997). *Household Welfare in Central Asia,* London: Macmillan.

Foley, M. (1997). 'Poverty in Russia: Static and Dynamic Analysis', in J. Klugman (ed.), *Poverty in Russia During Transition,* Washington, DC: The World Bank.

—— and Klugman, J. (1997). 'The Impact of Social Support—Errors and Leakage and Exclusion', in J. Klugman (ed.), *Poverty in Russia During Transition,* Washington, DC: The World Bank.

Frolova, E. (1996). 'Selected Economic and Social Indicators in the Russian Federation', Paper presented to meeting on Russian social policy, Paris: OECD, processed.

Goskomstat Rossii (1996*a*). *Rossiiskii statisticheskii ezhegodnik,* Moscow: Logos.

—— (1996*b*). *Uroven' zhizni naseleniya Russii,* Moscow.

Goskomstat SSSR (1991). *Sotsial'noe razvitie SSSR 1989,* Moscow: Finansy i statistiki.

Klugman, J. (ed.) (1997). *Poverty in Russia During Transition. Public Policy and Private Responses,* Washington, DC: EDI, World Bank.

—— and Braithwaite, J. (1998). 'Poverty in Russia during the Transition: An Overview', World Bank Research Observer, February.

Kolev, A. (1996). 'Poverty Analysis in Russia: What Can we Learn from the RLMS, Round 6?', processed.

Kovaleva, L., and Zubova, N. (1997). 'Public Opinion About Social Issues', in J. Klugman (ed.), *Poverty in Russia During Transition,* Washington, DC: The World Bank.

Le Houerou, P. (1994). 'Decentralisation and Fiscal Disparities among Regions in the Russian Federation', World Bank Internal Discussion Paper, January, Washington, DC.

Matthews, M. (1986). *Poverty in the Soviet Union,* Cambridge: Cambridge University Press.

McAuley, A. (1979). *Economic Welfare in the Soviet Union,* Madison: University of Wisconsin Press.

Mikhalev, V. (1997). 'Poverty Alleviation in the Course of Transition: Policy Options for Russia', EUI Working Paper RSC No. 97/20.

Milanovic, B. (1995). 'Poverty, Inequality and Social Policy in Transition Economies', Policy Research Department Research Paper Series, 9, Washington, DC: The World Bank.

Mozhina, M. (1992). 'The Poor: What is the Boundary Line?', *Problems of Economic Transition,* October.

Mroz, T., and Popkin, B. (1997). 'Monitoring Economic Conditions in the Russian Federation. The Russian Longitudinal Monitoring Survey 1992–96', Chapel Hill: University of North Carolina, processed.

Ofer, G., and Vinoku, A. (1992). *The Soviet Household under the Old Regime.* Cambridge: Cambridge University Press.

Popkin, B., Mozhina, M., and Baturin, A. (1992). 'The Development of a Subsistence Income Level in the Russian Federation', Chapel Hill: University of North Carolina, processed.

Ravallion, M. (1992). 'Poverty Comparisons: A Guide to Concepts and Methods', LSMS Working Paper 88, Washington, DC: The World Bank.

Rimashevskaia, N. M. (1990). 'Nash prozhitochnyi minimum', Sotsialisticheskii trud, no. 8.

Russian Economic Trends (1997). (nos. 1 and 2), London: Whurr Publishers Ltd.

Sarkisyan, G. S., and Kuznetsova, N. P. (1967). *Consumption and Income of Families: Level, Structure, Prospects,* Moscow.

Scherer, P. (1997). 'The New Social Policy Agenda', Paris: OECD, Social Policy Division, processed.

Shenfield, S. (1983). 'A Note on Data Quality in the Soviet Family Budget Survey', *Soviet Studies*, 35/4: 561–8.

Stewart, K. (1997). 'Are Intergovernmental Transfers in Russia Equalising?', EUI Working Paper ECO No. 97/22.

Tchernina, N. (1996). 'Economic Transition and Social Exclusion in Russia', International Institute for Labour Studies, United Nations Development Programme Research Series Number 108, Geneva.

UNICEF (1997). 'Children at Risk in Central and Eastern Europe: Perils and Promises', Economies in Transition Studies, regional Monitoring Report no. 4, International Child Development Centre, Florence.

Vserossiiskii tsentr urovnya zhizni (1996). *Monitoring sotsial'no-ekonomicheskogo potentsiala semei za III kvartal 1996g.',* Moscow.

—— (1997). *Monitoring sotsial'no-ekonomicheskogo potentsiala semei za IV kvartal 1996g.',* Moscow.

World Bank (1995). 'Poverty in Russia: An Assessment', Report No. 14110-RU.

17

The Health Sector: Illness, Medical Care and Mortality

CHRISTOPHER DAVIS

17.1. INTRODUCTION

Health in Russia is a topic that has attracted attention primarily because of the unanticipated large increases in illness and death rates during transition. The crude death rate rose from 11.2 deaths per 1,000 population in 1990 to a peak of 15.7 in 1994, dropped back to 13.6 in 1998, and increased again to 15.3 in 2000. The phenomena of rising mortality and falling life expectancy have stimulated numerous studies and debates over their causes.[1] Explanatory factors have included excessive

The author would like to thank the following Russian scholars and policymakers for their advice and assistance concerning the study of health in Russia over the past several years: Sergei Glaz'ev, Irina Katkova, Vladimir Mau, Igor Sheiman, Sergei Shishkin, Vladimir Starodubov, Vladimir Terekhov, and Anatoli Vyalkov. The research for this chapter also benefited from discussions with the Editors of the volume (Brigitte Granville and Peter Oppenheimer), Rifat Atun, Michael Borowitz, Andrea Cornia, Sarah Donaldson, Michael Ellman, Jonathan Harper, Tim Heleniak, Michael Kaser, Iain MacDonald, Judith Shapiro, Pekka Sutela, and Christopher Williams. The author's research has been supported by the Department of Economics and Queen Elizabeth House of Oxford University, the Social Policy Research Programme of the Institute for Development Studies at the University of Sussex, and the UK Department for International Development.

[1] A substantial Russian language literature exists on morbidity and mortality trends in Russia in the 1990s that should not be ignored by Western scholars. Among the informative works are MZRF (1993); Volkov (1993); Vishnevskii and Zakharov (1993); MZRF (1996); Vishnevskii (1997); Terekhov (1997); and Gerasimenko (1997). English and French language publications on similar topics include: Davis (1993abc); Ellman (1994); Nell and Stewart (1994); UNICEF (1994); Heleniak (1995); Meslé and Shkolnikov (1995); Shapiro (1995); Meslé et al. (1996); Williams (1996); Blum (1997); Shkolnikov (1997); Shapiro (1997); Davis (1998, 2000, and 2001); Chelleraj, Heleniak, and Staines (1998); and Cornia and Paniccia (2000).

alcohol consumption, deterioration of nutritional standards, morbidity patterns related to age-cohorts, and social stress linked to unemployment. Another issue of interest to economists has been reform of the health sector.[2] The Russian government has introduced numerous measures intended to improve the financing and performance of the medical system, such as the shift to compulsory medical insurance. Most of them have achieved only limited success. Thus, health reform remains an important item on the agenda of the new government of President Putin.

Many important health economic issues in Russia have been ignored. The complex nature of health production and its many interactions with general economic processes have not been analysed in a comprehensive manner. In the study of mortality trends, insufficient attention has been paid to the changing effectiveness of the medical system, which has been influenced adversely by macroeconomic developments as well as by disruptions in the performance of the medical supply network and pharmaceutical production. The economic implications of worsening health, such as lower labour productivity and growing demands for state-financed medical services, have not been adequately examined. Another neglected subject has been the size of the health sector in Russia in economic terms. The health share of Russian GDP in 1995 (taking into account state budget, compulsory insurance, and private expenditure) was about 5 per cent. In contrast, health shares of the traditional OECD economies in 1995 ranged from 5.8 per cent in Greece to 10.4 per cent in Germany to 14.2 per cent in the USA. Health expenditures in the USA in that year amounted to $989 billion, which was 49 per cent more than Russian GDP ($664 billion) (USDC SAUS 1997). Per capita US health expenditure of $3,756 was twenty-five times higher than that in Russia ($148). This large gap raises the question of whether it is realistic to project, as do the Russian government and various consultancy organizations, rapid 'catch-up' growth of both health spending and the domestic pharmaceutical market that will result in a 6–7 per cent health share of a much larger GDP by 2005 (see 'Kontseptsiya' 1997).

[2] Reforms of health financing and the shift to compulsory medical insurance in Russia are examined in Helmstadler (1992); Sheiman (1992); Davis (1993*bc*); Cherepov (1995); Polyakov (1995); Shishkin (1995); Chernichovsky, Barnum, and Potapchik (1996); Raison (1998); Sheiman (1998); and Shishkin (1998, 2000).

The chapter has six main objectives. The first is to define the health sector of the economy, which comprises a number of interrelated institutions that individually produce goods and services and collectively influence changes in the health status of the population (section 17.2).[3] The second is to place developments in Russia in the transition period (such as rising mortality) in historical perspective by reviewing the features and problems of the health sector in the Soviet command economy (section 17.3). The third goal is to identify the actual and potential impacts on health institutions of changes in the economic system, such as the shift to market co-ordination, and of general economic policies, such as macroeconomic stabilization, in the transition period (section 17.4.1). The fourth objective is to analyse the health reform process (section 17.4.2). This involves highlighting the complexity of inherited problems, identifying actual remedial policies, and assessing their effectiveness. The fifth aim is to evaluate the performance of health institutions in the transition era, taking into account changes in behavioural patterns, such as relationships between buyers and sellers, and trends in outputs, such as medical services (section 17.4.3). Last but not least, an assessment is made of the responsibility of the medical system and supporting institutions for the variations in mortality rates in the 1990s during the initial decade of transition in Russia (section 17.4.4).

17.2. HEALTH PRODUCTION AND MEDICAL SYSTEM EFFECTIVENESS IN COMMAND AND TRANSITION ECONOMIES: GENERAL CONCEPTS

Health production is a multivariate process that determines the population's health status (see Figure 17.1).[4] It involves the operations of

---

[3] In accordance with Davis (1987, 1997) the health sector is defined to include seven economic institutions that are involved in the productive, distributive and administrative activities that are directly related to health production: households, medical system, medical supply network (i.e. pharmacies), medical industry, biomedical R&D, medical foreign trade, and central health bureaucracy.

[4] The concept of the health production process is derived partly from ideas presented in Fuchs (1966) and Auster, Levenson, and Sarachek (1972). Health production can be expressed by the function $H = f(T, M)$, which relates health output indicators (H) to medical tasks determined by illnesses (T) and the supply of medical services (M). The shape of H is determined by two relationships: (1) for a given level of medical services health output diminishes as tasks become more complex ($\partial H/\partial T < 0$), and (2) for given tasks the health output improves as medical services are increased ($\partial H/\partial M > 0$). Health production in command and transition economies is discussed in Davis (1987, 1988, 1993b, and 1997).

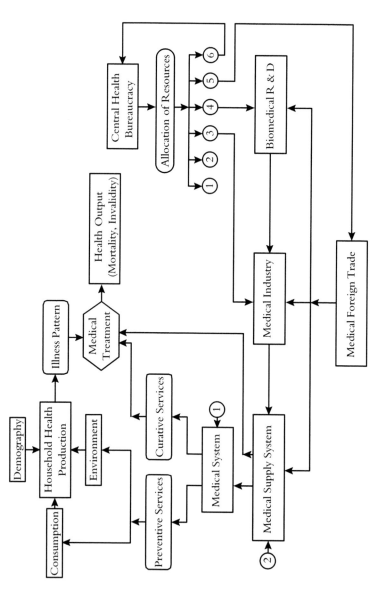

Figure 17.1. *The health production process in the USSR and Russia*

Source: Davis (1988).

numerous economic institutions in the health sector that produce health-related outputs (for example, medical services and medicines) and trade them in markets, while consuming inputs of labour, capital, and intermediate goods.[5]

Individuals (consumers) possess a 'stock' of health, which is influenced by demography (age, sex), genetic factors, and past experiences. Changes in the stock may be viewed in terms of a household health production function, which relates inputs of goods (food, medicines), services (education, medical), and household time to outputs measured by indicators of health and illness (degenerative, infectious, nutritional, and accidents) (Grossman 1972; Zweifel and Breyer 1997, ch. 3). The national morbidity pattern is an aggregation of individual illnesses.

In all countries, some illness that could be treated is not presented to the medical system. One reason is that people do not recognize the symptoms of illness and therefore do not perceive a need for medical care. However, consumer demand can also be suppressed by monetary and time costs. As a result, a 'morbidity iceberg' exists, with reported illness above the waterline and unreported, untreated illness as the submerged component. Even in countries with no price barriers to medical care, such as the USSR or UK, the scale of unreported illness can be large. All else being equal, the introduction of money prices for medical services, increases in costs of prescribed medicines, and the removal of transportation subsidies would inhibit demand and shift illness below the waterline.

The medical system plays a central role in the health production process. Hospitals and polyclinics produce preventive services that can diminish the incidence of illness, and curative services that can minimize

[5] According to research of this author, the seven institutions in the health sector are involved in 27 markets. Households sell their labour in general labour markets, as well as six in the health sector. They obtain inputs from the general retail market, medical services market (MSM), and medical goods retail market (PRM). Each of the other six health institutions obtains inputs from labour, intermediate goods, and capital goods markets. The medical system supplies services in MSM and obtains supplies from the medical goods wholesale market (PWM). The medical supply network sells goods in PRM and PWM and buys products in the medical industry wholesale market (MIWM) and foreign trade domestic market (FTDM). Medical industry sells goods for domestic consumption in MIWM and for export in FTDM. It buys imported technology in FTDM and domestic patents and processes in the biomedical R&D wholesale market (RDWM). Biomedical R&D sells in RDWM and FTDM and purchases imports in FTDM. Medical foreign trade sells imports and purchases goods for exports in FTDM and sells goods abroad in the foreign trade world market. The specific features of these markets depend upon the type of economic system within which they are embedded.

periods of sickness, invalidity, and mortality (Folland *et al.* 1997).[6] The volume and quality of services are determined by the organization, management, and financing of the medical system, as well as by the medicines, medical equipment, and other inputs received from the supply network (for example, pharmacies). Most of these medical goods are obtained from the domestic medical industry, which bases its technological innovation on the work of the biomedical R&D system. Additional inputs are obtained from medical foreign trade organizations.

Since health production involves all the institutions shown in Figure 17.1, performance problems in one of them can disrupt the process and adversely affect health output indicators. Even investigations of a specific issue (such as rising mortality) focusing on a single institution (such as households) or factor (such as alcohol consumption) should take into account developments elsewhere in the production chain. Furthermore, governments introducing reform programmes should consider in a comprehensive manner the problems and interconnections of the various health institutions in order to avoid inconsistencies in policies and unanticipated outcomes.

Measures of medical system effectiveness relate health outputs (H) to targets established by society (X) and can be of three types: medical, economic, and national health status. Medical effectiveness measures the success of medical services in achieving positive results using indicators such as patients' activity restriction and survival times (Culyer 1976). The economic effectiveness of a medical activity is determined by comparing the activity's inputs measured by costs with outputs produced by differing techniques or programmes expressed in non-monetary terms (cost-effectiveness) or in monetary terms (cost-benefit) (Folland *et al.* 1997).

National health status effectiveness is measured by assessing the contributions of the medical system to the achievement of target values of invalidity and mortality indicators. The usual mortality targets are:

(1) age-specific death rates should decline or remain stable;
(2) the infant mortality rate should be reduced to the levels found in OECD nations;

[6] This author recognizes that medical services and medicines cannot fully compensate for health-reducing behaviour, such as smoking or heavy drinking. So not all credit or blame for morbidity and mortality outcomes should be attributed to medical system performance. In fact, empirical studies by Auster *et al.* (1972) and others (see Zweifel and Breyer 1997, ch. 4) have found that in western countries medical services exert only a modest influence on developments in the health status of the population (i.e. $\partial H/\partial M$ is near zero).

(3) the crude death rate should decline or remain stable, despite the ageing of the population; and

(4) life expectancy at birth should be raised to levels achieved by OECD nations (Davis 1988).

If demographic, social, economic and environmental factors generate higher morbidity but the output of medical services is sufficient to ensure that the targets for mortality-related indicators are attained (H > X), then the medical system may be said to be national health status effective. Absolute effectiveness describes a situation in which health status improves despite worsening illness rates. If targets are not met (H < X), then the medical system is ineffective. Absolute ineffectiveness exists if medical service provision has worsened yet the illness pattern has remained constant or improved. Relative ineffectiveness means that the medical system performance has remained constant or improved, but the tasks are greater than it can control, and mortality rises.

17.3. THE LOW PRIORITY HEALTH SECTOR IN THE SOVIET SHORTAGE ECONOMY

The Soviet Union developed a large state-owned health sector that was successful in improving national health status indicators for much of the post-Stalin period.[7] However, the performance of health institutions was adversely affected by deficiencies in their organization and management and by their disadvantageous position in a flawed economic system. Although health institutions were governed by plans, central control over them was imperfect, in part due to the multiplicity of administrative bodies that managed them: Ministry of Health, Main Pharmacy Administration, Ministry of Medical Industry, Academy of Medical Sciences, and Ministry of Foreign Trade (Davis 1988). The health sector did not have a supra-ministerial body that co-ordinated activity between different ministries, such as the USSR Military-Industrial Commission in the defence sector. So decision making tended to be fragmented and often inconsistent.

---

[7] Although World Bank analysts and transitionologists working on Russian health topics appear to be unaware of any scholarly work on the Soviet health sector written prior to 1990, there is in fact a substantial, informative literature. Among English language books are Field (1967); Kaser (1976); Ryan (1978, 1990); and Knaus (1981). Thousands of Russian language books and articles have been published (see the bibliographies in Davis 1988, 1993a). Among those dealing with health planning and economics are Popov (1976) and Burenkov et al. (1979).

The centralized plans and rationing schemes of the Soviet government were influenced by its sectoral priorities. Special protection mechanisms ensured that the highest priority sectors, notably defence, achieved their objectives irrespective of general economic conditions. The health sector received a low priority for both pragmatic and ideological reasons. With respect to the latter, Marxist–Leninist political economy held that national income was generated by the productive branches of the economy, primarily industry and agriculture, and consumed by the non-productive sphere, which included all welfare institutions (Pravdin 1976).[8] A side-effect of this tenet was neglect of the economics of the non-productive sphere, including health economics.[9]

The low priority status of health care was reflected in both plan formulation and implementation (Davis 1989). Health received a low weight in the planners' preference functions, resource allocations were unresponsive to visible problems, relative wages were low, and financial norms beggarly. Central plans invariably were inconsistent and had to be revised as imbalances were revealed. The ensuing redistribution of resources was a zero-sum game that caused a tightening of constraints and made original health plans more difficult, indeed often impossible, to fulfil.

The Soviet Union developed the prototype of the shortage economy described by Kornai (1980, 1992) and maintained it throughout the command period.[10] Its features exacerbated the usual problems encountered

---

[8] Ironically, the armed forces belonged to the non-productive sphere, but pragmatic and strategic considerations determined that the military-industrial complex had a high priority standing.

[9] To some extent western economists have mirrored Soviet/Russian attitudes towards the 'non-productive sphere'. In the command era only a few scholars, such as Alastair McAuley, studied the economics of welfare in the USSR and eastern Europe. In the early 1990s most Western economists who analysed economies in transition and participated in economic policy debates neglected welfare (social safety net) issues because they perceived other topics to be of greater importance. Exceptions to this rule included Barr (1994), Ellman (1994), and Shapiro (1995). The same was true for most multinational institutions (IMF, World Bank, EBRD, OECD, EU). The UNICEF International Child Development Centre was one of the few western international organizations to devote attention to these problems at an early stage (UNICEF 1994). More recently there has been a substantial improvement in the coverage and analyses of health and welfare issues by western institutions, notably the World Bank.

[10] The shortage economy model is presented in Kornai (1980, 1992) and Davis and Charemza (1989). Its basic propositions are that the Socialist economies that existed in the USSR and eastern Europe were characterized by quantity (non-price) control mechanisms, such as central planning and rationing, pervasive shortages in retail and wholesale markets and rational, habitual responses by consumers and producers to shortage phenomena. Budget

in a situation where medical services are available 'free at the point of use', namely that the demands of the population exceed the supply capacities of the medical system. To cope with excess demand, the government made extensive use of rationing in accordance with socio-economic criteria through six sub-systems of medical care: élite, departmental, large city, medium city, industrial, and rural district (Davis 1988). Queuing was another instrument used to regulate demand.[11]

The legal markets connecting health institutions as buyers and sellers outlined in note 5 existed, but were highly constrained by the state. Demand and supply forces did not directly affect prices or production decisions. Despite the distortions, these markets involved 'transaction processes based on direct horizontal relations between supplier and recipient of the goods, even if price and money play little or no role' (Kornai 1980, p. 127). Transactions in legal markets were invariably dominated by sellers, whether they involved a medical facility interacting with a patient or the medical industry selling to the medical supply network (Davis 1989). There was also significant informal (black market) activity by institutions and their agents in the medical field (Ryan 1978, 1990; Knaus 1981).

The pressure on managers to meet the apparently insatiable demands of their customers resulted in continuous efforts to expand production (Kornai's 'quantity drive'). Although quality standards of medical care, drugs, and equipment improved over time, they did not keep pace with western developments due to sluggish technological innovation, which was characteristic of the closed, uncompetitive markets in the USSR.

The Soviet government made repeated attempts to reform the planning, management, supply, and behaviour of health institutions.[12]

constraints, on firms were soft, so there were weak financial restrictions on their demand for inputs. Firms operated in sellers' markets and produced goods and services of low quality and obsolete technical standards. On the input side, institutions experienced chronic difficulties in obtaining supplies and tried to maintain large inventories to minimize production disruptions caused by shortages of planned inputs.

[11] Aaron and Schwartz (1984) analyse the causes of shortages and the use of rationing in the British national health service. Their study confirms that these phenomena are not found only in the medical systems in command economies.

[12] Health sector reforms in the Soviet period are described and evaluated in Popov (1976, pp. 320–6); Ryan (1978, 1990); Burenkov *et al.* (1979, pp. 212–31); Korchagin (1980); Davis (1983*b*, 1987, 1993*a*); Sheiman (1991); and Schepin and Semenov (1992). Key Soviet government documents outlining proposed reforms are 'O merakh' (1977); 'O dopolnitel'nykh merakh' (1982); and 'Osnovnye napravlenie' (1987).

The most important measures are summarized in Table 17.1. They included decentralization of the management of medical facilities to republics and regions, attempts to introduce output-oriented health planning, economic experiments that devolved responsibility for the budget of medical facilities to their managers, and establishment of quasi-market relations between medical facilities by making polyclinics fund-holders. Almost without exception, health reform experiments in the command period were successful on a local level. But problems always arose when reforms were attempted on a wider scale, because it was impossible to provide all participants with preferential treatment. In general, health reforms suffered from the same flaws as economic ones in the Soviet era, namely that they were technocratic, failed to address the systemic deficiencies of the shortage economy, and were undermined by the bureaucracy (Schroeder 1979).

In order to furnish a necessary baseline against which developments in Russia's transition period should be assessed, Table 17.2 presents data on health conditions, illness patterns, performance of health institutions, and mortality rates in the USSR and RSFSR. The Soviet population increased from 230 million in 1965 to 290 million in 1991.[13] Although the birth rate declined over time, it still generated four million births per year. There were increases in the shares of the elderly in the population to 10 per cent, of males to 47 per cent and of urban residents to 66 per cent. Cohorts that experienced the Second World War and were supposed to have greater susceptibility to degenerative diseases than previous generations, entered old age.

The Soviet economy expanded at decelerating rates until 1988 and thereafter contracted. Improvements in income distribution, housing, and nutrition exerted positive influences on the disease pattern. Adverse developments included increases in cigarette smoking, alcohol consumption, and environmental pollution (Feshbach and Friendly 1992). However, the anti-alcohol campaign of the *perestroika* era (1985–8) resulted in a reduction in alcohol abuse (Meslé and Shkolnikov 1995).

Preventive medical services were effective in controlling many of the traditional threats to health. Most forms of infectious and social disease diminished, although Soviet rates remained significantly higher than those in the industrialized West and in leading east European countries

---

[13] Among the informative sources on health conditions, illness patterns, and mortality in the USSR are Dutton (1979); Davis and Feshbach (1980); Feshbach (1983, 1993); Ellman (1994); and Meslé and Shkolnikov (1995).

Table 17.1. *Health sector reforms in the USSR*

Health Reform Policy	Reform Implementation and Results
Devolve responsibility for managing medical facilities in regions from the Ministry of Health USSR to ministries of health in the republics.	A reform of this type was introduced in the Khrushchev era (1957–64) as part of the regionalization of the economy. The health service subsequently was re-centralized. In the late *perestroika* period (1989–91) greater powers in the health field were given to republican governments.
Cost containment programmes to hold down growth of real health expenditure.	The Ministry of Health, under pressure from Gosplan and the Ministry of Finance, made repeated attempts to contain costs in medical facilities.
Reform health planning and budgeting to make it more effective.	Throughout the post-1965 period reforms were introduced to update norms used in planning and budgeting and differentiate them to take into account specific features of regions. Largely unsuccessful attempts were made to base health plans on output indicators, rather than those of inputs (i.e. hospital beds).
Transfer ownership of industrial enterprise medical facilities to local government.	Unsuccessful attempts were made to introduce this reform in the Khrushchev period.
Improve the economic efficiency of medical system facilities by increasing the decision-making autonomy of managers and by providing them with new incentives to raise performance standards.	In July 1967 a two-year experiment with this type of reform was initiated, which involved 17 facilities. It was continued through 1976 and gradually extended to more hospitals and polyclinics. The final version of the bonus scheme was extended to the whole health service in 1977.
Optimize the allocation of resources in health districts by giving responsibility for patients' treatment and control of the budget to primary care outpatient facilities, which would purchase appropriate services from hospitals and other facilities in a health market.	This reform was introduced on an experimental basis in the late *perestroika* period in three regions: Leningrad, Kemerovo and Kuibyshev. Preparations were being made to extend it to the whole health service when the USSR fragmented in 1991.

Table 17.1. *(continued)*

Health Reform Policy	Reform Implementation and Results
Introduce fees for medical services in state facilities.	Throughout the Soviet period fees were charged for a variety of non-critical services provided by medical institutions, such as some work-related medical examinations. Managers of facilities were given greater freedom to introduce fees in the *perestroika* period.
Create self-financing out-patient facilities (polyclinics) that obtain their revenue by charging patients fees.	These facilities were established in the post-Khrushchev period but not allowed to develop to their potential due to ideological constraints. Plans were introduced to expand their numbers and increase their autonomy as part of a reform of consumer goods and services in late *perestroika*.
Legalize private outpatient practice by medical personnel.	Although private practice was legal in the Soviet period, it was tightly controlled and discouraged. However, in late *perestroika* the government removed some of the constraints on legal private medical activity.
Improve the management of medical facilities.	A new discipline of health service management was established in the 1970s and staff were given better training in this area.
Improve the utilization of the hospital bed stock by altering its structure, increasing technical support, and providing better incentives for rapid treatment.	Repeated technocratic reforms were introduced to achieve this objective throughout the Soviet period.
Improve the performance of pharmacies by making them truly self-financing.	This reform was started in the late *perestroika* period, but the collapse of the USSR hindered its implementation.
Improve the efficiency of pharmaceutical and medical equipment industry enterprises by making them market-oriented and self-financing.	All firms in the medical industry were shifted onto a self-financing basis in accordance with the 1988 Law on Enterprises. In late *perestroika* enterprises became increasingly autonomous.

Table 17.1. *(continued)*

Health Reform Policy	Reform Implementation and Results
Increase medically related exports and raise the efficiency of imports by allowing biomedical R&D facilities and medical industry enterprises to engage directly in foreign trade and to establish joint ventures with foreign firms.	In the *perestroika* period selected medical institutions were allowed to operate outside the state monopoly of foreign trade. The foreign trade organization Medeksport eventually was abolished.

Sources: Popov (1976); 'O merakh' (1977); Ryan (1978); 'O dopolnitel'nykh' (1982); Davis (1983b); 'Osnovnye' (1987); Davis (1987); Ryan (1990); Sheiman (1991); Schepin and Semenov (1992); Davis (1993a).

(Feshbach 1983) (see Appendix A). The combination of an ageing population, stress, and unhealthy living generated growth in degenerative diseases (Table 17.2, lines 13–14). Accidents and poisonings also rose. These developments in morbidity posed new challenges to the national health service.

The Soviet medical system provided curative services free of charge on a universal basis through a large network of polyclinics, hospitals, and other facilities (Field 1967; Kaser 1976; Ryan 1978, 1990). However, the government was committed to containing the costs of health, and the medical system remained subject to tight financial constraints (Davis 1983b, 1987). Although health outlays increased, their share of the government budget declined from 6.5 per cent in 1965 to a low of 4.3 per cent in 1986. The health share of GDP remained in the 3.0–3.5 per cent range.

The medical system adopted an 'extensive' development strategy: growing outputs of medical services of relatively low quality were produced using increasing quantities of inputs such as doctors and hospital beds (Davis 1987) (Table 17.2, lines 17–23). Efficient use of these inputs was hampered by the forces of the shortage economy and the general lack of incentives to economize. For example, the average length of stay in Soviet hospitals remained high by international standards: 15.9 days in 1970, 17.0 in 1980, and 17.2 in 1990. As Appendix A shows, visits to western hospitals were shorter and declined significantly over time.

Table 17.2. *Health production in the USSR and RSFSR, 1965–1991*

	Country	Health indicator	Units	1965	1970	1975	1980	1985	1990	1991
			Demography, health conditions and morbidity							
1	USSR	Population	Millions (beginning of year)	229.6	241.7	253.3	264.5	276.3	288.6	290.1
2	RSFSR	Population	Millions (beginning of year)	126.3	130.1	133.8	138.3	142.8	148.9	148.5
3	USSR	Birth rate	Births per 1,000	18.4	17.4	18.1	18.3	19.4	16.8	16.2
4	RSFSR	Birth rate	Births per 1,000	15.7	14.6	15.7	15.9	16.6	13.4	12.1
5	USSR	Abortions	Per 100 births	190.0	170.0	154.7	144.2	130.7	134.2	133.0
6	RSFSR	Abortions	Per 100 births	na	253.4	221.0	204.4	187.4	205.9	200.7
7	USSR	Share of males	%	45.7	46.1	46.4	46.7	46.9	47.2	47.3
8	USSR	Share of elderly	% 65 years and older	6.8	7.8	8.8	9.6	9.1	9.5	9.7
9	USSR	Alcohol consumption	Litres pure alcohol per adult	10.6	12.8	13.8	14.7	12.1	10.6	10.8
10	USSR	Typhoid	New Cases per 100,000	11.1	9.3	10.3	6.4	6.3	3.0	2.0
11	USSR	Measles	New Cases per 100,000	927.1	195.1	143.6	134.5	98.0	16.0	17.8
12	USSR	Viral hepatitis	New Cases per 100,000	204.0	167.0	276.0	302.0	337.0	317.0	268.1
13	USSR	Cancer morbidity	New Cases per 100,000	na	177.0	na	205.0	223.0	237.0	241.7
14	RSFSR	Cancer morbidity	New Cases per 100,000	na	198.0	218.0	232.0	248.1	264.5	266.0
16	USSR	Tuberculosis	New Cases per 100,000	na	na	na	50.2	45.7	36.9	36.0
16	RSFSR	Tuberculosis	New Cases per 100,000	na	72.4	58.6	47.4	45.2	34.2	34.0
			Medical system and health finance							
17	USSR	Doctors	Per 1,000 population	2.4	2.7	3.3	3.8	4.2	4.4	4.2
18	RSFSR	Doctors	Per 1,000 population	2.5	2.9	3.5	4.0	4.5	4.7	4.4

	Region	Indicator	Unit							
19	USSR	Medical wages	% of all economy average	81.9	75.4	70.2	75.1	69.9	68.0	66.0
20	USSR	Outpatient visits to doctors	Annual per capita	6.8	8.0	9.0	10.4	11.4	9.9	9.8
21	USSR	Hospital beds	Per 1,000 population	9.6	10.9	11.8	12.5	13.0	13.3	13.1
22	RSFSR	Hospital beds	Per 1,000 population	9.8	11.3	12.3	13.0	13.5	13.8	13.5
23	USSR	Hospitalizations	Per 100 population	20.6	21.5	22.7	23.7	25.1	22.5	20.4
24	USSR	Length of stay in hospital	Bed days per patient	14.9	15.9	16.8	17.0	16.7	17.2	18.6
25	USSR	Real health expenditure index (1985 roubles)	1970 = 100	66.7	100.0	123.8	160.6	192.3	240.2	206.0
26	USSR	Health share of state budget	%	6.5	6.0	5.3	5.0	4.6	5.6	5.4
27	USSR	Health share of GDP	%	3.0	3.0	2.9	3.0	2.9	3.6	3.5
Other Health Institutions										
28	USSR	Pharmacies	Thousands	19.9	22.9	25.3	26.6	29.2	30.5	30.6
29	USSR	Pharmacists	Per 10,000 population	1.6	2.0	2.4	2.8	3.3	4.1	4.2
30	USSR	Medicine sales	Roubles per capita	3.8	5.8	7.5	8.7	12.5	17.6	18.3
31	USSR	Output of medical industry	Million roubles	662.0	1,244.0	2,089.0	3,302.0	4,623.0	6,559.7	9,977.3

Table 17.2. *(continued)*

	Country	Health indicator	Units	1965	1970	1975	1980	1985	1990	1991
32	USSR	Output of medical industry	Roubles per capita	2.9	5.1	8.2	12.5	16.7	22.7	34.4
33	USSR	Imports of medicine	Million roubles	na	166.0	289.7	542.7	1,160.9	2,273.2	1,295.7
34	USSR	Imports of medicine	Roubles per capita	na	0.7	1.1	2.1	4.2	7.9	4.5
		Mortality								
35	USSR	Crude death rate	Deaths per 1,000	7.3	8.2	9.3	10.3	10.6	10.3	10.6
36	RSFSR	Crude death rate	Deaths per 1,000	7.6	8.7	9.8	11.0	11.3	11.2	11.4
37	USSR	Cancer mortality	Deaths per 100,000	123.4	127.3	134.7	140.3	155.3	166.6	na
38	USSR	Circulatory mortality	Deaths per 100,000	312.8	385.1	459.1	543.7	544.2	547.7	na
39	USSR	Maternal mortality	Deaths per 100,000 births	na	na	na	61.5	47.7	42.4	46.9
40	RSFSR	Maternal mortality	Deaths per 100,000 births	na	105.6	85.7	68.0	54.0	47.4	52.4
41	USSR	Infant mortality	Deaths per 1,000 births	27.4	24.4	30.6	27.3	26.0	21.8	22.3
42	RSFSR	Infant mortality	Deaths per 1,000 births	26.6	23.0	23.7	22.1	20.7	17.4	17.8
43	USSR	Population life expectancy	Years	70.4	69.4	68.8	67.7	68.4	69.3	69.1
44	RSFSR	Population life expectancy	Years	69.5	68.9	68.1	67.6	69.3	69.2	69.0
45	USSR	Male life expectancy	Years	66.1	64.5	63.7	62.2	63.3	64.3	64.0
46	RSFSR	Male life expectancy	Years	64.3	63.2	62.3	61.5	63.8	63.8	63.5

Notes: na = not available. Not all statistical series on health in the USSR are complete. Comprehensive publication of data only commenced in the *perestroika* period as a result of the Gorbachev regime's *glasnost* policy.

Sources: Detailed discussions of sources are presented in Davis and Feshbach (1980); and Davis (1983b, 1987, 1993ab, 1997, 1998, 2000). The main documents used for the USSR were: TsSU and GKS SSSR (various years) *Narodnoe Khozyaistvo*; GKS SSSR (1989) *Narodnoe Obrazovanie*; GKS SSSR (1990) *Okhrana Zdorov'ya*; GKS SSSR (1990) *Demograficheskii*; and GKS SSSR (1991) *Sotsial'noe Razvitie*. For the RSFSR the main sources were: GKRFS (1995a) *Meditsinskoe*; GKRFS (1995b) *Rossiiskii Statisticheskii*; GKRFS (1995c) *Zdravookhranenie*; GKRFS (1996a) *Demograficheskii*; GKRFS (1996b) *Zdravookhranenie*; Chelleraj et al. (1998); WHO HFA (2000); and WHO WHSA (various years).

Medical wages were well below average for the economy, labour productivity was low, and it was difficult to entice doctors to work in the
countryside. The overwhelming majority of the medical labour force was
female. Inadequate investment meant that many medical facilities lacked
basic amenities, such as central heating and water, were not properly
maintained, and were over-crowded. As economic difficulties mounted
in the 1980s, shortages intensified and the performance of the medical
system deteriorated (Davis 1993*a*).

Despite the free access to state-provided medical services in the USSR,
various factors acted to suppress demand, such as the time and travel costs
of treatment, informal charges, disutility of waiting, and deficiencies in
the quality of care. Soviet studies of morbidity, reviewed in Popov (1976)
and Davis (1988), estimated that one-third of illnesses in cities and two-
thirds in rural areas were not reported to doctors.

Substantial problems existed in the operations of supporting health
institutions (Davis 1987, 1993*b*). The medical supply network had inadequate storage facilities, made errors in planning the distribution of
supplies through wholesale and retail outlets, and was plagued by illegal
practices. The production of medical equipment and medicines by Soviet
industry was insufficient to satisfy the needs of the population and the
medical system. Biomedical R&D generated few important pharmaceutical discoveries. The main foreign trade organization, *Medeksport*,
was subjected to tight budget constraints and imported insufficient
quantities of foreign medical goods.

Medical effectiveness improved over time, but remained significantly
below international norms due to deficient diagnostics, financial constraints on medical treatment, poor conditions of health capital stock,
and inadequate supplies of medicines and equipment.[14] For example, the
risk of infections in Soviet medical facilities was higher than in the West
due to the absence of disposable medical technology (Knaus 1981).

Soviet studies of the economic effectiveness of specific medical techniques, medical efforts to eradicate certain diseases, and the medical
system as a whole consistently showed that their benefits exceeded costs

[14] In the Soviet period only limited amounts of information were published on indicators of medical effectiveness. No individual case history data sets were made available and it
was impossible to obtain consistent data for a given facility or district health system.
Furthermore, statistics on the transitions of patients to health, disability and death states
were very limited. Although hospital lethality data (deaths per 1,000 admissions) were routinely collected (on Form no. 266) and analysed by the Ministry of Health, these statistics
were not made available to the public.

(Kucherin 1978; Popov 1976).[15] The benefit-cost ratio of the eradication of poliomyelitis was 42/1, that for diphtheria 44/1. However, due to state censorship and a desire not to offend the Ministry of Health, Soviet health economists failed to evaluate medical programmes linked to illnesses with rising incidence, such as cardiovascular disease, cancer, traffic accidents, and influenza. Studies based on their methodology would have shown these activities to be economically ineffective.

Health status effectiveness varied by sub-period. In 1965–85 the national disease pattern in the USSR became more complicated and challenging. Health spending went up and most quantitative, distributive, and qualitative indicators of the medical system improved. But the medical system was not able to offset the negative impact of growing illness due to the problems and constraints discussed above. Virtually all adult age-specific death rates rose. The infant mortality rate increased from 22.9 deaths per 1,000 live births in 1971 to 31.1 in 1976 (Davis and Feshbach 1980).[16] The crude death rate went up from 7.3 deaths per 1,000 in 1965 to 10.6 in 1985, while total population life expectancy at birth declined from 70.4 years to 67.7 years (Table 17.2, lines 35–46). Thus, the medical system was relatively ineffective in these years.[17]

In the early *perestroika* period (1985–8) morbidity stabilized, with growth in degenerative diseases being offset by the beneficial impacts of

[15] Soviet health economists considered an activity to be economically effective if the benefits it generated by reducing illness, invalidity and mortality rates, measured by averted losses, exceeded its costs (Popov 1976, Kucherin 1978, Korchagin 1980). The averted losses from morbidity and invalidity reductions were calculated by taking into account possible lost production, lower productivity, curative medical expenditures, rehabilitation and retraining, and social security benefits. The economic effect of mortality reduction was calculated by multiplying the number of man-years saved by the estimates of annual national income produced per worker.

[16] Numerous other scholars subsequently investigated the infant mortality situation and reached differing conclusions concerning the reality of the phenomenon. A review of the debate is provided in Field (1986). The current opinion of this author is that one-half of the increase was due to improved statistical reporting and demographic shifts and one-half to deterioration in conditions affecting the health of pregnant women and infants.

[17] Davis (1990) compared the performances of similar national health services in different politico-economic systems: Britain (democratic society with a market economy) and USSR (dictatorship with a command economy). During 1970–90 the British NHS improved its technological capabilities and the quality of its medical services, maintained high standards in staff-patient relations, expanded the volume of services, and contributed to the lowering of morbidity and mortality rates while absorbing a low share of GDP by OECD standards (see Appendix A). In the same period, the Soviet NHS also increased the quantity of its outputs and served the whole population without direct charge. In contrast, it achieved minimal technological progress, produced low-quality medical services, had poor

the anti-alcohol campaign and other programmes. Medical service provision improved in most respects. All death rates fell through 1988 and life expectancy reached a historic peak of 69.8 years in 1987. As a consequence, the medical system became health-status-effective in a relative sense. However, during 1989–91 health conditions worsened, illness rates rose, and the shortage-related performance problems of the medical system intensified. Adult age-specific and the crude death rates increased again, while life expectancy declined. The medical system became health status ineffective in an absolute sense.

17.4. HEALTH CARE IN THE RUSSIAN FEDERATION, 1992–2001

17.4.1. *Economic and political environment of the health sector*

The shift from a Communist dictatorship to a more democratic government made Russia's rulers aware that they should be responsive to the preferences of citizens. However, the political system has been unstable and there have been recurrent conflicts between the main centres of power: presidential apparatus, parliament (Duma and Federation Council), ministries, and regions. The weakening of central government has led to the problem of 'state desertion' and deterioration in civic order, manifested by rising crime rates (Ellman 1995; World Bank 1997; Field *et al.* 1999). The Russian government has attempted to introduce simultaneously radical, democratic, and market-oriented reforms in all institutions, thereby diffusing scarce administrative and material resources. The inter-state and civil wars on the territory of the FSU have caused additional illnesses and deaths, damaged health sector assets, and generated growing numbers of refugees.

The transition to a market system has involved the decentralization of decision-making, the adoption of market-based co-ordination mechanisms and incentives, and transformations in the ownership of assets (Åslund 1995; Sapir 1996; IEPPP 1998 and chapters of this volume). However, institutional change has been slow and uneven, while programmes have been interrelated. A key example is that the government has announced many reforms that are dependent on adopted budgets,

staff–patient relations, and failed to ensure that either morbidity or mortality rates were consistently reduced. This differing experience suggests that a national health service financed by the state budget can be an efficient and effective way of organizing medical care in the appropriate political and economic system.

but has been unable to implement them because of its failure to collect sufficient tax revenue (see Chapter 9 in the volume). More generally, the poor performance of the economy in the 1990s undermined health conditions and seriously disrupted the work of all health institutions.

17.4.2. *Formation of the health sector and health reforms*

Of all the FSU successor states, the Russian Federation obtained the most complete set of health institutions (Davis 1993*bc*). However, numerous problems inherited from the past required correction through comprehensive reforms of the Russian health sector's organization, economic mechanisms, and institutions. Remedial measures would have been difficult to implement successfully, even if the politico-economic environment had not been in considerable flux and if resource constraints had not been so binding, because of three different, but related, challenges: to co-ordinate general economic and health sector reform policies; to co-ordinate policies affecting different institutions within the health sector; and to co-ordinate domestic policies with foreign technical and financial assistance programmes.

In order to meet the first challenge the Russian government should have acted to avert more of the potential problems posed by the economic transition policies to the health sector summarized in Table 17.3. The columns show the challenges of each policy to health institutions. The rows state the potential impacts of all policies on each institution. Effective reforms, rapid development of market mechanisms, and good economic performance could have ensured that these potential problems were not converted into actual ones.

Success in policy co-ordination has been difficult to achieve in Russia because of bureaucratic conflicts and weaknesses in leadership. The central health bureaucracy has been made up of policymakers in the presidential apparatus, government (Ministry of the Economy, Ministry of Finance), parliament, and Ministry of Health (Davis 1993*b*). Reform-oriented economic decision-makers in the government have had minimal competence in health economics, negligible knowledge of actual circumstances in the health sector, and limited understanding of the complexities of health production. They have viewed bodies such as the Ministry of Health as conservative and obstructive, and considered macroeconomic goals, such as reduction of inflation, to be of greater short-term importance than those in the health field, such as reducing illness. Top health sector managers, such as the ministers of health, have

Table 17.3. *Challenges posed by economic transition policies to health institutions in Russia*

Health Sector Institution	Economic transition policies					
	Price liberalization	Macroeconomic stabilization	Marketization	Privatization	Restructuring of capital stock	Foreign trade liberalization
Population (consumers)	Decreases in real income and consumption, higher prices of medical services and medicines	Anti-inflation policies result in lower wages, unemployment, and cuts in welfare programmes	Poor hygiene in private food markets causes illness. Problems in unregulated health markets	Private firms reduce their labour forces and cut their medical and welfare facilities	Inadequate capital investment in housing and social welfare	Problems with control of quality of imported medicines, decline in volume of imports
Preventive medicine	Rapid increases in prices of inputs of preventive medical establishments	Stingy budgets, low wages of staff, delayed wage payments, inadequate funds to obtain supplies	Rapid expansion of private trade in food and medicines makes it difficult to maintain hygienic standards	Private firms evade sanitary controls, criminal intimidation of state inspectors	Inadequate capital investment in water and sewage systems and pollution controls	Abolition of trade monopoly makes it more difficult to control quality of imported consumer goods
Curative medicine	Introduction of legal prices for medical services, rapid increases in prices of inputs of curative medical establishments	Stingy budgets, low wages of staff, delayed wage payments, inadequate funds to obtain supplies	Medical facilities forced to offer more services on a fee basis, elimination of central rationing of inputs	Best state medical facilities may try to privatize; emergence of two-tier medical system	Inadequate capital investment in buildings and equipment in medical system	Loss of state subsidies of medical imports, reduction in imports due to budget limits causes shortages

Table 17.3. (*continued*)

Health Sector Institution	Economic transition policies					
	Price liberalization	Macroeconomic stabilization	Marketization	Privatization	Restructuring of capital stock	Foreign trade liberalization
Pharmacies	Some price controls remain on goods for sale, but prices of inputs of pharmacies rise rapidly	Reductions in direct budget finance and in state subsidies of medicine prices	Growth of unregulated private medicine distribution network	Most pharmacies do not have suitable facilitities for private operations Danger of asset stripping and re-profiling	Inadequate capital investment in buildings and equipment in pharmacies and warehouses	Abolition of trade monopoly and CMEA disrupt traditional imports. Need to construct new private foreign trade system
Medical industry	Some price controls remain on goods for sale, but prices of inputs of industry rise rapidly	Reduction in direct budget finance Declines in demands of population and medical facilities for domestic industry's output	Need for producers to develop new marketing skills. Elimination of central rationing. Need to create wholesale trade system	Dangers of monopoly, asset stripping, foreign domination, cuts in firms' medical and welfare facilities	Inadequate capital investment in buildings and equipment to enable firms to develop competitive products	Reduction in imports of active substances and production technology. Loss of less competitive CMEA export markets

Notes: In order to show more clearly the impact of economic transition policies on the medical system, this institution has been divided into its preventive and curative branches. Due to space constraints the table does not include the institutions of biomedical R & D, medical foreign trade, and the central health bureaucracy.

Source: Based on analysis of the experiences of East European and FSU health sectors reported in Davis (1993*abc*, 1998, 2000, 2001).

tended to focus on the issues of relevance to their institutions (hospitals, pharmacies, pharmaceutical factories) and have had weak influence on the resource allocation decisions of the presidential apparatus and Ministry of Finance. Furthermore, decentralization to regional governments has reduced the power of federal authorities.

The second challenge has been equally daunting. Intra-sectoral co-ordination of reforms has been undermined by the carrying over from the command era of divisions of administrative responsibility. The bureaucratic reality is that most ministries and state committees that existed under Communism have survived under capitalism, usually with a different name (e.g. Ministry of Economics instead of State Planning Committee).[18] Lower level institutions (hospitals, pharmaceutical factories) are increasingly autonomous and incentives exist to reward self-enriching activities that often are inconsistent with the objectives of their superiors in ministerial hierarchies. A new complication has been the growth of health interest groups with links to private medical care, health insurance, pharmacies, pharmaceutical industries, and medical foreign trade.[19] As in the West, these groups disrupt health reform programmes likely to be of general benefit when they threaten to undermine their particular economic interests.

The third challenge has been to co-ordinate health reforms with the activities of the myriad foreign governmental, multi-national, and non-governmental agencies that have supported health projects in Russia. Western organizations often have been in conflict with the Russian Ministry of Health and other central governmental bodies, the former usually being more interested in market-oriented solutions than the latter. In such cases some western personnel have tended to assume that their Russian colleagues fail to understand the necessities and complexities of a market economy and are opponents of reform. Another daunting task has been to distribute efficiently and equitably the

[18] There has been continuity in the employment of key personnel from the Soviet era as well. Most of the staff in the state bureaucracies have remained unchanged, while reformist ministers have come and gone. Striking reminders of the power of the past were the September 1998 appointments by prime minister Primakov of Yuri Maslyukov (Russian Communist Party member and former chairman of Gosplan USSR) to the post of Deputy Prime Minister overseeing the economy and of Viktor Gerashchenko, former Chairman of the USSR State Bank, to the job of Chairman of the Russian Central Bank.

[19] See Rozhdestvenskaya and Shishkin (1996) for an analysis of health interest groups in Russia. Prekker and Feachem (1995, p. 17) mentions the influence of 'vested interests,' on health policy making. Klugman *et al.* (1996, p. 26) discuss the role 'stakeholders' play in the reform process.

substantial quantities of medicines and medical products delivered to
Russia through western aid programmes in the face of poor organization of the medical supply network, substantial theft, and rampant
corruption.

During 1990–2001 Russia has announced many health reforms and has
implemented successfully a sub-set of them. These are summarized
in Table 17.4. Some reforms are similar to those that were introduced
in the command period (see Table 17.1). Other reforms have been
unique to the transition period. These usually have involved a reliance on
market mechanisms, privatization, or movement away from collectivist
principles.

One reform with a long pedigree is cost containment (Davis 1990).
In the old days the Communist élite asked the population to accept
constraints on the provision of medical care while the perfect Socialist
system was constructed. Since transition commenced the new capitalist
élite has been asking the masses to make similar sacrifices in order to
construct a perfect future of democracy and market mechanisms. The
Russian government has attempted to hold down the growth of health
expenditures as part of its macroeconomic stabilization programmes. It
has introduced specific measures to restrain spending growth both in
institutions financed by the state budget and those receiving their funding through insurance reimbursement.

Management and finance have been decentralized to regional and local
governments with the goals of relieving pressure on the federal budget
and giving local authorities direct responsibility for medical establish-
ments on their territory.[20] Many health facilities formerly under the
control of industrial enterprises have been transferred to local governments, and all of them are supposed to be in the public sector by the end
of the year 2000. Attempts have been made to give managers of health
facilities full financial responsibility, hard budget constraints, and new
incentives to stimulate efficient behaviour. District health budgets are
being reallocated to primary care institutions (for example, polyclinics),
which then buy diagnostic and curative services from other facilities
(for example, hospitals). State facilities have been granted new rights
to charge fees for diagnostic and curative medical services, and have

---

[20] Interestingly, decentralization of the financing of the medical system to regional and
local governments also was a component of the Bolshevik government's macroeconomic
stabilization programme in the early years (1921–4) of the market-oriented New Economic
Policy. It was called the 'transition to local means' and is analysed in Davis (1983*b*).

Table 17.4. *Actual and proposed health sector reforms in the Russian Federation*

Health reform policy	Reform objectives and results
Health reforms introduced during 1992–99	
Shift financing of medical care from exclusive reliance on the state budget to a health insurance system based on compulsory contributions from enterprises for workers through a payroll tax and from the government for the non-working population	Reduce the health burden on state budget. Obtain supplemental funds from the business sector. Use the reimbursement process to exert pressure on medical service providers to improve their efficiency. A law on compulsory medical insurance was adopted in 1991 and subsequently revised. Only limited success achieved in this reform to date
Decentralize the financing and management of medical facilities from national to regional and local governments	Relieve health burden on federal budget. Bring decision-making closer to patients. The Ministry of Health has given up direct control of most medical facilities. This has resulted in growing differentiation across regions in the organization, financing, and provision of medical care
Cost containment programmes to hold down growth of real health expenditure	Keep state budget and insurance spending within agreed limits. Successive stabilization programmes have imposed tight constraints on health spending. Unpredictable budget sequestrations have disrupted the work of medical facilities
Increase autonomy of medical system managers by giving them responsibility for the budget of their institution and efficiency-promoting incentives	Enable managers to be more responsive to local demand and supply forces. Soviet-era incentive experiments have been continued in several regions and many related reforms have been introduced
Give the health budget of a district to primary care outpatient facilities (fundholders) and have them purchase services from hospitals and other facilities	Shift balance of resource allocation decision-making from hospitals to outpatient clinics that are closer to patients. Improve efficiency. Several regions have continued Soviet-era experiments with such reforms. Plans have been announced to introduce a reform of this type nationwide

Table 17.4. *(continued)*

Health reform policy	Reform objectives and results
Introduce fees for medical and dental services in state facilities	Revenue generation. Discourage over-use of state medical facilities. All health system managers have been given new rights to charge fees for services
Introduce or raise charges for prescription medicines related to outpatient care	Revenue generation. Overcome tight constraints on medical system budgets. This reform has been carried out in conjunction with the liberalization of prices of medicines in the retail pharmacy system
Legalize private outpatient pratice by medical personnel	Relieve pressure on state facilities, increase competition in medical care provision, and increase consumer choices. New laws guarantee doctors the right to private practice
Rationalize the hospital bed stock by reducing numbers while increasing unit support and throughput	Increase the efficiency of hospitals in their utilization of beds. Improve the quality of hospital care. Soviet-era reform efforts have continued. However, lack of funding has impeded progress
Enhance the ability of patients to choose their doctors	Increase consumer satisfaction. Use revealed preferences to indentify good and bad doctors. Several new laws and decrees passed on patients' rights
Introduce private voluntary medical insurance to pay for priority access to state medical facilities and for services not covered by state guarantees	Obtain extra funding for state facilities by charging insurance funds for the provision of services to their customers. New legislation has legalized private insurance, but few citizens have taken out policies
Establish private outpatient and inpatient medical facilities	Relieve the state of responsibility for financing all medical facilities. Raise revenue through auctions or profit-sharing schemes. Encourage competition from the private sector in order to raise efficiency. No state facilities have been privatized to date. However, *de novo* private clinics and hospitals now exist in Russia that primarily serve the domestic élite and foreigners

Table 17.4. (*continued*)

Health reform policy	Reform objectives and results
Privatize pharmacies	Recognize that pharmaceutical trade is a commercial activity best left to the private sector, subject to effective state regulation. To date, many pharmacies have been corporatized but only about 25% have become private
Reform medicine procurement practices, improve organization and management of medical supply network, and develop new regulatory mechanisms for pharmaceutical market	Improve the effectiveness and efficiency of the medical supply system. There has been a rapid growth of the private wholesale market in medical goods. More work needs to be done on state procurement procedures and regulation
Privatize pharmaceutical and medical equipment production enterprises	Recognize that pharmaceutical production is a commercial activity best left to the private sector, subject to effective state regulation. Virtually all medical industry enterprises have been privatized, mostly on an insider basis. Little progress has been achieved in restructuring facilities and in making them internationally competitive
Develop organizations to regulate emerging medical insurance and service provision markets	Ensure that the interests of consumers are protected in the new medical insurance and service markets. The Russian government has established a number of state bodies to regulate private activities in the health sphere

Health sector reforms proposed for the period 2000–5

Redefine health provision guarantees and exclude certain services (cosmetic surgery, sanatoria, prosthesis)	Relieve health burden on state budget. Focus resources on essential services. Provide citizens with a clear statement of the guaranteed types of medical services and of the related levels of care. These rights are to be enshrined in a new law 'On Patients' Rights' and in supporting government decrees

Table 17.4. *(continued)*

Health reform policy	Reform objectives and results
Transfer ownership of industrial enterprise medical facilities to local government	Open up closed facilities to the public. Relieve welfare burdens on privatized firms now subject to hard budget constraints. Transfer departmental facilities into the public sector
Base the provision of primary medical care on general practice (family) doctors, who are to be primarily located in existing polyclinics	This reform is intended to ensure better continuity in the care of families on the model of the GP, in the British NHS. It is a key component of the 'Kontseptsiya' document.
Encourage the development of more non-governmental organizations in the health field	This reform has the goals of improving the efficiency of preventive medical care, raising the public's knowledge of health issues, and providing supplemental goods and services to needy members of the population. There is supposed to be a substantial expansion of NGOs in 2000–5
Encourage the development of a significant private sector in health care	This reform should generate new forms of medical services and increase competition and efficiency throughout the medical system. A significant expansion of private medical care is supposed to occur in the period 2000–5
Reform the organization and performance of the medicine supply network	Clarify state guarantees of free or subsidized medicine in hospitals and polyclinics. Improve state regulation of the trade in medicine. Encourage improvements in the supply system to ensure that good-quality medicines are widely available and to raise the efficiency of retail and wholesale medical trade
Reform medical science by concentrating activities on high priority topics and by shifting the method of funding to one based on the competitive allocation of grants	The objectives are to eliminate duplication of work and research on issues of marginal importance, to streamline the medical research establishment and to accelerate technological innovation in the pharmaceutical industry

Table 17.4. *(continued)*

Health reform policy	Reform objectives and results
Develop a modern, internationally competitive pharmaceutical industry that is capable of providing 70% of medicines in Russia by 2005	Restructure the pharmaceutical industry to concentrate production in high-priority areas. Improve the financial conditions of enterprises through state loans and grants. Develop import-substitution programmes

Sources: Davis (1993*abc*); Preker Feachem (1995); Shishkin (1995); Klugman and Schieber (1996); 'Programma' (1997); 'Kontseptsiya' (1997); Davis (1998, 2001); Sheiman (1998); Federalnaya (1998); Shishkin (1998, 2000); 'Kontseptsiya' (2000).

been directed to generate revenue to supplement reduced budget allocations. Charges have been introduced or increased for dental treatment and prescription medicines related to outpatient treatment. Private practice by health professionals has been legalized. This has brought into the open some of the transactions previously conducted in the shadow economy. Technocratic reforms have included measures to improve information provision to health sector managers, to cut hospital bed stocks and increase patient throughput, to introduce quality assurance systems, and to raise the number of nurses in the medical system and enhance their professional capabilities.

Among measures unique to the transition period, an ideologically controversial proposal is to alter the coverage of the national medical system from universal to targeted. Efforts are being made to redefine state guarantees concerning health provision to exclude certain services (for example, cosmetic surgery, treatment in health resorts). The government has authorized the creation of private, fee-for-service medical subsystems to treat foreigners and national élites. These can be viewed as market-based equivalents of the former Communist party medical facilities run by the Fourth Main Administration of the Ministry of Health USSR. Indeed, some of these well-endowed élite polyclinics and hospitals are in the forefront of entrepreneurial medicine in the transition period. A major effort has been made to shift the financing of health services from the state budget to compulsory medical insurance (see the discussion in the next section). Reforms within medical institutions include the introduction of insurance-linked reimbursement based on capitation for outpatient care, or on norms derived from diagnostic related groups for inpatient treatment.

Privatization of health sector institutions is a revolutionary component of the new reforms. Although there has been discussion of the merits of transforming selected state hospitals and polyclinics into private commercial or non-profit units, none has been de-nationalized to date. In contrast, there has been privatization of pharmacies and pharmaceutical and medical equipment industrial enterprises (Ackerman and Smerkis 1997; Kokorina and Serebryakova 1997). In conjunction with this, prices of medical commodities have been liberalized and many reforms have been made of state procurement of medicines, of management of wholesale distribution remaining in state hands, and of state agencies regulating pharmaceutical trade.

Democratization has prompted the introduction of reforms with the goals of increasing patients' freedom to choose their doctor within the state sector and of providing them with better medical information. Finally, new organizations have been established to regulate the activities of health professionals, especially those in the private sector, and the operations of the new markets for private health insurance and medical services.

17.4.3. *The influences of state budget priorities and changes in the economic system on health institutions*

Hierarchical relations have become less important in capitalist Russia with the abolition of central planning and rationing, but low-level units, whether hospitals or pharmaceutical factories (most of them privatized), have remained dependent upon high-level state bodies for budget allocations, tax breaks, subsidies, and cheap bank credits. The current incentive system has changed to one based almost entirely on material rewards and market-driven sanctions. Health sector markets that existed in embryo or were severely constrained in the command era have become legal and active. In them, prices and production decisions are influenced, if only imperfectly, by demand and supply forces.

As in the command period, financial stringency and the existence of more important economic objectives (reducing inflation and the budget deficit, promoting rapid privatization) have prevented the new Russian government from allocating to health programmes the resources needed to solve existing, sometimes acute, problems (Korchagin 1997). The low priority status of the health sector has been reflected in real expenditure cuts and the unresponsiveness of state budget allocations to the mounting problems in it. The index of real health spending (1990 = 100) declined to 82 in 1992, recovered in 1993–4, and then dropped to 67 in 1999 (Table 17.5, line 37).

The behaviour of health institutions in the Russian transition economy has been somewhat different from that associated with the shortage economy. In markets for outputs, power has gradually shifted in favour of buyers; but the severe budgetary constraints imposed on the medical system, pharmacies, and biomedical R&D facilities have kept them in the position of supplicants relative to their suppliers, so sellers' markets have not yet disappeared. Many medical facilities have continued to neglect the quality of output and maintain quantity drives for the same reasons as in the past, namely excess demand for services at low or zero money prices and institutional inertia.

The medical system has remained financially disadvantaged. Official wage rates and benefits of state medical employees have remained low relative to other branches of the economy, despite their high educational qualifications. The work of medical facilities has been disrupted by payment arrears resulting from the government's practice of budget sequestration (holding back approved funds) in order to achieve stabilization targets (Sapir 1996, 1999). The inadequate and erratic funding has resulted not only in mass resignations of nurses but also in chronic shortages of current supplies (medicines, food) and insufficient capital inputs (equipment, spare parts, construction services). Moreover, it has proved difficult to obtain many traditional products at market prices because downstream supply networks have been adversely affected by the prolonged recession and the dissolutions of the CMEA and USSR. Medical system input indicators (for example, middle medical personnel, hospital beds) have diminished, albeit from high levels.

Most medical managers have recognized the need to upgrade the quality of medical services and products but have remained risk averse with respect to technological innovation due to the uncertainties concerning laws, health reforms, property rights, and incentives. In the early phase of transition there has been insignificant investment in health and negligible progress has been achieved in improving the capital stock. In 1995 32 per cent of hospitals required major capital repairs, 39 per cent had no hot water, and 19 per cent had no running water (Terekhov 1997, p. 55). Since medical facilities in the West continued to modernize in the 1990s, it is likely that technological gaps between them and their Russian equivalents have widened.

Table 17.5. *Health production in the Russian Federation, 1990–1999*

	Indicator	Units	1990	1991	1992	1993	1994	1995	1996	1997	1998	1999
			Demography, health conditions, and morbidity									
1	Population	millions (beginning of year)	148.0	148.5	148.7	148.7	148.4	148.3	148.0	147.5	147.1	146.7
2	Birth rate	births/1,000	13.4	12.1	10.7	9.4	9.6	9.3	8.9	8.6	8.8	8.3
3	Abortions	abortions/100 births	206.3	201.0	216.4	235.2	217.3	202.6	203.0	201.6	182.6	179.4
4	Male share of population	%	46.8	46.9	46.9	46.9	46.9	47.0	46.7	46.7	46.9	46.9
5	Elderly share of population	% 65 years and older	10.0	10.4	10.8	11.3	11.7	12.1	12.2	12.3	12.4	12.5
6	Refugees arriving in Russia	thousands	0.0	0.0	160.3	287.6	254.5	282	172.9	131.1	118.2	79.1
7	Industrial pollutants in atmosphere	millions tons	37.1	31.8	28.2	24.8	21.9	21.3	20.3	19.3	18.7	18.5
8	Pollutants in water supplies	billions cubic metres	75.2	73.2	70.6	68.2	60.2	59.9	58.9	59.3	55.7	54.8
9	Alcohol sales	litres per capita	5.6	5.6	5.0	5.9	6.8	9.3	7.2	7.5	7.3	na
10	Cancer	new cases per 100,000	264.5	266.0	271.8	276.3	280.2	279.1	288.1	294.7	302.4	304.1
11	Tuberculosis	new cases per 100,000	34.2	34.0	35.8	42.9	48.2	57.9	67.6	74.1	76.1	85.4
12	Gonorrhea	new cases per 100,000	128.0	190.7	169.6	230.1	203.8	173.7	139.2	114.2	103.0	120.2
13	Syphillis	new cases per 100,000	5.3	7.2	13.4	33.8	85.5	177.0	264.6	277.3	234.8	187.2
14	Accidents at work	cases per 1,000 workers	6.6	6.5	6.2	6.3	5.9	5.5	5.6	5.6	5.4	na

15	Salmonellosis	registered cases per 100,000	70.4	74.2	80.1	68.3	70.2	58.2	44.3	41.0	40.7	42.2
16	Diphtheria	registered cases per 100,000	0.8	1.3	2.6	10.3	27.1	24.1	9.3	2.7	1.0	0.6
17	Whooping cough	registered cases per 100,000	16.9	20.8	16.2	26.6	33.1	14.0	9.4	18.6	19.3	15.3
18	Measles	registered cases per 100,000	12.4	13.8	12.5	50.3	19.4	4.5	5.6	2.0	4.2	5.1
19	Scabies	registered cases per 100,000	28.6	43.0	99.3	237.4	389.7	395.0	315.0	229.0	182.2	na
	Medical system											
20	Doctors	per 1,000 population	4.7	4.4	4.5	4.5	4.6	4.5	4.6	4.6	4.7	4.7
21	Middle medical personnel	per 1,000 population	12.3	11.4	11.4	11.1	10.9	11.1	11.3	11.2	11.1	11.1
22	Polyclinic capacity	visits per shift per 10,000	217.4	220.6	223.9	220.7	233.2	235.6	237.1	238.1	239.0	241.4
23	Outpatient doctor visits per year	per person	9.5	9.3	9.0	9.2	9.2	9.1	9.1	9.1	9.1	na
24	Hospital beds	per 1,000 population	13.8	13.5	13.1	12.9	12.7	12.6	12.4	12.1	11.8	11.6
25	Hospitalization rate	hospital stays per 100	22.8	21.8	21.0	21.6	21.6	21.2	20.7	20.5	20.4	na
26	Length of stay in hospital	bed days per patient	16.6	16.7	17.0	16.8	16.8	16.8	16.9	16.6	16.7	na
27	Operations in hospitals rate	per 1,000 population	62.4	58.6	57.7	56.6	57.6	56.7	56.7	56.6	56.5	na
	Health finance											
28	State budget health expenditure	billion current roubles	0.01	0.03	0.47	5.4	19.7	41.0	56.2	77.1	64.4	103.0

Table 17.5. *(continued)*

	Indicator	Units	1990	1991	1992	1993	1994	1995	1996	1997	1998	1999
29	National health insurance exp.	billion current roubles	0.00	0.00	0.00	1.0	4.2	9.0	13.9	18.3	20.0	33.1
30	Private expenditure (low estimate)	billion current roubles	0.00	0.00	0.04	0.5	1.8	7.8	10.6	15.1	16.3	31.8
31	Private expend. (high estimate)	billion current roubles	0.00	0.02	0.3	1.9	7.4	39.1	53.1	52.8	70.8	81.7
32	Total health expenditure (low)	billion current roubles	0.01	0.03	0.51	6.9	25.7	57.8	80.7	110.5	100.7	167.9
33	Total health expenditure (high)	billion current roubles	0.01	0.05	0.81	8.3	31.3	89.1	123.2	148.1	155.2	217.8
34	SB + NIH Exp Share of GDP	%	2.4	2.4	2.5	3.7	3.9	3.2	3.3	3.8	3.1	3.0
35	Total HE Share of GDP (Low)	%	2.6	2.6	2.7	4.0	4.2	3.7	3.8	4.4	3.7	3.7
36	Total HE Share of GDP (High)	%	3.4	3.8	4.3	4.8	5.1	5.7	5.8	5.9	5.7	5.8
37	Real SB + NIH HExp Index	1990 = 100	100	101	82	109	100	75	73	85	68	67
	Other health institutions											
38	Pharmacies	thousands	14.8	14.9	14.5	14.0	13.7	na	na	na	na	na
39	Index of real output of medicines	1990 = 100	100.0	105.0	88.2	66.2	62.8	59.7	57.9	71.2	67.7	na

#		Unit										
40	Output of antibiotics	tons	4,672	4,524	3,577	1,898	1,556	1,582	1,468	1,038	na	na
41	Output of vitamins	tons	4,327	4,257	3,651	3,149	2,746	1,552	945	1,074	na	na
42	Output of anti-tubercular products	million ampules	93.1	85.0	80.4	73.4	47.5	54.8	42.8	28.3	9.6	27.1
43	Electrocardiographs	thousands	23.0	31.9	29.2	12.5	5.0	2.7	2.6	3.5	2.5	2.8
44	Imports of medicines	millions US$	na	na	1,008	299	1,184	965	1,083	1,538	1,194	761

Mortality and invalidity

#		Unit										
45	Invalidity rate	first diagnoses per 10,000	51.7	61.5	75.7	77.7	76.5	91.1	79.9	77.7	77.2	72.3
46	Crude death rate	deaths per 1,000	11.2	11.4	12.2	14.5	15.7	15.0	14.2	13.8	13.6	14.7
47	Male working-age death rate	deaths per 1,000	7.6	7.8	9.1	11.6	13.2	12.5	11.2	9.9	9.6	10.6
48	Male 40–4 years death rate	deaths per 1,000	7.6	8.0	9.8	13.3	15.2	14.1	12.2	10.6	10.2	11.5
49	Male death rate from murder	deaths per 100,000	23.2	24.9	37.6	49.5	52.6	49.5	42.2	37.5	35.9	na
50	Working-age male alcohol related deaths rate	deaths per 100,000	29.1	30.2	46.9	81.0	103.3	86.5	66.5	50.5	46.2	na
51	Cancer death rate	deaths per 100,000	191.8	195.5	199.7	204.6	204.5	200.8	198.3	199.9	202.5	205.0
52	Circulatory disease death rate	deaths per 100,000	617.4	620.0	646.0	768.9	837.3	790.1	758.3	751.1	748.8	815.7

Table 17.5. *(continued)*

	Indicator	Units	1990	1991	1992	1993	1994	1995	1996	1997	1998	1999
53	Maternal mortality	deaths per 100,000 births	47.4	52.4	50.8	51.6	52.3	53.3	48.9	50.2	44.0	44.2
54	Infant mortality	deaths per 1,000 live births	17.4	17.8	18.0	19.9	18.6	18.1	17.4	17.2	16.5	16.9
55	Life expectancy at birth	years	69.4	69.0	67.9	65.1	64.0	64.6	65.9	66.6	67.0	65.9
56	Male life expectancy at birth	years	63.8	63.5	62.0	58.9	57.6	58.3	59.8	60.8	61.3	59.9

Sources: Davis (1993b, 1998, 2000); GKRFS (1995a) *Meditsinskoe*; GKRFS (1995b) *Zdravookhranenie*; GKRFS (1996) *Zdravookhranenie*; GKRFS (1998a) Finansy; GKRFS (1998b) Promyshlennost'; GKRFS (1999a) *Demograficheskii*; GKRFS (1999b) Rossiiskii Statisticheskii; GKRFS (1999c) Sotsial'noe; GKRFS (2000a) 'Demograficheskaya'; GKRFS (2000b) Rossiya v Tsifrakh; GKRFS (2000c) Informatsiya; MZRF (1996, 1999) O Sostoyanii; Terekhov (1997); WHO HFA (2000); WHO WHSA (various years); and Shishkin (2000).

The transformation of the other institutions in the health sector can be reviewed only briefly here. At the start of the transition period, pharmacies were state-owned, often based in old, inefficient facilities, and financially insolvent due to a combination of rising costs and controls on sales prices (Davis 1993*b*). They were encouraged to become truly self-financing and their marketization proceeded rapidly. Changes in ownership were slower. By the end of 1995 34 per cent of retail pharmacies had become independent juridical entities, but only 16 per cent were private (Kokorina and Serebryakova 1997, p. 12). In wholesale trade, a number of large private companies emerged, chiefly importing foreign medicines to compete with the state firms that grew out of the Soviet-era *Farmatsiya* monopoly (Boston Consulting Group 1997). Pharmacy sales contracted to the equivalent of $1.5 billion in 1993, but then rebounded to $2.7 billion in 1995 ('Vnutrennyy' 1997, p. 8).

Medical industry enterprises were converted into joint stock companies and mostly were privatized (Davis 1993*b*). As in other sectors, this was done on an insider basis, so only weak mechanisms existed to ensure proper corporate governance (see Blasi *et al.* 1998 and other chapters in this volume). Demand for domestically produced pharmaceuticals and medical equipment was depressed by the tight budgets of the medical system, the destitution of much of the population, and the preference of the affluent minority for foreign medicines. By 1995 Russian firms supplied only 33 per cent of goods purchased in pharmaceutical markets ('Vnutrennyy' 1997, p. 8). Additional financial problems were that enterprises were not paid regularly by customers, especially if they were state medical facilities, and that prices of many medicines were controlled while the costs of most inputs, such as energy, rose substantially. Supplies of inputs from firms in Russia and in other FSU states and eastern Europe were disrupted. Investment in the pharmaceutical industry plummeted from 483 billion (constant 1996) roubles in 1994 to a negligible 39 billion roubles in 1996 ('Indeksy rynka: Osnovnye' 1997, p. 5). The index of real pharmaceutical output (1990 = 100) dropped to 58 in 1996 and then recovered to 68 in 1998. The physical output of most medicines and medical equipment declined in the range of 30–70 per cent (Table 17.5, lines 39–43).

State budget allocations to medical science were severely cut. The ratio of the approved to the requested budget of the Russian Academy of Medical Sciences fell from 78 per cent in 1991 to 15 per cent in 1995, while the ratio of actual to approved expenditure declined from 100 per cent to 88 per cent (Pokrovskii 1997, p. 26). This meant that actual expenditure in

1995 was only 13 per cent of the amount requested, and 14 per cent of that fraction was received late. Supplemental funding was difficult to obtain because there was insignificant demand for R & D services by enterprises in the pharmaceutical and medical equipment industries, many of which were technically bankrupt. In consequence, most scientific institutions were acutely under-funded and could not pay the low wages of staff with any regularity. Although the numbers of researchers remained high, many of the best young scientists departed for more lucrative employment in the commercial sector. Capital investment declined to near zero, despite the fact that 70 per cent of equipment was more than ten years old in 1995. The quality of medical research deteriorated from Soviet-era standards.

The state monopoly of medical foreign trade was abolished in 1992 and replaced by a mixture of state and private firms (Davis 1993*b*). Flows of goods from traditional suppliers in eastern Europe, other Soviet successor states, Finland, and India were severely disrupted. Imports of medicines plummeted in 1993 to $299 million, climbed to a peak of $1,538 million in 1997, and then dropped in the crisis year of 1998 to $761 million (Table 17.5, line 44). However, this was a small volume of purchases relative either to global trade in pharmaceuticals or to Russia's need for medicines. The demand for foreign products grew rapidly and by 1995 50 per cent of medicines sold in Russia came from EE and CIS countries and 17 per cent from OECD nations ('Vnutrennyy' 1997, p. 8).

Many of the reforms outlined in Table 17.4, though sensible in principle, have been undermined by lack of material resources, resistance of interest groups, conflicts with economic policies, and insufficient political and administrative support. An important example has been the attempt to shift the financing of the national health service from the state budget to compulsory medical insurance with employees' premia financed by payroll taxes.[21] This reform had serious flaws in its initial design and was introduced without adequate preparation at a time of acute recession and financial squeeze on enterprises.[22] Unsurprisingly, its

---

[21] See the references listed in note 2 as well as *Meditsinskoe* (1993); Kuznetsov and Chelidze (1997); and *O Meditsinskom* (1997).

[22] One critic of the shift to compulsory medical insurance, Korepanov (1992), argued that 'in conditions of widespread shortages of finance and material resources, no leaders of state enterprises, collective farms, state farms, joint-stock companies or private organizations will make significant payments to meet the needs of hospitals and polyclinics. Therefore, in my view, it would be highly dangerous to change suddenly and completely from state insurance.'

implementation has been chaotic and institutional developments have varied widely across Russia's eighty-nine regions (Shishkin 2000). It is likely that this reform contributed little positive to the actual management of the medical system during 1992–2000. Furthermore, it has added to health costs: 6–8 per cent of compulsory insurance funding has been spent on the programme's proliferating bureaucracy.[23]

It is true that some health reform pilot projects and experiments have produced encouraging results. However, these experiments usually have been carried out with above-average support from national governments or western agencies. This situation is similar to that of the Soviet period discussed in section 3. It can be predicted with certainty that identical difficulties to those encountered in the past will emerge in capitalist Russia when the sponsors of health reform pilot projects attempt to generalize their 'successes'.

Wide-ranging debates over the merits of existing health reforms, especially insurance financing, took place in 1996–7. Powerful groups within the Duma and Federation Council argued for a return to state budget financing of health. However, in November 1997 the government of Viktor Chernomyrdin issued a major decree on health designed to promote the compulsory insurance system and market-oriented reforms, entitled 'About Measures for the Stabilization and Development of Health Services and Medical Science in the Russian Federation' ('O merakh' 1997). According to it and a linked document, 'Concepts for the Development of the Health Service and Medical Science in the Russian Federation' ('Kontseptsiya' 1997), current reforms and structural changes were to be consolidated during 1998–2000 and then more radical reforms, such as developing the private medical sector, were to be introduced during 2000–5. A related decree devoted to reform of the medical industry was issued in June 1998 ('Federalnaya' 1998). The main proposals of these two decrees are summarized in the second section of Table 17.4.

The 1997 programme of reforms had minimal positive impact on the health sector due to acute political and economic problems in subsequent years. The post of prime minister shifted unexpectedly from

---

[23] Not all contemporary analysts of Russian health financing debates are aware that the USSR had an insurance-financed health system in the New Economic Policy period (1921–8). Davis (1983a) showed that it resulted in pronounced inequalities in health spending and medical provision across regions and social groups. For example, in 1927–8 health spending per capita for the urban insured (trade union members) and their families (14% of the population) was 19.8 roubles, whereas it was only 0.7 roubles for uninsured residents in the countryside, who made up 80% of the population.

Viktor Chernomyrdin to Sergei Kiriyenko (March 1998), to Yevgenii
Primakov (August 1998), to Sergei Stepashin (April 1999), to Vladimir
Putin (August 1999). Furthermore, Boris Yeltsin resigned as president
in December 1999 and his interim successor, Vladimir Putin, was elected
to the post in March 2000. These abrupt changes affected personnel,
decision-making, and resource allocation patterns in all sectors of the
economy. In the case of health, the minister of health was replaced in
this period.[24]

A second factor undermining the health reforms was the economic
crisis of August 1998. The budgetary situation of the Ministry of Health
deteriorated throughout the year, although its situation became extremely difficult in the autumn. Most health insurance organizations were
hit badly by the interrelated collapses of the GKO market (they had been
forced to purchase bonds by the government) and the banking system. In
1999 the resources allocated to health were lower than anticipated and
few of the 'Kontseptsiya' reforms could be financed. Although real health
spending recovered in 2000, the medical system still has not received all
the funds projected in the optimistic year of 1997.

The government of President Putin has demonstrated an awareness of
the nation's health problems and a determination to correct them. In
August 2000 its health strategy was outlined in the 'Conception of the
Safeguarding of the Health of the Population of the Russian Federation
in the Period up to 2005' ('Kontseptsiya' 2000). In contrast to the 1997
'Kontseptsiya', the new one bases its solution to current health problems
on 'the formation in the population of an appreciation of a healthy life
style, the increase in the level of sanitary-hygienic culture, that does not
demand significant financial expenditures, but may generate significant
socio-economic results'. The approved health promotion programme
contains measures directed at improving the health education of ordinary
people to get them to reduce unhealthy habits (smoking, alcoholism,
drug abuse) and to increase physical activity, reducing pollution,
improving diet and immunization programmes, and re-orienting the
work of the medical system. The last will involve restructuring curative
health care to give greater prominence to outpatient care, developing

[24] In an interview at the Ministry of Health of the Russian Federation in February 2000
this author was told by First Deputy Minister of Health Anatolii Vyalkov that the ministry
was planning to hold a large conference in March to review the ten years of experience with
health reforms. It then would prepare a new concept document and detailed plans for the
development of the health sector over the next five years. In the event, 'Kontseptsiya' (2000)
was approved by the government in August.

family doctors, and making sanitary–epidemiological work more effective. Priority attention will be given to certain population groups (for example, pregnant women and infants) and diseases (for example, hypertension). This inter-ministerial programme is being supplemented by specific ones developed by the Ministry of Health, which are outlined in a March 2000 document entitled 'Objectives of the Health Sector and Medical Science from 2000–2004 and through 2010'.

17.4.4. *Health production and medical system effectiveness in the Russian transition economy, 1992–2000*

Most health-related demographic variables worsened in early transition (1992–5) (Table 17.5, lines 1–6) (Heleniak 1995). Birth rates fell sharply, while those of abortions-to-births and divorces rose. Diets worsened for the majority of the population. Alcohol consumption rose, whereas that of tobacco declined. Although the flows of pollutants into the atmosphere and water supply declined because of the drop in industrial activity, Russia remained heavily polluted. According to Minister of Health Dmitrieva (1997), only 15 per cent of the urban population lived in cities with pollution within hygienic norms. Lack of investment and weakening state controls resulted in the deterioration of the quality of water and hygiene standards in food production and distribution. One-half of the population had access to drinking water that met state standards.

Cardiovascular and cancer morbidity rose throughout the 1990s, as did illnesses related to social conditions, such as tuberculosis and venereal disease. According to official statistics, just in the year 1995 morbidity of infants climbed by 6.2 per cent, of teenagers by 7.6 per cent, and of adults by 2.6 per cent (Terekhov 1997, p. 17). The incidence of many infectious diseases increased substantially during 1990–4, but then declined or remained stable (Table 17.5, lines 15–19). As is evident from Appendix B, Russia's disease rates have remained substantially higher than those of eastern European and OECD countries.

Trends in health output in Russia (see Table 17.5, lines 45–56) have been determined by the dynamics of morbidity and the performance of health sector institutions, discussed above. As a general rule, health indicators deteriorated during 1990–4 and improved over the next several years. Trends following the 1998 economic crisis are more varied. The invalidity rate rose from 51.7 registrations per 10,000 population to 91.1 in 1995, and then dropped to 72.3 in 1999. The infant mortality rate increased to 19.9 deaths per 1,000 live births in 1993, but then declined to 15.8 in 2000. Almost all adult age-specific death rates rose to peaks in 1994 and declined through 1998. For example, the rate for men aged 40–4 went up from 7.6 deaths per 1,000 in 1990 to a high of 15.2 in 1994 and then decreased to 10.2 in 1998. However, a number of male age-specific mortality rates went up again in 1999–2000. Maternal mortality increased from 47.4 deaths per 100,000 births in 1990 to 53.3 in 1995, and then decreased to a still high 44.0 in 1998. The crude mortality rate went up from 11.2 deaths per 1,000 in 1990 to a peak of 15.7 in 1994, declined to 13.6 in 1998, and then rose to 15.3 in 2000. Life expectancies at birth for the total population and for males have exhibited similar patterns of deterioration and improvement, and reversal. Male life expectancy dropped from 63.8 years in 1990 to a low of 57.6 years in 1994, recovered to 61.3 years in 1998, and then fell back to 59.9 years in 1999.

With respect to medical system effectiveness, the experience of Russia during the initial years of transition (increasing illness, deterioration in medical care, rising mortality) was similar to the pattern in the USSR during 1989–91, but different from that of 1965–85, when there were improvements in medical care. Given that the increased incidences of many diseases in 1992–5 were large and abrupt, it is likely that the medical system would have been overwhelmed even it if had maintained past standards and levels of financing. In this hypothetical case, the medical system would have been relatively ineffective in health-status terms. In reality, its worsening performance during 1992–4 made it ineffective in an absolute sense. In the words of a Federation Council report, one consequence was that 'patients suffering from many forms of chronic pathologies lived 8–10 years less than in countries of Western Europe' (Terekhov 1997, p. 17).

In 1996–8 health production in Russia remained problematic, but positive trends were evident. Although demographic, living standard, and environmental conditions continued to be unfavourable by OECD norms, most improved relative to previous years. The morbidity situation became more variable. Better health conditions and modest advances in preventive medical programmes helped to reduce the rates of most infectious diseases. Nevertheless, incidents of cancer, cardiovascular illness, and tuberculosis increased. Due to the continuing poor performance of the economy and recurrent fiscal crises, the financing of health care through the state budget remained inadequate. Most enterprises were unable to contribute anticipated funds to the compulsory medical insurance system. Nevertheless, the medical system expanded some elements of its capacity and continued to provide high levels of services

(Table 17.5, lines 20–7). The consumption of medicines by the population has increased. Overall, trends in health output, measured by indicators of invalidity and mortality, have turned positive. This suggests that the effectiveness of the medical system improved somewhat during, 1995–8, despite all the problems in this institution.

The 1998 economic crisis had a detrimental effect both on health conditions and the performance of medical institutions. In consequence, medical system effectiveness deteriorated in absolute terms, as in the initial phase of transition.

17.5. CONCLUSION

The study has found considerable continuity in the features and problems of Russia's health institutions over the past several decades due to economic factors and government policies. Health conditions for the majority of the population have remained poor, a uniquely challenging illness pattern (high incidences of infectious, social, and degenerative diseases) has been maintained, medical system performance has been inferior to that in the OECD region, and mortality rates have been high and have risen on several occasions.

Although the economic system in Russia has changed profoundly from that of the USSR, behavioural patterns of health institutions with respect to outputs, production, and inputs in command and transition economies are surprisingly similar. For example, sellers' markets and chronic shortages have survived as phenomena despite the shift to the market. This is largely due to the fact that health has remained a state sector with low-priority status.

The government has introduced numerous health reforms, ranging from technocratic ones, affecting specific processes within facilities, to systemic ones, such as the shift to compulsory medical insurance. However, Russian leaders in the transition have resembled Soviet predecessors in their general neglect of the health sector, ignorance of the inter-relationships between health institutions and tolerance of departmentalism. The government has not been effective either in co-ordinating economic and health reform policies or in developing consistent and feasible reforms for the health sector. The failures of the Russian government in the health policy field were partially responsible for the rises in mortality in that country. It seems clear that reductions in health spending and deterioration in medical care in the face of rising illness in both late *perestroika* (1989–91) and (1989–91), early transition (1992–5), and the aftermath of the 1998 economic crisis facilitated the increases in mortality rates.

An evaluation of Russian health developments in the future must take into account the inter-connections between economic and health processes and uncertainties surrounding both health production and the economy. In an optimistic scenario, the current economic crisis will be quickly resolved, the economy will grow at the high rates during 2001–5, health conditions will improve, morbidity rates will decline, and institutional reforms in the health sector will be consolidated. The health sector will expand rapidly in the Russian economy, the performance of health institutions will converge towards the standards established by their equivalents in OECD countries, and health output indicators, such as mortality rates, will improve considerably. In a more probable scenario, economic recovery will be slow and conditions within the health sector will remain strained for several years before slowly improving. In this case, the Russian population's health will continue to be poor during the initial five years of the twenty-first century and only modest progress will be achieved in reforming the financing and performance of medical institutions.

Appendix A. Health indicators in selected eastern European and OECD countries, 1970–1989

Indicator	Units	1970	1975	1980	1985	1989
	OECD Region					
	France					
Population	millions	50.8	52.7	53.7	55.2	56.2
Share of elderly	% 65 and older	13.4	14.0	14.3	13.5	14.4
Abortions	per 1,000 births	na	na	na	na	243.8
Measles	cases per 100,000	6.8	3.4	2.3	372.2	273.8
Tuberculosis	cases per 100,000	na	47.5	32.0	20.5	16.1
Hospital beds	per 1,000	7.2	na	11.1	10.5	12.5
Length of stay in hospital	average number of days	18.3	19.8	16.7	15.5	13.4
Doctors	per 1,000	1.3	1.7	2.0	2.7	2.6
Health share of GDP	%	5.8	7.0	7.6	8.5	8.7
Cancer mortality	deaths per 100,000	192.6	202.7	204.4	205.3	204.7
Circulatory mortality	deaths per 100,000	344.0	339.8	294.3	264.8	215.2
Maternal mortality	deaths per 100,000 births	28.2	19.9	12.9	12.0	8.5

Indicator	Units	1970	1975	1980	1985	1989
Infant mortality	deaths per 1,000 births	15.1	13.8	10.0	8.3	7.5
Crude death rate	deaths per 1,000	10.6	10.6	10.2	10.0	9.4
Male life expectancy	years	68.6	69.0	70.2	71.3	73.1
United Kingdom						
Population	millions	55.7	55.9	55.9	56.6	57.2
Share of elderly	% 65 and older	12.8	14.0	14.9	15.1	15.6
Abortions	per 1,000 births	na	na	185.3	203.3	235.8
Measles	cases per 100,000	616.5	283.5	264.5	185.1	54.2
Tuberculosis	cases per 100,000	25.4	22.6	18.8	11.8	10.6
Hospital beds	per 1,000	na	na	7.9	7.1	6.0
Length of stay in hospital	average number of days	25.7	22.9	19.1	15.8	14.8
Doctors	per 1,000	1.1	na	1.4	1.5	1.6
Health share of GDP	%	4.5	5.5	5.6	5.9	5.8
Cancer mortality	deaths per 100,000	216.9	217.4	220.3	224.8	220.4
Circulatory mortality	deaths per 100,000	557.6	529.5	483.0	434.9	378.0
Maternal mortality	deaths per 100,000 births	18.0	12.0	10.9	7.3	7.7
Infant mortality	deaths per 1,000 births	18.5	16.0	12.1	9.4	8.4
Crude death rate	deaths per 1,000	11.8	11.8	11.8	11.9	11.5
Male life expectancy	years	68.8	69.5	70.2	71.5	72.7
USA						
Population	millions	205.1	216.0	227.7	238.5	247.3
Share of elderly	% 65 and older	9.8	10.5	11.3	11.9	12.4
Abortions	per 1,000 births	na	328.9	430.2	422.5	387.8
Measles	cases per 100,000	23.1	11.3	5.9	na	na
Tuberculosis	cases per 100,000	18.1	15.7	12.2	na	na
Hospital beds	per 1,000	7.9	6.6	6.0	5.5	5.0
Length of stay in hospital	average number of days	14.9	11.4	10.0	9.2	na
Doctors	per 1,000	1.7	1.9	2.1	2.4	2.6
Health share of GDP	%	7.4	8.4	9.2	10.5	11.5
Cancer mortality	deaths per 100,000	129.9	na	132.8	134.4	134.5
Circulatory mortality	deaths per 100,000	340.1	na	256.0	225.1	196.1
Maternal mortality	deaths per 100,000 births	21.5	12.8	9.2	7.8	7.9

Indicator	Units	1970	1975	1980	1985	1989
Infant mortality	deaths per 1,000 births	20.0	16.1	12.6	10.6	9.8
Crude death rate	deaths per 1,000	9.5	8.8	8.8	8.8	8.7
Male life expectancy	years	67.2	68.8	69.6	71.2	71.7

Eastern Europe
Bulgaria

Indicator	Units	1970	1975	1980	1985	1989
Population	millions	8.5	8.7	8.9	9.0	9.0
Share of elderly	% 65 and older	9.6	10.9	11.9	11.6	12.6
Abortions	per 1,000 births	1027.1	991.6	1217.4	1098.5	1175.7
Measles	cases per 100,000	350.5	231.2	121.5	10.9	1.2
Tuberculosis	cases per 100,000	79.0	49.0	37.0	28.5	25.6
Hospital beds	per 1,000	7.7	8.9	8.9	9.1	9.7
Length of stay in hospital	average number of days	na	na	15.2	14.5	13.8
Doctors	per 1,000	1.9	2.2	2.5	2.9	3.1
Health share of GDP	%	2.3	2.4	2.7	3.1	3.4
Cancer mortality	deaths per 100,000	147.4	142.8	136.9	151.6	156.4
Circulatory mortality	deaths per 100,000	559.1	610.1	638.0	726.1	694.3
Maternal mortality	deaths per 100,000 births	44.7	27.7	21.1	12.5	18.7
Infant mortality	deaths per 1,000 births	27.3	23.1	20.2	15.2	14.4
Crude death rate	deaths per 1,000	9.1	10.3	11.1	12.0	11.9
Male life expectancy	years	69.1	68.7	68.4	68.3	68.3

Poland

Indicator	Units	1970	1975	1980	1985	1989
Population	millions	32.5	34.2	35.6	37.2	38.0
Share of elderly	% 65 and older	8.2	9.7	10.1	9.4	9.9
Abortions	per 1,000 births	na	na	199.0	199.3	141.5
Measles	cases per 100,000	386.4	429.0	69.9	95.9	19.0
Tuberculosis	cases per 100,000	na	76.8	72.5	58.2	42.6
Hospital beds	per 1,000	7.4	7.5	6.7	6.6	6.6
Length of stay in hospital	average number of days	na	na	na	na	12.5
Doctors	per 1,000	1.4	1.6	1.9	2.0	2.1
Health share of GDP	%	3.6	3.8	3.6	3.5	3.5
Cancer mortality	deaths per 100,000	178.0	180.6	194.8	206.1	211.0
Circulatory mortality	deaths per 100,000	494.8	493.6	577.5	611.4	587.5

Appendix A. *(continued)*

Indicator	Units	1970	1975	1980	1985	1989
Maternal mortality	deaths per 100,000 births	29.5	14.8	11.6	11.0	10.6
Infant mortality	deaths per 1,000 births	33.2	24.9	21.2	18.4	15.9
Crude death rate	deaths per 1,000	8.2	8.7	9.8	10.3	10.0
Male life expectancy	years	66.6	67.3	66.1	66.5	66.8
Romania						
Population	millions	20.3	21.2	22.2	22.7	23.2
Share of elderly	% 65 and older	8.6	9.6	10.3	9.5	10.1
Abortions	per 1,000 births	na	na	1035.6	844.0	522.5
Measles	cases per 100,000	611.1	521.1	47.2	22.0	16.7
Tuberculosis	cases per 100,000	137.4	110.0	54.5	45.8	58.3
Hospital beds	per 1,000	8.3	9.0	8.8	8.9	8.9
Length of stay in hospital	average number of days	11.5	11.4	11.1	11.1	11.1
Doctors	per 1,000	1.2	1.3	1.5	1.8	1.7
Health share of GDP	%	2.7	2.6	2.5	2.3	2.5
Cancer mortality	deaths per 100,000	146.0	145.8	149.4	148.0	148.5
Circulatory mortality	deaths per 100,000	671.5	645.3	768.9	773.0	712.3
Maternal mortality	deaths per 100,000 births	116.4	123.4	132.1	137.4	169.4
Infant mortality	deaths per 1,000 births	49.4	34.7	29.3	25.6	26.9
Crude death rate	deaths per 1,000	9.5	9.3	10.4	10.9	10.7
Male life expectancy	years	65.7	67.5	66.6	66.4	66.7

Notes: A more comprehensive presentation of health statistics for Bulgaria, Czechoslovakia, German Democratic Republic, Hungary, Poland, and Romania in the period 1970–89 can be found in Davis (1998).

Sources:
Population: WHO HFA (1998); WHO WHSA (various years); SEV (1981) *Statisticheskii*, p. 8; SEV (1989) *Statisticheskii*, p. 8; and USDC (1993) *Statistical*, p. 8.
Share of elderly: WHO HFA (1998); USDC (1979), p. 8; USDC (1993), p. 15.
Abortions: WHO HFA (1998); USDC (1993), p. 81.
Measles: WHO HFA (1998); WHO WHSA (various years).
Tuberculosis: WHO HFA (1998); WHO WHSA (various years).
Hospital beds: WHO HFA (1998); WHO WHSA (various years); SEV (1981), p. 443; SEV (1989), p. 445; OECD (various years) *OECD in Figures*, table on health; USDC (1993), p. 122; USDC (1997), p. 127.

Length of stay in hospital: WHO HFA (1998); OECD (1993) *OECD Health Systems*, p. 186; OECD (various years) *OECD in Figures*.

Doctors: WHO HFA (1998); WHO WHSA (various years); SEV (1981), p. 444; SEV (1989), p. 446; OECD (various years) *OECD in Figures*; USDC (1980), p. 115; USDC (1990), p. 101; USDC (1992), p. 108.

Health share of GDP: for the eastern European countries these estimates are based on an amalgam of the often inconsistent numbers presented in Kaser (1976), table 1.8; Davis (1989), p. 433; Chellaraj *et al.* (1996); UNICEF ICDC (1997), p. 135; WHO HFA (1998); and various statistical yearbooks of the east European countries. The shares for the OECD countries were obtained from: WHO HFA (1998); OECD (various years) *OECD in Figures*; USDC (1993), p. 107; and USDC (1997), p. 127.

Cancer and circulatory mortality: WHO HFA (1998); WHO WHSA (various years); USDC (1993), p. 90; USDC (1997), p. 95.

Maternal mortality: WHO HFA (1998); WHO WHSA (various years); USDC (1993), p. 89.

Infant mortality rate, crude death rate, male life expectancy: WHO HFA (1998); WHO WHSA (various years); Davis (1993*b*); SEV (1981), pp. 9–10; SEV (1989), pp. 11–12; USDC (1993), pp. 85, 87, 89.

Appendix B. **Health indicators in selected eastern European transition and OECD countries, 1990–1998**

Indicator	Units	1990	1991	1992	1993	1994	1995	1996	1997	1998
		Eastern Europe								
		Bulgaria								
Population	millions	9.0	9.0	8.5	8.5	8.4	8.4	8.4	8.3	8.3
Share of elderly	% 65 and older	13.0	13.4	14.0	14.4	14.7	15.0	15.3	15.6	15.9
Abortions	per 100 births	137.5	144.3	149.1	127.3	122.8	134.9	136.5	137.1	114.8
Measles	cases per 100,000	1.6	22.6	237.2	4.2	1.4	2.1	9.0	0.3	1.0
Tuberculosis	cases per 100,000	25.1	28.6	37.9	38.0	37.5	38.6	37.2	41.3	49.9
Hospital beds	per 1,000	9.8	9.8	10.2	10.5	10.2	10.4	10.5	10.3	8.4
Length of stay in hospital	average number of days	13.7	13.9	13.8	13.8	13.6	13.6	13.2	12.9	12.5
Doctors	per 1,000	3.2	3.0	3.2	3.4	3.3	3.5	3.5	3.5	3.5
Public health share of GDP	%	4.1	4.2	5.3	4.8	4.1	3.6	3.1	3.5	3.2
Real public health expenditure index	1990 = 100	100.0	94.1	110.0	98.4	84.2	77.4	59.9	62.7	58.8
Circulatory mortality	deaths per 100,000	691.4	699.2	677.9	705.8	706.4	726.0	749.0	814.0	816.0
Maternal mortality	deaths per 100,000 births	20.9	10.4	21.3	14.2	12.6	13.9	19.4	18.7	15.3
Infant mortality	deaths per 1,000 births	14.8	16.9	15.9	15.5	16.3	14.8	15.6	16.6	16.1
Crude death rate	deaths per 1,000	12.1	12.3	12.7	12.9	13.2	13.6	14.3	15.1	14.8
Male life expectancy	years	68.4	68.0	67.8	67.5	67.2	67.2	67.2	66.7	66.9

Appendix B. *(continued)*

Indicator	Units	1990	1991	1992	1993	1994	1995	1996	1997	1998
		Poland								
Population	millions	38.1	38.2	38.4	38.5	38.5	38.6	38.6	38.6	38.6
Share of elderly	% 65 and older	10.1	10.2	10.4	10.7	10.9	11.2	11.5	11.7	11.9
Abortions	per 100 births	10.8	5.6	2.3	0.3	0.2	0.1	0.1	0.8	na
Measles	cases per 100,000	148.1	6.3	9.6	3.7	2.2	2.0	1.7	0.9	5.9
Tuberculosis	cases per 100,000	42.3	43.1	42.8	43.4	43.2	41.4	39.8	36.2	34.4
Hospital beds	per 1,000	6.6	6.5	6.4	6.4	6.3	6.3	6.2	na	na
Length of stay in hospital	average number of days	12.5	12.3	11.8	11.4	11.0	10.8	10.6	10.4	na
Doctors	per 1,000	2.1	2.2	2.2	2.2	2.3	2.3	2.4	2.4	2.3
Public health share of GDP	%	4.6	4.7	4.8	4.4	4.4	4.4	4.7	4.4	4.2
Real public health expenditure index	1990 = 100	100.0	95.2	99.2	94.8	99.0	106.4	121.6	121.7	120.1
Circulatory mortality	deaths per 100,000	589.2	609.4	584.6	571.8	548.3	532.0	525.0	na	na
Maternal mortality	deaths per 100,000 births	12.8	12.8	9.9	11.7	11.0	9.9	4.9	5.8	4.8
Infant mortality	deaths per 1,000 births	19.3	18.2	17.3	16.1	15.1	13.6	12.2	10.2	9.9
Crude death rate	deaths per 1,000	10.2	10.6	10.3	10.2	10.0	10.0	10.0	9.8	9.9
Male life expectancy	years	66.5	66.1	66.7	67.4	67.5	67.6	68.2	68.7	68.8

Romania

Population	millions	23.2	23.2	22.8	22.8	22.7	22.7	22.6	22.5	22.5
Share of elderly	% 65 and older	13.6	11.9	11.4	11.0	10.9	10.4	10.2	10.5	10.6
Abortions	per 100 births	315.3	314.9	265.7	234.3	214.9	212.5	197.2	146.5	114.4
Measles	cases per 100,000	20.2	7.7	26.6	124.5	27.4	9.7	4.0	105	42.4
Tuberculosis	cases per 100,000	64.6	61.6	73.4	82.5	87.4	95.0	98.6	98.3	101.0
Hospital beds	per 1,000	8.9	8.9	7.9	7.9	7.7	7.6	7.6	7.4	7.3
Length of stay in hospital	average number of days	11.4	11.7	11.7	11.6	10.3	11.0	10.0	10.0	10.0
Doctors	per 1,000	1.8	1.8	1.9	1.8	1.8	1.8	1.8	1.8	1.8
Public health share of GDP	%	2.8	3.3	3.6	3.0	3.3	3.6	2.9	na	na
Real public health expenditure index	1990 = 100	100.0	100.4	100.6	86.4	99.4	115.6	96.1	na	na
Circulatory mortality	deaths per 100,000	705.7	729.5	751.1	753.0	739.3	748.0	794.0	757.0	730.0
Maternal mortality	deaths per 100,000 births	83.6	66.5	60.3	53.2	60.4	47.8	41.1	41.4	40.5
Infant mortality	deaths per 1,000 births	26.9	22.7	23.1	22.8	23.7	20.8	22.0	21.3	20.8
Crude death rate	deaths per 1,000	10.7	10.9	11.6	11.6	11.7	12.0	12.7	12.4	12.3
Male life expectancy	years	66.6	66.6	66.1	65.9	65.7	65.5	65.1	65.4	65.6

Appendix B. *(continued)*

Indicator	Units	1990	1991	1992	1993	1994	1995	1996	1997	1998
				Ukraine						
Population	millions	51.6	51.7	51.8	52.0	51.7	51.3	50.9	50.4	50.0
Share of elderly	% 65 and older	12.2	12.5	12.9	13.2	13.6	13.9	14.1	14.1	14.1
Abortions	per 100 births	155.1	151.7	156.2	154.5	153.1	150.2	147.1	134.8	125.3
Measles	cases per 100,000	13.2	10.3	25.6	45.2	19.0	3.8	17.1	13.9	10.2
Tuberculosis	cases per 100,000	31.9	32.3	35.0	38.5	39.9	41.8	52.8	56.2	55.5
Hospital beds	per 1,000	13.0	13.0	12.7	12.5	12.3	11.9	11.5	10.0	9.7
Length of stay in hospital	average number of days	16.4	16.5	16.8	16.8	16.9	16.8	16.8	16.2	15.7
Doctors	per 1,000	4.3	4.3	4.3	4.3	4.3	4.4	4.5	4.5	4.6
Public health share of GDP	%	3.0	3.3	3.5	4.1	5.4	4.9	3.9	4.1	na
Real public health expenditure index	1990 = 100	100.0	100.8	96.9	96.9	99.0	78.4	57.1	57.1	na
Circulatory mortality	deaths per 100,000	642.0	696.0	744.0	783.0	833.0	780.0	775.0	771.0	746.0
Maternal mortality	deaths per 100,000 births	32.4	29.8	31.3	32.8	33.1	32.3	30.4	25.1	27.2
Infant mortality	deaths per 1,000 births	13.0	13.9	14.0	14.9	14.3	14.7	14.3	14.0	12.8
Crude death rate	deaths per 1,000	12.2	12.9	13.4	14.3	14.7	15.4	15.2	14.9	14.3
Male life expectancy	years	65.7	66.0	64.0	63.5	62.8	61.3	61.7	62.4	63.3

OECD Region
France

Population	millions	56.7	57.1	57.4	57.7	57.9	58.1	58.4	58.6	58.7
Share of elderly	% 65 and older	14.5	14.7	14.9	15.1	15.3	15.6	15.8	16.0	16.2
Abortions	per 100 births	25.4	26.0	25.6	26.7	26.3	25.5	na	na	na
Measles	cases per 100,000	243.8	274.9	190.9	134.0	76.0	93.3	113.0	136.0	na
Tuberculosis	cases per 100,000	15.6	14.5	15.7	16.9	16.7	15.0	13.1	11.7	na
Hospital beds	per 1,000	9.7	na	na	9.4	9.0	8.9	na	na	na
Length of stay in hospital	average number of days	13.3	11.9	11.7	11.7	11.7	11.2	11.2	na	na
Doctors	per 1,000	2.6	2.7	2.8	2.8	2.9	3.0	2.9	3.0	na
Public health share of GDP	%	6.6	6.8	7.0	7.3	7.2	7.3	7.3	7.1	na
Real public health expenditure index	1990 = 100	na	na	na	na	na	na	na	na	na
Circulatory mortality	deaths per 100,000	205.6	203.7	195.1	193.8	182.8	183	182.0	176.0	na
Maternal mortality	deaths per 100,000 births	10.4	11.9	12.9	9.3	11.7	9.6	13.2	9.6	na
Infant mortality	deaths per 1,000 births	7.3	7.3	6.8	6.5	5.9	4.9	4.8	4.7	na
Crude death rate	deaths per 1,000	9.7	9.2	9.1	9.2	9.0	9.1	9.2	9.1	9.2
Male life expectancy	years	73.4	73.6	73.9	74.0	74.4	73.9	74.0	na	na

Appendix B. *(continued)*

United Kingdom

Indicator	Units	1990	1991	1992	1993	1994	1995	1996	1997	1998
Population	millions	57.4	57.8	58.0	58.2	58.4	58.6	58.8	59.0	58.2
Share of elderly	% 65 and older	15.7	15.7	15.8	15.8	15.7	15.7	15.7	15.7	15.8
Abortions	per 100 births	23.4	22.8	22.2	22.5	22.6	22.9	24.8	na	na
Measles	cases per 100,000	27.3	20.3	21.2	20.7	40.3	15.4	11.7	8.2	na
Tuberculosis	cases per 100,000	10.3	10.5	11.1	11.3	10.7	10.5	10.6	10.8	9.7
Hospital beds	per 1,000	5.7	5.4	5.1	4.8	4.6	4.5	na	na	na
Length of stay in hospital	average number of days	15.6	14.1	12.4	10.2	na	9.9	9.8	na	na
Doctors	per 1,000	1.6	1.6	1.6	1.6	na	1.6	na	na	
Public health share of GDP	%	5.1	5.5	5.8	5.8	5.8	5.9	5.9	5.8	na
Real public health expenditure index	1990 = 100	na	na	na	na	na	na	na	na	na
Circulatory mortality	deaths per 100,000	363.6	358.9	345.1	346.0	321.6	317.2	306.0	292.0	na
Maternal mortality	deaths per 100,000 births	7.6	6.9	6.7	5.7	7.9	7.0	na	na	na
Infant mortality	deaths per 1,000 births	7.9	7.4	6.6	6.3	6.2	6.2	6.1	5.9	5.7
Crude death rate	deaths per 1,000	11.2	11.2	10.9	11.3	10.8	11.0	10.8	10.7	10.6
Male life expectancy	years	73.1	73.3	73.7	73.6	74.2	74.1	74.3	na	na

		USA								
Population	millions	249.8	252.1	255.0	257.7	260.3	262.8	265.2	267.7	270.3
Share of elderly	% 65 and older	12.5	12.6	12.7	12.7	12.7	12.8	12.8	12.8	12.8
Abortions	per 100 births	38.9	37.8	38.0	37.8	36.4	35.1	35.1	na	na
Measles	cases per 100,000	na	na	na	na	na	na	na	na	na
Tuberculosis	cases per 100,000	na	na	na	na	na	na	na	na	na
Hospital beds	per 1,000	4.9	4.7	4.6	4.5	4.3	4.1	4.0	3.9	na
Length of stay in hospital	average number of days	9.1	na	8.8	na	na	8.0	na	na	na
Doctors	per 1,000	2.3	na	2.3	2.5	na	2.6	na	na	na
Public health share of GDP	%	4.9	5.2	5.7	5.9	6.1	6.3	6.3	6.3	6.3
Real public health expenditure index	1990 = 100	na	na	na	na	na	na	na	na	na
Circulatory mortality	deaths per 100,000	189.8	185.0	180.4	181.8	176.8	174.7	na	na	na
Maternal mortality	deaths per 100,000 births	8.2	7.9	7.8	7.5	8.3	7.1	7.6	na	na
Infant mortality	deaths per 1,000 births	9.2	8.9	8.5	8.4	7.9	7.6	7.3	7.1	na
Crude death rate	deaths per 1,000	8.6	8.6	8.5	8.8	8.8	8.8	8.7	8.6	na
Male life expectancy	years	71.8	72.0	72.3	72.2	72.3	72.5	73.0	73.6	na

Notes: More comprehensive presentation of health statistics for 23 eastern European and FSU transition countries can be found in Davis (1998, 2001).

Sources:

Population, mid-year: WHO HFA (2000); WHO WHSA (various years); UNICEF (2000); USDC (various years) SAUS.

Share of elderly: WHO HFA (2000); UNDY (various years); OECD (various years) *OECD in Figures*; USDC (various years) SAUS.

Abortions: WHO HFA (2000); UNDY (various years); USDC (various years) SAUS.

Measles and tuberculosis: WHO HFA (2000).

Hospital beds and doctors: WHO HFA (2000); UNICEF (2000); OECD (various years) *OECD in Figures*; USDC (various years) SAUS.

Length of stay in hospital: WHO HFA (2000); OECD (various years) *OECD in Figures*; OECD (1993) *OECD Health Systems*, p. 146.

Public health share of GDP: eastern Europe estimates are based on an amalgam of the often inconsistent numbers presented in Chellaraj *et al.* (1996, 1998); UNICEF (2000); and WHO HFA (2000). OECD data are from: WHO HFA (2000); OECD (various years) *OECD in Figures*; and USDC (various years) SAUS. In 1997 public shares were 74% in France, 84% in the UK and 46% in the USA.

Real public health expenditure index: The primary sources for the indices of east European countries for the years 1990–95 are Chellaraj, Heleniak, and Staines (1998) and Davis (2001).

Circulatory mortality (ICD8, A80–A88; ICD9, 25–30): WHO HFA (2000); Chellaraj, Heleniak, and Staines (1998); and WHO (various years) WHSA.

Maternal mortality: WHO HFA (2000); UNICEF (2000); USDC (various years) SAUS and IDB.

Infant mortality rate, crude death rate, male life expectancy: WHO HFA (2000); WHO WHSA; OECD (various years) *OECD in Figures*; USDC (1999) SAUS.

Crude death rate: WHO HFA (2000); UNICEF (2000).

Male life expectancy: WHO HFA (2000); UNICEF (2000).

The Health Sector 531

REFERENCES

Aaron, H. J., and Schwartz, W. B. (1984). *The Painful Prescription: Rationing Hospital Care*, Washington, DC: The Brookings Institution.

Ackermann, C., and Smerkis, V. (1997). 'Rossiiskie farmatsevticheskie distribyutory 2000', *Remedium*, 5 (June–July): 12–15.

Åslund, A. (1995). *How Russia Became a Market Economy*, Washington, DC: The Brookings Institution.

Auster, R., Leveson, I., and Sarachek, D. (1972). 'The Production of Health', in V. R. Fuchs (ed.), *Essays in the Economics of Health and Medical Care*, New York: NBER.

Barr, N. (1994). *Labor Markets and Social Policy in Central and Eastern Europe: The Transition and Beyond*, Oxford: Oxford University Press.

Blasi, J. R., Kroumova, J., and Kruse, D. (1998). *Kremlin Capitalism: Privatizing the Russian Economy*, London: Cornell University Press.

Blum, A. (1997). 'Cohort Determinants of the Mortality in Russia, East and Central Europe: Short and Long Term Evidence', Paper presented at a UNU/WIDER Project Meeting on 'Economic Shocks, Social Stress the Demographic Impact', 17–19 April, Helsinki.

Boston Consulting Group (1997). *Managing Change in Russian Pharmaceuticals Companies: Restructuring and Growth*, Briefing Book for a Conference for Senior Management of Russian Pharmaceuticals Distributors and Producers, Moscow.

Burenkov, S. P., Golovteev, V. V., and Korchagin, V. P. (1979). *Sotsialisticheskoe Zdravookhranenie: Zadachi, Resursy, Perspektivy Razvitiya*, Moscow: Meditsina.

Chellaraj, G., Adeyi, O., Preker, A., and Goldstein, E. (1996). *Trends in Health Status, Services and Finance: The Transition in Central and Eastern Europe Vol. II*, Washington, DC: World Bank Technical Paper 348.

—— Heleniak, T., and Staines, V. (1998). *Health Sector Statistics for the Former Soviet Union*, Washington, DC: draft of World Bank Technical Report.

Cherepov, V. M. (1995). 'Problemy reformirovanie zdravookhraneniya Rossiiskoi Federatsii', *Meditsinkoe Strakhovanie*, 12: 3–5.

Chernichovsky, D., Barnum, H., and Potapchik, E. (1996). 'Health Care Reform in Russia: The Finance and Organization Perspectives', *Economics of Transition*, 4/1: 113–34.

Culyer, A. J. (1976). *Need and the National Health Service: Economics and Social Choice*, London: Martin Robertson.

Davis, C. (1983a). 'Economic Problems of the Soviet Health Service: 1917–1930', *Soviet Studies*, 35/3: 343–61

—— (1983b). 'The economics of the Soviet Health System', in U.S. Congress, Joint Economic Committee, *Soviet Economy in the 1980s: Problems and Prospects*, Washington, DC: USGPO.

532   *Christopher Davis*

Davis, C. (1987). 'Developments in the Health Sector of the Soviet Economy: 1970–90', in U.S. Congress, Joint Economic Committee, *Gorbachev's Economic Plans*, Washington, DC: USGPO.

—— (1988). 'The Organization and Performance of the Contemporary Soviet Health System', in G. Lapidus, and G. E. Swanson (eds.), *State and Welfare, USA/ USSR*, Berkeley: Institute of International Studies.

—— (1989). 'Priority and the Shortage Model: The Medical System in the Socialist Economy', in C. Davis, and W. Charemza (eds.), *Models of Disequilibrium and Shortage in Centrally Planned Economies*, London: Chapman and Hall.

—— (1990). 'National Health Services, Resource Constraints and Shortages: A Comparison of British and Soviet Experiences', in N. Manning (ed.), *1989– 90 Social Policy Review*, London: Longman.

—— (1993a). 'The Health Sector in the Soviet and Russian Economies: From Reform to Fragmentation to Transition', U.S. Congress, Joint Economic Committee, *The Former Soviet Union in Transition*, Washington, DC: USGPO.

—— (1993b). *The Pharmaceutical Industry and Market in the USSR and Its Successor States: From Reform to Fragmentation to Transition*, Richmond: PJB Publications.

—— (1993c). 'Health Care Crisis in the Former Soviet Union and Eastern Europe: Overview', and Health Care Crisis: The Former Soviet Union', *Radio Free Europe/Radio Liberty Research Report*, 2/40, 8 October.

—— (1998). 'Morbidité, mortalité et reformes du secteur de la sante dans les États en transition de l'ex-URSS et de l'Europe de l'Est', *Revue d'Etudes Comparatives Est–Ouest*, 29/3: 133–85.

—— (2000). 'Transition, health production and medical system effectiveness', in G.A. Cornia and R. Paniccia (eds.), *The Mortality Crisis in Transitional Economies*, Oxford: Oxford University Press.

—— (2001). 'Reforms and Performance in Revival Systems in the Transitional States of the Former Soviet Union and Eastern Europe', *International Social Security Review*, 20/1: 2–3.

—— and Charemza, W. (eds.) (1989). *Models of Disequilibrium and Shortage in Centrally Planned Economies*, London: Chapman and Hall.

—— and Feshbach, M. (1980). *Rising Infant Mortality of the USSR in the 1970s*, Washington DC: U.S. Bureau of the Census, International Population Reports: Series P-95, No. 74.

Dmitrieva, T. B. (1997). 'O zdorov'e naseleniya Rossii', in N. F. Gerasimenko (ed.), 'Zdorov'e naselenie kak faktor obespecheniya natsional'noi bezopasnosti Rossii', *Informatsionno-Analiticheskii Upravleniya Apparata Soveta Federatsii: Analiticheskii Vestnik*, 10 (55).

Dutton, J. (1979). 'Changes in Soviet Mortality Patterns, 1959–77', *Population and Development Review*, no. 2.

Ellman, M. (1994). 'The Increase in Death and Disease under *katastroika*', *Cambridge Journal of Economics*, 18: 329–55.

—— (1995). 'The State under State Socialism and Post-Socialism', in H. J. Chang, and R. Rowthorn (eds.), *The Role of the State in Economic Change*, Oxford: Clarendon Press.

'Federalnaya tselevaya programma Razvitie meditsinskoi promyshlennosti v 1998–2000 godakh i na period do 2005 goda' (1998). *Rossiiskaya Gazeta*, 23 July.

Feshbach, M. (1983). 'Issues in Soviet Health Problems', in U.S. Congress, Joint Economic Committee, *Soviet Economy in the 1980s: Problems and Prospects*, Washington, DC: USGPO.

—— (1993). 'Continuing Negative Health Trends in the Former U.S.S.R.', in U.S. Congress, Joint Economic Committee, *The Former Soviet Union in Transition*, Washington, DC: USGPO.

—— and Friendly, A. jun. (1992). *Ecocide in the USSR: Health and Nature Under Siege*, New York: Basic Books.

Field, M. (1967). *Soviet Socialized Medicine: An Introduction*, New York: The Free Press.

—— (1986). 'Soviet Infant Mortality: A Mystery Story', in D. B. Jeliffe and E. P. Jeliffe, (eds.), *Advances in Maternal and Child Health*, Oxford: Oxford University Press.

—— and Kotz, D., and Bukhman, G. (1999). 'Neo-liberal Economic Policy, "state desertion", and the Russian health crisis', in J. Y. Kim, J. Millen, J. Gershman, and A. Irwin (eds.), *Dying for Growth: Global Inequality and the Health of the Poor*, Boston: Common Courage Press.

Folland, S., Goodman, A. C., and Stano, M. (1997). *The Economics of Health and Health Care*, London: Prentice-Hall.

Fuchs, V. R. (1966). 'The Output of the Health Industry', in M. H. Cooper, and A. J. Culyer (eds.), *Health Economics*, Harmondsworth: Penguin.

Gerasimenko, N. F. (ed.) (1997). *Zdorov'e Naselenie kak Faktor Obsepecheniya Natio-nal'noi Bezopastnosti Rossii*, Federal'noe Sobranie-Parliament Rossiiskoi Feder-atsii, Analiticheskii Vestnik: 10(55), Moscow.

GKRFS = Gosudarstvennyy Komitet Rossiiskoi Federatsii po Statistiki.

GKS SSSR = Gosudarstvennyy Komitet SSSR po Statistiki.

Gosudarstvennyy Komitet Rossiiskoi Federatsii po Statistiki (1995a). *Meditsinskoe Obsluzhivanie Naseleniya Rossiiskoi Federatsii v 1994 godu: Statisticheskii Sbornik*, Moscow: Goskomstat.

—— (1995b). *Zdravookhranenie v Rossiiskoi Federatsii: Statisticheskii Sbornik 1994*, Moscow: Goskomstat.

—— (1996). *Zdravookhranenie v Rossiiskoi Federatsii: Statisticheskii Sbornik 1995*, Moscow: Goskomstat.

—— (1998a). *Finansy Rossii: Statisticheskii Sbornik 1998*, Moscow: Goskomstat Rossii.

—— (1998b). *Promyshlennost' Rossii: Statisticheskii Sbornik 1998*, Moscow: Goskomstat Rossii.

Gosudarstvennyy Komitet Rossiiskoi Federatsii po Statistiki (1999*a*) *Demograficheskii Ezhegodnik Rossii 1999*. Moscow: Goskomstat.

—— (1999*b*). *Rossiiskii Statisticheskii Ezhegodnik: 1999*, Moscow: Goskomstat.

—— (1999*c*). *Sotsial'noe Polozhenie I Uroven; Zhizni Naseleniya Rossii: Statisticheskii Sbornik 1999*, Moscow: Goskomstat.

—— (2000*a*) 'Demograficheskaya situatsiya v Rossii v 1999 godu', in *Statisticheskii Byulleten'*, 5(68): 62–83.

—— (2000*b*) *Rossiya v Tsifrakh: 2000*, Moscow: Goskomstat.

—— (2000*c*) *Informatsiya o Sotsial'no-Ekonomicheskom Polozhenii Rossii: Yanvar'*— *Oktyabr 2000 goda*, Moscow: Goskomstat.

Gosudarstvennyy Komitet Statistiki SSSR (1987). *Narodnoe Khozyaistvo SSSR za 70 let*, Moscow: Ekonomika i Statistika.

—— (1988 . . . 1991). *Narodnoe Khozyaistvo SSSR v 1987 g. . . . v 1990 g.*, Moscow: Finansy i Statistika.

—— (1989*a*). *Narodnoe Obrazovanie i Kul'tura v SSSR*, Moscow: Finansy i Statistika.

—— (1989*b*). *Narodnoe Khozyaistvo SSSR v 1989: Statisticheskii Sbornik*, Moscow: Finansy i Statistiki.

—— (1990*a*). *Demograficheskii Ezhegodnik SSSR 1990*, Moscow: Finansy i Statistiki.

—— (1990*b*). *Okhrana Zdorov'ya v SSSR: Statisticheskii Sbornik*, Moscow: Finansy i Statistika.

—— (1990*c*). *Sotsial'noe Razvitie SSSR: Statisticheskii Sbornik*, Moscow: Finansy i Statistiki.

Grossman, M. (1972). *The Demand for Health: A Theoretical and Empirical Investigation*, New York: NBER.

Heleniak, T. (1995). 'Economic Transition and Demographic Change in Russia, 1989–1995', *Post-Soviet Geography*, 36/7: 446–58.

Helmstadler, S. (1992). 'Medical Insurance in Russia', *Radio Free Europe/Radio Liberty Research Report*, 1/31: 31 July.

IEPPP = Institut Ekonomicheskikh Problem Perekhodnogo Perioda.

'Indeksy rynka: Osnovnye pokazateli khimiko-farmatsevticheskoi promyshlennosti RF' (1997). *Remedium*, 4 (May), pp. 4–5.

'Indeksy rynka: Zdravookhranenie i potreblenie medikamentov v RF' (1997). *Remedium*, 5 (June–July), pp. 4–5.

Institut Ekonomicheskikh Problem Perekhodnogo Perioda (1998). *Ekonomika Perekhodnogo Perioda: Ocherki Ekonomicheskoi Politiki Postkommunisticheskoi Rossii 1991–1997*, Moscow: IEPPP.

Kaser, M. (1976). *Health Care in the Soviet Union and Eastern Europe*, London: Croom Helm.

Klugman, J., and Schieber, G. (with the assistance of Heleniak, T., and Hon, V.) (1996). 'A Survey of Health Reform in Central Asia', World Bank Technical Paper No. 344.

Knaus, W. A. (1981). *Inside Russian Medicine: An American Doctor's First-Hand Report*, New York: Everest House.

Kokorina, T., and Serbryakova, E. (1997). Rossiiskie apteki: trudnaya doroga k samostoyatel'nosti', *Remedium*, 6 (August), pp. 10–11.

'Kontseptsiya razvitiya zdravookhraneniya i meditsinskoi nauki v Rossiiskoi Federatsii' (1997), *Meditsinskaya Gazeta*, 19 November.

'Kontseptsiya okhrany zdorov'ya naseleniya Rossiiskoi Federatsii na period do 2005 goda' (2000). *Rossiiskaya Gazeta*, 13 September.

Korchagin, V. P. (1980). *Problemy Ekonomiki Zdravookhraneniya v Uslovyakh Razvitogo Sotsializma*, Moscow: dissertation for degree in Doctor of Economics.

—— (1997). 'Finansirovanie zdravookhraneniya: potrebnosti rastut, vozmozhnosti sokrashchayutsya', in N. F. Gerasimenko (ed.), 'Zdorov'e naselenie kak faktor obespecheniya natsional'noi bezopasnosti Rossii', *Informatsionno-Analiticheskoe Upravlenia Apparata Soveta Federatsii Analiticheskii Vestnik*, 10 (55).

Korepanov, V. (1992). 'Bol'noi ne dolzhen platit' dvazhdy', *Meditsinskaya Gazeta*, 21 February.

Kornai, J. (1980). *Economics of Shortage*, Amsterdam: North Holland.

—— (1992). *The Socialist System: The Political Economy of Communism*, Oxford: Clarendon Press.

Kucherin, N. A. (1978). *Ekonomicheskie Aspekty Zabolevaemosti i Proizvoditel'nosti Truda*, Leningrad.

Kuznetsov, P. P., and Chelidze, N. P. (1997). 'OMS: Itogi i perspektivy', *Meditsinkoe Strakhovanie*, No. 16.

Meditsinskoe Strakhovanie: Normativnye Dokumenty, Kommentarii, Strakhovye Kompanii, Slovar' Terminov (1993). Moscow: Izdatel'stvo PARTNER.

Meslé, F., and Shkolnikov, V. (1995). 'La mortalité en Russie: une crise sanitaire en deux temps', *Revue d'études comparatives Est–Ouest*, 26/4: 9–24.

—— —— Hertrich, V., and Vallin, J. (1996). *Tendances Recentes de la Mortalité par Cause en Russie 1965–1994*, Paris: Institut National D'Études Démographiques.

Ministerstvo Zdravookhraneniya Rossiiskoi Federatsii (1993). *O Sostoyanii Zdorov'ya Naseleniya Rossiiskoi Federatsii v 1992 godu*, Moscow.

—— (1996). *O Sostoyanii Zdorov'ya Naseleniya Rossiiskoi Federatsii v 1995 godu*, Moscow.

—— (1999). *O Sostoyanii Zdorov'ya Naseleniya Rossiiskoi Federatsii v 1998 godu*, Moscow.

—— (1998). *Zdorov'e Naseleniya Rossii i Deyatel'nost' Uchrezhdenii Zdravookhraneniya v 1997 godu: Statisticheskie Materialy*, Moscow.

MZRF = Ministerstvo Zdravookhraneniya Rossiiskoi Federatsii.

Nell, J., and Stewart, K. (1994).'Death in Transition: The Rise in the Death Rate in Russia Since 1992', International Child Development Centre, *Innocenti Occasional Papers: EPS 45*, December, Florence: UNICEF.

O Meditsinskom Strakhovanii Grazhdan: Sbornik Zakonodatel'nykh i Normativnykh Dokumentov po Sostoyaniyu na Iyul' 1997 goda (1997), Moscow: IPTs Bukvitsa.

'O dopolnitel'nykh merakh po uluchsheniyu okhrany zdorov'ye naseleniya' (1982). *Pravda*, 26 August.

'O merakh po dal'neishemu uluchsheniyu narodnogo zdravookhraneniya' (1977). in *Zabota Partii i Pravitel'stva o Blage Naroda*, Moscow, 1980.

'O merakh po stabilizatsii i razvitiyu zdravookhraneniya i meditsinskoi nauki v Rossiiskoi Federatsii' (1997). *Meditsinskaya Gazeta*, 19 November.

OECD = Organization for Economic Cooperation and Development.

Organization for Economic Cooperation and Development (various years). *OECD in Figures*, Paris: OECD.

—— (1993). *OECD Health Systems*, Paris: OECD.

'Osnovnye napravlenie razvitiya okhrany zdorov'ya naseleniya i perestroiki zdravookhraneniya SSSR v dvenadtsatoi pyatiletke i na period do 2000 goda' (1987). *Pravda*, 27 November.

Pokrovskii, V. I. (1997).'Vyzhivet li meditsinskaya nauka?', in N. F. Gerasimenko (ed.), 'Zdorov'e naselenie kak faktor obespecheniya natsional'noi bezopasnosti Rossii', *Informatsionno-Analiticheskoe Upravlenia Apparata Soveta Federatsii: Analiticheskii Vestnik*, 10 (55).

Polyakov, I. V. (1995).'Istoriya voprosa: Meditsinskoe strakhovanie i obosnovanie vybora putei razvitiya zdravookhraneniya v Rossii', *Meditsinkoe Strakhovanie*, 11, pp. 3–8.

Popov, G. A. (1976). *Ekonomika i Planirovanie Zdravookhraneniya*, Moscow: Izdatel'stvo Moskovskogo Universiteta.

Pravdin, D. I. (1976). *Razvitie Neproizvodstevennoi Sferi pri Sotsializme*, Moscow.

Preker, A. S., and Feachem, R. G. A. (1995).'Market Mechanisms and the Health Sector in Central and Eastern Europe', World Bank Technical Paper No. 293.

'Programma sotsial'nykh reform v Rossiiskoi Federatsii na period 1996–2000 godov', (1997). *Rossiiskaya Gazeta*, 12 March.

Raison, C. (1998). 'Regionalisation et crise sanitaire en Russie', *Revue d'études Comparatives Est–Ouest*, 29/3: 207–39.

Rozhdestvenskaya, I., and Shiskin, S. (1996). 'Reformy v sotsial'no-kul'turnoi sfere: v ch'ikh interestakh?', *Voprosy Ekonomiki*, 1, pp. 33–46.

Ryan, M. (1978). *The Organization of Soviet Medical Care*, Oxford: Basil Blackwell.

—— (1990). *Doctors and the State in the Soviet Union*, New York: St Martin's Press.

Sapir, J. (1996). *Le Chaos Russe: Desordres economiques, Conflits Politiques, Decomposition Militaire*, Paris: Éditions La Découverte.

—— (1999). 'Russia's Crash of August 1998: Diagnosis and Prescription', *Post-Soviet Affairs*, 15/1 (January–March).

SAUS = U.S. Department of Commerce.

Schepin, O. P., and Semenov, V. Yu. (1992). 'The Soviet Health Service System Reform', in O. P. Schepin, V. Yu. Semenov, and I. Sheiman, (1992). 'Health Care Reform in Russia', University of York, Centre for Health Economics, Discussion Paper 102.

Schroeder, G. (1979). 'The Soviet Economy on a Treadmill of "Reforms"', in U.S. Congress, Joint Economic Committee, *Soviet Economy in a Time of Change*, Washington, DC: USGPO.

SEV = Sovet Ekonomicheskoi Vzyaimopomoshchi.

Shapiro, J. (1995). 'The Russian Mortality Crisis and its Causes', in A. Åslund (ed.), *Russian Economic Reforms at Risk*, London: Pinter.

—— (1997). 'Health Care Policy and Russian Health', in S. White, A. Pravda, and Z. Gitelman. *Developments in Russian Politics*, London: Macmillan.

Sheiman, I. (1991). 'Health Care Reform in the Russian Federation', *Health Policy*, 19: 45–54.

—— (1998). *Reforma Upravleniya i Finansirovaniya Zdravookhraneniya*. Moscow: Izdatsentr.

Shishkin, S. (1995). 'The Metamorphosis of the Russian Health Care Reform', *Voprosy Ekonomiki*, 9 (translation from Russian original).

—— (1998). 'La reforme du financement du système de sante en Russie', *Revue d'Études comparatives Est – Ouest*, 29/3: 187–205.

—— (2000). *Reforma Finansirovaniya Rossiiskogo Zdravookhraneniya*. Moscow: TEIS.

Shkolnikov, V. (1997). 'The Population Crisis and Rising Mortality in Transitional Russia', Paper presented at a UNU/WIDER Project Meeting on 'Economic Shocks, Social Stress the Demographic Impact', 17–19 April, Helsinki.

SKSNG = Statisticheskii Komitet Sodruzhestva Nezavisimykh Godudarstv.

Smirnov, F. (1992). 'Na grani finansogo krakha', *Meditsinskaya Gazeta*, 21 February.

'Sotsial'no-ekonomicheskaya situatsiya v Rossii i razvitie farmatsevticheskogo rynka v 1 kv. 1997 g.' (1997). *Remedium*, 4, p. 23.

Sovet Ekonomicheskoi Vzaimopomoshshi (1981). *Statisticheskii Ezhegodnik Stran-Chlenov Soveta Ekonomicheskoi Vzaimopomoshshi 1981*. Moscow: Finansy i Statistika.

—— (1989). *Statisticheskii Ezhegodnik Stran-Chlenov Soveta Ekonomicheskoi Vzyaimopomoshchi*. Moscow: Financy i Statistika.

Statisticheskii Komitet Sodruzhestva Nezavisimykh Gosudarstv (1992*a*). *Mir v Tsifrakh: Statisticheskii Sbornik 1992*, Moscow: Finansovyy Inzhiniring.

—— (1992*b*). *Strany-Chleny SNG: Statisticheskii Ezhegodnik 1992*, Moscow: Finansovyy Inzhiniring.

'Tempy rosta rekordny i na udivlenie ustoichivy' (1997). *Remedium*, 1, pp. 7–9.

Terekhov, V. A. (ed.) (1997). 'Sostoyanie Zdorov'ya Naseleniya Rossiiskoi Federatsii', *Informatsionno-Analiticheskoe Upravlenia Apparata Soveta Federatsii Analiticheskii Vestnik*, 6 (51).

Tsentral'noe Statisticheskoe Upravlenie SSSR (1973, 1976, 1981, 1983, 1986). *Narodnoe Khozyaistvo SSSR v 1972 g.*, *1975, 1980, 1982, 1985*, Moscow: Ekonomika i Statistika.

TsSU = See Tsentral'noe Statisticheskoe Upravlenie SSSR, *Narodnoe Khozyaistvo.*

UNDY = United Nations Demographic Yearbook.

UNICEF, International Child Development Centre (1994). *Crisis in Mortality, Health and Nutrition.* Florence: UNICEF ICDC, Economies in Transition Studies: Regional Monitoring Report No. 2.

—— (1997). *Children at Risk in Central and Eastern Europe: Perils and Promises*, Economies in Transition Regional Monitoring Report No. 4. Florence: UNICEF.

United Nations (1997). *Demographic Yearbook 1995*, New York: UN.

—— (2000). *TransMONEE Database.* Download from the UNICEF website (http://www.unicef-icdc.org).

USDC = US Department of Commerce.

U.S. Department of Commerce (1997). *Statistical Abstract of the United States 1997*, Washington, DC: USGPO.

U.S. Department of Commerce, Bureau of the Census (1980...1999). *Statistical Abstract of the United States 1980...1999*, Washington, DC: USGPO.

—— (2000). *International Database* (IDB), Download from the USDC website (http://www.census.gov/ipc/www/idbnew.html).

Vishnevskii, A. G. (ed.) (1997). *Naselenii Rossii 1996 Ezhegodnyy Demograficheskii Doklad*, Moscow: Naselenie i Obshchestvo.

—— and Zakharov, S. V. (eds.) (1993). *Naselenie Rossii 1993: Ezhegodnyy Demograficheskii Doklad*, Moscow: Evrasiya.

'Vnutrennyy rynok: Tempy rosta rekordny i na udivlenie ustoichivy' (1997). *Remedium*, 1 (February).

Volkov, A. G. (1993). *Demograficheskii Perspektivy Rossii*, Moscow: RIITs.

WHO HFA = World Health Organization, Health for All Database.

WHO WHSA = World Health Organization, World Health Statistics Annual.

Williams, C. (1996). 'Russian Health Care in Transition', in C. Williams, V. Chuprov, and V. Staroverov (eds.). *Russian Society in Transition*, Aldershot: Dartmouth.

World Bank (1997). *World Development Report 1997: The State in a Changing World*, Oxford: Oxford University Press.

World Health Organization, Regional Office for Europe (2000). *Health for All Database*, June 2000 edition. Download from the WHO website (http://www.who.dk).

World Health Organization (various years). *World Health Statistics Annual*, Geneva: WHO.

Zweifel, P., and Breyer, F. (1997). *Health Economics*, Oxford: Oxford University Press.

Index

consumption 68
  energy 85, 86
  expenditure 16, 18, 19
  food 18–19
cooperative banks 95, 214
cooperatives 76 n. 33, 350, 370, 371, 398,
  413–14
  see also kolkhozy; sovkhozy
corporate assets, valuation of 243–6
corporate governance 64, 241–3
  oil industry 322–3
corridor, exchange rate *see under* exchange
  rates
corruption 35, 38, 47, 318
costs of production 72
Council of Ministers 22
CPSU (Communist Party of the Soviet
  Union) 21, 22, 23, 25, 30, 31
credits:
  directed 219, 220, 223–5
  technical 104–5
  to commercial banks 98, 99, 102
  to countries of the 'near abroad' 103–4
  to former Soviet republics 98, 99, 102–5
  to government 98, 99–100, 102, 140
  veksel 225–7, 230
crime 36, 356
Croatia 137
crude death rate 481, 490, 492, 493, 509, 516
culture, expenditure 158
Culyer, A. J. 480
currency:
  appreciation 278, 279, 281
  convertibility 79
  depreciation 79, 221, 280, 281
  devaluation 5–6, 20, 50, 119–21, 124,
    228, 236
  former Soviet Republics 104
  liberalization 5
  see also rouble; rouble zone
current account 282, 299
Czech Republic 1, 6, 137, 224, 349
Czechoslovakia 349

Dart Management 317
David, P. 387
Davidova, S. 389

Davis, C. 475–530
Dearden, J. 70
death rates *see* mortality
debt 94, 111, 112–15, 121, 123, 124, 125, 134,
  288–90
  corporate 251–3
  to GDP ratio 113, 114–15
  trade 23
debt default 214, 228, 258–9, 262, 289
debt market 239, 251–7
debt servicing 111, 113, 124, 127, 140, 156,
  157, 290
debt write-offs 374, 375
decentralization, of government sector
  163–6, 168
defence sector 80–3, 162, 242, 261
  expenditure 156, 157
  procurement 41, 421
deficit goods 74
'Democratic Russia' 26, 31
de-monopolization, in agriculture 367,
  378–9
de novo firms:
  and employment behaviour 330, 340
  ownership structure 179, 181, 185
depreciation 79, 221, 280, 281
Desai, P. 369
devaluation 5–6, 20, 50, 119–21, 124, 228, 236
Dhar, S. 177
directed credits 219, 220, 223–5
  agricultural 375
Dmitriev, M. 213–37
Dmitrieva, O. 369
Dolgopiatova, T. 367
dollarization 106
Duma 53
dwellings 81
  see also housing

Earle, J. S. 173–210
Easterly, W. 68
EBRD 6, 9, 10, 19, 229, 232, 233, 245, 349
education:
  expenditure 157, 158
  privatization 198
EFF loan (of the IMF) 288
élites 28–34, 59

QM LIBRARY
(MILE END)